10

PEOPLE, POWER AND PROCESS

SOCIOLOGY FOR CANADIANS

PEOPLE, POWER AND PROCESS

SOCIOLOGY FOR CANADIANS

ALEXANDER HIMELFARB
C. JAMES RICHARDSON
Department of Sociology
University of New Brunswick

McGRAW-HILL RYERSON LIMITED

Toronto, Montreal, New York, St. Louis, San Francisco,
Auckland, Beirut, Bogotá, Düsseldorf,
Johannesburg, Lisbon, London, Lucerne, Madrid,
Mexico, New Delhi, Panama, Paris, San Juan,
São Paulo, Singapore, Sydney, Tokyo.

PEOPLE, POWER AND PROCESS
SOCIOLOGY FOR CANADIANS

0-07-082865-2

1 2 3 4 5 6 7 8 9 10 D 1 2 3 4 5 6 7 8 9

Printed and bound in Canada

Care has been taken to trace ownership of copyright material contained in this text. The publishers will gladly take any information that will enable them to rectify any reference or credit in subsequent editions.

Canadian Cataloguing in Publication Data
Himelfarb, Alexander, date
People, power and process

Bibliography: p.
Includes indexes.
ISBN 0-07-082865-2

1. Sociology. 2. Canada—Social conditions.
I. Richardson, C. James, date. II. Title.

HM51.H55 301 C79-094101-5

to our parents:

Elizabeth and Abraham Himelfarb

Rose and Charlie Richardson

Acknowledgements

Robert K. Merton, p. 17:
"Now the Case for Sociology," *New York Times Magazine,* July 16. © 1961 by The New York Times Company. Reprinted by permission.

Horace M. Miner, p. 43:
"Body Ritual among the Nacirema," *American Anthropologist,* 58:504-505, 1956. Reproduced by permission of the American Anthropological Association.

Alvin W. Gouldner, p. 44:
The Coming Crisis in Western Sociology, p. 489. © 1970 by Alvin W. Gouldner Basic Books, Inc., Publishers, New York.

Frank Parkin, p. 52:
Class Inequality and Political Order, p. 42, MacGibbon & Kee Ltd./Granada Publishing Ltd., London, England, 1971.

Alvin Toffler, p. 55:
Future Shock, p. 10, Random House, Inc., New York, 1971.

Michael Harrington, p. 55:
The Accidental Century, p. 29. © Michael Harrington 1965, Macmillan Publishing Co., Inc., New York.

C. Wright Mills, p. 62:
The Sociological Imagination, p. 3, Oxford University Press, New York, 1959.

Jonathan H. Turner, p. 79:
The Structure of Sociological Theory, revised edition, p. 48, Dorsey Press, Homewood, Illinois. © 1978 by The Dorsey Press.

H. H. Gerth and C. W. Mills, p. 81:
Essays in Sociology, pp. 214, 216, Max Weber, ed., Oxford University Press, New York, 1958.

Robert K. Merton, p. 82:
Social Theory and Structure, p. 256, New York Free Press. © 1968 by The New York Times Company. Reprinted by permission.

Stanley Cohen, p. 116:
Introduction to Images of Deviance, p. 17, Stanley Cohen, ed. (Pelican Original, 1971). Collection © Penguin Books Ltd., 1971. Reprinted by permission of Penguin Books Ltd.

David H. Stymeist, p. 118:
Ethnics and Indians: Social Relations in a Northwestern Ontario Town. By permission of PMA Books, Toronto.

Judith A. Nagata, p. 242:
"Greek Working-Class Immigrants in Toronto," *International Migration Review* 4(3):53, Center for Migration Studies of New York, Inc.

Geoffrey Pearson, p. 254:
The Deviant Imagination: Psychiatry, Social Work and Social Change, p. 161, Macmillan Administration (Basingstoke) Ltd, 1975.

Stanley Cohen, p. 255:
With permission from *International Journal of Criminology and Penology* 1:p. 120, 1973. Copyright by Academic Press Inc. (London) Ltd.

S. Clark, J. Grayson, and L. Grayson, pp. 260, 266, 273:
Prophecy and Protest: Social Movements in Twentieth Century Canada, pp. 7, 32, 131-132, Gage Educational Publishing Ltd., Toronto, 1975.

N. Glazer and D. Moynihan, p. 241:
Ethnicity, p. 7, N. Glazer and D. Moynihan, eds., Harvard University Press, Cambridge, Mass., 1975.

Anthony Oberschall, p. 262:
Social Conflict and Social Movements, p. 33, Prentice-Hall, Englewood Cliffs, N.J., 1973.

Robert Brym, p. 267:
"Regional Social Structure and Agrarian Radicalism in Canada: Alberta, Saskatchewan and New Brunswick," *Canadian Review of Sociology and Anthropology* 15:3 (1978), pp. 339-351. Reprinted by permission of the publisher, Fitzhenry & Whiteside Limited.

W. J. Goode, p. 279:
World Revolution and Family Patterns, p. 7, Macmillan Publishing Co., Inc., New York, 1963.

D. H. J. Morgan, p. 286:
Social Theory and the Family, pp. 206-207, Routledge and Kegan Paul, Ltd., London, England, 1975.

Dorothy E. Smith, p. 289:
"Women, the Family and Corporate Capitalism," *Women in Canada,* revised edition, Marylee Stephenson, ed., General Publishing Co. Limited, 30 Lesmill Rd., Toronto.

M. Young and P. Willmott, p. 299:
The Symmetrical Family, p. 76, Pantheon Books (a division of Random House Inc.), New York, 1973.

D. H. Morgan, p. 303:
The Family and Social Theory, pp. 141-142, Pantheon Books (a division of Random House Inc.), New York, 1975.

Richard Sennett, p. 304:
From *Transaction,* Vol. 7, No. II. © 1970, by Transaction, Inc. Published by permission of Transaction, Inc.

B. Steele and C. Pollock, p. 305:
The Battered Child, 2nd edition, Helfer and Kemp, eds., University of Chicago Press, Illinois, 1974.

E. M. Lemert, p. 120:
Human Deviance, Social Problems, and Social Control, 2nd edition, p. 69, Prentice-Hall, Englewood Cliffs, N.J., 1972.

L. M. G. Clark and D. J. Lewis, p. 121:
Rape: The Price of Coercive Sexuality, p. 160, Canadian Women's Educational Press, 280 Bloor St. W., Toronto, 1977.

United Nations, p. 134:
Table based on statistics from *The Determinants and Consequences of Population Trends,* p. 11, United Nations, New York, 1953.

Paul R. Ehrlich, p. 136:
The Population Bomb, p. 28, Ballantine Books (a division of Random House, Inc.), New York, 1968.

Lorna Marsden, p. 139:
Table based on statistics from Dominion Bureau of Statistics, 1970-71, *Canada Yearbook,* Table 19, p. 309, and United Nations Statistical Office, *Demographic Year Book,* 1970, pp. 646-650.

L. Gertler and R. Crowley, pp. 141, 142:
Changing Canadian Cities. Reprinted by permission of The Canadian Publishers, McClelland and Stewart, Toronto, 1977.

Gad Horowitz, p. 151:
"Creative Politics," *Canadian Dimension* 3(1) 14-15, 1965.

T. B. Bottomore, p. 176:
Classes in Modern Society, pp. 16-17, George Allen and Unwin Ltd., London, England, 1965.

Kingsley Davis, p. 181:
Human Society, pp. 367-368, Macmillan Publishing Co., Inc., New York. © 1948.

Charles Anderson, p. 182:
The Political Economy of Social Class, pp. 84-88, Prentice-Hall, Englewood Cliffs, N.J., 1974.

Jane Synge, p. 213:
From *Education, Change and Society,* R. A. Carlton, N. J. MacKinnon, and L. A. Colley, eds., Reprinted with permission of Gage Educational Publishing, Toronto, 1977.

Ashley Montagu, p. 224:
The Concept of Race, p. 6, Macmillan Publishing Co., Inc., New York, 1969.

D. Hughes and E. Kallen, p. 228:
The Anatomy of Racism: Canadian Dimensions, p. 214, Harvest House Ltd, Montreal, 1974.

Wallace Clement, pp. 233, 234:
The Canadian Corporate Elite, pp. 232, 234. Reprinted by kind permission of the publisher, The Macmillan Company of Canada Ltd., Toronto, 1975.

PHOTOGRAPH CREDITS

Pages 1, 3, 41, 61, 86, 168, 253	*Ontario Ministry of Industry & Tourism*
Page 24	*Gulf Canada Ltd.*
Pages 39, 112, 251	*Miller Services Ltd.*
Pages 129, 276	*The New Brunswick Provincial Archives*
Page 131	*Naval Photographic Center, Washington, D.C.*
Page 199	*Board of Education for the City of North York*
Page 221	*Peter Thomas—Miller Services Ltd.*
Cover	*The Public Archives of Canada*

Contents

Preface

Like most books, this one emerged, initially, out of our own dissatisfaction with existing textbooks. We were teaching introductory sociology and found ourselves faced with the problem that Canadian texts did not cover adequately the conceptual issues at the interpersonal relations level with which we believe most people begin their course. At the same time, American textbooks, though very useful in the first half of our course, were embarrassingly irrelevant when we turned to substantive and theoretical areas such as social stratification, education, ethnic relations and collective behaviour. We set out, then, to write a book which would reflect both the rich social-psychological literature from American sociology and the growing body of literature taught in Canadian society courses. Moreover, we had, for some time, been concerned with how, in the space of one year, the link between the micro and the macro could be created. Existing textbooks, it seemed, resolved this problem in one of two ways. Either, they were essentially micro or macro texts *or* they were sociological compendiums which ignored the problem of integration by consciously avoiding taking a position.

In contrast, this book is an attempt to link the sociology of everyday life to the larger issues of social structure. Our mentors are, ultimately, Berger and Luckmann and C. Wright Mills, sociologists who, in our view, have come closest to welding the micro and macro into a unified perspective. We have, as much as possible, tried to view interpersonal relations within a larger structural context and tried to see within larger social structures how people make sense of and effect change within these self-same structures.

These are market issues and problems of pedagogy. But, the writing of this book has also forced us to look more closely at our background assumptions, our view of what ought to be. At the risk of sounding hackneyed, a central assumption in this book is that we like Canada and are concerned with its fate, especially at a time when it seems so vulnerable. Because ours is a critical perspective, we are inevitably forced to write at considerable length about the cultural and economic forces which threaten to split Canada and to see it subsumed within the American Empire. At the same time, our perhaps naive optimism cannot be entirely overwhelmed even by our own arguments. At some meta-theoretical level we cling to a prejudice that it would be best for Canadians, maybe even for Quebeckers, if separatism did not occur, if we could somehow shuck off the yoke of cultural and economic dependency on the United States.

Our background assumption in this text, then, is that we want Canada to retain both its autonomy and integrity. Having said this, we shall not, nor can we, attempt to defend our prejudice. Nor shall we raise it again explicitly. We have, now, stated our hope; the chapters in the text point to the obstacles, the social and economic forces, which make separatism appear not only rational, but inevitable, which make dependency seem a permanent fact of Canadian life. Nevertheless, running through this text is a note of optimism, a way out which is also implied in our choice of title for this book. We have called this book *People, Power and Process* because we believe that no matter how limited the degrees of freedom available to people, they nevertheless exist. People are, certainly, victims of social structures and blinded by ideologies, but they are also creators and interpreters of these social structures and ideologies. Sociology, in our view, is a humanistic discipline because it must, at once, recognize the myriad ways in which people impose or have imposed upon them delusion and how we all have the capacity to transcend our human condition. Sociology is both pessimistic and optimistic: it outlines both the structure of our imprisonment and the ways, however tortuous, out of it.

We make no claim with this book to have produced the Canadian equivalent of a Handbook in Sociology. By and large, we have written about topics, issues and approaches which interest us and which we teach to our students. Throughout, we have tried to maintain a position or theme, essentially an attempt to use insights of both what has been called conflict theory and symbolic interactionism. We outline our approach in Chapter I and develop it in Chapters II through VI. In Chapters VII through XII we apply our perspective to Canadian society and to processes of change. Because of our attempt at integration, the chapters in this book do, to a considerable extent, build upon one another.

At the same time as we are taking a position, we have also tried to do justice to alternative perspectives—theoretical as well as ideological—with sufficient force that students can react to rather than accept as textbook knowledge our position, our theoretical bias. We have, in other words, tried to be sensitive to the problem all textbook writers must face—that however tentative they may be, definitions and concepts when once presented become for students the definitive word; *a* reality becomes, in effect, *the* reality. Hence, as far as possible, we have tried to tie approaches and theories to real people living in real societies, the United States, Canada, Britain and France, at specific times. Inevitably, we present definitions but we have tried to do so through a variety of lenses. By taking a position, we hope to encourage discussion and enquiry, not to cut it off.

As is the case with most introductory textbooks, our bibliography grew large and is probably, for most students, forbidding. At the end of each chapter we present a number of works which we feel the student might want to explore. We have not tried to be comprehensive in our choice and many instructors will, no doubt, find glaring gaps in our lists. Our criteria for deciding what to include are twofold. First, we include works which we felt were representative of areas not covered very fully in the chapter. Second, we mention books that we like and which are written in a style we think is attractive to beginner students. Clearly, many of the books we mention as relevant to a particular chapter could have been repeated at the end of the other chapters.

We both feel a strong debt to Rex A. Lucas. He was, for both of us, an important teacher, a good colleague and, most important, a dear friend. We are better sociologists because of him. We have also been deeply influenced by Leo Zakuta and his special brand of symbolic interactionism. There is no doubt that much of what we say and do in this book will dismay him, make him wonder where he "went wrong" in his teaching. It is, however, he who taught us an appreciation for the sociology of everyday life.

Perhaps because we had these teachers in common, this book is, in the end, a genuine collaboration. It is conventional to assign credit (or blame) to individual authors for specific chapters or sections. It is true that initially each of us had responsibility for six chapters. But, the division of labour broke down after countless discussions, exchanges and revisions of drafts and the thrashing out together of chapters. Each of us must take responsibility for all of the chapters.

Both we and the text benefitted from the chapter by chapter reviews by Lorne Tepperman and Gottfried Paasche. As well, Robert Brym Very generously gave of his time to read and comment on an earlier draft of Chapter VII. We are especially grateful to our UNB colleague, Hugh Lautard, who not only has taken a lively interest in our work, but who also provided us with a number of previously unpublished tables from his own research. Margot Brewer read chapters, typed, gathered references and took on many other editorial tasks, jobs which lightened our burden considerably. We thank her, And, Himelfarb offers his thanks for so much more. Richardson adds a special thank-you to Rona, Michael and Rebecca who, inevitably, have been inconvenienced by and have had to cope with the extra demands the writing of this book has placed on them. He thanks them for their patience and their help. Finally, we would both like to thank Dianne Bawn and Liz Williams who, besides typing parts of this book, have made the UNB department such a pleasant and happy place in which to write a book.

Alex Himelfarb and Jim Richardson
Fredericton, New Brunswick, 1978

PART 1

Approaches To Sociology

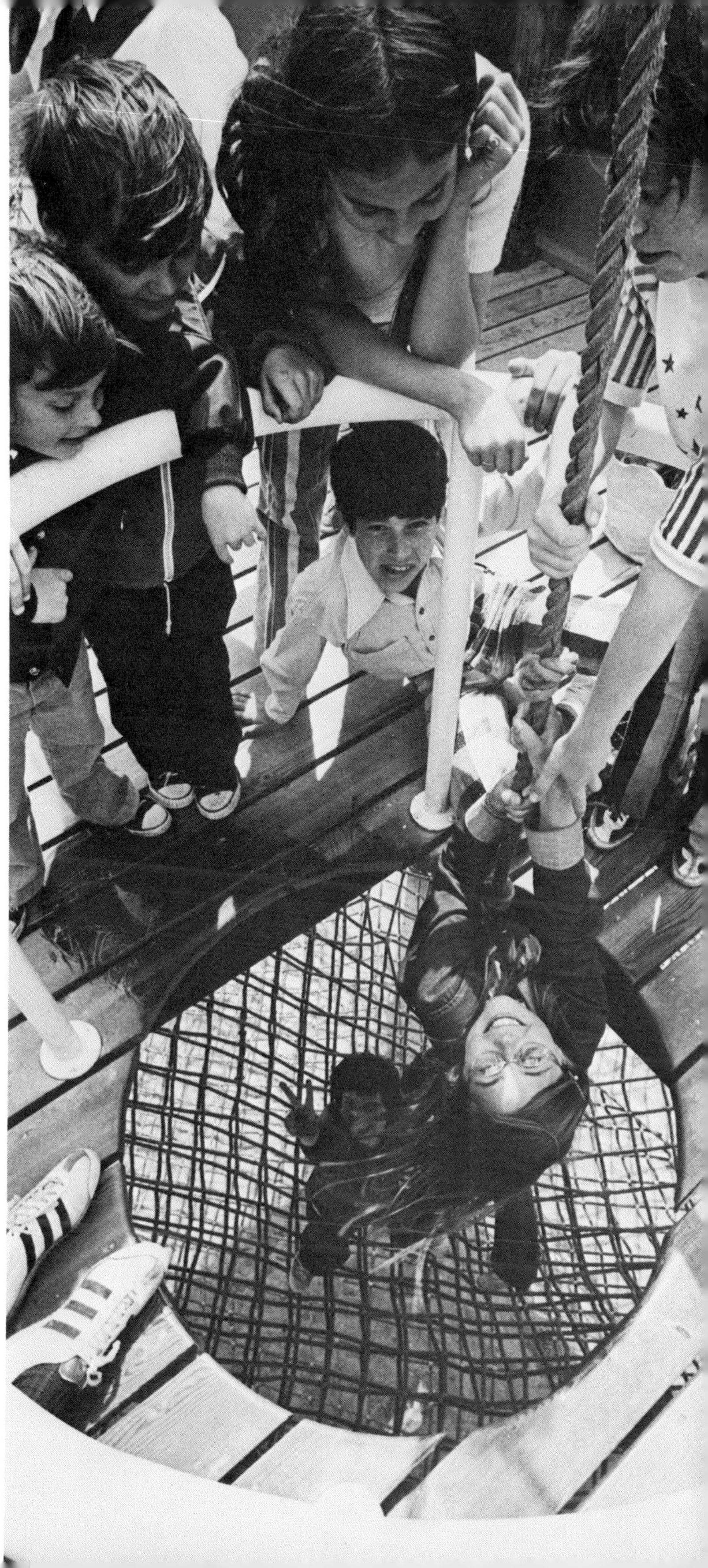

sociological perspectives
CHAPTER I

Sociology is the study of relationships among people, the study of society. In a sense, we all do something like sociology in our everyday lives. We learn or develop notions about what certain "types of people" are like. We imagine, or even think we know, the intentions or purposes of others. We all have our "theories" of how the media operate, what happens in schools, the workings of the government, who has the power and how they use it. This is the stuff of our everyday thinking, and, of course, of the arts. The *traditional knowledge* handed down to us by our parents and other teachers, *conventional wisdom*, that is, what "everybody knows," and the *everyday knowledge* that we gain through our own direct experience with life seem, to many, to be enough. It seems to work. So, why sociology? Part of the answer lies in understanding something of the preoccupations, concerns and perspectives of sociologists. Another part lies in understanding what sociologists do when they practise their "trade," the methods by which they do sociological research. In this chapter we shall be examining both.

Sociology has its roots in the eighteenth century, and, in particular, that intellectually and socially exciting period prior to the French Revolution—the Enlightenment. A variety of forces seemed to come together in the Enlightenment, ideas and assumptions which were critical to the development of the sociological perspective. During this time, social and political philosophers were much taken by advances in the physical sciences in the preceding century, above all, those of Sir Isaac Newton. Newton had almost single-handedly created a revolution in scientific thought. His laws demonstrated that reason and observation could be—indeed must be—united. Sir Isaac Newton supposedly "discovered" the law of gravitation when he saw an apple fall from a tree. What is significant here is not that Newton had access to this simple observation; many people had seen many apples fall. Newton, however, came up with the idea (however such thinkers come up with such ideas) that the same force which pulled the apple might also be the force that held the moon in its orbit around the earth; he looked for the *pattern* in his observations. Unlike many thinkers before him, Newton did not stop here, but tested his idea with more observations. His calculations confirmed what he had imagined. To look for the pattern in observations and to test the theory we build with more observations is the essence of the scientific method.

In the heady climate of the eighteenth century, it was a small step to recognize that the scientific method of Newton's physics could be generalized and employed to understand social phenomena as well as physical phenomena (Zeitlin, 1968:7). Basil Willey (1962:13), a British professor of English, summed it up this way:

> *When Newton bound together in one dazzling synthesis the great and the little, the stars in their courses and the fall of an apple, a thankful generation, at once scientific and pious, could exclaim with its spokesman, Alexander Pope:*
>
> *Nature and Nature's laws lay hid in night:*
> *God said,* "Let Newton be!" *and all was light!*

Such "light," it was soon recognized, might be applied to the social world as well.

BASIC ASSUMPTIONS

The implications of the scientific method coincided with two other changes in basic assumptions about man and society: (1) the notion that society was not divinely constructed, but was constructed by people and therefore could be changed—what we refer to as secularization; and (2) the idea that societies can be improved, that they "progress," that they could be made Utopian. There was, in other words, a growing sense that just as science could progress, so could there be moral and social progress. This view, though seriously shaken by two World Wars, by the Holocaust, by a growing ambivalence about the benefits of a technological society, is still very central to the sociological perspective.

But, almost from its beginnings, sociology has been divided into two deeply opposed perspectives, what are usually referred to as *order* and *conflict* theories. These are, in turn, based on two radically different assumptions about "human nature." We use the word "assumption" because neither view of human nature can really be tested or proved in a scientific way. As with the question of whether Heaven exists or not, human nature lies outside the realm of science—it is what we call a metaphysical question. The essential question asked is whether people are inherently good or inherently evil. As we shall see, it turns out to make a lot of difference which of these two positions one takes.

Throughout most of Western Civilization, the view that man is inherently evil has predominated. From the Judeo-Christian perspective, "Man" is a fallen creature who, though redeemable to some extent, can never attain perfection.[1] However, as social philosophers began to contemplate the origin of society they also began to contemplate what people might be like without all the trappings of society. What would people be like in "a state of nature"?

One famous and influential answer came from Thomas Hobbes (1588-1679), who, in his great work *Leviathan,* pessimistically maintained that without society, life would be solitary, poor, nasty and brutish. He started, then, from the assumption that people are basically egotistical, selfish, antagonistic and hostile to one another, that there would be a "war of all against all" if there was no state to keep people in check and make them conform.

In modified forms, the Hobbesian "solution" to the "problem of order" has permeated—some would say dominated—the sociological tradition even to the present and made sociology essentially a conservative tradition (Nisbet, 1967). It shows itself, for example, in Edmund Burke's (1729-1797) condemnation of the French Revolution (Burke, 1790). People, Burke argued, need the traditions of the church and of the aristocracy. To do away with these through revolution is to invite anarchy and the breakdown of civilization. Similarly, Auguste Comte (1798-1857), often called the "father of sociology," believed that while change was possible and while society could be perfected, order and progress must go hand in hand (Comte, 1893). And, as we shall see, Emile Durkheim (1859-1917) also viewed society as essential to people's well-being. When social constraints are insufficient, when order breaks down, people may, according to Durkheim, be more prone to commit suicide. Finally, following the work of Durkheim, much more recent theory of crime and deviance (see Chapter VI) begins with the idea that these are an outcome of social disorganization, social breakdown. It emerges also in the belief that children in the family and in the school require "structure": rigid schedules, set tasks and assignments, stern parents and teachers (see Chapters VIII and XII). Thus, in its most pessimistic versions this perspective becomes *reactionary*; it denies that society can be improved at all. In its more optimistic forms, we have conservatism at its best: things can be improved, but we must always move cautiously and carefully.

Jean Jacques Rousseau (1712-1778) is perhaps the most famous and influential spokesman for the opposite view of human nature. In Rousseau's hypothetical "state of nature," people are, if anything, intrinsically good. If today they seem to be corrupt and evil and greedy, the blame rests not on something innate in people, but on society. In this view, society, for the most part, represses rather than sustains people. This sentiment is most clearly captured in Rousseau's famous phrase which opens his *The Social Contract* (1762): "Man is born free; and everywhere he is in chains." For Rousseau, the "state of nature" is not a condition of selfishness, hostility and misery, but of freedom and great happiness. The evils of life are a direct consequence of society and the state, laws and institutions. In nature people are free—free to create and to enjoy life—and this freedom is necessary for human advancement. In society people have lost this freedom and therefore their happiness.

In *The Social Contract,* Rousseau moves on to the question of how people may gain freedom in organized society. Rousseau advances the notion of a community, a unity greater than the sum total of the individuals who compose it. Inherent individual rights would be transferred to the community as a whole, but individuals would not lose their rights as individuals because they comprise the community and share equally in its rights. Rousseau imagined a "community" which shares common ideals, shares a culture as well as rights, and which, as it takes control of its own destiny, comes to express "the common will." Rulers and governments are simply servants who must execute the general will; if they do not, they must be overthrown. In short, Rousseau believed that because men were basically good, a better society was possible, a society directed at enhancing individual freedom and fulfillment.

Unlike Rousseau, Karl Marx (1818-1883) never claimed that there ever had existed a primordial stage of history when people were actually free and happy. Yet, he did state that pre-capitalist societies were characterized by more cooperative, less competitive, social relationships. In Marx's view, human fulfillment is found primarily in work.

> *Far from being a sacrifice of one's time . . . truly human or "productive activity" is the mediating link between humanity and nature. It is through spontaneous, conscious, and creative labor that individuals express, realize, and develop their peculiarly human potentialities (Archibald, 1978:34-35).*

As well, in Marx's conception of human nature, man is not the antisocial creature painted by Hobbes, but, rather, is essentially social. Work inevitably involves humans in cooperative relationships with others. However, society, particularly capitalist society, has distanced man, *alienated* him, from his essence.[2] Men who must sell their labour for a wage, who must work for others, who become machine-like cogs in a complex division of labour become alienated from the all-important productive activity, the products of that activity, their fellow workers and themselves. They come to feel powerless and meaningless. Marx was confident, however, that the workers would finally revolt against the owners and, after a brief period in which they took power, the State would slip away and man would finally find his fulfillment in spontaneous and creative work. For Marx, like Rousseau, the evils in society were the consequence of society. To realize his potential, man would have to overthrow the social order which limited him, deprived him of his humanity. For Hobbes, like Burke and Durkheim, the social order is what protected man from himself, his antisocial and self-destructive nature. This cleavage between the perspectives of order and conflict persists today, but before we examine the recent versions, we shall briefly describe those early sociologists who contributed most to the development of a scientific approach, to the study of society and whose ideas remain a powerful influence in the discipline.

THE DEVELOPMENT OF SOCIOLOGY

Most discussions of the development of sociology are really attempts to trace the development of a particular kind of sociology—*positivist* sociology. "Positivism," as a philosophy of science, simply argues that the only things scientists should ask about are questions that can be answered with observable, that is, *empirical* data. All other questions are non-scientific. Just how much positivism is good for sociology, just how much this philosophy has led sociologists to undervalue or even stifle intuition are questions to which we will return. For now we shall simply trace the most powerful influence in contemporary sociology—the development of positivism.

As we mentioned previously, most sociologists recognize Auguste Comte as the true "father of sociology." Comte coined the term sociology which he thought of as a reform science. Writing just after the French Revolution, Comte was concerned with how societies might progress more slowly and cautiously, and thereby avoid the chaos and terror, the excesses which seemed to accompany revolutionary change. For Comte, progress must be achieved through the formulation of universal scientific laws of society. Using the methods of the other sciences—observation, experimentation and comparison—a new science, a "mother science," must emerge to study society as a whole, as a being in itself. To Comte, the social was more powerful than the individual; society, and its fundamental unit, the family, shaped the individual. To understand people, then, one had to understand the workings of society, its persistence and change. This notion of the primacy of social groupings is obviously the *raison d'être* of sociology. Although Comte's notion of a reform science did not develop much beyond the hope of a better age, he did a good deal to carve out a new scientific discipline.

One year after Comte's death, in Epinal, France, Emile Durkheim was born. We do not know the extent of Comte's influence on Durkheim, but Durkheim did concern himself with the same problem—the development of the scientific or positivistic study of society as a being in itself, as an "organism." Durkheim viewed society as based on and held together by interdependence, collective beliefs and ritual. What he wished to do was to study the social world in the same way that physicists and chemists study the natural world. In his own words, we must treat social facts as things, things which stand outside any one person and which can be studied in their own right. His first major work, *The Division of Labour in Society* (1893), described the changes in societies as they moved from simple to more complex. Simple societies are held together by common beliefs and common values, what Durkheim called *mechanical solidarity*. Complex society is held together by interdependence; with greater specialization of labour, people come to depend on others for the production of goods and services: *organic solidarity*.

The latter, organic solidarity, however, remained a future state, one which could only be brought about through the conscious intervention of those who possessed a scientific understanding of the social order and who could, then, assess what is "normal" and what is "pathological." His major concern, then, was with how moral order might be maintained in the France of his day, a society in transition from feudalism to industrialism and capitalism. In his major work, *The Elementary Forms of Religious Life* (1919), Durkheim analysed the role of religion, and particularly religious ritual, in promoting social solidarity.

We can see, then, that what Marx saw as alienating the individual, Durkheim saw as producing greater cohesion and social integration (Lukes, 1967). This view is perhaps clearest in Durkheim's most enduring study, *Suicide* (1897). We can see here, as well, Durkheim's view of human nature; society shaped the individual and protected him from his "natural state," from his antisocial and destructive "instincts."

Durkheim's *Suicide* and *The Rules of the Sociological Method* (1895) are the works which probably have most profoundly influenced the course of sociology. In the latter work, he describes the procedures which he then used in his examination of suicide. Because *Suicide* remains an excellent example of the application of positivism in social science research, it deserves a more detailed description.

Suppose you heard that one of your friends had committed suicide. After your initial shock you would no doubt wonder why. Why would anyone commit suicide? And, no doubt, you would think in individual terms. You would probably think of circumstances which might have created intense unhappiness. Perhaps your friend's business went bankrupt or perhaps he flunked out of college or lost a loved one. The common sense notion seems to be that suicides can be explained in terms of a personal tragedy, and obviously such factors do constitute part of the explanation. At the same time, however, much that is interesting and important is left out by these psychological explanations. If we examine suicide rates (that is, the number of suicides per 100,000 population), we find that certain categories of people are more likely to commit suicide than others. For example, men are more likely to do so than women. Nor does it seem that happiness can be the only factor operating. Durkheim set himself the task of accounting for these differences in rates of suicide.

In this study, Durkheim was concerned with demonstrating the importance and value of a purely sociological perspective. He, therefore, placed his emphasis on social or group factors. Durkheim did not simply go out and collect suicide data; he began with a hunch about what he would find. His hunch, his "theory" of suicide, was that too much or too little integration into social groups would produce high suicide rates. Once he started collecting his data to test his theory, he decided that no one explanation would explain all suicide. There were, he concluded, different types of suicide.

The first two types of suicide, *altruistic* and *egoistic,* are distinguished on the basis of the extent to which individuals are integrated into social groups. Suicide is described as altruistic if it occurs because people have over-identified with their group. Suicide is said to be egoistic if it is the result of an individual's lack of identification or lack of ties to his group. What Durkheim needed to test his ideas were suicide statistics for groups which had either very high or very low levels of solidarity or cohesion.

Durkheim's tests for his notion of altruistic suicide are a good example of his technique. If Durkheim was right, he should have found a high suicide rate for people in a situation in which their commitment to the group was excessively strong. The military provides an obvious example in that the value of the military group is always placed above that of the individual. Indeed, Durkheim found that in every European country suicide rates were higher for the military than they were for civilians. Now, this does not constitute very strong proof of Durkheim's ideas. A number of alternative explanations could be offered. Perhaps those in the military suffer more hardships. Perhaps they are unhappier, more fearful. If these alternative explanations were valid, we would expect enlisted men, who obviously suffer more hardships than officers, to be more prone to suicide. Durkheim found the opposite—officers had a higher suicide rate. The longer a man had been in the army, the more likely he was to commit suicide. Volunteer soldiers were more prone to suicide than those who had been drafted. Re-enlisted men were more prone than those who were in the army for the first time. Durkheim concluded that his idea was supported by the evidence. Those most attached to the army were most prone to suicide. Similar high rates of suicide are found in Japan and other cultures which place more importance on the group than on the individual. In such groups, the significance of life declines and the individuals might be provoked to suicide in situations which would not motivate others to do so.

Egoistic suicide is the other side of the coin. According to Durkheim, intimate group ties, emotional attachment to close (primary) groups, give individuals necessary support during times of stress and give meaning to individual goals. We would expect, then, and Durkheim found, higher rates of suicide for single people than married people, for childless couples than for families with children. Again, the evidence seems to support Durkheim's theory. Durkheim also used the notion of egoistic suicide to account for the differences in rates among various religions. Protestantism emphasizes the individual, self-reliance and self-control. The individual supposedly has a direct relationship with God. The Catholic Church places far more emphasis on ritual, which provides strong group support, and on organized group authority. In addition, while Catholics can depend on the Church for redemption if they have sinned, Protestants cannot. As we would expect from all this, Protestants have a higher rate of suicide than Catholics. Jews provide a particularly good test of egoistic suicide. Although nineteenth century European Jews supposedly had higher rates of mental illness than Catholics or Protestants, they had a lower rate of suicide than either. Durkheim argued that this was because of the higher degree of social solidarity of Jewish family life, of being a minority. Similarly, when Protestants were a minority, they too showed lower suicide rates.

Durkheim's third type of suicide he called *anomic*. In Durkheim's view, people are most content when their everyday behaviour is governed by clear and meaningful goals and when people lack these goals their lives become meaningless and suicide becomes more likely. In certain situations—a rapid change in society or in an individual's position in society—goals are destroyed and the result is a condition of anomie—normlessness.[3] Durkheim found, for example, that suicide rates were influenced by the business cycle. None of us are surprised to learn that suicide rates rise in times of severe depression. What is more striking is that economic prosperity produces more suicides. During times of sudden prosperity, people can supposedly no longer be certain about what goals they should reach for. They become confused because suddenly anything seems possible—there are no ceilings to their ambitions. If an individual has achieved his old goals easily he must create new ones and, according to Durkheim, the result is an endless upward spiral in search of the impossible—and perhaps suicide. Suicide, particularly anomic suicide, then, was for Durkheim an extreme symptom of the pathological condition of the society of his time. It was one example of the social disorganization which occurs when societies are in transition between two moral orders, that of mechanical solidarity and organic solidarity.

Durkheim's work on suicide has been subjected to many methodological and theoretical critiques (e.g., Douglas, 1967). Indeed, if we continued to read *Suicide* as a source of information and a thorough explanation of rates of suicide, we would have to count it as a rather minor contribution. His work remains important not because of what it tells us about suicide but because it has provided us with a model of the sociological perspective. He has influenced sociological thinking for at least three reasons: (1) he attempts to show that the feelings and actions of people are not solely psychological but derive at least partially from social forces "outside" of any one individual; feelings, including the desire to commit suicide are, then, affected by variations in the way society is organized; (2) by emphasizing the social, Durkheim attempted to carve out a distinct subject matter for sociology, one which could not be reduced to the psychological or biological; and (3) by maintaining the view that "social facts may be regarded as things" which can be studied as natural objects, Durkheim did much to create a positivist sociology—one which, like the natural sciences, is based on reason *and* observation and on the systematic collection of data. Durkheim, then, has had a greater influence on the direction of sociology than any social thinker other than Karl Marx.

Although most people know at least something of Karl Marx because of his contributions to political ideology and his role in the development of communism, he also has a very important place in the development of sociology. Marx was born in Germany in 1818. There, he studied philosophy and journalism and later, in Paris and Brussels, economics. He did his most important writing in London where he moved to escape hostility aroused by his political views and activities. Like Durkheim, Marx was attempting to understand the nature, the workings, the human implications of the industrial revolution and the rise of capitalism. At the core of his theory is the idea that the economic base of a society, the mode of production, determines the "social, political and spiritual processes of life." In other words, the way people earn their living profoundly affects how they think, how they relate to others, the very shape of the society and its culture. Although influenced by Georg Hegel, an idealist German philosopher, Marx was not an idealist but a materialist. This is caught in his famous phrase, "it is not the consciousness of men that determines their existence, but, on the contrary, their social existence determines their consciousness" (Feuer, 1959:43). That is, he did not see ideas or values as the moving force in history, but rather what men did, particularly in the production of material goods, determined all else.

What men do, their production activity, determines their attitudes. Thus, workers are different from owners. According to Marx, the very fact that some men own wealth and capital, the means of production, "forces" them to think in certain ways, to hold the world views which uphold the existing order, be it feudalism or capitalism. Moreover, they will attempt to impose these world views on others and make them the only conceivable reality. This is possible because those who possess the wealth of a society also possess control of the major agencies of socialization—the schools, the media, the church. Whereas Durkheim emphasized the positive contributions of religion in creating social solidarity and social integration, Marx saw religion as ideological, an "opiate" which not only blinded people to the real nature of their condition, but which also inhibited them from trying to change their miserable situation.[4] Either it was God's will that some should be poor and oppressed or one must endure privation now in order to find happiness in the next world.

For Marx, social history is the history of class struggle. He defines classes as those who share the same position in the production process. In capitalist societies, this means owners and workers, the *bourgeoisie* and the *proletariat.* Marx believed that class conflict existed in all spheres of society and that this conflict would lead to the inevitable decline of capitalist economy; the conflict would lead to greater class awareness, class consciousness and ultimately revolution. Marx's theory of social change was evolutionary. Society changes as the means of production change and these changes occur through progressive stages, the final stage being communism in which there is no individual ownership; private property would be abolished. With no more property distinctions, there would no longer be class distinctions and therefore no more class conflict.

While Marx believed that these changes were inevitable, man was not a totally passive observer. Rather, one could, as did Marx himself, seek through the use of a scientific study of society to understand how societies are organized and, most important, how they change. In this way, Marx hoped the social scientist could, perhaps, speed up evolution or at least act as a "midwife" to social change, make smoother the transitions which, like birth, are inevitable.

In Chapters VII and VIII we will have more to say about Marx; why, for instance, his exact predictions about the fall of capitalism have not been fulfilled. Nevertheless, his emphasis on how a society makes its living, its economic institutions, and how economy is related to other aspects of society has been highly influential. Nor was Marx a mere idealogue. In his concern with the careful gathering of empirical data to study if and how the mode of production in a society was related to the organization of that society, he too contributed to the development of positivist sociology.

Herbert Spencer (1820-1903) was born in Derby, England, where he was educated primarily in mathematics and the physical sciences. He had been a practising engineer before turning to sociology. His ideas were strongly influenced by the natural sciences and Darwin's theory of biological evolution. To simplify somewhat, Spencer held that societies were like biological organisms which would evolve naturally from simple to more complex and that this natural evolution should be allowed to proceed without interference from government or even well-meaning sociologists (like Comte, for example). He searched historical and anthropological data for evidence to support his theory and to encourage his *laissez-faire* ideology. Today, his ideas are seen largely as an ideology, as a way of justifying the *status quo* and particularly *laissez-faire* capitalism. Nevertheless, for a time his ideas received wide currency in Great Britain and the United States and were adopted by a number of American sociologists, among them Albion Small and William Graham Sumner. These two men brought to America, respectively, the first course in and the first department of sociology.

By the turn of the century Germany had produced a number of social thinkers who shared a concern with liberalizing German society while at the same time rejecting orthodox Marxism. The most influential of these was Max Weber (1864-1920). Like the others we have discussed, Weber was concerned with applying scientific methods. In this context, he argued for the development of sociology as a *value-free* discipline. By this Weber meant that while sociologists and historians must study people's values and how these values influence their behaviour, they cannot judge these values and decide whether they are true or not. Certainly, the sociologist has values to which he may be strongly committed. This was certainly true of Weber himself. And, these values will no doubt direct the sociologist to ask certain kinds of questions of the social world; the sociologist's values will usually define his area of investigation. However, the sociologist's analysis must adhere to the value-neutral rules of the scientific method.

Unlike the other social figures we have discussed, Weber gave a central place to empathy, intuition and individual motives. According to Weber, in order to understand patterns of behaviour, sociologists must first gain a subjective understanding, an understanding of how people themselves view their own behaviour. This kind of understanding, what Weber called *verstehen* (literally, "understanding") and what later sociologists call *taking the role of the other*, cannot be achieved through observation alone. Somehow the sociologist must imaginatively get into the heads of the people he is studying to see the world through their eyes. But *verstehen* means more than this. In order to build general laws, the sociologist must proceed to put this concrete understanding into the larger social context. Subjective understanding is not enough; sociologists must also gain causal understanding, an understanding of the causes of patterns of behaviour, causes which are outside and beyond the individuals themselves. So, while Weber emphasized individual motives, he shared with Durkheim and Marx the belief that these motives were socially derived.

Weber countered Marxian theory not by opposing it, but by modifying it. With his analysis of historical and comparative data, Weber tried to show that religious or cultural ideas are not simply the result of, or dependent upon, economic factors. He argued, instead, that "ideas become effective forces in history" (Weber, 1958:90). His theory about the rise of capitalism in Europe illustrates nicely this notion. Earlier, Marx had argued that capitalism emerged from technological developments of the industrial revolution and from the wealth which early expeditions to the New World brought back to Europe—from materialistic forces. Weber maintained that while such materialistic factors were no doubt important and were *necessary* conditions for the rise of capitalism, they were not *sufficient* explanations; we also need to take into account ideas and beliefs which make capitalism possible. He tried to show, for example, that there was a "reciprocal causality" between the economic system of capitalism and the ideas of Calvinism.

According to Weber, the "spirit" of capitalism was a combination of the values of hard work, thrift, asceticism and the willingness to pour profits into new investments and expansion. He went on to argue that the roots of this "spirit" could be found in Puritan Protestant sects of which Calvinism was the prime example. He demonstrated that modern capitalism first arose where these sects were strongest and that in other societies which he studied—ancient Judaism, China and India—modern capitalism did not arise because these values were absent. In his analysis, he rejected what had been taken for granted among most economists, that economic behaviour was governed by purely rational motives. The capitalist activities of Protestants were supposedly motivated by a sense of religious duty and by anxiety over eternal salvation.

> *In this belief system human activity "only has meaning in relation to God's purposes," yet these purposes cannot be comprehended by humans without His having revealed them, and He may choose not to do so! God chooses only a few people for eternal grace, and the choice has already been made, such that one cannot affect it, nor is there even any way of discovering whether one is in fact among the chosen! (Archibald, 1978:69-70).*

Thus, the member of the Protestant sect is left to his own resources to face his destiny, a lonely and unenviable position. And, according to Weber, his way of coping with his position was a constant attempt to prove to himself and others, through worldly success, that he was among the chosen, hence, the relationship between the spirit of capitalism and the Protestant ethic.

Weber was one of the most complex and far-ranging of the early sociologists. Throughout this text you will encounter his theories of, for example, power and stratification and bureaucracy. For now it is enough to say that Weber's emphasis on historical and comparative analysis and on *verstehen*, that is, understanding people's actions through the meanings they attach to their own and others' behaviour, remain important concerns in the discipline.

Sociology in America in the nineteenth and early twentieth centuries was far less rigidly positivistic. For example, Charles Horton Cooley (1864-1929) developed the notion of *sympathetic introspection*, putting oneself in another's position, as a technique for doing sociology. W. I. Thomas (1863-1947) emphasized the importance of people's *definitions of the situation* in determining their behaviour. In the words of Pirandello, "right you are, if you think you are"; people act on the basis of what they believe to be real. Thomas also helped develop the technique of participant observation whereby the sociologist learns about a group by observing it and by actually participating in its life. George Herbert Mead (1863-1931) developed the notion of *role-taking* to describe the *social act*, a process in which two or more people take one another into account, imagine one another's intentions and thus guide their own behaviour. All three men contributed to the development of the perspective of symbolic interactionism which we will discuss shortly.

Such a brief treatment of the development of sociology necessarily means a number of important theorists have been left out; their names will appear throughout the book in the areas of their special interest. Nor have we described the early development of Canadian sociology. As one would expect, Canadian sociology has followed the direction set by the discipline in America. Nevertheless, as we shall discuss in Chapter VII, there have been both early and recent attempts to develop a distinctive Canadian sociology. But even this brief discussion should illustrate that sociology has its roots in varied and conflicting sources. Each of these theorists is read today because he has tackled issues which transcend his own particular time and place. These are the issues of contemporary sociology. Recent sociology has, if anything, become even more diverse in the variety of perspectives offered. There is no one sociology.

CONTEMPORARY APPROACHES

Some writers have argued that the number of different and competing ways of doing sociology reflects the discipline's lack of a single unifying *paradigm* or strategy (Kuhn, 1962). Sociology does lack the kind of paradigm taken for granted in the natural and physical sciences which can rely on the time-honoured techniques of the laboratory. Sociologists must rely more heavily on *perspectives*, theoretical models of the world which guide their research activity, observations and analysis. As there are no "free-floating" intellectuals, the perspective the sociologist adopts, and his approach, will reflect his own interests, the groups in which he is or has been a member, his own personal and emotional needs. Nor are these approaches or perspectives subject to proof in the way that sociological theories must be. Perspectives can only be evaluated in terms of how useful they are in producing good social theory.

In any case, despite the diversity in sociology, about 90% of American sociologists have adopted, at least in part, what has been for years the dominant perspective in sociology: structural-functional analysis (Gouldner, 1970). Although not to the same extent, the influence of this perspective has been felt in Canada as well. In

Chapter IX, for example, we describe John Porter's (1965) functional approach to the role of educational institutions in Canada. The influence of this approach is also apparent in Rex Lucas' (1971) analysis of one-industry communities. In fact, whatever their approach, most Canadian sociologists have had to come to grips with structural-functionalism, and particularly its foremost American spokesman, Talcott Parsons.

When, for example, Emile Durkheim described how religion can serve to help integrate society, his approach was functionalist. His primary concern was how various aspects of society helped to hold that society together. This is the essence of functional analysis. Functionalists look at structured or patterned aspects of societies as necessary parts of a social system; they ask how a change in one part, for example, education, influences other parts, for example, social stratification, and how such changes influence the social system as a whole, for example, society. Their emphasis is on how each part contributes to the adjustment of the social system or its subsystems. We can, perhaps, make this clearer by analogy. Think, for instance, about a car engine taken apart and strewn randomly about a garage floor. We can study each of the parts, carburetor, heads, valves, pistons, etc., separately. We can even try to classify the parts, impose some sort of "taxonomic order" to these bits of metal. We may also ask what each part does. But, we may also want to understand the carburetor, not as a thing, but as a part having an integral function in relation to other parts (the fuel pump, the ignition system and so on) and as part of the total engine *as a system*. In short, we may be less interested in the actual components, more in what goes on between them as they contribute to the thing called an engine. Of course, much the same is true for the "parts"—the institutions—of society.

The particular feature of functionalism, then, is that it directs us to think about a total system and to view aspects of that system in relationship to the system. As the engine analogy suggests, the whole is greater than the sum of its parts. Put the parts together in the proper way and we have an entity—an engine—which is something more than any one of the parts—it is a system of interactions, interrelationships and, from a functionalist perspective, so is society. Clearly, when we are dealing with complex societies it is difficult, except in the most general way, to talk about the whole thing at once. The result is that most sociologists most of the time are concentrating on understanding one aspect of the society. Using our analogy (for the last time), some mechanics become carburetor specialists or experts on ignition systems. But, it is still necessary for them to think of these as part of the engine system and affected by other parts of that system. To lose track of this is to engage in what C. Wright Mills (1959) called "abstracted empiricism"—research carried out without a guiding theory. For example, as we shall see in Chapter IX, such has often been the case for the sociology of education.

According to Talcott Parsons (1951), every social system has certain needs which must be met. He describes these in terms of four general problems every system must solve:

Adaptation: All systems must develop ways to handle and adjust to circumstances that bring about change.

Goal Attainment: All systems must set goals for their members, provide means for achieving these goals and provide rewards to motivate the members to strive for these goals.

Integration: All systems must develop ways to insure harmony among the parts of a system.

Pattern Maintenance and Tension Management: All systems must have ways of transmitting established patterns of behaviour and ways of reducing strains in the system.

Parsons, then, proceeds to look at the parts of the system in terms of how they contribute to the fulfillment of one or another of these needs. We can see, for example, how the family contributes to pattern maintenance and tension management. The school, too, contributes to pattern maintenance and, to the extent that it is able to "cool out" failures, to tension management.

The way in which Parsons poses these problems is to put them at a very general and abstract level. He explicitly means them to be functional problems which all societies, groups, personalities, even organisms must solve if they are to survive in their environment. Robert K. Merton (1968), a contemporary of Parsons, has tried to develop a paradigm—a recipe—by which the functionalist perspective can be used to analyse concrete social phenomena such as social mobility, deviance, role behaviour, the nature of groups, prejudice and so on. He distinguishes among *functions*, which contribute to the adaptation of the systems, *nonfunctions*, which have no appreciable effect on the system, and *dysfunctions*, which contribute to the disintegration of the system. Because of their concern with what holds society together, most functionalists have given little attention to dysfunctions, nor, of course, are nonfunctions of much interest to them. Functional analysis, then, is generally the analysis of "positive" consequences. Merton also distinguishes between *manifest* and *latent* functions. Manifest functions are those consequences which are intended and recognized by the people being studied; latent functions are those consequences which are unintended and/or unrecognized by them. Not surprisingly, most functionalists concentrate on latent functions, those functions which people do not already know about.

One of the most interesting examples of functional analysis is Herbert Gans' (1972) treatment of poverty in America. It is particularly interesting because it is a work of irony; it follows the paradigm and yet at the same time manages to convey some of its deficiencies. The theme of his study is that poverty performs important functions for society and various groups within society; that is why it persists. For example, poverty ensures that the dirty work will get done. Who else but the poor would take on those jobs that most of us find disgusting or demeaning? The poor provide a market for inferior or unwanted goods and services—day-old bread, second-hand clothing, run-down housing, inept lawyers and doctors. The poor provide the rest of us with feelings of superiority, perhaps charity, and the welcome notion that we do not have it so bad, things could be worse. Poverty provides a whole range of occupations—social work, philanthropy and so on—which could not otherwise exist as they do. Poverty perhaps helps motivate the rest of us to try to strive for conventional goals as the poor are so often held up as examples of what happens to people who are lazy or otherwise inferior. These few examples should illustrate Gans' intent. Unquestionably, poverty is manifestly dysfunctional for the poor and, as we discuss in Chapter VII, for society as a whole in many ways. However, when trying to assess the *net balance of consequences*, we must ask, "functional for whom?" What is functional for some is dysfunctional for others. This may lead to conflict, and the most powerful group will prevail. But functionalists tend to emphasize, perhaps overemphasize, consensus and integration and to ignore conflict and power.

There has been a good deal of evidence recently of dissatisfaction with the traditionally dominant perspectives, particularly structural-functionalism, in sociology. Wilson (1970) writes of a *new* paradigm; Dawe (1970) speaks of "two sociologies." Reflexive sociology, phenomenological sociology, action sociology, for example, represent attempts to develop alternatives to the structural-functionalist perspective. At the same time, events of the last decade have again dramatized the question of how to treat values in sociological theory and research. In the United States, images of unrest and conflict have long since replaced the more benign and complacent views possible before the experience of the 1960s. Conceptions of the role of America abroad have also undergone a massive redefinition, bolstered, no doubt, by the emergence of Third World political and economic thought and action. Within Canada, too, this perspective can no longer cope with issues of rising national consciousness, the facts of American cultural and economic imperialism, the progressive alienation of Quebec, the dialectic of hinterland and metropolis, the persistence of inequality. Obviously, the functionalists' stress on value-consensus is well placed. How could a society exist without substantial agreement about what ends are desirable and important? But whose values? Who has the power to enforce their definitions on others? Are dissidents simply to be seen as deviants? Conflict theory, which has often arisen in opposition to functionalism, deals with many of these neglected issues.

Dennis Wrong (1961) has, in particular, criticized the functionalist's view of motivation. He argues that functionalists have assumed an "oversocialized" model of man.[5] For Durkheim, as you will recall, society constrained man and kept him in check. With societal breakdown, man became lost and perhaps suicidal. For functionalists, society's control is even more potent. Functionalists not only draw an image of man constrained by the institutions of society, they have also poured society and all its behavioural requirements into man's head. We, each of us, according to this view, "carry society around in our heads." We are all conformists and, in that functionalists emphasize value-consensus, we all conform pretty much to the same rules, and we conform because we have learned to want to. Ralf Dahrendorf (1958) argues that the functionalists' emphasis on harmony and consensus treats society as though it were a Utopia, free of conflict and force or coercion. He argues for a more balanced picture which recognizes that societies must have some stability, consensus and order if people are to live together, but recognizes as well that conflict is everywhere in society and that people do not always conform because they want to, but are sometimes forced to conform.

Following and modifying the works of Karl Marx, Dahrendorf views conflict as a natural part of any society, as a natural response to coercion and as an important mechanism of social change. While functionalism emphasizes *legitimate authority* to which people give their willing allegiance and obedience, the conflict approach emphasizes *power*, the ability of some groups to make others do their bidding. Society is divided by the different interests of the different groups or classes within it; it is held together by the coercion of the powerless by the powerful. The powerful have a *vested interest* in maintaining their power; the powerless have a vested interest in gaining power. From this perspective, conflict is not surprising. Rather, it is the absence of conflict that would be surprising and require explanation. The conflict approach, then, can be used to examine those situations in which some group challenges established authority (see Chapter XI) or those situations in which the powerful group controls or constrains the others.[6] The empirical work may range from studies of collective violence or the rise of social movements to the study of the manipulative uses of the mass media or the conservative influence of the schools.

Structural-functionalists claim that theirs is a value-neutral perspective, that it could be used for conservative or radical ends. We believe that it has an inevitable conservative bias. Its very language directs us to some issues and away from others, to legitimate authority and away from power and force, to consensus and away from conflict. Conflict theory, perhaps because it has so often arisen in opposition to functionalism, lays fewer claims to value-neutrality. Its concern has been much more explicitly with vested interests and the processes by which these are perpetuated and protected. It has, therefore, been less reluctant to advocate change *of* systems as compared to change *within* systems and, in effect, to put its values on the line. However, in its analysis of power structures and conflicting interests, it has, like functionalism, tended to ignore people's everyday activities, to ignore that society is built up by the meaningful activities of people. These are the issues addressed by the perspective of symbolic interactionism.

Symbolic interactionism is very much the product of the University of Chicago, particularly through the work of George Herbert Mead and his students, among them Herbert Blumer. Because many of Canada's early sociologists were trained at the University of Chicago, it has had a powerful influence on the discipline here. Central to this perspective is the theory of the development of self (see Chapter V). The child becomes human and is socialized by interacting with other humans. The individual learns and internalizes the perspectives of others, including how he imagines they see him. The perspectives of others are incorporated into the child's self and their view of him into his self-concept. Social interaction is possible because of shared symbols; because we can communicate shared meanings through language, we are able imaginatively to take another person's position, take his role and view ourselves as this other person views us.

When people interact, each tries to understand the other's perspective. Each tries to "read" the gestures, both verbal and non-verbal, of the other to try to figure out what he is thinking and what his intentions are. People, then, do not simply react to gestures, they interpret them. This interpretation process, thinking, occurs through an internal conversation, a conversation the individual has with himself based on his reservoir of past experience; he points out certain things to himself as significant. He responds, then, not to the objective features of the situation, but to his own interpretations, his *definition of the situation*. Interaction is a process of negotiation as the interactants try to define the situation, decide which rules or norms apply to such a situation and constantly adapt to and modify one another's behaviour. Symbolic interactionists have made important contributions to our understanding of the fluid and meaningful nature of interaction. People do not react to stimuli in some automatic robot-like fashion; they attach meanings to situations and act on the basis of those meanings.

There are many examples of symbolic interactionist studies in Canada, particularly in the area of deviance.[7] Perhaps the most fascinating example, however, is Rex Lucas' (1969) study of the behaviour of coal miners during a mine disaster. Lucas was part of a team which included psychiatrists and psychologists who went to a Canadian community after it had suffered a major mine disaster. The team wished to study responses to disaster. As part of the research design, miners who had been rescued were interviewed and were asked to reconstruct as faithfully as possible what had happened while they were trapped. They had been trapped in two separate groups: six men had been trapped for over eight days and 12 men for over six. Lucas shows how both groups behaved differently. In the group of six, there was virtually no way to escape close observation by others. There was high *visibility* in this group. The men in this group were concerned about how such expressive behaviour as crying, praying and singing might affect them and the group as a whole. They were worried, for example, that crying might be contagious, that if someone started crying they might join him and such behaviour would threaten their self-concept. Lucas shows how the men tried to control one another's behaviour and how they tried to exert self-control. In the group of 12, where visibility was not so high, there was more tolerance for expressive behaviour.

Lucas also shows how the behaviour of

all the miners changed as their definitions of the situation changed. For the first three days, the miners believed that their predicament was only temporary. All their activity was based on their belief that there was a way out, that they would soon be rescued. After about three days, their definitions changed and so did their behaviour. No longer convinced that they would be saved, their concern became survival. The objective situation had not changed, only their definitions of the situation.

In perhaps the most intriguing part of the book, Lucas describes how the miners came to drink their own urine. They had no water left and had exhausted all alternatives. One miner, in a joking and tentative manner, offered the suggestion that perhaps they would have to drink their own urine. Gradually the miners worked out new definitions of urine drinking, that others had done it or worse in similar situations, that anyone would do it, that they were "forced" to do it if they were to survive and, finally, that it was quite a natural thing to do in the circumstances. Even after the group had redefined urine drinking, each miner had to convince himself, through an internal conversation, that it was an acceptable thing to do. Finally, all the miners did drink their urine, acting on the basis of their definition of the situation. In all, Lucas provides us with an excellent example of how symbolic interactionism can provide rich insights into human behaviour.[8] Nor does Lucas succumb to some of the pitfalls of symbolic interactionism. Lucas begins his study with an account of the context of the interaction he studied, the community, its structure and culture. Unfortunately, most symbolic interactionists tend to ignore these larger issues. Too often they fail to relate the interaction to its social context. As well, like functionalism, symbolic interactionism is unable to account for power except through a similar assumption of value and norm consensus.

Clearly, sociologists do many different kinds of studies in many different ways and for different purposes. However, it seems that many people, not directly exposed to the discipline, have developed a narrow, one-dimensional image of what sociologists do.

CONTEMPORARY SOCIOLOGY: POPULAR IMAGES

About 15 years ago, Peter Berger (1963) wrote that sociology had not yet permeated the public consciousness. There were, he regretted, no jokes about sociologists. People did not know enough about sociologists even to joke about them. All this has changed. If the jokes and barbs on public affairs shows, situation comedies and in the popular press are any indication, sociology is coming of age. If this is true, it means that as you read this book you carry certain images, probably stereotypical images, of what sociologists do and how they do it. As these images are probably partly wrong or at least distortions, it is best to deal with them swiftly and firmly. It should be useful to examine, in this regard, Robert Merton's (1961) defence of sociology in the face of a critical article published in the *New York Times*. Merton begins his counterattack:

> *Once again the season of the anti-sociologist is upon us. The academic year has ended and professors are ready to turn from talking to writing. A self-selected few will dust off and publish yet again the litany that fiercely imprecates sociology and all its works. This year, the avowed conservative professor of political science, Russell Kirk, got in first. His version will serve to exhibit the curious admixture of illogic and sentiment that makes up the creed and canons of anti-sociology (1961:14).*

Just what are the canons of the anti-sociologists? Most people seem to view sociologists as almost solely manipulators of statistics, "as number crunchers." And, along with Kirk (1961), many seem to feel that the use of statistics is somehow inappropriate in the study of human behaviour, that statistics miss what is important about people's behaviour, that "no good can come of it." First of all, sociology has many varied research techniques, not all of them statistical. Indeed, many sociologists eschew statistical analysis, or at least avoid it. Sociology has its humanists and artists and many view sociology, ideally, as some combination of art and science. Nevertheless, some social statistics are likely to be found in almost any substantial piece of sociology, nor is this altogether a bad idea. Merton points out, for example, that many an amateur sociologist has tried to account for the increased rates of mental illness in North America. However, because of the careful statistical analysis carried out by some professional sociologists, we now know that the rates of mental illness are probably no higher today than they have been for the last hundred years. In other words, our amateur sociologist might well be explaining something that does not even exist. Now, this is not to say that some sociologists do not suffer from "quantophrenia," a slavish devotion to statistics. Some sociologists may well be so preoccupied with research techniques that they lose sight of the substance of sociology. And certainly there are a number of important sociological questions which do not lend themselves to statistical analysis. A sociology based purely on statistical analysis would indeed be sterile, but for the most part this is not the direction of sociology. As sociologists have at their disposal more sophisticated statistical techniques, *in conjunction with other methods*, they are more able to assemble systematic data for analysis.

Another common image of the sociologist views him as a jargon monger who invents unnecessary, usually ugly, words to complicate, mystify and impress. Sociologists do have a technical language. Sociology provides a way of viewing the social world that is different from other social sciences and different from how we view the world in everyday life. It "sees" different things and it must sometimes invent words to capture what it sees. As well, as with any discipline, sociology requires a technical language to facilitate precise communication, so that when several sociologists use the same words, we can trust that they mean more or less the same things. Again, however, the accusation has some merit. No doubt some sociology, perhaps much sociology, is jargon-filled and this can become a problem when some versions of sociology become incomprehensible even to other sociologists. In this text, we try to avoid jargon and technical language as much as possible. However, one must distinguish between jargon and technical language, and to learn a discipline one must learn its language.

What seems to upset the critics of sociology most, however, is their belief that sociology is attempting the impossible in trying to find regularities or uniformities in human behaviour, and that what they are doing is dangerous in that it puts people "in boxes," dehumanizes them. Sociological knowledge, the argument goes, is dangerous to society because it is the resource "through which men can be molded to fit a new and obnoxious social order" (Merton, 1974:15). There is an obvious inconsistency here. If it were true that sociology was destined to fail in its search for patterns or uniformities in human behaviour, it is difficult to see how it could be a danger to anyone. Sociology, as a relatively young discipline, has yet a long way to go and is still not producing the kind of knowledge easily converted into social policy (Birnbaum, 1971). Nevertheless, sociology has discovered a good deal which, as you will see, has not yet found its way into the public domain.

This brings us to a related accusation, only implicit in the debate between Kirk and Merton, that the findings of sociologists are trivial, that sociologists spend thousands of dollars to find out what everyone already knows or what journalists and film-makers seem able to find out more effectively and at much less cost. Part of the reason for this accusation rests in the fact that, as we have said, there seems to be an unfortunately long filtering process before sociological findings reach the public. In fact, however, sociologists are more likely to upset rather than to confirm popular or common sense notions. Peter Berger (1963) calls this the "debunking theme" in sociology. Many undergraduate students find sociology helpful not only in understanding society and others, but in understanding themselves. At the same time, many find that sociology can be upsetting as one after another of their beliefs is challenged or at least held up for investigation. Do the poor commit the bulk of crimes? How much upward mobility is there in Canada? Are Canadians witnessing the breakdown of the family? You may find that what you "know" about these things and the answers you find in this text are different.

In the same vein, basic to sociology is the notion of unintended consequences, that as people engage in social relationships their behaviour produces consequences which were not the intent of those relationships. For example, intensified punishment of criminals may produce more crime rather than inhibit it. Organizations which attempt to bring back into line such deviants as drug addicts, alcoholics and fat people may often make it harder for these deviants ever to think of themselves as normal. Behaviour that seems sensible in the short run may prove disastrous in the long run. Growing recognition of the importance of these unintended consequences has led to a demand for the services of sociologists in such fields as law, social work, medicine, education, city planning, business, labour, to name a few.

This is not to say that journalists and artists do not contribute valuable insights about human behaviour and society. On the contrary, journalistic writers and "pop sociologists" such as Hunter Thompson, Morton Hunt, Tom Wolfe, Philip Slater, Alvin Toffler and, of course, Vance Packard have the knack of zeroing in on what are the important social issues to most people in their society. Indeed, they reach a far wider audience than do "academic sociologists" and therefore likely have much greater impact. As well, because they are less constrained by the "rules of the sociological method," their analyses of social problems and social institutions are often more direct and hard hitting than conventional sociology. Jessica Mitford's (1977) analysis of American "death institutions" and in particular the undertaking industry is one of the most interesting and penetrating studies available on the topic. And, unquestionably, the artist provides countless insights for the sociologist.

However, it is important to keep in mind the distinction between these kinds of work and conventional sociology and to understand the distinctive role of sociological research. First, it is more difficult to replicate journalistic and artistic accounts and to tell what information was left out. Good sociological research, like good science generally, points out the "deviant" cases and indicates what hypotheses and hunches were not confirmed. Ideally, good sociological research involves a search for negative cases which the journalist or artist may ignore because they spoil the thrust of the argument.

Second, as we shall explore more fully in the next few chapters, journalists and artists, like the public generally, may not share the sociological emphasis on social structure—the larger context which frames our actions. Hence, as will become evident, things which seem personally alarming, such as unemployment of university graduates, may also be a social problem, the result of structural change in Canadian society.

SOURCES OF CONTROVERSY

We have described the controversies that rage about sociology and within sociology. Alex Inkeles (1964) suggests that a number of sociologists are concerned and dismayed about the amount of disagreement within the field. We have already suggested that these controversies might better be viewed positively, as necessary for the advancement of any science. In the following pages we shall review the major sources of controversy in sociology.[9] As you have seen, sociology has its roots in conflicting assumptions about human nature, a conflict which is still apparent in the diverse contemporary approaches. Because these assumptions about man which underlie current perspectives cannot be empirically tested, they must inevitably lead sociologists into ideological debate. There is an obvious temptation to avoid ideological debates and simply to go out into the world and gather data. This is, in essence, the solution offered by a number of sociologists whose primary concern is to produce objective, scientific findings. They have devoted themselves to developing and refining a variety of research techniques which lead to ever greater quantification and more sophisticated data manipulation. In the process, this "abstracted empiricism" (Mills, 1959) has, however, in ostrich-like fashion, evaded confrontation with the major dilemmas facing sociology and society. One cannot deal effectively with the ideological implications of sociological inquiry simply by ignoring them.

Another source of controversy in the field concerns the levels of analysis at which sociologists work. Some adopt a *macro-sociological* perspective, viewing society as a whole or comparing various societies. Some prefer a *micro-sociological* perspective, examining interaction and small-group behaviour. Functionalists and conflict theorists belong in the former group, symbolic interactionists in the latter. Symbolic interactionists are criticized for treating matters which are often trivial and they in turn criticize the others for missing too much and for dealing with questions for which they have no effective research techniques.

C. Wright Mills (1959) offers an alternative which falls in neither camp. He felt that the sociologist must be able to shift back and forth from the individual to the societal level. He must understand the history and structure of the society and the social psychology of the individuals he is studying, and he must be able to link the two. This analytic ability to relate individual problems to public issues Mills referred to as the "sociological imagination." According to Mills, sociology could, by relating the individual and the social, help people to understand their personal problems in social terms. This brings us to another source of controversy in sociology.

Traditionally sociologists have argued that sociology must be undertaken for its own sake. It should produce knowledge which people could use however they saw fit. The sociologist, they argue, should stay out of the question of how this knowledge should be used because concern about the uses of his knowledge might distort his research and analysis. C. Wright Mills and his followers advocated a more humanistic sociology, one which could help make a better society at both the micro and macro levels. He believed that sociology could help people to understand themselves and their problems and thus act as a liberating influence on people in much the same way as art and literature. At the same time, it could provide the scientific basis for societal reform. He argued, in any case, that sociological knowledge *does* have consequences for people and their lives, it does get used, and sociologists had better face up to the reality.

Mills seemed to feel that there was room in sociology for a hard scientific approach and a more humanistic artistic approach. He himself has often been criticized for relying too much on the latter, for relying too much on his insight and imagination. This brings us to the final source of controversy which we shall discuss—differences in methodological orientation.

Positivistic sociologists are still trying to emulate the hard sciences. They have adopted the hypothetico-deductive model employed by Durkheim, whereby hypotheses (tentative generalizations) are deduced from theory and are tested with precise quantifiable data. They are very concerned with precision and are likely to make use of official statistics, large-scale surveys using mailed questionnaires and so on. At the other end of the continuum, we have the more humanistic sociologist who argues that many important social issues do not lend themselves easily to quantification. They make the most of the fact that they live in the social world they are studying; they can empathize, draw on their own experience, to a greater extent than most other scientists can in their respective disciplines. These sociologists use methods such as participant observation, content analysis of documents, and case studies. In a sense, Glaser and Strauss (1967) offer a compromise position. They argue that sociologists have spent too much time testing theories, many of which may be outdated or irrelevant. The generation of new theory is at least as important as the process of verification; some version of the humanistic approach may be most appropriate for generating new theories, while the more positivistic approach may be best suited for verification.

For Glaser and Strauss, new theories are generated through a process of exploration; that is, research is undertaken without specific hypotheses. The positivist insists that his research begin with specific hypotheses; that is, he must deduce from some theory a tentative statement of how two or more concepts will be related (for example, the higher one's educational attainment, the more likely he is to vote in a particular way), and he must provide the operations for measuring these concepts and testing the relationship. Glaser and Strauss feel that the generation of new theory requires that hypotheses and concepts emerge from the research experience itself—the resultant theory they refer to as *grounded theory*, "grounded" in the empirical world. Through a process of constant comparison of different research settings, more general theories can be developed. The process of moving from specific observations to general theory is called *induction* (see Figure I.1). In any case, sociology is probably best viewed as some combination of humanism and positivism.

OUR APPROACH

It should be understandable from the foregoing discussion why some sociologists will switch from one perspective to another, depending on the nature of the question they wish to ask. Obviously, if we were interested in understanding why the trapped miners drank their own urine, we would not adopt a conflict perspective.

Figure I.1
THE SCIENTIFIC METHOD

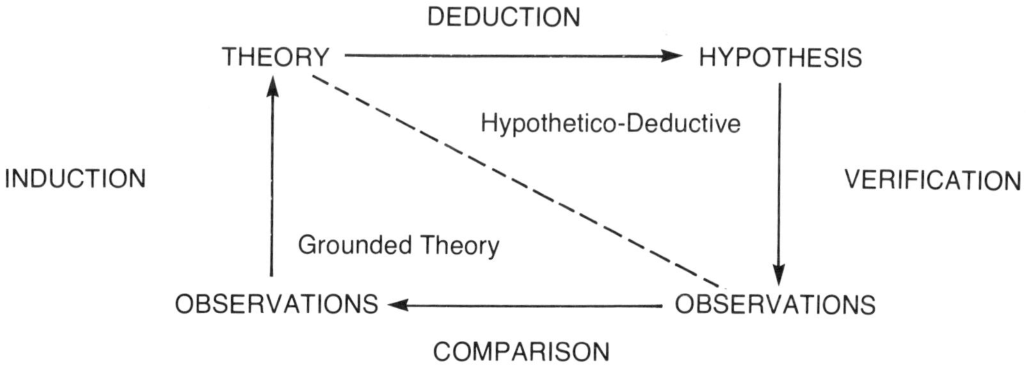

Different questions demand different approaches. Many sociologists use some combination of perspectives. To capture adequately Canadian society, we see no alternative but to adopt a conflict perspective and thereby to focus on power and inequality. But, we also believe in the value of symbolic interactionism to illumine our everyday lives, for most of us, most of the time, our only reality. This perspective, while stressing values and norms, emphasizes their ambiguity. It directs us to consider how norms are emergent from interaction rather than from social institutions, negotiated rather than fixed. Conflict theory and symbolic interaction theory represent for us opposite sides of the central paradox of social life: people are both product and producer of social structure (Berger and Luckmann, 1967). Throughout this book, then, we shall try to examine what people believe about their world and, at the same time, try not to exclude from our analysis what Dahrendorf (1959) calls "imperatively co-ordinated associations." A central theme running throughout this book is inequality, both real and perceived.

While we feel that scientific sociologists are mistaken in their attempts to remain neutral in the face of ideological and value debates, we are unable to condemn scientific sociology out of hand. We believe that the productions of the scientific method are as potentially radical in their implications as they are conservative. In other words, while the questions we ask are ultimately ideological, that is, value-laden, data emerging from the systematic application of the scientific method are not inherently biased one way or the other. The results of the careful use of statistical analyses equally with those of good qualitative analyses are what people make of them; they are as capable of transforming the social structure as they are of upholding the most oppressive forms of social inequality.

The orientation of the authors of this book is both humanistic and radical. We believe that sociology can provide its students with a new way of looking at the world that makes it difficult for them to say, "I have no choice" or "Things couldn't be any other way." Such "bad faith" is replaced by a new awareness of alternatives and possibilities—sociology becomes, in effect, liberating. As well, the analysis of social inequality and power may discourage the personalization or privatization of interests or problems. It is in this sense that we would use the term "false consciousness"—a lack of awareness of collective interests or of the relationship between personal interests and collective interests. Sociology, by linking personal problems and public issues, can provide the privatized student with a public sense. By its very nature, sociology must profoundly change those who become committed to it.

SUGGESTIONS FOR FURTHER READING

For those interested in gaining a fuller appreciation of the development of sociology and its social and philosophical roots, Robert A. Nisbet's *The Sociological Tradition* (1967) provides an excellent introduction. Other useful sources include: Raymond Aaron, *Main Currents in Sociological Thought*, Vols. I & II (1965); Lewis A. Coser, *Masters of Sociological Thought* (1971); Anthony Giddens, *Capitalism and Modern Social Theory* (1971); and Randall Collins and Michael Makowsky, *The Discovery of Society* (1978).

Collins and Makowsky also provide a useful introduction to contemporary perspectives and issues. Somewhat more advanced introductions to contemporary theorizing are: William Skidmore, *Theoretical Thinking in Sociology* (1975); J. H. Turner, *The Structure of Sociological Theory* (1977) and Percy S. Cohen, *Modern Social Theory* (1968). Later on in the course you might also want to read Peter Berger's *Invitation to Sociology* (1963).

To get the flavour of sociology, you

should glance through some of the academic journals. The two major English-Canadian journals are the *Canadian Review of Sociology and Anthropology* and *The Canadian Journal of Sociology*. Most Francophone sociologists publish in *Recherches sociographiques* and *Sociologie et sociétés*. The most important American journals are the *American Sociological Review* and the *American Journal of Sociology*. British sociologists publish in the *British Journal of Sociology; Sociology;* and *The Sociological Review*.

FOOTNOTES

[1]We shall be using "man," "he" and "his" a good deal of the time in this book. At times this is simply to conform to the conventions of English grammar which make "he or she" or "people" rather awkward and cumbersome. At other times we use "man" because women have not entered very much into sociological or social thought. For example, when Hobbes or Rousseau talk about the Nature of "Man" they may be using the word in its generic sense. More likely they were—if the truth were known—not particularly interested in the nature of women, because in terms of social philosophy women were not viewed as very interesting. Unfortunately, this view has, until very recently, persisted in most sociological research: it has been about men, man's work, male aspirations, male social mobility and so on. As Lyn Lofland (1975) has pointed out about community studies, women have been depicted much like servants in a murder story—they pad in and out of the scene (providing services) but are not really part of the plot, not part of the analytical action. Growing recognition of women's work, women's contribution to family and community and women's interests now pervades sociological research and has served to redirect the kinds of questions asked by sociologists. An excellent bibliography of women's studies is in Marylee Stephenson's *Women in Canada* (1977). For more recent material, look through *Atlantis*, a journal edited by women in the Atlantic Region.

[2]For an excellent discussion of Marx's views on alienation, see Archibald (1978).

[3]In a footnote of his own, Durkheim suggests a fourth form of suicide, *fatalistic* suicide, which occurs in situations where the goals are too clear and unchanging.

[4]An excellent summary can be found in Aron (1965). In Chapter III we shall discuss the concept of "ideology" in more detail.

[5]Harold Garfinkel (1967) raises similar issues in his discussion of man as "cultural dope."

[6]Lewis Coser (1956), a functionalist, does examine social conflict, particularly institutionalized social conflict, to show how it can contribute to the integration of a social system. His work serves as a useful reminder of the difficulties in classifying most sociologists in terms of their approach.

[7]See, for example, Vaz (1976) and Haas and Shaffir (1974).

[8]Other approaches which focus on interpersonal relationships (particularly "exchange" and "ethnomethodology") are treated in Chapter V.

[9]See Ritzer's (1972) excellent summary statement, "Sources of Controversy."

doing sociology

CHAPTER II

Perhaps one image of sociology we did not discuss in the first chapter is the sociologist as a poll taker, moving from door to door, clipboard in hand, collecting information about "background characteristics" such as educational attainment, income, marital status and so on, and "attitudes," such as voting preference and views about abortion, as images of Canadian identity. Poll takers, however, may well employ sociologists, but this by no means covers the variety and diversity of research techniques sociologists employ in trying to test their theories or generate new theories.

In Chapter I we talked briefly about the nature of social knowledge. Cooley (1926), many years ago, pointed out that we can't treat social knowledge as identical to physical knowledge. In Cooley's words, "social life is lived chiefly in the imagination." In other words, one cannot learn about the social simply by observing people's behaviour. Somehow we must get access to people's thinking processes, to how they think and feel about what they are doing. According to Cooley, the sociologist is in a uniquely advantageous position: he has access to his own thinking processes, to his own feelings and therefore, through a process of sympathy, can empathize with the people he is studying. For Cooley, then, "objective" research techniques, whereby the sociologist stands back from his subjects, must be complemented by "subjective" research techniques whereby the sociologist becomes involved with his subjects. Cooley was entering into one side of a long-standing debate, one which has continued until the present. This is, essentially, a debate between those who favour objective versus those who favour subjective research techniques. Each "school" has devoted itself to refining more specific techniques within one of those two basic traditions.

Those who favour objective techniques often decry the lack of rigour, precision and representativeness of more subjective—that is, qualitative—studies. "Objective sociologists" are prepared to ignore Cooley's injunction either because they feel people's inner "workings" can never be known with any precision or because they feel that these inner workings are relatively unimportant in determining people's behaviour. They are often prepared to assume that there is a similarity between observer and observed, that their subjects think and feel about a situation pretty much as they think and feel about it.

Objective sociologists have been concerned primarily with developing techniques which could produce reliable and reproducible findings; that is, two researchers using the same technique in the same situation should produce the same data. In this context, we can understand their concern with measurement and quantification. Ideally, they are trying to limit the influence of the sociologist's subjective perceptions, what he thinks he sees. This is not to say that they are ever so naive as to claim that they have achieved this goal; it remains an ideal.

Perhaps the most difficult problem sociologists, and scientists generally, confront is that their mere presence may change the social situation in ways they may never fully fathom. A particularly interesting example is provided by Allan King's documentary film on the family, *A Married Couple*. In this film King secured the permission of a couple to film their daily lives, their interaction together and with their child. King has produced an absorbing, and at the same time perplexing, film. What we see is moving and apparently true to life. But, the audience must inevitably ask, how much is "real," how much is acting for the camera and how much were these lives changed by the presence of the observers? The "married couple" ended up getting a divorce: would they have if the film had never been made? We can only speculate. This is precisely the problem confronted by sociologists doing research: how much of what they observe is "natural" or "true to life" and how much is the consequence of their own research activity.[1]

Unobtrusive Measures

Many objective sociologists have tried to minimize the observer's influence by developing techniques which *cannot* affect the people being studied. Webb and his associates (1966) refer to such techniques as unobtrusive measures. Some of these are rather amusing. For example, Webb suggests that if you want to know something of the lifestyle and status of people in a neighbourhood, you might simply go through people's garbage. In fact, this technique has been used with apparent success by journalists, biographers and, apparently, credit assessors. Or, rather than ask people which exhibit in a museum they like best, measure the wear on floor tiles. Obviously such techniques are limited in how much they can tell us, nor can they always be easily applied. But, a more conventional and frequently used unobtrusive technique is the analysis of historical documents—letters, diaries, newspaper accounts, etc.—often prepared for non-sociological purposes. For example, through the analysis of a variety of historical documents, William Acheson (1972 and 1973) was able to draw a picture of the social backgrounds and value orientations of Canada's industrial elite in the nineteenth century. This historical work has provided the basis for much of the contemporary analysis of the Canadian corporate elite. Also, Harold Innis and S. D. Clark, who, as we shall see, contributed most to the growth of sociology in Canada, made extensive use of historical materials. Similarly, census material, though in some instances initially collected obtrusively, when once collected, can tell us a great deal about the social composition and changes in any population. Clearly, such methods cannot be employed as easily if we wish to know about contemporary behaviour or attitudes in a systematic way.

Survey Research

In the minds of many, sociology is most closely associated with survey research.

Certainly this is a technique heavily used by sociologists. As the name implies, it involves a survey of a relatively large number of people. It makes use of sampling which allows for representativeness of the population being studied. This is because by definition a random sample is one in which everyone in the population has an equal chance or probability of entering into the sample. While we could, in principle, survey the whole population, we have learned, as sampling procedures and statistical techniques improve, that it is unnecessary and inefficient to do so. With careful procedures, we can use a sample to represent the entire population. For example, on the basis of a very small sample of the Canadian population, the Liberal Party decided in June 1978 not to call an election. On the basis of a poll of a carefully selected few, the Liberals felt that they knew the political preferences of the nation and that an election at that time would, at best, result in a minority.

Survey research involves the use of either a questionnaire or an interview schedule. Strictly speaking, questionnaires are research instruments which are self-administered. In doing research on students, for instance, self-administered questionnaires work well because the researcher can hand out the questionnaire during class time and can usually be present to answer any questions which might arise. Obviously, mail questionnaires are also self-administered questionnaires. These are especially likely to be used when the sample of people being studied is far flung geographically or when funds are very limited. Their main advantage is, then, that they provide a relatively cheap and quick method of collecting a good deal of data.

There are, however, several problems. First, response rates to mail questionnaires are often as low as 40% and probably, even with follow-up letters, seldom go much above 70%. Second, questions asked must be highly structured and close-ended; there is little opportunity for exploratory questions or elaborate answers. Finally, the interviewer is not there to evaluate the commitment that the respondent has to the questionnaire as a whole or to answer or elaborate on questions which the respondent has about specific questions and about the goals of the research project. Nor can the researcher "probe," that is, ask follow-up questions about limited or ambiguous answers.

For these reasons, most survey researchers probably prefer to be present, to conduct the interview. But, to do so is also to enter into a role relationship which in turn will influence the nature of the responses. We can expect, for example, that factors such as the age, sex and ethnicity of the interviewer will affect not only the probability of getting the interview but also how people go about answering the questions posed. Like participant-observation, to be discussed later, interviewing as a research technique is much more dependent on the skill of the interviewer and is as much art as it is science. In contrast, self-administered questionnaires are dependent on the skills of the researcher who constructs the research instrument.

Of course, when the project is a large-scale study, one which is based on a large sample and which, therefore, makes considerable use of what Roth (1974) calls "hired hand research," many of these same problems arise. That is, if there are a number of interviewers out in the field or if the field work has simply been contracted out to a survey research firm, the actual researchers may be as remote from the data collection process as if they had sent out a mail questionnaire. Even if they do conduct some of the interviewing themselves,they will still have to pre-test the interview schedule very carefully and eventually create fairly structured and close-ended or pre-coded questions. Not only will this cut down on the amount of coding at the end of the field work, it also helps to reduce some of the variation in interviewing techniques among those hired to carry out the interviews; all can then ask precisely the same question and in most cases code the answer using the pre-established logical or possible answers to the question.

Interviewing as a research technique is not, however, confined to large-scale studies of only random samples of the population. Frequently, the researcher simply has a list of topics which he plans to cover in the interview. The exact wording of the questions is left unspecified, to be put in a way and in an order which seems most "natural" at the time of the interview. They are followed up with other related and unanticipated questions when relevant and interesting. This approach is especially useful for exploratory research and for intensive interviews—what for some reason have come to be called "in-depth" interviews. Though unstructured interviewing is more likely to generate abundant case materials, it is best suited to small-scale studies where there is only one interviewer. As we might expect, because the questions are not set out in a formal manner, such research is hard to replicate.

Ideally, most researchers would like to be able to generalize their findings, to be able to say that their sample is representative of some universe—all secondary school teachers in Manitoba, all teenagers in Canada, all firms with sales under $2.5 million and so forth. Often, however, it is not possible to put together a random sample of the population we wish to study because no one knows its size or the exact location of its members. The most obvious examples come from studies of deviance. For instance, since we don't know the exact size of the homosexual population in Canada, it is impossible to give every homosexual an equal probability of showing up in our sample. This does not coincide with the definition of randomness. Any group we choose, then, is a non-random sample, one which we can never be sure is representative of all homosexuals. In fact, most researchers interested in deviant subcultures have used some variation of the technique called "snowballing" or "chain interviewing." This was partly the method used by Jean Veevers (1973) to interview voluntarily childless couples. The number of voluntarily childless couples in Canada is, of course, unknown. Thus, starting with couples she already knew, she correctly anticipated that they would know other couples who would put her in touch with others. Having made contact with one member of the group under study, the researcher then hopes that sufficient trust will be established so that one member will put him in contact with others, who in turn know still others. Of course, as useful as this technique may be, we must always keep in mind that findings of non-random surveying cannot be generalized beyond the group studied and must always be viewed with caution.[2]

LIMITATIONS OF SURVEY RESEARCH

The sample survey is, then, a very common and reasonably efficient method of collecting information on characteristics and attitudes of the people—the population—we wish to study. One particular advantage of survey research is that by the time the final research instrument is constructed, most things asked of people have become close-ended questions; respondents are given a list of responses and need only choose the one most appropriate to their situation. From there it is a very easy step to put these data onto IBM cards in a form that can be processed by computers. Thus, survey data can easily be summarized, analysed, manipulated and stored in data banks for later use by other researchers.[3] Because of this, however, some have questioned whether, in effect, the tail was beginning to wag the dog; are we perhaps forcing and delimiting our data so that it will fit into our programmes and meet the various assumptions which sophisticated statistical techniques require?

However, the most fundamental criticisms of survey research emerge from the objectivity-subjectivity controversy, from the basic problem raised by Cooley, that social knowledge and physical knowledge are not identical and cannot be studied in the same way. Despite its efficiency, then, survey research has a number of limitations. A major problem is that attitudes and behaviour are not always synonymous. There is, in other words, often a discrepancy between what people say they do, or will do, and what they actually do. For example, when people are asked if they wear seat belts when driving, a large majority say that they do. Yet, in one test (near Chicago), the investigators found that when drivers were stopped at a checkpoint, only about 40% were in fact wearing their belts. Or, when people are asked about neighbouring, many say that they really don't have much to do with their neighbours, that they "don't like to be in each other's pockets." But, observation of the neighbourhood shows that there is a good deal of interaction, that, in fact, people are constantly in and out of each other's houses (Young and Willmot, 1973).

Does this mean that people are lying to the interviewer? Probably not. What is more likely is that people are either talking about what they *think* is the ideal norm, what they wish that they did—smoke or drink less, for instance—or what they think the interviewer thinks is the "correct" or proper answer. For instance, many believe that they ought to use seat belts or that one should respect a neighbour's privacy. We might add, too, that when faced with actual social situations, hypothetical predictions based on ideal norms about how to act in that situation may, for a variety of reasons, go by the board. This is nicely illustrated by studies of prejudice and discrimination. Bartenders who claim that they won't serve a black because it's an all-white bar often do so when confronted with a real-life black customer. It turns out to be easier to do so; it avoids a scene or confrontation. Conversely, many who claim that they are not prejudiced turn out to be so in specific circumstances—deciding whether or not to pick up a hitchhiker or accepting easily that one's own son or daughter is planning a mixed marriage. Coxon and Jones (1978) have suggested that we face very similar problems when we ask people to undertake the very boring job of ranking, in terms of prestige or social standing, upwards of 200 occupations. They speculate that people may "react in one way to an occupational title which is encountered in the middle of a long and rather abstract task, but in quite another way when they meet someone whose job is covered by that same occupational title" (p. 31).

Obviously, there will be many instances where people will simply lie or deny any knowledge of the subject. Door-to-door research will not, for instance, tell us very much about who practises tax evasion or who in the population supplements their income by fencing stolen car parts. Thus, much that is of sociological interest simply cannot be asked in survey research because people have good reasons for denial or concealment. Either the activity is illegal or shameful or people do not have sufficient trust in the interviewer or aren't sure how information on, say, income will be used later. One of the authors of this book (Richardson: 1977) found in doing intensive interviewing of mobile people that once they had accepted the researcher into the home, most of these people were prepared to reveal all sorts of intimate information about themselves, whether it was relevant to mobility or not. But, when these same people were asked even basic information—occupation and residence—about their friends and relatives they became very tense and suspicious. They became even more alarmed and anxious when they were asked whether it would be possible to contact *their* fathers and administer a similar interview to them. Many refused outright. Some said that they would have to think about it but apparently never did. Others who did agree often warned that their fathers were old and crotchety and might not be very good respondents. (In fact this was very seldom the case.)

We do not know the exact reason for this reaction. Perhaps people felt that while *they* had nothing to hide, they were less sure of others and were not about to take the chance of putting a relatively unknown interviewer onto their friends and relatives. Maybe, too, they were concerned about getting caught in an unintentional lie—they feared two versions of the same story. To a considerable extent, an intensive interview is a conversation, in this case one which in effect asked people to tell their life story. When we do this in everyday life, perhaps on a plane trip with a stranger, we do so knowing that our story, how we describe ourselves, will not be checked up on later.

A third limitation on survey research is that the categories, the issues, the concepts which are, in effect, introduced to people we are interviewing may or may not have the same meaning or the same importance to them as they do to the sociologist. This has been especially obvious in studies of deviance. For example, studies of people who apparently engage in homosexual behaviour, who might objectively be categorized as homosexual, often find that they themselves do not so categorize their behaviour. Some deny the label of deviant or disagree that what they do is *really* homosexual activity. Some deny both while a few in effect agree with the objective categories.[4] Studies of social stratification and social mobility have also focused on the problem of whether subjective views about the class structure correspond at all to our objective measures, categories which derive perhaps from Marx.

Another aspect to this is that a good deal of the time people may not be very aware of what they "really" do and don't do and how often. It is not, in some instances, a particular desire to stretch the truth, or to please the interviewer or to talk about what ought to be. It is, rather, a simple question of not knowing. Think, for example, how you would answer questions such as, "How many times have you gone to the store or how many people did you 'interact' with in the past week?" It may be that the best answer people can give to certain kinds of questions may not, in fact, be a very accurate measure of their actual behaviour. Moreover, people may simply not be able to articulate exactly why they do something. During a trip to Greece, for example, one of the authors kept asking Athenians why (given high gas prices, narrow streets etc.) all the taxis were large American or German cars rather than the efficient Fiats of Italy. It appeared that no one had really given it much thought and could only answer that "I guess we like big cars," or, from taxi drivers, "If you don't use a big car, then you don't get any business," which tautologically puts things back at the beginning. More generally, it may be as with riding a bicycle—it is said that if you really think about everything you do, you'll crash to the ground. So, often, it is with social life. Martin (1954), for example, after exploring the relation between subjective and objective determinants of social status and social class, was led to ask whether terms like upper, middle and working class had the same significance for all who used them. Did they, in other words, share substantially the same mental map of the social scene? His conclusion was that there is only limited congruence between objective and subjective classes, a finding also borne out in a famous study by Elizabeth Bott (1971: 159-60). As she concludes:

> *Our data suggest, on the contrary, that people disagree profoundly in their views on class, so much that we sometimes wonder if they were talking about the same society. Our conclusion is that in certain important respects they are not . . . but . . . live in different worlds; they have different jobs, different neighbours and different family trees. Each bases his ideas of class on his own experience, so that it is hardly surprising that each had a different conception of the class structure as a whole.*

Similarly, Richardson questioned whether social mobility means the same thing to most people as it does to sociologists—how closely do personal definitions of mobility correspond to the conventional or objective measures of mobility? For sociologists, social mobility means the movement of people from one social class to another, status mobility as well as economic mobility. However, only a tiny minority of respondents shared this definition. For most, status mobility was either not considered or was viewed as unimportant. Rather, for them, mobility meant economic mobility, a better paying job, a bigger car, a better house and so on.

Related to this is the idea that people may not even have heard or thought about the issues, the categories, the concepts which we introduce in the interview situation. For instance, to ask people their position on the status rights of Indian women assumes not only that they have a position on this issue but also that they even knew this *is* an issue. Similarly, Lorna Marsden (1972) points out that to ask people what ought to be the population policy for Canada assumes far more technical and demographical knowledge than most of us have. In asking people whether they thought they had been socially mobile, it was sometimes difficult to avoid explaining to people what the concept means; many people had never heard of the term, even though objectively they had "experienced" upward or downward mobility (Richardson, 1977). There is, then, even with very careful and intensive "piloting" of our interview schedule and with well-trained interviewers, a real risk that we are going to "educate" our respondents about the very thing we are trying to learn about.

Participant Observation

To overcome some of these problems, many sociologists have advocated some variation of the technique known as *participant observation*. In Becker's (1958: 652) words, "the participant observer gathers data by participating in the daily life of the group or organization he studies either openly in the role of researcher or covertly in some disguised role, observing things that happen, listening to what is said, and questioning people, over some length of time." Participant observation as a research technique has been especially advocated by symbolic interactionists who believe that as researchers we can't remain aloof and act as "objective" observers of human action and behaviour. Rather, it is necessary to enter into "real-life" situations. We must try to catch the process of interpretation through which people construct their actions. We must, in other words, find ways to take the role of those we are studying, see the world from the standpoint of the actor and come to share his definition of the situation (Blumer, 1969). Participant observation seems to provide the most effective technique for fulfilling these objectives.

As Becker's definition suggests, participant observation can, in fact, range along a continuum from complete observation to complete participation (Figure II.1). As this figure shows, the main difference centres around the amount of role involve-

Figure II.1

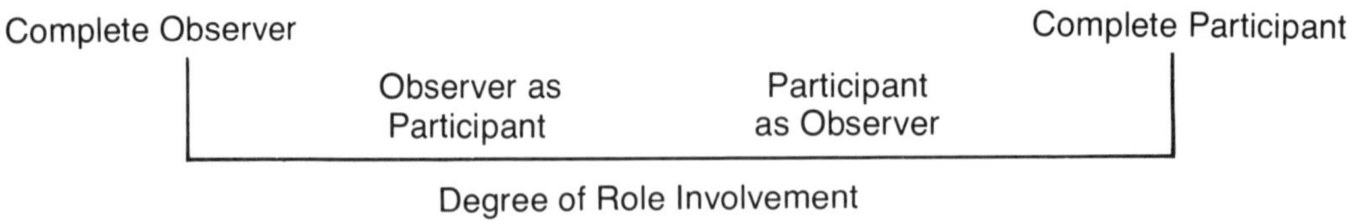

ment which the researcher has in the group he is studying. In most cases, the researcher is faced with the difficult task of managing, simultaneously, two roles, one as a member of the group, one as a scientist observing the group, recording what happens and eventually trying to make systematic sociological sense of his observations and experiences. But, as we move closer towards the complete participant end of the continuum, another element, that of concealment, perhaps "infiltration," is also involved.

We can find in existing sociological research examples of all four of these positions plus some which fall in between. Probably the most extreme example of pure or *complete observation* is work done by social psychologists using two-way mirrors. The hope is that "subjects" will not even be aware that they are, in fact, being observed. These are, of course, laboratory studies. In natural settings, it is seldom possible for the observer to be "invisible." Perhaps one of the best known studies very near the "complete observer" end of the continuum is one usually referred to as the "Bank Wiring Room." This research was part of the Hawthorne studies carried out by Roesthlisberger and Dickson in the 1930s. A detailed analysis of this study was later incorporated into George Homans' (1950) *The Human Group*.

Fourteen men were taken out of a larger department and put in a room by themselves. These men assembled, soldered and inspected banks of terminals used in telephone exchanges. An observer was placed in the back corner of the room as "a disinterested spectator." In an attempt to minimize his effect on the group, he was given a number of rules to follow. While he should remain on friendly terms with the men and not set himself apart from the group, he was not to give any orders, enter into any arguments, thrust himself into or infiltrate any conversations or seem eager or anxious to hear and see what the men said and did. Finally, he was not to violate any confidence or give any information to supervisors and managers. In short, he was to be as unobtrusive as a piece of furniture. Was he successful in this "role"? Homans concluded that he was, that he had very little effect on the behaviour of the group. But, in the final analysis we are in the same position as in considering Alan King's documentary film of a family. We have no way of knowing whether the same people not under observation would have behaved the same or differently.

In most situations even if one wanted to do so, it is extremely difficult to remain in the "role" of observer. In fact, as Blumer (1969) suggests, it is incorrect to do so since all the researcher ends up doing is practising "the worst kind of subjectivism." That is, the observer fills in the process of interpretation with his own surmises, his own interpretations, rather than trying to catch that process as it is experienced by the members of the group. Complete observation, then, suffers from many of the same limitations as does survey research: the aloof and "objective" researcher can never be sure that what he "sees" is what the people he is studying "see," that the meaning he gives to basic concepts is the meaning others give to these same concepts.

Anthropologists long ago abandoned the nineteenth century pretence that useful research could be done by remaining solely in the role of observer. Undoubtedly, one of the most sensitive and insightful accounts of the dilemmas and uncertainties associated with the position of *observer as participant* is Elenore Bowen's (1954) anthropological novel, *Return to Laughter*. As she shows, learning the language, crucial and difficult as this is, represents only the first step. She also had to work out a role acceptable to the community or tribe but which also allowed her to carry on as a scientist. She had to somehow maintain the thin balance between impartiality, avoiding taking sides in quarrels, and the need to become on intimate terms with people, to be part of the action.

She had to reconcile her human inclination to give medical aid when possible with the scientific need to get on with her research. Many of these same dilemmas are also described in William Whyte's classic sociological study of a Boston slum, *Street Corner Society* (1955). Like Bowen, he, too, found it difficult not to become "over-involved," to decide when and when not to interfere, and whether or not to lend money to members of the gang. Whyte's study also shows how crucial it is for the researcher to have the cooperation of at least one member of the group or community. In Whyte's case, "Doc," leader of the "Norton Street gang," was not only a key informant, he also vouched for Whyte to the community, that as Doc's friend he could be trusted.

Some of the best research in the participant-observation tradition has come from researchers who first of all were participants, active members in the group, and who then decided that the group or community should also be studied systematically. They tapped their own predicament, their own experience of the human condition. The obvious advantage of this *participant as observer* approach is that the researcher already has a vested interest in the group or is at least interested in the group's activity. Ned Polsky (1969) became interested in the subculture of poolrooms and the role of hustlers because from the age of 13 onwards he frequented poolrooms and, as an adult, played an average of more than six hours a week in various rooms. Similarly, one of the authors (Himelfarb, 1975) joined Weight Watchers to lose weight. As he became more familiar with Weight Watchers he requested permission of the group to make it an object of study. Thus, he moved from participant to participant-observer. He was, therefore, in a position from which he could empathize with fat people, how they viewed this common stigma and what it felt like to lose this stigma. He could also see beyond the group and recognize that many of the same sociological processes at work in Weight Watchers are also found in other self-help groups, indeed in any group which offers people some sort of physical or psychical renewal.

At the other extreme end of the continuum—*complete participant*—we can, perhaps, distinguish two aspects: retrospective analysis and infiltration. Clearly, there are many situations and many groups we have experienced solely as participants. Only in retrospect do these experiences seem worth reanalysing and rethinking. Often we are simply working outwards from our own personal experience. We begin to wonder whether our family life or our educational experience was unique or typical. Thus, it is probably a rare sociologist who does not at least illustrate his lectures, books and articles by retrospective analysis of his own experiences of social life. Gouldner (1970) suggests that it is, indeed, these prior experiences which make a given theory intuitively convincing or unconvincing. Hunches, hypotheses, the very questions we ask as sociologists emerge from the background assumptions which we all carry with us and which derive from our own store of social knowledge.

Retrospective analysis is, then, not only inescapable, but is also what enriches and creates social theory. "Infiltration," on the other hand, raises a number of ethical issues. By infiltration we mean the attempt by the researcher to pass as a genuine participating member of a group in order to observe unobtrusively. Given what we have said about the possible effect of the observer on what he is observing, it is, perhaps, understandable that many researchers have wanted to conceal their observer role, to act as if they were solely members of the group. Certainly, much of what we know about, say, deviance in the world could not have been obtained had the researcher revealed his "real" purpose in belonging to the work group. For example, one sociologist, while a summer employee in hotels, was able to see how the "fiddle" was worked against hotel owners and customers and was able to show some sociological reasons for its persistence. It is difficult to see how, as a genuine participant observer, he would have had access to this "inside" information.

Much the same could be said for Laud Humphreys' study of homosexuals, *The Tea-Room Trade*. However, this study raised considerable controversy and led to demands that his Ph.D. degree be revoked. Humphreys first played the role of "voyeur" and look-out in a public toilet. This gave him an opportunity to observe behaviour without anyone being aware that he was an observer. As the men left he also recorded the licence plate numbers of their cars. Several months later he interviewed them in their homes ostensibly as part of another study. At this time he made no mention that he had encountered them in the "tea room." They, apparently, didn't remember or recognize him. It is probable, then, that as an "infiltrator" Humphrey's presence had a very minimal effect on that which he wanted to study.

Nevertheless, the consensus is that Humphreys overstepped the bounds of ethical responsibility and respect for privacy. As a result of this and other similar studies, various sociological associations have developed professional codes of ethics. Generally, these require the researcher to reveal his observer role and to request permission of those he studies before using or publishing the research findings. In addition, people who are subjects should be given a reasonable amount of information as to the nature of the research, how the information revealed will be used and who else will have access to the data.

Is this to put ethical considerations before science? Perhaps. But, in most instances it is not at all clear that much the same information couldn't have been obtained without "infiltration." Ned Polsky (1969), besides his studies of poolroom subcultures, has also done similar research on professional criminals. He argues that there really is no need for concealment and recommends rather that the researcher be honest about his intentions and not pretend to be what he or she is not. In his view, criminal subcultures are not all that different from other groups one might choose to study. Both require that the researcher develop trust.[5] Both require the cooperation of an insider who will vouch for the researcher's integrity, that he is what he claims to be. Both depend on snowballing. We might note, too, that in infiltrating some groups it is problematic whether the researcher can escape "contaminating" what he hopes to observe. Festinger and an associate (1956) wanted to study a cult which claimed to be in touch with creatures from outer space who were to visit earth on a particular day. The researchers posed as "believers," as legitimate members of the group. But, we may well ask what effect the presence of two educated men, professors, had on a group of largely lower-middle-class people. Couldn't this be seen as validation of the group's beliefs? Festinger points out that they tried to remain "neutral" members but even a noncommital "hmm" is likely to be interpreted positively or negatively.[6]

ETHNOMETHODOLOGY

One of the more recently developed perspectives in sociology, ethnomethodology, has provided a critique of the assumptions which underlie participant observation. Ethnomethodologists ask what is obviously a crucial question: can an observer ever know what the people he is studying are thinking in any situation? Does not the sociologist, like every person, impute meanings to others based on his own experiences and interests? The ethnomethodologists, like symbolic interactionists, agree that meanings are central to the understanding of human behaviour. Unlike symbolic interactionists, however, ethnomethodologists are not willing to assume that sociologists can take the role of the other; instead they construct roles and impute them to the people they are studying. It is this constructing and imputing of roles and meanings, what ethnomethodologists sometimes refer to as *accounting procedures,* that these theorists make the focus of their study. They take what people say and do not necessarily as reflections of internalized values but as attempts to make the world appear rational and orderly to themselves and others. Talk, then, can be studied in itself, not for what it says about the content of people's thoughts about the world, but for what we can learn about the techniques or rules people use to account for themselves and the world. With this emphasis, ethnomethodologists do not try to become involved with the people they are studying, but try, rather, to maintain some detachment.

Harold Garfinkel (1967), for example, devised an experiment in which a number of undergraduates were told that they were to try out and evaluate a new counselling technique. They were to go into a room alone and through a device in the wall speak to a counsellor, ask him questions which could be answered with a "yes" or a "no," then speak into a tape recorder telling what they had learned from the answer. The counsellor and student would not see each other. The students, however, had been misled or duped. The counsellor was not at all a counsellor but a "stooge," a research assistant; his responses were based on a prepared list of random "yes's" and no's," so that the questions the students asked were irrelevant as far as the counsellor's responses were concerned.

Despite the randomness of the answers, the students were able to make "sense" of them, give "meaning" to them, even claimed to have learned from the experience. "Answers" that they could not easily "understand" they assumed would become clear sooner or later. In any case, the ethnomethodologist used the data produced in this experiment not to learn about the students' lives, but to get at how we impose order on chaos.

There are obvious ethical questions raised by such techniques as well. Having been deceived, many students may have felt embittered by the experience. Although they had given their consent to participate in the experiment they did not, by necessity, know what the experiment was. They had given their consent to participate in a different experiment. Perhaps this kind of trickery, although necessary for scientific purposes, shows a disregard for people and their rights to choose and would make many sociologists, including us, hesitate to employ such a technique no matter how productive it may be.

SOCIOLOGIST AS PARTISAN

Critiques of participant observation raise a particularly important and vexing issue for sociologists. Just what is the sociologist's responsibility to the people he is studying? Howard Becker (1967) demonstrated one position when he asked, "Whose side are we on?" His statement reflects the position of a number of sociologists in the 1960s who seemed to identify with the "underdogs." But it is not entirely clear what taking their side meant beyond trying to see the world through their eyes and to present their world to the public as legitimate. In other words, this work seemed essentially a call for understanding and tolerance. And, we believe these to be worthwhile aims indeed.

However, radical sociologists have voiced their dissatisfaction with this position because it does not explicitly point to the structured conditions of power and inequality that must be changed if the position of the underdog is to be improved. This raises, perhaps, the central issue: if the underdog perceives his problems in terms of his immediate *milieu* or perhaps doesn't even see himself as having any particular problems, does the sociologist "educate" him? Does the sociologist try to remedy "false consciousness"? Similarly, when people do perceive their troubles in terms of public issues, should the sociologist become their advocate, using his resources to help them achieve their aims?

Peter Berger (1963) warns that sociology is not for everyone because inevitably it upsets apple carts and many will suffer as a result of the new questions they come to ask. At the very least, we can take Berger's warning that it is quite a responsibility to impose or even offer one's viewpoint to others. Also, there is always the danger that the sociologist is replacing the group's false consciousness with his own distorted or partial view of reality. But to recognize these dangers is not to abrogate our responsibility to the people we are studying; it is only to understand that the exercise of this responsibility must be performed with care and empathy.

We argue throughout the text that the sociological perspective can be viewed as a resource for developing a critical understanding of society and for understanding one's position in society. Sociologists, then, do have a resource which they can offer those who wish to change their condition. It is difficult to imagine that a sociologist who has become involved in the lives of others could leave with no concern in helping. One way in which he can help and still respect the subjective world of these others is to learn from them what their problems, frustrations and dilemmas are and to put this information within a sociological perspective; in other words, to return to the people their own definitions of what is wrong in a way which makes it easier for them to see how to effect social change (see Bodemann, 1978).

On the surface this is not so very different a position from that of the "applied sociologists," many of whom claim to take a value-neutral stance. They argue that their job is to answer the questions put to them by their employers and to provide the best means to achieve their employers' goals. Those who buy this research are usually large corporations or the state. The stand of value-neutrality, then, generally translates into the, perhaps, unwitting defence of the *status quo.* That is, the resource of sociology is provided to those who have a vested interest in preserving the system. Even the applied sociologist who offers radical solutions, who challenges the goals of his employers, will have no control over how his information is being used. In any case, he's not likely to be hired very often.

For example, if an evaluation of an experimental programme turns in completely negative results, those who hired the social evaluator are not likely to abandon the programme or implement his more moderate suggestions. If the evaluator wishes to have some impact, his recommendations must be framed within the system of goals and programmes (Weiss, 1972: 115). It may be that applied sociologists, those directly involved in policy formulation and programme evaluation, are least effective in creating the kinds of changes which might be most important in terms of humanistic values. To take one example, Head Start programmes, along the lines of "Sesame Street," were inspired by the work of a number of sociologists intent on affecting social policy. Unquestionably, such programmes have much merit, but, as we see in Chapter VIII, they do not appreciably affect the structured inequalities which so drastically curtail the life chances of those to whom the programmes were directed.

It is in this sense, then, that we can appreciate Berger's (1971) insistence that sociologists remain unaligned, non-partisan. Only in this way, he argues, can the sociologist maintain a constant vigilance over the consequences of any human actions, of any group, which threaten human freedom and dignity. He is asking if, as the fortunes of groups change, sociologists may not find that the meaning of their partisanship also changes. To take the extreme example, in a successful revolution in which the dominated become the dominant, does the revolutionary sociologist now become the guardian of the new order? Will his partisanship limit his ability to maintain a critical consciousness and to defend the values which led to his original partisanship? What happens if the oppressed become the oppressors? The way out of this dilemma of whether the sociologist should be partisan, then, ultimately centres around partisanship to values rather than to groups.

The dilemma confronting sociologists is not whether they should be committed to values or attempt to be value-neutral; sociologists, we believe, must be committed to humanistic values, such as human dignity, equality and freedom, however difficult these are to articulate and to define once and for all. This is what we think of as *praxis,* theorizing as a way of life as we seek to understand these values, for ourselves and therefore for our discipline, in all our interactions, in our relationships—casual and intimate—and in our search through popular and classic literature and the bodies of knowledge which comprise the humanities. To John O'Neill, writing out of the traditions of phenomenology and Marxism, theorizing as a state of mind and way of life allows us to move beyond the confining circle of our own cultural worlds to imagine uncharted futures and leads us "to care for what is desperate in the human condition and the times through which it passes" (1972: 236).

Armed with an explicit ethical position rather than the pretence to value-neutrality, the sociologist can afford, perhaps is even obliged, to give himself up to the setting of his research. Only in this way can he learn the desires and frustrations, the obstacles and hardships in the lives of the people he is studying. He can learn of the constraints which prevent them from realizing their condition while, at the same time, avoiding these constraints in his own perceptions. By ignoring values and by pretending that we have dealt away with their influence or by ignoring the subjective worlds of those we study, we make ourselves vulnerable to being "cultural dopes" who ask only the conventional questions, or "paternalistic do-gooders" who enter the field thinking we already have the answers.

SUGGESTIONS FOR FURTHER READING

Norman K. Denzin's *The Research Act* (1970) is a good, general introduction to issues of social knowledge and research methods. A basic text is Claire Selltiz's and others' *Research Methods in Social Relations* (1976). Paul F. Lazarsfeld's and others' edited collection, *Continuities in the Language of Social Research* (1972) contains some of the seminal articles on quantitative research. G. J. McCall's and J. L. Simmons' *Issues in Participant Observation* (1969) along with the appendix to William Whyte's *Street Corner Society* (1955) will give you a good sense of the difficulties and advantages of participant observation research. Several recent edited collections describe and give examples of ethnomethodological studies. These include David Sudnow's Studies in *Social Interaction* (1972) and Hans Dreitzel's *Recent Sociology* Vol. II (1970). A good discussion of both methodological ideals and the reality of actual research practice is Abraham Kaplan's *The Conduct of Inquiry* (1964). Elisabeth Crawford's and Stein Rokhan's *Sociological Praxis: Current Rules and Settings* (1976) offers a collection of articles on *styles* of sociology and research. Many of the issues on the sociologist as partisan are discussed in J. David Colfax's and Jack L. Roach's edited collection, *Radical Sociology* (1971).

FOOTNOTES

[1]We are talking about sociological research, but obviously the same problems face social psychologists and, especially, anthropologists.

[2]At times, too, it may be irrelevant to have a random or representative sample because the behaviour to be studied is felt to be universal. A case in point is Gross's and Stone's (1970) study of "embarrassment." They simply interviewed friends and acquaintances and asked them to describe the kinds of situations which they found embarrassing.

[3]Various programmes or "packages" have been developed in recent years which make even the most mathematically "illiterate" social scientist an instant computer programmer. The most widely used of these is the *Statistical Package for the Social Sciences,* SPSS (Nie and others, 1975). This is, as well, an excellent introduction to the way in which social scientists go about analysing their data.

[4]An early study of the subjective perceptions of male prostitutes is Albert Reiss' "The Social Integrations of Peers and Queers" (1961). A more recent examination of the self-definition of homosexuals is Laud Humphreys' *The Tea Room Trade* (1970), a study of homosexuals who frequent public washrooms, "tea rooms." We describe this study further on, and the findings in Chapter VI.

[5]One unresolved problem is that when the sociologist is studying illegal behaviour he runs the risk of being an accomplice to the crime. Also, despite efforts to have their status changed, sociologists, like journalists, do not enjoy the same rights to privileged information as do lawyers, priests and doctors. Thus, the sociologists cannot in some circumstances give a promise of confidentiality.

[6]These issues are explored in a "sociological" novel by Alison Lurie, *Imaginary Friends* (1967).

PART 2

The Concepts Of Sociology

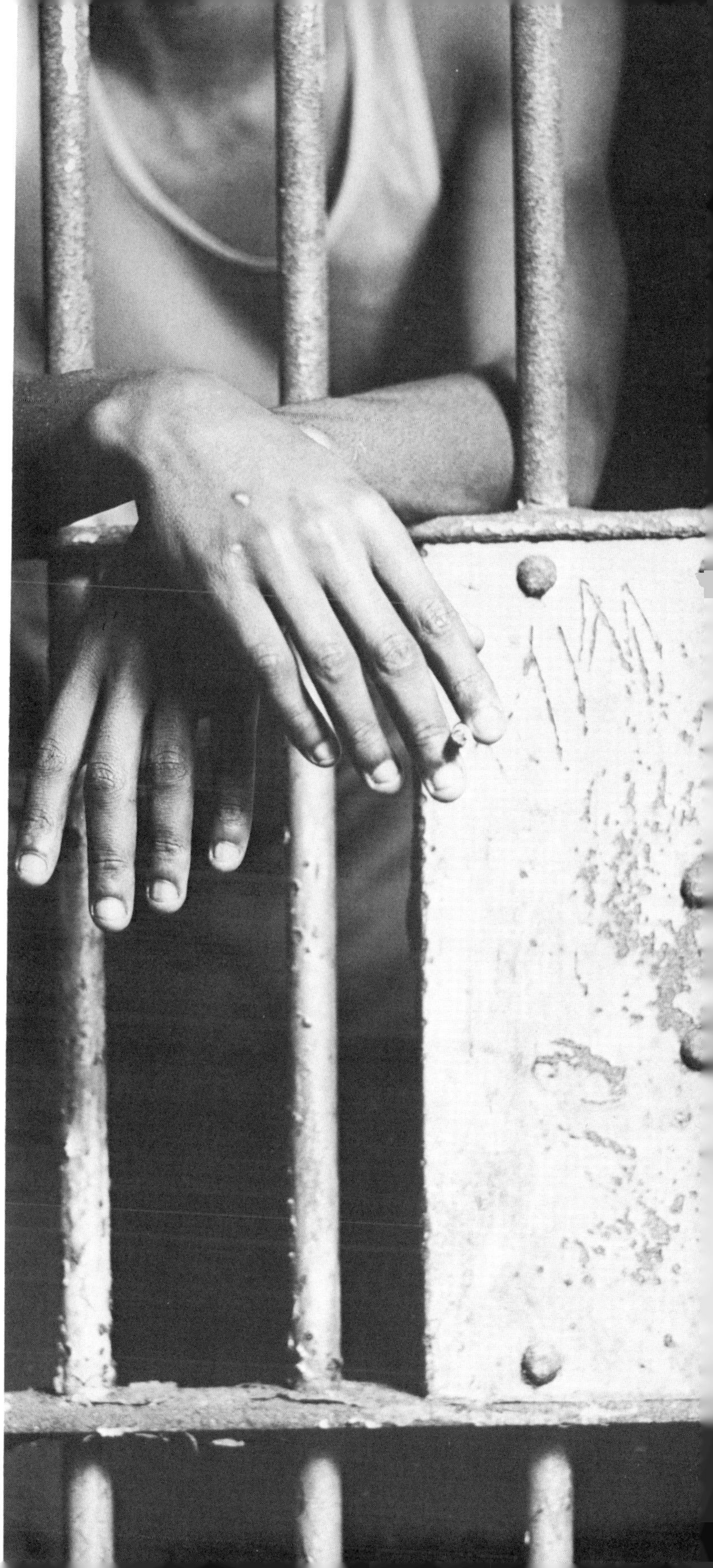

culture
CHAPTER III

Sociologists are sometimes accused of inventing words where they are not needed and of unnecessarily complicating the words that already exist. However, it must be recognized that the sociologists' subject matter—although we all live it, create it and experience its weight—is like the air we breathe, all around us but difficult to see. And, unless we can devise ways of "seeing" it, we cannot analyse it. In the following four chapters we will be introducing the central concepts sociologists have devised to carve out and slice up the social world. Sociology is characterized by a good deal of disagreement about just how to achieve this. Nevertheless, there is sufficient agreement about the basic concepts that, for the most part, sociologists are able to argue to the point and avoid talking past one another. So, on one level these concepts are useful in guiding sociologists' work in a similar direction. On another level, these concepts provide the forum for debate and controversy.

Culture, the subject matter of this chapter, is also a concept in our everyday thinking of the world. In common sense terms, we may think of people as having or not having culture. This use equates culture with the fine arts and as something to be acquired and valued. At the same time, the notion of "pop" culture—movies, Harlequin romances and comic books—that appeals to the "masses" has also entered the public consciousness. Others may think of culture as those patterns of behaviour which characterize remote and exotic societies. For example, as we shall see, people may often find the ways of life of, say, various Indian tribes or aboriginals interesting, or despicable, while at the same time taking for granted, never questioning, the way of life in their own society. Clearly, for social scientists, culture means all of these things and more. But, in part because it is such an all-embracing concept, sociologists, too, disagree about how it should be used.

There is some disagreement, for example, about whether the concept of culture should be restricted to describe the set of ideas of a group, or should also include the actual behaviour patterns of the group. We prefer to reserve the term "culture" to refer to behavioural *ideals* rather than to the behaviour itself. We feel that this helps to keep in focus the fact that the correspondence between these ideals and actual behaviour may be quite problematic. Culture is never the sole basis for behaviour; it simply provides the plans or recipes. Behaviour, moreover, is for the most part situational; the plans or recipes must be revised or modified according to the situation when people try to use them. Finally, as we shall emphasize throughout, people may have limited resources when they try to actualize the behavioural ideals of their culture. For example, in many cultures polygamy is a behavioural ideal; however, it is generally the case that few people can in fact afford to support several spouses. Polygamy may be the ideal, but monogamy the norm.

Furthermore, it is not always immediately clear in the social sciences what the differences are between "culture" and "society," "culture" and "social structure." These words or concepts are often used interchangeably or at least in an overlapping way, and are rarely used with any degree of rigour. This is largely because these are orienting words, orienting or sensitizing the sociologist to his subject matter. These are the words which define the field.

CULTURE AND SOCIETY

Sociologists use the term society in a variety of different ways. Sometimes society is taken to mean simply the people who share a culture. This use of the term makes no sharp distinction, then, between culture and society; culture and society are virtually interchangeable. More usually, however, society is taken to mean a web of relationships, a set of patterned relationships which existed prior to the individual and which will endure after him. In this sense, we can talk of a team or a class or whatever as a society—in other words, as a social system of two or more actors engaged in sustained and patterned interaction. While it makes sense from this perspective to distinguish between culture and society, it is difficult to conceive of a society which does not produce a culture or of a culture without a society. Perhaps the only time a culture exists on its own is in extinct societies whose cultural heritage is lodged in museums.

To add to the confusion, another use of the concept of society is to make it virtually synonymous with nation or country. It is, perhaps, in this usage that it makes sense to talk about subcultures and countercultures. The emphasis, here, is that while there may be one dominant set of ideas in any one country, in complex countries such as ours, these ideas will differ substantially from group to group and many groups may hold opposing ideas. This third usage is particularly relevant for sociologists. Anthropologists who have developed and refined the term "culture" have been able to treat culture and society as virtually synonymous because they have, for the most part, studied simple societies in which cultural consensus was extremely high. Moreover, many anthropologists have included behaviour in their definition of culture because in these societies there was a closer fit between real and ideal than we are likely to find in societies such as ours.

Finally, in an age of mass communication, travel and mobility, cultural boundaries, generally, become blurred. Much of the research on culture, particularly relevant to Canada, examines how some people may try to set up barriers to cultural intrusion and how these barriers may be permeated or crushed. To take a somewhat unusual example, the study of child socialization might be viewed as the progressive intrusion of adult culture on the seemingly private culture of children (see Opie and Opie, 1959).

CULTURE AND SOCIAL STRUCTURE

It is clear that not all cultural ideas lead to behaviour nor is there necessarily a close fit between culture and behaviour. Those behaviours which are based on shared meanings and patterns we refer to as social structure. That is, social structure is the outcome of people's use of cultural notions, ideas and norms to construct lines of action. Social structure, then, leads us to think of patterned behaviour, regular and repetitive behaviour which we are able to study. The process whereby cultural values become translated into specific rules which govern behaviour is called *institutionalization.* As Berger (1963) puts it, behaviour is compelled to run in ruts, patterns which are generally felt to be desirable but which may also be the only way deemed conceivable. This chapter will look at culture as an ideal; in the following two chapters we shall examine how these ideals are, through processes of institutionalization and interaction, translated into behaviour.

STUDYING CULTURE

Culture, then, consists of systems of ideals and ideas, ways of thinking and plans or recipes for behaving in any group of people, specifically those systems of ideas which are passed on from generation to generation. Anthropologists have also used the term to include the products and application of these systems of thought, that is, the tools and artifacts of the group—*material culture.* Sociologists, however, usually maintain the distinction between ideal culture and material culture.

People do not usually think of the systems of ideas passed from generation to generation in their own group as culture; rather, most of us think of these ideas as truth, reality, the best or even the only ways of thinking and behaving. People forget that the way they choose their spouse, raise their children, do their work and so on are all part of a long cultural tradition. Most people think of these activities as somehow natural. On the other hand, the traits of other cultures are often seen as unnatural. It is bizarre to worship many gods, to have more than one wife or husband, to marry, through a formal arrangement, someone you have never met. These are puerile, weird or amusing cultural traits. It is only right, natural, to worship one god, to have one mate and to marry for love. This way of thinking—judging other groups from the standards of our own culture—is called *ethnocentrism.* Most groups exhibit some degree of ethnocentrism, or more simply, most people hold the prejudice that their way of life is the best.

Horace Miner (1956:506) provides an interesting and insightful example of how such a prejudice can influence how we perceive other cultures. He describes the exotic and magic-ridden customs of the Nacirema. For example:

> *The Nacirema have an almost pathological horror of and fascination with the mouth, the condition of which is believed to have a supernatural influence on all social relationships. Were it not for the rituals of the mouth, they believe that their teeth would fall out, their gums bleed and their lovers reject them. . . . The daily body ritual performed by everyone includes a mouth-rite . . . which strikes the uninitiated stranger as revolting. . . . The ritual consists of inserting a small bundle of hog hairs into the mouth along with certain magical powders and then moving the bundle in a highly formalized series of gestures. In addition to the private mouth-rite, the people seek out a holy-mouth-man once or twice a year. These practitioners have an impressive set of paraphernalia, consisting of a variety of augers, awls, probes and prods. The use of these objects in the exorcism of the evils of the mouth involves almost unbelievable ritual torture of the client.*

If you have not already guessed, spell Nacirema backwards and read the passage again and you will get some idea of how an ethnocentric stranger might view the concern in North America about oral hygiene and our relationship with the dentist, and the bathroom.

Of course, the degree of ethnocentrism varies from person to person. A number of studies have shown that those people who are most ethnocentric are usually also least flexible.[1] Not only are they intolerant of other cultures, they tend to be intolerant of change and often find it difficult to cope with novel or ambiguous situations. Obviously, sociologists cannot afford to be ethnocentric; they must look at and compare cultures as objectively as they can. One of the goals of a liberal arts education, surely, is to broaden our perspective, to make us sufficiently flexible to be able to view new and different ideas with more tolerance or at least with more objectivity. The person who believes that he is the centre of the universe, rather than a representative of a long cultural tradition beyond his or any individual's understanding, is the greatest slave of culture. A person cannot liberate himself in any way from his dependence on culture until he recognizes and understands this dependence. The study of sociology can help in this liberation.

Others, however, often learn the hard way. Conventional wisdom has it that one of the best forms of self-education is world travel, learning different cultures first hand. This, however, can often result in *culture shock,* the feeling of unreality, confusion and anxiety that accompanies the realization that the ways of thinking and acting that we have always taken for granted are simply no longer appropriate. For many, this confrontation with new ways of life produces a sense, often an uncomfortable sense, of the fragility of right and wrong, of the fragility, even, of reality.[2]

Sociology is often referred to as the "relativizing" discipline, which makes everything appear right, nothing wrong. Many sociologists are *cultural relativists;* they argue that all cultures are equally worthwhile and that one should not judge other cultures from the basis of one's own culture. These sociologists have been concerned with avoiding the easy pitfall of disparaging other cultures, especially in comparison to their own. They have, for example, criticized Westerners' attempts to help modernize underdeveloped nations. They have felt that so-called modernization failed to respect the cultural integrity of these societies and, therefore, was likely to have unanticipated and disastrous consequences. Many sociologists are dissatisfied with this stance; indeed the issue of cultural relativism poses an important dilemma for sociology. Many, today, find extreme cultural relativism unsatisfying. They argue that if sociologists are going to have some input in social policy or, more generally, if they are to contribute to making society better, they must make some informed, though by no means certain, decisions about what changes would be best for whatever society they are studying.[3]

Of course, before sociologists can adopt this stance they must develop a set of criteria including normative standards for making these judgements. Indeed, a number of writers such as Alvin Gouldner (1970), Ivan Illich (1970) and André Gunder Frank (1969) insist that sociologists must develop and commit themselves to a set of standards for evaluating not only other cultures but their own. In essence they are arguing that evaluations (and recommendations based on such evaluations) are not only desirable, they are virtually inevitable and therefore must be made explicit. In other words, part of this task involves uncovering the unstated and often unrecognized background assumptions—world views which guide the sociological endeavour itself.[4] For some, such as Alvin Gouldner (1970), this has meant that we must develop what he calls a "reflexive sociology."

> *The historical mission of a Reflexive Sociology . . . would be to* transform *the sociologist, to penetrate deeply into his daily life and work, enriching them with new sensitivities, and to raise the sociologist's self-awareness to a new historical level.*

According to Gouldner, a reflexive sociology would have to be a radical sociology:

> *Radical, because it would recognize that knowledge of the world cannot be advanced apart from the sociologist's knowledge of himself and his position in the social world, or apart from his efforts to change these. Radical, because it seeks to transform as well as to know the alien world outside the sociologist as well as the alien world inside of him (p. 489).*

And, as we shall see in much greater detail in Chapter VII, there is an even greater need for a reflexive sociology—the explicit uncovering of our background assumptions—when as sociologists we attempt to understand a society other than our own. Thus, what Illich and Frank have both argued to be the case for American involvement in Latin America is also true more generally for sociologists trying to understand other cultures. Whether we are speaking of the American-trained sociologist studying Canada or the White Canadian sociologist studying native peoples, a reflexive sociology recognizes that both are confronted not only with methodological and theoretical obstacles, but with crucial questions of ideology and commitment as well.

Humanistic sociologists will often insist that sociology offers an opportunity for self-discovery. Reflexive sociologists, on the other hand, argue that this promise is seldom realized, that sociologists understand themselves too little, and that much of their work is guided by assumptions taken for granted, rarely made explicit or the subject for reflection.

As we have indicated, it is this very feature of culture—its taken-for-grantedness—that gives it much of its power to constrain and limit us. Indeed, the influence of culture is pervasive; it finds expression in our every thought and our every action, even in our most private moments. How and what we eat, whom and how we love, even what we daydream, are influenced by the culture into which we are born. While the genius, the artist, the revolutionary, for that matter all of us, add their own unique qualities to their activities, they must work with cultural tools—cultural notions of truth, beauty and goodness. We are all inescapably part of a long cultural tradition and we are able only on occasion to transcend it. Indeed, this potential for transcending culture is what Gouldner seemingly hopes will be the outcome of a reflexive sociology—the ability to locate, describe and subject to analysis our *background* and *domain* assumptions may enable us as well to transcend their influence.

It should be evident that culture is to some degree a cumbersome concept that includes too much. In the following pages, we shall look more closely at the elements that comprise any culture: symbols and values.

THE COMPONENTS OF CULTURE

In 1953, Jean Bruller, writing under the name of Vercors, wrote a best-selling novel in which an anthropological expedition discovers a group of strange creatures, Tropi, which seem to be something more than animals but less than human. In a fictional trial, theologians, biologists and social scientists offer their testimony about whether the Tropi are human. In so doing, they must come to grips with the age-old question—what is man? The Tropi are lovable and apparently loving; they seem curious; they use tools and are able to make a wide variety of sounds and gestures. They at least *seem* to have a society. What must we know about the Tropi before we can classify them as either people-like apes or ape-like people?

People do not always come off well in comparison to animals. There are animals with greater speed, greater strength. People, however, can think abstractly. They can think of ways to control or live better in their environment; that is, they come up with ideas which they can *share* with other members of their group and *transmit* to future generations. The mechanism for sharing and transmitting ideas is *symbols.* "Man's capacity to form symbols and words which represent phenomena of his external and internal worlds is his most distinguishing characteristic" (Mueller, 1973:19). Man is a symbol user. As sociologists, then, as long as we could not penetrate the language of the Tropi, that is, if we could not know that they used symbols, we would have to testify that they were not human. This is essentially the problem that we face when we impute to animals—for that matter to babies—human-like thoughts and sentiments. Both may, in their behaviour, appear to exhibit affection or guilt, for example, but unless we share a common universe of symbols, language in other words, we cannot know whether they are even capable of such emotions.

Symbols

Symbols are any objects to which people have attached some shared value and meaning. The Canadian flag, the Fleur de Lys, the dollar bill or a wave of the hand all have more or less shared meaning to people in our society. Clearly, these symbols are arbitrary. There is no reason why, for example, money must be represented by dollar bills and coins as we know them. But, once the symbol has been created and used and, particularly, passed down from generation to generation, it takes on a reality of its own and may in fact become sacred. The most important system of symbols for man is language. Language is also perhaps the most difficult of the symbols to subject to analysis. All of us depend upon language in virtually every aspect of our daily lives, in every interaction and transaction. Nevertheless, this dependence is taken for granted, in large part because of its pervasiveness.

Part of the complexity in studying language stems from the fact that it embodies cumulative human experience. Language, in effect, gives us a sense of what Berger and Luckmann (1967) call *historicity,* a sense that there has been a past, a past that somehow belongs to us. In earlier societies, the job of communicating and transmitting knowledge about the past rested largely with elders who informally passed on various beliefs, myths and superstitions through stories, wise sayings, rhymes and so on. This oral tradition is part of every society including our own—for example, the "myth" of Santa Claus—and is generally referred to as *folklore.* But today, knowledge is being increasingly produced and transmitted by "knowledge specialists" or "experts."

As societies became literate, as they moved from an oral to a written tradition, the nature of knowledge changed. For the first time, men were able to scrutinize, read over and over again and compare written documents. Their standards of evaluating knowledge therefore changed. No longer as free to create an imaginative, mythological history, literate societies made a greater attempt to distinguish fact and fiction. Nevertheless, part of the task of historians, knowledge experts, is to integrate past events into the culture. As they impose order on past events, they, in effect, create history and create for us a heritage of dramas, heroes and villains. Samuel Butler makes this point well in his unfair but witty description of historians:

> *It has been said that although God cannot alter the past, historians can; it is perhaps because they can be useful to Him in this respect that He tolerates their existence.*

We all know about the English conquest of New France in 1760, but what we know about the conquest, the battles and its heroes will depend on which text we have read and particularly on whether the text was written by a French Canadian or an English Canadian. The Royal Commission on Bilingualism and Biculturalism (1968) devoted a good deal of attention to the way history was presented in Canada. The Commission found that, typically, historical events were depicted very differently by the English- and French-Canadian texts. In fact, the two versions of Canadian history were often irreconcilable. Canada has a dual history and, as Richert (1974) shows, that duality is reflected in the attitudes of French- and English-Canadian students. For example, when students were asked which figures in history they most admired and who were their historical heroes, English Canadians most often chose English heroes, and even more markedly, French Canadians chose French heroes. While history may often be an integrating or binding force in a nation by providing the people with a rich heritage of which they can be proud, this obviously need not always be the case.

Rather, it appears that history in Canada may well be a divisive factor, one which may retard social and cultural integration (Richert, 1974:162).

In any case, it is language which provides us our link to the past. It is also through language that we can imagine the future and indeed influence the future by passing on our ideas. Language, then, gives us a place in the flow of history; it conveys to us that the world existed before us and will exist after us. Over a century ago, Marx and Engels wrote that "language, like consciousness, only arises from the need, the necessity, of intercourse with other men" (Feuer, 1963:251). Man's existence depends on language. At the same time, the ideas embedded in the language we learn shape our view of the world. One has no choice but to learn the language, therefore, the ideas of the group into which one is born.

There is substantial controversy about just how much language determines our thought processes. According to one view, language provides us with the labels (names), categories and concepts which enable us to think about the world at all. This is the view, for example, proposed by Benjamin Whorf (1956) in what has been termed the Whorf-Sapir hypothesis. Essentially the argument states that without language there can be no meaning. The labels or names that the child learns direct his selection process, that is, direct him to perceive only certain aspects of his environment; he will not recognize what he has no name for. As well, language provides the categories through which people come to conceptualize their world, think about it and therefore experience it; language forms our experience of the world. This does not mean that at some level we cannot experience some aspect of the world not contained in our language, but rather that we do not retain these experiences.

Whorf and Sapir, anthropologists and linguists, believed that the structure of the language of a people determined the whole of their culture. They derived much of their theory from a study of the Hopi, a peaceful and non-aggressive Indian tribe. The Hopi language, unlike our language, virtually ignores verb-noun differences. For example, rather than saying "the woman is leaving us," they would more likely say something equivalent to "leaving." Sentences in English, on the other hand, almost invariably portray something or somebody doing some action. In other words, English is a more active language which, according to Whorf's argument, is reflected in our concern with controlling nature and other people rather than simply accepting "life as it is" as do the Hopi. One could speculate that a similar deterministic relationship exists between the Inuit language and Inuit culture. The Inuit language contains no word to express the first person pronoun. So rather than say "I am hungry," the Inuit would say "Somebody is hungry."[5] Perhaps this is reflected in the greater appreciation of the community, of the collective, than of the individual.

Against this thesis is the perspective of structuralism, developed with particular force and clarity by the French anthropologist, Claude Lévi-Strauss. He describes his main thesis in, for example, *The Elementary Structures of Kinship* (1969):

Every new-born child comes equipped, in the form of adumbrated mental structures, with all the means ever available to mankind to define its relations to the world in general, and its relations to others (p. 93).

For Lévi-Strauss, then, infants' thoughts represent the "common denominator" of all thought and all cultures. If there are differences between Inuit and Hopi, or between Englishmen and Pakistanis, these are the results of what are ultimately *similar* kinds of responses to *different* kinds of ecological circumstances. Lévi-Strauss would not argue with Whorf's and Sapir's emphasis on the importance of language in transforming human thought; all would agree that it is language which distinguishes us from the lower animals. Lévi-Strauss, however, disputes the deterministic relationship proposed in the Whorf-Sapir hypothesis. When a child learns a language he learns to select among his mental structures, emphasizing some and rejecting others. And, while language does indeed allow people to communicate with one another, it also means that "the unlimited possibilities available to the child are irremediably lost" (Lévi-Strauss, 1969:94). Language, then, represents specialization. Structural linguists have proposed similar hypotheses. While Lévi-Strauss is concerned with understanding culture and particularly its elementary structures, structural linguists, notably Noam Chomsky (1957), have been interested in how all language is ultimately similar because it is the outcome of basic and universal cognitive processes. For structural linguists, then, languages, though "superficially" dissimilar, are identical at the level of "deep structure," because people of all cultures think in the same basic way.

It is difficult, perhaps impossible, to determine which of these hypotheses is correct, whether language determines our thought or thought determines language. What is clear is that all agree that language mediates our thought processes, guides our perceptions and allows us to establish relationships with the past, with others in our present, with the future, and even with eternity as in our symbolizations of our gods and other worlds.

Language and Freedom

As will be evident in Chapter V, symbolic interactionists often portray language as liberating. As children acquire language they are becoming progressively freed from their biological natures, their "instincts." They become more able to express themselves, to externalize their internal states and to manipulate the behaviour of others around them. And, because language contains cumulated past experience, people are able to profit from this experience and are freed from the necessity of creating new techniques to handle each situation that they encounter. They have the benefit of knowing how previous generations learned to control their environment and to cope with problems of geography and climate.

On the other hand, and this is particularly evident in the work of Sapir and Whorf, language is seen as constraining an individual's freedom. In a sense, the child becomes the heir to the linguistic stereotypes of generations. Another way of putting this is, as C. Wright Mills (1949) describes it, that we are heirs to a "vocabulary of motives" through which we "understand" our own and others' behaviour. In our society, for example, we learn to distinguish between madness and sanity, mental health and mental illness. The latter term has provided us with a residual category which we use to account for the apparently inexplicable. Thomas Szasz (1960; 1961), the social psychiatrist, has described how the term "mental illness" has been expanded to cover an increasing range of behaviours, until finally it is now used to describe virtually any behaviour which is unconventional. However, in earlier periods, people were constrained by a different vocabulary of motives. In the medieval period, for example, people usually accounted for bizarre behaviour in terms of possession by the devil. In later periods people were more likely to think in terms of "moral" and "immoral" behaviour.

> *. . . what formerly was thought of morally is in our time thought of esthetically or psychiatrically. Whereas formerly maidens and ladies spoke of "wicked" men and of "good" and "bad" conduct, today they speak of "decent" and "indecent" conduct, or of "neurotic" and "stable" persons (Gerth and Mills, 1953:123).*

Today, the notion of mental illness seems to have brought with it a wide-spread intolerance for the unconventional and seems to threaten our appreciation for human diversity. Our perception of others, then, is filtered through the linguistic symbols we have learned.

A more obvious example of what we mean by a linguistic stereotype is in the area of prejudice and discrimination. Once we have acquired language, we are able to learn about and think about categories of objects and people beyond our immediate perception. In fact, we can come to love or hate categories of people we have never met. These sentiments, then, do not emerge from our own direct experience of the people in question but are "inherited" prejudices. For example, many people who are not aware of ever having met a Jew will often feel that they know what Jews are like and, indeed, this "knowledge" may prove highly resistant to change. At the most taken-for-granted level, people who have not met Jews may still learn what it means to be "jewed down" in a financial transaction. People may learn prejudicial definitions without even being aware of what they have learned.

Even our conception of what constitutes a social problem to be dealt with is determined, in part, by the language we have learned. An excellent example is provided in I. A. Richards' study of Chinese culture and language in Mencius's period. The Chinese word for "aged" makes no distinction between age in the chronological sense and the ethical pattern of behaviour—deference and reverence—thought due the old. In Mencius's period, then, people could not think about whether they ought to treat the old with reverence; they did not "discuss or treat as open to discussion the rightness of paying respect to age as age" (Richards, in Mills, 1967:436) or, in the words of C. Wright Mills, "their language would not allow a definition of the problem" (pp. 436-437). While what to do about old people constitutes a social problem in our society, it could not in theirs.

It should be clear by now that as we learn the language of our group we are also learning the implicit rules and evaluations of our group. As Kenneth Burke puts it, "the names of things and operations smuggle in connotations of good and bad—a noun tends to carry with it an invisible adjective and a verb an invisible adverb" (Burke, 1965:224). In other words, as we are learning language we are learning much more—the social texture and context of life. What we are also learning is the stock of knowledge which has been created in the past and which includes everything which the members of the group "know" about every aspect of the world. To describe what we are learning as knowledge rather than beliefs implies a transformation process; ideas undergo a process Berger and Luckmann (1967) refer to as "objectification." They explain that when people create an agreed upon way of handling something in the environment, they are likely to recognize that their solution is arbitrary; it is simply a convention. But, when they pass on this convention to new members of the group—new-born children, for example—the convention is translated into the *reality*. What was simply a way of handling a problem becomes *the* way such problems are handled. For example, let us imagine that a man and woman on an island decide that their breakfast each day would, for reasons of convenience and taste, consist of fish. Their children would learn that breakfast means fish; people eat fish for breakfast. Indeed, to eat eggs for breakfast might for these children not only seem bizarre, it may in fact seem revolting. Convention becomes objective knowledge about reality. Very often, then, in transmitting a convention to their children, parents feel called upon to justify it, to make sense of it, perhaps to make it appear as the right and sensible way of doing things. According to Berger and Luckmann, one way of doing this is to explain what was simply a convention as being ordained by some supernatural being, a commandment of a god or gods. Eating fish for breakfast may become incorporated in the common stock of knowledge not only as a piece of information, but also as something sacred and inviolate. And, if this becomes the case, people are unwilling or unable to imagine alternatives.

How we think, then, is in large part determined by how the generations before us have thought. Language obviously captures the dialectic of man the creator and man the product because, at the same time, it is language which allows us to form relationships with others and therefore to engage in collective action. Language makes us part of the group, but it is also the resource we use for thinking of ways to change the structure or organization of the group. We might add that an understanding of the fundamental constraints inherent in language is a first step towards transcending these constraints. No doubt the wish to transcend the constraints of our language is implicit in the emphasis of liberal education on learning other languages. Perhaps, from the perspectives of these other languages, we can come to learn the limitations built into our own. In fact, language constraints may be more potent for North Americans who very often speak and think in only one language than for Europeans who more often have learned several languages. In some fundamental sense, Europeans may be more cosmopolitan, less prone to ethnocentrism, than North Americans.

Values

Language embodies values, those beliefs more or less shared by a group about what is desirable, what ought to be. Values help us guide our own and others' behaviour and guide us in the choices we make. Implicit in the language we learn are moral judgements, judgements about "good" and "bad." Very seldom, then, do we talk or think in purely descriptive terms. Rather, we are almost always evaluating. For example, when we describe someone as mentally ill we are not simply describing him, we are also evaluating him. However much the psychiatrist insists on the neutrality of the concept—its scientific status—it is pejorative. People are moral creatures likely to praise or condemn other people's customs and behaviour.

If you are asked to describe what makes French Canadians and English Canadians different, you would probably answer in evaluative terms rather than describe actual differences. Popular or stereotypical notions hold that the Francophones are more animated than Anglophones and have a greater *joie de vivre.* Certainly, as Pierre Berton (1975) has noted, the American version of French Canadians, as conveyed through Hollywood films, portrays them as "happy-go-lucky and high living" which probably, from an Anglophone perspective, implies that they are childlike and irresponsible. The Anglophone notion of himself as sensible and business-like is probably seen by the Francophone as cold and calculating. These characterizations are, for the most part, myths—they do not hold up under close scrutiny; however, they may tell us something about how the groups project themselves, that is, how the groups like to talk and think about themselves—their projected values.[6] What we are trying to illustrate here is that people make evaluations but they do so on the basis of shared notions of what ought to be; people judge behaviour on the basis of values that they have learned. (In Chapter VII we discuss the actual differences in values between French Canadians and English Canadians and in Chapter X among various ethnic groups in Canada.)

One of the most pressing questions facing not only Canadian sociologists but all Canadians is whether Canada has a distinctive identity. Another way of asking this is do we have our own system of values which somehow sets us apart from the two dominant English-speaking nations with which we have been most closely associated. We are certainly not any longer British, nor are we Americans. But who are we? What does it mean to be a Canadian? So much have these questions preoccupied us that there seems to be some truth in what many have said is the central feature of the Canadian identity—our everlasting preoccupation with our lack of a national identity. As Margaret Atwood (1972:33) observes, "Canadians are forever taking the national pulse like doctors at a sickbed; the aim is not to see whether the patient will live well, but simply whether he will live at all."

Perhaps, as we shall see in more detail in the second half of this book, we still manifest aspects of a "colonial mentality." We seem to value, for example, anything American. Who, for instance, had heard of Joni Mitchell before she became a "hit" in the United States? Who cared about Marshall McLuhan before he became an American "cult" figure? Canadian actors and actresses bemoan the fact that we ignore them unless they have been successful in London, or perhaps New York. Academics give more weight to publications in American or British journals than to those which appear in Canadian journals. We ignore Canadian films until they are declared "good" by foreign audiences. Though others marvel at the quality of CBC TV and radio, we routinely tune in American networks and listen to radio that emulates American sounds.

The values we use to judge how well "the patient is living" are American values. When judged by American standards and American values, we emerge as a conservative, elitist and authoritarian society. Americans living in Canada are often shocked by the number of issues resolved not by democratic process but by order-in-council, e.g., the handling of Japanese Canadians in the Second World War or, more recently, gun control.[7] They are similarly critical of the much greater secrecy in which governments and civil services carry out their business (see Shackleton, 1977). As Friedenberg, a Dalhousie professor and expatriate American, pointed out in a recent address, a central feature of Canadian society is our faith that, with a few exceptions, the state will protect us. It begins with the fact that we are the only country he knows of which defines itself in terms of loyalty to another country, something which is clearly repugnant to one who has, as part of his heritage, the "glorious revolution" of independence. We set up our identity in terms of other people and in other people's terms. This, he suggests, is illustrated by our lack of national symbols and heroes and by the fact that Canadian authors do not write about the struggle of individuals against the state, but against the "system."[8]

A more systematic example of the same judgements Friedenberg makes is S. M. Lipset's (1963) comparison of Canada's value system with that of Britain and the United States. Lipset, an American sociologist, suggests that Canada falls much closer to Britain than it does to the United States, particularly in terms of its elitism and respect for and deference to authority. As evidence, Lipset cites the lower proportion of students in higher education in Britain and Canada, the lower number of lawyers per capita in these societies and the fact that in Canada and Britain there has been an absence of populist movements and "witch hunting" as in the McCarthy era. What Lipset was trying to do, then, was to find a more systematic way of documenting what is fairly self-evident—that Canada has historically tended to follow the British pattern more often than it has the United States, that the American version of the liberal ideology is, in Canada, relatively weak.

As we might expect, Lipset's approach has been subject to considerable criticism. Truman (1973) has made what is probably the most thoroughgoing critique. Among other things, he questions whether Lipset's measures actually show what he says they do. For instance, is degree of lawlessness an adequate indicator of egalitarian versus elitist sentiments? As Truman points out, many very undemocratic and inegalitarian societies have higher crime rates than the United States. Horowitz (1973) argues that while Lipset may have depicted Canada's past, his analysis is not valid for contemporary Canada. Thus, as the on-going research by James Curtis and his associates at the University of Waterloo suggests, when we attempt to measure values of Canadians and Americans there may not, in fact, be much difference.

Arthur K. Davis (1971), a University of Alberta sociologist, has questioned the grounds on which Lipset is able to depict the United States as an open and egalitarian society. He makes the obvious point that equality of opportunity does not exist in America; race, sex, family background and religion do matter. This criticism challenges the approach of trying to understand a society through its values. Whatever the values, both America and Canada are characterized by a good deal of inequality of opportunity; values do not tell us very much about what seems to happen to people. Nevertheless, values do tell us a good deal about how people frame social action. There may be little chance for people to rise socially or economically in either Canada or the United States. But, if it were true that the United States stressed values of achievement and equality of opportunity more than Canadians do, then we would expect more upward striving among Americans. As well, the value system provides people with a way of evaluating what happens to them—are they satisfied or dissatisfied with opportunities?—and a way of explaining what happens to them.

Ideology

This latter function of values, that they help us to explain and justify what is happening to us and to society more generally, is of particular importance. The sociological question *par excellence* is "how is social order possible?" Why does society not fragment into a variety of warring groups? As we described in the first chapter, the conflict perspective has emphasized force or the threat of force; powerful groups in society, by definition, have a virtual monopoly on force and are thereby able to exact compliance to their wishes. Superficially, at least, most of us are likely to find this explanation implausible. We do not live in the kind of military dictatorship where we are constantly confronted with the symbols of force. For example, part of the horror many people experienced after the invoking of the War Measures Act in 1970 and particularly the image of machine-gun carrying military in the streets of a Canadian city may have been because it served as a reminder of the important role of force. Nevertheless, naked force can only be a temporary basis for compliance; it is an unstable basis for order. A society based solely on force would have to be a society in which "Big Brother" really could watch all of our actions and tap all of our thoughts. Most of the time force is not called into play because we more or less willingly cooperate in maintaining social order.

This, of course, raises the question—why, in the face of inequality, can force be left in reserve? Perhaps the most important and certainly most influential answer comes from Karl Marx. For Marx, certain ideas and cultural beliefs are of more consequence because they serve to justify the position of the privileged class—landowners in feudal times, capitalists when he was writing in the nineteenth century. He believed that only those in the owner class had the leisure time to develop ideas and, most important, the power and resources to communicate them to others. As Parkin (1971) puts it:

> *Marx's claim that the ideas of the ruling class are, in every age, the ruling ideas rests upon the fact that those who control the major agencies of socialization typically occupy privileged class positions. As a consequence, their definition of social reality, and their moral judgments, are far more likely to be blessed with the stamp of public legitimacy than are the social and moral constructs of those in subordinate class positions (p. 42)*

Most sociologists have followed Marx's

notion of *ideology* as a world view or belief system which corresponds to the interests and concerns of ruling classes and powerful groups in a society. At times, ideologies, then, are simply rationalizations for the existing state of affairs. Religious beliefs may be ideological because they, in effect, reconcile people to their low position in society, to their poverty. This is nicely illustrated in a verse from a nineteenth century Anglican hymn, "All Things Bright and Beautiful." It reminds parishioners that the inequality between lord and serf is part of God's plan and must, therefore, be accepted:

The rich man in his castle
The poor man at his gate
He made them high and lowly
And ordered their estate
All things bright and beautiful, etc.

A number of European sociologists have emphasized the ways in which the economic elite have used the media to manipulate symbols, to convince members of society that all is serene and as it should be (see Ossenberg, 1971:165-168).[9] This is hardly surprising since the owners of the media are also members of the economic elite. Such a view of the media often seems to portray "media-barons" fairly successfully "brainwashing the masses." Certainly, as Elkin (1971) and others have demonstrated (e.g., Caldwell, 1978), the English press has, at times, blatantly manipulated its somewhat captive audience by its misleading reporting of political events in Quebec.

However, for the most part, media influences probably operate much more subtly than in the Quebec case. No doubt the media offers a limited perspective but these limits do not always reflect a deliberate attempt to manipulate public consciousness, but may often simply reflect the limited perspective of those who control the media. And, as media control becomes concentrated in the hands of a few, it should not be surprising that they present one consistent and conservative point of view (Minifie, 1971). In response to the model of media as manipulative, a number of sociologists, particularly American sociologists, maintain that the media simply reflect societal views. But whose views? It seems clear that the media ask certain kinds of questions, make selections about what is important and what is not, report events as if they had no history, no social context, all within a framework which assumes that if a problem does exist it can be resolved within the system. Perhaps the most fundamental limitation of the perspective presented through the media is that only certain kinds of futures can be imagined; essentially their perceptions of "what is" frame their notions of "what might be." Whether deliberately manipulative or not, this certainly coincides with the ideology, with the world view, of the economic elite.[10]

So, while ideologies are often simply rationalizations—justifications or apologies—they are, as Marx was fully aware, much more than that. Perhaps, then, it is more useful to view ideology as a set of limits to consciousness rather than simply a set of justifications. Martin Shaw (1972), for example, describes ideologies in just these terms:

Ideology . . . is not apology, although it may and often does entail it. Ideologies are world-views which, despite their partial and possibly critical insights, prevent us from understanding the society in which we live and the possibility of changing it. They are world-views which correspond to the standpoints of classes and social groups whose interests in the existing social system and incapacity to change it make it impossible for them to see it as a whole (pp. 33-34).

CULTURE VARIATION AND CHANGE

In other words, for sociologists ideology is culture—the ideologies in society are the cultures of the various groups within that society. This does imply that some groups are more powerful and are able to achieve dominance for their culture—to make it *the* culture of the society. But it is wrong to assume that other cultures disappear. In any society as complex as ours, there are bound to be many smaller "societies," each with distinctive ideas, values and norms. These are generally described as *subcultures*. When the United States is described as a "melting pot," what is meant is that various diverse cultures come together to form a single integrated dominant culture. The popular image of Canada, however, is something quite different: a cultural mosaic, many different cultures coexisting, not only the dominant cultures of French and English Canadians, but also the "third force." We are supposedly a *pluralistic society*.

A variety of studies on Toronto alone, for example, have described the distinct subcultures of Jews, Italians and Greeks, to name a few. Ukrainians in Western Canada have fought for a long time for the teaching of their language in the public school system, no doubt as an attempt to preserve to some extent their own culture. The reaction of the Cree Indians of Northern Quebec to the James Bay project symbolizes a more general concern with the preservation of native cultures. Some sociologists argue that Canada has a built-in tolerance for other ethnic identities because we have two, rather than one, dominant cultures. Some, on the other hand, argue that this multi-culturalism is a myth, an illusion; that while these various ethnic groups might be allowed their unique dances, costumes and rituals, they can never maintain a "living culture" in the face of the dominant English-Canadian culture. These issues are taken up again in Chapter X.

Sociologists reserve the term *counterculture* to describe subcultures which exist in opposition to the dominant culture. What is often described as "the social movement" of the 1960s arose in opposition to what many felt was a materialistic, competitive and repressive establishment culture. They valued instead greater sexual freedom, "mind expanding" experiences and communalism. The study of deviance is, as we shall see, in large part the study of countercultures seeking legitimacy—seeking acceptance within the dominant culture.

Implicit in all of this is that cultures—ideologies—are never so monolithic or powerful as we may have portrayed up to now. Built into any culture at a variety of levels is cultural change.

Sources of Culture Change

While the major source of culture change is in the conflict within societies of competing ideologies, there are a number of other sources of change which we will examine first. One perspective emphasizes the importance of *technology* in determining culture change. Sociologists distinguish between ideal culture and material culture. Television, and typewriters, cars and snowmobiles, knives and forks, machines and computers are all examples of the material culture. Material culture is what makes its way into museums; archaeology is partly about reconstructing ideal cultures from the remains of past material cultures. Material culture includes the technology and material things used by any group to control its environment. It is how the knowledge of a culture is put into practice to achieve the goals of that culture. Technology, however, is not simply the product of culture; according to some perspectives, it is also the producer of culture.

One example of such a theory, made particularly relevant by Alvin Toffler's notion of "future shock," is William Ogburn's (1922) version of technological determinism. Ogburn argues that technological change always outpaces culture change; there is, then, in his terms, "cultural lag." Cultures change as people try to catch up, in their ideas, with the new technology. Because they do not catch up, cultures are always changing. Toffler argues that today the cultural lag is even greater and that we find the ever changing technology threatening and confusing. We have already described how travel may produce culture shock; today as we stand still and observe the rapid changes around us we may experience future shock.

Much that now strikes us as incomprehensible would be far less so if we took a fresh look at the racing rate of change that makes reality seem, sometimes, like a kaleidoscope run wild. For the acceleration of change does not merely buffet industries or nations. It is a concrete force that reaches deep into our personal lives, compels us to act out new roles, and confronts us with the danger of a new and powerfully upsetting psychological disease. This new disease can be called "future shock" . . . (1971:10).

This perspective seems to treat technology as a force in itself, as somehow self-perpetuating. This ignores what conflict theorists emphasize: that certain groups control technology and direct it in ways they believe will most benefit them. Very often these groups believe that what benefits them also benefits society. This is the idea behind many businessmen's apparent belief that profit means progress, that if business is healthy, society is healthy. In any case, the conflict theorists stress that it is the powerful groups in society that direct technology in their perceived self-interest. Nevertheless, we can understand the notion, implicit in the work of Ogburn and Toffler, that technology seems to have a life of its own, independent of any groups. Whatever the powerful may have intended, technology has quite apparently had far-reaching *unintended* consequences. Who, for example, could have imagined, social scientist or otherwise, the consequences for every aspect of our lives of the mass-produced automobile? Ironically, decisions made for short-term gain may have disastrous long-term consequences for everybody, including the powerful groups who made the decisions. Dumping chemical wastes into the Great Lakes may have seemed economically advantageous in the short run. In the longer run, of course, we are collectively faced with the massive—some estimate $100 million—task of cleaning up the lakes. This is not to say that those who did most of the polluting will foot the bill or be held totally accountable for their actions. Perhaps the more crucial point is that the exploitation of arable land, the polluting of our water and air, cannot, in the long run, be in anyone's best interests. Once technology is created and set in motion, it does indeed take on a life of its own and moves us speedily closer to what Michael Harrington (1966) refers to as the "accidental century." In this phrase, Harrington has captured an important notion: that even if we accept the view that emphasizes how the powerful use and control technology in their own best interest, we must also recognize that technology has gone beyond their control.

Each new invention, like the automobile, television, nuclear power, space rockets, was a triumph of the human intelligence. But the totality of these inventions, with all of their revolutionary consequences, was an increasingly puzzling, even mysterious, society. As the parts became more ingenious and minutely calibrated, the whole became more irrational to those who had unwittingly fabricated it. The legend of one of Goya's Caprichos *etchings—"The dream of reason produces monsters"—seemed as much social science as surrealism (p. 29).*

At the same time, Harrington recognizes that the direction of technology is based on the decisions of the powerful and, if we are to bring technology back into control, we must uncover the human power behind it. In other words, the unintended but increasingly well-recognized consequences of technology pose a crucial question for liberal democracies. It seems evident that no longer can individualistic or private goals determine the direction of technology. Its impact on the commons, on all of us, demands public intervention; we must give priority to the collective survival and this must inevitably mean public intervention in the affairs of individuals. The complexity of technology, then, requires the restructuring of human values. Because of this, public intervention can be viewed quite apart from radical ideology. In these terms it no longer makes much sense to worry about "creeping socialism." The concern might be better viewed in terms of creating an ideology of survival.

The technological argument emphasizes how material forces—climate, geography and the technological attempts to deal with them—shape the culture of any people. But, in focusing on the material, there is the danger that we may lose sight of how people in their everyday interactions influence, however minutely, the shape of culture. Sociologists refer to as *action* those behaviours which are guided by cultural prescriptions. The way in which cultural values are transmitted into norms which guide behaviour—the process of institutionalization—is described in the following chapter. But, at this point, it is important to emphasize that just as a house is different from and more than its blueprint, so is action different from the cultural "blueprint" for action. People act upon, modify, elaborate, re-create and even invent; culture provides the base but does not determine the outcome. Indeed, the way that these inventions and elaborations, these re-creations and creations of culture become routinized, justified and integrated into culture is the other side of institutionalization. Institutionalization describes the reciprocal process whereby culture shapes action and patterned behaviour affects culture. The examination of human action and interaction as we describe it in Chapter V is the study of man's creation of culture even while he is bound by it. As mentioned at the beginning of this chapter, cultures are historical products. In talking about human culture we are breaking in at one point of this production process and talking about the "product." Interaction focuses on the process itself. But this means more than simply the interactions of our daily lives, our interpersonal relations; culture is shaped primarily in the interaction between groups, in the interaction between different and competing cultures.

Particularly in this context, the concepts of counterculture, subculture, "shadow" culture, etc., become important. However dominant the dominant culture is, it is never the sole set of ideas in any complex society. In a variety of ways, groups within society will try to preserve their own subcultures: they may attempt to isolate themselves from the influence of other groups as in the case of the Hutterites in Western Canada; they may "go underground" such as the homosexual subculture centred around the "gay" bar; or, they may try to achieve the even more difficult task of maintaining their own symbols and values and at the same time developing some commitment to the dominant culture, the situation for most immigrant groups; and finally, they may confront the dominant culture in an attempt to provide either an alternative, as many believe was the case for communal living, or a replacement—revolution. We might view these various patterns, as in Figure III.1, as a series of adaptations to the dominant culture. The two extreme cases, 1 and 6, provide the most obvious examples of culture change. In the first case, the subculture is swallowed up by the dominant culture and ceases to be a living entity. In the latter case, it is the dominant culture which is changed either because, in whole or in part, the "revolution" was successful, or at least because the dominant culture had to confront the challenge and adapt to it. Even when the challenge is met with force, and the revolution is unsuccessful, "representatives" of the dominant culture will, eventually, have to use the cultural symbols to justify the use of force and explain the revolution. Indeed, the fact that the threat was overcome will probably become part of the culture, even institutionalized as a national holiday, a day of celebration. As we have seen, a cynical view of the historian's task holds that he integrates such events into the culture, preserving in his account some sense of the heroic defeat of villainous forces.

When we turn to the other attempts at adaptation to culture contact in Figure III.1, the implications for change may be

Figure III.1

ADAPTATIONS TO CONTACT WITH DOMINANT CULTURE

CULTURE CONTACT WITHIN SOCIETY

NATURE OF CONTACT	GOAL
1. Assimilation	Surrender to dominant culture
2. Isolation	Subculture preservation
3. Underground	Self-preservation
4. Dual committment	Structural assimilation without behavioural assimilation
5. Counterculture	Provide cultural alternatives
6. Contra-culture	Displace or radically alter the dominant culture

less obvious. One would think that isolation, for example, would protect the subculture while at the same time making it unlikely that it will influence the dominant culture. In fact, complete cultural isolation is impossible and such subcultures as Hutterites must be constantly vigilant against the inevitable intrusions and seductions of alternative lifestyles of the dominant culture (Peter, 1976). And, however negatively those within the dominant culture view the Hutterites, they at least know that the alternative exists. The Hutterite values, to some extent, enter the common stock of knowledge.

Clearly, this mutual influence becomes much more apparent when we talk about countercultures and underground cultures. Both are typically seen as threats and are directly challenged by the dominant culture; their survival is always precarious. At the same time, countercultures invite members of straight society to experience counter-institutions—free universities, communes, encounter sessions, etc. However short-lived these institutions or people's involvement in them, it is unlikely that once having experienced these alternatives, one can re-enter "straight" society quite so straight. There seems, as well, to be a certain attraction, a romantic appreciation of the "low-life" underground cultures. Indeed, a so-called "night on the town" may often involve, perhaps vicariously, a visit to what W. E. Mann (1970) calls the "underside" of a city. In a sense, it could be argued that underground cultures are useful to conventional society in that they provide a "safety valve" for the kind of behaviour and experience deemed dangerous to dominant values, but which no one supposes can ever be eradicated. But, as people move back and forth between the cultures, they transport cultural items; some of our most colourful and apt expressions originated in the gay bar, the jazz club and the poolroom (Polsky, 1969).

Finally, as we shall see in detail in Chapter X, it is impossible to maintain dual commitment without sacrificing either opportunities in conventional society (structural assimilation) or ethnic differences in behaviour (behavioural assimilation). In fact, both the dominant or host culture must, as they come in contact, influence one another. Clearly, the host culture is not static and will inevitably be influenced by its sub- and countercultures and its various immigrant groups. But, these changes are minor when compared to the extinction or gradual dissolution which is the fate of most competing or alternate cultures.

Much of the same processes occur between societies as within. At the most obvious level we are all aware of the process of *cultural diffusion*—a process which becomes more and more inevitable as, in Marshall McLuhan's terms, the world becomes a "global village." No culture can remain insular and therefore distinct.

There is a danger, however, in considering diffusion as the harmonious borrowing and lending of cultural traits and habits. Certainly this does occur and, at some level, countries of the world may share more and more cultural traits. However, the process is not one of simply exchange, nor is it necessarily a purely accidental process. As one speaks of dominant cultures within a society, one might, by analogy, describe the world powers as dominant cultures in the international sphere. While the dominant cultures, in these terms, do pick up cultural items—international cooking, fashions and folk art—what the dominant culture passes on—whole technologies, for example—will obviously involve these other societies in a much more fundamental cultural change. For example, it was generally hoped that as Third World nations incorporated the technology of industrialization, they would experience not only a drop in death rates but also a decline in birth rates. Improved standards of health and hygiene did, indeed, bring with them a decline in infant mortality and therefore death rates more generally, but not the anticipated decline in birth rates. What we seem to be witnessing in these societies, in exaggerated form, is the kind of cultural lag and future shock we have discussed previously.

Population explosion in the underdeveloped world underscores the kind of dilemmas culture contact entails. It seems that a society cannot adopt a part of the package, say, medical technology, without adopting pretty much the whole package—westernization. And, this inevitably involves massive and probably painful change in the fabric of the culture. It also seems that dominant cultures take for granted that they do have solutions to Third World problems without much consideration for these long-term consequences. They may even define these problems in their own cultural terms. Perhaps we can characterize the standard argument as "if these nations want to get ahead they will simply have to give up their culture, forget about their useless traditions, in essence, westernize." With increasing recognition of the dangers inherent in such a view, some theorists have sought ways in which Third World nations might benefit from Western technology without incurring such dramatic social and cultural costs. For example, some have suggested some form of "intermediate technology" which provides certain benefits but ideally poses fewer problems of cultural adaptation—people may not have to become Westerners overnight to benefit from some of the technological resources.

Marxist theorists are more likely to view the contact between dominant powers and other cultures in terms of imperialism. From this perspective, when a dominant culture contacts directly one of these other cultures it is almost always in a situation of exploitation. There is a clear parallel in what happens between societies with what happens within societies. As we have seen, the dominant culture in a society is, in part at least, an ideology of justifications. Similarly, those who are concerned with the nature and consequences of imperialism seek to understand not only the exploitation of one nation by another but also the ideology of imperialism which seeks to justify it. Perhaps the archetype of imperialistic relationships is South Africa. Whites entered South Africa principally to exploit its resources, including the labour resources, and they arrived with a more advanced technology for both exploiting resources and exacting compliance. As with all such relationships, the White ideology defined White dominance in terms of exchange between unequal partners. While the Whites might profit economically and otherwise, they have supposedly brought culture to the "uncultured," civilization to the "uncivilized" and salvation to the "heathen." Furthermore, the ideology maintains that what the Whites are taking does not deprive the host culture which was unable to benefit from the resources without White intervention. To put all of this much more simply, the ideology of imperialism is often some form of racism. Very often, too, the host culture will come to believe in their own "inferiority" and will internalize the racist ideology, and when this occurs the exploitative relationship is stabilized. In other words, when the host culture incorporates the beliefs of the dominant culture, that is, develops a *colonial mentality*, it adopts as standards of self-evaluation the values of the foreign power. However, just as we described the persistence of subcultures and countercultures within societies, pockets of resentment and antagonism inevitably persist. Imperialism, then, necessarily involves some interplay between legitimation and force.[11]

Finally, as we shall examine in more detail in Chapter VII, Marxist theorists maintain that the underdevelopment of Third World countries should not be attributed solely to their unwillingness or inability to adapt their culture to technological innovations. Rather, it is to the benefit of the dominant powers to keep these nations in some stage of under- or arrested development.

CONCLUSION

Culture is ideas, ideas about what is and what ought to be. These more or less shared ideas pervade every aspect of our lives, but like the air we breathe, we rely on culture without thinking much about it. To the extent that we take cultural ideas for granted, treat rules and values unreflectively and accept prepackaged knowledge, we are constrained by our culture. Sociology, by holding these ideas up to examination, by making explicit the taken-for-granted, by studying common sense knowledge, can be liberating.

At the same time, complex society inevitably means some degree of culture conflict, and culture change, particularly as urbanization brings more and more people from different backgrounds into close proximity, as people are inundated with media images of different lifestyles and new possibilities. But to understand culture and culture change is to recognize that cultures are historical phenomena, the products of past conflicts, and they reflect the achieved dominance of some groups over others.

We have described people as choice makers. They may, however, assume that there are no choices, that the ways they have learned are the only ways, or, they may believe that there are so many choices that there is no one right choice. Many sociologists seem to believe that the latter is becoming increasingly the case in Western society. Some see it in highly negative terms and describe man as alienated from himself and his fellow man; others see it more positively and describe man as protean, able to move from one social world to another with relative ease, to enjoy a fuller and broader range of experiences. But the ideas one has and the choices one makes can only be understood in the context of the structure of opportunities for realizing one's ideas and actualizing one's choices—the social structure.

SUGGESTIONS FOR FURTHER READING

Aside from the readings mentioned in the chapter, perhaps no better introduction to the concept of culture can be found than Elenor Smith Bowen's fictionalized account of her experiences among the Tiv of Northern Nigeria, *Return to Laughter* (1964). A classic sociological introduction remains A. L. Kroeber's and Talcott Parsons' article, "The Concepts of Culture and of Social System" (1958). Other early, and for the most part more interesting, works on "culture" include: F. Boas's *Race, Language and Culture* (1940); Ruth Benedict's *Patterns of Culture* (1934); Margaret Mead's *Coming of Age in Samoa* (1928); Clyde Kluckhohn's *Mirror for Man* (1949); E. B. Tylor's *Primitive Culture* (1958); Bronislaw Malinowski's *The Dynamics of Cul-*

tural Change (1945); A. R. Radcliffe Brown's *Structure and Function in Primitive Society* (1952); and Claude Lévi-Strauss's *Totemism* (1963). An excellent survey of "theories of culture" can be found in Marvin Harris's *The Rise of Anthropological Theory* (1968). Harris is also a proponent of a "materialistic" explanation of what he calls the riddles of culture. See, in particular, his *Cows, Pigs, Wars and Witches* (1974).

The relationship of technology to culture has been explored in a number of works, for example, Lewis Mumford's *Technics and Civilization* (1934); Jacques Elleul's *The Technological Society* (1967); Margaret Mead's *Cultural Patterns and Technical Change* (1955); and Alvin W. Gouldner's and Richard A. Peterson's *Technology and the Moral Order* (1962). An example of the highly controversial work of Marshall McLuhan, describing the relationship of communication and culture, is his *Understanding Media: The Extensions of Man* (1965). Two books which manage to get at many of the same issues, but without the constraints of academic sociology, are Carlos Castenada's *The Teachings of Don Juan: A Yaqui Way of Knowledge* (1968) and Robert Persig's *Zen and the Art of Motorcycle Maintenance* (1975).

Studies which have explored aspects of Canadian culture are Horace Miner's *St. Denis* (1939); John Seeley's and others' *Crestwood Heights* (1956); James Lorimer's and Myfanwy Phillips's *Working People* (1971); and Marcel Rioux's and Yves Martin's collection of articles, *French Canadian Society* (1964). W. E. Mann has edited a two-volume collection of articles on culture and cultural change in Canada, *Social and Cultural Change in Canada* (1960a). A radical and dramatic description of elite control of culture in Canada—news, television, art, education, sports—can be found in Ian Lumsden's *Close the 49th Parallel, etc.* (1970). Perhaps the most valuable insights into Canadian culture, up until now at least, can be found in the works of Canadian novelists and poets.

FOOTNOTES

[1]The most influential and controversial attempt to show how such "personality traits" cluster together is Adorno and others, *The Authoritarian Personality* (1950).

[2]B. Holzner (1968) provides a much fuller discussion of "reality shock." For some illustrations of "culture shock," read Hall's (1959) *The Silent Language*.

[3]Compare this to the discussions in Chapter I and II on value free sociology and partisanship.

[4]Gouldner makes a rather vague and confusing distinction between "background" and "domain" assumptions. While both are, in essence, world views, the latter appear to be those background assumptions which apply to particular situations or groups of people. Domain assumptions, then, are of more limited application than background assumptions.

[5]For a readable account of Inuit language and culture, see Hans Reusch's novel, *Top of the World* (1951).

[6]Rocher (1970) describes how these cultural differences are even expressed in two distinctive kinds of sociology—Francophone and Anglophone.

[7]Gun control poses a real dilemma for "small 'l' liberals." It is easy enough to view the Japanese-Canadian example as a violation of basic human rights and as testimony for the need to eliminate secrecy and elitism in government. The attempt to limit and control guns in Canadian society, however, probably has the backing of most of these same critics. They realize, too, that if put to referendum or parliamentary debate, gun control legislation will, as in the United States, be strongly opposed.

[8]This, in essence, is the thesis of Margaret Atwood's (1972) highly selective critique of Canadian literature. Canadians, she argued, are depicted by their writers as victims preoccupied with surviving rather than with controlling or dominating the vicissitudes of Canadian nature, climate, geography and, ultimately, social and economic forces.

[9]From a different angle, Vance Packard (1957) has examined the techniques employed in the media to manipulate tastes. One of the most fascinating, if controversial, studies of media technique is Key's *Subliminal Seducation* (1973). Right or wrong, you will never, after reading this book, look at a magazine advertisement the same way again.

[10]The extent to which there is a linkage between the economic elite and the media elite has been explored by Porter (1965); Clement (1975); Warnock (1970); Peers (1970)' and Baldwin (1977). Of interest also is the debate betwen Clement (1977b) and Baldwin (1977a) about the meaning of Clement's data on elite linkages.

[11]One of the now classic statements about cultural and economic imperialism is Franz Fanon's *The Wretched of the Earth* (1968).

social structure
CHAPTER IV

The idea of social structure suggests that human behaviour is patterned, repetitive and, to some extent, predictable. These patterns constitute the structure of opportunities (and limitations) which we must all confront. To get the sense of social structure, we can start by thinking about an opposite and hypothetical situation, one in which there is no social organization, no shared culture or language. What we do have is an organism—one which gets hungry, thirsty, cold and sexually aroused. "It" wants something and it goes after it. Now, to get what it wants it might well act like a bull in a china shop—smash its way through to its objective: food, warmth, sexual gratification. It could, in other words, "run amok," oblivious to things around it, unmindful of consequences, unaware of rules and of abstract norms about property, decorum and deference. Such a view of human beings—that this is what they are "really" like—is very close to that of William Golding, especially in his novel, *Lord of the Flies*. In this novel, children on a deserted island, accidentally placed outside of the constraints and norms of civilization, revert to savagery, bestiality and egoism. There is literally "a war of all against all" on Golding's fictional island.

Of course, such a picture of "man" is difficult if not impossible to conceive. There is, first of all, the obvious problem that the human organism is born helpless, undeveloped and unable to fend for itself. This means that even to survive there must be some rudimentary form of social order, some regularized forms of social activity. But, even aside from the biological necessity, man in a pre-societal state is a sociological absurdity. We are, as sociologists, always dealing with people as socialized organisms—this is, by definition, what is meant by "human." We are dealing with people who have "personalities" and who therefore may require affection, stimulation, praise and so on. Children raised in isolation or by animals—so-called feral children—either are not "human" or, as is the more likely case, they were partially socialized before being abandoned. Even Golding's children began to develop a social structure, however primitive and myth-filled it was.

SOCIAL ACTION

One starting point, then, for beginning to understand social order is a socialized human being who has learned goals, "energizers," the "subjective springs of action" (Gerth and Mills, 1953:114). In Charles K. Warriner's (1970) terms, the irreducible point from which we start is the *stream of action*, the continuous, ongoing activity that is characteristic of life. This is the primordial "given" of all the behavioural and social sciences. What does *action* mean? Essentially, the term action—usually social action—refers to behaviour which is meaningful to the person or social actor involved. It is social behaviour. In order to do something, we have to take into account not only the physical things (objects) in our environment, but also the social things. One problem of interest to sociologists is how we make sense of our social and physical environment—not how in some objective and external way is social order possible, but how is it that we are able to make the world outside seem to have order and stability?

The problem we pose in this chapter centres around the dilemma of the individual and the society. It is, in many respects, one of the enduring splits in sociology. The two sociological perspectives are well represented in the apparently conflicting views of Emile Durkheim and Max Weber (see Chapter I). Weber was concerned with action, subjectively meaningful behaviour; he emphasized how people use what is inside their heads to shape their own behaviour. Durkheim, on the other hand, was not really concerned with action, but with how behaviour is shaped by external constraints.[1] The question seems to be, do we view the social world as outside of people, independent of them, or are social phenomena only inside people's minds? As we hope will be apparent by the end of this book, these two views are not really opposite or contradictory. On the one hand, society does stand outside of us, limiting our actions and making us act in predictable and patterned ways. On the other hand, the social world is at the same time a subjectively shared world. By this we do not mean that you can wish away the social world any more than you can wish away winter. But, it may no longer affect you. If, in fact, someone achieves a state in which the social world no longer constrains him, this may often mean the same as "madness," unless of course he can get enough people to go along with his version of the social world. If so, he has created a counterculture, a social movement, perhaps a new cult or religion.

Indeed, the issue of madness serves as a useful illustration of the subjective and objective dimensions of structure. One *can*, subjectively, liberate oneself from the structural constraints of a particular society, step outside the patterns as it were. It is in this sense that the existential psychiatrist R. D. Laing has described the "mad" as "prophets of a new order." The crucial point, however, is that while the "mad" are supposedly subjectively "liberating" themselves, they are, after all, designated as mad and treated as such. In other words, they experience directly the weight of social structure, even at the same time as they subjectively free themselves from it. We, all of us, experience the weight of social structure in our everyday lives. In the words of C. Wright Mills (1959:3):

> *When a society is industrialized, a peasant becomes a worker; a feudal lord is liquidated or becomes a businessman. When classes rise or fall, a man is employed or unemployed; when the rate of investment goes up or down, a man takes new heart or goes broke. When wars happen, an insurance salesman becomes a rocket launcher; a store clerk, a radar man; a wife lives alone; a child grows up without a father. Neither the life of an individual nor the history of a society can be understood without understanding both.*

Indeed, most of us have, at least episodically, felt trapped. Things seem to have been laid out for us. There seem to be limits in how much we can ever hope to accomplish. Things seem to happen to us that shape our lives—events, circumstances, the workings of vast impersonal forces seem more powerful than us. Some of the problems we encounter, some of our troubles, seem to have no solution within our control. In essence, we have described the subjective experience of social structure. Indeed, social structure is defined as those patterns of social relationships into which we are born, which have existed before us, and which we "know" will persist after our deaths.

Social structure most of the time appears to us as something which is real and which stands outside of us, in almost the same way that the walls and corridors of a building limit and direct our physical movements. The very fact that these patterns have had such a long history may lead us to view them as somehow independent of human activities, that is, as if they had some life of their own. They may, indeed, seem overwhelming and unchangeable. Social structure, in part, then, constrains us through the sheer weight of custom and tradition. As Karl Marx puts it, "The past weighs like a nightmare on the living."

At best, in our everyday lives, we have only the vaguest notion of what these structures are. This is something we do not think about in our day-to-day relationships and it is, for us, these day-to-day relationships which are the paramount reality. Our awareness of the social world is bounded by the social scenes in which we live. The vividness of our face-to-face interactions, our close-up scenes—in the family, at school and at work—blind us to the context which frames these scenes. And, just as we recognize, in our everyday lives, that we may be "in a rut," we recognize that we may be having trouble seeing beyond our own experience, seeing outside the rut. Part of the weight of structure stems from our bounded awareness.

PRIVATE TROUBLES AND PUBLIC ISSUES

C. Wright Mills's distinction between personal troubles and public issues is an insightful attempt to recognize this aspect of social structure. We all know what personal problems are—problems of finding a job, getting along with one's mate, living within one's income. Public issues, on the other hand, are more difficult to understand and articulate. We all know about and may engage in debates about increasing unemployment, rising divorce rates and inflation. We find it harder, however, to talk about these issues in relation to our everyday lives. The ability to draw the link between the personal sphere and the public sphere is, for Mills, the sociological imagination. Public issues transcend our immediate environment, our personal milieu; they deal with the way in which many such personal milieux, society as a whole, are structured. For example, when one man is unemployed that is his personal trouble. We must look to his character, his background, his skills, to understand and deal with the problem. However, when many are unemployed, that represents a structural problem and therefore a public issue. This raises questions not of the character and skill of all these individuals, but of the structure of opportunities in society.

Even when unemployment rates soar, when unemployment has clearly become a public issue, the people who are unemployed are likely to worry not about the opportunity structure but rather about problems in their own milieu—how can they get other jobs, how can they feed themselves and their families, what are they going to do? In fact, in our society it may be part and parcel of the ideology that people are encouraged to see problems as personal troubles. And, most important, this focus leads them to blame themselves, to define the problem as some shortcoming in character, skill or what have you. Or, they will look to their immediate milieu and perhaps locate the problem in their family. It is the task of sociology, according to Mills, to help people make the distinction between private troubles and public issues in their own lives.

This, we might add, has been at least one of the tasks of the sociology of women. Connelly and Christiansen-Ruffman (1977), two Halifax sociologists, have, for example, explicitly studied women's consciousness of their problems in terms of public issues as private troubles. They used both formal interview data for 223 women from other studies and intensive interviews with a sub-sample of 25 women. According to their data, not all women are conscious of personal troubles as public issues. Among those who are, however, only a minority are able to link their own private troubles to the structural problems, the public issues, of being a woman in contemporary society. Apparently, a number of women, especially housewives isolated in their homes, see their unhappiness as something which is their own fault:

[These women] recognize their private troubles and are miserable, dissatisfied wives and mothers. They are obviously upset with their situation but do not see it resulting from their position as women. Their dissatisfaction is, therefore, usually couched in more personal terms. They often have little recognition of the structurally inequitable position of women in society and the personal interpretation usually given their problem by friends and doctors does not generally lead to such recognition (pp. 170-171).

Consciousness raising sessions, then, do not, as is sometimes alleged, necessarily create problems where none existed before. Rather, they are an attempt to make people aware that in seeking solutions to personal problems, it may be necessary to look beyond the personal *milieux* to the larger structural issues.

PERSPECTIVES ON SOCIAL STRUCTURE

To understand this larger social reality, we must first ask how the components of a society are connected to one another. There are three models, often thought to be competing models, sociologists use to answer this question. One views society as a system—emphasizing the integration of the parts and the role of values in holding the parts together. The second (the structure approach) sees social structure in terms of layers—emphasizing inequality—and sees society as held together by force and manipulation used by those on the top layer. The third model views society as symbolic interaction, as built up or constructed as people fit their lines of action to one another. The system model (functionalism) helps us draw the "blueprint" of society and, like any blueprint, it will exaggerate how harmoniously the parts connect; it is the plan, not the product. The structure approach tells us how the blueprint was created and, through focusing on contradictions within the plan, how it might be changed. Finally, the interaction approach, the subject of the following chapter, tells us how, in using the plan, people modify and elaborate upon it. In this sense, society is not the plan or even simply the result of the plan, but is *built up* out of the actions of people.

At the outset of this book, we indicated our approach to be a combination of the structure and interaction approaches (the conflict perspective and symbolic interactionism). The central questions, for us, are the role of power and inequality in creating the plan and the ways in which people actualize and modify it in their everyday lives. We believe, with Gerth and Mills (1953), that these two approaches allow us to link personal troubles and public issues. Nevertheless, we cannot blind ourselves to the utility, for heuristic purposes, of pretending that we can "stop" society at some point and describe it as an entity, a system with no history, one in which people are merely rule followers. We begin with the system approach because, at least in part, the other two approaches arose in response to it. Also, many of the concepts which now define conventional sociology and which are used to some degree, although somewhat differently, by all sociologists, emerged from structural functionalism, what we are calling the system approach.[2]

SOCIETY AS SYSTEM

The starting point for a system approach is to raise the question of system needs. This approach emphasizes that societies must meet certain basic needs—biological, economic and social—if they are to survive at all. These requirements are usually referred to as "functional prerequisites." Simply, all societies must reproduce themselves, they must make arrangements to care for infants, to teach them the language and culture and to turn them into functioning adults who will also reproduce and care for their young.

There must also be some sort of economy—people have to be fed, clothed and sheltered; goods and services must be produced and distributed to members of the society. Arrangements also have to be made to cope with physical and mental illness and injuries. Somehow, too, the various activities of the members must be organized and coordinated; some degree of social order is necessary if the other societal tasks are to be performed at all. One aspect of this is that there must be some provision for organizing "legitimate violence," either to keep members in line or to ward off external enemies. Finally, all societies, all groups, must face the crucial problem of providing their members with values which motivate them to carry out various activities required for social survival and which provide a rationale for the existing social structure. When put at a very general level, these functional requisites are Parsons's four general problems of adaptation, goal attainment, integration and pattern maintenance and tension management which we described in Chapter I.

In setting out these various prerequisites, we are in effect describing the major parts or *institutional orders* of a social structure. An institutional order consists of all those activities within a social structure which have a similar function. We can, then, speak of a kinship order, a religious order, an economic order, a political order, a military order, an educational order, a health and welfare order and so on. In a complex industrial society such as Canada, these various orders are fairly clearly separated and distinct from one another and may be further subdivided into specific institutions. In simple societies these orders may be less "visible" because they are overlapped and fused together. The medicine man may, for instance, also be the spiritual leader and in some instances the political and military leader as well. As Gerth and Mills (1953) point out:

> *We may isolate one aspect of a society from another for the sake of analysis, but we have to realize that often, as in the peasant village and the garrison state, this analytical isolation is not experienced; life is an inseparable fusion (p. 27).*

Thus, as we shall see later in this chapter, religious and/or kinship values may, in many societies, permeate all social relationships, all social orders, whether the activity in question is essentially economic, political, educational or medical in nature. This leaves open for the moment the question raised by Marx of whether the economic institutions are not the substructure—the basis—for the shape and order of all other institutions. This represents the central challenge by conflict theorists to the system view, a challenge which we take up when we consider the "society as structure" perspective later in this chapter.

There is a danger in confusing functional requisites with structural requisites, that is, in assuming that some feature of a society which serves a function cannot be changed. Part of the sociological imagination is to think up alternative ways in which needs may be met. While functional prerequisites set parameters to the ways in which societies can be constructed, they do not, of course, mean that no change is possible. Yet, one of the main arguments by conservatives is that if something exists, we remove it at our peril. There may, in other words, be dire consequences for social order and social integration if we try to remove or reform a particular institution. This, for example, was at the heart of Edmund Burke's critique of the French Revolution: the Aristocracy and the Church served important functions. To destroy them was also to invite chaos and anarchy. In fact, the "Reign of Terror" which followed the Revolution proved Burke to be right in at least the short run. But, what conservatives often forget is that there are functional *alternatives,* or, as the old saying has it, there is more than one way to skin a cat. Certainly the Church, however corrupt it had become, did have an integrating function in that it provided people with a sense of meaning and purpose. But other institutions, especially those connected with science and education, were, to some extent, supplanting the Church, and the state and secular ideologies became the focus of loyalty. Similarly, many of the traditional and necessary functions of the family have, in contemporary society, been parcelled out to other institutions, the educational system, for example, without necessarily destroying society in the process.

SYSTEM COMPONENTS

Status and Role

Probably the most important concept emerging out of the system approach is that of *role.* Essentially, a role is a set of obligations and expectations which serve to organize behaviour and, in effect, make it social. The concept of role has become central to the sociological perspective in a number of respects. First, as we shall see in Chapter V, the main way to understand the sociological meaning of personality and how it is developed is through an understanding of people as role-playing creatures. We are, from a system perspective, the roles which we play in society; the personality is little more than a composite bundle of roles. Second, roles are also seen as the major link between the individual and society. Roles, by definition, are interpersonal; that is, they are more or less regularized patterns of conduct in which we attempt to take into account another person or persons and to make our behaviour mutual with theirs. Third, the concept of role reminds us that interaction is seldom fleeting and ephemeral but, rather, involves actors in stable and persistent patterns of social relationships. Roles, then, are positions in interaction and in society. They are focal points around which norms cluster. Another way to put this is to say that a role relationship frames social action and therefore to some extent limits our range of choices.

Norms are simply rules. The rules receive their justification from the dominant value system, from the cultural system, but norms are more specific guidelines which people follow and which provide people with expectations about others' behaviour. Norms also imply social control, in terms of *sanctions*—rewards and punishments—which are applied to get people back in line. When our friends ridicule or praise us for what we do, we are experiencing informal social control. When we are arrested and convicted for an action, we have experienced formal social control. Roles, then, might be viewed as the bundles of norms and sanctions which adhere to a social position.

Traditionally, sociologists have distinguished two aspects of any social position or social relationship. Generally, the term *status* has been used to refer to a socially defined position in society. The concept of status directs us to the *rights* which go with a given position, what are sometimes described as the "perks" (perquisites) of a particular job or office. For example, in some firms, salesmen are given a regular Ford, Chevrolet or Dodge as a company car whereas sales managers are given a Buick or Oldsmobile; the Vice-President drives a Lincoln or Cadillac; the President has a chauffeur-driven limousine. These are rights which go with the social position, independent of who occupies the position.

Role, on the other hand, reminds us that along with rights or expectations go *obligations.* Status can be viewed as the passive side of a social position, role as the active side since it involves a performance. Role, then, is the pattern of behaviour expected or required of persons who occupy a particular status. In everyday life we are also prepared to make this distinction between status as position, role as performance. For example, even after the revelations of Watergate, some Americans were reluctant to impeach Nixon because they did not want to take the risk that in punishing his performance, as President, dirt would also fall on the position of the Presidency. For similar reasons, the medical profession has been loathe to take cases of medical malpractice and fraud to the courts because it believed that this would accentuate the "potential disgrace to the professions." Also, we seem able to distinguish between good popes and bad popes or among styles of prime ministers without necessarily affecting our respect (or lack of respect) for the statuses themselves.

Clearly, what is role from one point of view is status from another. For example, in our status as professors we expect that students will show interest in our subjects, that they will come to class, that they will address us as Professor or Doctor, not as "Pete" or "Hey you." As a student you expect that professors will be prepared for their lectures, that they will read and assess your work, that they will be available for consultation and so on.

More recently, this traditional distinction between the role and status aspects of a social relationship has broken down. Perhaps because status-role is awkward, most sociologists, including us in most instances, use role to refer both to the position and to the performance. Hence, we talk about the role of teacher, of doctor, of parent, etc. We are apt to say that in a particular situation we were not sure what role we were being asked to play. William Goode (1960) suggests that the term role is gradually replacing that of status because status has increasingly come to mean role relationships that have become more fully *institutionalized.* That is, while all social relationships are based on role and involve role performances, some relationships are based upon norms which are so widely held in the community or society that they become highly structured or routinized, whereas other role relationships are based on norms that must be worked out in interaction and require a good deal of negotiation and bargaining. The concept of status, then, directs us to the ways in which social interaction is *structured,* whereas the concept of role directs us to the *process* of interaction.

The concept of status also reflects two interrelated aspects of "status-role"; first, that roles are almost always reciprocal relationships. It makes no sense to talk of the role of husband unless we think of wife; employer means nothing without employee; teacher implies students; and so on. Second, a role relationship usually involves some degree of "structured" inequality. In everyday language we are apt to say that someone has gained a lot of status or that they do something for the status, not because they like it. Used in this way, we are recognizing that statuses are almost always ranked as more or less superior.

Indeed, the one case where this is not true seems to be friendship relations. Here, by definition, norms dictate that the situation should be one of equality and intimacy. We do not mean that all friendship relationships are, in fact, equal relationships. Obviously, in many relationships defined as friendship inequality exists; one person always takes the leadership, decides what is to be done, is thought to have more knowledge. But, the inequality in friendship relationships is *emergent*—it is not pre-defined by the partners in the relationship. The way in which inequality emerges out of interaction is one focus of exchange theory discussed in the following chapter.

Note that almost all statuses in society

involve some degree of structured inequality. As we have said, status implies "perks." But, what often is ignored by system theorists is that rights are not established in a vacuum. Powerful people lay claim to certain rewards—deference or a larger share of the pie. They claim that their position, their status, entitles them to extra rewards, to special treatment, and, as we shall see, very often their claims are successful. System theorists prefer to view unequal relationships as *authority* relationships as a result of people voluntarily submitting to normative prescriptions. For the system theorist, superordinate and subordinate share the same values and norms; there is value-consensus. Status is not problematic; both know who is on top and who is on bottom, both know what is coming to each and both know how to act. From this perspective it is assumed that parents, teachers or employers are entitled to their position as long as they fulfil their role because they supposedly have greater resources and knowledge than people occupying the reciprocal part of the role-status relationship. Statuses are, in these terms, authority relationships—they are unequal relationships in which power is legitimated by norms in the wider society and maintained by various forms of social control.

At one extreme we have relatively unstructured friendship relationships based on norms of equality and fairness. What lies at the opposite end of what we might call the authority continuum? As is suggested in Figure IV.1, the model for role relationships based on extreme inequality and a high degree of authority is what people have believed is their relationship to God, in some cases to the gods.[3]

The Equality Revolution: An Excursus

Admittedly, our relationships with our various gods have been so one-sided that they hardly qualify as a role relationship; a lot of messages, supplications and ritual sacrifices on our side; ambiguous signs, visions, portents and testimony from "false" and "true" prophets on the other side. But, traditionally and historically, kings and emperors have claimed either that they are partly gods or that the gods have spoken to them; historically a most powerful way, indeed, to insure that one's claim to deference, to power, to wealth and luxury will not be disputed.

Typically, rulers have been able to maintain immense social and physical distance from their subjects. They have been impersonal and seemingly oblivious of those over whom they rule. For their part, the ruled have had to be very sensitive to the moods, whims and capricious behaviour of their ruler. Often it was better not to come to his attention; chances of favours were balanced by chances of punishment or death. Interaction between ruler and ruled was also likely to be highly prescribed or ritualized. Even today, for instance, those granted an "audience" with the Queen are drilled in the proper forms of address and the proper protocol.

The patriarchal family also seems to have been modelled on traditional concep-

Figure IV.1
THE EQUALITY CONTINUUM

tions of god-human relationships. It is no accident, probably, that our Judeo-Christian God is often referred to as Father. Hence, children, ideally, were to speak only when spoken to and to maintain respect and fear for their father. Children, servants, even wives learned to stay out of the way when Father was in a bad temper, to anticipate his moods and to respond quickly to his wishes. As with rulers and slave-masters, the sensitivity in the relationship was very one-sided. Leo Zakuta has speculated on the rather neat parallel in Latin societies between the importance of the Virgin Mary and the patriarchal structure of families in these societies. Strictly speaking, one does not pray to the Virgin Mary but, rather, asks her to intercede on one's behalf with God. Similarly, mothers in Latin societies are the warm and affectionate parent, expected to act as an intermediary between children and the stern, remote father.

In sum, we can say that to the left of the authority continuum are highly prescribed formal and impersonal role relationships in which there is little room for negotiation of rules, for bargaining over rights and obligations. It simply would not do, in a patriarchal family, for a child to say something like, "I'll eat my meal if I can have an extra dessert," nor, for that matter, would parents find themselves saying things like, "If you want a story then you have first to get ready for bed." As we move to the right of the continuum, we find that while role relationships are still based on some degree of inequality, they become less rigid and formal, more personal and intimate. It seems, too, that the "inferior" in these role relationships feels more able to initiate bargaining with the "superior" and to enter into negotiations about the actual rules which will, in fact, structure the relationship. In turn, from the point of view of the "superior" person, there is a greater need to take the other person or persons into account, to think about their feelings and definitions of the situation. Clearly, authoritarian role relationships lack the sensitivity we typically find and expect in more equal relationships.

In the past few decades it seems that most role-status relationships have tended to shift closer to the right of the authority continuum. As Figure IV.1 suggests, this "equality revolution" has been especially pronounced in family relationships—the patriarchal family has given way to a more egalitarian and democratic family structure. Winch (1971) suggests that the family has gone from institution to companionship. He is referring mainly to the fact that husband-wife relations are no longer so clearly based on tradition. Rather, the tie between husband and wife is, ideally, an affectional tie, based on love, companionship and, therefore, a high degree of equality. It comes very close, then, to being a friendship relationship. Also, what becomes habitualized and routinized in the marriage is partially based on institutionalized norms, but is also partially worked out, emergent, from husband-wife interaction. Much the same seems true for parent-child relationships which appear to be far more egalitarian and democratic than in any previous era. Certainly, for people raised around the beginning of this century, today's children seem extremely disrespectful, cheeky and spoiled, and parents seem overly lax and indulgent.

In Chapter XII we shall look more carefully at some of the implications for marriage and family life of this shift towards greater equality. At the moment, what is particularly relevant is that this "equality revolution" has not stopped at the family but has, in varying degrees, permeated virtually all role relationships in modern society. Thus, just as the authoritarian father has disappeared, so too has the stern and demanding schoolmaster, lording it over his pupils, been relegated to educational history. Probably, too, the tyrant-boss of the Victorian times survives only in caricature form in the unending battle between Bumstead and Mr. Dithers and the unequal exchanges between Mutt and Jeff and a series of stingy, arbitrary and short-tempered employers. The general result of the "equality revolution" is that students, in Jerry Farber's memorable phrase, no longer view themselves as "Niggers," nor are they so viewed by their teachers and professors. And, as we shall see later in this chapter, workers have gone from being defined as units of production to "people," requiring motivation, fulfillment and personal recognition.

Another way we can consider the "equality revolution" is to consider the structural changes which have occurred. We cannot simply suppose that the superior member of the unequal relationship became, out of the goodness of his heart, more benevolent and more sensitive to his inferiors or that the inferiors became more "assertive," more "uppity." It is likely that the inferior member became aware of alternatives, that his structure of opportunities had expanded somewhat. The replacement of serfdom and peasantry with citizenship, and with free status came about partly because the industrial revolution created alternatives to being tied to the land. Similarly, emancipation of slaves in the Southern United States meant little until Blacks became aware of jobs in the North. Women are more able to seek equality in marriage when there are occupational alternatives and when it is possible to leave the home. Nor does the spectre of unemployment for workers have the same force when welfare and unemployment insurance exist. On the other side, the fact that alternatives do exist means that those in superior positions must now take into account some of the subordinates' wishes if they expect to maintain the relationship at all.

This does not, of course, mean that authority has somehow disappeared from these relationships. Rather, it is probably that the basis of authority has changed. In and of itself, a status, a social position, does not confer the same kind of traditional rights as in the past. Those in superordinate positions must earn, or seem to earn, their right to superiority; those in subordinate positions feel that they have the right, at least occasionally, to challenge the basis of that authority. It is not enough to say in answer to the question "Why should I?"—"Because I am your Father, or your Professor, or your Boss," as the case may be. Status, then, has become an ongoing accomplishment. In part, we are also dealing with a different *style* of authority. The ultimate power which parents have over children, professors over students, employers over employees is obscured by the *semblance of equality.*

Role Set and Social Structure

So far we have been thinking of the concepts of role and status as involving one reciprocal relationship, that between a teacher and a student, a doctor and a patient. However, each of us occupies a number of statuses and therefore plays multiple roles. Robert Merton points out that a particular status does not simply entail a single role but "an array of associated roles." This he refers to as a *role set,* "the complement of role relationships which persons have by virtue of occupying a particular social status" (1968:423). As Figure IV.2 illustrates, the status of teacher involves role relationships with students certainly, but also with colleagues, with the principal, with secretaries, with the public, with parents and so on. Each of these involves somewhat different sets of expectations.

In developing the concept of role set, Merton is also demonstrating the way functionalists, system theorists, think about social structure. A role set, for instance, creates "strains" on the "social fabric" which require "mechanisms" to reduce them. Clearly, it is impossible for teachers to meet the expectations inherent in all of these role relationships at the same time. One cannot, for instance, be "chewed out" by the principal and, simultaneously, maintain order in the

Figure IV.2
THE TEACHER'S ROLE SET

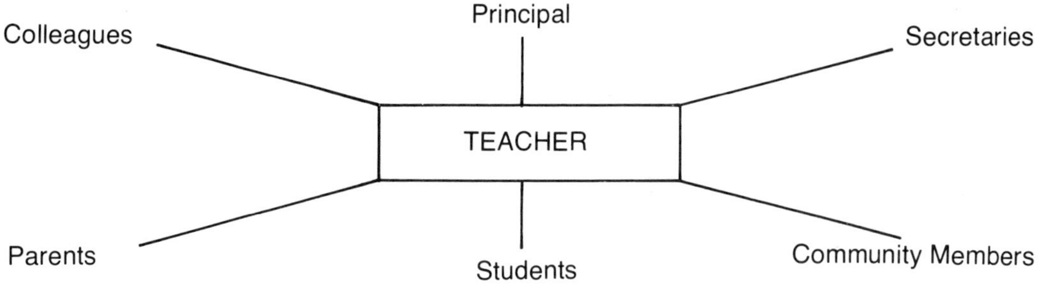

classroom. The board, made up of "pillars" of the community, may have expectations of teachers which are incompatible with what the principal or colleagues demand. Thus, in order to reduce the potential strain of trying at once to be different things to different people, some degree of *role insulation*, a social "defence" mechanism, will be required. The principal will not speak to one of his teachers in front of students but in the privacy of his office. Teachers speak to parents when the child is absent. Certain areas of the school, such as the faculty room, may be off limits to students, kept as a place where teachers can "be themselves" in the company of peers, their fellow teachers. In one sense, then, an institution is the interrelated and interlocking of various role sets.

Institutions

We have made reference throughout to the process of institutionalization, how behaviour does become patterned and predictable. The system approach, however, typically emphasizes *institutions*, the product rather than the process. In this view, just as norms tend to cluster about roles, so roles tend to cluster to form institutions. From a system perspective, the relationships among institutions—the family, education, industry, the state and so forth—is social structure. Even within the system approach, institution is used in two ways. In general, institution is meant to capture regular and patterned behaviour designed to achieve some goal. In other words, there are, in any society, patterned and regularized ways of gaining success, sexual gratification and so on. In fact, institutions have developed around how we handle even death. For example, Peter Marris (1973) has described how the institution of mourning provides clear-cut and supposedly beneficial ways of handling the death of people close to us.[4] The second use of the term institution captures, at a common sense level, that complex sets of relationships can literally be found within buildings. Hence, prisons, universities and corporations are, in both the common sense and sociological terms, institutions. Finally, system theorists typically group institutions together into what we have already described as institutional orders in terms of which of the societal needs they meet and which of the functional prerequisites they fill. And, as we shall see later in this chapter, when sociologists attempt to describe the kinds of changes which have accompanied industrialization they are, at least in part, describing ways in which institutional orders and their relationships change.

From the system perspective, then, institutions seem to be two things. First, they are the human equivalent of instincts. They guide and channel behaviour in more or less predetermined and predictable ways. This implies that institutions are the result of cumulative rationality—generations of people's best attempts to achieve goals. Second, institutions are viewed by system theorists as functionally necessary mechanisms to meet the basic needs of society and to keep it operating without undue friction, conflict or disruption. It is in this context, for instance, that Merton can talk about various mechanisms, practices and rules connected to a role set as institutionalized. Both are, or can easily become, conservative dimensions of functionalism. Both ignore that different groups have had different inputs historically in creating these institutions and both ignore the possibility that what exists works best, not in some objective or functionally necessary sense, or for society as a whole, but for the more powerful groups in society.

It is no doubt difficult to get a sense of what the system approach means in human terms; it seems detached from our everyday lives. But, the system approach has an implicit view of human biography. We are born into a set of patterns—the family—which ensures that we are socialized and regularizes the ways in which this occurs. We leave the family and enter the patterned set of relationships we call education, which furthers the socialization process and provides us with special skills to enter the regularized and ordered world of work. Because we have been successfully socialized, we fit into these patterns and can take our place. Even our leisure, our "free time," is institutionalized. The conflict we may have with our boss about wages and working conditions is institutionalized. Our sexual activity, our romantic relationships, the raising of our own children and, ultimately, our deaths occur within institutions. The corridors have been built and we simply walk through. However, to repeat ourselves, we know nothing from this perspective about how these corridors were constructed in the past and how they are changed in our everyday interaction or, more dramatically, through conflict and revolution.

The system approach, then, studies social organization. It is to the basic forms of social organization that we now turn.

The Nature of Groups

If pressed, most people would probably distinguish between sociologists and psychologists by saying that the latter study individuals, the former study groups. As we have seen, this is somewhat of an oversimplification since, essentially, sociology is about social action, of individuals, of groups, of organizations and societies. But, this distinction does contain elements of truth; many sociologists have started their work by viewing groups as building blocks of society in much the same way that cells are the basic unit of all living organisms. Thus, to understand how societies work, the argument goes, we have to start with groups and work upward to organizations and eventually whole societies. This, for example, was the approach used by George Homans (1950) in his well-known and pioneering study, *The Human Group.* Homans first tried to show that groups—whether at work, in the community or in an isolated tribe—have a very similar social structure. He then tried, somewhat less successfully, to show what is true for small groups is true for larger collectivities, such as organizations and communities. Sociologists, then, have been especially interested in both the nature and the internal structure of groups and the kinds of groups which can be found in modern society.

While the general idea of a group may seem fairly straightforward and obvious, it is, as with many concepts, more and more elusive the more we try to pin it down. According to Robert Merton (1968), "the concept of group refers to a number of people who interact with one another in accord with established patterns." Others have tried to narrow this broad definition by referring to *small groups:*

a plurality of individuals [two or more] who are in contact with one another, who take one another into account and who are aware of some significant commonality (Olmstead, 1959:21).

In terms of this definition, what we have called a role relationship is also a group—one which has only two people. In practice, however, a small group usually means a number of people who have established and shared interaction patterns and who define themselves as members of the group and who are so defined by others. Georg Simmel, a German sociologist, showed that something qualitative happens when we go from a two-person group—a *dyad*—to a three-person group—a *triad*. Whereas in a dyad, if one person breaks off interaction—goes to sleep, for instance—interaction, in effect the group, ceases at least temporarily. In a triad, interaction continues even when one member is "out of play." Also, in a triad, two can "gang up" on a third, one member can play the other two off against one another, or act as intermediary, strategies which children, indeed all family members, seem very adept at using. Who, for instance, cannot recall the feeling that parents were in league; who has not at one time or another practised "divide and conquer" in order to surmount what in concert would have been a "resounding no." It is, perhaps, for this reason that a baby represents one crisis point in marriage and family life. Triads, then, introduce the problem of *role conflict* as we try to be two different "people" at the same time. A familiar example of this is what often happens when we bring two of our friends together who have never met. We like them both, but as a threesome, things are sometimes awkward and we cannot figure out why. At other times we meet our friend's friend and wonder what one sees in the other. It may be that we are accustomed to taking the lead in one role relationship but tend to follow in the second relationship. In the triadic situation we cannot both be leader and follower at the same time.

Often we use the term group to refer to any collection of people whether or not they interact with one another or even take each other into account. For example, we are likely to talk about the various ethnic "groups" which make up Canadian society. Or, we read in a newspaper that a large "group" of people turned out to welcome home a winning football team. Strictly speaking, of course, these are not groups in the way we have just defined them, but *aggregates* and *collectivities* respectively. An aggregate is a grouping of people on the basis of some status characteristic such as age, sex, amount of education, type of residence, ethnic origin, religion and so on. An aggregate is a social category that may in fact have been somewhat arbitrarily created by a social scientist as is often the case with income groupings or occupational divisions. A collectivity, on the other hand, is simply a large number of people who have at least some values and norms in common but who do not interact with one another in any sustained and patterned fashion.

Both aggregates and collectivities have always the potential for group formation. In collectivities, ongoing and patterned interaction is likely to emerge simply because there are norms and values in common. Commuters on a bus are not a group but a collectivity. However, let the bus become stranded in a snowstorm for a few hours and a group is likely to form. Indeed, the coming together of strangers in the face of some emergency or disaster is a very common theme in movies and novels. Erving Goffman (1961a:7-14) has suggested that when people come together casually or unexpectedly, "focussed gatherings" is a better term than group, since group implies sustained and continuing activity.

Of equal interest is the process by which aggregates come to be collectivities and, perhaps, groups in the full sense of the word. What seems to occur is that under some conditions people become, or are made aware, that they have a shared situation, shared interests with others. For example, although sociologists are rather fond of creating categories, it is very unlikely that anyone imagined that out there in Canadian society existed the aggregate, "owners of rusty Fords." Nor, for that matter, had Ford owners probably ever thought of themselves in quite that way. Probably most of these people suffered silently, perhaps blaming themselves for not getting the car washed more frequently, until one day someone showed them that they were not unique, that they were not alone. A "private trouble" had become a "public issue."

Consciousness or awareness that some objective status or situation is shared with others is, then, often the starting point for collective behaviour. Because people in aggregates have shared statuses they may have shared interests. Potentially, they can be mobilized in defence of these interests. The most famous discussion of this process is Karl Marx's distinction between a class "in itself" and a class "for itself." Marx argued that it was easy enough to distinguish two main classes, capitalists (bourgeoisie) who own the means of production and workers (proletariat) who sell their labour. But, as long as workers remained unaware of their objective situation, they were simply members of an objective category, a class "in itself." Without awareness, not much change could be expected. For Marx, nevertheless, modern workers were potentially a revolutionary force in society. Instead of being scattered and isolated from one another, as were peasants in the previous era, workers under capitalism were more concentrated in large factories. They were beginning to develop trade unions and to interact politically with one another. Workers were on the verge of becoming consciously aware of their shared objective situation and of their shared interests. Workers were in the process of becoming a class "for itself," in short, a group.

In recent years, the idea of "consciousness raising" has become part of everyday language. It was especially common at the height of Women's Liberation. As the study by Connelly and Christiansen-Ruffman showed, consciousness raising groups were explicitly formed to bring women to a subjective awareness of their shared objective situation. Just as early Marxists hoped that class consciousness would eventually transcend national boundaries and unite workers everywhere, so it was hoped that feminism would transcend class and regional boundaries, that the status category of woman would be transformed into "sisterhood." We examine social movements in Chapter XI. In Chapter X we shall see how ethnicity has come to be perceived as the symbolic focal point for asserting and defending collective interests; how at times ethnic categories become genuinely ethnic groups.

Primary and Secondary Groups

Clearly, groups vary in size, in duration, in the degree to which norms and rules are routinized. One of the main distinctions between types of groups is that of whether the group is essentially a *primary group* or a *secondary group*. The term "primary group," and our appreciation of the importance of such groups, comes from the work of Charles Horton Cooley. Certain groups such as the family are primary, he suggests:

> *. . . in the sense that they give the individual his earliest and completest experience of social unity, and also in the sense that they do not change in the same degree as more elaborate relations . . . (Cooley, 1909:26).*

We usually think of primary groups as being relatively small, as involving warm, intimate ties and spontaneous interpersonal relations. Ideally, primary groups are ends in themselves rather than a means to other ends. That is, we enjoy interaction and activity within a primary group for its own sake, not simply because we want to get something done. In Simmel's terms, there is pleasure in sociability. Also, in primary groups, our relationships with others tend to be more all-inclusive, to involve our "total personality." We are not acting solely in terms of one of our statuses, but in terms of our "real selves."

Besides the family, friendship groups, gangs and often workers are examples of primary groups. Primary groups, then, provide us with the basic link between self or personality and society. They provide the context in which we are first socialized, made into human beings, and are, throughout life, the main way in which our identity—our sense of who we are—is sustained, maintained and sometimes transformed. It is within the primary group that we experience love, compassion, intimacy, care and caring. But it is also within primary groups that we are most likely to experience hatred, jealousy, sibling rivalry and rejection, the emotional pain which is the flip side of happiness and security.

Secondary groups can be defined roughly as the opposite of what we have just said about primary groups. Relationships among members are expected to be cool, impersonal and, perhaps, contractual. Typically, we are not expected to involve our whole personality, our whole self, but a "segment" of ourselves in secondary group relations. Finally, secondary groups are seen as means to other ends, rather than ends in themselves; people do not come together for the sake of "getting together," but because they want to accomplish some specific task. Professional associations, committees and shareholders' meetings are examples of secondary groups.

As these definitions suggest, the crucial difference between primary and secondary is not to be found in the nature of the group as such, but in the kind of social relationships which are supposed to occur in various social situations. The culture, in other words, tells us how, ideally, we ought to behave towards others in particular situations. At the same time, we must remember that no relationship is totally primary or totally secondary. Modern marriage, based as it is on love and companionship, probably comes as close as any to being primary. But even the most intimate and encompassing marriage will still be some distance from completely primary. We are likely, for instance, to show a somewhat different side of ourselves to other people than to our mate. There are things about ourselves that we may reveal to strangers, but not to our spouse.

The most extreme example of a secondary relationship is, perhaps, that between a customer and a cashier in a supermarket; the whole interaction sequence may be performed with only a simple phrase, about the total bill, being spoken. Probably we will not remember what he looked like, will not be able to place him if we see him in a different social setting—or he, us. But, even this relationship may become more primary. If we shop at the same store again and again, the check-out "boy" may become separated from his cash register in our minds. He may become someone we "know"—a name and a "personality." Primary and secondary, then, represent the extremes—what are often called "polar opposites"—on a continuum of social relationships.

Modern Western societies are unique in the kind of primary relationships and secondary relationships that co-exist and overlap one another. We move from the intimate and enveloping environment of the family to the more cool and unemotional setting of formal organizations or bureaucracies, school, university, the business firm. We learn to relate differently to those we think of as friends and relatives, those who are acquaintances, those who are strangers.

Simple and Complex Societies

As we have seen, sociology grew out of

the massive changes occurring in the eighteenth and nineteenth centuries. Robert Nisbet has argued that virtually all of the classical sociologists were trying to understand, to come to grips with, two revolutions, the French Revolution and the Industrial Revolution, two different kinds of revolutions which nevertheless had an enormous impact on social relations and on the nature of social structure or organization. Alvin Toffler, you will recall, maintains that Western society, for the past 300 years, has been caught up in a "firestorm of change" and that the rate of change is ever accelerating. We face the prospect of future shock—culture shock in our own society.

Hence, looking backward, it appears to us now that the two revolutions brought about changes that were in fact "evolutions" rather than "revolutions," that the change was rather slow in coming. Nisbet (1967:22) argues, however, that it did not appear so to those caught up in the change. As he says, "to intellectuals of that age, radical and conservative alike, the changes were of almost millenial abruptness. Contrast between present and past seemed stark—terrifyingly or intoxicatingly, depending upon one's relation to the old order and to the forces at work on it." As is so often the case, the human side of these changes emerges most clearly and dramatically in art, literature and poetry. W. B. Yeats, the Irish poet and playwright, captures in his remarkable poem, *The Second Coming* (1915), images which the social theorists were also attempting more prosaically to articulate. As he puts it,

things fall apart; the centre cannot hold;
mere anarchy is loosed upon the world.

It seemed for most social theorists that the bonds which had held society together for so long had given way to a new order, one which was ever-changing, unstable and "normless." Societies, it was argued, had been organized around the values of community, kinship, traditional hierarchy and authority and religion. The social integration and social organization of the past had given way to social disorganization, to *anomic* society, to a situation in which the traditional social constraints had been replaced by the totally new social order of a mass society, urbane, industrialized, scientific, rational and secular.

Particularly at the end of the nineteenth century, sociologists became convinced that something qualitatively different was occurring as societies became more complex. All seemed to have in mind a contrast between simple societies and complex societies. While most recognized that no society is completely one or the other, they did feel that the general direction of change was from the primary relations of peasant society, village and parish, to the secondary relations and associations of urban, industrial and bureaucratic society.

We can perhaps understand what these theorists had in mind by contrasting small-town or rural life with big-city life. Chances are that many of you have first-hand experience of small traditional communities in which, seemingly, everyone is either related to everyone else or, at least, everyone knows a good deal about others and about their past. Nicknames, acquired in youth, may stick with people throughout their lives. Statuses and labels may also be difficult if not impossible to lose as long as one remains in that community. For example, Mr. Jones may still be known as the "younger Jones boy, the wild one" well into his senility. The man who delivers the mail is not simply the postman, Mr. Johnson. He is Al Johnson, who married Ida Williams, your third cousin who had a son, Bill, who moved to Alberta, and is doing something on the pipeline, and who has a daughter who is supposed to be "very bright." And so it goes—a way of life which centred on kinship and community, one which in varying degrees has been the typical way of life for most people throughout most of the world throughout most of history. The contrast, of course, is the city.

In a very famous paper called "Urbanism as a Way of Life," Louis Wirth (1938), an American sociologist, described life in the city this way:

Characteristically, urbantites meet one another in highly segmental roles. They are, to be sure, dependent upon more people for the satisfactions of their life-needs than are rural people and thus are associated with a greater number of organized groups, but they are less dependent on particular persons, and their dependence on others is confined to a highly fractionalized aspect of the other's round of activity. This is essentially what is meant by saying that the city is characterized by secondary rather than primary contacts. The contacts of the city may indeed be face-to-face, but they are nevertheless impersonal, superficial, transitory, and segmental. The reserve, the indifference, and the blasé outlook which urbanites manifest in their relationships may thus be regarded as devices for immunizing themselves against the personal claims and expectations of others (p. 12).

Thus, one important difference in social organization has centred around the dichotomy between rural and urban. This was a peculiarly American perspective, particularly the view of the "Chicago School" of sociology. It grew out of that which was most obvious to these sociologists, that internal migration (urbanization) from the farm to the city and immigration from Europe were creating fundamental changes in the American city. In contrast to the rural life, cities seemed filled with wickedness and decadence. As Carl Sandburg said of Chicago, "They tell me you are wicked and I believe them, for I have seen your/painted women under the gas lamps/luring the farm boys."

In Europe, sociologists were also attempting to contrast the traditional and the modern by use of dichotomies. Perhaps the most famous of these was formulated by Ferdinand Toennies, a German sociologist, who spoke of a transition from *Gemeinschaft* to *Gesellschaft*—from community to society (or association). Emile Durkheim, focusing on the degree and scale of division of labour, spoke in terms of *mechanical* societies versus *organic* societies. Max Weber, writing at about the same time as Durkheim, argued that authority had moved from *traditional* to *rational-legal*. Robert Redfield wrote about two types of society, the *folk* society and the *urban* society. Like the proverbial seven blind men touching and then trying to describe an elephant as a wall, as a tree trunk, as a snake, etc., so various theorists were trying to present various aspects of what was perceived as a massive change in the way people relate to one another. Figure IV.3 shows these various dichotomies and the particular aspect of social structure each was considering.

What all of the classic theorists were responding to was what they felt was not only loss of community and kinship, but also loss of religion which seemed at some level to be the glue which held relationships together. So, modernization meant in part a *secularization* of relationships. The feudal society persisted so long partly because the traditional relationships were culturally defined in terms of *sacred* rites and obligations. Social bonds, then, were not simply between people but also with God—hence the strength of oaths, of fealty and of allegiance. To break these was to sin, to break one's word with God. Clearly, fealty long ago disappeared but the sacred has, until very recently, been apparent in marriage. Many still believe that the marriage vows are sacred vows which cannot be broken. It is at the same time apparent that while the marriage ceremony may still exhibit many of the trappings of the sacred, it has become essentially a civil ceremony to legalize a contractual relationship. Today people are even willing to talk about drawing up marriage contracts, perhaps even on a renewable basis. Secularization means that, increasingly, violating the vows is a legal matter, not a sin.

While we have suggested that the system approach cannot account adequately for change, the theorists have had to confront these kinds of dramatic changes.

Figure IV.3
SIMPLE AND COMPLEX SOCIETIES

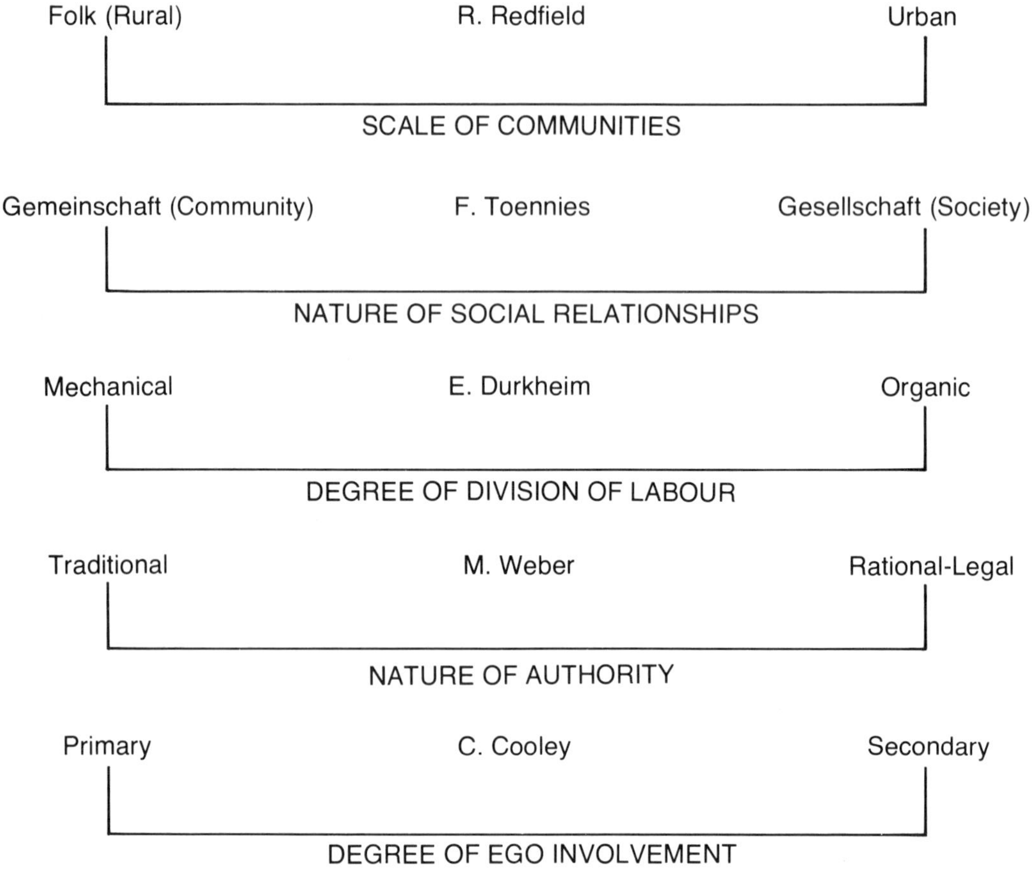

They have had to describe and account for modernization. Although they use the language of the conservative, they have managed to isolate some of the central dimensions of these changes. In their view, these changes are system adaptations. When one thing changes—industrialization—other things in the system must also change. And, not surprisingly, the system theorist will describe the major changes in positive terms, as functional adaptations. So, instead of talking about the alienation of man in mass society, they are likely to speak of the functional necessity of impersonality and personal detachment and of secularization. Moreover, these changes—loss of community, decline of kinship and religion, depersonalization in mass society—appear, in this approach, just to happen; there is little appreciation of the role of real people, powerful elites, determining the direction of these changes. Indeed, many twentieth century theorists seem to have lost sight of what was the impetus of much of the nineteenth century theorizing: the deep concern and fear about the direction of future society. The early theorists asked whether these changes were inevitable and, if so, what could be done to mitigate their consequences. Even if their answers were usually pessimistic, they did pose the questions.

One of the most famous contemporary attempts to describe these changes is Talcott Parsons's *pattern variables.* Parsons, too, thinks in terms of dichotomies. He argues that any role relationship or society as a whole can be described in terms of some combination of the pattern variables. These pattern variables are described in terms of two polar opposites, which are defined by Turner (1974:36) as follows:

1. *Affectivity—affective neutrality concerns the amount of emotion or affect that is appropriate in a given interaction situation. Should a great deal or little affect be expressed?*
2. *Diffuseness specificity denotes the issue of how far reaching obligations in an interaction situation are to be. Should the obligations be narrow and specific or should they be extensive and diffuse?*
3. *Universalism-particularism points to the problem of whether evaluation and judgment of others in an interaction situation is to employ standardized and agreed-upon criteria or subjective standards. Should evaluation be performed in terms of objective, universalistic criteria or in terms of more subjective, particularistic standards?*
4. *Achievement-ascription deals with the issue of how to assess an actor, whether in terms of performance or on the basis of inborn qualities, such as sex, age, race, and family status. Should an actor treat another on the basis of achievements or ascriptive qualities that are unrelated to performance?*
5. *Self-collectivity denotes the extent to which action is to be oriented to self-interest and individual goals or to group interests and goals. Should an actor consider his personal or self-related goals over those of the group or larger collectivity in which he is involved?*

These opposites represent dilemmas of choice and, according to Parsons, every system can be characterized in terms of the solutions it provides to each of these dilemmas. But of more importance, Parsons believes that as societies industrialize, they must change in particular ways: the system requires fundamental changes in values and orientations to achieve efficiency, perhaps even to survive. Basically what Parsons is arguing is that in industrialized societies, the kinds of relationships based on kinship are no longer appropriate, no longer functional. Rather, what is supposedly needed now are the kinds of values associated with bureaucracy.

In complex society, the child must supposedly learn to integrate the perspectives of a variety of groups; he must also learn to distinguish among kinds of relationships. In simple societies, most, if not all, of a person's social life is lived within the context of kinship. Community and kinship are almost synonymous. In complex societies, part of our life, certainly, is lived within the family, but we also participate in other institutions. In moving from family, to school, to work, we are also confronted with different kinds of social relationships and different patterns which supposedly represent the "best" ways of handling such relationships. The pattern variables provide one way of describing these different kinds of patterns and of summarizing the dichotomies we have discussed above.

Perhaps the easiest way to illustrate the pattern variables is to look at the university as an institution. According to the institutional blueprint, at least, students are admitted not on the basis of personal characteristics (ugly, obnoxious, etc.), family background (rich, poor, etc.) or social characteristics (sex, colour, religion, etc.), but on the basis of general rules which supposedly apply to all people in the same way and are based on performance or achievement in the past (high school grades). Moreover, students are to be evaluated in these same terms, that is, on the basis of general rules regarding performance. Also, the student-professor relationship is expected to be a "professional" relationship, with limited emotional involvement and specified focus of interest. In other words, it is expected to be a relationship restricted to the institutional sphere of the university. All this presumably provides the most efficient way of selecting, educating and evaluating students.

In the family, on the other hand, members are in fact expected to treat each other with warmth and with concern for each individual as a "total person." Nor should performance or lack of it affect the quality of the relationship. In the family, one should be responsive to individual differences and we are supposed to use subjective standards of evaluations. We would not expect to be called upon to justify, in terms of some general rule, why we love the people in our family.

Parsons is arguing that complex societies must be characterized by universalism, affective neutrality, achievement and specificity, whereas relationships in simple societies have been characterized by the polar opposites. These changes, for Parsons, were functionally necessary. When we look at social stratification in Chapter VIII, however, we shall suggest that while ideals may have shifted in these ways, there is a wide gap between these ideals and what actually happens to people. While industrial societies are supposed to be characterized by universalism and achievement in particular, they remain particularistic and ascriptive. All we are saying is that sex, colour, family background still matter, even while ideals may be shifting; we are more than some distance from full equality of opportunity. The gap between the ideals and the reality can easily be demonstrated empirically. More important, there may be theoretical reasons why the gap can never be bridged. No doubt the system theorists recognize that universalism and achievement (equality of opportunity) have not arrived, that discrimination persists. However, their belief that universalism and achievement are functionally necessary leads them to view inequality of opportunity as a "strain" in the system, a residue of the past, that is in the process of being overcome (see Collins, 1971). Alternatively, as we are stressing throughout this book, the persistence of ascription and particularism (inequality of opportunity) may be explained by the fact that we live in a layered or stratified society, one in which groups with different amounts of power are in conflict with one another.

Perhaps these issues can be made clearer if we focus on the nature of the institutions within society, rather than on complex society as a whole. In fact, many system theorists argue that this is the only approach because complex societies are too complex to subject to analysis. They argue, in other words, that what happens in large complex organizations is a model of what, if we could grasp the totality, happens at the level of society. And, understanding these organizations means understanding bureaucracy.

BUREAUCRACY

The starting point for any analysis of bureaucracy is Max Weber's distinctive formulation of it as a rational-legal model. How he constructed the *ideal type* of bureaucracy was through the accentuation and exaggeration of certain elements he perceived in his society and which, when magnified, became more apparent and comprehensible. In other words, what Weber meant by the ideal type was an heuristic device to help him understand bureaucracy and not a statement of the desirability of bureaucracy. As we saw in Figure IV.3, Weber saw the basis of authority as changing from traditional to rational-legal. By this he meant that rules or the right to create rules could no longer be justified by some statement such as "things are so because they've always been so," but instead in terms of formally stated principals which are thought to contribute to efficiency. Authority, then, derives out of technical competence.

This shift in the basis of authority is reflected in the characteristics Weber attributes to bureaucracy. The ideal type bureaucracy is organized into hierarchical positions, each with its own area of jurisdiction and guided by a general set of rules. These rules are formal, that is, written, and specify the precise amount of authority in each office. Authority is attached to the position, not the person. The various positions demand different kinds of skills and areas of technical competence and therefore require "thorough and expert training." The coordination and management of the bureaucracy is guided by relatively stable and exhaustive rules which everyone within the organization can learn. For Weber, the bureaucracy is an efficiency producing machine:

The fully developed bureaucratic mechanism compares with other organizations exactly as does the machine with the non-mechanical modes of production. Precision, speed, unambiguity, knowledge of the files, continuity, discretion, unity, strict subordination, reduction of friction and of material and personal costs—these are raised to the optimum point in the strictly bureaucratic administration. . . . (Gerth and Mills, 1958:214).

In addition to machine-like efficiency, Weber suggests that bureaucracy may also produce machine-like predictability:

Its specific nature, which is welcomed by capitalism, develops the more perfectly the more the bureaucracy is "de-humanized," the more completely it succeeds in eliminating from official business, love, hatred, and all purely personal, irrational, and emotional elements which escape calculation (Gerth and Mills, 1958:216).

Weber did, however, recognize that bureaucracy is janus-faced, that when people occupy the system of positions they also bring with them non-rational factors which inevitably affect the organization. In Weber's terms, they do bring with them their loves, hatreds and "purely personal, emotional, and irrational elements." Communication, for example, does not always flow along formal lines as specified in the organization chart; informal networks are inevitably part of any bureaucracy. Nevertheless, Weber emphasized and developed his analysis around the machine- or computer-like side of bureaucracy. And, for a long time, it was this emphasis that influenced organizational theorists.[5]

For example, what has now come to be called the classical school of organizational studies—"scientific management"—focused its attention on how the efficiency-producing machine might be perfected. They asked questions such as "What is the most efficient division of labour and mode of specialization?" or "What kind of and how much reward is necessary to induce workers to produce at maximum efficiency?" Out of these kinds of concerns emerged the now classic Hawthorne studies. In a series of experiments and observational studies, the researchers tried to find out how amount of lighting and length of work-breaks affected production at the Hawthorne plant of Western Electric. Their conclusions redirected future studies of bureaucracy.

Although their findings have been challenged in terms of poor research design and in terms of the influence of the investigators' values, these investigations do provide a rather interesting case of serendipity in sociological research. For instance, in one experiment, a number of female workers were segregated and, as they worked, the experimenters adjusted the amount of light in their room. They then observed their production, comparing it with the production of a "control" group, who worked under constant light conditions. What the investigators purportedly found was that, when segregated, both the experimental and control groups increased their production. The experimental group produced more regardless of changes in the lighting, even when the lighting was as dim as moonlight. The conclusion of the study was that "human factors" accounted for the increased production. Apparently, because these workers had been selected for the experiment and had by implication been singled out for special attention, they felt better about themselves and their work and therefore worked better. These findings were influential in creating a somewhat new approach to organizational studies—the "human relations" approach.

This new approach held that to understand bureaucracies one must take into account the non-rational factors inherent in social relations. Somehow the theorist must include in his analysis that, for example, the coffee-break is more than simply a way to reduce physical fatigue, but may also be the forum in which workers gain self-esteem, social support, the emotional satisfactions of sociability. The friendships that arise may provide important informal networks of communication. Still, this approach represents only a modification of scientific management. The goal is still the most efficient machine possible, now with the added recognition that the human factor must also be considered.[6]

In contrast to this approach, a number of social theorists have asked whether the human costs of this efficient machine were not too great. For example, Michael Crozier (1964:178) suggests that there is a contradiction, of which Weber was well aware, involving "a double belief in the superiority of bureaucratic rationality—in the domain of efficiency and its threatening implications in the domain of human values."[7] Robert Michels (1915), in proposing his "iron law of oligarchy," has argued that those with authority will always be willing to sacrifice the values of the organization as their prime concern becomes the preservation of their position within the organization. In the 1950s, William Whyte wrote what became a very popular book, *The Organization Man* (1957), in which he tries to capture some of the dehumanizing effects of life in complex organizations, where "organization men" come to lose their individuality, their capacity for creative work and are encouraged to be mediocre.[8] In Robert Merton's terms, bureaucracies unintentionally produce inflexible bureaucrats who typically lose sight of the goals of the organization; the rules and the regulations become ends in themselves; bureaucratic performance becomes a matter of ritual. It is no doubt this aspect of bureaucracy—red tape and impersonal treatment—that most of us typically think of.

Since functionaries minimize personal relations and resort to categorization, the pecularities of individual cases are often ignored. But the client who, quite understandably, is convinced of the special features of his own problem often objects to such categorical treatment. Stereotyped behaviour is not adapted to the exigencies of individual problems. The impersonal treatment of affairs which are at times of great personal significance to the client gives rise to the charge of "arrogance" and "haughtiness" of the bureaucrat (Merton, 1968:256).

On the other hand, in contemporary, highly complex bureaucracies only those who can handle and manipulate the new technology and who are flexible in the face of changing circumstances may survive. The new bureaucrat, then, may affect our lives not through bumbling and rigidity but through competence with a technology unavailable to us. The computer, a seemingly natural adjunct to bureaucracy, has provided the bureaucrat with what is to many of us an intimidating resource, but nonetheless a resource which allows the collection and storage of information which can be translated into power. These issues raise perhaps the most fundamental question about Weber's ideal type. What are some of the unanticipated consequences? Is the ideal type, in fact, the most efficient system?

Recently, Elliot Leyton has examined the workings of one bureaucracy, the Workmen's Compensation Board, and its effects on workers in St. Lawrence, a mining community in Newfoundland.[9] Leyton argues that this bureaucracy, by acting "rationally," ends up acting inhumanly, and without any regard for suffering and anguish. Since the early 1960s, it has been recognized that fluorspar mining leads to lung cancer. Hence, miners have about an 80% chance of contracting one of several work-related diseases. At some point, company doctors declare a man unfit for mining and therefore unemployable, at which point he must apply for workmen's compensation benefits. Some men declared unemployable receive full compensation; some receive only a portion; some receive nothing and must go on welfare. When these men die, as they inevitably do, their widows are subject to the same capricious rules as applied to their husbands. Some continue to have full pension; others are cut off the day their husbands die. Members of the community all "know" that their disability is a result of working in the mine and they expect the Board to compensate them. The Board, however, demands scientific (medical) proof of the link between the disease and the mine. This proof is not easy to provide so the rulings of the Board, apparently based on some attempted objectivity, are viewed by the local people as capricious and arbitrary. In this case, the bureaucratic rules ignore the needs and unique circumstances of the community which the Board is supposedly serving. What Leyton is describing, then, is the classic confrontation between the traditional values based on kinship and community and the "modern" values of the impersonal bureaucratic society.

There are, as many theorists have shown us, inherent contradictions and antagonisms within bureaucracies as within societies more generally. There are conflicts of interest between managers and workers, between professional staff and technical staff, between jurisdictional areas, between bureaucracy and bureaucracy, and, perhaps, between the bureaucracy and the public. And, these contradictions and conflicts demand a different perspective on both bureaucracies in particular and societies in general.

SOCIETY AS STRUCTURE

At this point, we shall give less attention to the structure or conflict perspective because it receives so much attention in the rest of the book. The structure approach centres our attention on the layers of inequality in society. In every society, there are some "who get most of what there is to get" and who therefore constitute an elite of sorts. Society is shaped in large part by the conflict between this elite, trying to maintain its position, and other groups, trying to improve theirs. Of course the elite have an advantageous position in this conflict and are able to exact compliance and solidify their position. As Harold Lasswell (1950) suggests, they do this through gaining control of the important societal tools: violence, symbols, practices and goods.

While dominant groups may temporarily use violence to maintain their position and influence others, and while force may never be too far below the surface in any social system, it cannot be the basis of social structure. However, by controlling the symbol-producing institutions, dominant groups are able to create a culture, or better, an ideology, to justify their position and therefore "structure" the inequalities. Further, in their control of the production and distribution of goods, they are controlling the sanctions, the inducements and punishments, which underpin these structures. Inequality becomes most fully institutionalized, most clearly structured, when it is formalized into a set of rules and laws and legal procedures for enforcement. The political system, then, creates these "practices" and the legal system and agencies of enforcement provide the last lines of defence against opposition to the structure.

The ability of the dominant group to maintain these structures, to impose their culture, is always problematic to some degree. Competing interest groups arise and, as we have shown, coalesce into groups offering alternative or competing ideologies. Revolutions, as well as the more frequent minor insurrections, do occur. Even when these do not occur, the elite must accommodate itself to the pressures and even anticipate them. It is for these reasons that Karl Marx viewed history as conflict and change.

Neither the system analogy nor the structure approach helps us understand how people in their everyday lives view social structure and how they are, more or less, constrained by it. This is the goal of interaction approaches to social structure. In the next chapter, we examine how people learn these structures through socialization and modify them through a continuous process of interaction.

SUGGESTIONS FOR FURTHER READING

In our view, to understand social structure you can do no better than C. Wright Mills's *The Sociological Imagination* (1959). An excellent collection of his articles is *Power, Politics and People* (1967). An interesting textbook which uses Mills's insights and perspectives is Hans Gerth's and C. Wright Mills's *Character and Social Structure* (1953).

Probably the best all-round demonstration of the system approach at work is the various essays by Robert K. Merton in his *Social Theory and Social Structure* (1968). Another readable collection which also views social structure and role theory from a system approach is W. J. Goode's *Explorations in Social Theory* (1973). Michael Banton's *Roles* (1965) provides a useful introduction to role theory. For a slightly satirical critique of role theory, indeed of sociology generally, see Stanislav Andreski's *Social Sciences as Sorcery* (1974). An excellent but more difficult critique of system perspectives on role theory is Aaron Cicourel's article, "Basic and Normative Rules in the Negotiation of Status and Role" (1970).

A basic book on the nature of groups is Michael Olmstead's *The Small Group* (1959). Another is W. J. H. Sprott's *Human Groups* (1958). And, of course, George Homans's *The Human Group* (1950) remains one of the most important statements on group structure. Finally, we urge you to read Rex Lucas's *Men in Crisis* (1969), one of the finest studies pulling together data on real-life groups with research on laboratory groups.

Robert Nisbet (1967), whom we mentioned in Chapter I, is also a very good source for a depiction of modernization and its impact on sociology. See also his *Social Change and History* (1969). For a highly readable, but conservative, reaction to these changes, we suggest José Ortega y Gasset's *Revolt of the Masses* (1932).

Throughout the second half of the book we shall be suggesting readings within the structure or conflict approach. Aside from the Mills readings, some easy and valuable introductions are: Harold Laswell's *Politics: Who Gets What, When, How* (1950); Charles Anderson's *Political Economy of Social Class* (1974); Frank Parkin's *Class Inequality and Political Order* (1971); Pat Marchak's *Ideological Perspectives on Canada* (1975); and Peter Archibald's *Social Psychology as Political Economy* (1978).

FOOTNOTES

[1]The distinction we draw here is a matter of emphasis; it would be a distortion to say that Weber did not understand the importance of external constraints or Durkheim the importance of subjective meanings (particularly in his later works). See Farberman and Stone (1970). See also Rocher's (1972:13ff.) discussion of Durkheim and Weber.

[2]Although the "system approach" is, in essence, functionalism, we refer here to "system" because many others share similar assumptions about how to view social structure and use the concepts we present here.

[3]Although he should not be held responsible, much of the discussion of role and inequality, as well as Figure IV.1, derives from the largely unpublished lecture notes on "Sentiment and Social Structure" of Leo Zakuta, of the University of Toronto.

[4]Marris also points out the process of "de-institutionalization"; traditional ways of mourning are breaking up, making death increasingly difficult to handle.

[5]There is a very large body of writing on bureaucracy. A sample of early literature can be found in Robert Merton *et al., Reader in Bureaucracy* (1952). A more recent review of bureaucratic and organizational literature can be found in Charles Perrow's *Complex Organization: A Critical Essay* (1972) and N. P. Mouzelis's *Organization and Bureaucracy* (1967).

[6]Probably the most detailed account of changes in ideologies of management and of research perspectives is Reinhard Bendix's *Work and Authority in Industry* (1963).

[7]He also points out to us that bureaucracies work differently from culture to culture.

[8]Various writers have recognized these features of bureaucracy and, with great insight, have made them a matter of humour and satire. See especially C. Northcote Parkinson's *Parkinson's Law* (1957) and, more recently, Lawrence J. Peter's and Raymond Hull's *The Peter Principle* (1969).

[9]See Handelman and Leyton (1978).

socialization and interaction

CHAPTER V

INTERACTION

As we have suggested, one of the things in our environment or situation which we have to take into account and interpret is other people. Imagine a blind date organized by a third party who tells you nothing about the person at all. Liekly, things will be awkward at first. Before you can really interact you have to get to know one another. There may be some long pauses, perhaps because of shyness, but maybe because you have no idea what to talk about. But, at the same time, you are not out on a date with an alien intelligence. Chances are you share a language in common and are both Canadians. Presumably your date is of the opposite sex. You can estimate pretty quickly whether he or she is younger, older or about the same age as yourself. Finally, the situation in which you find yourself is a relatively well-defined situation—it is a date, not a job interview, nor a business engagement. Not only is it a date, but it is a *first* date, and a blind one to boot.

In short, while it may be a very trying, perhaps even disastrous, experience, you do start out with some idea of how to act in this situation. It is not, in other words, completely unstructured. You can, as it were, call on the culture for help. Vague as they may be in actual practice, there are cultural norms about how to act with someone of the opposite sex. There are norms about how to act with someone your own age compared to someone older or younger or of the opposite sex. There are also norms about how to behave on dates generally, maybe about blind dates specifically.

At the same time, neither of you is a programmed robot, obviously. Nor, for that matter, are you stage actors with memorized scripts from which you know exactly what to expect from the other person, what the final outcome will be, as in Figure V.1. Rather, you are improvising and estimating as you go along. This turns out to be true for all social situations, all social interaction. What seems to occur is that whenever we encounter another person, we are immediately posing a number of questions: Who and what is this other person relative to me? Who and what am I relative to him or her? What do I want from this encounter? What does this person think I want? What does he or she want? What does he or she think I think he or she wants? What sort of situation is this anyway? Does the other person agree with what I think this situation is? We could go on. And, to make things even more complicated, we must remember that the other person is asking exactly the same kind of questions. Interaction even between two people is, then, a complex business of estimating and negotiating, as shown by Figure V.2. Interaction is, it seems, a never-ending series of estimates of trying to see the situation from two points of view—our own and the other person's.

Faced with these questions and complications, we might well ask how social interaction ever gets started. Why are we not suspended or paralysed, afraid to act at all? Or, once started, how can we speak about social order, patterned social activity and relationships? Part of the answer is that despite a great deal of ambiguity, the questions we ask in social situations are structured questions. There is a common stock of knowledge which we can make recourse to; it is a safe assumption that a good deal of the time others will also make recourse to this same knowledge. Most important, people tend to *routinize* interaction so that even though each interactional situation is in some ways unique, it is also in some ways patterned, and these newly created patterns may enter the common stock of knowledge. Otherwise, as Peter McHugh (1968:26) points out, "No one would be able to get out of bed and dressed in the morning; rather he would think until bedtime of every alternative procedure and potential happenstance."

A more formal way to put this is to say that all social behaviour involves *norms.* Social order and social action are possible because of two related factors: (1) that the culture provides us with values which are translated into norms which, in turn, become the rules which govern interaction, and (2) that to *some degree,* at least, social actors share a common culture and therefore a common value system. For example, a cultural value may be that it is wrong for women to be promiscuous. Translated into a norm, this may take the form that one should be cautious about entering into a sexual relationship. Translated into a rule, this may be specified as one should not go to bed with a man on the first date, especially a blind date. The hope, then, is that there will be some agreement about this value, that the other person (in this case, the man) will not only have knowledge of this value but will believe in it as well.

There is a chance, however, that in this specific case, the man has learned a somewhat different set of values. While the culture may say that women should not appear "too easy and willing," it may, rather contradictorily, say that men should get as much sexual experience as possible and that they should be aggressive in heterosexual relationships. The

Figure V.1

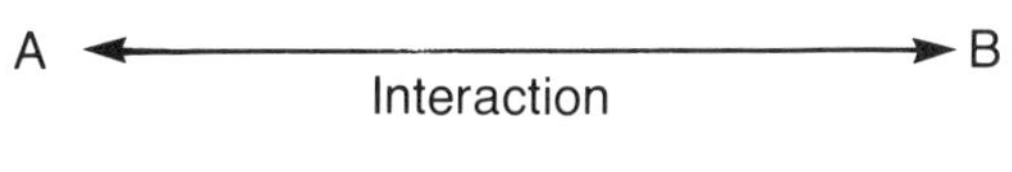

Figure V.2

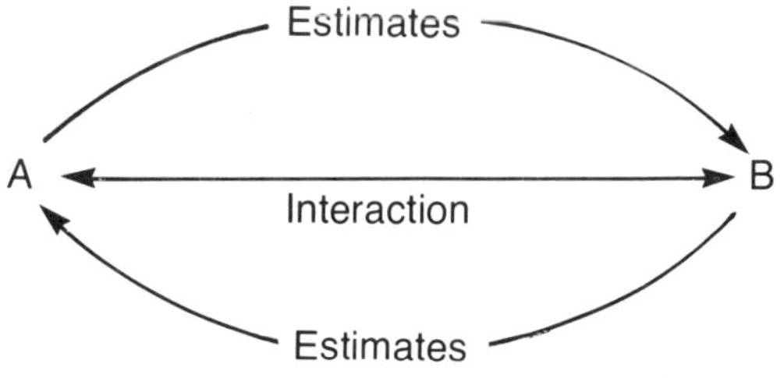

culture may, in fact, have a "double standard"; one set of norms for women and another for men. This may or may not mean conflict in the relationship. For instance, one outcome may be that the woman, actually desiring to make love with this new "find," feels constrained by the norms not to do so. Similarly, perhaps the man, though desiring the woman, does not agree with the double standard. Perhaps he believes that all people ought to wait until they are married. Or perhaps he believes that this is what the woman believes. Nevertheless, he may still feel that he ought to conform to the norms of the double standard, to make a try, because *she* might accept (and expect) the double standard. She expects him to make a pass; he realizes that he is expected to; she says no. He expects her to say no. And so it goes. As we can see, even a relatively simple encounter turns out to be highly complicated, the outcome far from certain. In varying degrees, all social relationships contain elements of *Mad* magazine's "Spy-Counterspy" series. This provides one reason why we cannot view social interaction as ever completely structured or totally predictable. Another reason is that norms and rules may become modified through interaction and as circumstances seem to demand. And, as we have seen in Lucas' study of the mine disaster, new norms can be created in interaction.

Nevertheless, in every situation, we bring with us a norm and some idea of how to use it. Though rule-governed, we are also rule users. In chess, for instance, the books provide us with rules, some specific, some very general, which we must interpret and try to use, given our definition of how the game is going. At the same time, we are far from free to make any move we want. Faced with a more powerful opponent than ourselves, a wrong move may have very objective consequences: we lose our queen and must resign; we are checkmated. As it is with chess, so it is with social life. Social norms also constrain us and, in many instances, to violate them is to invite disaster—imprisonment, death, ostracism, poverty, scorn and ridicule. In sum, social behaviour is, in its essence, an effort to conform to rules and norms. Our attempts to live up to them and the efforts of others to make us conform are what make situations social.

SOCIALIZATION

Anyone who has had prolonged contact with young children has no doubt been stung—physically and psychically—in any number of unexpected ways. One soon discovers that, unlike most adult acquaintances, the child cannot be trusted. He is unpredictable; he may, for no reason we can understand, poke us in the eye or tell us we are fat. Our adult friends are more predictable because they have acquired the culture, the symbols, norms, values and beliefs of our society. They have, in other words, been *socialized*. Socialization is the interactive process whereby people acquire and internalize the culture of a group. We say "interactive process" because socialization requires interaction with already socialized people. It presupposes society. It is through such interaction that the child becomes human in a social sense and it is through such continued interaction that we are all socialized throughout our lives.

Primary Socialization

Many sociologists, and certainly functionalists (system theorists), have viewed child or primary socialization as the process whereby the child learns to want or even to need to conform to social rules. According to this view, the child *internalizes* social norms, that is, makes them part of his personality; he carries society around in his head and follows the rules of society in almost every situation. A similar and usually complementary view emphasizes how the child learns to value or to need social approval from others, particularly those he likes and respects. In either case, socialization is seen to produce conformists. Predictably, such a view encounters problems when trying to account for the many instances in which many people violate rules, even rules which they have "internalized." The following chapter on deviant behaviour deals with these issues. We should, therefore, begin the discussion of socialization with some caution. First of all, while we are all socialized, we are probably never fully socialized. We are, after all, biological beings born with differing capacities and drives. While sociologists will all emphasize the social, they will, as we saw in Chapter I, come at it in different ways, depending on their basic or background assumptions about the nature of man. For some, other drives or motives—materialism or sex—seem as important wellsprings of social action as our need to conform, to gain social acceptance (Wrong, 1961).

A second caution to keep in mind is that while we talk about how the child learns to conform to rules, we must always ask whose rules. Certainly we all do learn to conform to rules to some degree, but we do not all learn to conform to the same rules. Much of the chapter on deviant behaviour discusses how some groups attempt and succeed in enforcing their standards on others. We may often conform because we must.

The infant is born into a ready-made world which will shape him far more than he shapes it. If we are born in Canada, for example, we will inevitably share certain features with others who were also born and raised in Canada. However, we are not all exposed to the same aspects of Canadian culture. It will make quite a difference, for example, if one is born in New Brunswick or in "Upper Canada." These regional differences are made more complex by internal subcultures along ethnic, religious and class lines. The family unit itself does more than simply relay the larger culture to the newborn. It also selects aspects of social reality, modifies and interprets the culture for the child. It presents the world outside as a social milieux to be feared or trusted. Indeed, the family must be treated as a social system in itself. The socialization of the child will be different in a one-parent family. It will differ from large families to small families. It will differ for the first born and the second born. And so on.

Obviously there are many sources of heterogeneity in socialization. These differences will influence what and how much the child learns about the social world and, in turn, will influence the child's life chances. To take one example, Basil Bernstein (1961), a British socio-linguist, has demonstrated that the linguistic backgrounds of working-class children can account, in good part, for these children's poor school performance. Working-class parents use a restricted or limited language code which makes it difficult for their children to become sensitive to differences in interpretation and nuance of meaning; they often seem to confuse the word for an object with the object itself. The middle-class parents will more likely use an elaborated language code which prepares their children to be more sensitive to the possibility that different people will interpret the "same" thing in different ways. If Bernstein is correct, this would obviously mean that, for the most part, middle-class socialization experience gives children a distinct advantage when they enter school.

Finally, even if we have been socialized, even if we have learned the rules and are seeking approval from those around us, conformity is still an accomplishment. Just think of the countless times that you have miscued, committed a social blunder, made a fool of yourself, Successful socialization is often defined in terms of how well the individual "fits" in his social group, how well he can interact with others. However, the rules one learns are only guidelines for behaviour, nor is it always clear which rules to apply when. Interacting with other people always involves some effort, some thought, some negotiation. It is in this sense that socialization never quits. Nevertheless, it is in childhood, through the process of primary socialization, that we become human. It is in this stage that the child develops interactive skills, particularly through his development of a self-concept.

Development of Self

Although much has been written about the psychological processes involved in primary socialization, little is known for certain. Obviously we cannot "get into the heads" of the children going through this process, certainly not in the early stages. Many of the sociologists who have specialized in this area have based their theories of observation on their own or a small number of children. Nevertheless, however difficult to test, this work has been extremely important in helping us to understand social interaction more generally.

Many psychologists and social psychologists agree that the key aspect of primary socialization is the child's development of *self*. Initially, the child is apparently unable to distinguish himself from the rest of the world; it is all one. Much of the first year or so of the child's development is spent in learning that there is a world out there and, often painfully, the rough shape and feel of that world. As the psychologist James Mark Baldwin argued, the child learns first the "not-I" before he becomes conscious of himself as an "I" (in McCall and Simmons, 1978:205). Gradually the child learns that he is distinct from the rest of the world, including other people. As the child engages in what is largely a trial-and-error exploration of the world, he soon discovers, for example, that it feels rather different to strike himself than to strike mother.

One of the early and influential contributions towards understanding development of self is Charles Horton Cooley's theory of "looking glass self." Children are obviously dependent on the others around them for all forms of comfort. According to Cooley, children become keen observers of these others and soon discover that they can influence them, that certain actions bring attention or food or anger. They learn that they have the power to influence others.

> *A girl six months old will attempt in the most evident and deliberate manner to attract attention to herself, to set going by her actions some of those movements of other persons that she has appropriated. She has tasted the joy of being a cause, of exerting social power, and wishes more of it. She will tug at her mother's skirts, wriggle, gurgle, stretch out her arms, etc., all the time watching for the hopeful effect (Cooley, 1902:197).*

The child soon learns to do different things and be different people for others. The child becomes deeply concerned about how these others view him. Thoreau wrote that it takes two to speak the truth, one to speak and one to listen. This "need" for an audience to tell us that what we speak is true, that our accomplishments are worthwhile, that we are beautiful, good or, of course, otherwise is the essence of Cooley's "looking glass self." We see ourselves through the eyes of others; we imagine how others see us, how they judge us, and this reflected image evokes some self-feeling such as pride or shame.

Cooley pointed out that not everyone's judgement is equally important. Some people are more *significant* than others. According to Cooley, we find our most significant "mirrors" in primary groups (groups in which we have intimate face-to-face interaction). In early life the family is our most important looking glass. The child's self-image at this time is typically rudimentary; he is learning what his parents expect and is able to see and evaluate himself in terms of these expectations. But, as the child becomes immersed in the world outside the home, plays with other children and meets other adults, the sense of self quickly becomes more rich and complex.

The most compelling and most complete account of the self-development process was provided by George Herbert Mead (1934) whose work is clearly influenced by Cooley's formulations. For Mead, as for Cooley, self and other are inseparable concepts; self and society are bound together. Mead describes how the child gradually comes to acquire a self as he comes to learn and use language. Mead agreed with Cooley that what distinguished human socialization from animal learning was the ability of humans to shift perspectives, to see the world from another's vantage point. This is only possible when we learn language, symbols that mean much the same to others as they do to us. Mead's most important contribution is perhaps just this—his understanding of the importance of the symbolic process. Animals respond to one another on the basis of natural *signs* rather than significant (meaningful) symbols. Imagine, for example, that someone reaches his hand out to you and in his upturned palm there is something you want. You do not simply respond to the stimulus; you interpret the gesture. You imagine what is in the other person's mind; you imagine his *intentions.* In Mead's terms, for humans, the gesture stands for the completed act. Humans interpret the intentions of others before they themselves act. This is the basis of the symbolic interactionist perspective which we shall discuss later on. For now, we are interested in how the child learns this interpretive process. The child may at first grab what is in the upturned hand, but he soon learns not to.

For Mead, the process occurs through three stages of increasing complexity. In the first stage, the *preparatory stage,* the child simply imitates the actions of those around him. He may, for example, like his father, "read" the newspaper, though he cannot yet read. In this stage, then, he is engaging in actions which he does not really understand. Nevertheless, he is learning a good deal about the relationship between his actions and the actions of others towards him. In the second stage, the child begins to *play* the roles of others. He may, for example, play at being mother and scold himself for being naughty. The child can do this as he acquires language because it is through language that he is able to think of himself abstractly, to "get out of himself" and respond to himself as others do. It is in this stage then that the child is learning *to take the role of the other,* to respond to himself as others do. Through actually playing out the role of mother, father and so on, the child is learning to take their roles, learning to imagine how they see a particular situation and, most important, learning to respond to himself as they would. He can ask himself, "Am I being bad, naughty?" It is through such role-taking that one develops a self-concept and learns to exert self-control in terms of the imagined expectations of others. During the play stage, however, the child's role-taking is unorganized, he takes one role at a time, one after another. Because he has no single organized standpoint from which to view himself, he has no organized conception of self.

In the final stage, the *game* stage, the child learns to take a number of roles simultaneously, to see himself from a generalized standpoint. Mead uses the example here of a baseball game. To play the game the child must imagine the expectations of all the others in the game simultaneously and he must develop a composite, generalized set of expectations of all the others in the game on the basis of which he can act. Mead referred to this as the development of the "generalized other," or the learning of group norms. In this stage, then, the child no longer things of himself only in relation to particular *significant* others, but also in relation to the *generalized* other, his synthesis of the group or community as a whole. The child has now learned to think in terms of a set of standards—group norms—which he can apply consistently across a wide variety of situations. This marks the development of self; the child can now respond to, control and organize his own behaviour.

Role Learning

As the child is playing at certain roles he is learning not only about himself and how he is seen by others but also about roles which he may play in the future. He is engaged in a process of *anticipatory socialization.* He is playing at roles that one day he will play for real. He is learning what is expected of mothers, teachers, older brothers, men and women, as well as a host of other roles—cowboy, fireman, astronaut—that he is less likely to play as an adult. When parents buy their daughters dolls, cooking sets and so on, they are encouraging their daughters to practise certain roles. As parents tell their children stories, relate myths, encourage daughters to help in the kitchen and sons in the garage, they are providing their children with the resources and direction for their early role rehearsal. And although children are usually given a good deal of leeway in their play, parents will generally attempt to "correct" the child who is consistently practising the "wrong" roles. Even today, many mothers who are pleased to see their sons rehearsing roles traditionally female, playing with dolls, for example, find that the son often meets with ridicule when he goes into the outside world.

From the time of the child's birth, parents and others place the child in a number of roles. And for a long time the child is unaware of these ascribed roles. Immediately, for example, a male child is given a male name, dressed in male clothing and encouraged to participate in "male activities." He is also ascribed roles on the basis of his parents' religion and class standing. These ascribed roles, and particularly the sex roles, come to be taken for granted by the child and form the backdrop for all other role learning. The female child learns that only certain kinds of play and games are deemed appropriate for her; while her brother pretends to be a football player, she may pretend to be the cheerleader; while a young boy pretends to be Prime Minister, the young girl may pretend to be his wife or secretary.

As far as we know, children do not naturally act in sex appropriate ways. Girls, for example, *learn* to walk, talk, dress and so on "like little girls." Our sex role becomes a core feature of our self and a taken-for-granted basis for our actions. Others respond to the child (and adult) in terms of their sex role performances. The child modifies his performance in terms of these reactions and, as we have said, comes to see himself as these others see him. Clearly role and self are closely related. Some of the roles we learn, though not all, will become an important part of our self-concept and will influence much of adult behaviour. Just how this early role learning influences our adult role performances is quite variable. Anticipatory socialization is often very useful in preparing one for adopting new roles. In fact, anticipatory socialization continues throughout adulthood. People are constantly preparing themselves for, anticipating, new roles. On the other hand, the early role learning of some children may have created obstacles for them and may make it hard for them to take on some roles. The child's early experiences may have led him to develop unreasonably high expectations which make it almost inevitable that he come to see himself as a failure. Conversely, the child may have developed unreasonably low expectations which make him reluctant in the future to take on new and demanding ventures (see Atkinson and McLellan, 1948; and Hoffman, 1972). Early socialization, then, can influence in later life our desire or even our willingness to achieve.

Moral Development

Child socialization describes the gradual

process whereby the child overcomes his initial egocentrism. The young child "is at first enclosed in his own point of view and sees all things from within it" (Lindesmith and Strauss, 1968:258). As the child acquires language, he participates in a wider range of social relationships and, as we have shown, begins to take on other people's perspectives. This aspect of socialization has received its greatest emphasis and most meticulous description in the works of the Swiss psychologist Jean Piaget (1948; 1952; 1954). Although Piaget does not use explicitly the term role, nor does he fully appreciate the role of language acquisition, his detailed study of lower-class children in Geneva lends a good deal of support to the sociological work we have described. His emphasis has been on the expanding cognitive ability of the child, on how the child develops increasingly more sophisticated understanding of the physical and social world. One area, in particular, in which his work complements that of Mead's is his treatment of moral development.

Piaget describes the development of children's moral judgements as they move from egocentric to relativistic standards. According to Piaget, the child up to the age of four or five is a *moral absolutist;* right is right and wrong is wrong and those who do wrong must be punished regardless of the circumstances. Later, up to the age of about nine or ten, the child comes to realize that moral rules do not possess the same kind of reality as the physical world; they are a product of the group into which the child is born. The child realizes this as he gains some sense of the varied perspectives of others around him (similar to Mead's "generalized other"). Finally, the child becomes a *moral relativist;* he comes to see rules as somewhat flexible and some rule violations, under mitigating circumstances, as forgivable. A number of other studies lend support to Piaget's findings (see Brown, 1965).

There is more question, however, about Piaget's explanation for these findings. Piaget argued that absolutism in the young child was the result of the authoritarian parent-child relationship, a relationship based primarily on punishment and reward in one direction. The child's view becomes more relativistic and general as he comes to participate in more egalitarian and cooperative relationships, particularly with his peers. This explanation probably underemphasizes the importance of the child's increasing language and role-taking skills, quite apart from the nature of the relationships he is in. Nevertheless, Piaget has been used by a number of educators to justify their pleas for more "freedom," less authoritarianism and structure, in the school setting (see Nyquist and Hawes, 1972).

Piaget has also inspired a good deal of research on moral development and a particularly interesting example is provided by Lawrence Kohlberg (1963; 1964). Kohlberg's cross-cultural study of children's moral judgement seems to show the influence of both Piaget and Mead. The study consisted of asking children varying in age from seven to 17 a series of questions that contained some moral dilemma. He asked, for example, whether it would be right to steal under the following circumstances:

A woman is near death. Doctors believed that one particular drug might save her and this drug was available at the local druggist's. But the druggist was charging very much for the drug and the woman's husband could only collect half the price. He told the druggist about the wife's condition and asked him to lower his price or allow him to pay the rest later, but the druggist refused. The man finally broke in and stole the drug. Should he have done this?

On the basis of the children's answers to this and similar questions, Kohlberg distinguished three levels of moral judgement, each level divided into two stages. These levels and stages represent increasing complexity and relativism similar to Piaget's findings. The levels, then, represent stages of moral development.

Kohlberg calls his three stages *preconventional, conventional* and *postconventional.* In each of these stages, the child is often "well-behaved," responsive to the cultural notions of good and bad, but in each stage the basis of his conformity varies. At the preconventional level, the child is concerned with the rewards and punishments his actions bring. In stage 1, the child is primarily concerned with avoiding punishment; this is how he judges good and bad. For example, his answer to the moral dilemma posed might be, "The man should not steal the drug because his mother will be mad and punish him." In stage 2, the child becomes more concerned about rewards for his actions. The child might answer in this stage that indeed the man should steal because he needs his wife to cook for him.

The second level, the conventional level, involves a concern with living up to the expectations of, and gaining the approval of, significant others. In the first stage at this level, the child is concerned with gaining the approval of others; he wishes to be viewed as good or nice. He might answer the experimental question in terms of how others would react to the husband, whether he would be seen as bad for stealing. In the second stage, children are characterized by a "law-and-order" orientation. They have learned respect for authority, and rules are seen as inflexible and a matter of duty. The child might answer simply that the man should not steal "because it is against the law."

The final level, the postconventional level, represents the most sophisticated moral judgements; the child is developing moral values and principles. In the first stage, the child is concerned about general community standards and procedures for evaluating behaviour. He might answer the question in terms of what is best for the community as a whole and might consider means of legally changing the laws so that the man might be able to get the drugs he needs. The child is concerned about law and order, but is willing to consider changes to the order in terms of some general principles. At the second stage the child is most concerned with personal conscience. At this stage he has developed some universal ethical principle, recognizes that it is a self-chosen principle, and that these abstract principles require a good deal of reflection and deliberation before a moral decision can be made in any given situation. The stages are presented as follows:

1. *Obey rules to avoid punishment.*
2. *Conform to obtain rewards, have favours returned, and so on.*
3. *Conform to avoid disapproval, dislike by others.*
4. *Conform to avoid censure by legitimate authorities and resultant guilt.*
5. *Conform to maintain the respect of the impartial spectator judging the terms of community welfare.*
6. *Conform to avoid self-condemnation. (Kohlberg, 1970)*

One of Kohlberg's major contributions was his recognition that not all people achieved the "highest" levels of moral development; children could become "stuck" at lower levels. He believed that conflict, having one's beliefs challenged, allowed one to see new possibilities.

In modern mass societies people may assume perspectives of groups in which they are not recognized members, sometimes of groups in which they have never participated directly and sometimes of groups that do not exist at all (Shibutani, 1955:569).

What this means is that constructing lines of action becomes increasingly complex as we come to use the standards of our own groups and the groups to which we aspire and continue to encounter groups which use different standards to evaluate our behaviour. These *reference groups* provide us with different perspectives which we must sort through and choose among.[1] Exposure to conflicting beliefs is essential for moral development. Mead, too, believed that an individual achieved his highest level of humanity when he could continue to develop his own personal syntheses of the conflicting expectations and interpretations he encountered. In the 1960s, a number of sociologists argued that too few of us were achieving this level, that too many of us were unreflective conformists. If this has been true in the past, perhaps the changes in content and patterns of socialization are also contributing to changes in moral development.

Most sociologists agree that the socialization process, both its form and its content, is changing rapidly in contemporary society. One argument is that these changes are leading to a greater permissiveness in the range of roles children are allowed to play. Bronfenbrenner (1970), for example, points to a number of changes in the family structure, many of which result in less parental attention and supervision for children. Certainly, in our society, both parents work (often because they must) and the family unit is less likely to include other adults to take the parents' place. Families are less likely to include three generations within the same community. Increasing numbers of children, it seems, are being raised in single-parent families and parents more generally, particularly middle-class parents, seem to be spending more time away from their children. All of this may mean that socialization by the nuclear family will be supplemented by new alternatives, not only day-care centres, but also informal neighbourhood cooperatives. Perhaps men, old people and the child's peers will become increasingly influential in the child's socialization (Symposium, 1973). Already, the school has become very important in child socialization since much of any teacher's time is devoted to teaching children to value education, to become "good citizens" and to conform to a large array of rules which may have little to do with education *per se*. These issues are treated much more fully in Chapter IX. On the other hand, some sociologists point out that despite these changes, the smaller family size in contemporary society means that parents have more rather than less time with their children (Bane, 1976).[2] People are not solely the rules and roles they have internalized. They are more than the internalized perceptions and expectations of others. What this "more" is necessarily involves us in some discussion of human nature.

Human Nature and Socialization

In his discussion of the social self, Mead distinguishes between two aspects of self: the "I" and the "me." Mead does not see them as two entities, but rather as two modes of interacting with or relating to people. The child's behaviour is dominated by the "I"—the impulsive tendencies of the individual. As the child is socialized, his behaviours are increasingly influenced by the "me"—the internalized meanings and expectations, the standards, of the group. According to Mead, the "I" and the "me" complement one another—the "I" initiates actions and gives impulse, while the "me" gives direction to the impulse. The "I" and "me," taken together, constitute the self-process. While the balance between "I" and "me" may vary from individual to individual and from culture to culture, all socialized humans have both. Action is based on a "conversation," or at least interplay, between the two.

This view of self has important implications for understanding human behaviour. The "me" is the part of self which represents the social roles the individual has internalized. This is the rule-following conforming aspect of the individual. The "I," on the other hand, thinks beyond social roles to possible futures beyond what has been learned. For Mead, it is what allows us to defy socialization. It is the spontaneous, creative aspect of self. For example, the "I" may tell a student to complain to his professor that his classes are boring or that he does not devote enough attention to his students. The "me" will act as something of a critic of this line of action, cautioning the student to consider the consequences. How will the teacher and others in the class react? What will his parents and friends think if he fails the course?

And how will all this make him feel about himself? The "me" helps us understand the stability and predictability of much of our behaviour. The "I" allows us to recognize, at the same time, human spontaneity and creativity that we also find. Mead then gives us a view of individual and society in which the individual does not completely disappear. Self cannot exist apart from society. Only through his interaction with others does the child gain the resources to think about himself and his relationship to the world. But society is not simply poured into our heads. We are shaped by the social world into which we are born, but we also act upon that world and help to shape it. With the resources they have learned, people are able to imagine futures they have not learned. And they may act upon these images.

Mead's distinction between the "I" and the "me" is often compared to Freud's discussion of the "id" and the "ego." The comparison, however, is not a very apt one. According to Freud, the "id" is the impulsive part of a person's personality, the part which must be brought under control by socialization. The "id," however, unlike the "I," is antagonistic to the social; it is a bundle of sexual and aggressive drives which must be brought under control if society is to exist. Freud's view is clearly much more pessimistic than Mead's. The former's view of human nature implies that the child is an unwilling participant in his own socialization, that he resists it. Socialization involves the *repression* of the child's natural tendencies and this is achieved only with the greatest pain. The socialized human has learned to *sublimate* these natural drives of sex and aggression into social pursuits which do not threaten society. To be human, then, means to live in an unnatural and therefore potentially explosive state; nor did Freud have much hope that the situation could be otherwise.

Obviously, the assumptions that we make about human nature will influence not only our theories of socialization, but also our views about how best to socialize children. Those who view man as essentially bad will emphasize the importance of supervision and discipline. Those who view man as essentially good will advocate greater permissiveness, less supervision. Obviously, the assumptions that the parents make will greatly influence the child's socialization. Mead's position, that man is neither inherently good nor inherently evil, falls somewhere in between. According to this view, supervision and discipline are necessary for the development of the "me," and the freedom to engage in unsupervised play is important for the development of the "I." Mead emphasized neither the individual nor society, but social interaction—how people take one another into account, take each other's role, respond to one another's gestures and intentions and thereby influence one another. Man is, then, essentially a symbol user. Mead has been influential in encouraging sociologists to examine the process of social interaction and has "fathered" a sociological approach to interaction—*symbolic interactionism.*

APPROACHES TO INTERACTION

Symbolic Interactionism

Howard Becker (1964) has distinguished three major uses in the social sciences of the term interaction: (1) At the simplest level, interaction is viewed as the reciprocal influence of individuals. According to this view, interaction is the virtually automatic response of individuals to stimuli. No sharp distinction is drawn between human interaction and the communication of gestures which characterizes animal interaction. In this view, interaction is equated with *stimulus-response*. We shall return to this use of the term in our discussion of exchange theory. (2) The second view sees human interaction as *symbolic interaction*. This view stresses the difference between animal behaviour and human behaviour in that symbolization transforms interaction. Because of symbolization, individuals do not respond directly to one another, to stimuli, but to their own interpretations of other. Interaction, then, is mediated by symbols, particularly linguistic symbols; stimuli are never directly apprehended by the interactants. In this use of the term, interaction is equated with communication and communication always means interpretation. This is related to the third use of the term. (3) Interaction is also used to describe the *internal dialogue* people engage in, communication not only with others but with oneself. This use of the term equates interaction with the self-other process, that is, the process of making indications to oneself about the social world in terms of what others think.

It is these last two uses of the term that are central to the symbolic interactionist perspective. As we mentioned in Chapter I, symbolic interactionism is one of the dominant perspectives in North American sociology. This is due primarily to the work of Herbert Blumer (1969a), whose writings have served to keep alive the ideas of George Herbert Mead and to illustrate their implications for sociology. Blumer describes symbolic interactionism in terms of three basic premises: (1) People "act toward things on the basis of the meanings that the things have for them." (2) "The meaning of such things is derived from, or arises out of, the social interaction that one has with one's fellows." (3) "These meanings are handled in, and modified through, an interpretative process used by the person in dealing with the things he encounters" (Blumer, 1969a:2).

The first premise simply restates what we have been saying all along about the importance of symbolization: people do not respond to stimuli, but to the meaning those "stimuli" have for them. Blumer notes that while few social scientists would argue with this premise, they persist nevertheless in underplaying meaning. Human behaviour is treated too often, according to Blumer, as simply the product of internal (psychological) factors—attitudes, unconscious and conscious motives and the like—or of external forces—roles, rules, social pressures and the like. In order to understand human behaviour, Blumer argues, we must give priority to how people themselves define these internal and external "forces." It is on the basis of these meanings that people act.

The second premise states that meanings are a social product, a product of social interaction. "The meaning of a thing for a person grows out of the ways in which other persons act toward the person with regard to the thing (Blumer, 1969a:4). A central aspect of the process of interaction, according to this view, is the creation of shared meanings. This definitional process was particularly well illustrated in Lucas' study of the trapped miners (Chapter I). The emphasis here is clearly on interaction, not the individual.

The third premise is perhaps the one that most clearly distinguishes symbolic interactionism from other perspectives in sociology and social psychology. Here, Blumer is emphasizing the fluid nature of interaction. People do not simply apply the meanings they have acquired in some automatic way; because they have selves, they are able to engage in an internal dialogue in which they make indications to themselves and point out what is meaningful. People do not simply apply meanings, they handle them, select among them and modify them in terms of the perceived demands of the situation. The use of meanings, then, is an interpretative process.

What is meant by an interpretative process? Consider, for example, tying up a dog which has never been tied up before. Chances are that the dog will resist, in response to the *stimulus* of the rope. But, what happens if we tie up a human being? One response, of course, is simply to resist. But, suppose that this is explained to him as part of a game, or, for his own reasons, he interprets this as a game. Or, if he is on a ship on a rough sea, he believes (interprets) that he is being tied up for his own safety. In these cases, he will not likely resist; he will respond to his *interpretations*, not simply to the stimulus of the rope. This process of interpretation is the focus of studies in symbolic interactionism.

No doubt the central concept of symbolic interactionism is "definition of the situation" (see Stebbins, 1967). At the simplest level, what this means is that we must place people and objects and ourselves into meaningful categories in any situation before we are able to formulate a plan of action. In any situation, we must socially place the others we are interacting with, attach an *identity* to them and, at the same time, we must establish our own personal identity. As Foote (1951) has pointed out, our own situational identity, who we are in any situation, is not automatically given, but is always more or less problematic. For example, how would you define the situation if, while dining out, you found that you were being waited on by a close friend? Does the situation call for the kinds of actions appropriate between friends or those which we think define the waiter-customer relationship? Who is it you are interacting with and who are you in this situation? Does one leave a larger tip or perhaps no tip at all?[3] Chances are that whatever you do will involve some degree of embarrassment because of the identity ambiguity. A good deal of symbolic interactionist research examines how people *negotiate* definitions, and particularly identities, in problematic situations. Wilfred Martin (1976), a sociologist at the University of New Brunswick, has provided one of the most systematic attempts to apply a "negotiation framework." In his study of interaction in the school, he has, for example, shown the different degrees and kinds of negotiation practices in interaction between "equals," on the one hand, and "unequals," on the other. He argues that the negotiation framework, the study of how people work out shared meanings, is able to cover a broad range of human associations: "for example, conflict, domination, exploitation, consensus, disagreement, indifferent concern for another, and closely knit identification" (Martin, 1976:157-158).

Symbolic interactionists, then, see people not only as shaped by social situations, but also as shaping them. Whatever a person's objective, it is to his advantage to try to control the behaviour of others, particularly how they respond to him. This is achieved primarily by controlling other people's definitions of the situation. A person will conduct himself and express himself, "in such a way as to give [others] the kind of impression that will lead them to act voluntarily in accordance with his own plan" (Goffman, 1959). One particular brand of symbolic interactionism, "dramaturgy," uses the analogy of the theatre to help us understand people's attempts to control the definition of the situation.

The Dramaturgical Model

The dramaturgical model views social life in terms of actors performing to audiences, wearing masks, using props and, finally, reading the reviews. The analogy is not really to the classical theatre's rigidly followed scripts (as in conventional role theory), but to improvised theatre where the actors work out the script as they go.

> *To the role theorist, the archetypical role is that seen in ritual or classic drama, in which every line and every gesture of every actor is rigidly specified in the sacred script. In our view, the archetypical role is more nearly that seen in improvised theatre, such as is provided by the Second City Troupe, which performs extemporaneously with only the broad outline of the sketches and of the characters assumed (McCall and Simmons, 1978:7).*

Much of the inspiration for this perspective comes from the work of Cooley. He believed that a dramatic turning point in a child's socialization is the child's realization that he can to some extent control the conduct of others. Initially, the child's attempts to "impress" others are obviously just that; the child has not learned to be subtle. As adults, we learn to hide the fact that what we are trying to do is impress others, to affect how they view us. We learn to do so without appearing to do so. This has been the point of departure for much of the work of Erving Goffman, who has done most to develop the dramaturgical model.

According to this view, whatever the situation, we are trying to convey a particular impression of who we are. In other words, much of our interaction is devoted to *impression management*. Goffman describes the "stage-craft" and "stage-management" techniques we all use in everyday life.

Think, for example, of the performance of a professor lecturing to his class. He may stand behind a podium with his typed lecture notes or he may deliberately move the podium to one side and walk among the students. In either case, he has manipulated, or at least made use of, some aspects of the social setting, the *scenery*, to convey some information about what he is like. He will give additional information about what he is like through the *props* he has chosen—suit, tie and briefcase or denim and shoulder-bag. Gregory Stone argues that in everyday life we tend to socially identify one another largely in terms of appearance, the clothes we wear and how we wear them; so, the clothes we choose become an important statement of who we are. "By appearance, a person *announces* his identity, shows his value, *expresses* his mood, or *proposes* his attitude" (Stone, 1962:101). Finally, as part of the performance, the professor will adopt a particular manner in playing his role—he may try to "relate to" the student or maintain maximum distance from him.

In all of this, the professor is an actor performing to students, the audience (and perhaps to internal audiences, imagined audiences of family, colleagues and so on). And the students too are actors, performing to one another and to the professor. Moreover, the students' performances are likely to be very different within and outside the view of their professors. If we consider students performing for the professor (audience), we can distinguish, as in the theatre, two regions of performance: the *back region* and the *front region*. In the back region, outside the view of the audience, the student can to some extent drop his "front." Here he can prepare his performance, rehearse, check that his appearance is suitable for the front stage. He may, as well, confer with fellow students—members of his *team*—about how he is doing, how he might do better and how they might help. We typically enlist the aid of others in giving a performance and establish "teams" of mutual cooperation. Only team members are allowed into the back region. Back region, front region, team member and audiences are, of course, variable, matters of definition. The student may think of his fellows as team members as he prepares his front-stage performance, and they will be privy to information not made available to the professor, but, at the same time, they will be an audience which the student is seeking to impress. Movement from back stage to front stage is an interpretive rather than a physical shift.

The distinction between back and front regions underscores a crucial element of impression management—information control. At the same time that we seek to give certain information about ourselves, we withhold other information. Typically, actors try to "schedule" their performances so that "outsiders" cannot observe and thereby see a performance not intended for them. Many students, for example, might be made uncomfortable if their roommates observed their interaction with their parents (or vice versa). Similarly, many professors might find it more difficult to perform their classroom role in the presence of an outside observer such as a colleague or spouse. These and similar "information leaks" are a continuing source of embarrassment in everyday life.

Clearly, actors do not have complete control over their performances or, more precisely, over how others respond to their performances. As Goffman puts it, not only do we *give expressions,* we also *give off expressions.* People do not simply observe what we knowingly present to them, they also observe and judge us on the basis of unintended gestures; "nervous mannerisms" such as trembling knees, sweaty palms, blushing, slips of the tongue and so on. In fact, as people have learned to be somewhat cynical, they may use the impressions given off, thought to be beyond the control of the performer, to judge the sincerity of the performance. The audience will often check the fit between expressions given, thought to represent the performance, and expressions given off, thought to represent the person behind the mask, the "real" meaning of the performance.

In short, as we give a performance, claiming and staking out an identity, there is no guarantee that the identity we are claiming will be validated by our audience. We have all, at one time or another, received bad reviews. Our identity may be discredited because the audience may decide we are "phonies," that we do not have the credentials—the *content*—to justify our identity claim. Or, our identity might be discredited because the audience views our performance as inept. We do not have the *style*. This is nicely illustrated by the audience response to two people playing the role of professor. One, Thorstein Veblen, was the author of the witty and insightful work, *The Theory of the Leisure Class*. Because of this book, Veblen attracted large crowds of students to his lectures. Unfortunately, students found him to be a bad and boring lecturer. The result, according to one of his students, was that his course would begin with 250 to 300 students and would end with only one or two persistent ones. Veblen was high on "content," extremely low on "style." Indeed, had it not been for the written evidence of his intellect, he would likely have been declared incompetent. We can compare this case with "MacDonald," a psychology professor at Lakehead University in the mid-1960s. MacDonald was well-liked by both students and colleagues. One of the authors of this book, during a visit to the nearby Teacher's College where MacDonald also taught a course, was told that he was one of the best teachers that Lakehead had ever sent over. Then, to everyone's horror, it was learned that "MacDonald" was an imposter; he had assumed the identity and credentials of another person, someone who had graduated from a university in the Southern United States. The point is that the "performer" was discredited not because he was found to be "incompetent," but because, by sheer accident, the *real* MacDonald discovered and pointed out the fraud. In other words, whereas Veblen had content, but no style, the imposter had style but supposedly lacked content.

In other words, our identities may be discredited in terms of our performances rather than in terms of what we *really* are. For example, in one of his works, Goffman (1963) describes how people who possess some *stigma*—for example, a physical deformity, "personal problems" thought to lead to behaviour such as alcoholism or mental illness or membership in a particular religion or race—may find that their identity as normal human beings is challenged.

Goffman is often criticized for developing too cynical a model of man and interaction. To talk about people as actors seems to imply that they are always playing parts, not themselves. All the language seems to imply pretence, phoniness and calculated manipulation. There seem to be two elements to this criticism. First, many people infer from the model the view of man as an anxiety-ridden, sweaty-palmed actor concerned only about how he is coming across to others, and this does not jibe with their own experience. Second, there seems to be some concern that dramaturgy implies that we are insincere in our everyday relationships. These criticisms, however, do an injustice to the model.

Goffman and others who use the perspective do not imagine that we are necessarily preoccupied with our own performances. This may be the case in some rare circumstances such as a first date or a job interview, but for the most part we are able to take for granted our performances, and those of others. From our socialization as children, we have been taught how to perform for audiences and to change our performances as the audiences change. None of this is new to us. As well, we give most of our performances over and over again until they become routine and require little thought. We tend to become aware of our performances only when they have been challenged, when our identity has been discredited or when we are confronted with an ambiguous situation.

Furthermore, the dramaturgical model does not imply that actors are insincere. According to this model, an actor is sincere if he believes in his own performance and he is insincere if he does not. A further analogy, then, might be provided by the "method actor." Perhaps the sincere performer, like the method actor, is the one who cannot perform a role unless he believes it. These are the situations when self and role fit in together. Nevertheless, Goffman recognizes that we are often called upon in everyday life to perform roles which we find distasteful, or simply lacking congruence with our self-concept. In these situations, the actor may exhibit *role distance*,[4] giving expressions to others and perhaps to himself to convey that he does not really mean what he is doing.

Finally, Goffman himself warns his readers that the language of the stage is simply a device, a rhetoric, a way of helping us to understand what we find so difficult to understand—our own interaction. The dramaturgical model is an analogy, scaffolding, and "scaffolds, after all, are to build other things with and should be erected with an eye to taking them down" (Goffman, 1951:254). It is important to emphasize again, however, that this perspective which views man as the negotiator of identities does not capture all aspects of human behaviour, nor necessarily the most important aspects. If man were simply the negotiator of identities, the actor, the wearer of masks (and different masks for different audiences), he would be rather an empty being. He would be much like one of T. S. Eliot's "Hollow Men," who asks:

Let me also wear
Such deliberate disguises
Rat's coat, crowskin, crossed staves
In a field
Behaving as the wind behaves

Goffman's dramaturgical approach seems to work best when we are considering what he calls "brief encounters" —secondary relationships—between sales person and customer; waiter and customer; professional and client. It is less useful when we are examining the sustained interaction of a primary relationship. No doubt, as Eric Berne (1964), the father of transactional analysis, has argued, people play games in even the most intimate of relationships and put on fronts and hold back information, but in a more limited and restricted manner than is possible in brief encounters. For example, while husbands and wives may perform for one another, they are also a team, constructing a shared definition of reality; they are often engaged as team members along with the rest of the family to present a particular performance, a particular definition of the situation to "outsiders" (Berger and Kellner, 1964). In other words, when people are "back stage" does it make any sense to talk about an "audience" for their "performance"? Goffman does not very adequately capture the kind of interaction which we think of in everyday life as intimacy.

Another analogy applied to social interaction which also emphasizes man as a rational manipulator of social symbols, but which focuses on competition and conflict in interaction, is the game perspective.

The Game Perspective

As we have mentioned, Mead recognized the importance of games in child socialization. Through games, children learn to read the cues offered to them by others, to take the roles of others and to fit their lines of action with the actions of others. A number of sociologists and social psychologists have followed this lead and have argued that games provide an apt analogy for social interaction more generally. They use games as a perspective for looking at social interaction. If we define games as those interactions in which one party is seeking some end at the expense of another party, but bound by some agreed upon rules, the comparison between games and a good deal of social interaction seems apparent. In a game, poker say, the pay-off or outcome depends not only upon one's own performance, but also upon the performances of others in the game, upon the performances of one's opponents. And, because of this, we must try to imagine, beforehand, what our opponent is going to do. In other words, we must take his role before we form our own line of action. Similarly, in everyday interaction, our behaviour depends upon the behaviour of others and we must try to imagine the other's intentions, what other is going to do, before we act. As well, both in games and in everyday interaction, the behaviour of all the participants is bound by a set of rules, agreed upon norms, for "playing the game." We might distinguish two types of rules: *constitutive rules* are the rules without which the game (or interaction) could not be played at all; *preferred rules* are the rules which describe how the game is usually played and the expectations about how players will play.[5] Constitutive rules describe the taken-for-granted rules that form the basis of the game—in poker, for example, the number of cards that are necessary, the notion of following in order, the idea that people will not look at one another's cards and so on. Preferred rules are the rules which describe the etiquette and style. Similarly, in interaction there are some rules which, if violated, disrupt interaction entirely and other rules which simply indicate preferred styles and manners in interaction. If, for example, you were constantly to ask people what they meant when they offered conventional messages such as "How are you?", you would no doubt be violating a constitutive rule and disrupting interaction (Garfinkel, 1967; Cicourel, 1964). People take for granted that when they ask us how we are, we will understand the question, just as in poker the players will assume that the others in the game will wait their turn, and so on. In interaction, there are also a number of rules which direct us in how to answer such conventional questions. For example, we are not expected to tell someone about all of our ailments and physical difficulties when they ask us, "How are you." This, however, is a preferred rule as its violation would not likely disrupt interaction entirely. Finally, both games and social interaction are "probabilistic"; we can never be certain that our action will bring about the required response in others, though the "odds" are probably much easier to work out in game situations. Much of our gaming behaviour is the plotting and devising of strategies to maximize the probability that we will be successful in bringing about the desired response in our opponents (Brittan, 1973).

A number of laboratory studies have devised game situations in order to study the kinds of strategies people employ. The classic laboratory game involves three (and sometimes more) subjects who are asked to play a board game for some reward, for example, points which can later be converted into money. The object of the game, much like Parcheesi, is to move around the board before one's opponents. Each participant moves his man a number of spaces, depending on the roll of the dice. Unlike Parcheesi, however, all participants move their men on each roll. The reason that they do not all finish at the same time, in a tie, is that each is assigned a different "weight" or value at the beginning of the game. For example, one might be given a "three" and the other two "two" each. What this means in the game is that the "three" would move his man three times the roll of the dice, while each "two" would move his man twice the roll of the dice.

The outcome of the game is obviously predetermined by the experimenter—those with the highest "weights" will always win. However, the experimenter encourages the participants to form coalitions to alter the predetermined outcome. He explains that any two participants can unite and form a team. Say a "three" and a "two" formed such a coalition. Each member of the coalition would move his man the roll of the dice multiplied by the combined total of their two scores—in this case five times the roll of the dice. They would, then, win the game and somehow divide the spoils. In the example we have given, any coalition would win: "three" and either one of the "two's" or both "two's."

The experimenter is interested in examining what kinds of coalitions the players will form in order to change the predetermined results of the game. Clearly, each "two" would lose if he did not form some coalition with one of the other two players.[6] The players in these experimental games will usually bargain with one another to decide which coalition will be most effective in winning and they will bargain about how to divide the spoils once the game has been won. For example, a "three" coalescing with a "two" might ask for a greater share of the winnings. A number of conclusions have been drawn from this experiment and many variations of it. People will usually try to form a coalition in which the power difference is in their favour, that is, in which they have more "weight" than the others in the coalition. If this is impossible, they will try to avoid situations in which the power difference is too great. They will try to maintain some "minimal power" (Caplow, 1956). In other words, the players are trying not only to win the game, but also to have some dominance over their partners. As well, it seems that the players will form the smallest coalition necessary to win the game (Gamson, 1961). In other words, they will try to form a winning coalition which nonetheless does not mean that they have to divide the pie in too many ways.

Of course, the forming of coalitions is only one of the many possible game strategies employed either in games or in everyday life. One central feature of most game strategies is "concealment." In games, it is important to conceal our strategies, our techniques, our plots from our opponents. Success usually depends on concealing such information, perhaps even upon misleading our opponent deliberately. Again, we can find many analogies in everyday life. Obviously, the game model paints humans as primarily calculating and manipulative. In everyday life, we are quite willing to look at some interactions in these terms. Many of us seem to view politics as primarily a "game."

> *Politicians are seen as being engaged in a deadly pastime of moving strategic pieces so that they place their opponents at a disadvantage. Strategic advantage is obtained by playing the game in as economical and calculating a manner as possible (rational efficiency). The players who can amass the greatest number of pieces (indoctrinated supporters, resources, offices, etc.) can be considered to be in a position of relative strength* vis-à-vis *the other players (Brittan, 1973:129).*

Most of us are reluctant to apply such a model to our own interaction or to the interaction of those close to us. Nevertheless, surely you can find a number of analogies in "the family game," "the dating game," "the course assignment game" and so on. In families, for example, one often finds children forming coalitions to stand against their parents, plotting together in the "back stage," and concealing their strategies from their parents. They develop techniques to gain certain ends—money, or special privileges—and more generally to gain greater autonomy, greater control over their parents and therefore their lives. Similarly, parents will often form coalitions "against" their children, devising strategies to get the child to go to bed at "bedtime" or "to behave" in front of "the visitors," in order to gain more control over their children's behaviour. The gaming perspective can be useful, then, in helping us to understand the struggle for power and control in social interaction. Implicit in this perspective is the notion that cooperative solutions can be demonstrated to be more advantageous than individualistic solutions, though a number of experiments have shown that people do not typically make the "rational" or "logical" decision.[7]

As with dramaturgy, it would be dangerous to take this analogy too seriously. It does not capture all aspects of social interaction. Not all interaction can be characterized as the participants' attempts to maximize their own ends, nor is all interaction strategic in the sense of games, nor is it necessarily premised on concealment. Just think, for example, of the importance you attach to your friendships, or certain friendships, in which you are able to disclose certain of the most secret and private features of yourself, to reveal yourself. This is the essence of the psychotherapeutic relationship and perhaps one of the reasons that it is so initially painful and highly emotionally charged and ultimately valued by the participants. In fact, we often seem to find great release in those encounters with strangers, on a bus or a plane, for example, in which we use the episodic and transitory nature of our interaction, the fact that we are not likely to see these people again, to "bare our souls." Such interaction is not very well captured by the game perspective.

There are perhaps even more important differences between game situations and everyday life. In everyday life we are less likely to be as sure of the rules of interaction as we are of the rules of a game. Indeed, in interaction two "players" may well be playing different games with different rules. And, in everyday interaction, rule violation is probably much more frequent than it is in game situations. In a game, the rules apply in the same way to all the participants. In everyday life, the rules are selectively applied and enforced and some people have more power in creating, applying and enforcing these rules (see Chapter VI). Finally, games are a matter of fun and enjoyment and, while much of our interaction is intrinsically pleasurable to us (Simmel, 1964), not all of our interactions are voluntarily entered into and most of them, whether pleasurable or not, affect our lives in ways in which games cannot replicate.

Another perspective which also emphasizes man's rational attempts to maximize his ends through bargaining in interaction is the exchange perspective.

The Exchange Model

The exchange perspective represents a substantial departure from symbolic interactionism, the perspective with which we introduced these various models. Although there are a number of versions of the exchange model in social psychology and sociology, we shall focus on the works of George Homans (1958; 1961) who has done most to bring exchange principles to the attention of sociologists. Homans has been concerned with the development of deductive theory: a set of general principles which would allow sociologists to predict human behaviour in a wide variety of situations. While sociologists look to historical, structural or cultural factors to explain human behaviour, Homans insists that the most general explanatory principles can be drawn through focusing on individual motivation. Homans, drawing his principles primarily from B. F. Skinner's highly influential behaviouristic psychology and from elementary economics, intends his exchange theory to apply to "all" human interaction.

The guiding idea is that people behave

in a way to maximize rewards and minimize costs. This does not mean that people are simply concerned with gaining immediate gratification. People's behaviour, according to this perspective, is governed by *enlightened self-interest*; they seek only to make some profit in any interaction (Homans, 1961:79). Of course, the basic ideas of exchange theory have existed for a long time, as Homans himself points out, both in the work of early social thinkers and in our common sense view of motivation. What Homans has tried to do is to present these ideas in an explicit and systematic way so they can be subjected to some testing. At the same time, he tried to develop a model of man that people could recognize in terms of their everyday experience.

Homans enumerates five basic principles or axioms which underpin the theory of exchange:

1. *If, in the past, a particular stimulus has accompanied rewards for an individual's behaviour, the more similar later stimuli are to these early ones, the more likely the individual is to perform the same or similar activity.*
2. *The more often a person's activity is rewarded, the more often he will perform that activity.*
3. *The more valuable the reward an individual receives, the more often he will perform the activity so rewarded.*
4. *The more often an individual has in the recent past received a rewarding activity from another, the less valuable any further unit of that reward becomes to him.*
5. *If an individual's expectations of the rewards and costs of his activity are not met, if he feels the exchange has not been "fair," he will become angry and behave aggressively. (Homans, 1961:53-75)*

The first three principles derive directly from the psychological work of Skinner. The first axiom describes the learning theory principle of *generalization*. Take, for example, a coach in hockey. When the combination of players that he has used in the game produces a victory, the coach's activities in that situation have been rewarded. In the next game, we may find that the coach tries to use exactly the same players, that is, he performs the same activities, seeking the same reward. Some coaches have been known to wear the same clothing that they wore the last time their team achieved a victory. If the situations are the same, people will behave in ways that "worked" in the past.

The second proposition is basic to learning or reinforcement theory. This proposition simply states that people will continually perform activities that have met with rewards in the past; the more often the activity has been rewarded, the more frequently people will engage in that activity. If studying hard has consistently brought a student good marks, he will more often study harder than one who has tried and failed.

The third proposition recognizes that there is substantial variation in what people find rewarding. Rewards are *variables*. Some people may value highly the reward of good marks, others may not. The more valuable the reward, the more likely it is to produce reward-seeking behaviour.

The fourth proposition derives from both reinforcement theory and elementary economics. It introduces the notion of *satiation*: people can get too much of a good thing. At the simplest level, this simply means that food is not as valued a reward to a well-fed person as to a hungry one. More generally, it means that after a time, rewards will decrease in value. If you eat steak every day, steak will lose some of its value as a reward. In elementary economics, this is known as the principle of *marginal utility*. The value that an individual attaches to any commodity depends on how much of that commodity he already possesses. The value that an individual attaches to any reward, then, depends on his past history, how much and how often he has been rewarded in the past.

In the fifth proposition, Homans introduces a new concept, essentially an elaboration of Skinner's work—the concept of *distributive justice*. Skinner observed that when pigeons do not receive their expected rewards, they exhibit behaviour which seems to reveal anger and frustration. Homans argues that people will respond in much the same way, but, being more sophisticated than pigeons, they make some calculation before they exhibit anger or frustration. They weigh the "cost" of the activity against the rewards they have received and thereby determine whether the "net reward" or profit was fair and just. In other words, when people receive punishment when they expect rewards, or assess the rewards as insufficient repayment for their investment (other rewards they have sacrificed), they will become angry and behave aggressively[8] (see Turner, 1974:235-237). This, then, is the core of exchange theory. Before we examine its failings, we shall briefly illustrate how it is applied to explain interaction.

Homans has used these ideas to analyse the interaction in a federal law enforcement agency (first reported in Blau, 1955). These agents had the task of making prosecution decisions about legal cases and, as with most legal matters, their task entailed a good deal of ambiguity. Although official bureaucratic policy forbade consultation among agents, this became a routine practice. There was general agreement among the workers about who were the most and the least skilled among them. Typically, workers would ask the more skilled among them for advice about their cases. The rewards these less skilled workers received are obvious: help in their work, social support from respected others and training. But the more skilled workers also received rewards in the exchange. When friends help us move, we often give them a good deal of beer in exchange. Similarly, the less skilled workers might offer to buy the more skilled a "free" lunch. But, more often, and more important, what they gave to those who offered help was respect and social esteem. Simply, if you ask someone for help and you do not do this in a deferential manner, and you do not show proper respect and gratitude afterwards, you are not likely to receive help from this person in the future. Homans characterizes interaction among law enforcement officers as this kind of social exchange.

In the agency, the demands made on the time of the more skilled workers came to affect their own work—their sense of distributive justice was violated. In turn, they raised the price for the help they gave; they demanded more deference, more gratitude, more respect. As well, they raised the price, according to Homans, because they were becoming satiated with the reward of self-esteem from their colleagues. Because the less skilled workers were often unwilling to pay the price—the costs were too great—they asked these experts for help less and less often. The law enforcement officers were supposedly continually calculating the rewards and costs of these exchanges.

The most interesting and potentially fruitful application of exchange principles is Peter Blau's (1964) analysis of *power*. Blau defines power as the ability of an individual (or group) to extract compliance in an exchange relationship. According to the exchange perspective, people *allow* others to influence them because it is in their best interest to do so. Power is tied to the notion of dependency. If a person cannot, or believes he cannot, get something that he "needs" from any other source, he will continue to interact with the source of these rewards even if the costs seem great and the exchange unfair. To put it in another way, those who possess a highly valued and scarce resource have power over those who feel they need the resource. When this resource is something that gets used up or constantly needs replenishing—money, food and sex, for example—power is at its greatest. People will incur high costs to get these rewards. But, according to exchange theory, power is never absolute. There is usually some other source for the reward and, if people realize this, they will shop around for the source which exacts the lowest costs. This does not mean that the power relationship is eliminated, but rather that the power is constrained. Even if no other source of the reward seems to be available, those in the weak position are still likely to have some power, though considerably less, over those in the stronger position. In the exchange perspective, power is always to some degree reciprocal.

Let us take again the example of the student-professor relationship. The professor has power over the student in that he controls something the student "needs"—grades. To some extent, then, the professor can exact compliance from the student—influence him to sit through his lectures, do assignments, write exams—even if the costs are great. However, the student can drop out, switch courses or, most subtly, try to work it so that the professor comes to value the student's respect and goodwill and thereby comes to be careful about what he demands. The student, then, in this situation, supposedly has at least some influence as well.

Exchange theory obviously has a good deal of face validity when we think of many of our everyday life situations. When we give someone a gift it seems generally the case that we expect to receive in return a gift of similar or equal value. When we have been invited to dinner we will often think in terms of "owing" a dinner invitation in return. When people fail to meet our exchange expectations, we may hesitate to trust them in future interactions. Nevertheless, despite its obvious appeal, exchange theory has a far more limited applicability than Homans intended and is also fraught with conceptual problems. First of all, exchange theory is probably not very useful for handling situations involving force or coercion. Exchange does not seem to enter the picture when we have been forced to engage in some activity; our calculations of costs and rewards are certainly less relevant. As Blau (1964) himself has recognized, exchange principles do not seem to apply very well in situations in which people are acting out of fear. When people are acting, say, out of a fear of eternal damnation or of losing their jobs or of arrest, they may well be calculating costs, but there is no exchange. It would appear that game theory's work on coalition formation and particularly symbolic interactionism would be more useful in these situations. When people are acting on the basis of fear, they are imagining the responses of others, viewing themselves as objects and controlling their behaviour in terms of these symbols. Furthermore, the exchange assumption of "the essential ubiquity of the hedonistic calculus" may also limit the range of situations for which it can be applied (Brittan, 1973). When someone gives an anonymous donation to charity or, more generally, when somebody behaves altruistically, is he simply seeking to maximize his own self-interest? One might certainly answer that he is doing this so that he will feel good about himself, but to say that this is simply a particular example of exchange-reward is to stretch the term beyond reason. Again, we would argue that symbolic interactionism and its emphasis on the reflexive nature of self offers a more useful perspective. This brings us to our final criticism of exchange theory—its behaviouristic orientation.

Skinner, the psychologist who so influenced Homans, has argued that social scientists should avoid the inclusion of mental processes in developing their theories. While this may do very well for the psychologists' highly controlled observations of animals in the laboratory setting, it will not do, as we have argued, for the symbolic interaction of humans. Homans has framed his propositions without reference to mental processes; they reflect a somewhat sophisticated version of the stimulus-response model. For example, in Homans's propositions, he makes reference to the notion of "similarity of situations" or "similarity of stimuli." But, just when are two stimuli similar? However much Homans may wish to avoid it, the proposition would be better phrased in terms of what people *think* of as similarities. In this way, the propositions would be made to refer to the conscious actions of people and meaningful behaviour. There is much more to interaction than the exchange of rewards. Indeed, the meaning of Homans's central concept—rewards—cannot be treated as given. Surely what people define as rewarding and the value they attach to rewards are not meanings that have been learned in the past and then applied in some automatic fashion; as people interact, they no doubt negotiate, handle and modify these meanings as well. In these terms, it seems clear that exchange theory would benefit from a closer alliance with symbolic interactionism (see Singlemann, 1972).

Exchange theory developed largely as a response to the dominant conventional sociological theories we discussed in Chapter I. The intent was to explain social and cultural processes in terms of the principles of individual motivation and exchange; from these building blocks we could supposedly understand how societies are constructed and maintained. In this they have, as yet, been unsuccessful. Nevertheless, exchange theory has provided an orientation to interaction which has influenced many social psychologists and some sociologists and has, thereby, helped to bring within one framework many diverse studies and scattered findings.

Another perspective which offers an even more radical alternative to conventional sociology draws on the work of George Herbert Mead, and also from phenomenology, particularly the works of Alfred Shutz (1964). This is the approach of ethnomethodology.

Ethnomethodology

Superficially, at least, ethnomethodology seems in many ways similar to symbolic interactionism. Norman K. Denzin (1969) has gone so far as to argue that they are sufficiently similar to be quite easily synthesized. Both are interested primarily in the negotiation of symbols in everyday interaction. Denzin, however, has failed to recognize the full extent of ethnomethodology's departure from conventional perspectives. Symbolic interactionism, like all sociological perspectives, views interaction in the context of society; symbolic interactionism seeks to explain how people fit their lines of action together and pattern their interac tions, on the basis of more or less shared meanings. The symbolic interactionist assumes that these patterns exist and he seeks to account for them. Ethnomethodologists, on the other hand, refuse to make this assumption. They do not assume that social order exists "out there." They ask a rather different question: how do people, including sociologists, produce and maintain for one another the *presumption* that the social world is real and orderly (Garfinkel, 1967)? In other words, they ask how people plan and explain their behaviour to themselves and others in the process of interaction; how they make their behaviour and the behaviour of others *appear* rational and orderly. For the ethnomethodologist, consensus or agreement in interaction does not refer to the actual meshing or fitting together of meaning, but to the interactant's *belief* that this has been accomplished. According to this view, social order, or, more accurately, a *sense* of social order is created and maintained in interaction. The ethnomethodologist's goal then is to uncover the methods people use to make sense of the world and to make the world appear sensible to themselves and others with whom they are interacting.

In fact, the cement that holds society together may not be the values, norms, common definitions, exchange payoffs, role bargains, interest coalitions, and the like of current social theory, but people's explicit and implicit "methods" for creating the presumption of a social order (Turner, 1974:322).

Ethnomethodology, then, is the study of people's *accounting procedures*, the methods people use for making the world visibly rational and orderly for themselves and those they are interacting with. Ultimately, they hope to uncover the rules whereby people construct these accounts.

However, these rules are difficult to study because they are implicit. One of the ways that ethnomethodologists have tried to overcome this problem is by the technique of "disruption" (Garfinkel, 1967:37). The general idea is to start with the commonplace, familiar scenes, and to make trouble, to force the "subjects" to make explicit what they usually take for granted. For example, Harold Garfinkel, the major proponent of ethnomethodology, asks his students to perform an assignment in which, in their everyday interaction with others, they ask for clarification of the meanings of commonplace remarks that they would be expected to understand. One student provided Garfinkel with the following report:

On Friday night, my husband and I were watching television. My husband remarked that he was tired.

Wife:	*How are you tired? Physically, mentally, or just bored?*
Husband:	*I don't know. I guess physically, mainly.*
Wife:	*You mean that your muscles ache or your bones?*
Husband:	*Don't be so technical.*
(After more watching.)	
Husband:	*All these old movies have the same kind of old iron bedstead in them.*
Wife:	*What do you mean: Do you mean all old movies, or some of them, or just the ones we have seen?*
Husband:	*What's the matter with you? You know what I mean.*
Wife:	*I wish you would be more specific.*
Husband:	*You know what I mean! Drop dead!*

This, and similar experiments such as the one described in Chapter II, provide ethnomethodologists with a good deal of their material for theorizing. In this particular example, the husband obviously *assumed* consensus; he assumed that he and his wife were using shared meanings, that they understood one another. In everyday life, we are always saying only a fraction of what we mean, and we assume that others can fill in the rest. In this case, when the wife challenged this assumption, the husband became indignant. No doubt he assumed that she was doing this strange thing deliberately. In this and similar experiments, people try to *normalize* the situation and try to make it appear sensible. The husband will, for example, impute motives to his wife to account for her bizarre behaviour. Perhaps she is teasing him because she is angry. Perhaps she is tired or drunk. Perhaps she is going mad. Or perhaps with more information everything will soon come clear. We use these techniques in everyday life as we are continually imputing motives to others and ourselves in order to make sense of behaviour (Blum and McHugh, 1971). Children, however, may be more willing than adults to tolerate highly "unstructured" situations. This is the thrust of John Holt's (1964; 1967; 1969) various books on the socialization and education of children.

It is also of significance that people who find themselves in ethnomethodological experiments typically react with such vehemence. In the example cited, the husband was not simply confronted with an awkward or annoying situation, he was confronted with a threatening one. When our assumption of shared meanings, of consensus, is challenged, we realize how difficult communication really is. We realize how imprecise and problematic is our use of language. We realize the precariousness, the fragility, of "social order."

Thus far, ethnomethodologists have done little more than demonstrate that such interpretative rules as we have described do exist. As well, the problems that they will encounter in developing an adequate methodology to uncover these rules and a general theory of these rules are substantial. This is particularly the case since these interpretative rules may well be situation specific, created anew in each interaction situation. In any case, ethnomethodologists have provided sociologists with new questions and have contributed to conventional perspectives on interaction in their description of accounts and people's attempts to normalize the apparently abnormal (see Scott and Lyman, 1968).

CONCLUSIONS

We have described a perhaps confusing number of images of man and interaction. All of these images are simply perspectives with which to view interaction; none is complete, and none is entirely wrong. Man is probably an actor, a game player, a bargainer, an explainer of the world and much more. People sometimes follow rules in a relatively unthinking way; they sometimes use rules to guide their interaction and they sometimes use rules to account for interaction. All of these perspectives emphasize in one way or another man's active and creative role in shaping his world. But, perspectives on interaction alone never adequately deal with how the world "acts back" on people. They form one side of the dialectic which we have described in Chapter I.

It is our belief that symbolic interactionism in particular is important because an understanding of how people view the world and how they act in terms of their own perceptions helps us link micro and macro, "the private and the public, the innermost acts of the individual with the widest kinds of socio-historical phenomena" (Gerth and Mills, 1963:xvi). In the following chapter, we shall examine how symbolic interactionism, when combined with conflict theory, can help us to understand "deviant" behaviour.

SUGGESTIONS FOR FURTHER READING

An excellent introduction to the area of socialization and interaction is Alfred Lindesmith's and Anselm Strauss's *Social Psychology* (1968). Jerome Manis and Bernard Meltzer have compiled a collection of readings which include the classic works of Mead and Cooley, as well as the work of more recent symbolic interactionists and ethnomethodologists, *Symbolic Interaction: A Reader in Social Psychology* (1967; 1972). G. J. McCall's and J. L. Simmons's *Identities and Interactions* (1968) also provides a good general introduction. J. W. Berry and G. J. S. Wilde have collected together articles of research in social psychology in Canada, *Social Psychology: The Canadian Context* (1972).

Useful sources on child socialization include: Frederick Elkin and Gerald Handel, *The Child and Society: The Process of Socialization* (1973); Elia Zureik's and Robert Pike's two-volume collection of articles, *Socialization and Values in Canadian Society* (1975); and David Goslin's *Handbook of Socialization Theory and Research* (1969). Secondary socialization is examined in O. G. Brimm's and S. Wheeler's *Socialization After Childhood: Two Essays* (1966) and in several articles in Jack Haas's and William Shaffir's *Shaping Identity in Canadian Society* (1978).

There is a large and growing interest in socialization into sex roles. The Royal Commission on the Status of Women (Canada, 1970a) gives a good overview of some of the central issues and findings. A recent textbook is Anne-Marie Ambert's *Sex Structure* (1976).

Erving Goffman's *Presentation of Self in Everyday Life* (1959) is probably the most compelling introduction into dramaturgical sociology. You might also wish to look at his *Asylums* (1961), *Stigma* (1963a), *Behaviour in Public Places* (1963) and perhaps his most recent work, *Frame Analysis* (1974), in which he shows the influence of ethnomethodology. Kenneth Burke has also been important in the development of dramaturgical sociology. See his *A Grammar of Motives* (1969). Peter Blau's *Exchange and Power* (1964) is no doubt the best and most readable statement on exchange. It is hard to suggest any reading that provides a clear statement of ethnomethodology. You can, however, get the flavour of this approach by reading Harold Garfinkel's lengthy analysis of "Agnes" in his *Studies in Ethnomethodology* (1967). Finally, for approaches to interaction not discussed in this chapter, see Edwin Hollander's and Raymond Hunt's collection, *Current Perspectives in Social Psychology* (1971).

FOOTNOTES

[1]For a sample of the extensive literature on reference groups, see Hyman and Singer (1968).

[2]While many of us may carry a number of romantic "myths" about what the large families of the past were like, we do not really know very well the socialization implications of family size. It may well be that being born into a large family will present children with a number of disadvantages in their life-chances (Blau & Duncan, 1967).

[3]See Leo Zakuta's (1970) insightful analysis of money and the imputation of motives.

[4]See, in particular, Goffman's (1951) essay on "role distance."

[5]These concepts emerge from the perspective of ethnomethodology which we discuss later in the chapter.

[6]This approach owes its inspiration to Simmel's (1964) discussion of cooperation and competition in triads.

[7]See, for example, the "Prisoner's Dilemma Game" in R. D. Luce and H. Raiffa (1957:95ff). For a critique of these games experiments, see Vinacke (1971).

[8]In a later revision, Homans (1974:39) also considers responses to unexpectedly high rewards and to situations in which individuals expected but did not receive punishment. In these situations, the individual is, predictably, pleased and is likely to continue to engage in those activities.

deviance and control
CHAPTER VI

The last three chapters have shown why people conform to institutionalized standards of behaviour. One view is that people internalize these standards of behaviour which guide their actions. It is impossible to imagine interaction without such standards. At the same time, however, which of us has never felt an impulse to do something we "knew" to be wrong? It should be no surprise that sociologists have given a good deal of attention to those who act on these "deviant" impulses, who steal, kill or eat too much, for example. If, as we have said, social control is largely self-control, why is it that the mechanisms of self-control are not sufficient to keep these people "in line"?

Some sociologists seem to find these "deviants" rather a nuisance—a tiresome exception to otherwise quite neat theories of "ordered interaction." Perhaps, they argue, something went wrong in their socialization, or maybe they were subjected to some unusual social pressures; the implication seems to be that there is something wrong either with these deviant people or with their immediate environment.

Some sociologists, on the other hand, seem to find great delight in studying and theorizing about deviants (Gouldner, 1970). To them, deviants are a nice illustration of the paradox of human nature—that we are determined but also free. These theorists are not surprised that people often do unusual things. In fact, they seem to expect it. They are more interested in what happens to the deviant. Why are some deviants selected for special treatment? How are they affected by this treatment, be it informal social control—ridicule, rejection—or the more elaborate formal social control—arrest, prosecution and incarceration?

Both perspectives, the focus on deviants and the focus on social control, have produced theories and empirical data which have enhanced our understanding, not only of deviant behaviour, but of behaviour more generally.

THE DEVIANT BEHAVIOUR PERSPECTIVE

In the 1930s, American sociologists began to move away from the notion that deviants and non-deviants were two different types of people. Most sociologists rejected the earlier theories which held that deviants were biologically or psychologically defective. Moreover, in attempting to develop social theories of deviant behaviour, they rejected the earlier notion that some acts were inherently improper or wrong—inherently deviant—as judged from some absolute moral standard.[1] What is considered deviant changes over time and varies from place to place. Not surprisingly, these sociologists defined deviance in sociological terms—the violation of a social norm, rule-breaking. In later writing, R. K. Merton said that deviance "refers to conduct that departs significantly from the norms set for people in their social statuses. It must be related to the norms that are socially defined as appropriate and morally binding for people occupying various statuses" (Merton, 1968:723-724). In other words, what is deviant for a woman, say initiating sexual contact, may not be deviant for a man. Or, what is deviant for an adolescent, drinking alcoholic beverages for example, may not be deviant for an adult. While the use of morphine might be considered appropriate behaviour for the "sick role," it is otherwise viewed as deviant behaviour.

In their efforts to move away from biological and psychological theories, some sociologists may have gone overboard in their emphasis on the social. Dennis Wrong (1961), you will recall, has accused sociologists of developing "an oversocialized conception of man"; once an individual has internalized the norms and values of his society, he becomes a purely social animal, "a cultural dope" (Garfinkel, 1967), incapable of independent, creative action. He is a rule-follower par excellence. Moreover, system theorists have emphasized the consensus about norms and values that exists in most societies. Thus, we have a picture of the members of the society not only following rules, but also following pretty much the same rules. Now we have a problem—where do deviants come from?

Anomie and Social Structure

Robert K. Merton (1939) provides one solution which until recently has dominated the field. Drawing on the work of Durkheim (1897), Merton developed the *theory of anomie*. It holds essentially that the social structure can exert *pressure* on some social groups to commit deviant acts.

He argues that all societies teach their members cultural goals and the means appropriate to achieving these goals. Some groups, however, may not have access to the legitimate means to achieve the goals they have learned to value. It should be obvious that, in North America, some groups—non-whites, the poor—are in a disadvantaged position in the competition for the scarce and desirable resources – power, prestige and particularly money. They are likely, for example, to encounter discrimination in the educational and occupational structures, the institutionalized means of acquiring power, prestige and money. This disjunction between cultural goals and institutionalized means leads to anomie—a state in which norms lose their power to regulate behaviour. The strain of anomie can lead to a search for new, often illicit, means of achieving "success." Merton, for example, was struck by the disproportionately high rate of crime among the lower classes. Much of this crime, goes the argument, can be understood as an example of *innovation*—the attempt to achieve conventional success in unconventional ways (theft). Innovation is particularly common in North America, where greater emphasis is placed on the importance of economic success than on the legitimate routes to success. It does not matter so much how you get there as long as you get there. Merton suggests that there may be a grudging admiration for those who cheat their way to the top. To some extent, the "con-artist" may be an American folk hero. While the innovation of new means to success may be a common response to anomie, it is not the only response.

Some people may give up or lower their

Figure VI.1

A TYPOLOGY OF MODES OF INDIVIDUAL ADAPTATION

Modes of Adaptation	Cultural Goals	Institutionalized Means
I. Conformity	+	+
II. Innovation	+	−
III. Ritualism	−	+
IV. Retreatism	−	−
V. Rebellion	±	±

+ = acceptance; − = rejection; ± = rejection of prevailing values and substitution of new values.

SOURCE: Merton (1968:194)

desire to achieve cultural goals, but continue to abide "almost compulsively" by the rules. Conformity may become an end in itself, a response Merton calls *ritualism*. An example might be the officious and rule-nit-picking bureaucrat—the "bureaucratic virtuoso." For him, the rules of the game are more important than winning.

Merton suggests two other possible adaptations to anomie besides innovation and ritualism. *Retreatism* occurs when the individual rejects both the goals he once held and the means for achieving these goals. He withdraws from the game. The skid row alcoholic and the drug addict are often cited as examples. *Rebellion* occurs when people not only reject their old goals and means, but also substitute new goals and means, a new value system. Revolutionaries and political activists are in this sense rebels.

Tepperman (1975:200) has suggested that Merton's typology of the range of adaptations to thwarted aspirations can be useful for understanding Canadian society.

There is in Canada as in other industrial societies, a bad fit between culturally induced aspirations—such as the predominant aspirations for high status jobs that are in short supply—and the potential for realizing these aspirations in socially approved ways. There are various adaptations to the sense of failure and frustration felt on being denied one's goals. The frequency with which one or another adaptation is selected varies from society to society, and varies over time. An individual may even try many adaptations in his lifetime. The denial of aspirations and the attendant sense of failure are widespread in Canadian society and may continue as such into the foreseeable future. In this respect, failure and the psychological and social adaptations to it represent a major problem in our society.

Differential Association

For Merton, then, deviants are "normal" members of society; they have internalized the appropriate norms and values. They have become deviant because of the pressures exerted by the social structure. This view, however, represents only one of the streams of the deviant behaviour perspective. Edwin Sutherland (1939) offers a different solution to the "problem of deviance" with his theory of *differential association*. Like Merton, Sutherland focuses on the process of socialization. Unlike Merton, however, Sutherland emphasizes the differences in norms and values among the various sub-groups in society. For Sutherland, deviants, like the rest of us, are rule-followers. They are simply following the rules of their own group. Deviant behaviour is learned in the same way as any other behaviour. All of us are exposed to patterns of behaviour and definitions which both favour law violation and which discourage it. What determines if one engages in deviant behaviour is the balance between deviant and conventional contacts. In short, we learn deviant behaviour from the people around us—primarily through interaction in close, intimate groups. In light of this, for example, it should be no surprise that many researchers have come to see the prison as a place of higher education for criminals. More generally, Sutherland's theory would predict a higher crime rate in urban rather than rural society. The city is characterized by diversity; there are many different subcultures and different ways of life. Urban life also involves a good deal of geographic mobility. The diversity and mobility of urban societies are likely to create more possibilities for pro-criminal associations—contacts which encourage law violation.

Several theorists have explicitly attempted to bring these two theories together. Cloward and Ohlin (1960), for example, have argued that in order to understand why any group is likely to turn to crime we must ask about the availability of *both* legitimate opportunities—access to legitimate means—*and* illegitimate opportunities, for example, the availability of criminal role models.

This emphasis on opportunity is well-placed. The desire or felt need to commit a deviant or criminal act is, in itself, not enough. One must also have the opportunity—the ways and means.

It would be extremely difficult, if not impossible, to embezzle if one were not strategically located in a work system, perhaps as a bookkeeper or purchasing agent. A would-be confidence man needs confidence and salesmanship, just as those who would engrave counterfeit plates need artistic ability. A successful "society" jewel thief would obviously need "society" contacts and a degree of savoir faire. *To "crack" a safe takes skill, and one can hardly steal atomic secrets if one has no access to such secrets. Similarly, an unknowledgeable middle-class housewife who wished to "sample" marijuana might have to pass up the experiment since she might not know where to obtain the "pot" (Bryant, 1974:8).*

To become a deviant, then, one must learn the appropriate attitudes and skills, one must have the opportunity to act on these attitudes and use these skills and one must learn to recognize these opportunities. The fact that different groups have different opportunities is certainly a large part of the explanation of why different groups engage in different kinds of deviant and criminal acts.

The "deviant behaviour" approach, then, is the perspective which has dominated the study of deviance in North America. Researchers have been concerned, for example, with documenting and explaining the high rates of crime, or at least certain kinds of crime, among the poor, Indians, Blacks and other oppressed social groups. With this increasing research has come a corresponding increase in the awareness of just how complicated deviance is.

Deviance is an extremely slippery concept. What in one context is deviant is, in another, conformity. In a complex society with a variety of reference groups, with more than one set of institutions, people may, indeed, not be out of step but, as Thoreau put it, merely marching to a different drummer.

Recently a number of sociologists have suggested that the search for the causes of deviance may have taken sociology in the wrong direction or at least that there are other equally important questions. Surely everyone has done something, at one time or another, that can be termed deviant. Most children, for example, know the guilty pleasures of eating candy stolen from the counter or bought with money from mother's purse. As well, most have known the shame of being found out. Perhaps such behaviour is "polygenetic" and has many different causes which can never be captured by a single theory of deviance causation (Lemert, 1972). There are, however, other important questions that sociologists might ask about deviant behaviour.

LABELLING PERSPECTIVE

The labelling perspective was developed primarily by Edwin Lemert (1951), Howard Becker (1963) and, more recently, Edwin Schur (1971). For labelling theorists, deviance is a matter of social definition, and "deviant behaviour is behaviour so labelled" (Becker, 1962). In formulating "new" questions about deviance, labelling theorists have drawn on both conflict theory and symbolic interactionism.

Creating Deviance

The cornerstone of this most recent perspective is skepticism. The sociologists must not take for granted and must question society's labelling of certain forms of behaviour as deviant. Societies, or more precisely powerful groups within society, create deviance by creating and enforcing rules. Here we can see labelling theory's debt to conflict theory.

To say that society creates its deviance and its social problems is not to say "it's all in the mind" and that some nasty people are going around creating deviance out of nothing. . . . But it does mean that the making of rules and the sanctioning of people who break these rules are as much a part of deviance as the action itself. . . . So, whenever we see terms such as deviance and social problem, we must ask: "Says who?" (Cohen, 1971:17).

We must ask who has the power to designate certain acts as deviant and how do they achieve this.

Howard Becker, for example, studies the development of anti-marijuana legislation in the United States. He points out that anti-marijuana laws were passed without any consultation with marijuana users—those best able to provide "expert testimony." He concludes that the most significant pressure to criminalize marijuana smoking came from narcotics agents themselves. They had a *vested interest* in expanding their jurisdiction. In a similar study, Shirley Cook (1969) traces the development of Canadian narcotics legislation. She describes the conflict between Chinese immigrant groups and English-speaking Canadians and the power of English-speaking Canadians to legislate their morality.

Becker has coined the term *moral entrepreneur* to describe those individuals or groups who attempt to *criminalize* (Schur, 1965) behaviour which they feel threatens their way of life and their morality. Conventional wisdom has it that law reflects the moral climate of the community. But which constituents do legislators listen to? Some may be louder than others. For example, psychiatrists are among the most powerful moral entrepreneurs.[2] Not only do they define the conditions under which a person should be regarded as insane, certainly a most consequential label, but they also influence legislators in deciding which acts should be viewed as criminal (Vaz, 1976).

Moreover, once some behaviour is made illegal it may also come to be seen by most people as immoral (Henshel and Henshel, 1973:59-65). Law, then, serves a symbolic function; it designates certain behaviours as morally inferior.

The area which best illustrates the conflict of values is what some sociologists refer to as *victimless crimes.* Prostitution, homosexuality and marijuana use, for example, are forms of deviance in which the participants are willing, no one is directly injured and those involved are unlikely to bring complaints. These acts are criminalized because some people, not directly involved, do not approve. Similar arguments have been raised regarding abortion, narcotics use and many other "crimes," an illustration of the potential of the labelling perspective for challenging the legal structure (Henshel and Henshel, 1973:65).

The question of whose rules define deviance inevitably involves an examination of economic and political power, issues which are discussed at length in future chapters. For now, it is enough to indicate that in very many ways, men make the rules for women; whites make the rules for non-whites; the middle class make the rules for the poor; and so it goes.

. . . much of what is considered deviant in society (e.g., types of mental illness, prostitution, abortion, drug addiction, vagrancy, etc.) represents little more

than the special brand of morality of the prevailing power holders in the society (Vaz, 1976:46).

Creating Deviants

At another level of analysis, labelling theorists also ask who has the power to label particular people as deviant. Becker (1963:9) has defined the deviant as "the one to whom that label has been successfully applied." The point is that rules are enforced selectively. Certain groups in our society—police, psychiatrists—play a key role in social control; they are the "master labellers." A good deal of empirical evidence has been collected on how they decide who is "criminal," "mentally ill," etc. These decisions are influenced by a number of factors, the most important of which seems to be the social position of the "deviant." Werthman and Piliavin (1967), for example, have found that police in a San Francisco ghetto operate on the basis of a number of stereotypical criteria in deciding which teenagers are "delinquent enough" to be arrested. What does the boy look like, how is he dressed, what is his family background, what is his attitude during interrogation? The central conclusion of this and numerous other studies is that *political criteria* play an important part in police decisions. The "good pinch" is an arrest that is politically all right, that does not meet with community disapproval. This is best achieved when there is a good deal of consensus that the crime involved is serious (sexual crimes for example), and when the "criminal" is already seen as disreputable.[3]

Perhaps the disproportionately high rate of crime among the poor, Indians, etc., can best be understood in terms of the social organization of social control. That is, official crime statistics may tell us more about the ideologies which support official social control and the activities of agents of social control than they do about criminal behaviour. In Saskatchewan, for example, Indians comprise 50% of the prison population and only 10% of the total population. Does this mean that they are more likely to engage in crime or that they are more likely to get arrested? We are not suggesting that policemen are going around arresting Indians whether or not they break the law. What we are saying is that if two boys, one an Indian, the other a White, break the same law the Indian may more likely be arrested.

Just how much the police are influenced by political criteria is open to question. First of all, it is well to point out that the majority of the policeman's time is not spent in crime detection or apprehending criminals, but in other aspects of police work, for example, traffic control and public assistance. In any case, part of the reason that the powerless groups are more likely to be arrested can be found in the actions of the ordinary citizen. An excellent example is provided by David Stymeist (1975) in his study of "Crow Lake," the name of a fictitious town in Northern Ontario. In Crow Lake, as elsewhere in Canada, Indians are frequently arrested, and almost always for public drunkenness (see Table V.1). Stymeist describes how the police routinely park outside of the Crow Lake Hotel, the town's largest tavern, around closing time, waiting for "arrests." The waiters will often ask a drunken White patron who may be a friend or a steady customer if he wishes them to call a cab. The White customers, then, are often picked up at the rear entrance and driven home unseen by the police. Indians are not accorded this kind of treatment and must leave by the front entrance where they are often picked up.

Despite the debate among criminologists, it seems evident that police, like most of the rest of us, will have learned and incorporated cultural stereotypes and these stereotypes will influence how they treat people in various social positions in their day-to-day activities (see Thornton, 1975). Indeed, Jock Young (1971), a British sociologist, argues that the police are more vulnerable than most of us to the stereotypes presented in the mass media because they are isolated from the rest of the community and have few friends outside of the police. Accounts by Blacks in cities

Table VI.1

COMPARISON OF REASONS FOR ARRESTS IN CROW LAKE FOR NATIVES AND NON-NATIVES

	Native	Non-Native
Intoxication	58	11
Speeding	—	13
Impaired Driving	2	8
Assault	3	7
Fighting	4	—
Theft under $50.00	4	1
Failing to Yield	—	3
Failing to Have Clean Windows	—	2
Failing to Report an Accident	—	1
Liquor in a Place other than Residence	2	1
Minor Consuming	1	—
Prohibited Person Consuming	1	—
Obtaining Benefits by False Statement	—	1
False Affidavit	—	1
Break and Enter	—	3

Sample Size: 127 cases (3 court sessions, winter 1971)

SOURCE: Stymeist (1975:67)

in Canada, the United States and Britain would indicate that they are more likely to be stopped at night by police for routine checks and are, therefore, at much greater risk of being arrested for impaired driving, illegal possession, etc. Another example of selective labelling is provided by Edmund Vaz (1965) who interviewed a number of middle-class Canadian high school boys to find out how many of them had committed delinquent acts. While very many of them admitted that they had performed such acts, very rarely had they been labelled as delinquent.

Labelling theory makes us aware that not all those who have broken a rule are labelled deviant; nor can we assume that all those who have been labelled deviant have broken a rule. What "deviants" do have in common is that they have been negatively labelled and such negative labels—crook, nut, fool—can exert a powerful influence on their lives.

Latent Consequences of Social Control: Victimless Crimes

A related set of questions addressed by labelling theorists concerns the unintended consequences of social control. What are the consequences, for example, of the criminalization of drug use? Edwin Schur (1965) has attempted to demonstrate that the narcotics laws have "made things worse." Because of the high risks involved in the manufacture, importation and distribution of narcotics, these drugs are scarce and the price is high. Drugs become an attractive commodity to organized crime. The addict feels forced to engage in other crimes to support his habit. Narcotics legislation has aggravated the narcotics problem and has compounded the difficulties in law enforcement.[4]

Also, the addict is edged out of the conventional society. The need for secrecy, the fear of reprisal and the need for illegal contacts all encourage the addict to restrict his interaction to those who are also engaged in prohibited activities. Obviously, the prohibition of certain activities will change the way in which those activities are carried out.

The Deviants' Perspective

Finally, labelling theorists, drawing on symbolic interactionism, have focused on the interaction between the labeller and the "deviant." To examine this interaction, it is important to know how the deviant views himself and his actions. A good example of an attempt to get at the "inner lives" of deviants is Humphreys' (1970) study of *Tearoom Trade,* homosexual behaviour in public washrooms. Humphreys found great variation in how the men who engaged in such homosexual behaviour defined themselves and their actions. We can use his data to develop a typology of deviants. One of his most interesting findings was that not all of the men who engaged in such homosexual behaviour saw themselves as homosexuals. Some seemed to be saying that while homosexuality is deviant, the label does not apply to them. They claimed that the tearoom provided them with a source of quick impersonal sex; they went for the orgasm, not the company. (Because they did not get involved with their tearoom partners, this kind of sex did not threaten their family lives.) They might be termed the "falsely accused."

On the other hand, some of the men claimed that there is nothing wrong with homosexuality in general. Homosexuality, they claimed, is a perfectly natural act. These men were generally immersed in a homosexual subculture with values different from those of conventional society. Some homosexuals may actively invite the label "come out of the closet" in an attempt to change societal values. Others may be more concerned with leading a "normal homosexual" life among other homosexuals (see also Sawchuck, 1974). The former group might be termed "dissidents," the latter "subcultural deviants." Subcultural deviants are isolated or isolate themselves from conventional labels.[5]

Of course many of the tearoom participants believed both that homosexuality was immoral and that they were homosexuals. Except for their limited tearoom contact, they generally avoided other homosexuals, in "gay bars" for example, and consequently had not learned to justify or rationalize their behaviour. Unlike the former categories, they were likely to feel guilt and self-hatred. They are the "pure deviants."

In short, the people being labelled may disagree with the labellers. There may be a conflict of *values* (for example, the social desirability of homosexual behaviour) or *definitions* (for example, the applicability of the label "homosexual"). Looking through the deviants' eyes, then, we can distinguish the types of deviant listed in Figure VI.2.

Figure VI.2

THE DEVIANT'S PERSPECTIVE

		VALUE CONFLICT	
		Behaviour is Deviant	Behaviour is not Deviant
DEFINITIONAL CONFLICT	Label is Accepted	PURE DEVIANT	ACTIVE DISSIDENT
	Label is not Accepted	FALSELY ACCUSED	SUBCULTURAL DEVIANT

The dissident and the subcultural deviant, immersed as they are in a deviant subculture, are less vulnerable to the negative reactions of others than are those deviants who are still attempting to maintain a commitment to conventional norms and values.

DEVIANT CAREERS

Labelling of individuals as deviant seems to have a self-fulfilling effect.

Indignation, punishment and segregation from the community might mark the person out in a special way, and together with others in a similar position, he might eventually act in ways that resemble society's stereotypes of him (Cohen, 1971:17).

The negative label often denotes a *master status*. The individual comes to be seen as first and foremost a deviant. He is seen in a completely new light. When the labelling is public, the "deviant" becomes a symbol—the dramatization of evil, a reminder of the importance of the rules and the consequences of violating them.

The general principle at work is a simple one: when others decide that a person is non grata, *dangerous, untrustworthy, or morally repugnant, they do something to him, often unpleasant, which is not done to other people. This may take shape in hurtful rejections and humiliations in interpersonal contacts, or it may be formal action to bring him under controls which curtail his freedom (Lemert, 1972:68).*

Imagine that you have discovered that your friend is a homosexual. Initially this is rather a shock, but soon you begin to "recall" certain of his past peculiarities which "should" have made his homosexuality obvious to you. In retrospect, you say that you can certainly find a number of instances which "fit" and, now, everything he does seems to confirm his homosexuality. In short, our perception becomes selective. In reacting to the deviant, the social audience engages in a process of *retrospective interpretation* on the basis of *common sense stereotypes*.[6]

Often these reactions will have a profound effect on how the deviant views himself. This will be the case particularly when most of the people the deviant encounters respond to him and his behaviour in similar ways. The deviant may feel degraded by the reactions of others. He may feel a dramatic loss of status and dignity. Even the deviant who believes he has been falsely accused may begin to experience self-doubt and guilt. Often he incorporates the negative label into his self-conception. Once an actor has developed a deviant self-concept, he is well on the path to a deviant way of life, or what Lemert calls *secondary deviation*. The deviant may find that he has limited alternatives in choice of friends, occupation and so on. At this point, he may begin to seek out the only people he believes can give him the support and understanding he needs—other deviants.

It is also of interest that societies have rather elaborate rituals and "ceremonies" to mark the *status passage* (Glaser and Strauss, 1971) from citizen to convict, from sane to insane, from normal to deviant, but virtually no public statement of the reversal (Garfinkel, 1956; Goffman, 1961; Gusfield, 1971).[7] Public flogging and now "trial by the press" make the public aware that justice has been served and the guilty have been punished. And, in the process, the accused is transformed. However, there are no comparable statements from the press when a convict is released from prison. Perhaps, as Durkheim argued, punishment is more an example to others—one way in which the collective conscience is shored up—than deterrence, rehabilitation or retribution.

As the outcast comes to restrict his associations to other "deviants," he may learn to justify his behaviour, to neutralize his feelings of guilt and even to redefine the activity in positive terms. The labellers—conventional society—may become the "outsiders"—corrupt, hypocritical, square, what have you. These learned justifications may allow not only further participation in the deviant activity, they may even encourage it. So, for example, fat becomes beautiful, "a sign or result of character, spirit, love of life, or some other rare and desirable quality" (Himelfarb and Evans, 1974:231). Membership in the organized deviant group—subcultural deviance—is the final stage in the *deviant career.* At this point, *the process of becoming deviant* may be virtually irreversible. People become deviant because they have been labelled deviant.[8]

On the other hand, some organized deviant groups, the Gay Liberation Front, for example, have taken an active part in trying to change public definitions and social policy. At this point, whether their actions are seen as political protest in the form of dissidence, or deviance, depends on the ideology of those doing the labelling. In any case, it would appear that "deviance" might in fact be seen as a source of important social change. Some groups have a vested interest in maintaining the status quo, others in changing their society, and so we return to the initial question of the labelling theorists: which groups have the power to enforce their values on others?

The labelling perspective, then, among other things, emphasizes the role of power in defining what is a deviant act. This is, perhaps, best illustrated in official reactions to rape. Courts do not treat rape as simply a case of assault. Rather, it seems that the rape victim will be asked to demonstrate that she behaves in a sexually "moral" and "proper" way. In other words, it seems that, to the courts, only certain kinds of women can be raped. Lorenne Clark and Debra Lewis (1977) at the Toronto Rape Crisis Centre have, for several years now, been analysing rape cases—those which come to trial, those reported but not tried and the very many which are never reported officially. Clark and Lewis find that the police decision to pursue a rape case is based essentially on their perception of the victim. They are less likely to put forward a case for prosecution, for example, if the victim lives alone or if she has been drinking, or if she is from the lower class. Clark and Lewis do not blame the police for these decisions because they are in a structural bind. On the one hand, they get into trouble if their arrests consistently fail to produce convictions. On the other hand, they are often frustrated because many of the cases they "know" to be crimes are unlikely to produce convictions. They know that successful cases usually demand that the victim be middle class, "morally upright" and living "under the protection" of parents or husband. Clark and Lewis conclude from their research that women are viewed by the courts as property and rape is not assault but a crime against the property of men.[9]

Men have defined rape as a sexual offence because it is an attack on their sexual property. One of the worst consequences of this definition is that it leaves no harm to be punished unless a "valuable" woman is physically damaged by the rape attack. If no economic harm is done, or if this harm is very minimal, there appears to be no theoretical basis for treating rape as a legal offence or for punishing the rapist. The rapist commits a wrongful act because he damages or "steals" another's property; his crime is sexual because the property stolen is sexual. But when the victim does not belong to somebody else, or possesses qualities which make her potentially valuable, then her rape cannot be perceived as wrong (Clark and Lewis, 1977:160).

Before we leave labelling theory, it is important to emphasize that labelling, categorizing others, is a fundamental feature of how people think about the world. Labelling theorists simply encourage us to examine the labels we use, to question what we may have taken for granted, to ask how the labels emerged and what are the consequences of their use. They also encourage us to question and even challenge the prevailing legal system.

CRIME AND DELINQUENCY

Just as deviance varies from society to society and time to time, so too does criminal behaviour. To take one example, in Inuit society, acts become criminal only when they threaten the survival of the community, not when they threaten an individual. In virtually every modern society, however, those actions which are thought to involve "some serious violations of person and property" are held to be criminal (Hagan, 1977:20). Of course, just exactly what constitutes such "serious violations" is not always clear. Groups will define this differently and, as we have shown, interest groups will often compete to get their definitions enacted into law.

Behaviour defined as crime falls into three broad categories. We have already described the category of victimless crimes. Laws against drug use, pornography, many forms of sexual deviation and so on are supposedly enacted to protect us (see Goode, 1973:121-124). It seems likely that the law makers and pressure groups do not feel the need for such protection themselves but for the mass of people "less able" to manage their own affairs. And, as we have suggested, underlying this paternalism are the concerns of powerful groups with maintaining the status quo, protecting vested interests and preserving their own lifestyle by legally enforcing their morality.[10]

However, when most of us discuss and worry about increasing crime we are thinking about crimes against person and against property. Certainly, no crime captures the public imagination like murder, even though as we can see in Figure VI.3 Canada is a relatively non-violent country, particularly in comparison to the United States. Indeed, Canada is a less criminal nation in general (Hagan, 1977). Few would quibble with the notion that murder and other forms of violence against people must be dealt with as crimes. However, given that most murders occur in the home among intimates, it is unlikely that greater police vigilance or the expansion of the police force would make much difference.

Certainly, more court and police time is taken up with crimes against property—theft, shoplifting, vandalism and so on. Indeed, most of the laws in the Criminal Code are in one way or another concerned with the protection of property. In a society such as ours, where we are all bombarded by campaigns encouraging us to buy, to own, to accumulate material possessions, it is not surprising that those "who have" are preoccupied with the concern that those "who have not" will take. It is in this context that we can understand the pressures on agencies of law enforcement to come down hard on what may be trivial crimes of property. Also in this context we can understand why white-collar criminals, for example, embezzlers, are less likely to be "processed" as criminals. White-collar crimes are more often dealt with out of court (Sutherland, 1961). Polluters, price-fixers and tax evaders are breaking the law but are rarely designated as deviant. They are likely to see their behaviour as a legitimate part of the business enterprise, and legal intervention as State intrusion into private affairs.

These processes emerge clearly when we examine juvenile delinquency in Canada. Canada passed its first juvenile delinquency act in 1908. While there is some debate about the direction of influence between Canada and the United States regarding approaches to and legislation on juvenile delinquency, both American and Canadian legislation appear to have had a similar development and certainly have been closely connected (Hagan and Leon, 1977).

An excellent text on the development of juvenile delinquency legislation in America is Anthony Platt's *The Child Savers* (1969). According to Platt, feminists at the turn of the century provided the impetus for special juvenile delinquency legislation. He points out that these feminists did not challenge basic structures or assumptions, as contemporary feminists have done, but were primarily concerned with extending the woman's role outside the home and with reforming society, particularly in such areas as the education and treatment of children outside the home. Many were particularly concerned with the predicament and future of lower-class youth who, of course, were the most likely

Figure VI.3

MURDER RATES PER MILLION POPULATION, CANADA, UNITED STATES, AND ENGLAND AND WALES, 1961-1970

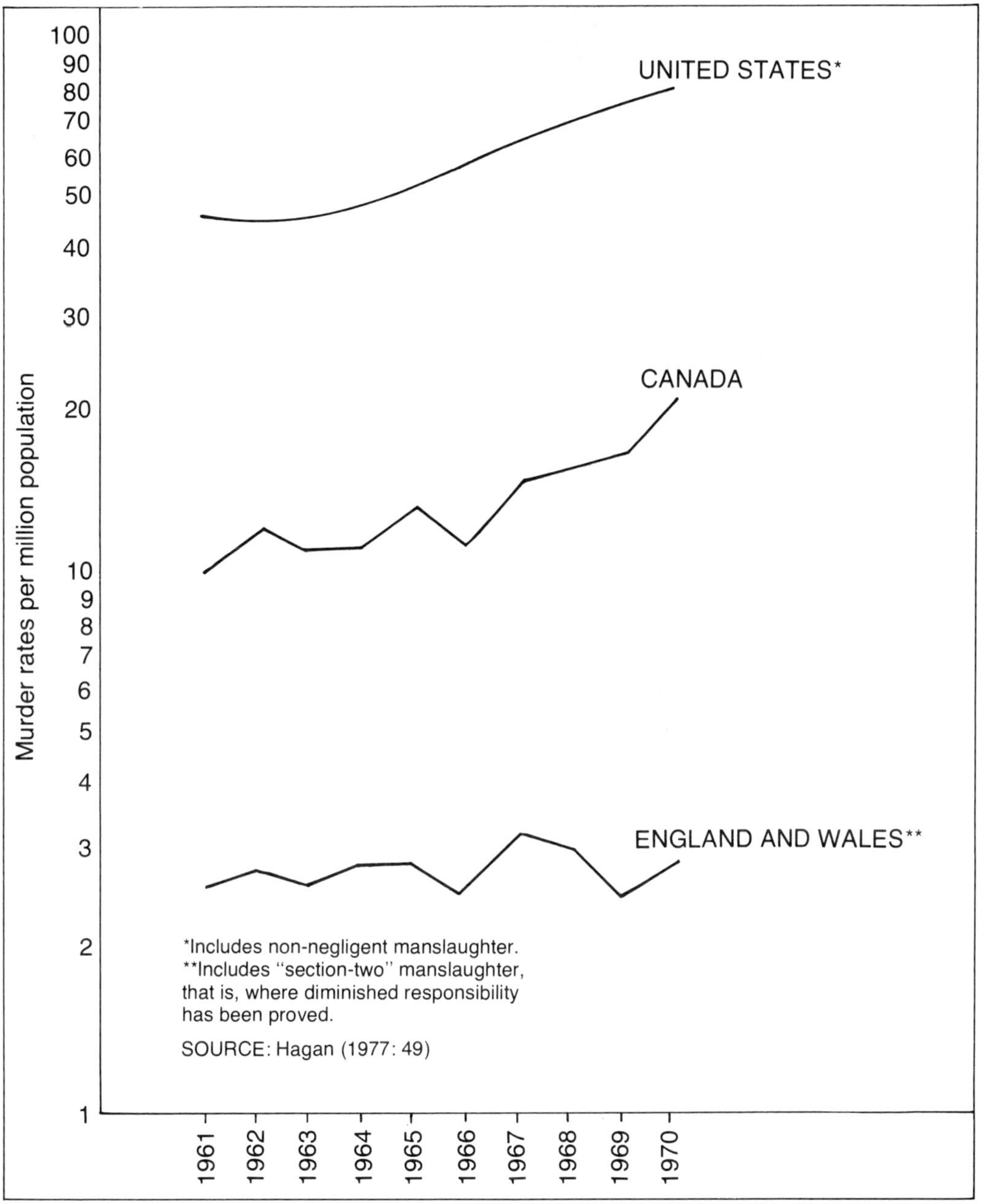

to come into contact with the courts. The "child-saving movement" clearly reinforced, rather than challenged, dominant values revolving around motherhood and the role of women. In any case, this movement was able to influence legislation and to create and occupy a range of court-related treatment occupations—counsellors, court workers, social workers. The central theme of this new approach to juvenile delinquency, a theme objected to by many law enforcement officers, was that juvenile delinquents should be treated, not punished. In Canada a similar movement (or movements) emphasizing separation of juvenile and adult offenders and treatment and probation for juveniles, rather than punishment, had similar success (Hagan and Leon, 1977).

Under the Juvenile Delinquents Act of 1908 (revised 1929), a child is considered to be delinquent if he violates any provision of the Criminal Code, provincial statutes or municipal by-laws. But, the definition of juvenile delinquency is much broader than that of adult criminality. The definition of a juvenile delinquent also includes any youth "who is guilty of sexual immorality or any similar form of vice, or who is liable, by reason of any other act, to be committed to an industrial school or juvenile reformatory under the provision of any Dominion or provincial statute." As we have suggested, it is difficult to imagine any youth who could not be sentenced under the broad terms of this act. We have already described the influence of political criteria on police decisions to arrest. This is no less true of the sentencing activities of judges. For example, as Tepperman (1977:85) argues:

Judges tend to come from a particular social stratum: they are well-educated and relatively prosperous besides generally having professional, social, and political attachments to the elite. Their sentencing patterns often reflect the concerns of any prosperous person for life and property when dealing with poor people, especially during a period of social discontent like the Depression. The judiciary has a political and not only rational-intellectual activity in which written rules and community standards are applied to information about behaviours. Like the others engaged in maintaining order, judges tend to support the status quo. Some evidence shows that judges are selected because they are in sympathy with the ruling class.

Clearly, judges have a particularly high degree of discretion in the handling of juvenile cases. This discretion is legitimated in terms of "individualized justice" and in the name of treatment. But what does this mean for the juvenile who comes in contact with the juvenile court? For one thing, the juvenile who sees the variability in court decisions, in convictions and sentencing, may well develop a "sense of injustice" which may further alienate him from conventional society (Matza, 1964). This sense of injustice is likely to be enhanced because delinquents in Canada are not guaranteed the same degree of protections against the court, for example, in their rights to legal counsel, as are adult criminals. Further, the juvenile accused, say, of "joy riding" will no doubt come to recognize the contradictions built into a system which continually encourages him to evaluate himself in terms of whether he has a car and the type of car he owns and, at the same time, punishes him for "borrowing" a car for a while. In fact, the great bulk of juvenile crimes involve cars.

As well, the emphasis on "treatment" in juvenile justice may be misleading. First of all, "treatment" may often mean little more than incarceration—"doing time"—in a reformatory or training school. For example, the only training school in New Brunswick has a professional treatment staff of one social worker. More important, however, there is a good deal of question about whether the treatment programs which are offered work (Hagan, 1977:182ff). Indeed, Matza (1964) points out that social workers are often the ones who teach the juvenile how to justify his delinquency as they explain to him that he is not really accountable for his actions, that the delinquency is not really his fault but rather a result of his poverty, his broken home, his alcoholic parents or what have you. All of these factors—the growing sense of injustice, the learned justifications and, of course, the official public labelling of the juvenile as delinquent—probably encourage rather than discourage further delinquent activity (see Vaz, 1976:167-169).

In the last few years the Law Reform Commission has drafted new legislation and proposed alternative approaches to juvenile delinquency which suggest a growing awareness of the problems in the organization of juvenile justice. Their "Young Persons in Conflict With the Law" bill would not only provide the juvenile with more legal protection but also emphasizes the juvenile's accountability for his actions.[11] This represents an attempt, then, to bring the juvenile justice system closer to the adversary relationship of the adult criminal system. The new proposal asks, for example, for an end to long, indefinite sentences and for automatic review of juvenile cases. It is interesting to note that the Mental Health Association has traditionally opposed such modifications to juvenile delinquency legislation. They argue adamantly for a treatment approach, an approach which treats delinquency essentially as a sickness. Clearly, treatment personnel, particularly psychiatrists, have gained a powerful role as labellers, not only within the criminal justice system but more generally. As we mentioned, psychiatrists play an important role in defining both what is deviant and what is criminal, in labelling deviants and in enforcing their labels through compulsory treatment. We might see their opposition to the reform of juvenile delinquency legislation in terms of their vested interests as master labellers. Thus far, their view, the treatment approach, has prevailed.

At the same time, there has been a growing emphasis on finding alternatives to incarceration and compulsory treatment. The Law Reform Commission has described the basic elements of a programme of "diversion" which would minimize or even eliminate the contact offenders have with the justice system. Many, though certainly not all, offences could be dealt with informally within the community, some charges might simply be dropped and many cases could be settled out of court. And often alternatives to incarceration could be found. Certainly it is not clear exactly where to draw the line, that is, which crimes might be handled by such diversion, but what we have described as victimless crimes and many of the "non-criminal" acts defined as juvenile delinquency may be the places to start. In essence, a policy of diversion or non-intervention argues that, whenever possible, leave deviants and criminals alone (Hagan, 1977:196).

We should reiterate that official labelling or, more generally, official social control activities are not *the causes* of delinquent or criminal behaviour. It is hard to argue with the thesis that poverty and obstacles to mobility produce unusual pressures to commit certain criminal acts. However, it is probably true that we cannot provide a general theory of the causes of deviance or crime; different kinds of deviant and criminal behaviour probably require different kinds of explanations. What we have tried to show, however, is that a general understanding of deviance and crime requires an examination of how rules are made, applied and enforced—the activities of social control. As we have shown, the weight of law falls more heavily on some groups than others. Powerful groups have more say in creating the rules and laws for the rest of us. Police and the courts do, at least to some degree, apply these laws selectively. Some groups are more likely than others to get arrested, to get convicted or to get committed for mental treatment. Public labelling, incarceration and "treatment" may serve to alienate, or at least further alienate, many people from conventional society. And, this alienation may, in turn, for many, lead to commitment to a professional criminal career.

Finally, as Vaz (1976:169) cautions us:

Those groups and agencies responsible for the control and prevention of deviance are themselves likely to break rules in the course of their duties. Neither formal nor informal control agents are special kinds of people, nor are they immune to the forces and processes operating to produce deviance in society. Therefore, we should not be surprised when we hear of the cruelty of parents towards their children, of the viciousness of prison guards and the staffs of correctional institutions towards their inmates, or of the immorality of priests. Nor should we be shocked to learn about corruption among our law enforcement agencies, that inspectors and politicians as well as judges can be bribed, that cheating, malingering, favoritism and wickedness are found among the institutions designed to watch over us. As Albert K. Cohen suggests ". . . we have travelled full circle and are confronted with the problem of the social control of the agencies of contol." The question is: "Who will guard the guardians?"

SUMMARY AND CONCLUSION

Two persistent themes of the literature on deviant behaviour are the importance of *socialization* and the importance of *inequality*. The deviant behaviour perspective suggests that deviant motives, attitudes, skills, etc., are acquired through interaction; deviant behaviour is simply a manifestation of deviant socialization. The labelling perspective, on the other hand, suggests that deviant motives, attitudes, skills, etc., may be acquired as a response to being labelled; people may learn to be deviant *after* their initial act simply because they have been set apart and "forced" to interact with other deviants.

The deviant behaviour perspective emphasizes how unequal access to the legitimate means of success may produce pressures on some groups to engage in certain non-conforming acts. The labelling perspective emphasizes the unequal distribution of power—power to impose definitions of appropriate behaviour, to label and to resist labels. Significantly, groups which are labelled deviant will have unequal access to the legitimate means of success. And so we see the "vicious circle" of deviance and control.

We suggested at the outset that some sociologists find in the area of deviance reassurance of man's individuality and creativity. Indeed, at least implicit in the work of many labelling theorists is the suggestion that we ought to be more tolerant of deviance and of human diversity. The extreme of this view can be found in the later work of R. D. Laing (1967), a British psychiatrist, who describes the mentally ill as the "prophets" in an insane society, psychiatrists as the new police, guardians of the status quo. He decries the conservative ideology and dehumanizing tendency of the social sciences. Our discussion hopefully demonstrates that sociological discourse can be cast in distinctly human terms, can challenge conventional wisdom and can contribute to our understanding of even what appear to be the most individualistic of acts.

SUGGESTIONS FOR FURTHER READING

For a good general overview of approaches to deviance see Howard Becker's *Outsiders* (1963); Albert Cohen's *Deviance and Control* (1966); David Matza's *Becoming Deviant* (1969); Paul Rock's *Deviant Behaviour* (1973); Edmund Vaz's *Aspects of Deviance* (1976); John Lofland's *Deviance and Identity* (1969); and Edmund Lemert's *Human Deviance, Social Problems and Social Control* (1972). Edwin Schur's *Labelling Deviant Behaviour* (1971) shows how the labelling approach draws from conflict theory, functionalism, symbolic interactionism and phenomenology. His *Crimes without Victims* (1965) is a provocative discussion of some of the social policy implications of the labelling approach. John Hagan's *The Disreputable Pleasures* (1977) is probably the best and most recent introduction to deviance in Canada. For a more general account see also Richard Henshel's and Ann-Marie Henshel's *Perspectives on Social Problems* (1973). Most of the important theoretical statements and empirical findings are to be found in collections. Some of the more important and interesting of these include Carl Rubington's and Martin Weinberg's *Deviance: The Interactionist Perspective* (1968); Howard Becker's *The Other Side* (1964a); Paul Rock's and Mary McIntosh's *Deviance and Social Control* (1974); and Clifton D. Bryant's *Deviant Behaviour: Occupational and Organizational Bases* (1974). There are, as well, excellent recent Canadian collections including Craig Boydell and others, *Deviant Behaviour and Societal Reaction* (1972); Jack Haas and Bill Shaffir, *Decency and Deviance* (1974); and William E. Mann, *Social Deviance in Canada* (1971).

For an introduction to the work in crime and delinquency see Gwynn Nettler's *Explaining Crime* (1974). Although somewhat dated, David Matza's *Delinquency and Drift* (1964) provides an excellent critical review of the delinquency literature and a useful approach to delinquency research. A radical approach to criminology is Ian Taylor, Paul Walton and Jock Young, *The New Criminology: For a Social Theory of Deviance* (1973). One of the finest studies of the interpretative process at work in the criminal justice system is a Canadian study, John Hogarth's *Sentencing as a Human Process* (1971). Other useful sources of crime in Canada include: Craig Boydell and others, *The Administration of Criminal Justice in Canada* (1974); W. T. McGrath's *Crime and Its Treatment in Canada* (1972); R. Silverman's and J. Teevan's *Crime in Canadian Society* (1975); and Lorne Tepperman's text, *Crime Control* (1977).

Some of the most controversial work in deviance has raised questions about the meaning of mental illness and the role of psychiatrists. Thomas Szasz, himself a psychiatrist, raises many of the important questions in *The Myth of Mental Illness* (1961) and *Psychiatric Justice* (1965). The Scottish psychiatrist R. D. Laing provides a different kind of challenge to psychiatry in *The Politics of Experience and the Bird of Paradise* (1967). For a vivid and angry rebuke to Laing, see Mark Vonnegut's *The Eden Express* (1975).

FOOTNOTES

[1]C. Wright Mills (1942) offers an excellent critique of the moral bias in these early theories of deviance.

[2]Thomas Szasz (1961), a psychiatrist himself, has produced a highly controversial analysis of the power and moral authority of psychiatrists.

[3]Gigeroff (1968) shows in a similar way how the police in Toronto decide whether two people in a parked car are breaking the law, that is, engaging in a sexual crime.

[4]In Great Britain, where narcotics have been defined as a medical problem, not a legal problem, there is little connection between addiction and crime (Lindesmith, 1965).

[5]An interesting account of "subcultural deviants" is Easto's and Truzzi's (1974) article on the carnival.

[6]John Lofland (1969) has examined this process of "retrospective interpretation" in the media. He demonstrates how in newspaper accounts of murders, reporters look for features of the "murder's" past which they believe are consistent with the label "murderer." Their reporting is selective.

[7]An exception to this is the various self-help groups such as Alcoholics Anonymous and the John Howard Society which are in the business of "de-labelling" and "re-labelling" deviants and finding ways of celebrating their return to conventional society. This process, however, seems far less successful than the labelling process (Ray, 1961; Himelfarb, 1975).

[8]A particularly vivid illustration of the self-fulfilling effects of labelling can be found in Giffen's (1966) description of the "revolving door" of alcoholism.

[9]The exceptions to these generalizations are rape cases where there is demonstrable violence. Then, it is not clear whether it is assault or rape which is being tried.

[10]Very often to legitimize this paternalism the law makers emphasize that there are indeed victims—the children exposed to pornography, homosexuality or drugs, the families of the addicted and ultimately society. For an interesting illustration of this, see James Gray's *Booze* (1972), a study of temperance in Western Canada.

[11]This bill has been revised and is now simply called "Young Offenders." The status and future of this bill is still uncertain at the time of this writing.

PART 3

Focus On Canada

perspectives on canadian society

CHAPTER VII

In the first half of the book, in each chapter, we have tried to convey the dominant images of society which constitute sociology. In this half of the book, we shall be looking at how these competing images can be used to understand Canadian society. This chapter is partly an introduction to what we will be discussing in later chapters, partly a context in which to place the more specific processes and institutions which we will be examining. We do two things in this chapter. First, we will try to describe some of the distinctive demographic, cultural and political features of Canadian society. Second, we will be concerned with the general question of how we can go about understanding Canada, how we can make sociological sense of this puzzling society. As we shall see, there is no single or easy answer to the questions we have posed. Rather, there are perspectives or approaches which various sociologists have used to try to understand Canadian society and to contemplate its eventual fate. However, whatever the perspective, sociologists must start with basic data, such as that provided by demographers.

DEMOGRAPHIC PERSPECTIVES

Perhaps the most straightforward and neutral way to analyse any society is in terms of its *demography*—the systematic analysis of population phenomena. Demographers, though often using complicated and sophisticated measures, are essentially concerned with very basic information about a population: births, deaths, movements of people, the distribution of the population and social characteristics of individuals and families. Demographic data provide a good starting point for a study of society for several reasons. First, most of the information is collected by governments on a regular basis and comes closer than any other form of data to complete coverage of the population. Because people are legally bound to provide census information, it is probably also the most accurate information which social scientists have at their disposal.[1] Second, demographic data are about "vital" processes—literally life and death matters—birth, marriage and divorce rates, geographical mobility and mortality rates (rates per 100,000 population).[2] In other words, they are about things that affect all of us individually and collectively. Third, what is happening to our population has important social, political and economic consequences; it sets basic structures or parameters in which a good deal of social behaviour takes place. For example, Figure VII.1 provides clues as to why there is such a thing as Western and Eastern alienation from Central Canada, why regionalism is an issue in Canadian society, why (as we shall see) it makes sense to talk about conflict between metropolis and hinterland. As Bercuson (1977:2) points out:

The Power of Quebec votes and the necessity of the federal government to pay as much heed to Quebec as it does to Ontario reveals the existence of one region—Central Canada—with common characteristics. It is industrialized, populous, part of the St. Lawrence heartland, the holder of an absolute majority of seats in the House of Commons, and the major beneficiary of national, economic, cultural and social policies.

The crux of the matter is, of course, population, or, in politicians' terms, voters. Similarly, the rise of separatism in Quebec and the various language bills (Bill 22 by the Bourassa Government and Bill 101 by the Lévesque Government) are, in part at least, beleaguered responses to the stark demographic facts that in less than two decades Quebec has gone from having one of the highest birth rates in the Western World to one of the lowest, and that unless the immigrant population can be pulled towards the Francophone population, the French-Canadian presence in Canada will diminish absolutely and proportionately (Caldwell, 1974).

Figure VII.1

ISODEMOGRAPHIC MAP OF CANADA

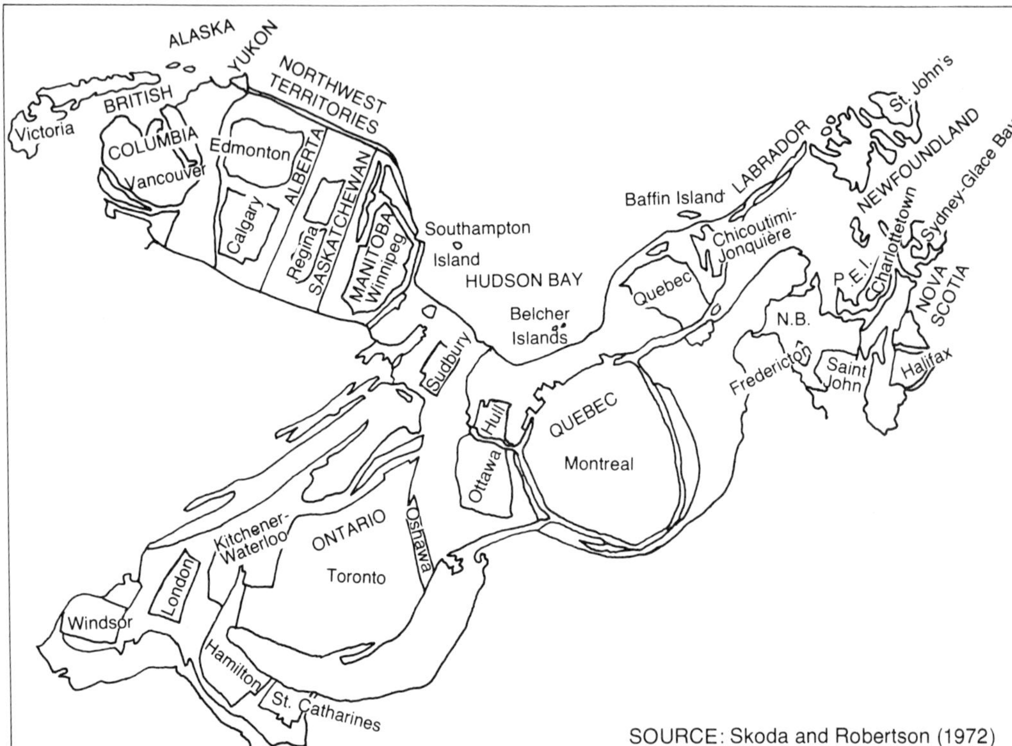

SOURCE: Skoda and Robertson (1972)

More generally, of course, there is unlikely to be consensus about what an increasing, static or declining population may mean for our economic and social life. To examine again the Quebec situation, politicians, whatever their position, have looked with alarm on the prospect of a declining population. However, some demographers in Quebec have adopted a more radical stance and argued that these demographic developments provide the opportunity for creative policies based on a philosophy of non-growth. On the other hand, conventional wisdom, of both political leaders and the public, has long held that we should welcome an increase in population because it is the basis for economic development and prosperity. Nevertheless, faced with chronic energy shortages, a rapidly expanding world population, pollution, noise, congestion and shrinking amounts of productive land, a majority of Canadians apparently no longer see continuing population growth as being desirable. Thus the position of the Quebec demographers no longer seems so radical. A recent Gallup Poll, for example, found that only about 28% of Canadians favour a larger population for Canada, whereas three decades ago, some 63% felt Canada should have more people.

At the same time, it is not at all clear that we have social and economic institutions capable of coping adequately with a static or declining population and the non-growth economy which would inevitably go with it. For instance, until the creation of the Anti-Inflation Board, an annual percentage increase in profits, wages and, of course, prices had become taken for granted. Universities, besides facing the tighter budgets which accompany falling or stable enrolments, must also cope with what has recently been called "stable state stagnation"—the decline in intellectual stimulation brought about by the fact that faculty are no longer so mobile, that there is less turnover of people and that the decade of growth and expansion has come to an end. In short, while it has for some time seemed that most of our problems are the result of overpopulation, an end to population expansion will produce problems totally different from those we presently face. Still, except for the threat of thermonuclear war, the most compelling problem confronting mankind is, undoubtedly, population growth—population explosion, as it is usually described.

World Population

Collectively, as members of the human race, we are faced with the plain fact that the present annual rate of world population growth is 2%. At first glance this may seem a rather innocuous figure, a very modest growth rate which, if translated into an interest rate, would have us searching very quickly for an alternative investment. But, a 2% growth rate means that the world's population (estimated at about 3.86 billion in 1973) will double in about 35 years; by 2008, there will be some 7.7 billion people in the world. We do not have to look very far for an explanation. We are dealing with exponential growth (2, 4, 8, 16, 32, etc.), not arithmetical or linear growth (1, 2, 3, 4, etc.). Rather than simple interest, we have the equivalent of the "miracle" of compound interest.[3]

The real dangers of exponential growth were vividly demonstrated a few years ago by the Club of Rome in its first publication, *The Limits of Growth* (Meadows and others, 1972). One illustration was in the form of a riddle: A farmer observes that a lily pad in his pond is doubling in size every day. He calculates that in 30 days it will have filled the whole pond and decides to cut it back when it has filled half the pond. The question is what day must he take action. The answer is not, as linear growth might suggest, on the fifteenth day, but on the twenty-ninth day, since it is the last doubling which will fill the pond. The parallel to world population growth is fairly obvious. After centuries of slow and uneven growth, we have reached the point where further doublings will have drastic, only partially understandable and imaginable, consequences. Yet, like the farmer, we have only "minutes" to avert what, by the middle of the next century will, under present conditions, be catastrophic.

While demographers can make only crude estimates of the size, distribution and growth of world populations in the past, it seems fairly certain that for most of human history, population growth was slow and erratic. However, from about 1650 onwards, we have what appear to be fairly reliable estimates of world population. According to Weinstein (1976), in the industrializing societies—Europe, North America and Japan—traditionally slow growth rates began to accelerate. After 1900, the growth rate in these countries began to decelerate and, with some exceptions such as the "baby boom" of the 1950s, has continued to do so. However, in the rest of the world, Asia, Africa and Latin America, in particular, growth rates remained slow and fluctuating until this century. Then, they began to accelerate, and, for the most part, have continued to do so until the present. As can be seen in Table VII.1, it is the high rates of population growth in Third World countries which account for the major share of the population explosion. Thus, like the farmer, we have very little time to avoid the drastic consequences of successive doublings, to seven billion by the turn of

Table VII.1

ESTIMATED POPULATION OF THE WORLD AND OF THE CONTINENTS, 1650-1973

	Population in Millions							
Continent	1650	1750	1800	1850	1900	1930	1950	1973
Africa	100	95	90	95	120	154	217	374
Asia (excluding U.S.S.R.)	327	475	597	741	915	1080	1355	2204
Latin America	12	11	19	33	63	109	162	309
North America	1	1	6	26	81	135	166	236
Europe and Asiatic U.S.S.R.	103	144	192	274	423	531	572	722
Oceania	2	2	2	2	6	10	13	21
World Total	545	728	906	1171	1608	2019	2485	3860

	Percentage Distribution							
Continent	1650	1750	1800	1850	1900	1930	1950	1973
Africa	18.3	13.1	9.9	8.1	7.4	7.6	8.1	9.7
Asia (excluding U.S.S.R.)	60.2	65.2	65.7	63.1	57.8	53.5	53.8	57.1
Latin America	2.2	1.5	2.1	2.8	3.9	5.4	6.6	8.0
North America	.2	.1	.7	2.3	5.1	6.7	6.8	6.1
Europe and Asiatic U.S.S.R.	18.7	19.8	21.4	23.5	25.4	26.3	24.2	18.7
Oceania	.4	.3	.2	.2	.4	.5	.5	.4
World Total	100	100	100	100	100	100	100	100

SOURCE: Wrong (1976: Table 1, p.16). See Acknowledgements for source of statistics.

the century and to a staggering 14 billion people only 35 years later—within the lifetime of most readers of this book.

The Demographic Transition

For some time now demographers have pinned their hopes for population control on Third World countries replicating the three-phase European and North American pattern of slow growth: accelerating growth, decelerating growth, what is usually referred to as the *European Demographic Transition.* In order to understand what is meant by a demographic transition it is necessary to keep in mind the simple arithmetic of population increase. Simply, if births exceed deaths, then population increases; if deaths exceed births, population decreases. Clearly, there are four possibilities: (1) high birth and death rates; (2) high birth and low death rates; (3) low birth and high death rates; and (4) low birth and low death rates. Situation number three is, of course, ultimately disastrous and does not seem to have occurred very often in recorded history at least. Situation one seems to have been true for most of the world for most of human history and is still true for the most underdeveloped areas of the world, e.g., Central Africa. Most of the Third World appears to be in situation two: birth rates, though beginning to fall, now far exceed the death rate which has fallen drastically because of improved medicine and nutrition. Hence, population in these societies is increasing very rapidly. Most industrialized or developed societies are in situation four, having birth rates only slightly higher than death rates.

Why did the birth rate decline in industrial societies? No one knows for sure, but a major hypothesis underlying the concept of the demographic transition is that as societies industrialize and urbanize, people begin to have fewer children. Figure VII.2 shows the three-phase cycle of the demographic transition as it occurred in Europe and North America. It is important to remember, however, that the third part of Figure VII.2 is really a hypothesis rather than a fact. That is, we know that birth rates have fallen in industrialized societies but we do not know for certain what is the precise reason for or cause of lower fertility levels.[4] In any event, the expectation was that if Third World countries could be transformed from underdeveloped to developed societies, then their birth rates would also fall. In fact, to some extent, this has occurred. In Latin America, for example, birth rates, though still very high, have fallen slightly. However, in Southern Africa, the Indian sub-continent and Southeast Asia, birth rates remain very high despite the fact that death rates have fallen considerably (Wrong, 1976; Weinstein, 1976).

Demographers have suggested a number of reasons why the demographic transition has yet to occur in these societies. One reason may simply be a matter of time. High death rates are usually due to high levels of infant mortality; the most dramatic increases in life expectancy arise not through extending the lives of old people but through keeping babies alive during childbirth and during the first two or three years of life. While developments in medicine were fairly gradual in European and North American society, they were introduced almost overnight into many Third World countries and only a short while ago. It may be that people simply have not had enough time to change their attitudes sufficiently to bring their birth rates into line with actual decreases in infant mortality. Accustomed to losing several babies, people may now, in fact, be ending up with more children than they have ever had or ever wanted.

A related problem is that increased life expectancy does not simply mean that people die at an older age but that more babies survive to adulthood. Thus, as life expectancy increases in a population, the average age of the population falls—there are more younger people who, naturally enough, want to marry and have children.

Figure VII.2

THE THREE-PHASE DEMOGRAPHIC TRANSITION

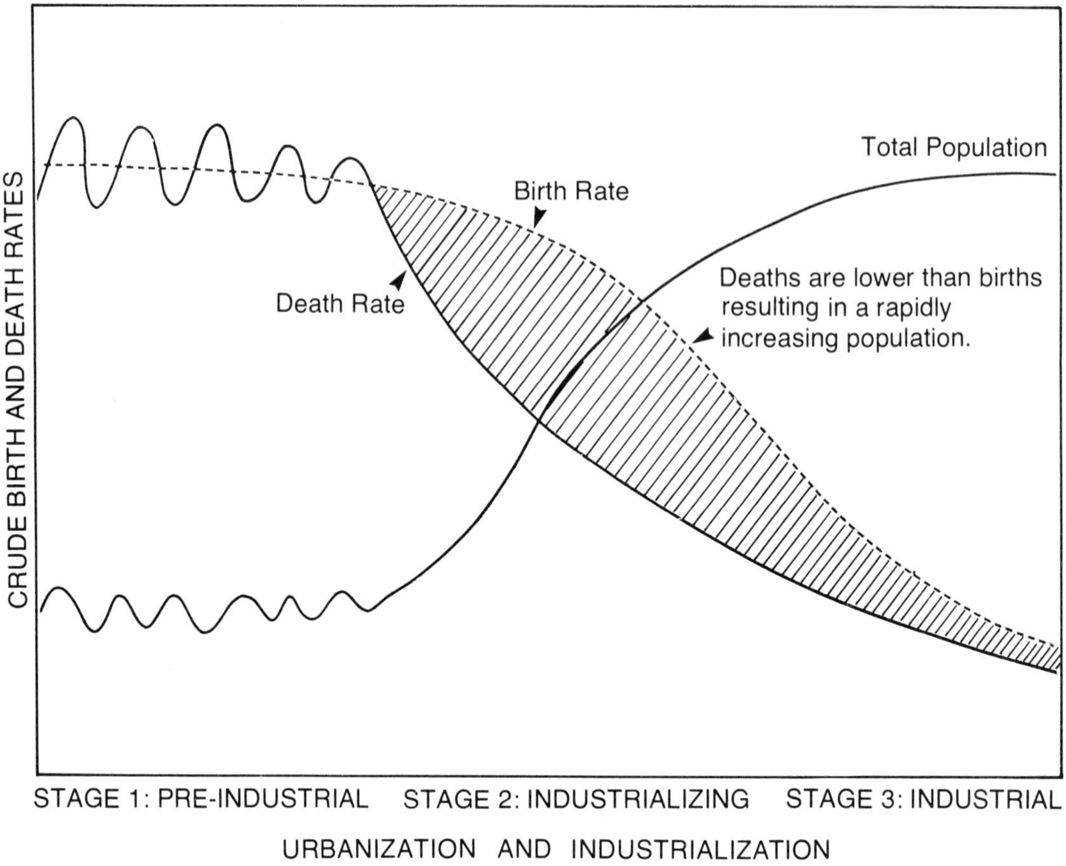

Thus, in the short run, even if birth rates do fall, birth rates within particular societies are still likely to increase for some time. As Paul Ehrlich (1968:28) warned some years ago:

> *One of the most ominous facts of the current situation is that roughly 40% of the population of the underdeveloped world is made up of people* under 15 years old. *As that mass of young people moves into its productive years during the next decade, we're going to see the greatest baby boom of all time. Those youngsters are the reason for all the ominous predictions for the year 2000. They are the gun-powder for the population explosion* [*emphasis in original*].

Short of wide-scale plague, famine, war or genocide, the world's population will, whatever policies are implemented, have to double to at least seven billion before it can begin to stabilize and, hopefully, decline. This, so demographers tell us, takes upwards of a century.

Even if the precipitating factor in declining fertility is, in fact, industrialization, we are no further ahead because most of the Third World has been unable to replicate the kind of development experienced by Europe, the United States and Japan. Why development has been arrested in these societies is a matter of considerable controversy. Some argue that the answer lies in the lack of resources of these societies and

Table VII.2

COMPONENTS OF GROWTH OF THE CANADIAN POPULATION FOR INTERCENSAL INTERVALS SINCE 1871 (IN THOUSANDS)

Census Interval	Population at Beginning of the Interval	Births	Deaths	Natural Increase	Immigration	Emigration	Net Migration
1966-1971	20,015	1,845	771	1,074	838	359	479
1961-1966	18,238	2,249	731	1,518	539	280	259
1951-1961	14,009	4,468	1,320	3,148	1,543	462	1,081
1941-1951	11,507	3,184	1,214	1,970	548	379	169
1931-1941	10,377	2,294	1,072	1,222	150	242	−92
1921-1931	8,788	2,415	1,055	1,360	1,203	974	229
1911-1921	7,207	2,338	988	1,350	1,612	1,381	231
1901-1911	5,371	1,931	811	1,120	1,759	1,043	716
1891-1901	4,833	1,546	828	718	326	506	−180
1881-1891	4,325	1,538	824	714	903	1,109	−206
1871-1881	3,689	1,477	754	723	353	440	−87

Note: Emigration figures are estimates only and include residual and error values.

SOURCE: Kubat and Thornton (1974:18)

their inability to produce surplus capital for reinvestment. Others maintain that for development to occur there must be a dramatic change in attitudes and social structures. As we shall see later in this chapter, for some it is the outcome of imperialism; it has been in the interests of the developed societies to keep major portions of the world in a state of underdevelopment.[5]

CANADIAN POPULATION TRENDS

As Table VII.2 shows, Canada's population has grown fairly steadily, though at a rate somewhat below that of much of the rest of the world. Both Canada and the United States have growth rates higher than most comparable countries in Europe (from 1970 to 1975 Canada grew at a rate of 1.6% per year; the United States had a growth rate of 1.8%). Specific forecasts of the future population are, of course, very difficult to make. The best we can do is make estimates using various kinds of assumptions. Stone and Marceau (1977) have recently made some projections using two different assumptions about what is likely to occur with respect to fertility and net migration between now and 1985 (in industrial societies, death rates have become more or less constant). They estimate that by the time of the 1991 Census there will be somewhere between 26 and 30 million people in Canada.

Is this good or bad? Probably—from the point of view of a European, living as he does in a country only a fraction the area of Canada, 20 to 30 million people is a miniscule figure, easily absorbed in the seeming vastness of our country. Significantly larger than the United States, we nevertheless have about one-tenth as many people. But, as Marsden (1975:24) has recently pointed out, to adopt this kind of perspective is to ignore the harsh realities of Canadian climate and geography.

Canada is not a vast, uninhabited country. Canada is a tiny habitable country embedded in a vast uninhabitable country, which while bearing the advantages of mineral resources, is not a resource for human habitation or food production. In that tiny seven percent of Canada that is habitable, everything to do with human habitation is in escalating competition. Into that space must go cities, agricultural land, highways, airports, pipelines, grazing and recreational land.

We do not know the carrying capacity of the world but what Marsden is suggesting is that Canada's capacity to sustain population is, given present technology, far below that of Europe and the United States. We need, then, an overall population policy, one which would, in turn, provide a more informed and more humane basis for immigration policies of the future.

Fertility and Mortality

Table VII.2 shows also that fertility rates in Canada are the lowest that they have ever been. Although there is little doubt that Canada has passed through the demographic transition, few demographers would be willing to predict that the downward trend shown in this table represents the shape of future population trends.[6] For example, population experts in the 1930s were convinced that the low birth rates of the depression years posed real threats to the future of industrial societies; yet, birth rates shot back up to pre-depression rates during the "baby boom" of the late 1940s and 1950s. Nevertheless, it does appear that, for the time being, Canadians are having fewer children and they are having them fairly early in life. Kubat and Thornton (1974:36) point out that this has important implications for the situation of women in the Canadian society and economy:

The impact of this compact childbearing on the social structure is bound to be profound, if for no other reason than it frees a great number of women from staying at home and makes them socially "visible", be it in the marketplace of jobs or in the marketplace of daily encounters. After the age of thirty-five or forty, most women become functionally "childless"; that is, their children are grown up enough to free them from daily childrearing preoccupations. As happens to any human behaviour once this becomes visible it becomes institutionalized, which in turn allows for natural childlessness to become accepted. Perhaps one may argue that inasmuch as the older-age "childlessness" has preceded the late-teen-married decline in childbearing, alternate models of behaviour for women were visible a while before they became actively emulated by the youth. This again contributes to the dissociation between marriage and parenthood and is bound to bring zero population growth to Canada smoothly and without much of a future shock.

According to Geoffrey Hawthorn (1970), we are some way from having a satisfactory sociological explanation of fertility behaviour. At some point people make decisions about how many children *they* want. No doubt fears about the size of the Canadian and world population or their rates of growth *may* enter into their decision, but, so do many other factors of more immediate and direct concern—the increasing desire or need for two incomes in the family, for example. Sometimes, as Veevers (1977) has shown, the decision to have no children, to be a voluntary childless couple, comes, so to speak, after the event. People intended to have children, but after putting it off for a while find that they do not want to alter so radically their lifestyle, their standard of living or their freedom to travel. Mortality rates, on the other hand, are for the most part independent of individual decisions and therefore tend to be fairly stable over time. Hence, Kubat and Thornton (1974) note that minor changes in birth rates must be interpreted cautiously; they may be only minor fluctuations in a longer term trend. Changes in death rates represent true changes over time.

Mortality

In any event, compared to fertility, mortality has, in Canada, ceased to be a very important variable in the demographic equation. Indeed, since 1960 we have had the lowest level of mortality among countries with mainly European populations (Kalbach and McVey, 1971). As we have seen, the main contribution to a high mortality rate is infant mortality. In Canada, infant

Table VII.3

INFANT MORTALITY COMPARISONS FOR THE YEAR 1968

Country	Rate per 1,000 Male Live Births	Rate per 1,000 Female Live Births
Canada	22.9	18.6
Newfoundland	28.2	19.8
Nova Scotia	22.3	20.6
New Brunswick	21.0	19.5
Prince Edward Is.	38.8	13.7
Quebec	23.6	19.6
Ontario	21.0	16.8
Manitoba	23.8	17.6
Saskatchewan	28.9	22.4
Alberta	21.9	18.3
British Columbia	21.1	18.0
Northwest Territories	67.3	62.1
Yukon	33.3	26.3
	Rate per 1,000 Live Births	
Netherlands	13.6	
Sweden	13.1	
Iceland	14.0	
England and Wales	18.3	
United States	21.7	
France	20.4	

SOURCE: Marsden (1972:60). See Acknowledgements for sources of statistics.

deaths have shown marked and consistent decreases. For example, in 1921 the rate was about 90 for each 1000 live births. By 1971 this rate had fallen to about 19 per 1000 (Kubat and Thornton, 1974). Still, as Table VII.3 shows, there are marked differences between regions of Canada.

What is also evident from Table VII.3 is that males have, everywhere, a higher rate of infant mortality than do females. Men, it seems, "get it" at both ends. They are involved in more accidents, are more likely to have a heart attack and are more likely to commit suicide. If we then take all of these factors together, at birth men have a life expectancy of about 68 years whereas women can, on average, expect to live slightly more than 74 years. Birth rates and death rates are only two of the components of population change. Migration into and out of nations or regions has obvious effects on population change and less apparent effects on the age and sex composition of a population.

Migration

In other words, when we deal with any population unit smaller than the world, we must add two further components to the equation of population change—immigration and emigration—the flow of people into and out of nations and regions. The formula, then, becomes:

$P_2 = P_1 + \text{Births} - \text{Deaths} + \text{Immigration} - \text{Emigration}$

Where P_1 *= Population enumerated at time 1*
P_2 *= Population enumerated at time 2*
and births, deaths, immigration and emigration refer to the number of events occurring during the time interval $t_1 - t_2$ *(Kalbach and McVey, 1971:31).*

Numbers of immigrants into Canada have fluctuated considerably, sometimes adding to natural population growth. At other times, they have been more than offset by the outward flow of people, to the United States mainly but also a smaller trickle of immigrants returning to their country of origin. If we turn, again, to Table VII.2, we can see that, on balance, migration has had a positive effect on Canada's population growth. Except for the depression years, we have, since the turn of the century, gained more people through immigration than we have lost through emigration. Yet, at not time since Confederation has net migration comprised more than half of the change in population between decennial censuses. Growth of the Canadian population, then, has been mainly (85%) a result of an excess of births over deaths rather than the result of immigration. This has been especially true for Quebec which grew with almost no immigration from about 60,000 people at the time of the Conquest to about 6,000,000 French-speaking Canadians today.

Migration statistics give some substance to the notion of Canada as a "jumping off place" for the United States; immigrants who cannot get into the United States come to Canada and may eventually move on to the United States. They also lend substance to the fear that those who emigrate are part of a "brain drain" (Kalbach and McVey, 1971:42-44). The work of Sorokin and others in 1927 suggests that this problem is not new. In fact, much of this debate is only conjecture. The reason is that while the Canadian government keeps a careful count of immigrants, it keeps no record of out-migrants, those who leave the country.[7] In all likelihood, however, those who left Canada were not simply transients passing through Canada on their way to the United States. Many were American immigrants since about 40% of Americans who emigrate to Canada "return home." Others were British and Europeans who, for various reasons, chose not to stay on in Canada (about 20% of immigrants). Clearly, Canada has lost talented and educated people to the United States. But, as Kalbach and McVey point out, this has probably been counterbalanced by immigrants with specialized qualifications and skills.

While net migration has not had a substantial effect on the growth rate of the Canadian population, migration has, at times, altered the age, sex and ethnic composition of the Canadian population. As we shall see in more detail in Chapter X, immigration of Southern and Eastern Europeans, and in recent decades of West Indians and Asians, has to a considerable extent supplanted British migration and, in effect, has undermined the primacy of British ethnic groups and created a third ethnic "force" in Canadian society. In the past, too, immigrants tended to be young and, at times, predominantly male. More recently, sponsorship of older relatives and the immigration of married couples has meant that immigration probably does little to alter the age and sex structure of the Canadian population (Gertler and Crowley, 1977:58).

Internal Migration

Figure VII.1, the isodemographic map of Canada, shows very vividly that Canada's demographic development is highly uneven. Despite policies to the contrary, immigration has contributed to this imbalance. Most who have emigrated to Canada have been drawn to cities and towards the centre and its wider range of opportunities. In fact, the attraction of centres has not been lost on native-born Canadians, either. We are, it turns out, a mobile lot, so much so that the number of internal migrants has, in the past 15 years, far outweighed the number of international migrants. In 1966-67, for example, the number of interprovincial migrants totalled 450,000 whereas immigrants totalled only 215,000 (Gertler and Crowley, 1977:64).

Table VII.4 shows what most Canadians already know: the growth areas are Alberta, British Columbia and Ontario. Both internal and international immigrants are more likely to be attracted to these three provinces. Moreover, much of the internal migration is between these three. For example, while Alberta has had, for many years, a high degree of attractiveness to people in other provinces, Albertans, if they moved, tended to go to Ontario and, secondly, to British Columbia (Stone, 1967). Gertler and Crowley (1977:66) conclude that:

The mobility of Canadians is therefore expressed through interprovincial migration towards those parts of the country where incomes are high, where the number and variety of jobs are greatest and where the range of social amenities—educational facilities, health services and recreational opportunities—is most appealing. Although variations are apparent for internal and international flows, the predominant focus of both flows on Ontario. Alberta and British Columbia gives rise to the suggestion that the forces that govern the directions of internal migration may be the same as those that influence the choices of immigrants.

However, migrants, whether Canadian or from abroad, do not migrate simply to a region. They move, rather, to a city. Thus, one of the major changes in the distribution of the Canadian population is that it has become increasingly urban.

Urbanization

Like most of the world, Canada has, in the past 100 years, undergone massive urbanization, an almost symmetrical turnabout from a predominantly rural society to a predominantly urban society (Figure VII.3). Around the time of Confederation less than 20% of the Canadian population lived in towns and cities. In contrast, by 1971, 100 years later, more than three-quarters of Canadians are classified by the census as urban.[8] Nor does this trend show any signs of abating. Demographers generally agree that by the time of the 2001 census, no more than 5% to 10% of Canada's peoples will be rural dwellers.

Whether, in fact, this minority will be rural in orientation is another matter. In the nineteenth century, urbanization essentially meant rural-urban migration, the movement, on a large scale, of young people out of farming and into urban-based occupations. In recent years, however, urban areas have expanded largely as the result of movements of people from city to

Table VII.4

CANADA, INTERPROVINCIAL AND INTERNATIONAL MIGRATION FLOWS, 1961-75

Province	(1961-66) Net Inter-provincial Migration	(1961-66) Net Inter-national Migration	(1961-66) Net Total Migration	(1966-71) Net Inter-provincial Migration	(1966-71) Net Inter-national Migration	(1966-71) Net Total Migration	(1971-75) Net Inter-provincial Migration	(1971-75) Net Inter-national Migration	(1971-75) Net Total Migration
Newfoundland	−15,300	− 7,400	− 22,700	− 19,300	− 4,900	− 24,200	− 2,500	− 7,500	− 10,000
Prince Edward Island	− 3,000	− 1,600	− 4,600	− 2,800	− 800	− 3,600	+ 3,200	+ 200	+ 3,400
Nova Scotia	−27,000	− 8,900	− 35,900	− 16,400	− 1,000	− 17,400	+ 7,200	+ 3,400	+ 10,600
New Brunswick	−25,700	− 7,700	− 33,400	− 19,600	− 7,900	− 27,500	+10,200	+ 2,300	+ 12,500
Quebec	−19,800	+ 13,700	− 6,100	−122,700	+ 70,000	− 52,700	−65,000	+ 48,900	− 16,100
Ontario	+85,300	+157,700	+243,000	+150,700	+353,500	+504,200	−17,400	+295,100	+277,700
Manitoba	−23,400	− 3,500	− 26,900	− 40,700	+ 25,500	+ 15,200	22,600	+ 21,700	− 900
Saskatchewan	−42,100	− 9,600	− 51,700	− 81,400	+ 3,700	− 77,700	−46,600	+ 4,300	− 42,300
Alberta	− 2,300	+ 1,500	− 800	+ 32,000	+ 44,000	+ 76,000	+34,000	+ 40,100	+ 76,100
British Columbia	+77,800	+ 26,900	+104,700	+115,000	+ 90,600	+205,600	+96,700	+ 87,500	+184,200

Notes: Figures are rounded to the nearest hundred. Annual counts are for the period June 1 to May 31 the following year. Data for emigration and interprovincial migration are estimates. Estimates of interprovincial migration are based upon family allowance data, which are derived from the count of change of address cards received in the Department of Health and Welfare, Government of Canada.

SOURCE: Gertler and Crowley (1977:65)

city. Indeed, the small proportion (9.4%) of all interprovincial migrants who did move from rural areas to urban areas was almost offset by the "counterflow" of urban dwellers to rural areas (Gertler and Crowley, 1977). It makes sense, then, to think of Canada as an urban society. Most people actually live in large cities; even those who live in small towns or in the countryside have for all intents and purposes become *urbane*. Clearly, this statement is more or less true depending on which part of Canada we are examining. By 1971 over 80% of Ontarians and Quebeckers were classified as urban. In contrast, only 38% were urban in P.E.I. and 53% in Saskatchewan (Figure VII.3).

While Canada may have been a country of small towns (Lucas, 1971), urbanization increasingly comes to mean concentration of growth in Canada's largest urban areas. Rather than simple moves from farm to village or town, the concern is with the mushrooming growth in a few metropolitan agglomerations: Southern British Columbia, Central Alberta, Southwestern Ontario and Southern Quebec. Thus, the proportion of urban Canadians in small towns (1,000-4,999) has dropped from 29% in 1901 to about 10% in 1971. The population of 100,000-plus cities has, at the same time, increased twentyfold, from 25.5% of the urban population in 1901 to 62.4% in 1971. In short, most of the growth in Canada's population is taking place within a very few centres and areas of Canada (Table VII.5). Gertler and Crowley (1977:48) note that:

Of the one and one-half million people added to the Canadian population in the latter half of the 1960's,

Figure VII.3

PER CENT OF POPULATION IN URBAN CANADA BY PROVINCE, 1871-1971

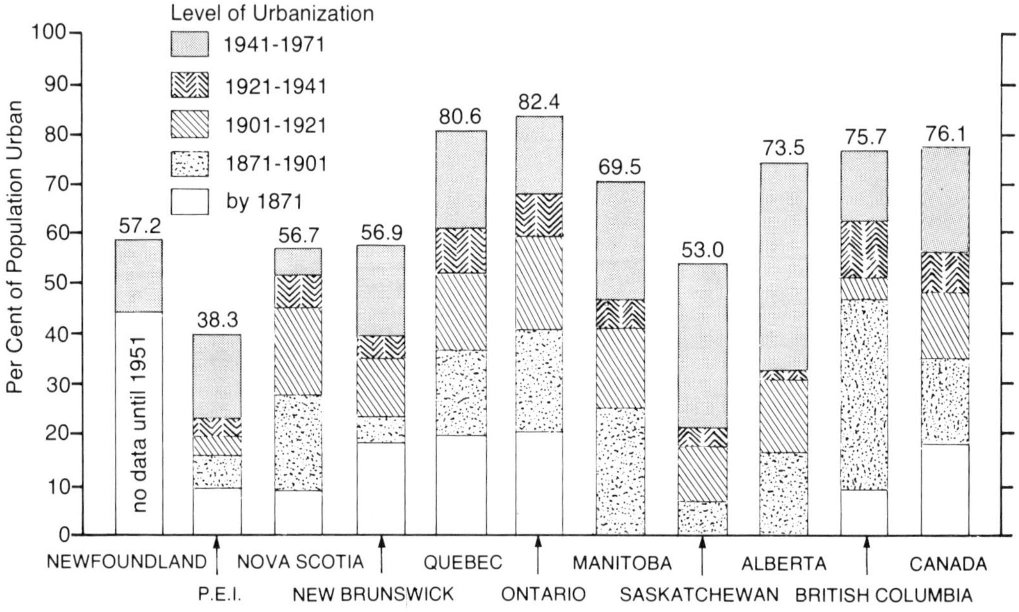

SOURCE: Gertler and Crowley (1977:46)

almost two-thirds were located in the three largest metropolitan areas—Montreal, Toronto and Vancouver. For Calgary, every 100 people residing there in 1966 were joined by twenty-two additional people in 1971. Only slightly lower increments were recorded for Edmonton (16.5), Vancouver (16.0), Toronto (14.8) and Ottawa-Hull (13.9) during the same five-year time span.

Ironically, perhaps tragically, metropolitan agglomerations are not located on barren and infertile soil but on some of the best agricultural land to be found in Canada. Progressively, we seem to be paving under one of our scarcest and most finite of resources, arable land. The Niagara Peninsula, for example, an area with unique climate and soil, one of the few areas in Canada capable of producing fruit and tobacco, is also a "growth area," rapidly becoming one long suburb from Hamilton to Niagara Falls. Urbanization, then, involves a vicious circle of expansion and growth of that which is already large and overdeveloped, with, at the same time, further decay and decline of those parts of Canada most in need of development. There is, then, a reciprocal relationship between urban growth and economic development. Migrants leave less developed areas in order to participate in the wider structure of opportunities which big cities provide. But migrants, themselves, add further fuel to these already superheated economies as additions to the market of consumers. At the same time, outmigration from hinterland regions of Canada diminishes further the economies of these regions. Not only are there fewer consumers to be supplied by local producers, there is also a "thinner" labour supply which further diminishes incentives for industry to decentralize. We find ourselves in the ludicrous situation that in a country as vast as Canada, over three-quarters of our people must compete for space, amenities and facilities on about 1% of Can-

Table VII.5

POPULATION OF URBAN CENTRES BY SIZE GROUP, CANADA, 1901-71 (NUMBER IN THOUSANDS AND PERCENTAGE)

Size Group	*1901*	*1911*	*1921*	*1931*	*1941*	*1951*	*1961*	*1971*
100,000 and over	476	1081	1659	2328	2645	5222	8401	10426
	(25.5)	(35.9)	(41.8)	(45.1)	(45.2)	(59.2)	(64.0)	(62.4)
30,000-99,999	343	489	496	697	928	1231	1647	1931
	(18.4)	(16.3)	(12.5)	(13.5)	(15.9)	(14.0)	(11.8)	(11.8)
5,000-29,999	503	783	1058	1305	1370	1198	1641	2593
	(26.9)	(26.0)	(26.6)	(25.3)	(23.4)	(13.6)	(12.7)	(15.8)
1,000-4,999	545	655	765	831	910	1167	1595	1641
	(29.2)	(21.8)	(19.1)	(16.1)	(15.5)	(13.2)	(11.5)	(10.0)
Total Urban	1867	3008	3977	5161	5854	8818	13972	16411
	(100.0)	(100.0)	(100.0)	(100.0)	(100.0)	(100.0)	(100.0)	(100.0)

Notes: This information only gives a broad indication of the secular trend. The definition of "urban" employed in the respective census years are utilized. From 1951 onward, the smaller-sized centres included within the boundaries of census metropolitan areas, major urban areas (1961) and census agglomerations (1971) are allocated to the larger centre.

A Census Metropolitan Area (CMA) is defined as the main labour market of a continuously built-up area having a population of 100,000 or more.

SOURCE: Kubat and Thornton (1974:20)

Table VII.6

CANADIAN LABOUR FORCE, BY OCCUPATION DIVISION, 1931-1971 (%)

Occupation Division	1931	1941	1951	1961	1971
Managerial	5.7%	5.7%	8.0%	8.3%	7.9%
Professional and Technical	6.2	6.9	7.3	9.7	12.5
Clerical	7.0	7.5	11.0	12.9	14.8
Sales	5.3	4.9	5.4	6.4	6.1
Service and Recreation	9.2	10.4	9.7	12.3	11.6
Transport and Communication	5.2	5.1	6.3	6.1	5.0
Farmers and Farm Workers	28.6	25.7	15.7	10.0	5.8
Loggers and Related Workers	1.1	1.9	1.9	1.2	0.6
Fishermen, trappers, and Hunters	1.2	1.2	1.0	0.5	0.3
Miners, Quarrymen, and Related Workers	1.4	1.7	1.2	1.0	0.7
Craftsmen, Production Process, and Related Workers	17.8	22.4	24.7	23.6	20.8
Labourers	11.4	6.4	6.7	5.3	4.7
Not stated	0.0[a]	0.3	1.2	2.6	9.0
Totals[b]	100.1%	100.1%	100.1%	99.9%	99.8%
(Number in thousands)	(3,908)	(4,184)	(5,277)	(6,458)	(8,609)

[a]Less than 0.05%.
[b]Does not equal 100.0% due to rounding error.

SOURCE: Canada. Statistics Canada. 1978. 1971 Census of Canada, Vol. III, Part 2 (Bulletin 3.2-2). Occupations: Historical for Canada and Provinces (Cat. 94-716). Ottawa: Printing and Publishing, Supply and Services. Table compiled, especially for this book, by Hugh Lautard, University of New Brunswick.

ada's land. The result is, on the one hand, all of the familiar problems of big cities—congestion, pollution, high land prices and a deteriorating housing stock and, on the other, an accentuation of regional disparities in income and opportunities. Cities, faced with mushrooming growth, become less pleasant places to live but so do smaller spaces.

Occupational Structure

Clearly, urbanization and industrialization go hand in hand and are complex components of the general process of modernization discussed in Chapter IV. As the above discussion of urbanization implies, the major and most persistent change in the Canadian labour force is the shift away from agriculture to urban-based occupations. At the turn of the century about 40% of the labour force was engaged in agriculture. The most dramatic shift, however, is between 1931 and 1971. During this period, farmers and farm workers declined in number to about one-fifth of their 1931 level (Table VII.6), less than 6% of the total labour force. The significance of this change can, perhaps, best be appreciated by looking at Figure VI.4. If the 1931 pattern had not altered, we would, in 1971, have had about 2,500,000 farmers and farm workers whereas, in fact, there were about 500,000.

Table VII.6 shows, more generally, the major changes which have taken place in the distribution of the labour force since 1931. By 1951, the proportion of workers in agriculture and primary occupations finally fell below that of industrial workers.

Figure VII.4

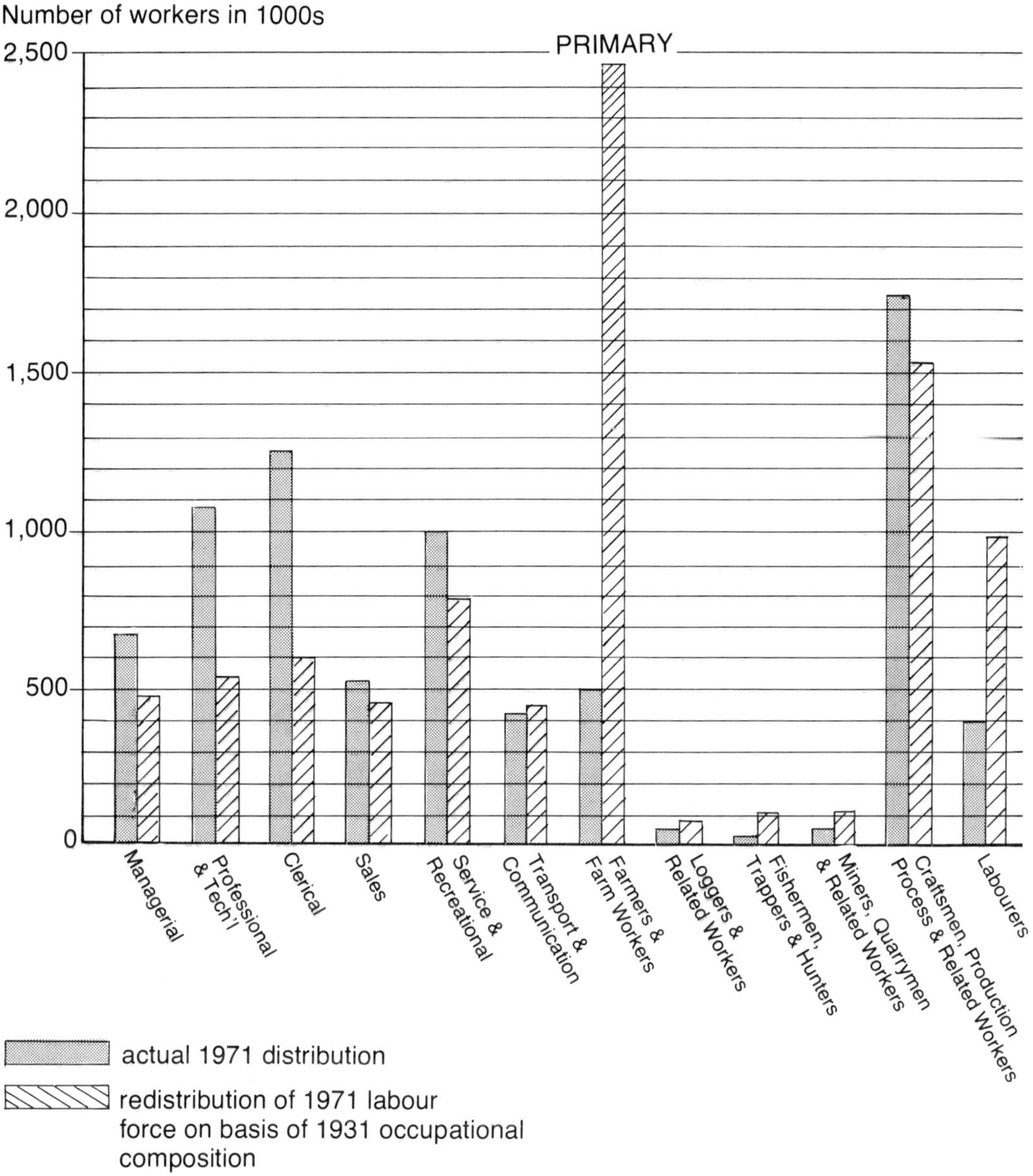

Figure 01. Comparison between actual occupational distribution of labour force as of 1971 and redistribution of 1971 labour force on the basis of 1931 occupational composition.

SOURCE: Based on data in Table VII.6. Prepared especially for this book by Hugh Lautard.

We had, it seems, become an "industrial society." This shift was, however, overshadowed by the phenomenal growth in the white-collar work force: "together, the professionals, the managers, the clerks and the salesmen formed the largest single occupational sector of the working population" (Ostry, 1967:14). Again, Figure VII.4 illustrates how much smaller a proportion of the labour force professional, technical and clerical workers would have been had the 1931 pattern remained. In fact, these three categories all doubled as a proportion of the total labour force between 1931 and 1971.

Canada then moved rapidly from primary industry to secondary industry to tertiary industry, from a producer of raw materials, to manufacturing, to a service economy. We became, like the United States, what some call "post-industrial" rather than an industrial society. Manufacturing, though a crucial component of the economy, is overwhelmed by the more elusive and invisible industry of symbol manipulation, the utilization in both private and public sectors of specialized skills, knowledge and professionalism.[9] A case in point is Calgary, Alberta. Despite its formidable growth over the past two decades, the "industrial" section of the city seems to have changed very little; it may actually have declined. It is in the centre of the city with its many office blocks where most people find employment. It turns out, for instance, that a large proportion of the data processing for the oil industry in Western Canada and the United States is done in Calgary. These and other "hidden industries" account for a large portion of Calgary's growth and prosperity.

Women in the Labour Force

A second important change in the Canadian labour force is the dramatic increase in female participation. Table VII.7, for instance, shows that while the number of men in the labour force almost doubled between 1931 and 1971, the number of females increased four and a half times. Over this same period, the participation rate for women, as well as the female percentage of the labour force, doubled. The increased participation of women in the labour force either coincides with or is the result of a variety of structural factors which we have described in this section. Clearly, the low fertility rate of the Canadian population coupled with early marriage means that women are free earlier to enter or re-enter the labour force. Urbanization, too, has meant that many women previously in unpaid labour on farms are able to seek paid jobs outside of the home. Probably most crucial has been the massive increase in the service sector and, in particular, the dramatic growth in clerical occupations. In fact, in 1971, over one-half (53%) of all women in the labour force were concentrated in clerical and service jobs (Table VII.8). In other words, women have not entered all occupation divisions equally, but have been segregated into sex-typed occupations, jobs which are, in effect, extensions outside of the home of what inside the home was traditionally women's work—elementary teaching, nursing, secretarial work and cleaning. Thus, as Table VII.9 shows, women are under-represented in managerial jobs, in blue-collar jobs in the primary industries, and are over-represented in clerical, sales, service and recreation. And, if we remove nurses and teachers from the professional and technical category, women would probably be under-represented here as well.

At this point it would, perhaps, be useful to point out how to read tables so that we are not abusing our statistics. Table VII.8, for example, presents data on the *concentration* of males and females in certain occupations. The columns have been percentaged downwards. In other words, for each year given, the percentage in any cell is based on the total number of males or females in the labour force. This table

Table VII.7

CANADIAN LABOUR FORCE, BY SEX, SHOWING PARTICIPATION RATE[a] AND SEX COMPOSITION: 1931-1971

	1931		1941		1951		1961		1971	
	Male	Female	Male	Female	Male	Female	Male	Female	Male	Female
Number (in thousands)	3,245	663	3,666	832	4,114	1,162	4,694	1,764	5,649	2,960
Participation Rate (%)	87.5	19.6	85.8	20.7	83.8	24.1	77.7	29.5	75.7	39.2
Sex Composition (%)	83.0	17.0	81.5	18.5	78.0	22.0	72.7	27.3	65.6	34.4

[a]Percentage of the adult population employed or seeking work.

SOURCE: Canada. Statistics Canada. 1974. 1971 Census of Canada, Vol. III, Part 1 (Bulletin 3.1-2). Labour Force and Individual Income: Historical—Labour Force, for Canada and Provinces, 1911-1971 (Cat. 94-702). Ottawa: Information Canada, Table 1. Prepared especially for this book by Hugh Lautard.

Table VII.8

CONCENTRATION OF MALES AND FEMALES IN OCCUPATIONAL DIVISIONS: CANADA 1931-1971

Occupation	1931		1941		1951		1961		1971	
Division	Male	Female	Male	Female	Male	Female	Male	Female	Male	Female
Managerial	6.5%	1.6%	6.6%	2.0%	9.3%	3.4%	10.2%	3.3%	10.5%	2.9%
Professional and Technical	3.9	17.7	4.7	15.7	5.3	14.3	7.6	15.4	10.7	16.1
Clerical	4.7	18.0	4.8	18.5	6.2	27.8	6.9	28.8	6.5	30.5
Sales	5.0	7.0	4.4	7.1	4.5	8.6	5.6	8.4	5.7	7.0
Service and Recreation	4.2	33.7	4.5	34.1	6.5	21.1	8.5	22.4	8.6	17.4
Transport and Communication	5.8	2.4	6.0	1.7	7.2	2.8	7.5	2.2	6.9	1.3
Farmers and Farm Workers	33.7	3.6	31.5	2.3	19.3	2.8	12.2	4.3	7.1	3.4
Loggers and Related Workers	1.3	0.0	2.3	0.0	2.5	0.0[a]	1.7	0.0[a]	0.9	0.0[a]
Fishermen, Trappers and Hunters	1.4	0.1	1.5	0.0[a]	1.2	0.0[a]	0.7	0.0[a]	0.5	0.0[a]
Miners, Quarrymen and Related Workers	1.7	0.0	2.1	0.0[a]	1.6	0.0[a]	1.4	0.0[a]	1.1	0.0[a]
Craftsmen and Production Process Workers	18.5	14.0	23.7	17.0	27.1	16.3	28.2	11.6	27.2	8.6
Labourers	13.3	1.7	7.6	1.4	8.0	1.8	6.9	1.2	6.6	1.2
Not stated	0.0[a]	0.0[a]	0.3	0.2	1.2	1.1	2.6	2.4	7.7	11.5
Totals[b]	100.0%	99.8%	100.0%	100.0%	99.9%	100.0%	100.0%	100.0%	100.0%	99.9%
(Number in thousands)	(3,245)	(663)	(3,352)	(831)	(4,114)	(1,162)	(4,694)	(1,764)	(5,649)	(2,960)

[a]Less than 0.05%.
[b]May not equal 100.0% due to rounding error.

SOURCE: Canada. Statistics Canada. 1978. 1971 Census of Canada, Vol. III, Part 2 (Bulletin 3.2-2). Occupations: Historical for Canada and Provinces (Cat. 94-716). Ottawa: Printing and Publishing, Supply and Services. Prepared by Hugh Lautard.

does not tell us whether males or females are over- or under-represented in any occupation. Table VII.9, however, does provide statistics on *representativeness*. It describes the proportion of males and females in each occupation. The percentages have been recorded across the table. In other words, each cell is a percentage based on the total in any occupational division for any given year. For example, if we look at 1971, we can see that females hold 13% of the total managerial positions; men, of course, the other 87%. Now, if we compare this breakdown to the proportion of men and women in the total labour force, we can see clearly that women are under-represented in managerial occupations: women comprised 34% of the total labour force in 1971 and only 13% of the managerial labour force.

Hence, as a recent study by Pat and Hugh Armstrong (1978) documents, rapidly growing numbers of women in the labour force do not signify any fundamental change in attitudes, or in the position or status of women. Rather, because of sexual segregation, there has not been a fundamental alteration in the division of labour by sex or in the nature of women's work (p. 14). Using different and more elaborate measures, Lautard (1978) comes to similar conclusions. While he finds some decline in sexual segregation as Canada becomes a more industrialized society, he also concludes that at the present rate of change, we will have a completely

Table VII.9

PROPORTION OF MALES AND FEMALES IN OCCUPATION DIVISIONS: CANADA, 1931-1971 (%)

Occupation Division	1931 Male	1931 Female	1941 Male	1941 Female	1951 Male	1951 Female	1961 Male	1961 Female	1971 Male	1971 Female
Managerial	95	5	93	7	91	9	89	11	87	13
Professional and Technical	52	48	55	45	57	43	57	43	56	44
Clerical	56	44	51	49	44	56	39	61	29	71
Sales	78	22	72	28	65	35	64	36	61	39
Service and Recreation	38	62	35	65	52	48	50	50	48	57
Transport and Communication	92	8	94	6	90	10	90	10	91	9
Farmers and Farm Workers	98	2	98	2	96	4	88	12	80	20
Loggers and Related Workers	100	0	100	0	100	0[a]	100	0[a]	98	2
Fishermen, Trappers and Hunters	99	1	99	1	100	0[a]	99	1	98	2
Miners, Quarrymen and related Workers	100	0	100	0[a]	100	0[a]	100	0[a]	100	0[a]
Craftsmen and Production Process Workers	87	13	85	15	86	14	87	13	86	14
Labourers	97	3	96	4	94	6	94	6	91	9
Not stated	81	19	85	15	80	21	74	26	56	44
Total Labour Force	83	17	80	19	78	22	73	27	66	34

[a]Less than 0.5%.

SOURCE: Canada. Statistics Canada. 1978. 1971 Census of Canada, Vol. III, Part 2 (Bulletin 3.2-2). Occupations: Historical for Canada and Provinces (Cat. 94-716). Ottawa: Printing and Publishing, Supply and Services. Prepared by Hugh Lautard.

desegregated labour force in about 450 years![10] While women doubled their representation in the labour force as a whole from 1931 to 1971, their representation in professional and technical occupations has actually declined.

Clearly, demographic analysis can only take us so far. Even questions of why there is a decline or increase in birth rates necessarily involves us in questions of culture—what are the prevalent ideas about having children, birth control, abortion. Whether or not women enter the labour force and in what capacities is, as we have seen, mainly due to structural changes. Radical change in the status of women involves changing values, changing conceptions about men and women and about the kind of political economic system we want to live in.

The kinds of raw data which we have presented provide only a backdrop for understanding Canadian structure and culture. In the first chapter we outlined the major approaches to understanding society. Some early Canadian sociologists seemed content to adopt the dominant American perspectives—functionalism and symbolic interactionism—and to assume that these would fit the Canadian case. More recently, however, there has been a growing emphasis among Canadian sociologists on recognizing Canada's unique history and structure and on adopting approaches consistent with it. Before examining Canadian sociology, we must recognize that sociological ideas also emerge out of the dominant ideologies of society at large. It is these ideologies, as well, which define the social issues and problems for sociological analysis.

CANADA AND THE LIBERAL IDEOLOGY

As we discussed in Chapter III, Canadian society has generally been depicted as conservative in its traditions and politics. According to George Grant, in his book *Lament for a Nation* (1965), one way that we sought, historically, to maintain a separate identity was through what he calls "Conservative Nationalism." It was this which linked English Canada to French Canada. Thus, what was in Ontario stuffy and stodgy Presbyterianism was, in Quebec, repressive and archaic Catholicism. Others have agreed with Grant. John Porter (1967:56), for instance, has argued that "English and French Canadians are more alike in their conservatism, traditionalism, religiosity, authoritarianism and elitist values than the spokesmen of either group are prepared to admit." He asks, then, if Francophone and Anglophone cultures are not simply "subcultural variants" of a single culture in which the core values are conservative. S. D. Clark (1968:236) has also argued that we clung to these traditions because they made us different from the more "open" and "liberal" climate of American society.

Until recently, the dominant ideology in Quebec was the ideology of conservatism which defined Quebec primarily as the bearer of a culture; the task of the Québecois was to preserve the symbols and values handed down by their ancestors. Gerald Fortin, a sociologist from Laval, has described the traditional values these Québecois wished to preserve and to pass on to their descendants:

> *[This ideology of conservation extolls] the merits of the French language, the Catholic religion, the spiritual culture, the national history, rural life, and the family: it warns of the dangers of English imperialism, industrialization, urbanization, and the means of mass communication . . . (in Rioux, 1973:269).*

More recently, for many Québecois, the emphasis has shifted; they no longer see Quebec as primarily a cultural unit, but also as a modern industrial society which must become the master of its own political and economic destiny. This change in ideology is discussed more fully in Chapter X, Ethnic Groups.

For Grant, the failure of conservatism in Canada since the 1960s is also the defeat of Canadian nationalism. Both, in his view, were swept away by the twin forces of "technology and empire" (see Grant, 1969). Writing more than a decade ago, he warned that:

French-Canadian nationalism is a last ditch stand. The French on this continent will at least disappear from history with more than the smirks and whimpers of their English speaking compatriots—with their flags flying and, indeed, with some guns blazing. The reality of their culture and their desire not to be swamped, cannot save them from the inexorable facts in the continental case (Grant, 1965:76).

Separatism, an independent Quebec, is in many respects not a "problem" for French Canadians at all. Culturally and politically, it is a critical issue for the rest of Canada; it is not clear that without Quebec in Confederation the rest of Canada could withstand the juggernaut of American economic and cultural imperialism. This is not to say that we necessarily can continue to do so buttressed by Quebec. Written several years before the October 1970 events in Quebec which led to the invoking of the War Measures Act and long before the victory of the Parti Québecois, Grant's message still has relevance. As René Lévesque is well aware, maintaining a distinct Quebec culture and also fulfilling Quebec aspirations for an American-style standard of living are, perhaps, incompatible ends.

As we have become more closely affiliated with the United States and more distant from Britain, the American version of liberalism has come also to be the standard by which we judge ourselves. This, in essence, is the main thrust of John Porter's important study of class and power, *The Vertical Mosaic* (1965). Canada, in Porter's view, emerges as ethnically fragmented, inequalitarian, an immobile society with an almost caste-like elite. Rather than the vigour and innovation of the American melting pot ideology, we settled for a mosaic ideology, one which left the British (specifically English and Scots) at the top of the Canadian social hierarchy and other ethnic groups somewhere below. Thus, Canada appeared to be "behind" not only the United States but also perhaps other liberal capitalist democracies in Europe. Porter (1965:557-558) concludes that we have

a long way to go to become in any sense a thorough-going democracy. . . . Even into the 1960's Canadian educational systems have yet to become democratized through to the university level. The possibilities for upward social mobility are reduced and, at the same time, shortages of highly trained people for the new occupational structure continue. In this respect Canada is behind twentieth-century democracy elsewhere.[11]

Even if we have "a long way to go," according to Pat Marchak (1975:12), the dominant ideology in Canada has become the liberal ideology.

[It] assumes that each child may choose his way of life, determine his own future, arrange his itinerary, that all are equal in this opportunity. . . . The liberal ideology rests on the premise that the individual is more important than the society and that the society does not have the right to limit his freedom to pursue happiness as he chooses to define it.

In other words, from a liberal perspective or ideology, the just society is not one of equality of condition, one where resources are distributed more or less equally, but one in which there is alleged to be equality of opportunity: people, it is believed, should have the equal right, regardless of race, ethnicity, sex or family background, etc., to rise in the social hierarchy, to compete for scarce resources—power, prestige and money. Marchak calls these beliefs an ideology because, as she shows, even by this limited definition of "equality," i.e., equality of opportunity, we fall far short of the ideal. So, of course, does the United States. We will look further at this in the next three chapters. In addition, liberalism places considerable emphasis on individual fulfillment even if this is at the expense of others. Robin Mathews (1973:214) argues that:

The human product, in human terms, of the liberal ideology is the Robber Baron of free enterprise and the cop-out hippie/yippie of the so-called counter culture. . . . The liberal ideology supports all manifestations of liberal anarchist individualism, whether that of the rich free enterpriser who manipulates the community for his own profit or the so-called disengaged *rejecter of community who denies it.*

In sum, the liberal ideology espouses what C. B. MacPherson (1962) calls *possessive individualism*. Rather than collectivism, the emphasis is on freedom to rise (and fall) in the class and status hierarchy. Generally, it has also taken for granted the efficiency and "rightness" of free enterprise over public enterprise and of private property over collective property. Indeed, any other form of social and economic organization may be seen as inconceivable.

We are likely, then, to think of liberalism as either midway between the opposite poles of conservatism and socialism or, perhaps, ranged alongside socialism in opposition to conservatism. At the risk of some oversimplification we can say that conservatism places considerable emphasis on historical values, the importance of traditional forms of hierarchy, social inequality and stable, integrated social structures. A conservative, for example, is likely to argue that traditional closed elites, such as the European aristocracy, served important functions for society, in that they acted as "culture bearers," a means by which social continuity and social order could be maintained and anarchy and chaos forestalled. In contrast, socialism has denied that hierarchy, class and status inequality are either inevitable or even desirable. Rather, "it stresses the good of the community as against possessive individualism; equality of condition as against more equality of opportunity; the cooperative commonwealth as against the acquisitive society" (Horowitz, 1965a:13).

Simply, the socialist solution to elites would be to do away with them as much as is possible. The liberal would argue that since you cannot do away with elites and may not even want to do so, the next best thing is to make them open, no longer hereditary aristocracies but meritocracies—aristocracies based not on birth but on talent.[12]

SOCIALISM AND CONSERVATISM

At the same time, Horowitz and others have observed that socialism and conservatism come together in their emphasis on the primacy of society—the view that the collective takes precedence over the individual.

The liberal sees life in society as a competition among individuals; the prize is individual "achievement" or "success"; equality is equality of opportunity in the struggle for success. The individual is thought of as self-determining, autonomous, rather than a member determined by the class and community of which he is a part. It is because *the socialist has a conception of society as* more *than an agglomeration of competing individuals—a conception much closer to the tory view of society as an organic identity—that he rejects the liberal idea of equality as inadequate. Socialists disagree with liberals about the essential meaning of equality* because *socialists have a tory conception of society (Horowitz, 1965:14).*

George Grant (1965) has long held that conservatism and socialism are alike in their willingness to use governmental control to protect the public from free enterprise. Not only did we open up the west differently than in the United States, but more modern public institutions such as Ontario Hydro, the CNR and CBC were created by conservative governments (p. 71). One could, of course, add many others to this list ranging from provincially-owned telephone companies, to Air Canada, to such unique and innovative institutions as the Canada Council. In many respects then, we have what John Meisel (1977) calls a public enterprise ethic rather than a free enterprise ethic.

Thus, various manifestations of the Welfare State—medicare, social security, regional development and other social innovations—have been implemented far more quickly and easily in Canada than in the United States. The irony, of course, is that in judging ourselves by the standards of the American liberal ideology and in worrying about "catching-up" with the United States, we sell ourselves short. We remain slaves to colonial thought patterns. Herschel Hardin argues that:

Canada, in its essentials, is a public enterprise country, always has been, and probably always will be. Americans have, or at least had, a genius for private enterprise; Canadians have a genius for public enterprise. As long as we describe Canada in terms of the American model, we will continue to see ourselves as second-rate Americans, not being Americans at all (Hardin, 1974:140).

There is a danger in this kind of discussion that political ideologies will appear to be disembodied idea systems existing independent of people, without a historical and structural context. Nor can we, as the historian Hartz (1964) maintained, understand Canadian ideologies simply by tracing which fragment of the spectrum of Old World ideologies the original settlers of French Canada and English Canada brought with them. Certainly they will have brought ideologies with them, ideologies which reflected their position and experience in Europe. However, these ideologies will have changed to reflect the facts of Canadian life—its late development, its regional disparities, the hurdles to transportation, its hostile climate and geography, its changing patterns of immigration and its changing occupational structure. Moreover, it would be misleading to imagine that only one ideology was imported to the "New World." And, as always, in the competition of ideologies we must ask which groups had the most resources to make their ideology the dominant one. This is not to say that only one dominant ideology will emerge, nor even that the dominant ideology can ever exist in "pure form," "uncontaminated" by competing systems of ideas. Gad Horowitz (1966) makes this very point:

The three components of the English-Canadian political culture have not developed in isolation from one another; each has developed in interaction with the others. Our toryism and our socialism have been moderated by liberalism. But by the same token, our liberalism has been rendered "impure," in American terms, through its contacts with toryism and socialism. If English-Canadian liberalism is less individualistic, less ardently populistic-democratic, more inclined to state intervention in the economy, and more tolerant of "feudal survivals" such as monarchy, this is due to the uninterrupted influence of toryism upon liberalism, an influence wielded in and through the conflict between the two. If English-Canadian liberalism has tended since the depression to merge at its leftist edge with the democratic socialism of the CCF-NDP, this is due to the influence which socialism has exerted upon liberalism, in and through the conflict between them.

THE STATE AND CAPITALISM

Clearly, then, to understand a society, we must look not only at its ideas, but also at its material base. At this point, two features of Canadian society deserve attention: (1) however much Canadians are willing to consider socialist ideas, we live in a capitalist society and this has important consequences for us; (2) the form our capitalism takes is shaped by the fact that much of our economy is owned and controlled by foreigners.

A major difference between socialist and capitalist societies centres on the greater potential power of the State in communist societies to change the course and direction of society. According to Karl Marx, the State under capitalism is "nothing more than the form of organization which the bourgeoisie [capitalist class] necessarily adopt for the mutual guarantee of their property and interests" (Marx and Engels, 1965:78). Leo Panitch (1977:85) suggests that in some people's minds this translates as follows:

It is assumed that what one really *means, in the modern Canadian context, is that E. P. Taylor, after having eaten two or three babies for breakfast, calls Pierre Trudeau every morning and, amidst satisfied belches, gives the Prime Minister instruction on what the government should accomplish that day.*

Obviously, the relationship between the State and the dominant or ruling class is more complex than this. But, as Panitch goes on to show, most of it is correct in its essentials: the State does, for the most part, act on behalf of (rather than at the behest of) capitalist interests in situation after situation, case after case. In part, this is because there is considerable and, indeed, increasing "interpenetration" between the corporate elite and the State elite (Clement, 1975:34). But, even without some people active in both spheres, there is, according to Leo Panitch (1977:95):

"a confraternity of power" of such dimensions as to permit the clear employment of the term ruling class in the political as well as the economic sense in the Canadian case. It suggests, above all, an ideological hegemony emanating from both the bourgeoisie and the state which is awesome, which is reflected in the sheer pervasiveness of the view that the National interest and business interest are at one, and which certainly ensures the smooth functioning of the relationship between the state and the capitalist class.

What Panitch, and indeed Marx long before him, is suggesting, then, is that there is no need for a telephone call between Taylor and Trudeau. Both, in fundamental respects, already share a world view or ideology which is not only highly similar but which precludes any other way of thinking. For instance, John Turner, a former Finance Minister and strong rival to Pierre Trudeau as leader of the Liberal Party, was able to leave Government and make a smooth transition into a very lucrative job in the corporate world. It is not unlikely that in the future he will make an equally effortless return to Federal politics.[13]

Because of this relationship and because there is a very large degree of action which is beyond public control, the State in liberal capitalist democracies is relatively impotent to bring about fundamental structural changes. When, as in Quebec, there is a conscious attempt to restore sovereignty, the perils may be great. Large companies, for example, Sun Life, pull up stakes and move to Toronto, thereby making an additional threat to an already vulnerable economy. René Levesque, for example, must somehow create change and yet convince Wall Street financiers that there really is not any *basic* change in the offing. Quebec will, despite separatism, still be a capitalist society offering a warm welcome to multi-nationals. In a communist society, on the other hand, the shape and direction of the society is, in theory at least, within the control of the State.

What exactly does this mean in human terms, at the level of everyday life? It is probably true that most Canadians assume that living in Russia, say, would mean a very different kind of lifestyle, not only in terms of standard of living, and not only in terms of quality of life, but also subjectively different, different in terms of how happy they could be. No doubt life would be different but it is also clearly true that most Canadians are likely to exaggerate these differences. In fact, some social scientists have argued that it probably does not make much difference at all that all industrial societies, whether capitalist, mixed or communist, are converging towards what is a pretty similar kind of society, perhaps post-industrial society. It seems unlikely that a Soviet worker, say on the assembly line, is more satisfied in his work and with his compensation because the State, rather than shareholders, benefits from the surplus of his labour. Life on the assembly line is likely to be deadening, boring and perhaps dangerous, whatever the economic system. Similarly, though many in the middle mass of Canadian society may well feel dissatisfied with their incomes, this is probably not because they measure themselves against the economic elite—against K. C. Irving or E. P Taylor. Rather, like their Russian counterparts, they are more concerned with the privileges and standard of living of those just above them in the social and occupational structure (Runciman, 1966). And, we know that in the Soviet Union certain strata, notably those white-collar workers associated with the party, have for some time now received more material and social privileges than those of other strata (Parkin, 1971:151; Djilas, 1959).

None of this is to suggest that the differences which do exist are unimportant. Canadians are able to take for granted certain freedoms, not available to those living in the Soviet Union. But, it is wrong automatically to equate these freedoms with capitalism or repressions within communism. Repression did not come to the Soviet Union along with communism; repression preceded communism and, obviously, the facts of life in Russia shaped the particular brand of socialism with which it is associated. At the same time, it is probably the case that the dominant ideology in Canada serves to exaggerate the extent to which Canadians, individually and collectively, shape their own destiny.

In sum, if, in a communist society, there is a hierarchy of prestige and differences in income comparable to Canadian society, this is at least partly the result of political decisions rather than the outcome of a market system or of decisions made by an economic elite to serve its special interests. As Clement (1977a:289) notes:

> *The power contained in these companies [multinationals] is private power, exercised by sets of people in ways they feel to be most beneficial to themselves and their companies, with very limited accountability for their actions to the people directly affected. Those who own and control these enormous operations are not subject to popular elections, nor are they often brought to account publicly for their decisions. They are a self-selecting, self-perpetuating set of people who have wide-ranging control over the lives of Canadians and the shape of Canadian society.*

Thus, it is probably the case in all capitalist societies that political decisions will seldom run counter to the interests of corporate capitalism and of big business.

As we have said, Canadians face the additional problem that much of our economy is, in fact, owned and controlled by foreigners, notably Americans. We are, in effect, a branch plant economy intertwined with and highly dependent on the United States and on the decisions of multi-national companies. Until recently, concern about the "American take-over" of Canada has been obscured by the general belief that what Canada needs is foreign investment, foreign capital, if we are to prosper and grow. Indeed, successive governments, especially liberal governments, have actively sought foreign investment and have, at times, bent over backwards to insure that the flow of American capital into the country would not in any way be checked (Levitt, 1970). As John O'Neill (1975:109) puts it:

> *It is hard to establish the case for rape where the victim has such a long history of seduction and sellout. . . . After all, Canada has no desire to be left on the shelf, an industrial virgin, excited by nothing but the unconsummated call of her nature lovers.*

Kari Levitt goes one step further, however, and shows that the real irony is that Canadians have, to a great extent, financed their own take-over. In fact, as she points out, American funds to expand U.S.-controlled industry in Canada comprise only a small portion of the money invested (5% to 20% depending on the industry). Rather, the major portion of funds for expansion came from profits gained in Canada, depreciation allowances and borrowing from Canadian banks and other financial institutions. Moreover, while foreign investment in Canada may have been of benefit in the short run, in the longer run it leads to underdevelopment of the economy because more capital is drained out of Canada than is invested. Levitt finds that, by the 1960s, Canada was losing more than it gained from the United States:

> *"In the period 1960-67 remitted profits of American subsidiaries in Canada ($5.9 billion) exceeded new capital inflows ($4.1 billion) by $1.8 billion" (Levitt, 1970:94).*

The most recent and thoroughgoing analysis of American economic penetration in Canada is Wallace Clement's (1977) study, *Continental Corporate Power*. Like Levitt, and others, Clement is concerned with the implications of being locked into a continental economy for national sovereignty, regional development and the shape of Canadian society more generally. In short, because we are unequal to the United States, the existence of multi-national corporations—foreign ownership—reduces even further the potential power of the State to bring about any kind of fundamental change in Canadian society (p. 301). These issues are explored further when we consider dependency theory later in this chapter.

CANADIAN SOCIOLOGY

What we have presented to this point is little more than a catalogue of some of the issues and factors Canadian sociologists must consider to understand our society. By the beginning of the twentieth century, sociology was already well developed in the United States; however, S. D. Clark (1976:120) estimates that as late as 1958 there were probably only about 15 to 20 sociologists in the whole of Canada—five or six at the University of Toronto, about the same number at McGill, another five or six working alone at various universities across the country. Today, there are more than 600 sociologists teaching and working in Canada, in universities, community colleges and Government. At least a dozen universities offer Ph.D. degrees, and the majority offer M.A. degrees in sociology.

This increase is largely the result of importing academics from outside of Canada. And, importing talent from outside the country also means importing perspectives, approaches and concerns which come from abroad and which may or may not be relevant to the Canadian situation. S. D. Clark, who has been teaching sociology in Canada since the 1930s, has decided that:

A review of the history of the discipline of sociology in this country leads to the almost inescapable conclusion that what has developed here is not a Canadian sociology but a sociology that is American. Not only have Canadian universities recruited their sociology staffs largely from the United States, but also most of the Canadians we have had teaching sociology in this country have acquired their training across the border (Clark, 1976:132).

In its worst forms this has meant, at times, that sociologists have in their teaching taken all of their examples and illustrations from the United States so that students end up writing term papers about "our" Black Problem or the impact of Watergate on "our" political system and so forth.[14] The more subtle and contentious effect of this centres on a question we raised in Chapter III: What constitutes knowledge? Does a sociological principle found to be true in Boise, Idaho, necessarily have validity in Moncton, New Brunswick, or Haifa, Israel? Sociologists are deeply divided about this issue. Some would argue that scholarship knows no national boundaries, that like chemistry or biology, sociology will only become a science when its "laws" and generalizations are applicable to any society at any time. While we agree that this may be the ultimate goal of social science, we tend to follow C. Wright Mills's (1959) argument that sociological theories, to be useful, must also be historically and culturally specific. That is, we must always take into account the historical factors which have led to the present-day society. All of the sociologists whom we now think of as classical sociologists—Marx, Weber, Durkheim, Toennies—were intensely and passionately concerned with the nature and fate of their own societies. They were, in Robert Nisbet's (1967) words, "moral philosophers" who were desperately attempting to interpret and evaluate changes which they felt were occurring around them.

Whatever the reason, we have "inherited" an American sociology and that has generally meant functionalism, or what we call the system approach.

In Chapter I, we outlined some of the problems of functionalism. In addition, it has been criticized more specifically as inadequate for understanding Canadian society because it also assumes that there are common values *between* as well as *within* societies. Stolzman and Gamberg (1975:102), for instance, suggest that:

In the Canadian context functional theory easily translates into some form of the now familiar ideology of continentalism. In this view, Canada and the United States are by history and culture joined in a mutually beneficial arrangement that enables both countries to achieve high levels of industrial prosperity. Insofar as the United States is acknowledged to be slightly ahead in the developmental process, this is seen as a temporary advantage accruing to the senior partner as a result of any number of minor differences between societal neighbors of the same structural type. In short, the North American continent is depicted as a functionally interdependent whole founded upon a harmony of interests between its constituent parts. The possibility that the routine operation of the system works to the advantage of one unit and to the relative detriment of the other is alien to functional logic.[15]

Accordingly, recent years have seen a conscious effort to develop a critical Canadian sociology, grounded in our particular historical development as first a colony and then a nation in the shadow of a powerful empire. In this regard, two perspectives are of especial importance: the historical perspectives of Harold Innis and S. D. Clark, and the work of dependency theorists.

Historical Perspectives

Understanding of the structure and development of Canadian society has been largely left to historians, geographers and economists. What sociological work has been done on Canadian society has been strongly influenced by the writings and teachings of Harold A. Innis, who until his death in 1952 was head of the Department of Political Economy at the University of Toronto.[16] In a series of essays and books, Innis (1930; 1940; 1956) developed what is known as the "staples" approach to understanding the Canadian economy. Unlike Britain's, the United States' and advanced European economies, the Canadian economy, he argued, developed not from manufacturing but from the export of raw materials, staples, fish, fur, lumber, timber, mining products and now, of course, energy to successive imperialistic empires: France, Britain and finally the United States. The consequence of this was that the economic and therefore sociopolitical development of Canada was shaped and restricted by the interests of empires. We were, in other words, unable to transcend our historic status as "drawers of water," "hewers of wood," dispensers of raw or unfinished products. While export of these resources enriched and accelerated the economies of Britain and the United States, it did little to transform us into a producer of manufactured goods for the world economy. We could not and cannot (goes this argument) use the profits from selling resources to build an industrial society because we have had little control over where these funds go.

Without doubt, the major sociological spokesperson for a historical approach to understanding Canadian society is S. D. Clark, a former University of Toronto professor and one of the first and still best known sociologists in Canada. As a student and then colleague of Harold Innis at Toronto, Clark was obviously influenced by the "staples approach." But, as a sociologist, his work complements rather than extends the Innis tradition. That is, he is less concerned with economic factors, than with sociological issues such as religious sectarianism, protest movements and urban and rural poverty in Canada. For the most part, Clark is sympathetic to functionalism but has also recognized that in its bias towards order, equilibrium, consensus and integration, it is prone to charges of being conservative and seeming to maintain and uphold the *status quo*. Nevertheless, up until the 1960s functional theory was, in his view, a satisfactory way for Americans to study their own society. In part this was because functionalism fitted American assumptions about itself as a stable and consensual society. Partly, too, as Clark argues, American sociologists could take for granted their society.

The task of explaining how it had come into being could be left to the historian. The major concern of the social scientist was with how it worked (Clark, 1976:4).

According to Clark, Canada was never in this situation and was never a society which could simply take itself for granted; its very survival was and is problematic. Therefore, the present concern about national unity and identity has long historical roots which go back long before Confederation. Like John Porter and George Grant, Clark also recognizes the conservatism of Canadians, the emphasis on tradition, the lesser concern with progress and individualism, which link English and French Canadians and which set them apart from Americans and the American dream. Clark argues that it is precisely for this reason that we have remained rather "stodgy and backward," reluctant to give up traditional institutions. Conservatism, from the time of the Loyalists onwards, represented our main defence against assimilation and absorption into the American empire.

In particular, Clark argues that the Western frontier developed very differently in Canada than in the United States. We have, for instance, no equivalent mythology in Canada to the raw, lawless, anarchic West, the staple of thousands and thousands of American "Westerns." For Americans, the West was a safety valve, an escape from the confines of civilized society. In contrast, as Clark points out:

The claims to the interior of the [*Canadian*] *continent were staked not by advancing frontiersmen, acting on their own, but by advancing armies and police forces, large corporate economic enterprises and ecclesiastical organizations, supported by the State (Clark, 1968:214).*

In part, of course, this was simply because Western Canada, the "North-West," was a far less hospitable place to escape to. One could not, as Huck Finn decided, avoid the confines of civilization by simply "lighting out for the territory." From the fur trade onwards, some rudimentary organization was essential if people were to survive Canadian winters and Canadian wilderness. More crucial, however, was that both Eastern and Western Canada, in turn, were not regarded as places to settle, but places to exploit. As Ralph Matthews observes about Newfoundland, "although tens of thousands of fishermen came annually to fish Newfoundland's waters, almost none chose to settle" (Matthews, 1976:13). Similarly, at times, "settlement interfered with rather than furthered the interests of the fisheries, the fur trade, and later the timber industry" (Clark, 1976:56). Thus, rather than groups of people going out to Western Canada, it was the Hudson's Bay Company and what became the Royal Mounted Police which, as it were, set the scene. Later, it was the CPR and the CNR.

In other words, Canada was a hard frontier in which resources, whether fish or furs or lumber, were hard to get at.

What was called for in the opening up of this Northern half of the continent were massive accumulations of capital, large scale forms of economic organization, long lines of communication and transportation, and extensive state support (Clark, 1976:55).

People, then, were never freed entirely from the bureaucratic and legal controls of Eastern Canada; seldom did law and order have to be created on the spot as in the American West. As Clark points out, this control—though somewhat less effectively—extended even into the disorderly and disorganized "Gold Rush" societies of the Yukon and Klondike. The result was to bring about law and order more quickly than in Alaska where there was no equivalent of the federally-backed North West Mounted Police (Clark, 1968:97).

When settlement did occur, it was still controlled by political and economic interests in Eastern Canada. As Porter (1965) notes, this meant that "less favoured" immigrants to Canada, particularly Ukrainians, were given less favourable land in the northern parts of the Prairie Provinces; the better land was saved for British and Northern European immigrants (p. 68). Certainly, as a trip across Western Canada will reveal, the stamp of bureaucracy, of central control, is evident even in the placement of towns. Since most were created after the coming of the railroads, they are spaced along the track roughly every 9 miles (Robertson, 1973). Roads, too, are set out in grid-like fashion every two miles (north and south), every mile (east and west). Also, sections of every township in Alberta (for instance) were initially Hudson Bay or CPR land, and are still labelled as such by farmers who now own them. Finally, it is also of some consequence that, unlike Texas and Oklahoma, the oil boom in Alberta did not create instant millionaires out of farmers who had oil on their land. Rather, shortly after its creation as a province the Alberta government "bought up" mineral rights from existing farmers and did not give them out later with homesteaded land. Alberta has obviously benefitted collectively from oil. Individuals who have an oil well on their land, however, receive only a small payment for right of entry and rental of three or four acres of land, enough, perhaps, to pay the taxes for the quarter section of land. We can speculate, at least, that these policies had a strong influence on the way capitalism developed in Western Canada.[17]

Criticisms of Clark's work have come mainly from Marxist sociologists. Without necessarily denying his contribution to Canadian society, they argue that while influenced by Harold Innis, he (and others at the University of Toronto) ignored or underplayed the themes of nationality and imperialism which are at the core of the Innis tradition (Drache, 1976:10). Thus, while Clark sees Canada as subject to a great deal of influence by the United States, he does not view this as systematic domination (Stolzman and Gamberg, 1975). It can also be argued that though espousing a historical perspective, he nevertheless maintains an essentially functionalist perspective. In fact, he chooses to treat changes as episodic, as a series of events not necessarily tied together (lacking a systematic theory) such as Marxian theory would have provided (Watson, 1975:357).

While Marxist sociologists have often been critical of Clark's approach and assumptions, others argue that he has provided us with a good empirical, perhaps theoretical, starting point on which to build a relevant Canadian sociology (Felt, 1975). In addition to this, Clark has made two general contributions. First, he has consistently avoided the pitfalls of "abstracted empiricism," the study of particular institutions or social phenomena as if they existed in a social, cultural and economic vacuum. In other words, Clark's sociology is essentially holistic: he shows that to understand a particular aspect of a society, one must also understand the total society and the relationship of the parts to the whole. Clark's second contribution lies in his emphasis on doing historically informed sociology. This, of course, stands in marked contrast to the ahistorical orientation of functionalism which for several decades dominated Canadian as well as American sociology.

The development of a Canadian sociology is not, then, as the Symons Report implies, simply a matter of teaching more Canadian content and putting more Canadian illustrations into American models and frameworks. Rather, as some have argued, we have to go further than Clark and bring about "a thoroughgoing intellectual revolt against imported modes of American sociology, a revolt that would tail, parallel or perhaps even guide the struggle for full national independence" (Stolzman and Gamberg, 1975:99). Although this task is far from complete, many believe that the most promising approach is that provided by a Marxist-oriented dependency theory, what Laxer (1973) calls "the political economy of dependency." An important aspect of this theory is the metropolis-hinterland perspective.

METROPOLIS AND HINTERLAND

As an alternative to functionalism, Davis (1971) has argued that an appropriate perspective for understanding Canadian society is the metropolis-hinterland perspective, developed originally by Innis, Lower (1964) and others.[18] Hinterland refers to relatively underdeveloped or colonial areas which provide raw materials or semi-processed goods, and sometimes people, to relatively developed centres of economic and political control—cities, regions, nations. Since the metropolis both dominates and exploits its hinterland, conflict is at least inherent in the relationship between the two. Davis points out that conflict may, for a considerable time, be latent. Nevertheless, there is "a tendency on the part of hinterland groups and interests to fight back eventually against their metropolitan exploiters in order to gain a larger place in the regional or national or international sun" (p. 13). For this reason, the metropolis-hinterland perspective fits within the conflict approach.

Davis suggests that to understand Canadian society both internally and in relationship to the rest of North America and the world, it is necessary to think of a hierarchy of metropolis-hinterland relationships which, like Chinese boxes, nestle one inside another. For example, during the fur trade era, the Northwest was a hinterland of Montreal. But, Montreal and, in turn, the whole of Canada was a hinterland dominated by Paris and then London. Today, what Maritimers still refer to as Upper Canada and Westerners simply as "Down East"—Southern Ontario—is a metropolis for both. Subjective impressions of hinterland-metropolis also vary. For example, though Albertans may view Quebec as part of the metropolis, Quebeckers in turn have reason to view their society as a hinterland under the thumb of English Canada. Both objectively and subjectively, when we widen our focus, Canada can be seen as a hinterland of the United States, Toronto and Montreal as intermediaries in this large metropolis-hinterland nexus.

Single Industry Towns

Perhaps the archetypal case of hinterland-metropolis conflict is provided by studies of one-industry towns.[19] While most of us think of social change in Canada in terms of larger and larger urban conglomerations, Canadian industrial expansion has depended, in great part, on the proliferation of small isolated towns created to extract resources. As resources are being exploited, corporations have had to move increasingly farther away from the metropolis. The towns that have been created share three features: they are small, they are isolated and they are dependent. They therefore share many features with other communities in the North of Canada and in the wilderness areas of Newfoundland and British Columbia. Similarly, many Canadians, in fact about half the population, should be familiar with the features of small-town life in these communities; more Canadians than we typically imagine live in communities of less than 30,000 (Himelfarb, 1977).

A central fact of life in single industry towns is dependency. The residents are dependent on a sole employer and on the often unrenewable resource being exploited. The community as a whole is dependent on decisions made at corporate headquarters in the metropolis, often a foreign metropolis. Decisions crucial to the life of the community are then often made by people far removed from that community. Not surprisingly, the residents can be characterized as resigned and fatalistic—feelings of powerlessness prevail. Nor do the residents know whom to blame; there seems to be little class consciousness and most residents seem to share the feeling that the company, its managers and employees and the rest of the community are in the same boat, all dependent on vast and impersonal forces over which they have no control. This may, in part, result from the fact that the decision-making processes are remote and invisible. The workers only see the consequences of the decisions, never the decision-making process or even the offices in which decisions are made.[20]

Lucas (1971), influenced by functionalism, seems to portray these communities and their culture and structure as an inevitable outcome of Canada's industrialization and unique geography. Indeed, Australia with a similar set of geographical hurdles has similar communities with similar problems (UNESCO, 1974). However, more recent theorists have tended to view the problems of one-industry towns as the inevitable outcome of the exploitation of the hinterland by the metropolis;[21] as political events in Australia in the past decade show, Canada and Australia must both deal with dependency as well as aspects of geography.

DEPENDENCY PERSPECTIVES

More recently, a number of young Marxists have been dissatisfied with the extent to which the metropolis-hinterland perspective catches the essence of conflict and exploitation in Canada. Dependency theory has been developed mainly by economists, economic historians and political scientists.[22] For dependency theorists, the critical issues are twofold. First, we live in a liberal democratic society which not only upholds the concept of private property but which enjoins the State to create a climate favourable for capitalism to flourish. Second, and here is where the concept of dependency enters the picture, Canada has from its conception been a colony, a dependent society and economy, first of France, then of Britain. Now it is an economic satellite, in effect a colony, of the United States. As Laxer (1973:6) puts it, "Canada is a dependency moving towards colonial status in the American empire," thereby echoing Innis's earlier conclusion that we have gone from colony to nation to colony. Thus dependency theorists draw upon both Marxist perspectives and the staples approach of Harold Innis and his students.

Dependency theory departs from Clark's historical perspective both in emphasis and in its basic theoretical orientation. In general, Canada's development is not seen simply as the result of a unique geography and climate or of a series of unrelated events, but as the systematic outcome of imperialism and economic domination and exploitation by a succession of metropolises acting in their own economic interests. While, like Clark, Innis's staples approach provides valuable clues as to how to go about understanding Canada, dependency theorists have increasingly looked to Marxist writers such as André Gunder Frank for the appropriate analytical tools. Frank's (1967 and 1969) work on Latin America has led him to the conclusion that

> *. . . underdevelopment is not due to the survival of archaic institutions and the existence of capital shortages in regions that have remained isolated from the stream of world history. On the contrary, underdevelopment was and still is generated by the very same historical process which also generated economic development: the development of capitalism itself (1969:9).*

Frank, therefore, shares with other Marxist thinkers the view that the nature of economic, political, social and cultural institutions in underdeveloped countries (hinterlands) must be as much the outcome of capitalism as are those of developed societies, the metropolises which dominate them. This means that underdevelopment will not simply "go away" and Third World countries will not simply "evolve over time." Nor can they simply incorporate or assimilate into their cultures the skill, knowledge, values and technology which made the imperialist nations economically successful; it is not simply a process of catching up. Rather, according to Frank, policies which will be effective in creating economic development and cultural change will be those which are politically revolutionary, which, in other words, involve the destruction of capitalism in these societies and its replacement with another system, one based on socialism (1969:78).[23]

Canada is not, of course, Chile or Argentina. Nevertheless, dependency theorists find in the Canadian situation a number of parallels and are led to very similar conclusions about the kinds of options available to Canadians if they wish to "win back" control of their economy and culture.[24] First, as we have already seen, the main lines of our economy and social institutions were moulded by the fact that Canada from the outset was a hinterland, a place to extract staples—partially finished raw materials for manufacturers in Britain and the United States. We have remained, goes the argument, a branch plant economy, arrested in our development because it was and is in the interest of a succession of metropolises that we should remain so.

This is the argument presented in Naylor's (1972) work on the emergence of capitalism in Central Canada. Capitalism, in Canada, he argues, was never an independent development but was always lock-stepped into the context of colonialism and dependency. This meant, in particular, that Canadian businessmen did not, for the most part, become involved in manufacturing or resource extraction but instead confined themselves to mercantilism and finance. Where the elite did venture into manufacturing, they were willing and eager to sell out to American interests, to replace control with comprador elite status.[25] As Mel Watkins (1973:257) puts it, "the Canadian capitalist class is a financial bourgeoisie which did not control industrial production in Canada. Hence, bankers are the most powerful section of the Canadian bourgeoisie. They make money financing the foreign take-over of Canada."[26]

Naylor, then, like other dependency theorists, is arguing that the degree and pattern of development in the hinterland is directly and indirectly conditioned by, dependent on, what is occurring in the metropolis. Internal changes in the class structure, capital accumulation and rate of expansion in the metropolis are "the immediate cause of socio-economic reorganization in the hinterland." One consequence is arrested economic development. Another may be actual de-industrialization.

De-industrialization

One of the more important theses of dependency theory is that Canada, as a hinterland economy, is being systematically de-industrialized. Robert Laxer (1973:9) holds that "de-industrialization is the most important result to Canada of integration in the American Empire." Imperialism, or in the American lexicon, "continentalism," not only keeps the hinterland in a state of underdevelopment, but may, at times, also result in an absolute decline in manufacturing. Such is likely to be the case when economic conditions in the metropolis begin to deteriorate. To save jobs in the metropolis, branch plants in the hinterland are closed down or allowed to have excess productive capacity.

> *The drive to de-industrialize Canada is not only a strategic aim of U.S. government policy as it tries to solve the crisis of over-production, now aggravated by its inter-imperialist rivalries with Japan and Western Europe. Such a policy to shift manufacturing and jobs to the U.S. has received official support from the top leadership of American labour (Laxer, 1973:9).*

As we shall see later, evidence to support the de-industrialization thesis for Canada as a whole is slim and somewhat elusive. One problem is that when we speak of Canada as an industrialized society we are really speaking about that part of Canada linked by the MacDonald-Cartier Freeway—Windsor to Montreal. The rest, as Clement (1977:296) points out, is better described as a resource hinterland. This, he suggests, is at least partially the outcome of these hinterland regions being tied to the economies of national and international metropolises. Acheson (1977) has provided impressive historical evidence that within the nation, metropolis-hinterland relations can work to the detriment of the hinterland and can bring about de-industrialization.

According to his research, prior to Confederation Nova Scotia and New Brunswick had a flourishing and growing industrial base. But, after the Maritimes joined into Confederation with Upper and Lower Canada, Central Canadian businessmen bought out many of these businesses and systematically shut them down in order to reduce competition with their Ontario firms. This was made possible, perhaps augmented, by policies of the federal government, especially with respect to tariffs and freight rates. Gradually, suggests Acheson, the Maritimes have been driven into a condition of dependency and now have an economy reliant upon federal transfer payments. Alexander (1977) makes a similar argument in describing the disastrous results of Confederation for the Newfoundland fish industry.

In effect, the culture of the Mother country, of the metropolis, rides in "on the coat-tails" of economic invasion and take-over. It acts both to legitimate economic domination and to "soften" the hinterland for further rounds of exploitation. Typically, the ideas and the culture of the metropolis take precedence over those of the hinterland and become, in effect, the standards of excellence by which members of the dependent society come to judge themselves. The result, as we have seen, is a kind of collective "inferiority complex" in which we debase as second rate our own cultural productions and literally believe that those of the metropolis are inherently superior. Mathews suggests that this process has been hastened by the acceptance in Canada of the liberal ideology in both its British and American versions:

> *It [the liberal ideology] insists that the ideas of mobility put forward by the imperial centre are "progressive." To resist those ideas is "reactionary." It insists that all history is going in one direction, led by the imperial centre. Inasmuch as the colonial country is like the imperial country it is "advanced." Inasmuch as it is different, it is "underdeveloped." It insists that ideas created for and propagated from the imperial centre are ideas of universal interest and importance. Inasmuch as the colonial country permits those ideas to be superimposed, and permits them to be superimposed by immigrants from the imperial country, the country is "liberal." Inasmuch as it insists upon the integrity of its own ideas and people, it is, of course, "chauvinistic," "narrowly nationalistic," "navel gazing" and so on (Mathews, 1973:219).*

It is in this context, then, that we can best appreciate George Grant's (1965) concern over the demise of Canadian conservatism. Nationalism, the attempt to recover control of our economy and of our culture, is antithetical to the American liberal ideology. It simply becomes translated as racism or facism. The reason seems fairly clear. Nationalism, especially when accompanied by socialism, is a significant example of the hinterland fighting back. It threatens, as in Chile, the continuing freedom of multi-nationals to do as they like in the hinterland economy. Thus, even cultural concerns, in and of themselves "harmless," may, if left unchecked, become motivating forces, well-springs of social action and conflict in the economic sphere as well.

Dependency theory, then, leads to the pessimistic conclusion that our ability to shape an independent culture and national identity is limited. It is not simply that we are perverse and ambivalent. Rather, fundamental cultural development cannot occur without fundamental change in our economic structure. We cannot, as it were, simply pull ourselves up by our intellectual and cultural bootstraps and create a distinctive national identity while, at the same time, remaining an economic satellite of the United States. It follows, too, that we cannot, as Porter (1965) hoped, simply institute policies to end pluralistic conflict and increase equality of educational opportunity—in a word, "catch-up"—unless basic structures of dependency are first eradicated. In a nutshell, this is also the major dilemma facing Quebec: will separatism without socialism do more than make Quebec society even more vulnerable to outside economic and cultural domination (Milner and Milner, 1973)?

Critiques

Several of the basic assumptions of dependency theory have been challenged. In particular, Moore and Wells (1975) argue that the thesis of de-industrialization in Canada is largely "myth." They present statistics which show that Canada is not unique. Rather, the decline in manufacturing in Canada is part of an international trend, a trend which reduces the relative importance of manufacturing as a percentage of the Gross Domestic Product. While Canada has shown a marked decrease in the percentage of manufacturing, the same can be said of the United States, Britain, France and Sweden. In absolute terms, manufacturing has increased but not as fast as the super-growth in the public and private service sector. In short, according to Moore and Wells (1977:40), "Canada compares well with other countries in rate of growth of manufacturing labour productivity."

A second issue (also raised by Moore and Wells) centres on where exactly Canada fits in the system of world capitalism. Saul and Heron (1977:10), for instance, note that

. . . the reality of the powerful American grip on the Canadian economy and culture seems to make us look a lot like a dependency. Yet, at the same time, we lack the most obvious attributes of underdevelopment, and possess classes and a state which resemble those of the most advanced capitalist nations and which participate eagerly in various "central" schemes designed to further subordinate the "Third World."

Thus, it appears that Canada is in the paradoxical position of being both things at once, a kind of "hybrid" or incomplete form of capitalism, what Daniel Drache (1977:16) calls "advanced resource capitalism." Some theorists have suggested that dependency theory has given insufficient attention to the intricacies of world capitalism largely because of its focus on the exchange relationship between two nations rather than on production relations which transcend national boundaries (Friedman and Wayne, 1977).[27]

Clearly, the analysis of Canada's position in world capitalism is far from complete. Nor do we fully understand the role of Canada's economic elite. However, Clement's recent study (1977; 1977a) of multi-national corporations in Canada suggests that there is enough variation, enough complexity, for both the dependency theorists and their critics to be "right." His research suggests that there is both an indigenous elite *and* a comprador elite. The former has, in effect, appropriated a "turf"—finance, transportation and utilities. The *dominant comprador* elite, on the other hand, is "active in manufacturing and resources, is both national and international, and is located in branch plants of foreign-controlled multinationals" (1977a:25) because each has "staked out" different sectors of the economy; Canada is partly foreign controlled, partly Canadian controlled. There is, nevertheless, interdependence between the two.

The upshot is that the power of Canadians to make decisions about specific economic activities in Canada has regressed to a state of underdevelopment of economic well-being, with control over future development and stability lost because of the lack of an indigenously controlled base in manufacturing and resources. In the overdeveloped finance, transportation and utilities sectors . . . the dominant indigenous capitalists now in control still remain powerful components of the total class. In other words, the process of compradorization has been sector specific and took place in the presence of traditionally powerful capitalists rather than displacing them. The effect on weak capitalists in production was, of course, to bring about their downfall (1977a:293).

Finally, while intuitively there seems little doubt that Canadian culture has been heavily influenced by American culture, some have questioned how different we would be if we were not economically dependent on the United States, how in a scientific way we could prove the assertions of the neo-colonialist or dependency perspective. Archibald (1978:243), for instance, points out that:

We know that Canadians have had a higher rate of

job turnover but we can hardly jump to the conclusion that American ownership of industries in Canada necessarily makes jobs more alienating. (It is conceivable that a more rapidly expanding economy provides Canadians with more job opportunities.) We know that Canadian politicians make, and certainly, administrate, policy decisions with much greater concern for the reactions of Washington than vice versa, but it is unclear that these decisions would be very much more in the "general public's" interest without this concern. We know that Canadians take out more life insurance, but we don't know that foreign control of their life chances is the source of the difference.

CONCLUSION

Clearly, the debate about Canadian unity and Canada's dependency is far from resolution or conclusion. No one could deny the significance—economically, culturally and politically—for Canada of living next door to the most powerful nation on earth. But, we agree with Archibald that there is little to be gained in viewing everything that occurs in Canada as the fault of the United States. Victims we may be, but in the very fact of recognizing that condition and in beginning to understand the extent of our dependency, we go part way towards the development of a new and stronger national character and identity. In other words, materialistic forces shape and constrain us and set parameters to what we can do and be. But we must also keep in mind that ideas are also powerful forces which in the Canadian context may already have taken us beyond "Survival."

Canada has unique historical, climatic and geographical features which have clearly contributed to the shaping of Canadian society. While we believe that dependency theory offers the most promising perspective within which to view Canadian social structure, the subject of remaining chapters, no single perspective or level of analysis can account for the shape and direction of Canada or any other society, for that matter. We have said little about Quebec society and Quebec's quest for identity and self-realization (though we do say more in Chapter X). This is partly because of the complexity of the question and partly because of the questions still hanging in the balance. There are two sociologies in Canada, English Canadian and Québecois, and clearly the latter provides the best source for understanding Quebec society.

In the following chapters, we view Canadian society from the general perspective of power and inequality. But we do so largely from the viewpoint of Canada as an independent, capitalistic and industrialized society, similar in its broad outlines to other western liberal democracies and in some respects similar to industrialized societies of the communist world. However, students should recognize that, as we have tried to show in this chapter, Canada is in many ways unique both in its development and in its place in the world capitalist system. How unique and how much the obvious facts of dependency have affected our development, our social structure, our culture and our identity is, at this time, still open to investigation and to empirical question.

SUGGESTIONS FOR FURTHER READING

While much sophisticated work has been done in the area of demography and particularly in refining statistical measures, a useful general introduction is Dennis Wrong's *Population and Society* (1976). In addition to the books by Kalbach and McVey (1971; revised in 1979) and Kubat and Thornton (1974) mentioned in this chapter, other useful sources for Canadian demographic data include: *Perspectives Canada II* (1977) published by Statistics Canada; Lewis Auerbach's and Andrea Gerber's *Implications of the Changing Age Structure of the Canadian Population* (1976); and Michael Barrett's and Chris Taylor's *Population and Canada* (1977).

Some of the best discussions of Canadian political culture can be found in various issues of *Canadian Dimension* and *Canadian Forum* and, of course, the *Canadian*

Journal of Political Science. The historian Louis Hartz provides a provocative account of the origins of Canadian political ideologies in his *The Founding of New Societies* (1964). S. F. Wise, also a historian, takes up some of the issues raised by Hartz in two articles reprinted in S. F. Wise's and Robert Craig Braun's *Canada Views the United States, Nineteenth Century Political Attitudes* (1967).

With the advent of the "Quiet Revolution" in the 1960s and the recent victory of the Parti Québecois, studies of Quebec have taken on a new urgency. Some of the more important works include: Marcel Rioux's *Quebec in Question* (1971); Pierre Vallière's, *White Niggers of America* (1971); R. N. Morris's and C. M. Lanphier's *The Three Scales of Inequality: Perspectives on French-English Relations* (1977); Gérard Pelletier's *The October Crisis;* Dale Posgate's and Kenneth McRobert's *Quebec: Social Change and Political Crisis* (1976); Pierre Elliott Trudeau's *Federalism and the French Canadians* (1968); and, obviously, from a different perspective, René Lévesque's *An Option for Quebec* (1968). Some useful recent collections include D. C. Thomson's *Quebec Society and Politics* (1973); Dimitrios Roussopoulos, *Quebec and Radical Social Change* (1973); and G. L. Gold's and M. A. Tremblay's *Communities and Culture in French Canada* (1973). Papers from a major conference looking at the implications of separation for English Canada have been published by the University of Toronto in a collection called *Options* (1977).

S. D. Clark's brief *Canadian Society in Historical Perspective* (1976) is a useful introduction to his own contribution to Canadian society and to the development of Canadian sociology more generally. Harry Hiller's *Canadian Society: A Sociological Analysis* (1976) describes dominant perspectives which have been used to understand Canadian society. Major statements of dependency theory have appeared in a succession of edited collections of papers, themselves the outcome of a number of seminars and conferences held over the last decade. In order of appearance, these are Ian Lumsden's *Close the 49th Parallel, etc.* (1970); Gary Teeple's *Capitalism and the National Question in Canada* (1972); Robert M. Laxer's *Canada Ltd.: The Political Economy of Dependency* (1973); and John Saul's and Craig Heron's *Imperialism, Nationalism and Canada* (1977).

More general introductions to Canadian sociology and Canadian society include: Dennis Forcese's and Stephen Richer's *Issues in Canadian Society: An Introduction to Sociology* (1975); Steward Crysdale's and Christopher Beattie's *Sociology Canada: An Introductory Text,* 2nd ed. (1977); and G. N. Ramu's and Stuart D. Johnson's *Introduction to Canadian Society: Sociological Analysis* (1976).

FOOTNOTES

[1]Though we do not have the oldest census in the world, the Canadian Government has been conducting regular decennial censuses since 1851. From a sociological point of view, it is probably one of the most extensive censuses.

[2]Most contemporary demographers use more sophisticated measures than crude birth and death rates, for example, age-adjusted death rates and infant and perinatal mortality rates. For definitions, see *Perspective Canada II* (Canada, 1977).

[3]Strictly speaking, compound interest (interest on the principal *and* on the accumulated interest) is an example of geometrical growth. This is because interest is calculated annually or semi-annually. Exponential growth depicts continuous compounding, a better approximation of actual changes in population. Doubling times, of course, depend on the growth rate.

[4]Many sociologists believe it has something to do with changing labour force demands, for example, as we describe later in this chapter, the massive movement from farming.

[5]Frank, whom we discuss later in this chapter, has discussed these and other positions on social change and development in an essay entitled "Sociology of Development and Underdevelopment of Sociology" (Frank, 1969:21-94).

[6]For a detailed description and discussion of Canada's demographic transition, see Marsden and Harvey (1979).

[7]This is why emigration in Table VII.2 is given as an estimate. Demographers calculate the rate of emigration by what is known as the "residual method." That is, to calculate emigration from Canada between (say) two census periods, we need two populations plus statistics on birth, deaths and immigration. A variation of the basic demographic equation provides an estimate of emigration:

Emigration = P_1 + (Births − Deaths) + Immigration − P_2

Clearly, emigration is only an estimate because none of these statistics has ever been totally complete. Especially for earlier decades, emigration, then, was an educated guess based on assumptions about births, deaths and immigration. For recent decades, estimates of emigration are probably much more accurate.

[8]For census purposes, "urban" means incorporated towns, cities and villages and unincorporated places and built-up fringes with a minimum population of 1000 and a population density of at least 1000 per square mile. "Rural" includes all the remaining non-urban population (Gerther and Crowley, 1977:70). Obviously, these definitions do not always capture what sociologists mean by an urban and a rural way of life.

[9]For a detailed analysis of the concept of post-industrial society, see Bell (1973). An important critique of the post-industrial thesis is Johnson (1977). For an empirically-based critique of this concept, see Hamilton and Wright (1975).

[10]An important aspect of the Armstrong study is that women are not only segregated, they are also slotted into occupations characterized by low pay, low skill requirements and low prospects for advancement. We will return to this in the next chapter when we consider sexual inequality.

[11]As Gad Horowitz (1965) puts it, Porter, a sociologist, essentially gave up the notion of equality of condition for the goal of equality of opportunity (see Chapter VIII).

[12]We appreciate that this and what follows do not fit very well with conventional or popular notions of these political positions and may be confusing. One source of confusion is that a number of things which were conservative policies in the nineteenth century are now tenets of the Liberal party. Another is that as capitalism has grown, so has the perspective of the Liberal party. What it was championing in the nineteenth century—the individualism of small entrepreneurs—has, in this century, become a conservative cause. To add to the confusion, we might add that Archie Bunker espouses a kind of bastardized conservatism, what many refer to as "Red Neck Conservatism."

[13]Panitch recognizes that this relationship is even more complex than what we have described here and gives a fuller discussion in his long essay on the State in Canada.

[14]Not too long ago, a Canadian history textbook was published with a picture of Abraham Lincoln on the cover. The most comprehensive study of Canadian studies is Symons's *To Know Ourselves* (1975), in paperback known simply as *The Symons Report.* Two very insightful and informative reviews of this report, by Stephen Clarkson and by John Woods, can be found in the November 1976 issue of the *Journal of Canadian Studies.* For recent discussion about Canadian sociology, see Felt (1975) and Stolzman and Gamberg (1975). In addition to Clark (1976), Tepperman (forthcoming) describes the state of Canadian sociology in the last five years.

[15]That there is much greater sensitivity to American "provincialism" is suggested by the fact that Washington no longer speaks about a Continental Energy Policy as it was in the habit of doing in the past.

[16]Sociology, until the early 1960s, was part of this department at the University of Toronto.

[17]As Clark admits, readily, the West did not totally escape the lawlessness and disorder which characterized the American frontier. This is shown by the high rates of crime and divorce, possible indicators of a higher degree of anomie in the West than in the East (Cohn, 1976).

[18]Warnock (1974) provides a historical account of the metropolis-hinterland perspective in Canadian writing.

[19]Lucas's (1971) *Minetown, Milltown, Railtown* is a comprehensive examination of these communities.

[20]Some of these same processes are described in Matthews's (1976) study of relocation of people from Newfoundland outposts.

[21]A number of planners have argued that one-industry towns need not be an inevitable outcome of industrialization, that there are, in fact, alternatives (Himelfarb, 1977).

[22]Some are, of course, sociologists, who claim as their field of expertise and specialization political sociology, historical sociology and Marxist (or critical) sociology.

[23]It is probably for this reason that Frank has, on various occasions, been refused visas to speak in the United States and, more recently, in Canada. A conference at Queen's University in March 1977 was cancelled because Frank, the keynote speaker, was refused admittance to Canada.

[24]In 1969 a group within the NDP party known as the Waffle Group presented a Manifesto calling for an independent socialist Canada. At the Winnipeg conference, the Waffle Manifesto received 36% of the votes cast. However, in 1972, the Waffle Group was formally expelled from the party because its alternatives were seen as too radical and too opposed to the dominant ideology of the NDP party and its aim to remain, like the liberal party, pragmatic.

[25]According to Clement (1975:119), the term "comprador" comes from an analysis of China in the

1850s. Compradors were used by foreign powers as mediators between themselves and the Imperial System. In Canada, "comprador elites are top ranking managers and directors of branch plants who follow directives and policies of multinational headquarters."

[26]This position has, however, been criticized by MacDonald (1975) in an article entitled "Merchants Against Industry."

[27]For some insights into Canada's place in world capitalism, see Daniel Chirot's *Social Change in the Twentieth Century* (1977).

social stratification
CHAPTER VIII

Few sociological topics have been of such abiding and pervasive concern as those relating to the general problem of social inequality. The personal and social consequences of poverty and racial and sexual discrimination are vivid reminders of what we have already seen in earlier chapters: that while social reality is built up by people and can, in principle, be "reconstructed" or changed, society often confronts us in ways that make it seem objective and unchangeable. Inequalities are key "facts" of social life. They set out the parameters to our structures of opportunities; they constrain us and limit what we might be and do.

The study of social inequality suggests, too, that it would be very useful indeed if we could "choose" our parents, our sexual role and our race or ethnicity. Of course, we cannot. They are what sociologists refer to as *ascribed* statuses. Our sexual role is biologically and socially determined; we inherit the ethnicity of our parents; we are born into families holding more or less favourable positions with respect to wealth, prestige and influence.

Yet, despite their not being of our choosing, these ascribed characteristics have important social, economic and personal consequences for us. For an Indian or Métis, for example, "racial" inequality means to be born poor and to face limited opportunities to improve that condition. It may mean, also, that relative to white Canadians, his life is shorter and more unhealthy. To grow up in poverty, whatever one's ethnic or racial background, may be to face narrowed horizons and to have one's imagination, curiosity and talents systematically blunted. It is, also, to know, at first hand, powerlessness and humiliation, the price paid by those who must deal with and depend upon the welfare system of our country. To be a woman is to learn that some jobs are officially or unofficially male jobs; that men often receive more pay for the same work; that women are "not taken seriously" or are regarded as inherently incompetent to do "man's" work.

Even those "lucky enough" to be born male, white and with the proverbial silver spoon in mouth are constrained by the social fact of inequality. To maintain our advantageous position we may have to believe and behave in *bad faith;* that is, to "pretend something is necessary that in fact is voluntary" (Berger, 1963:143). Bad faith, in other words, is to believe in our own ideologies, the "film of lies" by which we maintain and rationalize our secure or privileged positions. To accept the privilege and power of being white in a racist society, then, may be to believe in racial superiority—to hold, in effect, beliefs which fly in the face of scientific evidence and humanistic values. To be male and to conform to the norms of a sexist society is another example of bad faith. It is also to deny oneself the pleasures and pains of child rearing and the range of emotional responses humanly possible but forbidden by traditional stereotypes of masculinity. In other words, while the injustices which flow from being labelled or defined as "inferior" are fairly obvious ones, it should be remembered that there are also costs attached to advantaged positions.

In the preceding chapter we examined Canada as a dependent society subject to imperialism. But, we also pointed out that Canada is internally stratified, an unequal society perhaps not very different from other industrial societies. This chapter is mainly concerned with various general theories about the origin and maintenance of structured inequality and of social stratification. Indeed, for most sociologists, to understand the system of stratification of any society is to understand its social structure, and when sociologists classify societies they do so on the basis of their particular form of stratification, their system of patterned inequality.

As we have seen, sociology emerged out of the tumult and unrest of eighteenth century France. Sociologists and social philosophers had to come to grips with the fact that the two revolutions, the French Revolution and the Industrial Revolution, were undermining what had for centuries been taken for granted—that some people, by virtue of birth, were entitled to more power, more wealth, more deference than others. Sociology, then, emerged at the point in history when hereditary aristocracies could no longer be tolerated. But what was to replace them? If the mere fact of being born to wealth and privilege was no longer viewed as just, what then was social justice? This, more than any other question, continues to plague us and remains central to the sociological tradition.

In the nineteenth century, in France, Britain, the United States, indeed anywhere that capitalism took root, the dominant answer was that provided by liberalism. Essentially, liberals argued that traditional forms of inequality could no longer be tolerated, not because there was so much disparity between lord and serf, but because hereditary aristocracies impeded progress and allowed no place at the top for the new class of industrialists or capitalists. In the eighteenth and nineteenth centuries, America was viewed as a Utopia, not because everyone was happy or affluent—of course, they were not—but because it was a new society which had no aristocracy to impede the upward movement of the ambitious and ruthless "Robber Barons," the new aristocracy of capitalism. In short, the liberal answer to traditional forms of inequality was not to do away with inequality but to change its basis.

As a kind of counterpoint to the liberal ideology and its emphasis on equality of opportunity, there have developed two other perspectives. One is conservatism which, as we have seen, was concerned with the costs for the social fabric and social order of eradicating traditional forms of inequality. For conservatives, the main thing is stability and order; the fact that some ambitious people are denied upward mobility or that many people live in squalor and privation is a small price to pay for avoiding chaos and anomie. The second counterpoint to liberalism is, of course, socialism, especially, though not exclusively, as embodied in the work of Karl Marx. Socialists are not, as are liberals, concerned with who should have more than others but with why there should be inequalities between people at all. Whereas liberals are concerned with *inequality of opportunity*, socialists are mainly concerned with *inequality of condition*.

EQUALITY OF CONDITION

Those who advocate equality of condition question whether there should be social inequalities between people at all. Why, it is asked, should some people receive more money and social benefits than do others? Equality of condition does not necessarily mean that everyone gets exactly the same amount as everyone else. If in a family, for instance, all receive equal portions of dessert, then there is *absolute* equality between the members. In practice, however, equality is likely to be seen in relative terms. It may be that teenagers in the family are thought to "need" more food, including dessert, than do adults. Small children may be believed to have a greater "desire" for dessert. Merit often enters the picture as well. People may be expected to live up to certain norms, such as cleaning up their plate. Not as much may be expected from small children as from older children.

Even in a family, norms about what is a "fair" or "just" distribution of valued and scarce resources are involved. Lenski (1966) suggests that only in simple hunting and gathering societies, existing at a subsistence level, is there likely to be absolute equality of condition. In such societies, *need* for some minimal amount of food, clothing and shelter results in an equal sharing of what is brought into the tribe. He points out, however, that while economic goods are distributed equally in such societies, prestige (social honour) and power are not. Less able members reward the more skilled member with prestige and influence in exchange for a share in the game he kills (Lenski, 1966:104-105).

Societies at or near a subsistence level have little choice about equality of condition; they must share to survive. However, communal societies such as the *kibbutzim* of Israel or the Hutterites of Western Canada have made conscious efforts to put into practice egalitarian and socialistic philosophies.[1] Property in these societies is held in common, distribution of goods is based on need and everyone is expected to contribute, to the best of their ability, to the work of the community. The various accounts of these communal societies suggest that they have come very close to realizing a socialist version of the just society; one in which each contributes according to his ability and receives according to his needs. While there are differences, certainly, in social honour and influence, these do not appear to be very pronounced.

Generally, it appears that the price to be paid for an egalitarian society is the foregoing of industrialization on any very elaborate scale. Nevertheless, contemporary industrial societies, though far from egalitarian, differ considerably in the amount of inequality which they are prepared to tolerate. Communist and socialist states, such as China and Sweden, for instance, believe that equality of condition is both a desirable and, ultimately, an achievable goal. In Canada and the United States, attempts to redistribute income through progressive taxation and guaranteed annual income programmes reflect social and political pressures for a more egalitarian and, in socialist terms, a more just society. Similarly, as we noted in Chapter IV, the rise in the past decade of Women's Liberation movements, Black Power, Red Power and Students Groups suggests that a number of traditional forms of inequality were being questioned and were under attack and that we were, apparently, in the throes of an "equality revolution" (Gans, 1968).

EQUALITY OF OPPORTUNITY

For the most part, the debate about inequality has not been about equality of condition but about what constitutes the best basis (justification) for inequality. What is sometimes called the "meritocratic" critique of inequality assumes that social inequality is inevitable. Those who hold this view, essentially the view of the liberal ideology, are concerned with how people are *recruited* to favourable positions and with the *processes* and *justifications* by which inequalities are transmitted from one generation to another. At least since the beginnings of the sociological tradition in the eighteenth century, the main concern has been not with equal rewards but with equal opportunities to compete for those rewards (Parkin, 1971:13). Traditionally, the battle has been between merit on the one hand and hereditary privilege on the other, between liberal and conservative, respectively.

According to the liberal ideology, then, the just and equal society is one in which there is equality of opportunity. That is, each person through his own abilities and drive will *achieve* his position in society, regardless of his social origins. As we saw in Chapter VII, Canadians are, paradoxically, sympathetic to both conservatism and socialism. But, most also share the liberal *ideal* that *ascribed* statuses, such as sex, race, ethnicity and family background, should not be relevant in assigning people to various positions in the social hierarchy. People who advocate the ideal of equality of opportunity are not, therefore, challenging the existence of a social hierarchy. Rather, their concern is with the extent to which these unequal positions are open to everyone in the society; to what extent they are reserved for the children of those who already hold these positions. In other words, to what extent are societies likely to be characterized by *social stratification?*

SOCIAL STRATIFICATION

To say that a society is stratified is to say that it can be divided into unequal or hierarchical categories or social strata which may persist for a long period of time. The study of social stratification is about both *structure* and *process.* A concern with structure leads the sociologist to descriptive accounts of the nature and type of social stratification existing in a particular society, to comparative analyses of stratification systems and to questions about how social strata within a given society differ from one another. The concept of process, on the other hand, directs us to look at how privileges (or lack of privileges) are transmitted from one generation to the next and how this is justified or legitimated. It may, too, lead us to examine how various groups or strata in the society act collectively to improve their position and reduce the gap between themselves and those more privileged. In many respects, this is the theme of the chapters on ethnic groups and collective behaviour which follow later in the book.

It is the element of continuity of particular forms and patterns of social inequality which distinguishes a stratified society from one in which there is simply social inequality. Dennis Wrong (1964), for example, has pointed out that while the Catholic Church is hierarchical and inegalitarian, it is not, strictly speaking, stratified. This is because the priestly vow of celibacy means that inequalities begin afresh in each generation and do not necessarily depend on one's social origins. Thus, popes and bishops have sometimes come from very lowly beginnings.

The Family and Social Stratification

Normally, however, inequalities tend to become crystallized into specific social strata because of the existence of the family and the kinship structure. Families do not create inequality; rather they respond and adapt to it, attempting to pass on to their children the same positions and privileges they have enjoyed. As Michael Young, a British sociologist, pointed out some years ago, social reformers must ultimately come to grips with the fact that parents will want to leave their wealth and property to their children and not to the

State. This is likely to be true even when there is a widely shared belief in equality of opportunity and in the "meritocratic" view that the best people should be recruited for the job on the basis of merit and ability rather than on the basis of inheritance:

As members of a particular family, they want their children to have every privilege. But, at the same time, they are opposed to privilege for anyone else's children. They desire equal opportunity for everyone else's children, extra for their own (Young, 1958:31).

At the core of almost all systems of social stratification is the family or the kinship structure.[2] Social strata, then, consist not of individuals, but of groupings of *nuclear* or extended families hierarchically ranked according to the power they have to control their own and their children's *life chances.* It is because of this connection between the family and inequality that those who have wanted to create Utopias—perfect societies—have usually begun by abolishing the family as we know it. Only by turning over to the State the responsibility for child rearing, it has been argued, could privilege and influence be eliminated and all children be given an equal start in life.

The *kibbutzim* of Israel provide one of the best known attempts to eliminate the family as we know it. From a very early age children are raised in separate quarters from their parents. At the same time, nearly everyone is involved in some way with the care and education of the children. Milford Spiro, one of the first to study the *kibbutzim,* concluded that the family had not been abolished. Rather, the society was, in effect, one large extended family. The *collective* interests of the community and the *private* interests which ordinarily are contained within the family had, in this case, coalesced (Spiro, 1958). As evidence of this, many observers have noted that young people raised on the same *kibbutz* seldom marry one another, tending rather to view their peers almost as brothers and sisters.

Open and Closed Societies

In the vast majority of societies, past and present, private interests of the family have prevailed over the collective interests of the total society or of parts of the society. Thus, almost all known societies have been stratified societies. Nevertheless, there are important differences in the degree to which social positions are likely to be determined by particularistic-ascribed (family-type) relationships. In industrialized societies there has, apparently, been a marked transition from *closed* to *open* systems of stratification.

In closed systems it is difficult, sometimes illegal, to leave the social stratum in which one is born. Social position is fixed at birth so that one does not expect to rise or to fall in the social hierarchy. Open systems, on the other hand, permit a good deal of movement from lower social strata to higher social strata and vice versa. In open systems there is both a greater chance to "rise" and a greater risk of "falling." In a completely closed system of social stratification all members of each stratum would be recruited from that stratum, usually by inheriting their parents' status and occupation. There would, therefore, be "perfect" social stratification. At the other extreme we can conceive of a society in which there is "perfect" equality of opportunity. This would mean that the family has no influence on the individual's eventual social position. In this case there could still be social inequality but, because it is renewed afresh in each generation, there would be no social stratification.

To clarify this somewhat, it may be helpful to think of a very simple and hypothetical society in which there are exactly 1000 fathers who have exactly one son each. Let us suppose, too, that like most other societies, past and present, our imaginary society is also a sexist society; women are allowed to hold no other positions in society besides that of wife and mother. Hence, women's status, their social and economic fate, is totally dependent on what happens to their husbands. Finally, imagine that this is a two-class society: an elite of 100 families and a non-elite of 900 families.

Figure VIII.1 presents three hypothetical situations with respect to social movement. In Case A, a totally closed society, there is no social mobility— every elite son would inherit his father's position; every non-elite son would remain a member of the non-elite. There is, then, no social mobility at all. Now, let us suppose that in this hypothetical society a law is passed which forbids any sons of elite fathers from inheriting an elite position (Case B). Because of the law, *all* sons of elite fathers are downwardly mobile and are replaced by 100 sons of non-elite fathers. Note, however, that even with "complete mobility," 800 sons will have to settle for a non-elite position. There is not room in the elite for everyone. Finally, Case C shows what would happen if there was full equality of opportunity, that is, if family background had no influence on what happens to people in terms of their social position. As we can see, 10 sons of elite fathers could be expected to "inherit" an elite status and 90 sons would be downwardly mobile. At the same time, 90 non-elite sons would be expected to move upward and 810 would remain non-elite. Simply, the elite comprises 10% of the population and therefore full equality of opportunity leads us to expect that the elite in the next generation would consist of the same proportion—10%—of elite sons.

Obviously, no society is as simple or as neat as to fit any of these cases. For instance, in reality, not all fathers will have a son while others will have several. Generations do not split quite this easily either. Further, as various things happen, the size of the elite may change. A war may create a need for more leaders and for a larger elite. Or, at the same time as there is a decrease in positions for non-elite members, there is an increase in need for people to manage the society. Both the failure of the elite to reproduce itself and changes in the composition of the labour force create a demand for *structural mobility.* But, even if conditions remain pretty much the same, some non-elite sons will have sufficient ability and drive to "push" their way upwards. Similarly, some elite sons are likely to be incompetent or lack the desire to assume an elite position and will "fall" to a non-elite position.

Our hypothetical example does, however, illustrate two important points. First, even as in Case B, where no one is allowed to inherit a favoured position, we do not have equality of condition but what Pareto called a *circulation of elites.* Second, even with full equality of opportunity, the liberal ideal, not everyone can be upwardly mobile. There is, in other words, only so much room at the top. Only a minority can expect to rise and, unless the structural conditions are changing, a number of those born in advantaged positions must expect to lose that advantage. Some structural changes in the Canadian labour force—more white collar workers and fewer factory workers and farmers—were outlined in Chapter VII. These changes clearly have produced a good deal of the social mobility in industrial societies. This illustration will also have further relevance when we consider the nature of the Canadian elite later in this chapter and when we look at education in Chapter IX.

CASTE, ESTATE AND CLASS

No society has ever been either perfectly closed or perfectly open. It is usual, however, to consider caste and estate as examples of relatively closed systems, and class systems of modern society as examples of relatively open systems. Since all three are, however, unequal societies—ones in which some have control of resources and others do not—we can also think of these as different systems of justification for in-

Figure VIII.1

CASE A
A TOTALLY CLOSED SOCIETY

Son's Generation

Father's Generation	Elite	Non-Elite	Total
Elite	(1) 100	(2) 0	100
Non-Elite	(3) 0	(4) 900	900
Total	100	900	1000

CASE B
TOTAL CIRCULATION OF ELITES

Son's Generation

Father's Generation	Elite	Non-Elite	Total
Elite	(1) 0	(2) 100	100
Non-Elite	(3) 100	(4) 800	900
	100	900	1000

CASE C
FULL EQUALITY OF OPPORTUNITY

Son's Generation

Father's Generation	Elite	Non-Elite	Total
Elite	(1) 10	(2) 90	100
Non-Elite	(3) 90	(4) 810	900
	100	900	1000

equality. In other words, these three systems also represent three types of ideology of justification.

Caste

The main, and perhaps only, example of the caste system is found in the ancient system of stratification of India. Castes are hereditary ranked divisions of Hindu society which are religiously and traditionally sanctioned. Membership is based on the fact that one is born into a particular caste so that movement into or out of a caste is prohibited. Since castes are also endogamous (marriage occurs only within the caste), they have in their broad outlines been able to exist, unchanged, for several thousand years.

Although castes are often viewed as a "limiting case" of social stratification, there is considerable doubt among sociologists and ethnologists whether this is a correct interpretation of the caste system. Louis Dumont, for instance, argues that caste inequality begins from different premises about man and society than those which we in the Western World take for granted (see Dumont, 1970). For our purposes, however, the distinguishing feature of caste systems as opposed to other systems of stratification is their systematic reliance upon religious, philosophical and genetic explanations to maintain and justify inequality.

Estates

The estate system of stratification stands somewhere between a caste system and a class system. Historically, the feudal system of medieval Europe provides the most specific example of this form of stratification. Like the caste system, estates were essentially closed social strata in which intermarriage and social movement were virtually impossible. Estate systems were based on an agrarian economy in which one's social position was intimately tied to the ownership and non-ownership of land. At the top was a hereditary aristocracy or nobility, followed by merchants and craftsmen. At the bottom were free peasants and then serfs who were tied to the land. The clergy, though most closely associated with the aristocracy, was, itself, arranged into a hierarchy interacting with the secular hierarchy at various levels. Although the estate system was not formally upheld by religious beliefs as is a caste system, but by laws and custom, the Church certainly did nothing to undermine the system and, as we have seen, often acted as an ideological tool of the ruling classes.[3] Thus, the estate system upheld by legal means and by tradition the belief that it is legitimate and proper for people to inherit both the privileged and less privileged positions. With some few exceptions, it was assumed that people would remain in the stratum or estate in which they were born.

Vestiges of the estate system can still be found in South America and Spain. Russia, up until the Revolution of 1917, remained essentially an estate system. However, in those countries most affected by the industrial revolution—Germany, France, England and Holland—the estate system began in the late eighteenth and early nineteenth centuries, to be replaced by what is called class stratification.

Classes

Despite what we have said, in all societies, including caste systems, some families and individuals have, by legal or deviant means, managed to improve their social position. In all societies, too, some families have been unable to maintain privileged positions and have "sunk" into the anonymous strata lying below or have simply died out. But, the distinctive feature of class systems of stratification is that *social mobility*, the movement of individuals and their families from one social stratum to another, becomes institutionalized and expected. Instead of the rigid boundaries of castes and estates, classes, by definition, are sufficiently permeable so as to allow for movement into and out of them. As Bottomore points out, wealth, rather than birth, becomes in a class system the more important criterion stratifying members of the society:

. . . social classes, in contrast with castes or feudal estates, are more exclusively economic groups. They are not constituted or supported by any specific legal or religious rules, and membership of a particular class confers upon the individual no special civil or political rights. . . . The individual is born into a particular social class, just as he is born into a caste or estate but he is somewhat less likely to remain at the social level in which he is born than is the individual in a caste or estate society. Within his own lifetime an individual, or his family, may rise or fall in the social hierarchy. If he rises, he needs no patent of nobility, no kind of official recognition to conform his new status. It will be enough for him to be wealthy, to have a particular economic and occupational role, and perhaps to acquire some of the secondary cultural characteristics of the social stratum into which he has entered (Bottomore, 1965:16-17).

THEORIES OF CLASS INEQUALITY

Present day thinking about social stratification and social class has been mainly influenced by the theories of Karl Marx and Max Weber. Perhaps because they wanted to believe that the United States was a "classless" society, American sociologists traditionally looked more to Weber than to Marx for their ideas. European sociologists, on the other hand, have more explicitly been influenced by Marx and have, therefore, tended to emphasize *class* inequality rather than *status* inequality concepts which we discuss later in this chapter (Westergaard, 1974). Although Canadian sociologists in the past followed the American approach, in recent years there has been a renewed interest in viewing Canadian society from a Marxian perspective.

Karl Marx

The work of Karl Marx dominates all other theories of social inequality and social stratification. Deeply sensitive to history, Marx provided a brilliant and sweeping synthesis of all that had gone before. One hundred years later the broad outlines of this theory still inform and influence social and political thought. His sociological contributions, though extremely important, are somewhat dimmed by the immense influence his ideas and visions have had upon the shape of the political world.

Because a large part of his life was spent in England, Marx was able to view at first hand the extreme poverty and oppression generated by one of the most "advanced" industrial and capitalistic societies of the nineteenth century. While he admired the fact that capitalism had achieved more in one hundred years than any previous economic system, he concluded that it was also an inhumane system shot through with contradictions. Capitalism, he maintained, contained within it the "seeds of its own destruction."

The central theme of Marx's theory is that the social institutions and cultural features of every society are essentially determined by the relationships and economic institutions which emerge from private property and from the "dominant mode of production." The family, religious, political and philosophical beliefs, education and the media are all shaped and influenced by economic factors. Moreover, as agencies of socialization, these institutions and beliefs convey definitions of social reality and standards of judgement which are at least compatible with the interests of the ruling class—those who own the means of production, the land or wealth of the society.[4] Thus, Marx began his analysis by looking at the nature and function of *ideologies,* that is, the ideas and beliefs which serve to legitimate inequality. In other words, whose definition of social reality is likely to dominate? How do the major institutions of society shape and direct our thinking, our definition of what is just, our values about what ought to be and our perceptions of what is possible?

Bourgeoisie and Proletariat

Marx contended that in every period of history, society breaks down into two basic and inherently hostile classes—a ruling class which owns the means of production and a class that is ruled or oppressed. As Marx put it in his most famous work, *The Communist Manifesto:*

The history of all hitherto existing society is the history of class struggles. Free man and slave, patrician and plebeian, lord and serf, guild master and journeyman, in a word, oppresser and oppressed, stood in constant opposition to one another, carried on an uninterrupted, now hidden, now open fight, a fight that each time ended either in a revolutionary reconstitution of society at large or in the common ruin of the contending classes (Feuer, 1959:7).

Within capitalist societies, the two main and opposed classes are the *bourgeoisie*—capitalists and the large land-owners who had survived—and the *proletariat*—the class of modern wage earners who, having no means of production of their own, are reduced to selling their labour power in order to live. According to Marx, the material condition of the proletariat could only worsen, what is often referred to as the "law of increasing misery." At first, this "pauperization" leads only to misdirected conflict and struggle. Unaware yet of their revolutionary potential, the proletariat are distracted from direct confrontation with the bourgeoisie. Workers compete among themselves for better conditions; they attack the factories rather than the factory owners; they fight the remnants of the aristocracy, "the enemies of their enemies" rather than the capitalists. In time, Marx anticipated, these distractions are set aside. Workers become conscious of their class interests, their shared predicament. The proletariat becomes a revolutionary class.[5]

Marx and Modern Capitalism

As far as Western industrial societies are concerned, Marx's prediction of revolution has not been borne out by history. In fact, Marxist or Communist revolutions have occurred in societies which were essentially estate or feudal systems—Russia and China—and which had not yet become capitalistic and highly industrialized. Similarly, other societies today hovering on the brink of communism, such as South-East Asia and South America, still possess strong remnants of an estate system of stratification. We must ask, then, "why no revolutions in capitalist society?"

In answer to this, many sociologists have suggested that Marx underestimated the power of capitalism to provide such affluence for the majority of its citizens. They also point out that Marx failed to recognize the importance of the middle class. They argue that instead of "sinking" into the proletariat, as he anticipated, the middle class has, in industrial society, actually grown in size, providing what Lopreato and Hazellrig (1972:36) call a "sort of 'demilitarized zone' standing formidably between bourgeoisie and proletariat." Others point out that living and working conditions for the mass of working people have improved immeasurably over what they were in the nineteenth and early twentieth century.

At first glance, capitalism of today does seem very different from the capitalism Marx knew and studied. Workers, after a long struggle, did win the right to form unions and to bargain collectively. Compulsory education and legislation finally brought an end to child labour. A series of acts progressively shortened men's and women's working hours and brought some improvements in the conditions and safety of mines and factories. People do think they are better off than they were in earlier generations.

But, many sociologists would argue that capitalism has undergone only a superficial face lifting; in its basic features it remains unchanged. Wealth in Canada still is highly concentrated, held by a very tiny minority of the population. As we shall see, a closer look at the actual incomes of Canadians makes questionable whether there is a growing middle class and whether very many people can afford the package depicted by the media as the middle-class way of life. Overall, inequalities in income and life chances have not been reduced and may have worsened. Lower paid workers are actually experiencing increasing impoverishment. Poverty, rather than disappearing, seems a pervasive—perhaps necessary—phenomenon of capitalist society. Factory work may be as tedious and alienating as it was in Marx's time. Finally, we must remember that a good deal of the affluence of capitalist societies has been at the expense of "Third World" countries, which partially explains why Marxism and communism appeal to these societies; they have grown conscious of their oppressed relationship to the developed world.

It is closer to the truth to say that Marx underestimated the ability and power of capitalism to justify itself, to give the illusion of change without affecting the basic structure. Legalizing collective bargaining gives workers the semblance of power but actually institutionalizes conflict, contains it and renders it harmless as a potential for revolutionary change. "Progressive taxation" supposedly redistributes income from the rich to the poor but in fact seems to make very little difference at all. The media, by focusing attention on the middle class, present us with images and affluence, not of impoverishment. Credit cards, consumer loans and endless mortgages allows families to appear more middle class, more affluent than they actually are. Married women who are working, not out of desire but need, serve to mask some of the impoverishment of lower paid workers. The dominant ideologies tell us to view poverty not as a problem of the system but of individuals who will not work and who prefer to live on welfare.

In short, Marx's prophecy of a communist revolution has, in capitalist societies, turned out to be a "suicidal prophecy": once people hear about a theory or prophecy they are able to take steps to avoid what it predicts, thus putting off, perhaps destroying, the prophecy. Threatened with the possibility of revolution, the ruling classes of capitalist societies have acted to reduce and redirect that potential danger. They have done so without removing the underlying problem—class inequality.

Max Weber

It is sometimes argued that Weber's theory of social stratification represents a refutation of Marx's theory. It is more correct, however, to view Weber's work as an academic "rounding out" of Marx's obviously more political and largely unfinished contribution (Zeitlin, 1968:112).

As we have seen, Marx put great emphasis on the importance of economic factors in determining the fundamental basis of social stratification. Weber shared with Marx the view that ownership and nonownership of property are crucial determinants of class formation and position. He agreed, also, that under some circumstances, groups of people sharing similar economic interests might form into a coherent and conscious class. But, he argued, economic interests do not form the sole basis for social stratification. Ideas and attitudes held by people are also important determinants of how society is organized. While ideas are likely to be conditioned by economic institutions, ideas and ideologies are themselves social forces which must be taken into account.

Weber's theory of stratification centres around the notion that social stratification derives from an unequal distribution of power or *life chances,* that is, everything from the chance to stay alive during the first year after birth to the chance to view fine art, from the chance to remain healthy and grow tall, and if sick to get well again quickly, to the chance to avoid becoming a juvenile delinquent (Gerth and Mills, 1953:313). While a family's economic power is an extremely important determinant of these life chances, Weber argued that power can be expressed in more ways than simply the economic dimension.

Class, Status Group and Party

Weber contended that individuals and their families are, at once, members of three different orders of stratification—class, status and party (or power as it is usually translated). Class or class situation refers essentially to economic stratification and is fairly close to Marx's use of the term. Status or status situation refers to the way in which social honour or prestige is distributed. Status situation comes not only from wealth but from *lifestyle*—in effect, how one spends his money and how one thinks and behaves, and from ascribed factors, in particular, family background. Status is based not so much on what we possess as upon how others treat us. By party, Weber seemed to mean the distribution of "pure" political power in a society. As with status, political power may arise independently of economic power and be valued for its own sake.

Ordinarily, people are likely to be located at roughly the same place in each of these three hierarchies. In that case, the distinction between the three is *analytical* rather than *empirical*. But, it is also easy to find examples where the three are incongruent so that individuals are quite differently ranked on each dimension. Ministers and priests, for instance, enjoy considerable prestige within a community and may have considerable power. But, generally, they have little or no wealth.[6] The present leader of the opposition, Joe Clark, has considerable political power, but he is neither rich nor is he an established member of the Canadian social elite. Extremely rich men, such as the late Howard Hughes, may seek anonymity and therefore be almost unknown among those who determine social standing. Film and "pop" stars may become very wealthy and enjoy considerable prestige, but possess little or no political power.

Classes, for Weber, are essentially economic groups. People can be placed objectively in terms of whether they are owners or non-owners of the means of production, whether they possess wealth or not. Status, on the other hand, is more subjective: how does the individual see himself; how do others define him? As Weber showed, under ordinary circumstances, *status situation* rather than *class situation* is likely to create in people a sense of "group consciousness." Nor is money, in and of itself, sufficient to give a person access to certain status groups. Winning a million dollars in Loto Canada, for example, will not necessarily mean that one is invited to join an exclusive golf and country club. Similarly, a substantial loss in income does not necessarily mean an equivalent loss of social status. Often, as Warner (1963) found, old established families may possess higher social status than the *nouveaux riches* even when the latter are in fact richer.

Weber's third dimension, party, refers to the fact that people do not necessarily require high status or great wealth in order to wield considerable political power. Hitler would seem to be such an example as are the "Mandarins," the higher civil servants in the Federal government. For Weber, then, class, status and party are the three basic resources people have available to them to control their own and other people's life chances. In most cases, however, it is difficult to think of Weber's major concepts separately. Indeed, Weber was clearly aware that class, status and party usually come together. But, he was arguing that the degree to which they intersect is an empirical question. It is this issue which C. Wright Mills addresses in *The Power Elite* (1956) when he tries to demonstrate the interlocking of the political, military and economic elites in America. John Porter (1965) has tried to put these ideas to the test in Canada in his examination of the relationships among the economic elite, labour elite, political elite, bureaucratic elite and what he calls the ideological elites who dominate the media, higher education and organized religion. More recently, many theorists and researchers on power have concentrated almost exclusively on the economic (or corporate) elite, presumably because economic power underlies any other form of power; indeed economic power is seen as the only power.

Power is one of the trickiest notions in sociology because it has been used to describe so many different things. We are all likely to understand the notion at the level of everyday life. Children know the power of their parents; employees the power of their bosses; students the power of their teachers and so on. We know that there are people who have more influence over our actions than we have over theirs. We also know that there are a number of people who, because of their status, can influence us to do even what we do not wish to do. And, as we have described, probably all of us have encountered the power of the bureaucrat who can make recourse to official practice to justify his cavalier treatment of us. All of these examples have in common the ability of the "powerful" to mobilize resources—as Weber described them, economic resources, status resources and political resources (practices). At the same time, this kind of power is situation specific and depends, in large part, on our own volition. Their power is not absolute and it is exerted within the existing social structure.

At another level, power has been used to describe the ability of some groups to actually shape the structure and direction of a society. More precisely, power, in this usage, refers to the ability of some groups to shape society in their own best interests. Some American sociologists (e.g., Reissman, 1950; Pilisuk and Hayden, 1965) have argued that there is no single "power elite," but rather a plurality of "veto groups," each with its own sphere of interests and whose power is highly constrained by the competition of elites and by the need of these elites to enlist the support of the public. Reissman calls these elites veto groups because they act only when their particular interests are challenged. Against this, Marxists and neo-Marxist theorists argue that there is a single unified elite which can at times act in concert to promote and defend its shared interests. While it may at times appear that there are a number of elite groups and that they are in conflict with one another, these theorists argue that this may only be true for relatively trivial issues, those which do not represent a fundamental threat to the existing social structure. As the research in this tradition shows, there cannot be very serious conflict between these elites because, to a large extent, they are indistinguishable from one another—there is a high degree of interpenetration between elites, what Panitch (1977) calls a "confraternity of power." In other words, powerful people in one sphere either sit on the governing bodies of other spheres or they have relatives who do so.

Because of the very nature of power itself, this debate is far from resolved.[7] Power is the least known aspect of stratification because, as Mills (1956) has shown, it is hidden in at least partial secrecy. People who seem to be part of the power elite may deny it. Some, perhaps believing their own propaganda and the prevailing ideology, fail to recognize how much power they do in fact possess. Moreover, the most that researchers such as Porter, Clement and Panitch can do is locate those who they *think* have power by virtue of their position. But, because they have only limited access to these "higher circles" (the boardrooms of large corporations, the inner group around a prime minster), we generally obtain only glimpses, only circumstantial evidence, of how power is distributed and employed. In short, as we shall see, it is relatively easy to determine people's class situation and status situation; it is less easy to determine how much power goes with these positions.

More Recent Theories

Marx and Weber were both in somewhat different ways emphasizing how inequality and conflict are closely related. Marx concentrated on the inherent conflict existing between those who own private property and capital and those who do not. Weber stressed the fact that groups are in a constant struggle, not only for wealth, but also for status and power. Weber's perspective on stratification suggests that status is not a passive characteristic of groups. Rather, status groups attempt to appropriate or have a monopoly over certain symbols, lifestyles, occupations and kinds of education (Collins, 1971).

A more recent conflict theorist, Ralf Dahrendorf (1969), shares some of Marx's views, but denies that complete equality between people is ever possible or, for that matter, even desirable.[8] Dahrendorf disagrees with Marx that with the end of private ownership of property, conflict will disappear. He argues instead that there are many relationships between people and groups which involve inequality and which can give rise to conflict. These he calls "imperatively coordinated positions" or power relationships (Dahrendorf, 1959). Although this inequality will be justified by the more powerful group, there will always be a counter-argument by those less favourably placed in society. They will try to impose a system of norms promising them a better rank. In turn, those favourably placed have a vested interest in justifying and maintaining the existing situation. Thus, relationships of inequality are inherently seen as conflict relationships. For Dahrendorf, much that is good as well as much that is bad about social life comes from these potentially explosive relationships. Inequality is, on the one hand, the source of injustice and deprivation. On the other hand, it is the well-spring from which flow innovation and culture change. Seen from this perspective, deviance might for example well represent innovation or a counter-ideology by groups who feel they are labelled and discriminated against, unfairly or unjustly (see Chapter VI).

The Functional Theory of Stratification

An alternative and more benign view of social stratification was developed by two American sociologists, Kingsley Davis and Wilbert Moore, in the 1940s (Davis and Moore, 1945). This view, usually referred to as the functional theory of stratification, begins with an argument which most people might make if they wished to defend inequality.

All societies, they argue, must have a way of assigning people to the various positions or occupations in a society. Once allocated to a position, people must be motivated to perform their roles adequately. If all positions were equally important or if everyone were equally talented, then it would not matter much who did which job. But, say Davis and Moore, this is not the case. Talent is scarce. Some positions are more important or functional for the survival of a society. Some jobs which must be done are more demanding, requiring more skills and more training.

In short, the functional theory holds that a society must offer differential rewards as incentives to get people to take on these jobs and to carry them out properly. Davis and Moore suggest that these rewards will consist of money, prestige and leisure which go with the position itself.

In contrast to the Marxian perspective, inequality from a functionalist perspective is viewed not only as inevitable but as necessary or *functional* for the survival of any society.

> *Social inequality is thus an unconsciously evolved device by which societies insure that the most important positions are conscientiously filled by the most qualified persons. Hence every society, no matter how simple or complex, must differentiate persons in terms of both prestige and esteem and must therefore possess a certain amount of institutionalized inequality (Davis, 1948:367-368).*

Most sociologists now regard the Davis-Moore argument as a "rationalization" for inequality rather than as a theory of inequality.[9] Nevertheless, there are three important aspects of this theory that make it worth considering. First, the Davis-Moore argument is very close to that which most businessmen, for example, are likely to use against egalitarian or socialist proposals. Who, for instance, has not heard arguments along these lines: the trouble with socialism is that it takes away people's drive and ambition; if you work hard and have what it takes, you *deserve* more; we need good doctors and businessmen and to get them we have to be prepared to pay for them?

Secondly, as we will see, functionalism has influenced much of the thinking about education and social mobility in industrial societies. Finally, despite considerable criticism of their theory, no one has been able to refute, empirically or logically, the Davis-Moore argument that if positions *are* to be filled adequately there must be *some* minimal amount of inequality of rewards (Wrong, 1964).

One of the major criticisms of the functional theory of stratification is that it is difficult, if not impossible, to say for certain which are the more important positions in society. Are lawyers more important than farmers? Are accountants more valuable than coal miners? In other words, can we make the functionalist assumption that values and norms are widely shared and that there is a good deal of consensus about what constitutes the grounds for inequality and what positions are most important? From the functionalist perspective, these judgements are assumed to be part of most people's socialization; they will have internalized values which hold that, for instance, a doctor is entitled to more social honour and more income than a factory worker. To hold a different view is, therefore, to be inadequately or improperly socialized.

Conflict theorists do not necessarily deny that these values or moral judgements are widely shared by members of a society. They ask, however, *whose* value judgements are likely to dominate? Where do these values come from? In other words, whose definition of the situation determines what is thought to be an important or valuable position (Parkin, 1971:42)?

A second criticism is that even if the importance of a position could, somehow, be established, there is no guarantee that the "best" people are, in fact, recruited to these positions. As we have already seen, high status families will want to pass advantages on to their children, thus creating social stratification rather than social inequality. As a result, "important" positions may come to be reserved for those born into high status positions and be closed to members of lower social strata. Davis and Moore, then, neglected to consider the dysfunctions—the negative consequences—that may accompany the positive functions of inequality.

Finally, many critics have posed the question of how unequal the rewards need to be in order to motivate people to carry out the tasks of a society. Anderson, for example, asks:

> *Must there be billionaires and paupers? Idle rentiers and poverty-line workers? Or only six figure vs. four-figure income spreads? Or something even less unequal? Put another way, how much of a reward is necessary for society to bribe its members into becoming high-ranking administrators and executives, physicians, scientists, and professors, generals and admirals, large stock- and bondholders, presidents, consultants, corporate lawyers, university deans, movie stars and so on? . . . and for positions of relative "insignificance" what is the size of the shrunken pittance society dangles before the eyes of the unqualified? Subsistence wages? Welfare? Nothing? (Anderson, 1974:83-84).*

In sum, the functional explanation of social inequality raises more questions than it succeeds in answering. While it was probably not intended as such, it serves as a rationalization and justification rather than as an adequate explanation of social inequality and social stratification.

Figure VIII.2
STRATIFICATION IN CAPITALIST SOCIETIES

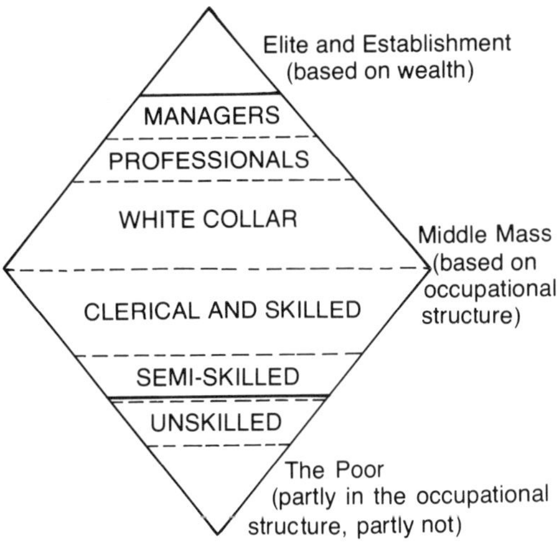

Class Inequality In Canada

These theories of stratification which we have just described fall on different sides of the debate with which we introduced the chapter. Marxian theories direct us to two types of questions that emerge from an examination of inequality of condition. First, many researchers have focused on power—who has it and how much do they have? Others have studied poverty, emphasizing the sharp economic disparities in capitalist societies and the social and social-psychological consequences of inequality. Functionalism has been the most important influence on liberal sociologists. Their concern has been to establish the degree of inequality of opportunity in any society and the social and social-psychological consequences of blocked mobility. Many sociologists, Porter for example, have been influenced by both approaches. Finally, Weber's discussion of status has influenced a number of American sociologists who have chosen largely to ignore the very top and bottom of the stratification system, to ignore questions of poverty and power and who have, instead, focused on the status and income differences, the cultures and lifestyles, of the large middle mass.

What we believe is the nature of class in Canada depends, then, on which questions we ask, on what portion of the stratification system we are focusing upon and whether our interest is in social status, wealth and power or poverty. Figure VIII.2 presents a rough picture of the stratification profile of capitalist societies, including Canada. At the top are the rich and the tiny minority which comprises the Canadian economic and social elite. At the other extreme are the 20% to 35% of the population who, depending where we draw the line, find themselves living below or at the "poverty line." Yet, to most Canadians, Canada is a middle-class society, with little poverty and a wide distribution of power.

This is reflected in levels of Canadian class consciousness. Richard Apostle (1977) finds, for example, that when forced to do so, most people can place themselves in a social class. But, a majority (51%) interviewed in a 1974 study did not think of themselves as belonging to a social class nor did they believe that class conflict is bound to occur. Apostle concludes that

> *. . . Canadians have rather weak conceptions of class structure or of cohesive social classes engaged in conflict, and their opinions regarding the class structure do not form a coherent set of beliefs which might approximate a clear perspective or ideology concerning that class structure (1977:15).*

When we look at the top of Figure VIII.2, then, we are asking questions about power—the concentration of wealth and the ownership of the means of production in Canadian society. When we look at the bottom of the diamond we are asking questions about powerlessness—the inability of the poor, individually or collectively, to create change and to improve their own and their children's life chances. Just as Canadians, generally, may often be blinded to the top and bottom of the stratification system, so, too, may sociologists be blinded to the issues of power and poverty by the perspective that they have adopted and their background assumptions. Nevertheless, although sociologists who concentrate on questions of status and income difference do not capture the structure of stratification, they do tell us a good deal about the middle mass and about inequality as it is expressed in our everyday lives.[10]

INEQUALITY OF CONDITION: THE MIDDLE MASS

Occupation

One of the first questions we are likely to ask of a stranger is what he does for a living. Occupation tells us, generally, what to expect from a person. We use occupational roles to build up "hypotheses," and eventually to define typifications. Occupation tells us how much a *man* earns, how well he is educated, where he is likely to live and what his standing is likely to be in the community. To learn that a man has been given a large promotion is to assume that he will also move up a step or two in the social hierarchy. Unemployment, in turn, may mean downward mobility. Thus, occupations are perhaps the best single indicator of status or power within the middle mass (Runciman, 1968).

Note, however, that we are less likely to ask a woman the same question and more hesitant to assume her occupation provides us with the full story. We are more likely to ask her marital status. If married, we may want to know, as well, what her husband does for a living. If she is single we may wonder about her father's occupation before deciding where she fits in the class structure. Occupational prestige, it seems, works differently for women than it does for men. The tradition that the man is the head of the household and the woman is the dependent dies hard and slowly. The result is that women who do work and have careers are still categorized on the basis of their husband or father; they are not accorded status in terms of their own achievements. As Margaret Eichler (1973) argues, women are subject to a kind of double ranking. When they participate in the labour force they derive, as do men, an independent status from their occupation but with an additional factor, "femaleness," included. At the same time, they also have a derived or dependent status based on the male to whom they are attached.

The dependent status of women emerges most clearly when we consider the unpaid position of housewife. A later study by Eichler (1977) finds that while people on average rank housewife at about the same level as stenographer and typist, there is considerable discrepancy in reponses. Apparently, the answer "I'm *just* a housewife" in and of itself provides a few clues as to where in the status hierarchy that person should be placed. Table VIII.1 from this study shows that people, by and large, regard housewives as deriving their status from their husbands. Indeed, the prestige of a housewife married to a physician (81.5) is almost comparable to that of a female university professor (82.9) (Eichler, 1977:162). In short, our measures of social class apply mostly to men and to the family. The problem of how to measure the position women hold independently in the class structure is as yet unresolved, and perhaps will remain so until women are accorded full equality with men.

More generally, it seems people mean several things when they talk about the "prestige" of an occupation.[11] Some, certainly, use the Davis-Moore argument and give high prestige to the jobs they think of as most useful to the community or which they think require the most skills and training. Others put more emphasis on the income the job earns. For others, the main criterion is how pleasant and interesting the job is or how much autonomy it offers. As it happens, the specific criteria do not seem to matter very much; in the end people come up with what on average are sim-

Table VIII.1

MEAN PRESTIGE SCORES OF HOUSEWIVES WITH HUSBANDS' OCCUPATIONS SPECIFIED

Housewife whose husband is a physician	81.5	170
Housewife whose husband is a social worker	62.5	170
Housewife whose husband is a plumber	57.2	171
Housewife whose husband is a commercial farmer	56.4	171
Housewife whose husband is an elevator operator	37.1	172

SOURCE: Eichler (1973:162)

ilar rankings of the prestige of occupations.

For example, Pineo's and Porter's (1967) Canadian study of occupational prestige yields a scale fairly similar to what researchers have found in the United States, Britain and elsewhere. A part of their scale is shown in Table VIII.2. Blishen, in 1967 and again in 1976, has tried to measure the socio-economic status of occupations by adding an average income and educational level to prestige. There is close agreement between his scale and the Pineo-Porter scale. Table VIII.3 gives Blishen scores for some selected occupations.

We should not be too surprised by the fact that people are in general agreement about occupational prestige. What these scales show is that most Canadians have internalized the same criteria for evaluating occupations. We learn that professions are "superior" to trades; that skilled jobs are "better" than unskilled jobs; that white-collar work ranks "higher" than blue-collar work. Thus we do not need to know much about a specific occupation in order to rank it. Pineo and Porter (1967) found, for example, that many people could rank even fictitious occupations such as "biologer" and "archaeopotrist."

However, researchers find important differences when people are first asked to rank occupations the way they think most people would and then as they personally feel. Many manual workers feel lawyers and accountants are overrated and coal miners and farmers are not given their just due (Richardson, 1977:Ch. 4; Coxon and Jones, 1978). In other words, while people know what they are supposed to think—what are the relevant criteria—lower-class people have not necessarily internalized the values of the upper classes.

Sexual Inequality

As we have seen in Chapter VII, one of the main changes in the occupational structure is the dramatic increase in participation of women in the Canadian labour force—from about 17% in 1931 to over 34% in 1971. It is fairly obvious, however, that women do not earn as much from their work as do men. MacDonald (1975:4) points out that "women who work full-time in Canada earn, on the average, about 60 percent as much as male full-time workers. . . . The gap in wages and salaries between women and men is *increasing*—in all the provinces, and anyway you look at it." These discrepancies have traditionally been rationalized by employers, males and, often, sociologists (see Hamilton and Pinard, 1977) by arguing that women may justifiably be paid less because theirs is a second income. First of all, this ignores the many women who choose not to marry, have not yet married, have divorced or have been widowed or deserted—any of whom may suffer economic hardship because of this second income assumption. More generally, and more fundamentally, the notion of "second income" reflects the lower status of women in our society, that so many of us

Table VIII.2

OCCUPATIONAL PRESTIGE SCORES FOR SELECTED OCCUPATIONS

Occupational Title	Score
Physician	87.2
University Professor	84.6
Lawyer	82.3
Architect	78.1
Bank Manager	70.9
Public Grade School Teacher	59.6
Real Estate Agent	47.1
Stenographer	46.0
Farm Owner and Operator	44.1
Trailer Truck Driver	32.8
Construction Labourer	26.5
Cod Fisherman	23.4

SOURCE: Pineo and Porter (1967)

Table VIII.3

BLISHEN SCORES FOR SELECTED OCCUPATIONS

Occupation	Score
Dentists	74.70
Managers (Science and Engineering)	74.44
Physicians and Surgeons	74.22
Lawyers	72.73
University Teachers	72.30
Architects	71.95
Elementary Teachers	65.85
Printers	50.30
Real Estate Salesmen	50.07
Typists	45.46
Foremen (Construction)	42.42
Truck Drivers	29.74
Labourers (Manufac.)	29.02
Farmers	23.02
Fishermen	18.63

SOURCE: Blishen and McRoberts (1976)

Figure VIII.3

PERCENTAGES OF MALE AND FEMALE LABOUR FORCES IN THE UPPER THREE, AND THE LOWER THREE, CLASSES OF THE BLISHEN OCCUPATIONAL SCALE: CANADA , 1951-1971.

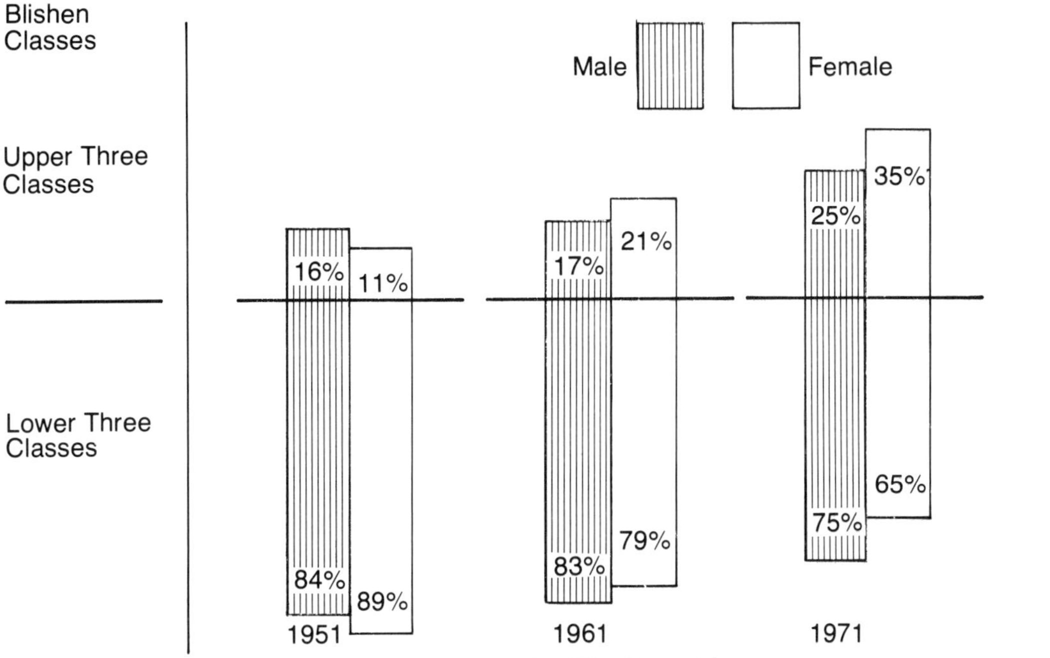

SOURCE: Special compilation by Hugh Lautard, University of New Brunswick

will virtually automatically think of the husband as the breadwinner and the wife as one who works for the pleasure, the diversion or the extra frills. On the contrary, the ongoing research by the Armstrongs (1975 and 1978) shows quite conclusively that women work for the same reasons as men; not "to fulfill themselves" but because they must.

So pervasive is sexual inequality that some sociologists argue that along with the other dimensions of stratification we also need to think in terms of sexual stratification (Collins, 1971a; Acker, 1973). However, as we have suggested, these are issues of inequality, not issues of stratification. If we forget, for the moment, the discrepancies between male and female incomes, we can view the problem in structural terms, as an outcome of our particular form of stratification. As Figure VIII.3 vividly shows, most jobs in our capitalist society are "low-class" jobs. Most men, as well as most women, in the labour force hold jobs of low income and low prestige. As more women enter the labour force, it is these jobs which they will be taking; equality with men in the labour force means that most women will be getting the same kinds of "bad" jobs as most men. Clearly, income discrepancies between men and women in the same occupation are a social injustice which cannot be tolerated. But, we are asking whether there is not a much larger question facing the women's movement and all others who seek greater equality: Is equality between males and females the primary

Table VIII.4

FAMILIES AND UNATTACHED INDIVIDUALS BY INCOME GROUP, 1973

	Families	Unattached Individuals	All Units
Under $1,000	1.1	9.2	3.3
$1,000-3,999	7.9	41.4	16.8
$4,000-6,999	14.1	23.1	16.5
$7,000-9,999	17.2	13.9	16.3
$10,000-14,999	29.2	8.8	23.7
$15,000-24,999	24.6	3.0	18.9
$25,000 and over	5.9	.6	4.5
TOTAL	100.0	100.0	100.0
Average Income	$12,716	$5,149	$10,694
Median Income	$11,533	$3,927	$9,441
Estimated Nos. (000's)	5,222	1,906	7,135

SOURCE: *Perspectives Canada II* (1977:160, Table 8.1)

Figure VIII.4

AVERAGE INCOME OF FAMILIES, UNATTACHED INDIVIDUALS, AND ALL INDIVIDUALS BY SEX

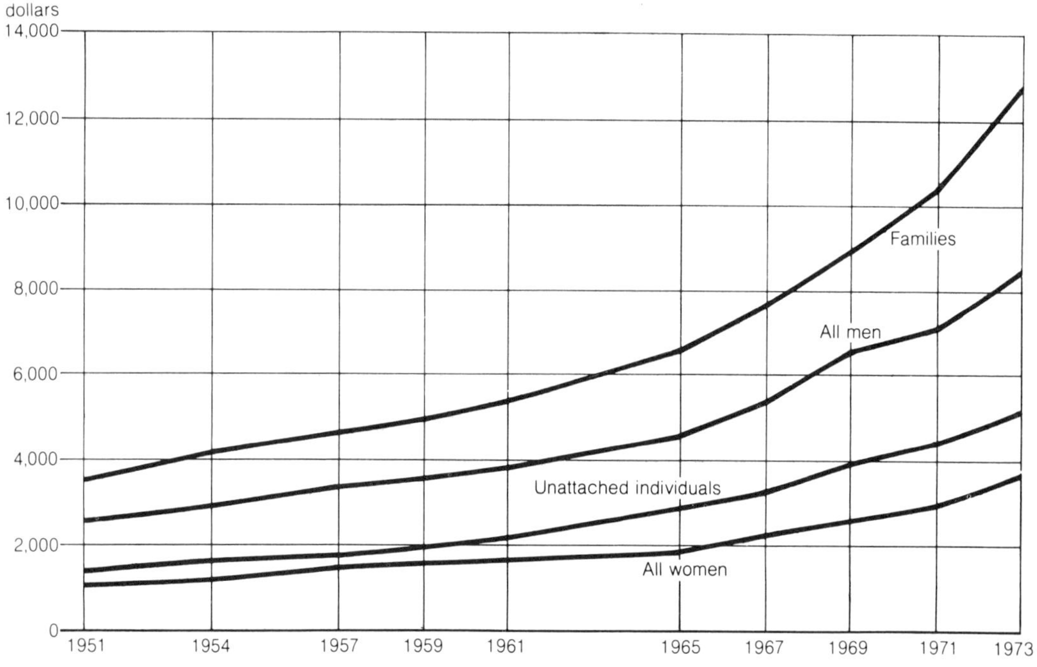

SOURCE: *Perspectives Canada II* (1977: Chart 8.2, p. 160)

Figure VIII.5
INCOME GROUPS IN CANADA, 1973

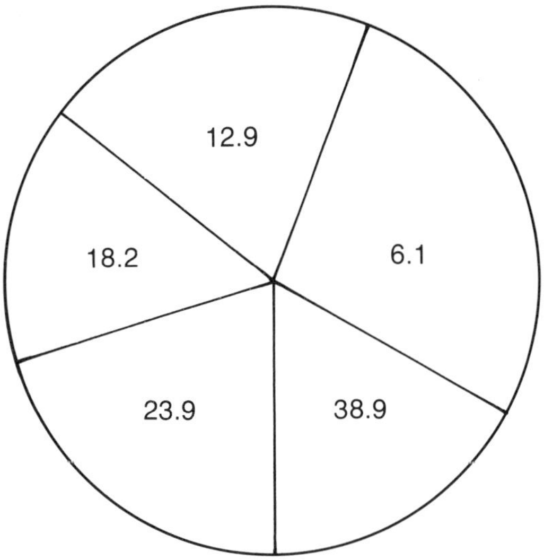

SOURCE: Adapted from Table 8.3, *Perspectives Canada II* (1977: 161)

issue or is it, as we believe, more important to ask about the stratification system more generally?

Income Inequality in Canada

The structural approach becomes even more relevant when we consider the extent of income inequality in Canada. Again, we should emphasize that income studies do not directly tell us about the concentration of wealth, the ownership of the means of production or capital or, for that matter, about discrete social classes. Nor are such data easily come by; although wages and salaries are almost completely reported, investment income may be unreported by as much as 50%. Nevertheless, even from these more narrowly defined studies, it is evident that there are large and marked inequalities in Canadian society. Table VIII.4 shows that fewer than 6% of Canadian families earned $25,000 or more in 1973; whereas over 23% earned less than $7,000 per year. And, the percentage of unattached workers who earn less than $7,000 per year is even more dramatic. Figure VIII.4 shows changes in average income from 1951 to 1973 and illustrates the relative deterioration of women's income.

Income distribution in Canada is most effectively seen when we divide the population up into quintiles, equal fifths of the population. If everyone earned roughly the same in Canadian society, each quintile would receive roughly 20% (one-fifth) of the income. This is most emphatically not the case in Canada. Figure VIII.5 shows that the bottom one-fifth of the Canadian population receives only 6% of the total income; the bottom 40% receives only about 19%. At the top end, 20% of the population earns nearly 40% (38.9%) of the total income.

Nor is there any evidence that conditions are improving. In fact, they may be worsening for the lowest paid people in society. Leo Johnson (1973) has shown that while incomes have increased dramatically in the last 20 years, the lowest paid people in society have experienced a dramatic decline in purchasing power while the more highly paid people have shown increases of 50% or more (Johnson, 1973:3). There is truth to the old adage that the rich get richer and the poor get poorer.

The main response to this growing impoverishment has been a large increase in the number of wives working outside the home (Armstrong and Armstrong, 1975). Table VIII.5 shows both the growing inequality in income distribution and how families have managed to maintain their position in the class structure. From 1951 to 1971, individuals in the three lowest quintiles received a decreasing share of the total income while those in the top two quintiles increased their share. As the bottom rows show, supposedly "progressive" taxation made little difference to the final distribution of income. But, when we look at the income of families, we find that the two lowest quintiles have experienced only a slight decline in their share of total

Table VIII.5

PERCENTAGE DISTRIBUTION OF TOTAL INCOME BY QUINTILES, 1951-71

Year	Lowest Quintile	Second Quintile	Third Quintile	Fourth Quintile	Highest Quintile
All individuals					
1951*	3.2	9.2	17.4	25.2	45.0
1961*	3.1	8.9	17.2	26.0	44.8
1971	2.0	7.2	15.5	26.0	49.2
1971**	2.3	9.2	15.8	25.8	45.8
Wage earners					
1951*	4.2	12.0	18.6	25.0	40.3
1961*	3.7	11.7	18.7	25.6	40.3
1971	2.3	10.1	17.8	25.8	44.0
Families					
1951*	6.1	12.9	17.4	22.4	41.1
1961*	6.6	13.5	18.3	23.4	38.4
1971	5.6	12.6	18.0	23.7	40.0
1971**	6.4	13.5	18.5	23.8	37.8

SOURCE: Adapted from Armstrong and Armstrong (1975:381)
*Excludes farm income
**Represents income after income taxes, but no other taxes have been removed

income while the middle groups increased their share. The top quintile has actually shown a slight decline. The Armstrongs argue that the reason for this is that wives work in order to help the family maintain its financial position. This camouflages the increasing impoverishment and income inequality occurring among individuals—whether male or female.

Of course, quintiles are a sociologist's device for making income comparisons. Nevertheless, it is safe to say that at least the bottom quintile does constitute a unique category. This quintile is clearly below the poverty line. There are various definitions of the poverty line. The Economic Council of Canada said that families spending 70% or more of their income on the basic necessities of life were at or below the poverty line (ECC, *Fifth Annual Review*, 1968). Adams, on the other hand, suggests a relative poverty line set at 50% of the average living standard of Canadians and a "near" poverty line set at two-thirds of the living standard of Canadians. Thus, estimates of how many Canadians fall below this line vary from 20% to 35% and more.

Nevertheless, it is often argued that Canada has no classes to speak of or that nearly everyone is more or less middle class. Certainly, popular images of Canadians in magazines and on television give just this impression. Because people, through the "magic" of credit cards and consumer loans, seem able to afford colour televisions, rooms of furniture and new cars every two or three years, Canadians appear to be very affluent. There is undoubtedly pressure to conform to these unrealistic images and expectations. In order to do so, families begin to curb their fertility, to depend perpetually on having two incomes and expect to be involved forever in expensive consumer credit plans. This is especially true in less wealthy provinces such as Quebec where fertility has rapidly declined and consumer debt has soared dramatically in the past decade (Caldwell and Czarnocki, 1975). For many, however, even this way of "keeping up" is closed—credit is not available to everyone.

Poverty by and large is hidden. We do not see those who cannot afford even the cheap imitations of the middle-class lifestyle. Hofley (1971) points out that we are insulated from both extremes in Canadian society—the poor and the rich. We do not see the pockets of poverty in Canada. If it is rural poverty, we are likely to see the poor as quaint, their regions—the Gaspé, Northern Ontario, New Brunswick—as unspoiled. In the city, expressways take us over the poorer sections. Poor people whom we do encounter are seen as "depraved," "lazy," unwilling to work. For example, a survey taken in 1971 found that about half of all Canadians believe that poverty is self-imposed (Adams and others, 1971). Yet, poverty studies indicate that most of the poor are employed or want to work. We are dealing not with "welfare bums" but with the casualties of class inequality. Poorly paid occupations begin to look like a pervasive feature of capitalist society.

It was essentially this realization, that the causes of poverty are at least partially structural, that led Ian Adams, William Cameron, Brian Hill and Peter Penz to leave the Special Senate Committee on Poverty. They explain:

> *Any attempt to discuss the actual production of poverty in Canada—the roles played by the tax system, corporate autonomy, collective bargaining and the rest—was systematically eliminated from the drafts of the report (Adams and others, 1971:v).*

In other words, in their view, the Senate Committee would only ask questions *within* the system rather than *of* the system.

Certainly, changes in the welfare system, for example, do nothing to eliminate poverty, nor does the present system of "progressive" taxation redistribute income. Welfare and tax legislation offer personal solutions to what is a collective problem and treat as personal troubles that are public issues. As well, none of these "solutions" come to grips with the powerlessness, helplessness and entrapment which are the real meaning of poverty. While at the common sense level poverty obviously means lack of money, it is more useful to view the poor as those who can mobilize no resources. The poor are those who are not heard. Few studies in Canada have explored the social-psychological consequences of poverty; nevertheless, the army of unemployed and those in the "marginal work world" must face not only material deprivation but also the psychic costs of insecurity and instability and the widespread belief that poverty is an individual problem, the result of individual inadequacy.[12]

The poor must also live with a future which promises no improvement and with the probably realistic picture that they will die poor and pass on their poverty to their children.

Discussions of mobility are not about the poor nor, as we shall see, are they about the elite. In the middle of the occupational structure there is clearly a good deal of social mobility. Goyder and Curtis (1977), for instance, find that over four generations, family influence disappears almost entirely. This is not the case at the upper end of Canadian society, nor at the bottom.

Clement (1975) has updated and extended Porter's (1965) famous study of elites and power in Canada. He finds that, if anything, there is a slightly greater tendency for the Canadian Corporate Elite to be closed and self-perpetuating. That is, there is a greater chance that sons will inherit a position today than in the past. Tepperman (1977a) has examined Toronto's elite and comes to similar, but even more pessimistic, conclusions. According to his data and calculations, it has been possible for all members of the elite to pass on a high ranking position to their children. Upward mobility into the elite occurs because with economic growth there are more elite positions available. Also, elite families do not always reproduce themselves or, at least, not at a high enough rate to match the growth in the elite.

SOCIAL MOBILITY

The conventional answer in North America to inequality has been to try to assure the opportunity for mobility. There have been two streams in this liberal solution. The first is based in the "rags to riches myth," the Horatio Alger stories, the notion that "anyone can make a million." If people work hard, have the right values and perhaps a bit of luck, they can rise to the top. Sociologists have called movement up or down the stratification system within one's lifetime *intragenerational* or *career* mobility. A second, somewhat contradictory, theme is that everyone should start out the race on an equal basis. This is the *meritocratic* principle that those who win are the best. Social and economic advantages should not be passed on to children. The measure of the extent to which children are able to rise above or fall below the level of their parents is referred to as *intergenerational* social mobility by sociologists.

Strictly speaking, people can be mobile upwards or downwards in any one of Max Weber's three dimensions of social stratification—class, status or power. In fact, the third dimension, power, has not received very much attention for the same reason outlined earlier in the chapter—it is difficult to pin down and measure. Rather, most sociological interest in mobility has centred on changes in "class" situation (economic mobility) and status situation (changes in prestige) in the middle mass of society. Indeed, in its fullest sense, social mobility seems to mean that people have experienced both economic mobility and status mobility. They have experienced a change in lifestyle, attitudes and, most crucially, patterns of social relationships. For example, first prize in Loto Canada is obviously economic mobility and will certainly affect the winner's life chances, lifestyle and social life. But, will winning a million dollars make him or her a "millionaire"? Will it give him or her entry into establishment circles?

In most cases the answer is probably no. Money, it seems, is not enough. On the one hand, it is almost impossible as an adult to shed the habits, viewpoints, tastes and speech patterns of a lifetime for those of another, perhaps higher social class. On the other hand, there is snobbery. Higher status groups may, as they have often done, refuse to accept the *nouveaux riches* on the grounds that their family background is "questionable" or that they went to the "wrong" schools or that they lack "refinement."

Occupational Mobility

Of course, few people come into sudden wealth or, for that matter, have large fortunes to lose. For most, changes in occupation are the result of promotion or demotion or through starting out their work life in a "better" occupational position than their parents. In deciding whether a society is "open" or "closed," the amount of intergenerational occupational mobility is of greatest interest and relevance. However, it is probably intragenerational or career mobility which most people have in mind when they think of "moving up in the world," as well as social mobility. Generally, it seems, we base success not so much on how we have fared relative to our parents but on how we have fared over our own lifetime. Hence, we look for jobs with a career ladder and with built-in mobility rather than dead-end jobs, those we describe as having "no future."

Traditionally, occupations within bureaucratic organizations—banking, finance, government, large corporations—have come closest to an "ideal-type" conception of a career. These organizations offered a series of related, definable and more or less predictable steps. People entered at the bottom levels and with experience, age and training moved gradually up the hierarchy until they reached the top levels, resigned or died (Tepperman, 1975:74). This partly explains why white-collar jobs have generally carried more prestige than blue-collar jobs. But, we should also remember that in the past some who became managers or business owners started out working on the shop floor or on an assembly line and progressed slowly up into the higher ranks of the organization.

However, one consequence of educational expansion is that on-the-job promotions may have become much more rare. Managers and executives are far more likely to have an engineering or a business administration degree and to enter the firm as a junior executive. Time spent in the factory or in the field is likely to be defined as part of a training programme. And, as a number of business magazines have been reporting, promotion to the top may also be far more rapid than in the past so that, increasingly, those in the top echelons are in their thirties and early forties. In short, as the bond between education and occupation tightens and as the educational levels of executives rise, the likelihood of factory workers becoming managers diminishes. A traditional mobility route, promotion through the ranks, becomes cut off; intragenerational mobility has, as we shall see, given way to intergenerational mobility through the educational system.

Of course, at no time did the majority of workers have much chance of rising from foreman to executive. Educational expansion has, however, increased the likelihood that manual workers, indeed most white-collar workers, will be locked into what are essentially dead-end jobs. At the same time, the educational system is only partially successful in deciding whom to "cool-out" and whom to "warm-up" (Hopper, 1971). Undoubtedly, as Jencks (1972) has shown, education is not a guarantee of success and failure. Luck, drive and ambition will, for some, overcome formal and informal obstacles which school and society may place in their way. Others will not succeed even though they do receive a good education. These are the issues explored in the next chapter.

Social Mobility in Industrial Society

During the past 20 years a number of countries have carried out mobility studies to determine just how open or closed their society is. The most recent of these is the Canadian National Mobility Study by a team of sociologists at Carleton, McMaster and the University of Waterloo. In most cases what these studies actually measure is intergenerational occupational mobility. Since many occupations have a very similar social standing, it is common to think in terms of occupational categories or divisions (see Table VIII.6). Often, in order to make comparisons more consistent, these occupational categories are collapsed even further into manual and non-manual and sometimes farm classifications.

When this is done we only consider as social mobility intergenerational changes which cross the manual/non-manual line. This has usually been justified on the grounds that manual and non-manual are rough equivalents of working class and middle class. Thus, to move from one to the other may involve social as well as occupational mobility. Certainly, affluence has blurred the historical distinction between blue-collar and white-collar lifestyles but it has not destroyed them completely. Rather, there is convincing evidence that manual work is less interesting, less involving and less secure than non-manual work. Seldom does it offer a "career ladder" or comparable fringe benefits (Richardson, 1977). And, to achieve middle-class incomes, manual workers must usually work overtime.

Previous mobility studies have provided us with a remarkably consistent set of findings about trends and rates of social

Table VIII.6
FATHER'S OCCUPATION BY SON'S OCCUPATION FOR NATIVE-BORN MALES AGED 35-50, in 1973

FATHER'S OCCUPATION	SON'S OCCUPATION				
PMT	53.5	24.0	21.9	1.0	100.4
WC	30.3	37.1	31.8	1.0	100.2
BC	13.5	26.8	58.5	1.3	100.1
FARM	9.2	16.2	52.4	22.2	100.0

(N = 3664)

PMT = Professional, Managerial and Technical
WC = White Collar
BC = Blue Collar
FARM = Farmers and Farm Labourers
SOURCE: Jones and McRoberts (1977)

mobility in industrial society. The more recent Canadian study, then, contains few surprises and provides a picture for Canada very similar to that found in Britain, the United States and elsewhere (Jones and McRoberts, 1977).

First, most mobility is short distance mobility. It appears that the changes in occupational status which people experience are usually quite modest; few rise from the very bottom to the very top of the social hierarchy, even fewer make long falls downwards. Second, there is less social mobility than there would be if there was complete equality of opportunity. To put that another way, parents' status still influences what happens to sons and daughters. This is especially so at the top (professional, managerial) and at the bottom (unskilled). Both tend to be more "closed," more subject to "inheritance" than are categories towards the middle of the occupational hierarchy.

Previous national mobility studies have usually neglected the mobility patterns of women in the labour force. Monica Boyd (1977a), however, has analysed the data on women interviewed for the Canadian National Mobility Study. She finds that although the gross patterns of female mobility seem to parallel those of males, there are important differences. Because fathers have less influence on the occupational attainment of their daughters than on their sons', it seems that women neither suffer the worst consequences nor reap the greatest benefits of occupational inheritance. That is, women continue to be under-represented at the very top and bottom of the occupational structure; they get neither the best jobs nor the worst jobs which Canadian society has to offer.[13]

Consequences of Social Mobility

We need to ask whether social mobility is actually something to be desired. The usual liberal-functional answer is that it is. Strictly speaking, of course, a high rate of downward mobility should also be beneficial in terms of social and economic efficiency and may actually be a more crucial test of whether the society is meritocratic (Richardson, 1977b). The fact that there is downward mobility in a society implies that more privileged classes are not simply selecting additional talent from below but are also rejecting from their midst those who, despite being born in favoured circumstances, are incompetent to hold important positions.

Probably because no one cares to think of oneself or one's children moving downwards, politicians and sociologists have seldom had much to say about downward mobility. In any event, few fall from the top of the class structure. Evidently very few children of elite families are so lacking in ability that they cannot acquire some of the credentials and social polish required to maintain a position similar to their parents'. When difficulties do arise, private schools and special tutoring may offset the threat of downward mobility. In fact, most of the downward movement which we measure in mobility studies probably originates in families which are not very well assimilated into the middle class, that is, families which have moved upwards but who have not been able to translate economic mobility into social mobility (Richardson, 1977b).

Negative Consequences

While recognizing that there may be positive benefits associated with mobility, sociologists have also pointed out that there are personal, social and political costs which may outweigh its value. Durkheim, in his classic study of suicide, pointed out that when stratification systems are closed, there is a degree of security since social restraints act to limit the aspirations of everyone and to regulate the distance which one may fall. As society becomes more open and mobility is encouraged, the moral order is weakened. There is no longer a ceiling on ambitions. People cease to know what is possible and impossible, just and unjust. Whatever their actual achievement, they are never satisfied and are constantly seeking for more. Thus, social conditions which make social mobility possible may also create a strain towards *anomie,* a weakening or breakdown in the moral and normative order. Durkheim argued that this in turn contributes to an increase in the suicide rate.

Another early student of social mobility, Pitirim Sorokin (1927), was also ambivalent about what happens to people who are socially mobile in "a society mad in its mobility and futile strenuousness" (p. 510). Along with certain positive contributions, he maintained that there were also psychic costs: mental strain, mental disease, superficiality and skepticism. It seemed to him that at the interpersonal level, social mobility diminishes intimacy and increases isolation, restlessness and loneliness.

Later sociologists agreed with Durkheim and Sorokin that social mobility might be disruptive. They sometimes viewed mobility as a process akin to migration; changes in social class create problems and dilemmas very similar to those which occur when one moves to another country or region. Thus, both social and physical movement were believed to disrupt and sever kinship, friendship and community ties and leave the individual isolated, uprooted, and anxious. The mobile person is, in this view, caught between two worlds, neither at home in his or her original class, nor completely accepted in the new class. Unable to consolidate their status positions and to form longlasting friendship ties, mobile people, according to some sociologists, may experience a sense of discontinuity with their past and become unsure of just who and what they really are.

Social mobility became a way of explaining such things as prejudice, political extremism, social isolation and alienation. Sociologists were, in effect, warning that there were unanticipated costs associated with the mobility ethos of "onward and upward." A number of studies in the 1950s and 1960s did seem to bear them out. For example, upwardly mobile as well as downwardly mobile people were found to be more prejudiced, more isolated and more alienated than the non-mobile. Mobility did seem to create in people a sense of anxiety and confusion which sometimes worked itself out in the form of scapegoating, sometimes as withdrawal from social life (Blau, 1956). However, more recent research has been unable to replicate these findings. These studies suggest that social mobility *per se* is not especially disruptive and may, in some instances, produce "healthier and happier" people (Richardson, 1977).

We can suggest a number of reasons for this. First, mobility is far more acceptable and "visible" than it was in the past. At the same time, except for the very top and the very bottom of the status hierarchy, social classes have less *status rigidity,* that is, status distinctions have become less obvious and sharp. Also, those who have the "right" educational qualifications cannot so easily be excluded—their claim to acceptance and to high status is harder to counteract. Perhaps the simplest and most obvious reason is also the best: people when they do rise or fall do not usually move very far so the adjustment is a small one. Social mobility rarely means "rags to riches."

We should note, too, that sociologists have at times placed too much emphasis on status striving. For many people an improvement in economic position is quite sufficient. Either they do not recognize that they have not experienced status mobility or they do not much care. They define mobility mainly in economic terms—a bigger house, a better car, more money for holidays and so on—and seldom as a change in social status. In other words, to feel deprived, people must perceive that they have been "blocked" from achieving their goal or that there is a discrepancy between their goals and achievement. This, of course, can happen to people whether they are socially mobile or not.

Political Consequences

As we have seen in previous chapters, political and moral values make some theoretical perspectives more compatible to us than others and influence what questions we ask and which ones we fail to ask about various social phenomena. So it is with views and theories about social mobility. For instance, the speculations, hypotheses and empirical findings about the negative consequences of mobility stem mainly from what is ultimately a conservative impulse or bias in the sociological tradition; that is, the assumption that people require stability, hierarchy, social restraints and strong community and kinship ties if they are to be emotionally healthy and feel secure. The liberal ideology, on the other hand, starts from a different set of premises thereby putting far greater stress on individualism, achievement and economic efficiency. The result is that it has seldom questioned whether mobility may be in the best interests of the society or of the individual.

In direct contrast are radical sociologists who have seldom found much that is positive about social mobility. Whereas conservatives worry about what social mobility might do to social integration, radicals are concerned with how it dilutes social conflict and undermines the forces of social change. They point out that there need not be, and there probably is not, any necessary connection between a high rate of upward mobility and a reduction in inequality of condition. In fact, it might just be the opposite. If the society is relatively open, then there may be little sympathy or concern for those who do not or cannot better their economic situation. The self-made businessman, the successful career woman, the upwardly mobile French Canadian or Indian may feel a sense of gratitude to the system which has treated them so well. They are apt to wonder why all the "fuss" about class, sexual and ethnic inequality. Even those who, in effect, inherit their favoured position may view those at the bottom as personal rather than social failures—others have made it, why can't they?

A high rate of social mobility also gives the illusion of equality. Since fewer people are at the top than at the bottom, it may seem from the point of view of the former that "everyone" has been upwardly mobile. But, even if there was complete equality of opportunity, not everyone could be upwardly mobile. Only a portion of people at the bottom could expect to improve their position even under these circumstances, and there would have to be a much higher rate of downward mobility than actually occurs. In fact, it is only from the perspective of the top of the social hierarchy that there seems to be a lot of social mobility in Canadian society. However, perhaps because sociologists and policy makers are also looking "down," not "up," the social hierarchy, and perhaps because of the unpopularity of downward mobility, this aspect of social mobility has conveniently been ignored or downplayed.

Finally, radicals argue that mobility inhibits structural change. Certainly, an open society allows some in the lower classes who possess ability, drive and ambition to rise into positions of power and influence. But, in doing so, those who rise must also take on the values, beliefs and world view of the existing ruling class. Not to "co-opt" them in this way would be, for the existing elite, to run the risk of their forming a group which, if not revolutionary, is at least antagonistic to the system. Radical sociologists point out that mobility has, among other consequences, the effect of retarding the development of class consciousness and awareness of class interests. Also, mobility striving deflects people away from collective action to improve the lot of everyone towards privatized or individual efforts to raise oneself and one's family in the existing class structure. Similarly, from a radical perspective, it can be argued that upward mobility siphons off the most articulate and most competent of the lower and working classes, thus leaving them without effective leadership or spokespeople.

In sum, the assumptions made and the questions asked about social mobility will ultimately depend on our values and moral assumptions. Liberal democracies are premised on capitalism which is, in turn, premised on inequality of condition. Within that general framework or world view, equality of opportunity is, from a variety of perspectives, preferable to inequality of opportunity. A stratified society which permits social mobility is clearly a better place to live than a stratified society which does not. But, as we have stressed, equality of opportunity and equality of condition are separate issues; the first does not and cannot lead to the second. Social mobility implies that there is inequality of condition. If we believe that inequality is wrong for people and for society, then it makes no sense to promote or encourage social mobility. Our battle will be with the existing system, not with people's varying capacities and opportunities to rise within it to positions where they may exploit others.

SUGGESTIONS FOR FURTHER READING

There are an enormous number of texts and books on social stratification and inequality. We recommend, in particular, Frank Parkin's *Class Inequality and Political Order* (1971) and Charles Anderson's *The Political Economy of Social Class* (1974). Dennis Forcese's text, *The Canadian Class Structure* (1975), addresses specifically Canadian issues. A sample of Canadian research on social stratification can be found in James Curtis's and William Scott's *Social Stratification: Canada* (1973). A revised version of this reader will appear shortly. The controversies inspired by C. Wright Mills's studies of power and status in *The Power Elite* (1956) and *White Collar* (1951) are still with us.

Two recent collections on sexual inequality in Canada are *The Working Sexes* (1977), edited by Pat Marchak, and *Opportunity for Choice* (1976), edited by Gail Cook. Pat and Hugh Armstrong's *The Double Ghetto* (1978) is a highly readable account of their research on sexual segregation and inequality in the Canadian labour force.

Tables and statistics give one perspective on class inequality and social mobility. The human side, the personal and social consequences of inequality are caught in a number of works: Ian Adams's *The Poverty Wall* (1971); Terry Copp's historical account of working-class conditions in Montreal, *The Anatomy of Poverty* (1974); Richard Sennett's and Jonathan Cobb's *The Hidden Injuries of Class* (1972); and articles in John Harp's and John Hofley's *Poverty in Canada* (1971). Anselm L. Strauss's *The*

Contexts of Social Mobility (1971) provides a non-statistical and provocative enquiry into the meaning and nature of social mobility. Lorne Tepperman's *Social Mobility in Canada* (1975) examines mobility from a number of perspectives and gives accounts of various forms of career mobility.

The two most important Canadian works on elites are John Porter's now classic study, *The Vertical Mosaic* (1965) and Wallace Clement's updating of Porter's research, *The Canadian Corporate Elite* (1975). Peter Newman's *The Canadian Establishment* (1975) gives lively accounts of the personal lives of the Canadian elite.

Writings about Marx and his work are voluminous. Samples of his and Frederick Engels's writing can be found in Lewis Feuer's *Marx and Engels* (1959); Tom Bottomore's and Maximilian Rubel's *Karl Marx* (1963) and Robert Tucker's *The Marx-Engels Reader* (1978). Erich Fromm's *Marx's Concept of Man* (1961) provides a useful introduction and a sample of Marx's early humanistic and philosophical writing.

FOOTNOTES

[1]The *kibbutz* movement is described in Spiro (1958). For a brief description of Hutterite society see Forcese (1975).

[2]This view has been criticized in recent years because of its failure to take into account the status of women. See, for example, Acker (1973) and Eichler (1975). These authors argue that, for problems related to sexual inequality, the individual rather than the family may be a more useful unit of analysis. We will discuss this further when we discuss inequality later on in this chapter.

[3]See Barber (1957:54-55) and Lenski (1966:Ch. 9).

[4]This perspective is caught in Marx's phrase that "the ideas of the ruling class are in every age the ruling ideas." It is because of this that we describe the various systems of stratification—caste, estate and class—as different ways of legitimating inequality.

[5]Marx recognized the existence of other classes in society. He suggested, however, that the middle classes would have to choose sides in the eventual conflict. In the case of small shopkeepers and tradespeople, this decision would be made for them. Unable to compete with the larger capitalists, they would "sink gradually into the proletariat" (Feuer, 1959:15).

[6]By wealth, we do not simply mean income but the ownership of capital.

[7]Indeed, it is essentially over this issue rather than findings that Clement's (1975) study departs from Porter's (1965) study of power in Canada.

[8]This view has led many Marxists to see Dahrendorf's work not as an extension but as a denial of Marx's work.

[9]Some of the major critiques, especially the one by Tumin (1953), as well as the original statement, can be found in Bendix and Lipset (1967).

[10]Indeed, traditionally, most of the work on inequality in America and Canada has not been concerned so much with the system of stratification *per se* but with the more subtle and gradual distinctions in income, status and "power" of this middle mass. These studies have taken occupation as the crucial empirical indicator of social class. Some studies have examined income differences, again an approach which views class as continuous rather than layered. We prefer to view these studies as examinations, not of stratification, but of inequality in the middle mass. As well, as we shall see, studies of social mobility tend to be studies of movement *within* this middle mass.

[11]Perhaps the best discussion of what people have in mind when they rank occupations is the recent book by Coxon and Jones (1978).

[12]The term "marginal work world" comes from a long-term study of low-paid workers in the periphery of the labour force by the Institute of Public Affairs in Halifax. See Clairmont and Wien (1974).

[13]It should be noted, as Boyd herself comments, that the results might be different if income or power, rather than status, measures were used.

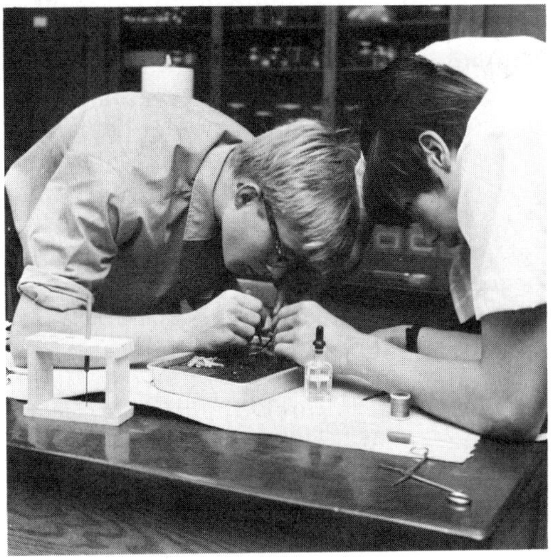

education and inequality

CHAPTER IX

When we think of opportunity we are likely to think of education. At one time or another we have all heard that it pays to stay in school or that even to get in on the ground floor of most firms you need a degree. But we also hear that a university degree these days is not worth the paper it is printed on, that there are Ph.D's driving taxis, qualified teachers working at Dominions, that the best thing to be is a plumber or an electrician. We pick up one newspaper which tells us that despite all the changes which have taken place most university students still come mainly from wealthy backgrounds, seldom from poor families. Another day we read that, in future, students will have to pay for a greater share of their education. Contradictions abound. Some say that the only way Canada can survive is to spend more on education; others argue that expenditure on education is unproductive, a wasteful squandering of resources.

Everyone, it seems, has an opinion about education and a personal and ideological stake in what happens to it. Accompanying this is an almost boundless faith that educational change will bring about social change. From Plato's time to the present, utopian and social reformers have seen in education a panacea for personal, social and economic ills. They have argued that to create a better society we must first create "better" people and that schooling can potentially put right what parents at times do so badly. Thus, there have been countless experiments with open classrooms and non-graded elementary schools, with a myriad of evaluative and teaching devices, with "cafeteria-type" curricula and with "multi-media" approaches. Recently there has been a countermovement back to a greater emphasis on the "basics," to more structure, to more rigorous standards, the very things seen previously as "restrictive," "repressive" and "discriminatory." There have been even more passionate and devisive debates over whether curricula should include or exclude such contentious things as religious instruction, evolution, sex education, socialism and communism.

For those who have equated equality of educational opportunity with equality of opportunity, the issue is not what is learned in school but with who gets there—the "inputs" to the system. Human capital theorists, on the other hand, have been more concerned with the "outputs" from the system and with the role of the educated in economic development and efficiency. Conservatives, too, have had their say, sometimes opposing mass education on the grounds that effective and competent leadership is best produced in separate elitist schools and universities.

Lurking behind these issues is the deeper controversy about what education is all about. Is it a means to an end, a place where we acquire the skills, values and credentials necessary for a good job? Or, is it an end in itself, a place where non-conventional ideas may be preserved, where alternative futures may be imagined and even tried out, where people can develop and learn critical perspectives on society, where people learn to think? In other words, ought education to be vocational or humanistic? The debate is a complex one with more than two sides. For example, many who oppose the increasing emphasis on job-specific education are simply arguing that to train people to be good citizens and integrated members of society requires that they be provided with more general skills and the ability to think, as well. Conservatives often worry that these more general skills can be assimilated by only a select few and may be "misused" in a dangerous way by the "masses." They advocate two educational systems—one for the masses, one for the elite. Educational critics worry, on the other hand, that education as it exists provides few ideas that could be dangerous to the *status quo,* that there is no such thing as the free market place of ideas or the community of scholars who pursue knowledge for its own sake. Instead, many argue, education produces unreflective conformists.

Both radicals and humanists bemoan the state of the educational institutions in our society. Radicals point out the role of education in justifying and preserving the *status quo,* the institutionalized inequalities in society. Education is a superstructure. Humanists, on the other hand, are likely to emphasize the liberating potential of education and knowledge, a potential largely unrealized because of the increasing emphasis on technical and vocational training. The radicals do seem to capture the role of education in capitalist societies. Indeed, this represents the major theme of this chapter. However, we share with the humanists the "ideal" of education as liberating; to understand the constraints we live under is surely the first step to removing them. This ideal, however, is being overshadowed as most people—educators, parents and students—increasingly come to view education as a means to an end, specifically, a good job, a better job than one's parents. Educators experience pressure to make their courses "relevant" not in political but in occupational terms. And, they may succumb to these pressures as they are increasingly called upon to play the numbers game. Students demand that courses be justified in terms of their employment potential as they are increasingly called upon to play the credentials game. Parents worry about whether their children's educational choices are "sound" and "practical" as they have come increasingly to believe that their children's life chances are determined by their educational achievement. The equation of education with occupational mobility is, ultimately, a false equation. It has, nevertheless, changed the shape of education and education research.

SOCIOLOGICAL PERSPECTIVES

As we might expect, these controversies have also found their way into the sociology of education. Mainly, the split has been between *liberal-functional* theorists and *conflict* theorists. However, interpretive sociologists—ethnomethodologists and some symbolic interactionists—have also begun to develop a third approach to understanding what education is all about and what it does to people and to society.

Until very recently, the most pervasive influence on sociological thinking about education came from the liberal-functional perspective. It provides a view of education which is both optimistic and familiar to most Canadians. Essentially, education is seen as a good thing for the individual and for society and as an effective lever by which to bring about social change. From this perspective, education is the key to success and opportunity, what the authors of *The Learning Society* called "an ascending ladder of social and economic mobility" (Ontario, 1972). The goal, one shared by most sociologists, has been to remove the barriers standing in the way of equality of educational opportunity and to create equal access at all levels of education for those who want to or can benefit from it. Thus, for most sociologists, educational reform and expansion have been the means by which family and class influences can be counteracted and society made more open, meritocratic and efficient.

However, in recent years conflict theorists have begun to challenge the traditional assumptions and approaches to the sociology of education.[1] These sociologists point out that although we have spent a great deal of money on educational expansion and put a lot of effort into educational reform, not much has changed. The basic patterns of inequality of condition and inequality of opportunity are largely unaffected by what happens to the educational system. Indeed, from a conflict perspective, education seems to reproduce, not alter, the basic form of social stratification in terms of both selection and what happens within the school. You cannot, say these theorists, change society by changing education because the problem does not lie with education but with capitalist society, with class and status inequalities. Unlike liberal-functional sociologists who view educational systems as at least partly an independent variable, able to effect social change, conflict theorists view education as dependent on what is happening economically and culturally in the wider society outside of the school.

At the same time, the approach and method of interpretive sociology has forced attention back to what goes on inside the school, what is sometimes called the "hidden curriculum." The approach of one group of sociologists neatly parallels what labelling theory has done to the study of deviance and criminality (Young, 1971). Sociologists interested in deviance used to accept what the police, the courts and middle-class agencies regarded as social problems. However, labelling theorists began to treat as sociologically problematic not only the deviant but also those who label him or her—the police, the courts and middle-class agencies. Similarly, sociologists who used to accept what administrators, principals and teachers saw as a problem—dropping-out, truancy, low motivation and achievement, lack of discipline—have begun to ask different sorts of questions. For example, rather than ask why lower-class students "drop out," they turn it around to ask why, despite limited opportunities and social pressures to leave school, do some of these students continue? Others have begun to examine assumptions and goals which lie behind what is taught in school, who is defined as "bright," who is "dull" and so on. Some have begun to look more carefully at how student and teacher definitions of situations and rules vary and are worked out through "negotiation" (Martin, 1976).

There is, then, a good deal of rethinking and re-evaluation of the traditional assumptions about the role and function of education in society. We call this chapter "Education and Inequality" because all of these sociological perspectives on education ultimately reflect sides of the debate considered in Chapter VIII: equality of opportunity versus equality of condition. We will consider in this chapter theories about the relationship of education to social mobility, social stratification and industrial society. As we will see, education is like other institutions in that it cannot be studied in a cultural and economic vacuum. It, too, must be viewed in the context of power and inequality.

EDUCATION IN INDUSTRIAL SOCIETY

However we might want to interpret or explain it, the fact remains that education has become one of the key institutions of industrial society. Much that was previously done by the family—passing on the culture to the next generation, teaching adult skills—is now almost exclusively the province of the educational system. Education also plays a very central role in what might be called the "total selection process," sifting and sorting people into various roles in the social hierarchy and, more importantly perhaps, making people accept as just their position in that hierarchy. As the bond between education and occupation grows ever tighter, we become a "credentials society," one in which knowledge and ability do not "exist" unless there is a degree attached and in which the main way to move upwards or to avoid downward mobility is through formal education.

Growth of Education

Education is such a pervasive and taken-for-granted part of our lives and a degree seems so obviously the path to a good job, that we forget how rapidly this has occurred. We forget that what was the general rule, illiteracy, has become a rare phenomenon. While most would probably be shocked at the persistently high rate of illiteracy in Canada (perhaps as high as one in 13 adults), we forget that not long ago *most* Canadians were completely illiterate. Until nearly the end of the nineteenth century, education at even an elementary level was reserved almost exclusively for the rich. The majority of children simply stayed at home until they were old enough to work on the farm, in the factory or down a mine. Even with compulsory education (1870-1900), most left at the minimum age of 14 or 15 since it was easy to circumvent the laws. Many parents took their children out of school early on various pretexts or allowed them to attend only a few weeks a year. Later, when resistance to compulsory attendance had abated somewhat, World War I, then the Depression, intervened. Thus, it was not until the end of World War II that compulsory education until 14, 15, or 16 was firmly entrenched in Canada (Phillips, 1957).

Secondary schooling as a place for more than the rich was even slower to develop. The Depression of the 1930s and World War II meant that a high school diploma for most people was a rarity, perhaps equivalent to what in the 1970s is a B.A., perhaps even an M.A., degree. As Table IX.1 shows, in the 1950s we lagged far behind the United States in secondary enrolments and despite great increases we have not yet caught up.

The decade of the 1960s saw massive and unprecedented growth in the Canadian educational system. Elementary and secondary systems were swelled by the "baby boom" of the post-war years. In response, new schools, especially for vocational training, were constructed and existing facilities were upgraded. It was, however, at the post-secondary level that the truly massive expansion occurred. Existing universities embarked on large-scale building programmes and faculty recruitment. New universities and community colleges were founded and staffed, sometimes making do with warehouses, old secondary schools and office blocks, until new buildings could be constructed. In other cases, ultra modern buildings, seemingly created instantly, emerged in suburbs, on mountain tops, in the midst of forests. Post-secondary enrolments shot from a 1960 low of 165,348 to 474,418 in 1969-70, an increase of 187%. Costs of post-secondary education rose even more

Table IX.1

SECONDARY AND UNIVERSITY ENROLMENT RATIOS, CANADA AND THE UNITED STATES

	Actual 1956-57	1960-61	1967-68	Projected 1975-76
Secondary Enrolment	As Percentage of 14-17 Age Group			
Canada	56	67	86	94
United States	83	86	93	98
University Enrolment (Full time)	As Percentage of 18-21 Age Group			
Canada	10	13	20	31
United States	14	15	21	24
University Enrolment (Full-time Equivalent)	As Percentage of 18-24 Age Group			
Canada	6	8	14	21
United States	16	18	23	27

SOURCE: Harvey (1975:46)

drastically, going in the same period from $315 million to nearly two billion dollars, an increase of 467% (Porter and others, 1973). Thus, budgets seemed, to those working at all levels within the educational system, virtually without upper limits. Extras were added to new construction which, according to one estimate, raised the price per student in Ontario from a 1960 figure of $1360 to over $3580 by the end of the decade, only half of which was due to inflation (Martel, 1974:6).

The 1960s, then, were indeed an exciting time to be a student, teacher or administrator. By the early 1970s, the "party" seemed to have come to an end. And, like all "good binges," the morning after is a time for sober recriminations and for facing the inevitable mess. Perhaps we grew too quickly and did not need quite such elaborate secondary schools, nor so many new campuses. Certainly, we find ourselves in the 1970s with under-utilized physical facilities and insufficient funds to run them. Student enrolments have failed to expand as anticipated, creating further budget restrictions and a tight job market for teachers at all levels. We must also live with the fact that many of our senior and middle-level university faculty are not Canadian citizens and apparently do not intend to become so, and that some who were hired in the 1960s did not have the appropriate qualifications or were hired into universities essentially as teachers rather than for their research capabilities.

THE TECHNICAL-FUNCTIONAL MODEL OF EDUCATION

Why this rapid growth in education? The usual and traditional answer was from the liberal ideology with its emphasis on economic efficiency, mobility and achievement. Collins (1971), an American sociologist, has labelled this approach to education a technical-functional model and suggests that it is a more specific version of Davis's and Moore's functional theory of stratification described in Chapter VIII. According to this model, education comes to be so important in industrial society because the skill requirements of jobs are constantly rising due to technological change. Formal education is necessary so that the more highly skilled occupations can be filled adequately. Hence, educational requirements for employment must also constantly rise causing larger numbers of people to stay in school for ever longer periods of time. This, then, explains why education becomes the key to mobility and to maintenance of a high family status. In other words, expansion of education has typically been seen as serving a dual role. On the one hand, key occupational roles could be filled more adequately and performed more efficiently. On the other, extending and expanding the educational system would increase mobility by making access more available to all members of society.

In Canada, the most influential and persuasive argument for the technical-functional perspective was John Porter's *The Vertical Mosaic*. Although this important book was not published until 1965, various findings from his lengthy and ambitious research emerged in the early 1960s and no doubt provided considerable impetus and rationale for the expansion which followed. His message was clear. In retaining what were essentially British elitist attitudes and practices, Canada had failed to develop an educational system capable of producing the skills required in an industrial society. Rather than train Canadians for skilled positions, we had limped through the first half of the century by bringing in skilled people from elsewhere—notably Britain, the United States and Europe. This created an illusion that we were, somehow, coping with industrialization. Canadian society emerged, then, as one characterized by considerable inequality of opportunity and a much lower level of economic productivity than in the United States. Porter concluded that the educational system would have to be drastically expanded and reformed. We would have to abandon the British *elitist* model for the *egalitarian* model of the United States. As he pointed out:

> *Modern education should be examined against the kind of model which is here being suggested—that is, a society in which the allocation of individuals to social tasks and access to educational resources is determined by ability. Thus two ends are served: the occupational structure will reflect a more rational allocation of ability; and individuals will have the greatest opportunity to develop their talents and make their contribution to the social good. . . . The principle of equality and the principle of the rational use of economic resources thus have a mutually reinforcing function. Now, more than ever, education means opportunity. A system which does not provide equal opportunity is also inefficient (Porter, 1965:167).*

Criticisms of the Technical-Functional Model

In recent years many of the basic and underlying assumptions of the technical-functional model have been under attack. First, as students have increasingly become aware, education does not automatically guarantee a high status job. Education, like most other things it seems, is subject to "inflation." That is, the occupational status one could "buy" 20 years ago with a high school degree now requires a university degree, perhaps a second degree. A study of graduates from four Ontario universities provides impressive evidence of this process (Harvey and Charner, 1975). The study compares the occupational success of 1960, 1964 and 1968 graduates. Those who graduated in 1964 were in the most advantageous position whatever their degree or academic record. By 1968, graduates needed a second degree to get an equivalent job to what a 1964 graduate could obtain with only one degree. More recent evidence both confirms these findings and suggests that in the 1970s the process of inflation has continued so that soon one will need a

Ph.D. to "buy" the kind of job an M.A. "bought" in the past.

The authors of this study suggest that "rates of return" on education have fallen because of an over-supply of graduates and a shrinking labour market. They do not question whether there was actually a need for a better educated work force. Others, however, have argued that in industrial societies, educational requirements have risen much more quickly than have technical or skill requirements of most jobs. For example, Randall Collins suggests that educational inflation arises because high status groups use education as a kind of status resource, a way of excluding those who challenge their favoured position, and not because the jobs have become more difficult or complex. So, as lower classes begin to get degrees, they find that the rules have changed. Suddenly, a second degree is required or the only degree which counts is one from an elite university financially beyond most people's means.

Other assumptions of the technical-functional model of education have also been under attack. Ivor Berg (1970) writes about what he calls "the great training robbery." He concludes that education makes very little contribution to individual productivity and performance. In fact, in a number of occupations, he finds that highly educated employees are not more productive and, in some instances, may be less productive than those with less education. Other research suggests, too, that educational qualifications are not very closely connected to the actual demands of the job. For example, large organizations generally require more education than small organizations for exactly the same work. Also, educational requirements for jobs are higher in the spring (when there are a lot of graduates in the market) than they are in the autumn. In short, educational requirements do not seem to be based on fixed demands of the job. Rather they are worked out through "bargaining" between employee and employer, the outcome depending on the balance of power between the two (Collins, 1971).

Finally, there is increasing evidence that the connection between what is learned in school and what one eventually does is very loose. It now looks like formal education may often be irrelevant and inefficient as a way to teach vocational skills. According to George Martel (1974:8), vocational schools were created and expanded in the 1960s both to reduce unemployment and to increase our industrial capacity. Yet, neither of these goals has been achieved. Rarely do "graduates" of vocational and technical schools go on to jobs for which they have been trained and unemployment remains high.

FUNCTIONS OF EDUCATION

If education is not about job training and does not increase productivity, what does it do? One answer, essentially a functional explanation, is that schools teach the norms of industrial society. One American sociologist, Robert Dreeben (1968a) suggests that we should focus not on what children are taught—the formal curriculum—but on the nature of their experiences as they face the particular organization of schooling—the hidden curriculum. He starts with what we have already considered in Chapter IV, that norms appropriate within the family are inappropriate in an industrial and bureaucratic society. As education becomes separated from the family, children, in going off to school every day, move from primary group norms to secondary group norms.

In the early grades, a formal and prolonged process of separating children from the family begins. It does not involve severing or renouncing kinship ties nor relinquishing the normative principles of family life since most members of society, after all, remain part of some kinship unit throughout most of their lives. Schooling does, however, put demands on pupils to adopt principles of conduct different from those they have come to accept as family members—more precisely, to restrict the premises governing family life to conduct among kinsmen, and to learn new pre-

mises that apply to settings outside the family. It is a process in which children learn both to generalize principles of conduct from one setting to another and at the same time to specify what principles are appropriate to which setting (Dreeben, 1968:29).

In particular, he singles out four norms as having particular relevance to industrial society: independence, achievement, universalism and specificity, essentially what were discussed in Chapter IV as "pattern variables." In common sense terms, we are expected to act one way at work, another way at home. Marital and family relationships are expected to be primary relationships. They are, ideally, warm, personal and diffuse. Spouses and children are seen as unique and irreplacable, i.e., particularistic. At home, the good parent is one who continues to love and accept children whether they are successful or unsuccessful, high achievers or low achievers. In other words, the role of son or daughter is ascribed, not achieved. Finally, family members are expected to act collectively, not independently, helping one another and sharing equally with other members.

In contrast to the world of the family is the world of the school. As Dreeben points out, even in the early grades children learn not to invest too much emotional involvement in one adult. Unlike parents who are more or less fixed for all time, teachers change each year, only in rare cases following children up through the grades. Later, instead of classroom teachers, students begin to go to various teachers who perform highly specific roles—teaching art or mathematics or physical education. Similarly, students normally move in age cohorts through the grades so that "Johnny" is not a unique son but a category; he is now in grade 4 and aged 9. Certain universal things are expected of him. Test results, for instance, suggest whether he is "normal," "above-average," "slow for his age" and so on. Children, then, are encouraged to view themselves not as a "special case," as in the family, but as members of a category. Streaming—ability grouping—probably contributes to this since it reduces the need of teachers to treat certain students as "special cases"—the child with emotional problems or a reading disability and so on. Gradually, too, children are not expected to help one another but to work on their own, to be independent and individualistic. Indeed, students who try what is normal in the home, helping one another, may be accused of "cheating." Dreeben (1968:35) suggests that:

The irony of cheating in school is that the same kinds of acts are morally acceptable and even commendable in other situations. One friend assisting another in distress, a parent helping a child—both praiseworthy; if one lacks the information to do a job, the resourceful thing is to look it up. In effect, many school activities called cheating are those in which customary forms of support and assistance in the family and among friends are expected.

Finally, the child's performance begins to be judged in the concrete language of grades. Status in school, then, comes to be achieved rather than ascribed as it is in the home.

For functionalists, education is the mechanism by which people learn the norms appropriate for an industrial society. Since stratification is seen as inevitable, education is important because it creates a degree of consensus about the rightness and justice of inequality. Similarly, since bureaucracy is also inevitable we must learn to cope with it. Hence, functionalists do not question whether we ought to teach children these norms. However, seen from a radical perspective, what is learned in school takes on a quite different tone. As Herbert Gintis (1972:57), a Harvard economist, puts it, "The social relations of education produce and reinforce those values, attitudes and affective capacities which allow individuals to move smoothly into an alienated and class-stratified society." From this viewpoint, then, schooling is mostly about producing compliant and docile workers who will respect authority and accept the fact that society is hierarchical. Ivan Illich (1971), author of the controversial book, *Deschooling Society*, goes further and suggests that education schools people "down to size," robs them of their creativity and forces them to discount their own experience and to believe that the only valuable knowledge is that which is certified by degrees and diplomas.

Earl Hopper, a British sociologist, suggests that for those moving upwards from lower classes, the appropriate term to describe *their* education is "status training." This, he maintains, may be a more crucial component of their educational experience than the technical skills imparted. He points out that

> *. . . the upwardly mobile are taught through both formal and informal means to speak "properly," to use the "correct" accent, to dress "well," to make friends with the "right" kinds of people, etc. They are taught to extricate themselves from friendship-networks containing people from their own initial economic and status positions and to exercise authority over those below and to submit in the appropriate manner to authority from those above (Hopper, 1971:296).*

Of course both functionalists and radicals may be exaggerating the actual effect of education. Actually, as Carl Bereiter (1972) has pointed out, we only assume but cannot prove that schooling teaches norms of industrial society and/or turns out "alienated" people. The problem is much the same as is involved in assessing the impact on people of television or the car—we do not have a "control group" which has not been exposed to these influences.

One attempt to find such a group is a study by Davis (1975). He found a sample of students in the interior of British Columbia who had done all their schooling by correspondence. He reasoned that if schooling does have an effect on norms and values these students should differ from those who attended a regular school. However, he failed to discover any differences which led him to conclude that the norms Dreeben claimed are learned in school may be part and parcel of our culture. It may be, then, that educational experiences strengthen or augment these norms but do not create them in the manner suggested by Dreeben and others.

Selection Function

The selection and allocation function of education admits less controversy. It seems evident, and could hardly be otherwise, that in an unequal society people are going to enter the educational system from different levels in the social hierarchy. Just as clear is that if inequality in the wider society is to persist, the outcomes of education will also have to be unequal. That is, educational systems are at least partially responsible for deciding who is likely to make it to the top, who will be at the bottom of the social hierarchy, who will be motivated to achieve and who will be "cooled-out" of mobility striving.

These are not, of course, problems unique to industrial society. Indeed, all societies must somehow solve the problems of selection, allocation, training and regulation of ambition—sub-problems of the total selection process. In previous eras, however, these were largely resolved through inheritance and ascription. It was expected that men would generally follow in their fathers' footsteps and take up an occupation, if not identical, then very similar to theirs. Women were expected to become wives and mothers. Perhaps because they are more complex and because of the liberal tradition in Western society, these problems are, in industrial societies, mainly resolved by the educational system.

Of course, family background is still very important. But, people from privileged backgrounds cannot in industrial societies simply "inherit" their parents' position. They must also show that they "deserve" it by achieving a university degree. For instance, as we saw at the end of Chapter VIII, the Canadian corporate elite did not become more open between 1950 and 1970. In fact, a slightly higher proportion of the present elite had fathers who were also in the elite. The difference is that these men were far better educated than their fathers. The sons did not enter the elite because of their educational credentials; they got their credentials because higher degrees, which supposedly signify greater ability and intelligence, have increasingly become the basis for justifying privilege. "Credentials" have in part replaced moral, religious or legal justifications of the past. Similarly, even for those who take over smaller family businesses, an engineering degree, perhaps a Master's degree in business administration, becomes increasingly essential.

Industrial societies, in other words, are increasingly becoming *meritocracies* in which one of the main ways of legitimating or justifying inequality is by the possession of educational credentials. Michael Young (1958), who coined the term "meritocracy," meant by it that those who form the elite and fill the most important roles in society would be those who are most intelligent. But, he also pointed out that meritocratic rule would be one of the hardest justifications to counter. If people did, in fact, rise and fall on the basis of talent and ability, as proponents of equality of opportunity have always desired, how would those at the bottom cope with their "failure"? No longer could they put the blame on the "system" and claim that they did not have the opportunity or that they were discriminated against. "Failure" becomes a "private" trouble rather than a "public" issue. More recently, Ivan Illich has made this same point even more forcibly. He points out that:

The hidden curriculum of schools . . . teaches all children that economically valuable knowledge is the result of professional teaching and that social entitlements depend on the rank achieved in a bureaucratic process. The curriculum transforms the explicit curriculum into a commodity and makes its acquisition the severest form of wealth. Knowledge certificates—unlike property rights, corporate stock, or family inheritance—are free from challenge (Illich, 1971:46).

Sponsored and Contest Mobility

While educational systems are intimately related to the selection process, they do not necessarily operate in exactly the same manner in every society. One problem is when should selection occur? Are people to be "sorted" at the end of elementary school or high school or, perhaps, in university? Whatever point is chosen is likely to be controversial. It may be seen as unfair or premature to "stream" children at age 11 or 12 because it does not leave room for "late bloomers." At the same time, late selection is likely to be criticized as inefficient, as creating "lower standards" and as "holding back" the bright students.

Probably, the actual outcome has less to do with educational policy and theory than it does with norms and values about social mobility and assumptions about the nature and source of ability. One attempt to summarize norms about social mobility and to show how they affect the organization of educational systems is the work of Ralph Turner, an American sociologist. He labels American norms about mobility as "contest" norms; those of Britain, "sponsorship" norms. He suggests that mobility in the United States corresponds to a race or contest in which elite status goes to those who have, as it were, run the hardest or shown the greatest perseverance:

Contest mobility is like a sporting event in which many compete for a few recognized prizes. The contest is judged to be fair only if all the players compete on an equal footing. The most satisfactory outcome is not necessarily a victory of the most able, but of the most deserving. Applied to mobility the contest norm means that victory by a person of moderate intelligence accomplished through the use of common sense, craft, enterprise, daring and successful risk-taking is more appreciated than victory by the most intelligent or the best educated (Turner, 1960:857).

In contrast, sponsorship mobility as found in England favours a controlled selection process:

Elite recruits are chosen by the established elite or their agents and elite status is given on the basis of some criterion of supposed merit and cannot be taken *by any amount of effort or strategy. Upward mobility is like entry into a private club, where each candidate must be sponsored by one or more members (Turner, 1960:856).*

Although the orthodox way to move upward in the United States is through education, innovative or irregular ways of achieving success are also admired and often attempted. For example, myths about mobility in the United States put a great deal of emphasis on the self-made man who, through "ingenuity and drive," finally reaches the top. And, as we suggested in Chapter VI, the mobility ethos in its extreme form may lead to such "innovations" as robbing a bank. For example, the film *The Godfather* is ultimately about upward social mobility of those prohibited from rising through legitimate channels.

Under sponsorship norms, ambition is not legitimate until selection occurs. This does not, of course, mean that people in Britain do not do things such as starting a business unless they are selected by the educational system. But, it does mean that their success will not smell so sweet. They may not be accepted by members of the higher classes who view them as "pushy," or perhaps as "uncultured" or "uncouth." Thus, the path upwards for those who are sponsored is likely to be an easier one than for those who move upwards without education (Richardson, 1977).

The Nurture-Nature Debate

Part of the difference between contest and sponsorship norms is the result of different assumptions about the amount and source of talent and ability in society. Indeed, they seem to reflect different sides of what has come to be known as the "nurture-nature" or environment-heredity debate. Contest mobility implies that differences in ability are the result of differences in the social and physical environment. People, according to this view, are very much alike at birth. Later differences can be explained by inequalities in life chances which work to the detriment of some and to the advantage of others. From the nurture perspective, it is worthwhile trying to give disadvantaged children a "head start" and to try to cancel out the differences which inequality creates. It also makes sense to educate people as long as they will put up with it because perhaps they will benefit from it and begin to develop their abilities.

Sponsored mobility starts from opposite premises. It is assumed that there is a limited pool of talent in society and that heredity rather than environment explains differences in ability. For this last reason, it makes no sense to try to educate everyone exactly the same. Rather, higher education should be reserved for those who have the ability to benefit from it. Others in the society—the majority—should have a different education, one suited to their lower abilities—a terminal vocational or commercial programme. Finally, where contest mobility tries to equalize opportunities for everyone, sponsored mobility is more concerned with "wasted talent"—those who have ability but are held back by social and economic factors.

CANADIAN EDUCATION

Where does Canada fit in Turner's scheme? One clue is that sponsorship and contest mobility mean approximately the same thing as *elitist* and *egalitarian* ideologies respectively. We have already examined the latter in Chapter VII when Canada was compared to Britain and the United States. As it happens, Turner was interested not only in describing these norms but also in showing how they affect the organization and selection procedures of educational systems. He assumed that educational systems are the main modes of upward mobility in industrial societies. Thus, he suggests, there are constant efforts to shape the educational system to conform with whichever mobility norm is prevalent in a particular society.

Turner points out that despite a number of reforms, British education still attempts to make an early selection of those who are bound for elite status from those who are not. From about age 11 or 12, when selection occurs, a minority of students attend grammar school, the only educational route which leads to university and the professions. They are therefore segregated from the majority who leave school at age 15 or 16 and enter more or less directly into the labour force. Since education is assumed to be only for those who can benefit from it, the education of this second and larger group tends to be rather half-hearted. In contrast, American schools have generally avoided an obvious separation of superior and inferior students. Since selection comes at the end of the contest, students in the United States are kept in school (and therefore in the running) as long as possible. Those who may eventually comprise the elite receive essentially the same education as those who will eventually have to settle for lesser positions. In most states, for example, virtually all students who complete high school are eligible to attend either the state university or a junior college. It is only then that selection occurs. One result of this is that in Britain very few who enter university fail, whereas in the United States a very large proportion of the first year class does not complete the full programme (Clark, 1960).

As there are 11 separate systems of education in Canada, it is difficult to generalize about Canadian education. However, at the university level, Western Provinces have tended to model their universities more on those south of the border. Those in Ontario and the Atlantic Provinces have more often been set up along the lines of British universities. Quebec's educational system, until very recently, reflected an essentially elitist ideology though it was obviously not consciously influenced by British traditions.

At lower levels, streaming has always been part of the Canadian educational system. While in recent years academic, commercial and technical students have usually been housed in the same building, the programmes seldom overlap. Channels across exist in theory but, in practice, few students move from the commercial and technical streams to the academic stream.

Nor at the university level has there been the same pressure for open admissions as there has been in the United States. If entry standards have relaxed in recent years, this is probably to do more with the financial problems of universities than with any drastic change in ideologies. Further evidence that the elitist ideology is still important in Canada can be found in the Ontario community colleges (colleges of applied arts and technology) and the similar institutions in most other provinces. They were set up to provide post-secondary education to students not in a senior matriculation or academic stream. These could have been modelled on the California system of junior colleges which offer two-year programmes, some of which lead to university. Instead, the deliberate decision was made in Ontario to make these terminal diploma programmes and not "back-door" entries into university.

"CAATS" were, from the beginning, slotted into an openly acknowledged hierarchy of post-secondary institutions with graduates expected to enter similarly stratified positions in the occupational structure (Garry, 1975). Interestingly enough, the opposite decision was made in Quebec. CEGEPs (Collège Enseignement Générale et Pratique) right from the start were intended to be "social levellers" mixing potential lawyers and potential plumbers in the same classroom (Denis, 1975). Everyone, whatever his level of ability or future plans, was expected to attend a CEGEP for two years. To insure this, some professions in Quebec require that the individual have a diploma before he or she is allowed to practise in the province.

INEQUALITY OF EDUCATIONAL OPPORTUNITY

Despite a great deal of effort and expenditure, the liberal goal of equal access to higher education is still distant and unfulfilled. Ascriptive factors such as class, ethnicity, sex, even the region of Canada where one grows up, have not diminished in importance and, indeed, seem to be persistent and patterned obstacles which lower aspirations and limit actual achievement. So pervasive are these that Breton (1972) concludes that any study which did not find these factors at work would be suspect. We are, of course, some way from being able to predict educational and occupational achievement. Studies which use more complicated statistical techniques show that there are still many factors which we have been unable to measure. The most readable account of these techniques is probably by Christopher Jencks and his associates (Jencks, 1972). In the end they conclude that a good deal of what happens to people is due to "luck" rather than systematic factors like class or ethnicity.

Tables IX.2 to IX.5 provide evidence that inequality of educational opportunity is still very much the case in Canadian society. Undoubtedly the most important influence on educational aspirations and actual achievement is the social class background of students. Generally, those from higher-class backgrounds have higher aspirations. This remains true even among those who have the same level of measured intelligence (Breton, 1972; Porter and others, 1973). Of course, the higher the income of parents, the more likely are their children to attend university (Table IX.2). It is also of interest that students from lower social classes who do go on to post-secondary education are more likely to attend a community college.

As we might expect, educational opportunities follow quite closely the pattern of economic inequality between provinces. For instance, Martin and Macdonell (1978) have shown that educational expenditures, teacher qualifications and retention of students (Table IX.3 and IX.4) are lowest in the Atlantic Provinces and Quebec, highest in Ontario, Alberta and British Columbia.

Sex is also an important determinant of aspirations and of who goes on to university. While girls often do better than boys in the early stages of school, women are less likely to go on to university and even

Table IX.2

DISTRIBUTION OF POST-SECONDARY STUDENTS BY PARENTS' INCOME, ACADEMIC YEAR 1968-1969

Family Income Group	% University Graduate	% University Undergraduate	% Community College
Less than $2000	1.4	1.0	0.9
2000-2999	5.1	4.1	4.3
3000-3999	6.7	4.9	6.3
4000-4999	4.8	6.2	8.8
5000-6999	21.1	20.7	29.7
7000-7999	21.7	24.6	27.0
10,000 and over	39.2	38.5	23.0
	100.0	100.0	100.0

SOURCE: Hiller (1976:Table 2.6). (Eighth Annual Review, Economic Council of Canada (1971). (May be replaced by Secretary of State Data.)

Table IX.3

EDUCATIONAL ATTAINMENT OF THE CANADIAN POPULATION AND LABOUR FORCE BY REGION, APRIL 1972[a]

		REGION				
	Canada	Atlantic	Quebec	Ontario	Prairies	British Columbia
Grade 8 or Less						
Population 14 years of age and over	29.4	36.2	37.1	25.6	26.8	19.5
Labour force	24.4	30.2	33.0	21.2	21.9	14.1
High School						
Population 14 years of age and over	52.6	47.2	45.5	57.1	53.5	58.1
Labour force	53.6	47.7	45.4	58.2	54.7	60.1
Post-secondary						
Population 14 years of age and over	18.1	16.6	17.4	17.2	19.7	21.4
Labour force	22.0	22.1	21.5	20.6	23.4	25.8

[a] Since labour force characteristics are subject to seasonal fluctuation, it is appropriate to note the month in which data were collected.

SOURCE: Martin and Macdonell (1976)

Table IX.4

ENROLMENT IN GRADE 9 AND HIGHER OF ELEMENTARY AND SECONDARY SCHOOLS, BY SEX, AND PERCENTAGE OF 14-17 AGE POPULATION

Year and Sex	Atlantic Provinces	Quebec	Ontario	Western Provinces	Canada
1960-61					
Male	53.6	43.9	63.1	79.4	66.1
Female	60.0	43.9	82.9	80.4	66.8
1972-73					
Male	75.8	104.8	105.6	91.5	86.5
Female	81.1	104.4	102.9	92.5	93.3

SOURCE: Martin and Macdonell (1976)

more unlikely to do graduate work than are men (Tables IX.5 and IX.6). Synge (1977) suggests that there are different kinds of expectations and pressures on men and women which act to depress female aspirations and eventually to limit their desire to go on to university. Class also affects women differently than men. Parents of lower income are less likely to make the same kinds of sacrifices to educate a daughter as they would for a son. At the same time, women are less able than men to earn enough to put themselves through university without parental assistance (Breton, 1972:130-133).

CLASS AND EDUCATION

Until recently we did not have to explore very far to discover what was the major barrier to equal educational opportunity. Sheer poverty seemed to overwhelm any other kinds of explanations of why some children do not get very far in school. Obviously, extreme poverty, whether due to unemployment, poor wages, a large family or a single parent family, is bound to have an important effect on the child's ability to learn and to concentrate. For example, as a British study found, overcrowding and bad living conditions are strongly related to academic performance and measured intelligence; children who scored low on these tests did much better after their families had been moved by the government to larger and more modern homes (Douglas, 1964). Compulsory education has, of course, kept children whether rich or poor in school until age 15. As we have seen, it is at the secondary and post-secondary levels that economic factors have had their most dramatic impact. In the past, few low income families could afford to forego the earnings of young people. Thus, there were parental pressures to leave school and get a job.

Table IX.5

EDUCATIONAL ASPIRATIONS FOR UNIVERSITY OF HIGH MENTAL ABILITY STUDENTS IN GRADES 12 AND 10 BY SOCIO-ECONOMIC STATUS AND SEX

	SOCIO-ECONOMIC STATUS							
	High		Medium		Low		Total	
	Male	Female	Male	Female	Male	Female	Male	Female
Grade 12	77	56	55	47	47	34	55	42
Grade 10	70	61	55	49	46	36	52	44

SOURCE: Porter, Porter, and Blishen (1973:123)

Table IX.6

PERCENTAGE OF MALES AND FEMALES IN FULL-TIME UNDERGRADUATE, GRADUATE, AND OTHER POST-SECONDARY EDUCATION

	18-21 Age Group Undergraduate		22-24 Age Group Graduate		18-21 Age Group Other Post Secondary	
	M	F	M	F	M	F
1960-61	16.2	5.4	1.6	.3	2.9	7.1
1970-71	25.8	15.5	4.9	1.4	7.6	7.5

SOURCE: Synge (1976:303)

Yet, even with rising affluence and with grants, loans and scholarships, working-class children are still more likely to drop out of school than are middle-class children. While, as a recent Canadian study (Porter and Others, 1973) suggests, "money still matters," particularly for university, research attention has, in general, shifted away from economic factors to other kinds of class and family influences which operate to the detriment of lower-class children and to the advantage of middle-class children. Why, when access to secondary and even post-secondary education is nearly universal, do so many lower-class children leave school and enter the labour force? Why do those who do go on "drop out" more often than their middle-class counterparts?

Intelligence

A traditional answer was that lower-class children are of lower potential ability and IQ than middle-class children, that, in fact, the educational system is selecting those with high ability and, in effect, rejecting those of lesser ability. Certainly, it is true that there are some differences between classes in measured intelligence but the difference is not great (perhaps not more than 15 points from top to bottom) so that there is in fact nearly as much internal variation within social classes as between them. While upper classes will have some people of higher measured intelligence than found in lower classes, a large proportion of people at the bottom of the social hierarchy will have higher measured intelligence than some of those at the top. The difference in IQ between classes is not large enough to account for differences in educational aspirations or performance.

The long and recently heated controversy about what IQ scores measure and where intelligence comes from provides a good illustration of how ideology influences the kinds of questions sociologists ask. Whatever IQ means, these scores have been increasingly used as the justification for selection decisions in education. Most liberal social scientists have held, for some time now, that differences in measured intelligence among social categories can be explained in terms of differences in physical and cultural backgrounds. Educational discrimination on the basis of IQ, they argue, is unjust because it simply reinforces and perpetuates the disadvantaged position of some groups. These sociologists were given rather a shock to which they responded with extreme hostility when Arthur Jensen (1969) took what was to many a backward step by arguing that IQ differences by "race" and "class" were mainly the result of genetic differences. It is probably safe to say that neither camp has succeeded in making its case empirically.[2]

Nor do we wish to enter a debate which is essentially among psychologists, except, perhaps, to suggest that the attempt by Jensen and his followers to "prove" that these genetic differences exist *and* the reaction to this work are misdirected. Whichever is "right," inequality justified on the basis of intelligence remains inequality. That is, whether intelligence is the result of environment or heredity, it is, in either case, beyond the control of the individual to do much about. It is, in other words, an ascribed, not an achieved, characteristic. Preoccupation with the meritocratic ideology has led, as well, to a preoccupation with how to measure who is "best"; the persistence of inequality is taken for granted. But, as Jensen himself admits, job allocation decisions based on IQ do not truly reflect job demands; there are probably few jobs that demand the "highest level of intelligence." And, there seems to be little correlation between intelligence and job performance (Jensen, 1969:16; Gintis, 1973:58).

In any case, studies in a number of countries have shown that there are large class differences in educational achievement even among those of high ability. For example, when people of the same measured intelligence but different class background are compared, those from higher social class backgrounds are more likely to be in an academic stream. At the same time, children of lower ability but from middle- or upper-class backgrounds will also be in the academic stream in large proportions. In other words, while IQ is an important factor, class background may be even more important in determining who goes on to university (Porter and others, 1973). Other studies, particularly in the United States, suggest that while class influences diminish among those who go on to college or university, they do not disappear entirely. Even at this stage, social class still has a direct effect on graduation rates (Corwin, 1974).

Cognitive Poverty

A better answer than intelligence differences is that students from different class backgrounds bring with them to the school different kinds of resources. It has become obvious that children raised in families where there are good books, conversation and discussion, stimulating toys and so on are likely to have a "head start" over those raised in a more limited and more impoverished environment. There is increasing recognition that poverty is not simply lack of money. It is also, at times, a world view or a subculture which leads to a kind of cognitive poverty—a world with narrowed horizons, limited aspirations and inadequate knowledge and social skills. Indeed, poverty and low status may even affect the way in which people use language and ultimately how they think. You may recall that in Chapter V we discussed Bernstein's concept of *restricted* and *elaborated* codes of language—the former being the main speech mode of the lower classes, the latter that of the middle class. According to Bernstein, working-class language tends to be a more "public" language in which sentences are short and grammar is simple. Traditional phrases and stereotyped responses predominate. On the other hand, middle-class children learn a "formal" language which is both more complex and more subtle, more capable of dealing with symbolic and conceptual issues. The implications of this for educational achievement are fairly obvious. Since the school environment is mainly middle class, those limited to the "restricted" code are at a distinct disadvantage, especially in their relations with teachers. Whereas middle-class students who use the "elaborated" code will be in tune with teacher expectations, working-class children are likely to be defined as "slow" and inarticulate. And, indeed, these students are likely to score low on IQ tests which reflect middle-class modes of thought and speech.

Bernstein points out, as well, "that a middle-class child learns *both* linguistic modes and uses them according to the social context, whereas a lower working-class child is restricted to a *public* language" (Bernstein, 1961:292). Thus, class factors may operate in quite subtle ways to put working- or lower-class children at odds with the school culture. For instance, as we have seen earlier in this chapter, when children leave home for school they enter what progressively becomes the "non-familial" world of bureaucracy; they must abandon primary group relations for secondary group relations. Yet, there is plenty of evidence that in working-class subcultures people are likely to behave mainly in terms of "traditional," that is, family-type norms. We know that in contrast to the middle-class, lower-class people depend mainly on kinship and friendship ties to find jobs and housing and for help and advice. Migration, too, is likely to be chain migration—lower-class people do not move because of a specific job but because they already have relatives there who can help them find a job and a place to live.

The lower-class subculture, then, seems to be an adaptive response to poverty, uncertain employment and low status. But, it is also likely to be in conflict with the middle-class culture of schools. Parents, for example, who do not themselves have good memories of school may feel ill at ease in talking to teachers and principals who treat them in a "professional" manner. Children, too, may find the cool and impersonal world of school with its regulations and norms about social order very different from what happens in their home and community (Willmott, 1969).

Value Differences

Probably, too, we should not assume that all lower-class people share middle-class values about the goodness of education and are simply repressed. Indeed, as John Porter (1968) points out, the real problem may not be how to increase opportunities but how to induce people to take advantage of those which presently exist. For example, as we have seen in the previous chapter, people at lower levels in the occupational hierarchy do not always agree about which jobs are most important. Many manual workers have a very low opinion of "office jobs" compared to skilled trades and are less likely to encourage children to stay on in school if the result will be "an unproductive desk job." Some parents, too, may be concerned that too much education will change the child's attitudes and, in effect, cause him or her to move psychologically and physically away from the family.

Finally, working-class parents may be more willing to accept teachers' evaluations of their children than are middle-class parents. When they learn that their child is not doing well in school they may encourage him or her in different directions in an effort not to put too much "pressure" on the child. In contrast, middle-class parents may consult with the teacher, try a different school, hire tutors and, as a last resort, perhaps put the child in a private school. In short, what may seem like indifference, even antagonism about education, may, from the parent's perspective, be an attempt to be tactful and accepting of the child whatever his or her level of achievement (Richardson, 1977).

In sum, creating complete equality of educational opportunity is not an easy task. While it is true that the school has taken over many of the socialization functions of the family, the first five or six years of life remain very crucial in the formation of attitudes, values and behaviour. And, of course, most children continue to live with their parents throughout their school years. Hence, family influences as well as the class influences of peer groups and the community are likely formidable barriers overwhelming what is often the very limited involvement in the classroom.

Nevertheless, *educational* opportunities have obviously improved dramatically since World War II. Certainly, university students still come disproportionately from wealthy families, but no longer is university exclusively the preserve of the rich. Large numbers of young people from lower-class backgrounds do make it either to university or to a community college. But, as many sociologists have begun to realize, educational expansion and reform do not appear to make much difference as far as equality of opportunity or equality of condition is concerned. To understand why this should be the case requires that we widen the focus beyond simply the educational system. We need to look again at the nature of social mobility and its relationship to education in industrial society.

EDUCATION AND SOCIAL MOBILITY

The most surprising findings about social mobility emerged when it was finally possible to compare various societies and to look at mobility trends within the same society. For American sociologists raised to believe that the United States was, indeed, the land of opportunity, the expectation was that there would be more mobility in the United States than in Europe. In fact, there is not a great deal of difference between any of these societies and what differences there are do not appear to be related to social and educational policy or underlying ideologies (Miller, 1960). For example, despite the fact that there are nearly four times as many people in higher education in the United States than in Britain, rates of social mobility for the two countries are pretty much the same. Although Canada falls somewhere between, it has a very similar rate of social mobility. Thus, in terms of equality of opportunity, it does not seem to matter very much whether a society is elitist or egalitarian, whether it tends towards sponsored or contest norms about social mobility.

Nor do rates of social mobility appear to have changed much over this century; they may, in fact, have worsened in some societies. Again, given the massive expansion in education, these were surprising and, to some, disheartening findings. After all, since the turn of the century, liberal faith in educational reform and expansion rested on the hope that the outcome would be greater equality of opportunity. That this has not resulted has, of course, forced a reassessment and evaluation of the place of education in industrial society.

Part of the reason that mobility rates do not change very much should have been obvious but was not. It is simply that not everyone can be upwardly mobile. In an unequal society some will rise to the top; most will end up in less favoured positions. In short, no matter what happens in terms of social and educational policy, the majority cannot expect to be socially mobile.

There is no doubt that educational opportunities for lower-class children have improved dramatically in recent decades. But, they have also improved for everyone; as those at the bottom begin to get more education so do those at the top. In fact, most policies designed to help out the disadvantaged—head start programmes, kindergartens, scholarships and bursaries, counselling and so on—probably do help. It is just that other classes benefit from them even more. As far as social mobility is concerned, the end result is a static situation and "educational inflation": the educational system expands without narrowing relative differences between groups or changing the underlying structure of opportunities (Karabel, 1972).

In sum, education seems relatively impotent to bring about changes in social mobility. Those most likely to benefit from a "good education" are those who had a head start in the first place. This means two things: (1) we have not achieved equality of educational opportunity—lower-class students do not do as well or go as far, and (2) equality of educational opportunity, even if it were a reality, is not the same thing as equality of opportunity. A good education does not guarantee a good job. Although education has come to be seen as a resource for improving one's social and economic position, it is better viewed as a resource of the powerful for assuring their position and the position of their children.

EDUCATION AND CHANGE

Especially in the past two decades social reformers pinned many of their hopes for a better society on educational reform. But, in the context of the 1970s, these now seem optimistic, unrealistic and non-sociological. Education, it turns out, is not a cure-all. Nor is it even a very effective lever to bring about social change. As we have seen in this chapter, educational systems are shaped by, but do not shape, social arrangements; they respond to social and economic forces in the wider society. Educational reform and expansion cannot create equality of condition or produce a more efficient society. Rather, the main function of education seems to be to reproduce and legitimize inequality. Change and innovation within the educational system, therefore, must wait for more fundamental changes in the wider society.

This partly explains the demise and failure of the free school movement and of experimental university programmes. Like most utopian solutions, they failed to confront the fundamental issues of capitalism and bureaucracy; they ignored "structure" and acted as if they were in a social and economic vacuum. Few, today, would disagree with the ideals of a "liberated education": freedom from the constraints and repression of the hidden curriculum with its grades and rules and structures and, instead, learning as an end in itself, not a means to other ends. But, as Bowles and Gintis (1976) show, free schools have so far been little more than "isolated havens for the over-privileged"—escapist enclaves for those who can afford to ignore for a while the demands of the credentials society. They have simply been irrelevant, sometimes harmful, for those who need educational qualifications if they are to cope with the economic and social reality of a hierarchical and authoritarian work world. So, as Pomfret (1976) points out, most educational innovations have little or no impact on the society as a whole and may even strengthen the *status quo* by rechanneling and diffusing discontent.[3]

Yet, as bleak as the prospects for change are made out to be, few have been willing to abandon education or to adopt Ivan Illich's (1971) drastic solution that schools should simply be abolished and that society should be "deschooled." Many continue to see education as at least potentially liberating and as ultimately a force for social change. Guy Rocher (1975), for example, suggests that education has, in fact, changed much more rapidly than the rest of society. Hence, educational systems serve as a kind of social laboratory which eventually introduces a dynamic element into society. They are institutions where planned change can be implemented and studied and "alternative futures" explored (Fullan, 1972).

Also, compared with business and industry, universities are relatively free, non-authoritarian and unstructured. They are, therefore, fertile grounds for the creation of social movements and new ideologies—the "quiet revolution" in Quebec and the counterculture are recent examples (Westhues, 1975). Of course, we can question whether the counterculture has had any real or lasting impact on society. But, while most students probably shaved their beards, cut their hair and put on ties in anticipation of job interviews, they could not so easily shed the values of the counterculture. Inevitably, the sense of liberation, tolerance and distrust of established authority which marked the counterculture had to spill over into the workworld and alter relationships there as well (Ondrack, 1973).

We must remember, as well, that the outcome of even the most repressive system is always uncertain and can only be partially anticipated. Bowles and Gintis (1976:12) remind us that "the authoritarian classroom does produce docile workers, but it also produces misfits and rebels. The university trains the elite in the skills of domination, but it has also given birth to a powerful radical movement and critique of capitalist society." Finally, these same authors argue that if schooling can teach the norms of capitalist society, then it is also capable of teaching equality and social justice.

The sociological study of education is, in the end, a vivid example of what we mean in this book by humanistic sociology and of the paradox that people are both products and producers of social structure. In this chapter we have emphasized the intimate and complex relationship between the educational system and the inequality of the wider society—what might be called the *latent consequences* of education. But, we have also tried to show that these emerge more or less clearly, are interpreted differently and seem more or less inevitable and taken-for-granted as we move from one value position to another. In the process we have largely ignored what education is *manifestly* about—the teaching of skills, values and ideas. We have done so because the main contribution of the sociological perspective is to make us aware of what can be changed and what cannot. Thus, in education as in social life generally, we cannot simply will social change into being—the mistake of the free school movement. We must first come to understand the limits to freedom of action which economic and social structures impose and eventually the choices open to us. It is only at this point that education can be liberating instead of repressive.

SUGGESTIONS FOR FURTHER READING

Just as the 1960s saw an expansion in education, the decade also saw an expansion in writings on this field. Many of the positions and authors we have mentioned are represented in Holger R. Stub's and Robert R. Bell's *The Sociology of Education: A Sourcebook* (1968). Two other useful collections are Michael F. D. Young's *Knowledge and Control* (1971) and Earl Hopper's *Readings in the Theory of Educational Systems* (1971). Some basic textbooks include: Burton R. Clark's *Educating the Expert Society* (1962); Olive Banks's *The Sociology of Education* (1968); and Ronald G. Corwin's *A Sociology of Education: Emerging Patterns of Class, Status and Power in the Public Schools* (1965). Also of interest is his *Education in Crisis* (1974).

During this period a number of social scientists and educators were experimenting with and writing about educational reform. Drawing explicitly on the socialization theories of Jean Piaget, a number of educators tried to find ways of giving students greater autonomy in their own education. A sample of these efforts can be found in a collection compiled by E. B. Nyquist and G. R. Hawes, *Open Education* (1972). Other reformers and critics drew their inspiration from philosophers and theorists ranging from Plato to Montessori, and this is reflected in the varieties of reform proposals. One of the most controversial experiments remains the English school, Summerhill, founded by A. S. Neill (1960). A representative sampling of "new" approaches to school reform is R. Gross's and B. Gross's *Radical School Reform* (1969). Two important works out of this period are Neil Postman's and Charles Weingartner's *Teaching as a Subversive Activity* (1969) and Charles E. Silberman's *Crisis in the Classroom* (1970). Perhaps even more controversial are the works by Ivan Illich which are cited in this chapter. Inevitably, new educational ideologies produce counter-ideologies. For a recent set of critiques of the educational innovations of the 1960s, see Cornelius J. Troost's *Radical School Reform: Critiques and Alternatives* (1973). Samuel Bowles's and Herbert Gintis's *Schooling in Capitalist America* (1976) is a powerful Marxian critique of existing education and attempts, to date, at reform. Michael B. Katz's *Class, Bureaucracy and Schools* (1971), an historical account of the development of education, takes a similar position to Bowles and Gintis.

The issue of inequality of opportunity has stimulated a great deal of research. A landmark study in this area is what is usually called the *Coleman Report,* James S. Coleman and others, *Equality of Educational Opportunity* (1966). A very readable and important book is Christopher Jencks and others, *Inequality: A Reassessment of the Effects of Family and Schooling in America* (1972). British researchers have, it seems, been more successful in capturing the subtle relationships between the home, the community and the school. In particular, we recommend Brian Jackson's and Dennis Marsden's *Education and the Working Class* (1962); Brian Jackson's *Streaming: An Educational System in Miniature* (1964); and Peter Willmott's *Adolescent Boys of East London* (1969). However, Bel Kaufman's *Up the Down Staircase* (1964); Jonathan Kozol's *Death at an Early Age* (1967); and David Roger's *110 Livingston Street* (1968) are important American examples of this more humanistic and non-quantitative tradition in educational research.

An important Canadian study is Raymond Breton's (in collaboration with John McDonald and Stephen Richer) *Social and Academic Factors in the Career Decisions of Canadian Youth* (1972). Studies which focus on post-secondary education in Canada include Edward Harvey's *Educational Sys-*

tems and the Labour Market (1974); Marion Porter and others, *Does Money Matter?: Prospects for Higher Education* (1973); and Robert M. Pike's *Who Doesn't Get to University—and Why: A Study on Accessibility to Higher Education in Canada* (1970). Heather Robertson's *Reservations Are for Indians* (1970) is a powerful indictment of the effects of "white man's" schooling on native peoples. Various articles in Elia Zureik's and Robert M. Pike's *Socialization and Values in Canadian Society* (1975) develop this and other themes about the effects of schooling. Alison Prentice and Susan Houston have put together an interesting and useful collection of their research on the history of Canadian education, *Family, School and Society in Nineteenth-Century Canada* (1975). See also Prentice's book, *The School Promoters* (1977). A recent and very thorough textbook is Wilfred Martin's and Allan Macdonell's *Canadian Education: A Sociological Analysis* (1978). A sample of recent research in Canada can be found in Richard A. Carlton, Louise A. Colley and Neil J. MacKinnon, *Education, Change and Society* (1977). For more radical perspectives on Canadian education, see Randle W. Nelson's and David A. Nock's *Reading, Writing, and Riches* (1978). Finally, some of the most provocative and critical writing on Canadian education appears in *This Magazine* (formerly, *This Magazine is About Schools*).

FOOTNOTES

[1]In particular, see Collins (1971; 1974); Carnoy (1976); and Bowles and Gintis (1976). A summary of these with implications for Canadian society can be found in Richardson (1977a).

[2]Similar arguments to Jensen's have been made by H. J. Eysenck (1971) in Britain, and Richard Herrnstein (1971) in the United States. Criticisms of their positions can be found in Richardson and Spears (1972); Gartner and others (1972); and in a special compilation of *Harvard Educational Review* (1969) articles.

[3]For an interesting study of a Canadian free school, see Mark Novak's *Living and Learning in the Free School* (1975).

ethnic groups
CHAPTER X

If one substantive area has captured the interest of Canadian sociologists, it is the study of ethnic groups and ethnic relations. Certainly most Canadians experience Canada as a multi-ethnic nation. They hear different languages, eat in ethnic restaurants and attend ethnic folk festivals. They are also preoccupied by language conflicts, questions of the rights of native peoples and fear of accusations of prejudice and discrimination. Part of the consciousness of being Canadian is to realize that Canada is a society of immigrants.

For sociologists, one of the key issues has been whether this apparent ethnic diversity is "real," that is, more than the superficial remnants of ethnic groups which no longer exist in Canada. Is Canada an ethnic mosaic? If the differences are real, why do they persist? Whose interests do they serve? And, what are the social consequences of these differences? If these differences are only apparent, perhaps even trivial, then why have so many attached such importance to them? Some would argue that the trivial differences became important because real differences, ethnic diversity, are impossible in the face of the intrusions of the dominant culture. Others have argued that Canada in particular, because it has two dominant cultures, has been more tolerant of ethnic diversity than countries such as the United States. Most liberal sociologists, however, have understood the question as a matter of degree. They frame the question in terms of a dilemma faced by all immigrant groups: Do they assimilate or do they preserve their cultural heritage? In part, then, this is seen as a dilemma of choice. If immigrants are to compete equally with other Canadians for the scarce resources, that is, if they are to be structurally assimilated, how much of their cultural heritage can they preserve? To what extent does structural assimilation require behavioural assimilation? In other words, the liberal is again asking questions about equality of opportunity. To what extent do ethnic differences impede opportunities for social mobility?

To understand these views, the differing kinds of questions sociologists ask, we must understand the normative and ideological stances on ethnicity. Do social scientists view ethnic diversity as good or bad? For the most part, the conventional answer is that ethnic diversity is to be valued. When Canadians speak of their country as a mosaic rather than as a melting pot, they often do so with pride. Canada, in these terms, is described as having a particularly rich and diverse culture, possible only in the placid Canadian context of tolerance. Canadians do not have a "race problem," for example. Indeed, the promotion and encouragement of ethnic diversity and ethnic pluralism, has, for a long time, been a deliberate policy of the Federal government.

Many social scientists would agree with such a policy but for somewhat different reasons. For many, ethnic groups serve, at least in part, to fill the gap created by secularization, the breakdown of traditional authority and the loss of community. They may even celebrate the fact that within the homogenizing confines of mass society, ethnicity—the clinging to and, perhaps, rediscovery of one's "primordial ties"—flourishes. Even if this diversity creates conflict, they argue, it is a small price to pay if the rediscovery of ethnicity serves as a bulwark against the dullness and predictability of Howard Johnson's, McDonald's and Holiday Inns. Perhaps ethnicity provides one way we can do battle against the impersonality of a technological and bureaucratic society.

On the other hand, many liberals find the preoccupation with ethnicity repugnant: to talk about human diversity is simply to rekindle the flame of racism and racial conflict; encouraging ethnicity is to invite the continuation of ethnic inequality. Ethnicity is bad because it stands in the way of achieving a more meritocratic society. Clearly, the liberal position on ethnicity reflects their preoccupation with equality of opportunity.

Radical sociologists have, for the most part, ignored ethnicity. They would argue that the promotion of and preoccupation with these issues are misdirected. Ethnicity, like education, is a superstructure—a mechanism for maintaining the *status quo*. Ethnicity obscures the real cleavages in society, those which centre around class inequality. In other words, ethnic conflicts inhibit class consciousness. Ethnic conflict is usually conflict about mobility opportunities rather than about structural class inequality.

Nevertheless, there has been a growing recognition that ethnicity may be a valuable *resource* for the rallying and expression of collective interests. Indeed, many would argue that more people will initially perceive shared interests in terms of ethnicity than in purely class terms. Ethnic conflicts might be viewed as a kind of primitive political expression of what are ultimately class conflicts. As we shall see, social movements tend to fragment into factions, in part at least, because collective conflict has a radicalizing potential. Whatever the initial issues, some, at least in the experience of confrontation and in interaction with others who share their grievances, will come to recognize not only the troubles of personal milieu but also the larger structural problems. Hence, questions of ethnic identity and national character may become transformed into questions of political economy.

A radical perspective also allows us to see that ethnicity as a resource is double-edged. Just as ethnicity may be a useful resource in expressing the collective discontent of disadvantaged groups, so, too, is it a resource available to the powerful to minimize and channel social discontent. From this perspective, then, ethnic conflict is resource management; ethnicity is a resource which can be used either to organize dissent or to divide and rule.

We find the resource conception of ethnicity a particularly useful device for viewing the diverse theoretical and empirical work on ethnic relations. We can view ethnicity as a resource used by "those who have" to block the mobility of "those who have not." We can view it as a resource used by the disadvantaged to protect themselves from the effects of discrimination and as a lever for individual and collective mobility. And, on the level of personal identity in everyday life, ethnicity is a cultural resource, part of the common stock of knowledge which we can call on in particular situations.

Indeed, by this point in the book, there is not a great deal we can say about ethnic relations which is "new." Ethnicity serves as another illustration of how power and inequality shape interaction, of how people make sense of their world, give meaning to their experiences and come to act back on the structures which constrain them. Viewing ethnicity as a resource keeps in the forefront that people create and maintain social structures. This chapter, then, examines how, in Canada, this resource is managed by the powerful, the less powerful and all of us in everyday life.

ETHNIC DIVERSITY IN CANADA

As we saw in Chapter VII, a major preoccupation of Canadian history, politics, sociology and literature is the now 200-year-old conflict between the English and French. But, as Table X.1 shows, the balance of power between these groups has shifted somewhat and has become more complex by the addition of other ethnic groups into the Canadian social structure. One of the major changes in this century is that we have progressively moved from a dual-ethnic society to a multi-ethnic society. Whereas in 1871 virtually everyone in Canada was either French or British, today somewhere between one-quarter and one-third of Canadians are, for census purposes at least, members of some other ethnic affiliation. Of course, none of these "other ethnic groups" is even close in size to the two charter groups. Nor are they, by any means, collectively, a cohesive or united "third force." Nevertheless, the pattern of post-war immigration does have the effect of eroding the supremacy of both English and French in Canada. Moreover, since most of these ethnic groups are assimilating towards English-speaking culture, French-Canadian influence, federally, is progressively undermined. We should note, as well, that claims by any one ethnic group—Ukrainians, for example—for special status are likely to kindle other similar claims from other ethnic groups.[1] Indeed, some of the growing consciousness of Indians in Canada has, undoubtedly, been fuelled by the growing presence in Canada of ethnic pluralism and ethnic conflict.

RACE AND RACIAL THINKING

Race, ethnicity and minority group are often used rather loosely and interchangeably. And, as with most sociological concepts, there is often a discrepancy between

Table X.1

PERCENT DISTRIBUTION OF POPULATION BY ETHNIC GROUPS IN CANADA FOR SELECTED DECADES

GROUP	1871	1901	1931	1961	1971
British	60.5	57.0	51.9	43.8	44.6
French	31.1	30.7	28.2	30.4	28.7
French	31.1	30.7	28.2	30.4	28.7
Other European	6.9	8.5	17.6	22.6	24.1
Asiatic	–	.4	.8	.7	1.3
Native People	.7	2.4	1.2	1.2	1.4

SOURCE: Adapted from *Report of the Royal Commission on Bilingualism and Biculturalism*, Book IV, 248 the technical definition and what people mean by the term in everyday life. Leaving aside for the moment sociological definitions, common sense definitions of race and ethnicity and how people use these terms have a profound influence on how the various groups interact. For example, racial beliefs have had a profound influence, even in this century, on who is likely to be admitted to this country. Particularly in the nineteenth century, race became an unquestioned means of classifying people. Not only could people be put in one of several racial categories, but it was also assumed that mental and social characteristics were closely associated with certain physical characteristics. A very easy, perhaps inevitable, step was to assume that races could be ranked from superior to inferior.

We have yet to escape fully the effects of the myth of racial differences and racial superiority. We are, for instance, still living with, trying to cope with and understand the kind of madness which lay behind The Holocaust—the deliberate and systematic murder of 12 million Jews, Slavs and Gypsies, a programme of genocide without precedence and which was based on a totally erroneous belief in the superiority of the so-called Aryan Race. That many people believed that Aryans constituted a race at all was clearly powerfully influential even though no technical definitions—not even nineteenth century thinking—would have accepted or condoned Aryan as a racial category.

Understandably, since World War II, the concept of race has been subjected to very close scrutiny. The overwhelming conclusion is that race is a meaningless, unscientific and ultimately dangerous notion, whether considered in terms of biology or anthropology. Ashley Montagu (1969:6), a prominent American anthropologist, has this to say about race:

The process of averaging the characters of a given group, knocking the individuals together, giving them a good stirring, and then serving the resulting omelet as a "race" is essentially the anthropological process of racemaking. It may be good cooking but it is not science, since it serves to confuse rather than to clarify. When an omelet is done it has a fairly uniform character, though the ingredients which have gone into its making may have been variable. This is what the anthropological conception of "race" is. It is an omelet which corresponds to nothing in nature. It is an indigestible dish conjured into being by an anthropological chef from a number of ingredients which are extremely variable in the characters which they present. The omelet called "race" has no existence outside the statistical frying-pan in which it has been reduced by the heat of the anthropological imagination.

Tumin (1969:5) also agrees that race is not a scientific term since all it means is that a group of humans possesses a distinctive gene frequency. But, since no one can agree on how many distinctive physical traits a group must have to be called a race, there could be thousands of races of humans, depending on where we draw the line and what physical traits we choose to include as relevant—blonde hair, brown eyes, what have you. Clearly, most definitions of who is and who is not a member of a race are socially determined. Otherwise, why would someone who is one-third, maybe only one-fifth "Negro," be called "Black"? Why are "half-breeds"—Métis—lumped together by most "Whites" with Indians?

What is crucial is that any classification of races biologists may devise has no sociological relevance; it will not allow us to say anything about group or personal characteristics (Tumin, 1969:5, 6). Does it, then, make sense even to speak of races and race relations? Montagu argues that it does not, that virtually all of the issues which we are likely to talk about in this chapter are better dealt with by using the term *ethnic group*. In his view, social scientists have a moral obligation to challenge lay thinking on race and that the way to do this is to avoid talking about it at all and to use the less loaded "ethnic group." The latter, he suggests, encourages the passage from ignorant or confused certainty about what groups are like to thoughtful uncertainty.

For the layman, as for others, the term "race" closes the door on understanding. The phrase "ethnic group" opens it, or at the very least, leaves it ajar (Montagu, 1964:24).

Montagu is, of course, correct in his view that one of the tasks of social scientists is to "re-educate" people away from erroneous and, as in this case, dangerous beliefs. Montagu also points out how well a belief in racial differences fits with an exploitative capitalist society. But it is also the case that to *understand* behaviour, it is necessary to take belief systems as given. For some purposes—interpreting social action—we must take seriously W. I. Thomas's dictum that if situations are defined as real, they are real in their consequences. For example, to understand why nineteenth century sailors feared sailing beyond the sight of land, we have to keep in mind that for all intents and purposes the world was "flat" and there was a good chance of falling off the edge. As Tumin (1969) points out, racial *thinking* must also be viewed in this way—as a set of unscientific and erroneous beliefs which have nevertheless had dangerous and devastating consequences. We have to cope with the fact that people do think in terms of races and that, at a minimum, most people would say that there are three, perhaps four, basic races—Yellow, Black, Red and White even though we know that on the basis of skin colour or any other characteristic, they would often be unable to place a given individual into one of these broad categories. Furthermore, we have to cope with the equally incorrect belief that appearance and behaviour are hereditary; that these "inherited" differences are almost always evaluated as good or bad—never just different, thus giving rise to some notion of superiority and inferiority; that very often those in the "inferior group" begin to accept as true the negative (sometimes positive) stereotypes placed on them by the "superior group." Some Indians, for example, come to believe the white stereotype which lies behind the Indian Act. They accept as "truth" that there is some genetic or biological reason why they cannot "handle liquor" and must be controlled (cf. De'Ath and Padbury, 1977).

As a result of racial thinking, people are likely to have characteristics or attributes imputed to them which may or may not be true. This is what is meant by stereotyping: the assumption that what we have observed or only heard about some members of a group—whether racial or ethnic—applies to all members of that group. Racial thinking also leads to discrimination, the selecting or rejecting of people on the basis of some physical characteristic which is associated in people's minds with some stereotype. Rather than taking people on their individual merits, they are treated favourably or unfavourably on the basis of skin colour, religion or presumed ethnic background. The end result is the vicious circle of segregation, an attempt by one group to maintain social distance from another.

In other words, the processes of stereotyping and labelling which we discussed in the chapter on deviance are also the essence of racial thinking. Race, like deviance, is a matter of social definition. People are categorized in terms of some racial designation with implicit and often explicit stereotypes and moral evaluations. Individuals are labelled as belonging to one of these categories and are then treated in terms of the label. And, some people will have the power to make their labels and stereotypes "stick." A teacher assumes that his Indian students are inferior to the white students. However subtly, this assumption influences not only how he responds to the Indian but also, perhaps, how he evaluates his work. Where a White student's failure may indicate the need for special attention, the Indian student's failure may be taken as evidence for the appropriateness of the stereotype. The Indian student may be edged out of the school, may come to view the White educational system with antagonism or, perhaps most serious, may come to accept the label and stereotype imposed upon him by the teacher.

This suggests that there are a number of responses to racial thinking, just as there are to any negative labelling. Some may accept and even welcome the racial designation, the imputation that they are different, but deny the conventional stereotypes and moral evaluation. So, Black, or Red, is beautiful. Others may deny the label and dissociate themselves from the racial category. So, Blacks may straighten their hair; Jews may get a "nose job." And, if they think that they are able, some may try to "pass" as members of the dominant group. As will become evident in our discussions of ethnic assimilation and ethnic diversity, whatever the rewards, there are substantial costs in any of these adaptations to racism.

Perspectives on Prejudice

Perhaps inspired by the ideal of ethnic diversity without conflict, many liberal social scientists have tried to discover the sources of prejudice and discrimination. There are at least three positions, each with its own prognosis. The psychological viewpoint looks for the source of prejudice in individual personality. Prejudice is irrational and there must be something wrong with the person who could hold such a belief. Either that, or prejudice is a "defence mechanism" and ethnic groups the "scapegoats" for the failures of others. The prognosis, at least implicitly, is pessimistic.

A second position, a somewhat more optimistic perspective, is that prejudice is one of the earliest learned attitudes. Children may learn in the home to view as inferior and to hate groups they may never have encountered. This line of argument usually holds that just as people learn prejudice, they can learn tolerance. Changing people's beliefs and attitudes, "resocialization," will probably be more difficult, but it is possible. A now famous and much debated illustration is the Hilltown study of a bi-racial housing project (Merton, 1968:488-490). Prior to moving into the project, most people expected a good deal of friction in a community made up of equal numbers of Blacks and Whites. However, fewer than one-fifth of the Whites and one-third of the Blacks reported friction along racial lines. Many have concluded from this that continued peer interaction breaks down stereotypes. Others, even more optimistic, have argued that as our knowledge increases and as we become more aware that race is a meaningless concept, prejudice will diminish. Certainly, not all "experiments" such as this have succeeded and, from the evidence, it seems premature to be optimistic. In any case, it is difficult to assess such studies except in the context of larger social conditions. For example, how much unemployment is there in the community undergoing "integration"? Or, to put it another way, to what extent is the "inferior" group seen as an economic threat? Similarly, "busing" in the United States may actually increase interracial conflict, not so much because of prejudice but because it threatens people's notions of individual rights and freedoms.

A third position holds that prejudice is not a result of personal pathology but of social pathology. For example, this position would hold that dominant group members are more likely to hold prejudicial attitudes in times of economic instability. In this case, prejudice reflects their economic and status interests which may appear to them to be threatened. According to this argument, they begin to look for a reason, a scapegoat, to explain their deteriorating position. One might understand the British response to recent immigrant groups, at least in part, in terms of Britain's economic problems. None of this is to suggest that prejudice is simply a fabrication, a resource people use to protect their interests. Certainly, ideas reflect interests, but they also become the definitions of reality which guide people's conduct, and as definitions of reality they may become self-perpetuating. From a sociological point of view, it is the latter two perspectives which offer the most promise.

We agree with Schermerhorn (1970) that it is somewhat unproductive to try to prove that prejudice is a personality trait, some flaw in people or in their socialization which has made them hold, sometimes act upon, what looks from the outside as irrational beliefs. As he points out:

> *If research has confirmed anything in this area, it is that prejudice is a product of* situations, *historical situations; economic situations; it is not a little demon that emerges in people simply because they are depraved (p. 6).*

From a sociological perspective, we might begin by looking at the *structural conditions* which intensify and may actually create prejudiced attitudes and sentiments. From this viewpoint, prejudice and racism are not the monopoly of any one type of individual or any one group. Blacks as well as Whites may act and feel the same if they find themselves in similar situations. Peter Carstens (1971), for example, suggests that the reservation system for Indians in Canada is structurally very similar to the South African Coloured Reserves and leads to very similar results. Both systems segregate members of the indigenous population from the mainstream culture, create a sense of paternalism in Whites and tend to perpetuate a system of inequality and a sense of powerlessness on the part of those living on reserves. Similarly, David Stymeist has tried to use some of Carstens's insights by showing how, in a small Ontario town, hostility to native people is a product of historical and economic factors which on a day-to-day basis, formally and informally, exclude Indians from town life. Dominant groups will always try to justify exclusion and inequality. As Stymeist shows, segregation reinforces and perpetuates the various stereotypes Whites have about Indians and Indians have about Whites.

This kind of structural approach also helps in understanding language conflict in Canada. Our Canadian experience suggests that Anglo-Saxons are generally intolerant about other languages and even in Quebec, until very recently, Francophones had to speak English at work. But, in Belgium, French-speaking people, though in a numerical minority, make up the dominant language. This was also the case in Algeria where Arabs became bilingual and the French remained unilingual. Hence, as Lieberson (1970) shows, with particular reference to Canada, the more economic power one has, the less likely is he or she to be bilingual. In Canada this has meant that French Canadians learn both languages and the English speak only English. Storekeepers in Sherbrooke, Quebec, for instance, have to speak English if they hope to do business with English Canadians, this despite the fact that Anglophones today make up only about 10% of the population of the Eastern Townships.

Racial thinking, then, is best viewed as an ideology to justify structural conditions. Once this ideology becomes part of the common stock of knowledge it will be passed on to future generations through the process of socialization. And, as many of us are "cultural dopes," we will accept the labels, the stereotypes and the evaluations and act in terms of them. In fact, when racial thinking is part of the culture, even those who reject it must come to grips with it. We might take as an analogy Fred Davis's (1964) study of the interaction between "normals" and the visibly handicapped. In this study, Davis points out the double bind of the normal. Imagine, for example, that you are interacting with someone with a severely scarred face. You believe, or wish to believe, that this makes no difference to you. You wish, as well, to convey this to the other. You know that you should not stare at the scar because not only is it rude, it also makes it appear that you think the scar important. Of course, it is just as bad to self-consciously avoid looking at it. Does one talk about it or self-consciously avoid any mention of this scar or scars in general? This is, of course, only an analogy but it does convey how a racist culture must inevitably influence us all at the level of everyday life. When we have learned the racial categories, that racial distinctions are important whether we like them or not, we are also likely to often wonder how to avoid seeming to be prejudiced when interacting with others.

An illustration of the double bind of prejudice and discrimination is provided by Donald Dutton's (1972) study. Dutton performed an experiment involving a number of the more expensive restaurants in Toronto and Vancouver. He selected restaurants which required men to wear ties. Each restaurant was then visited by two couples. Both members of one couple were Black, the other White. Sometimes the Black couple would enter first and sometimes the White. The males were not wearing ties. Dutton found that restaurateurs were more lenient with the Black couples; that is, few of the Black couples were refused service. The restaurateurs, then, treated Whites and Blacks differently—discriminated—perhaps to avoid seeming prejudiced. Ironically, the restaurateurs acted in terms of the racial distinction apparently to show that the distinction was not important to them.

Just why some people seem more inclined to cling to prejudicial beliefs and attitudes is still very much an open question. To understand a specific individual's prejudice, we must understand his experience and biography. From a sociological perspective, we are more concerned with racial thinking as part of the culture of the society, serving as justification of the structural arrangements in that society, perpetuated and perhaps solidified through socialization, and interpreted, handled and modified through interaction in everyday life. So, for example, prejudicial attitudes and beliefs about Indians may well have arisen to justify the power relationships and structural arrangements of the reserve system. But, these ideas of Indian inferiority do, in a sense, take on a life of their own and are passed on from generation to generation as though they are *the* reality rather than a man-made reality.

Canadians, for the most part, have prided themselves on not being prejudiced. Most would say that racial thinking is not part of our culture. The simple fact is that up until recently, we have not, as a nation, really been put to the test. While there have been Blacks (sometimes slaves) in Canada since long before the conquest, they have been largely "invisible" because they are so limited in number, partly because they became structurally segregated into pockets of poverty in much the same way as Indians (see: Clairmont and Magill, 1974; Spray, 1972). With respect to other immigrant groups, racist policies in earlier decades, designed to keep Canada "White," insured that we did not have a race problem.

But, as a number of studies in recent years have shown, we have little reason for smugness. Whenever there is contact between White and non-White in Canada, Canadians do not turn out to be much different from Americans or anyone else for that matter. This seems to be true whether we consider the treatment given Japanese Canadians in World War II (Adachi, 1976), Indians throughout Canada, Sikhs in the Vancouver area (Ferguson, 1975; Ames and Inglis, 1975) or Blacks in Nova Scotia (Henry, 1971). Thus, a recent study concludes that racism is as "deeply rooted in the Canadian hierarchy of ethnic inequality as it is in the American system." It differs only in that it is less overt.

> *Canadians, it appears, are "polite racists." They* politely *move slightly away from a Black co-passenger on the subway; they* politely *refuse to rent to or hire a Black; they* politely *refer to Blacks as negroes rather than "niggers," and, in general, they* politely *continue to discriminate against and segregate themselves from all but the most impersonal, formal contacts with their Black fellow (or potential fellow) Canadian citizens (Hughes and Kallen, 1974:214).*

As recent events have shown, Canadians are not always so polite or covert in venting their hostility. For example, the Task Force on Canadian Unity in its tour of Canada received many reports by Blacks and Asians of violence (especially on subways) and property damage. Sikhs in British Columbia continually risk having rocks and eggs thrown at their cars and homes (Ferguson, 1975:193). Though we pride ourselves on the fact that, unlike American cities, our streets are safe to walk on at night, a Pakistani in Toronto will tell a very different story.

While discussion and research on race have tended to be heated, this has not been the case when sociologists use what they hope will be the more neutral terms, ethnic group and ethnic relations. Indeed, this term has led many sociologists to emphasize cultural differences, perhaps often at the expense of ignoring material and power differences. As we shall see, however, ethnic relations must be understood within the larger structural conditions, in terms of the distribution of power, prestige and wealth.

Ethnic Groups

There is almost as much ambiguity and confusion about the meaning of ethnic groups as there is about the now discredited concept of race. Isajiw (1974), a University of Toronto sociologist, has been able to ferret out some 70 definitions of ethnicity and ethnic group. For anthropologists such as Montagu (1969:25) ethnic group is used in a very wide and general sense. In his words,

> *. . . an ethnic group may be defined as one of a number of breeding populations, which populations together comprise the species* Homo Sapiens, *and which individually maintain their differences, physical or genetic and cultural, by means of isolating mechanisms such as geographical and social barriers.*

However, Hicks (1977) limits this broad definition by suggesting that at least three ideas have usually been involved when we talk about ethnicity: (1) reference to common origins; (2) a conception of distinctiveness; and (3) the necessity that ethnicity is relevant only when two or more categories of people are involved in the same social system (p. 3). Thus, for an earlier generation of sociologists, ethnic group had no meaning in a culturally homogeneous society. Nor, for that matter, did Europeans think of themselves as ethnics until they became immigrants and found themselves treated as distinct from the host or mainstream culture. Very often they also discovered that they were part of a *minority group*, conforming to Louis Wirth's famous definition:

> *We may define a minority as a group of people who, because of their physical or cultural characteristics, are singled out from the others in the society in which they live for differential and unequal treatment, and who therefore regard themselves as objects of collective discrimination (Linton, 1945:347).*

This definition of minority group is broad enough to include, besides ethnic groups, women, homosexuals, the handicapped, groups which numerically may or may not be a minority. The concept of minority group has, in fact, nothing to do with numbers but with the way in which a collectivity may be disadvantaged with respect to the power it has to control its own destiny (Elliott, 1971:3). In terms of ethnicity, it clearly puts the focus on the inequality of condition and opportunity an ethnic group may face relative to others in the mainstream culture.

Minority group and ethnic group are so intertwined that at times it seems they have meant the same thing. Indeed, for Anglo-Saxon Canadians, ethnic group has often only had a meaning when one was talking about immigrant groups who spoke a different language and who were at the bottom of the occupational hierarchy. Cabbage rolls and lasagna were regarded as "ethnic" foods, roast beef and Yorkshire pudding apparently were not. But, in recent years, ethnicity has been a term applied not only to minority ethnic groups but also to dominant and mainstream groups as well. Recently, Anglo-Saxon Canadians have been labelled

"Wasps" by European and Asian ethnic groups and as "Les Anglais" by "Les Québécois," now themselves a group attempting to strengthen their sense of ethnic identity. They have, as Geertz (1963) argues, embarked on the same search as many other people for their primordial ties: "the giveness that stems from being born into a particular religious community, speaking a particular language, or even a dialect of language, and following particular social patterns" (pp. 109-110). It has recently been argued, therefore, that all groups who claim some ancestral and cultural affinity become, for all intents and purposes, ethnic groups. We will return to this when we consider processes of assimilation and acculturation.

ETHNICITY AND SOCIAL CLASS

To speak about ethnic relations is to speak about ethnic inequality. In most multiethnic societies, including Canada, it appears almost inevitable that one's ethnic background will be an important determinant of one's social position; where ethnic differentiation exists we usually also find ethnic stratification, the ordering of ethnic groups into a hierarchy of inequality. Indeed, ethnic identity may well retain its importance and saliency precisely because people come to realize that they are not participating equally and obtaining their fair share of the societal pie. John Porter (1975:295) points out that ". . . the revival of ethnicity has come about precisely because of the failure of universalistic and achievement values to take hold, and thus create a society of equality of opportunity and condition."

Because of the obvious relationship between ethnicity and inequality, sociologists have been divided as to whether there is any need to treat ethnic groups as a separate concept from social classes. That is, does ethnicity give people a separate and distinct status from that received from such factors as occupation, income and education, or are ethnic groups ranked in a hierarchy simply because their members possess more or less of these attributes? Pineo (1977) detects at least three positions which sociologists have taken on this issue. Some argue that in using the term ethnic relations we do more to confuse than to clarify. In this view, ethnicity is simply another manifestation of power and inequality, another way in which powerful groups legitimate social closure and maintain existing patterns of class inequality. Thus, it is merely academic hairsplitting to speak of ethnic groups and social classes as distinct phenomena.

While agreeing that ethnic groups may at times be hierarchical, others argue that this is far from inevitable. Rather, ethnicity may crosscut class lines as we show below in Figure X.1. It appears that ethnic groups may at times be status groups which have at least the potential to stand in, more or less, equality to one another.

The third, and probably most widely accepted, view is that ethnic groups and social classes form two co-existing systems of social stratification. In pluralistic societies such as Canada, we must talk about ethnic stratification as well as social stratification. According to Van den Berghe (1974:3):

> *To the extent that a society is divided both into ethnic groups and into classes, neither of the two kinds of groups can be reduced to the other. Ethnicity is not simply a minor complication or special case of class, nor can ethnicity be understood outside the total context of inequality which includes class.*

Ultimately, the problem becomes: Under what kinds of circumstances are people more likely to be aware of class interests and when are they more concerned with ethnic interests—and why? Both Marxists and liberals have, for different reasons, predicted that ethnic differences would disappear—Marxists, because they thought that ethnic differences simply mask and divide the underlying class interests and people would come to realize this; liberals, because it was believed that with assimilation and prosperity, ethnic distinctions would disappear.

In fact, we are in need of considerably

Figure X.1

FROM ETHNIC STRATIFICATION TO STRUCTURAL ASSIMILATION

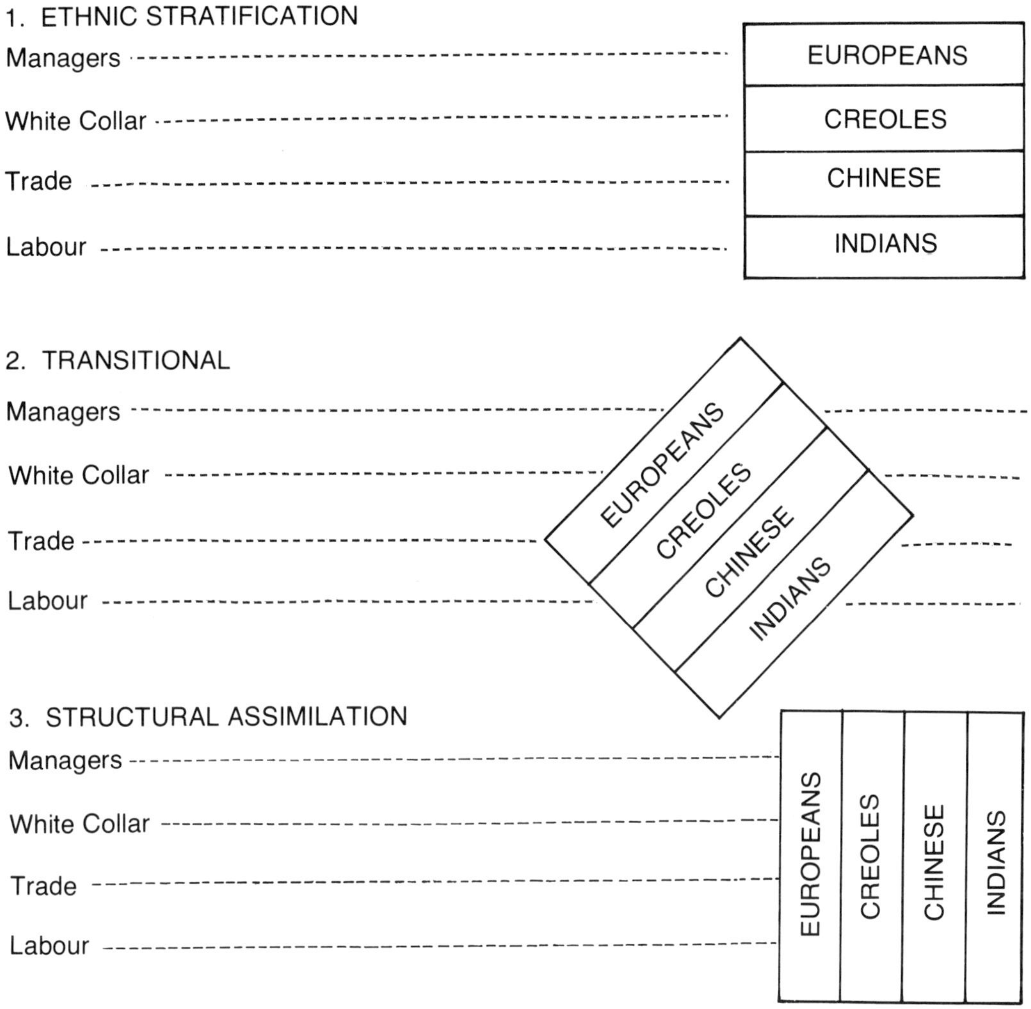

SOURCE: Schermerhorn (1970:47)

more research before we can conclude that ethnicity is distinct from or simply a manifestation of class inequality. Pineo's study, for instance, suggests that occupation is somewhat more important than ethnic membership in determining a person's status. Similarly, Stevenson (1977) finds that in Winnipeg the "ethnic vote" (for NDP) disappears as Ukrainians become middle class. But, as we shall see, research in the United States suggests that ethnicity rather than class is the most important source of identity and a focal point around which to organize interests (Greeley, 1974).

ETHNIC INEQUALITY AND MOBILITY

In contrast to a melting pot ideology, the mosaic ideology upholds the ideal that in Canada people are encouraged to perpetuate the language, religion and culture of their forebears. The ideal is that there should be *social differentiation* but not ethnic stratification; ideally ethnicity as an ascribed attribute should not enter into the ways in which people are allocated to various positions in the society. Another way to put that is to say that a multi-cultural society is one in which there is *structural assimilation* without *behavioural assimilation*—people do not have to submerge or renounce their ethnic identity and lifestyles and completely adopt those of English Canadians or French Canadians in order to participate equally in the economic, political and social life of Canadian society. Structural assimilation, then, would mean that if a particular ethnic group comprises, say, 10% of the population, then we would expect that over time about 10% of university students, doctors, lawyers, members of parliament, members of the corporate elite, skilled and unskilled workers and so on would be members of that ethnic group. This is essentially what the contentious quota systems in the United States—reverse discrimination as some call it—have sought to achieve.

Of course, some ethnic groups have been able to change their initial entrance status. As in the case of social mobility, generally, we have to distinguish between individual and group mobility. Studies which focus on actual ethnic *groups* are obviously concerned mainly with group mobility. Studies which use census data, on the other hand, are dealing with both group mobility and mobility of individuals who, at the time of the census enumeration, may be "pressured" to declare an *ethnic affiliation* even though they may no longer think of themselves as "Greek" or "Italian" or "Ukrainian." Thus, some members of ethnic groups move upwards simply by disappearing from the group, perhaps by Anglicizing their names and moving away from areas where there is a concentration of immigrants. Probably this is a relatively common practice for those who make it to university since it is often possible for graduates to change their names for their diplomas. More generally, it has been noted that in Manitoba alone more than 2000 Slavs made name changes from Slavic to Anglo-Saxon in the years 1937-1957 (Radecki and Heydenkorn, 1977).

Clearly, this is not an easy decision to make. Herbert Gans (1962), for instance, has drawn a neat parallel between the problems of upward mobility from an Italian community and those of moving out of a traditional working-class community as is found in Britain. In both cases the general view is that it is acceptable to improve economically but one should not start to adopt middle-class ways. Those who do so are criticized and eventually ostracized for having gone "high society." Attemps at upward mobility are likely to be interpreted as a repudiation of traditional values. Somewhat unrealistically, young people are encouraged to get an education and a better job, but, at the same time, they are told that they should not change in the process.

Studies of specific ethnic groups have generally concentrated on how the group as a whole has fared. The recent study of

Polish Canadians by Radecki and Heydenkorn (1977:182) concludes:

> *. . . between 1951 and 1961 the Polish aggregate "shook off" their long-held entrance status as agricultural workers and unskilled labourers. The arrival of a large number of better-educated and highly qualified people and the entrance into higher occupations by the second and third generations totally changed the occupational composition of the Polish group in Canada. There are now significant proportions of the Polish labour force in Canada who are doctors, dentists, lawyers, professors, engineers, scientists, architects and highly skilled technicians. . . . Thousands have established their own businesses while others are managers or executives for larger concerns. . . . The Polish group is now well represented in the higher socio-economic occupations.*

Isajiw and Hartmann (1970) came to a similar conclusion about Ukrainians in Canada. They suggest that three steps are involved in ethnic mobility. The first is cultural assimilation. In moving off the farms, Ukrainians begin to take over the values and behavioural patterns of the Canadian Anglo-Saxon society. The second pattern is related to the process of structural assimilation, "a reach for equality of opportunities through participation in what popularly is defined as 'decent' jobs" (p. 105). In the third stage, what they call "a process of structural modification," the ethnic group comes to be part of the establishment, thereby having power and influence meaningful in the society as a whole. But, while Ukrainians may have advanced through two of these stages, the authors of this study point out that they have not reached this third pattern of occupational change. Similarly, Radecki and Haydenkorn temper their optimism about Polish structural integration by noting that "the doors to the corporate elite remain at present closed to them, as they are largely closed to many other immigrant groups . . ." (p. 182).

This is shown somewhat more systematically in Table X.2, taken from Wallace Clement's *The Canadian Corporate Elite* (1975). As can be seen, the elite is still mainly composed of people of British descent; other ethnic groups and the French are vastly under-represented. Also, Clement cautions that the changes between 1951 and 1971 do not represent a greater degree of openness but are, rather, reflections of changes in the demographic composition of Canadian society. This is shown in Table X.3. The British, in other words, have not lost any ground to the French or other ethnic groups over these two decades. Similar conclusions emerge from Kelner's (1970) study of the Toronto elite. Though non-Anglo-Saxons have made important steps upwards in Toronto's social structure, she finds that the core or nucleus of the elite remains, in

Table X.2

PROPORTION OF ETHNIC REPRESENTATION IN THE ECONOMIC ELITE, 1951 and 1972*

	Economic Elite		Canadian Population	
	1951	1972	1951	1971
Anglo	92.3%	86.2%	47.9%	44.7%
French	6.7	8.4	30.8	28.6
Other	1.0*	5.4	21.3	26.7
TOTAL	100%	100%	100%	100%
N	(760)	(775)		

* According to Porter (1965:286), 0.78% of his sample is Jewish; other "third" ethnic groups were hardly represented at all.

SOURCE: Clement (1975:232)

Table X.3

INDEX OF ETHNIC REPRESENTATION IN THE ECONOMIC ELITE, 1951 and 1972*

	ECONOMIC ELITE 1951	1972
Anglo	1.93	1.93
French	0.22	0.29
Other	0.05	0.20

* A figure of over 1.00 denotes over-representation and an index below 1.00 shows under-representation.
SOURCE: Clement (1975:234)

many instances, entirely Anglo-Saxon.

The best known Canadian study of ethnic mobility is Richmond's (1967) research on post-war immigrants. He finds that the pattern of immigration has tended to reinforce the connection between ethnicity and social class. This is especially the case for sponsored immigrants from countries such as Italy who, in pre-war years, started their Canadian work-life in low-paid and low-prestige jobs. Both British and non-British immigrants experienced some downward mobility on coming to Canada, though about half of those who fell were able, eventually, to recover or improve on their former position. However, his data show that British immigrants are far more likely than non-British immigrants to experience upward mobility after spending some time in Canada. "English speaking immigrants added to the existing association between British ethnic origin and high social status in Canada" (Richmond, 1970:90). Nevertheless, his overall conclusions about ethnic mobility share the same optimism Radecki and Heydenkorn express about the changing situation of Polish Canadians:

The Canadian Mosaic is undoubtedly a vertical one, but it is not necessarily rigid. Although recently arrived immigrants of all nationalities tended to experience some status dislocation, avenues of upward social mobility and family income advancement appeared to be open to all immigrants, despite initial educational, linguistic or other handicaps (p. 94).

Relative to their entrance status, movement upward has been impressive, or at least seems impressive. No doubt, stories of individuals who have "made it" add to the sense that if one really wants to succeed in Canada, ethnicity need not stand in the way. But, it is also apparent that most ethnic groups in Canada have some way to go before it could be said that there is full structural assimilation. To date, the best data are still those collected by the Royal Commission on Bilingualism and Biculturalism. In the 1960s, at least, all ethnic groups, except Jews, fell below the English in income, level of schooling, enrolment at university and occupational status. What was particularly surprising in these findings was the disparity between the British and the French with respect to these various measures; on most, the French—one of the two Charter groups—fell below other ethnic groups in Canada. As Table X.4 shows, this was also true for French Canadians *within* Quebec.[2]

As conventional wisdom would have it, ethnic group members are faced with a choice: participate equally in the competition for resources and give up ethnic group identification or maintain commitment to the ethnic group at the risk of blocked mobility. In more technical language, equal participation in opportunity structures seems to require *acculturation*, acquiring the culture of the dominant ethnic group, and acculturation seems to lead

Table X.4

MEAN ANNUAL INCOME OF WAGE-EARNING MALES IN QUEBEC BY ETHNIC ORIGIN IN 1961

Ethnic Origin	Income in Dollars	Index
Total	3469	100.0
British	4940	142.4
Scandinavian	4939	142.4
Dutch	4891	140.9
Jewish	4851	139.8
Russian	4828	139.1
German	4254	133.6
Polish	3984	114.8
Asian	3734	107.6
Ukrainian	3733	107.6
Other European	3547	102.4
Hungarian	3537	101.9
French	3185	91.8
Italian	2938	84.6
Indian	2112	60.8

SOURCE: Canada Census, 1961—Special compilation for Rioux (1971:95)

to *assimilation,* absorption into the dominant group (Shibutani and Kwan, 1965). In the following pages we will examine these processes in light of the paradoxical trend in Canada and the United States towards increasing emphasis on ethnicity.

ASSIMILATION AND ETHNIC IDENTITY

John Porter takes the conventional position in his discussions of ethnicity. In the decade since the publication of *The Vertical Mosaic,* he has maintained a consistent argument against the mosaic ideology. In his view, the revival of ethnicity in recent years creates a high risk of ethnic stratification and the perpetuation of ethnic inequality (Porter, 1975:289). Indeed, he argues that the kind of ethnic mix which we depicted in Table X.1 is at least partially an artifact of Statistics Canada's insistence that at census time we must pin an ethnic label on ourselves, since "Canadian" is not a valid answer to questions on ethnicity—for census purposes both those born in Canada and immigrants had to have a non-North American ethnicity (Porter, 1975:279). He suggests, then, that a large number of people may no longer think of themselves as Polish, Hungarian, Italian, Irish and so on, but as simply Canadian. If so, assimilation of Canada's immigrants has proceeded much further than the mosaic ideology implies.

This is also, essentially, the conclusion of another influential Canadian sociologist, S. D. Clark. In a series of papers, he argues that, in fact, behavioural assimilation to a "middle-class culture" is fairly advanced.

What has happened since the second World War is that those cultural differences associated with ethnic origin have been on the way of disappearing, to be replaced by cultural differences associated very much more with social class, but as well with occupation, religion, education and with the pursuit of such cultural interests as music, art and literature. The university, the highrise apartment buildings of the city, the city suburbs, but as well the modern business and industrial enterprise, have become centres of powerful forces of assimilation in our society (Clark, 1976a:2).

Thus, in Clark's view, cultural barriers have, in Canada, been largely broken down by the forces of economic development to the extent that "Canadians have become more like Americans in coming to live in an urban middle class world, just as French speaking Canadians have become more like English speaking Canadians, or Ukrainians or Italian Canadians, like Scottish or Irish Canadians" (p. 7).

In sum, the mosaic ideology and the policies encouraging ethnic diversity which it generates are viewed as regressive and unproductive. Hence, Frank Vallee (1960) argued, some years ago, that minority groups cannot, on the one hand, strive to maintain an ethnic language and culture and, on the other, successfully prepare their members for competition in the larger or mainstream culture of which they are a part. Vallee is referring to what Breton (1960) calls the degree of institutional completeness of an ethnic group: the extent to which the ethnic community can perform all the services required by its members. It is, for example, possible for an Italian immigrant in Toronto or Hamilton to carry out virtually all aspects of his or her life from shopping, banking and legal advice to entertainment and often even employment, without speaking English or needing to interact with people outside the ethnic group. As we would expect, Breton finds that institutional completeness limits interaction with those "outside" the ethnic community. It is a barrier to assimilation, something which will eventually disappear: "with time—and it may be quite long—the ethnic organizations will themselves disappear or lose their ethnic identity, completing the life-cycle of the community." This is, then, a view in accord with what Metzger (1971) calls an assimilationist bias—the expectation that, over time, immigrants will give up their former ways and be drawn into the social and cultural mainstream.

This was especially believed to be the case in the melting pot of the United States, much less so in Canada. But, as S. D. Clark suggests, despite ethnic associations, behavioural assimilation has already occurred in Canada, and, like it or not, we have all been homogenized into a North American culture devoid of ethnic distinctions. Certainly, there is a good deal of evidence around us that this is the case. For example, English-Canadian businessmen in Quebec are often heard to wonder what all the "fuss" is about. They point to French Canadians who work for or with them and note that, aside from their "irrational" desire to speak French, they live in the same kinds of houses, eat the same food, drive the same cars, want the same things and perhaps even think like "everyone else" in Canada and the United States.[3]

But, as these sociologists readily admit, we are faced with the paradox that at the very moment when many of the most obvious differences between ethnic groups disappear, a new and sometimes very self-conscious sense of ethnicity has emerged in Canada and the United States. Glazer and Moynihan (1975:4) suggest that we have to change our thinking about ethnic groups.

Formerly seen as survivals *from an earlier age, to be treated variously with annoyance, toleration, or mild celebration, we now have a growing sense that they may be* forms *of social life that are capable of renewing and transforming themselves.*

Several things seem to be happening at once. As we have suggested, even while cultural differences based on ethnicity may be disappearing, ethnicity is becoming an important resource both to dominant and dominated groups.

ETHNICITY AS RESOURCE: DOMINANT GROUPS

As we have seen, despite considerable progress, many ethnic groups have not been successful in achieving structural assimilation. It is not, as the institutional completeness approach would have it, simply a question of stubborn refusal to "become like us" on the part of ethnic groups. The dominant charter groups have, either directly through discrimination, or indirectly through *nepotism*. effectively excluded other ethnicities from full participation in Canadian society. No doubt, people will use kinship influences—nepotism—when it is to their advantage to do so. As with nepotism, so it is with ethnicity, whether we are talking about succession to elite status or who gets the better jobs in communities of single industry. As Lucas (1971:135-136) shows, ethnicity and nepotism are so closely intertwined on the railroad that after some 60 years of hiring, the "British represented 100 percent of the managerial group, 91 percent of the train crews, but only 15 percent of the labourers" (p. 136). News of an upcoming vacancy circulates informally among the running trades group which is almost entirely British. A son or a friend is told to drop in and see the "super" and others put in a good word for him. Nepotism becomes ethnic sponsorship.

If a man of French or "other" ethnic background applies for a job, the superintendent tells him with perfect honesty and sincerity: I'm sorry but there are no openings in the crews. . . . When the job is posted formally, it has already been filled informally (p.136).

Also, from a Marxist perspective, the resurgence of ethnicity might be interpreted as evidence of the success of capitalism—of the ruling class—in diffusing the underlying conflict inherent in class inequality. From this perspective, ethnicity is a kind of false consciousness diverting attention away from the objective interests which lower classes, whether of Italian, Indian or Portuguese ancestry, have in common. Ethnicity may, then, have important functions for the dominant or mainstream culture as well as for minority groups. It may take some pressure off the system. As we have said, class and ethnicity are not exactly synonymous but they are intimately related. Focusing on ethnicity rather than poverty, as in the case of Indians, provides a neat rationalization of why some people are poor or without power. The problem, we are able to say, is that they will not assimilate or change their ways. It is a process akin to castigating those on welfare or those who are unemployed because "they won't work." It makes it the individual's fault, his problem, rather than a weakness of society. When we blame ethnicity, then, we are saying, if only people would assimilate, then their troubles would be over. Marcel Rioux (1971:17) points out that it is a common explanation of Quebec's problems: Quebeckers are "the outlaws of their own misfortunes." The Church held them back; they have outmoded attitudes about work and business; they elect reactionary and corrupt politicians and so on. But, what is seldom asked is why these values and traditions developed and are maintained. As Quebeckers have come to recognize, these are, in part, adaptations and responses to 200 years of political and economic domination and exploitation.

Perhaps the clearest illustration of the use of ethnicity can be seen in both the early and present attempts by charter groups to control immigration. John Porter bases his analysis around two key concepts, *charter group status* and *entrance status*. A charter group as the first ethnic group to enter a previously unpopulated territory has the most say about who else may later enter and what jobs they are allowed to have. In Porter's words:

A given ethnic group appropriates particular roles and designates other ethnic groups for the less preferred ones. Often the low status group accepts its inferior position. Through time the relative status positions, reinforced by stereotypes and social images—the Irish policeman and the Irish maid, for example—harden and become perpetuated over a very long time. In the general scheme of class and status that evolves with economic growth and immigration there exists an "entrance status" to be assumed by the less preferred ethnic groups. Entrance status implies lower level occupational roles and subjection to processes of assimilation laid down and judged by the charter group. Over time the position of entrance status may be improved or it may be a permanent caste-like status as it has been, for example, with Chinese in Canada. Thus most of Canada's minority groups have at some time had this entrance status. Some, but not all, have moved out of it (1965:63-64).

As Porter suggests, it was easy enough in the nineteenth century for the two charter groups, and particularly for the English, to justify immigration policies which were explicitly racist and discriminatory. The seeming complexity and high level of social and economic development of Britain, France and Germany were taken as clear evidence of innate superiority over nationalities in the east and south of Europe. More generally, the reports of anthropologists and others who visited and studied tribal societies seemed to confirm the idea that societies *evolve* from the "savage" and "primitive" to the "civilized" and "complex." Thus, what we now refer to as preliterate societies were of interest mainly for the clues they seemed to provide about our own prehistorical past.

As another generation of anthropologists with different views about how to do research went out into the field, this simple evolutionary model began to look more and more implausible. What mainly shattered it was that, unlike their predecessors who had been content simply to observe, later anthropologists held that one could not stand outside of social action; it was necessary to participate, to attempt to understand the culture on its own terms, not those of the researcher. The first step in that process is, of course, learning the language. This, in turn, led to an awareness of just how complex and difficult it is to learn about any culture. As Lévi-Strauss (1956:159) notes about marriage, "apparently ignorant and savage peoples have been able to devise fantastically clever codes which sometimes require, in order to understand their workings and effects, some of the best logical and even mathematical minds available in modern civilization." Or, as Elenore Smith Bowen describes it in her anthropological novel, *Return to Laughter,* the subtle knowledge even small tribal children possess of things in their environment such as plants and leaves, etiquette, etc., rivals in complexity what children must know and take for granted in our society. In other words, whatever the culture, taken-for-granted knowledge—what "everybody knows"—is never simple to strangers.[4]

Nor, as we now recognize, is there anything innately inferior or even different about one ethnic group from another. All of the evidence points to the fact that differences between groups are due to differences in physical and cultural demands. African tribesmen are not what we were several milleniums ago. Rather, we are all "modern" people who have developed in somewhat different ways in response to what was demanded of us. A vivid illustration of this is the relative ease with which the Third World students are able to obtain degrees in Western universities. For instance, one of the writers recalls a fellow graduate student from Kenya who had the permanent facial scars of his puberty rite. In his wallet were pictures of his parents standing in front of a grass hut, the father wearing only a loin cloth and carrying a hunting spear. In one generation, it seems, people can adopt sufficient Western ways of thinking to earn a Ph.D. degree. Rather than a straight-line evolutionary process, the more accurate model seems to be one of separate parallel development, as in Figure X.2.

Which society should be regarded as superior? Clearly, there is no simple solution to that question. Obviously, cultural relativism only goes so far; there are many aspects of non-literate and underdeveloped societies which are repugnant to us—the high mortality rate, malnutrition, the fatalism and callousness which often characterizes such societies.[5]

However, Westerners typically judged pre-literate societies as inferior not simply in terms of these consequences, but in terms of the very different cultural ways of

Figure X.2

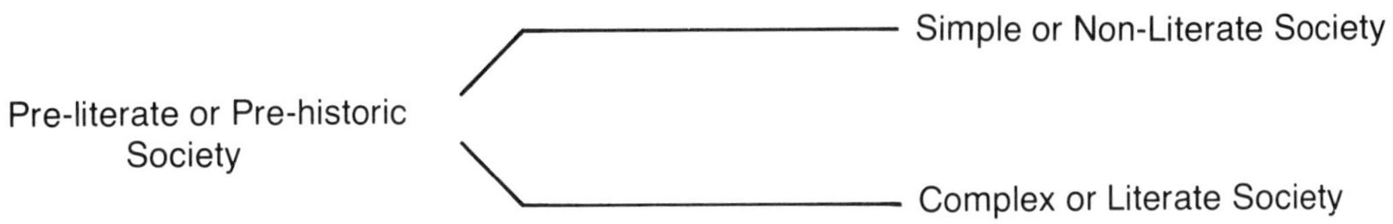

the people. Lévi-Strauss (1969) offers a provocative explanation of this kind of ethnocentrism. He reminds us that not only did many Indian and African tribes seem child-like to Europeans, but the reverse was often true. For example, the European anthropologist was often viewed as a child by those he was studying. To Lévi-Strauss, if you recall, cultures are the products of the interaction of adumbrated structures in the child with the physical problems people must face. Cultures, then, select among these already present mental structures, inhibiting some and encouraging others. In this sense, Lévi-Strauss would argue, all cultures are child-like but in different ways because each has selected differently among the mental structures of the child. Specifically, those things that a child is taught not to do and those things a child is taught not to think in one culture are precisely the things that will be emphasized in some other cultures.

Nevertheless, nineteenth century views about "racial" or national superiority still haunt us. For example, despite occasional reversals, Canadian immigration policy has right up to the present been implicitly, sometimes explicitly, racist. Earlier in this century there was an outright preference for Northern European immigrants and rejection of "too many" Southern Europeans. Asians and Africans were inconceivable as regular immigrants and potential Canadians. By the time the Green Paper on immigration emerged in 1975, only the language had changed—to vague references to the "resilience" of Canadians in accommodating so many "foreign migrants." Since all migrants are, by definition, foreign, this was obviously a euphemism for non-white immigrants or "visible minorities" as some prefer to call Asian and Carribean migrants.

The Green Paper simply took for granted that assimilation of these groups would be more difficult. Government policy seemed to be reflecting vague and as yet unproven fears that non-White immigrants pose some kind of threat to Canadian society.[6] Yet, as Paul (1975) points out, immigrants from Third World countries are more likely than their European or British counterparts to have qualifications which allow them to be employed in professional occupations. As well, they are, after three years in Canada, more likely to state that they are "at home in Canada" than are British or American immigrants. Richmond (1975), an expert on immigration, feels that the former point may be part of the problem; in the 1970s job opportunities in the professions have been severely restricted, meaning that Third World immigrants are in direct competition with middle-class Canadians for their jobs. Concern about the rate of immigration—though not necessarily about who immigrates—has recently come more from this group than from the working class, the group traditionally most opposed to immigration.

ETHNICITY AS A RESOURCE: SUBORDINATE GROUPS

Ethnic groups may, over time, give up many aspects of their culture, but, in the process of living and working in North America, they may sometimes invent new attributes which bear only vague resemblance to what the original immigrants brought with them. This is nicely illustrated by what is happening to the Italian language in Toronto. Rather than give up speaking Italian entirely, immigrants have created "Italiese, a brand-new hybrid tongue somewhere between Italian and Inglese." Basically, English words are given Italian pronunciation and spelling: hurry up—*arriapa;* backyard—*bacchi-iarda;* city hall—*sitialla;* report card—*reportacarta* and so on (Clivio, 1977). Apparently, Portuguese has been undergoing a very similar transformation as Azorean and mainland immigrants cope with the Canadian environment—people *usam o snowshovel* and *pogam os bills* (pay the bills), for example (Anderson and Higgs, 1977:179).

Some members of an immigrant group may have vested interests in maintaining ethnic differences. They may find in ethnicity a resource for individual mobility. Breton (1964) points out that when immigrant groups come to Canada with limited skills and resources, there is an important gap to be filled by social entrepreneurs. "His rewards would be either monetary profit, prestige in the community, more members for his church, or more buyers for his newspapers" (p. 93). Similarly, Beiler Brettel (1977:179) argues that "ethnicity is partially sustained in urban areas as a good business venture." She is referring to the profusion of Portuguese travel agents in the Kensington Market area of Toronto, examples of what she calls "ethnic entrepreneurs." As well as selling travel, these agents read mail, write letters, place phone calls, fill out forms for people, thereby assuring themselves of a steady flow of Portuguese clients. Such entrepreneurs act simultaneously as a communication link between the ethnic group and the wider society. In this way, the boundary between the two is sustained and sometimes created (Nagata, 1974). In some senses, then, "ethnic entrepreneurs" or "brokers" are seen as contributing to the isolation of the ethnic group (De'Ath and Padbury, 1977). Clark (1976:9) points out that

> *the vested interests of ethnicity, represented by such bodies as the ethnic church, the ethnic press, and the ethnic associations of various sorts, anxious to maintain the identity of the ethnic groups they serve, seek by various stratagems to erect cultural impediments to the full and free participation of the individual in the social world about.*

This, we might add, has long been the situation of English Canadians in Quebec. Vested interests—the media, the educational system and business—have often operated so as to keep their English-speaking constituency ignorant of what is happening politically and socially in Quebec society and incapable of participating fully in the society. There is, for instance, good evidence that the two English newspapers, *The Gazette* and *The Montreal Star,* have in their reporting of political developments, such as Bill 22 and Bill 101, often misled their English readership with biased, sometimes downright incorrect, reporting of facts (Elkin, 1970; Caldwell, 1975). Similarly, the English-speaking school system has been very slow and reluctant to begin programmes which would prepare its students for full participation—linguistic, social, cultural and economic—in Quebec society as it has developed and is developing. The difference, of course, is that, unlike other "minority" groups, the English in Quebec have been economically a majority group within the province and linked to the wider North American mainstream culture. Again, this emphasizes the importance of consideration of power variables in the examination of ethnic group relations. Clearly, the English minority group in Quebec is a minority only statistically, certainly not in terms of economics and power.

This, however, does not explain why there may be a continuing market for ethnic entrepreneurs and ethnic associations. Clearly, ethnic entrepreneurs and institutions are supported because people feel that they have something to gain by ethnic affiliation. They may feel that complete assimilation in private life as well as public life undermines values which seem worthwhile sustaining. People may, in other words, want to have the best of both worlds—they want the material advantages of Canadian society but not at the cost of giving up the important and positive things about, say, family life. What Kurt Danziger (1974) describes about Toronto Italians illustrates the problems and tensions involved in acculturation. As he shows, it is not simply that Italians do not want to mix with others or that they prefer to "stick together." Just the contrary—like just about everyone else in Canada, they want to enjoy the material advantages which this society offers. But, such conformity also poses a threat to traditional core values about family, about the place of women, courtship and so on. The solution, he suggests, is to let men "bear the brunt of the acculturation process and to take steps to protect the girls, in the hope that they will become the guardians of the core values of the traditional culture" (p. 134).

Italian girls, for example, are encouraged to retain traditional expectations about domestic and mothering roles. Efforts are made to supervise whom they see, where they go, and to insulate them from the "winds of change" such as feminism. This is, in varying degrees, probably true of many ethnic groups. Hence, in public life, immigrant groups may appear to be highly assimilated and acculturated. In the privacy of family relationships, however, ethnicity remains of considerable symbolic importance (McCready, 1975: Nagata, 1974).

Thus, people become ethnics partly because they are so defined by the larger society, partly because it is in their own interests to become ethnics. And just as people are not equal, neither are ethnic groups. Dahrendorf (1969) holds that the origin of inequality resides in the inability of some people to fulfill adequately society's norms. The same thing applies to ethnic groups whose members find that, individually and collectively, they have different levels of success in attaining that which has been defined as desirable. Clearly, Dahrendorf is not talking about universals but about norms which are highly relative and dependent on who has the power to decide what constitutes the appropriate values and norms—the goals worth striving for and the legitimate means of getting there. In looking back on their own famous study, *Beyond the Melting Pot* (1963), Glazer and Moynihan (1975:7) conclude that ethnicity, as well as class, becomes a resource to focus on and mobilize, for the pursuit of group or individual interests.

One of the striking characteristics of the present situation is, indeed, the extent to which we find the ethnic group defined in terms of interest, as *an interest group. Thus, whereas in the past a religious conflict, such as that which is tearing Northern Ireland apart was based on such issues as the free and public practice of a religion, today it is based on the issue of which group shall gain benefits or hold power of a wholly secular sort.*

We might add as well that the rules of the game are also constantly changing. We have already seen this when we considered educational inflation in the previous chapter: as various groups begin to achieve the educational credentials traditionally held by the elite, new definitions of what constitutes a "good" education emerge. Similarly, as ethnics finally are able to move to a "fashionable" neighbourhood, they find it has become unfashionable—the dominant group has moved on to a more "exclusive" area of the city. In sum, we can expect that ethnicity and ethnic conflict will continue to be a central issue in Canada as long as one strategy of closure by dominant groups revolves around norms directly or indirectly tied to ethnic origin (Parkin, 1976). Quite apart from this "imposition" of ethnicity, we must also appreciate that, under certain circumstances at least, these primordial attachments may provide a symbolic focal point for collective action and the formation of interest groups.

ETHNICITY AS A RESOURCE: INTERPERSONAL RELATIONS

Some anthropologists and sociologists focus on the meanings of ethnicity in everyday life. They suggest that we should concentrate on *ethnicity* as an interpersonal resource, rather than as a fixed or objective status; ethnic identity is a *processual* and *subjective* status. Ethnicity is seen as one of a number of symbolic "props" with which we present ourselves, and, like other roles we play, it is *situational.* Our use of the prop depends on the context in which we find ourselves. While one's objective cultural or ethnic background may be important in how we view the world and how others treat us, Frederik Barth (1969) argues that it is by no means crucial in how, ethnically, we choose to present ourselves to others. Hicks (1977:17) suggests that "people often have a repertoire of ethnic attributes from which they can select the ones most suitable to a given situation. The possibility is opened for people, as it were, to leap back and forth across several ethnic boundaries."

This is also Judith Nagata's experience from doing research on Greek immigrants in Toronto. She finds that there is considerable discrepancy in ethnic behaviour between public performances and those in the privacy of the family. As she points out:

> *What apparently emerges is not so much a "unilinear" model of acculturation, whereby individuals become progressively "less Greek" or more "Canadian," and from which no reversal is possible, but a "situational" process in which sometimes Greekness prevails, sometimes Canadianness. The norms and behaviours that prevail on any particular occasion depend as much on expediency as on loyalties to either culture (1969:53).*

Situational ethnicity reaches some sort of extreme in David Stymeist's (1975) study, *Ethnics and Indians.* Stymeist went to "Crow Lake" expecting to find different ethnic groups arranged in some sort of order. Rather, what he found was that ethnicity was not very pervasive, nor was it very closely connected to position in the community. He found that sometimes people would state they were, perhaps, Scottish or Ukrainian, even Indian. But, on other occasions and in different situations they would deny these labels and attach another ethnicity to themselves. How is this possible? The key seemed to be that under, say, the general heading of Ukrainian and Polish, someone who referred to himself and was considered "Ukrainian" would, on being pressed, admit that in fact both his parents were born in Poland; it was just more convenient—more meaningful in the community—to call himself Ukrainian. It was also more convenient for others in the community to be able to lump him in with Ukrainians. Moreover, in relationship to Indians in the community, people tended to downplay and ignore their ethnic differences, identities which in other contexts could be fairly important and divisive.

Probably many of us have practised situational ethnicity at one time or another. When we travel to Europe, for instance, our various ancestries may give way to the label "Canadian" as we seek to distinguish ourselves from Americans by sticking Maple Leaf flags on pack-sacks and suitcases. At other times, when we are travelling through the country of origin of our parents or their parents, we may become more conscious of our ethnic roots. Someone who ordinarily does not think of himself as Jewish may, in talking to some people, want to make it known that he has Jewish ancestry. In still another setting, the fact that he is also of Hungarian descent may overwhelm his identification with Jews.

The idea of situational ethnicity, then, moves the concept of ethnicity from a highly objective category of people who have a common cultural heritage to a more subjective emphasis on identification or self-labelling. Barth (1969:13-14), for example, holds that "to the extent that actors use ethnic identities to categorise themselves and others for purposes of interaction, they form ethnic groups." The notion of situational ethnicity emphasizes that people are not determined by their ethnic origins and are not passive recipients of an ethnic culture, but rather they use ethnicity as a resource to achieve a number of purposes. It may be a private resource to maintain the solidarity in the family, as a source for familial rules and ritual. Similarly, it may be a resource for maintaining a sense of community. And, as we have seen, it may be a resource in the public sphere, a rallying point for collective interests.

Viewing ethnicity as resource allows us to capture more clearly some of the complexity of ethnic relations. For example, it allows us to recognize that ethnic conflicts may be nominally ethnic, in fact a reflection of deeper structural cleavage. As well, someone who seems to be holding fast to an ethnic identity or apparently rejecting it is acting in a situation and in terms of the perceived demands of that situation. Such a perspective seems particularly apt for the Canadian case.

Compared to some societies, ethnic diversity and processes of assimilation are, in Canada, especially complex. It makes sense in the United Kingdom, for instance, to talk about a host population and an immigrant group, but much less so in Canada. Here, it is not at all clear who is doing the assimilating. Who, for instance, constitutes the host population in Canadian society? Those who claim British descent? Both French and English? Francophone and Anglophone Canadians? In either case, how do we deal with relationships between French and English? Furthermore, how do we deal with native peoples since they are neither an immigrant population nor part of the mainstream culture—French or English?

All of this suggests the need of new terms to replace the static and deterministic concept of ethnic group. Ironically, these issues have been most effectively addressed by the American sociologist, Andrew Greeley (1974), who developed the concept of *ethnicization.* He describes the concept as follows:

> *Implicit in this perspective is the notion that ethnicity is not a residual social force that is slowly and gradually disappearing; it is, rather, a dynamic, flexible social mechanism that can be called into being rather quickly and transformed and transmuted to meet changing situations and circumstances (p. 301).*

The approach recognizes that ethnic boundaries are permeable, that the bases of ethnicity are not fixed and that over time and through interaction with one another, both the dominant and subordinate ethnic collectivities change. In these terms, as in ours, ethnicity is a resource, ethnicization the process of resource management. The utility of such an approach for bringing together apparently conflicting accounts of assimilation and the rediscovery of ethnicity can be illustrated in the Quebec case.

QUEBEC SOCIETY

The mobilization of ethnicity as a resource will depend on the availability of other resources, both human and material. In this context, Quebec is in rather a unique position, simultaneously the host culture to immigrant groups, and the subordinate culture to English Canada. Even within its own boundaries, power rests in the hands of the Anglo "minority." Québecois have had limited experience with the absorption and assimilation of immigrant populations. Typically, immigrants who settled in Quebec have moved towards Anglophone rather than Francophone culture (Caldwell, 1974:112). Until the 1960s this did not matter since the "battle of the cradle" was obviously being won by French Canadians. The dramatic fall in the Quebec birth rate has changed all that; whether as a separate state or a province with special status in Confederation, Quebec society is demographically threatened unless the shortfall in births can be made up through immigration. Both Bill 22 by the Liberal government of Bourassa and the equally famous Bill 101 which ushered in the Parti Québecois government of Lévesque were at least partially intended to insure that immigrants become part of French rather than English culture in Quebec.

Official policy is to encourage assimilation. But, it is not at all clear that Quebec society is, at this point, capable of assimilating immigrants. Compared to the concept of "Canadian," *Canadien* (now Québecois) is unambiguous—it means that one can trace his or her roots back to what Jones (1972:40) calls the "primordial event of the conquest." The result is that Quebec society views itself not only as a charter group but also as a *nation,* a community of people who see themselves as linked together by a common culture, history and language (Ryerson, 1972). Just as it is impossible for an Englishman, a German or an Italian to conceive of someone "becoming" one of these, so ultimately it is impossible for someone to become Québecois except in the limited sense of citizenship. Ultimately, of course, Quebec will have to come to grips with the same processes of ethnicization (and change of the host population) which have occurred in other multi-ethnic societies. No doubt this will be one of the major problems which Quebec, as one of the "two nations" making up Canada, must face in the next few decades.

When we consider the relationship of Quebec to the rest of Canada, an "ethnic group" perspective seems no longer useful or applicable. Marcel Rioux (1971:78) argues that French Canadians in Quebec have ceased to think of themselves as an ethnic community and have, rather, begun to see themselves simply as an industrial society of the twentieth century. Assertions of collective equality and self-determination, it appears, have become taken for granted and are no longer questioned by most Quebeckers. It seems, too, that English Canadians have, however reluctantly, come to accept this definition as well. They no longer assume that with time and economic development Quebeckers will simply become neutral Canadians and North Americans. To use Lower's phrase, the people of Quebec have gone from *Colony* to *Nation.* In the process they no longer find it necessary to take refuge in the past, to call upon ethnicity as a resource. Like other industrial societies, Quebec seeks its Utopia in the future rather than in some bygone era in its own history.

This argument, perhaps, ignores the extent to which ethnicity has been a powerful resource in mobilizing people towards nationhood. Ethnicity, as we have seen, is a powerful means to focus interests, pull people together and bring them to an awareness of their shared economic or class position. According to Milner and Milner (1973:230):

> *. . . the presence of a different ethnic and cultural group at the top of the social structure facilitates the recognition of power relationships and class distinctions on the part of the lower classes within the population. Added to this are cases of outright discrimination and expressed attitudes of disdain towards the French Canadians and their culture which aggravate and expose the social class distinctions.*

Rioux's wish to underplay the role of ethnicity is understandable. He has taken the radical position that the focus on ethnicity obscures the real bases of conflict which are always economic. So, for Rioux, ethnic consciousness and class consciousness developed along parallel lines, an argument which does not share Milner and Milner's optimism that ethnic consciousness is a mechanism which may lead to class consciousness. However, Rioux does capture the other side of the coin, that dominant groups may use ethnicity in different ways. Certainly, as we have shown, it may be used to obscure class differences and inhibit class consciousness. At the same time, it may provide a mechanism for exploitation. It is, for example, no accident that during the Quiet Revolution, companies like Labatt's Breweries were able to multiply their sales by tying their products to the historical heritage of the province, or that countless *brasseries* throughout Quebec have adopted a "*Habitant*" decor and menu; it made good economic sense to tap what was latent and unfulfilled in the culture (Elkin, 1971).

At this point, we cannot, of course, predict what will be the final outcome of the National Unity debate. Current events have the habit of making liars of us all. Obviously many—some would say most—Québecois are, in fact, anxious to have structural assimilation without behavioural assimilation, acculturation but not assimilation; this despite the fact that bilingual French Canadians have, generally, fared worse in Quebec and Canada than unilingual English in Quebec and Canada. They would, in other words, prefer the precarious status of being an ethnic group, admittedly a special ethnic group, to the uncertainties of being a separate nation. But, it is unlikely that we can ever return to the "catching-up" ethic of the Quiet Revolution, to the notion that if Quebeckers get enough education, etc., they will throw off thoughts of separatism in order to compete and be mobile individually in North American society. Whether intended or not, in Quebec, the quest for ethnic identity and self-realization, perhaps even class consciousness, reached some sort of climax with the election of a Parti Québecois government. November 15, 1976, is a historical watershed after which things will never be quite the same in Quebec or Canada.

Where does this leave French Canadians in the rest of Canada? At present, federal policy is still to give these groups a special status denied other ethnic groups in Canada. But, given the kind of sentiments expressed to the Task Force on Canadian Unity, it is questionable how long these constitutional rights would remain when Quebec separates and there is no longer reason to "woo" the Quebec vote. From a Quebec standpoint, French-Canadian communities in the rest of Canada seem doomed to extinction. However, this view may be both too objective and too premature. It ignores the concept of situational ethnicity, the fact that groups may construct or reconstruct an ethnic identity. Certainly, the increasing alienation of Quebec from the rest of Canada does remove an important form of political and emotional support. Ironically, it has also forced these groups to re-evaluate what they had come to take for granted—their continuing existence as a cultural group in Canada. This seems to be as true for the French in Alberta, Manitoba and New Brunswick as it is for Acadians in New Brunswick and Nova Scotia, who have in recent years also talked of separation. In short, we suspect that with or without policies designed to further bilingualism and biculturalism, French Canadians will remain an important ethnic force in the Canadian mosaic.

What we know about ethnicization applies mainly to European immigrant groups. While, as we have seen, ethnic diversity is still a major factor in Canada and the United States, it is conceivable that individuals, even collectivities, could "disappear" into the mainstream culture. Indeed, as immigrants to this country, it is easy enough to make the case for, at least, acculturation, that these people have some sort of obligation to become "Canadian" and to learn the language—be it French or English. However, no such case can be made for Canada's native peoples. They did not contract to become Canadians, they did not choose to cut ties with their original culture, they did not emigrate to a new land.

The nineteenth century justifications for segregating Indians and assigning them an inferior status no longer hold up for most Canadians. There may even be developing among Canadians a collective guilt about the history of abuse and the contemporary situation for native peoples. In any case, as we learn more about the history of white-native relations, it is less and less clear that native peoples owe any allegiance to Canadian legal and political institutions. It is conceivable that treaties signed a century or more ago are between Indians and the British Monarchy and, legally, have nothing to do with Canada at all. Ultimately, it may even turn out that the proper place to settle disputes over treaties will not be in British or Canadian courts but in the International Court of The Hague. As the land claim dispute in the State of Maine suggests, these are not simply legalistic fantasies, but very practical issues which will be before the courts for a very long time and which will have far-reaching consequences for native peoples and for everyone else in North American society as well. In both the United States and Canada we are likely to be in for a long and protracted period of legal and political conflict.

NATIVE PEOPLES

Virtually all of the ethnic groups which make up the Canadian mosaic have benefitted from the general growth and prosperity of Canadian society. Again, the exception is Canada's native peoples who, from all accounts, experience poverty, hardship and mortality rates which in many ways surpass what is typical of the poorest Third World countries. Writing more than a decade ago, Alan Borovoy (1966:13) described the plight of Indians:

The poverty of Indians staggers the imagination of white men. It simply drains our mental resources to conceive of how in the technological Canada of 1966 over 80% of Indian homes are devoid of such elementary facilities as sewers, septic tanks, flush toilets, running water, and telephones. . . . The suffering occasioned by their poverty is intensified by temperatures of 40 and 50 degrees below zero. Being so far removed, we cannot feel the horror which lies behind the fact that Indian pre-school mortality is eight times the national average and school age mortality, three times the national average.

Unfortunately, there is no evidence that the situation of Indians and Inuit has changed much in the last decade. Frideres (1974), in what is, to date, probably the most comprehensive study of Canadian Indians, shows that on virtually any measure we might choose, Indians are severely disadvantaged compared to the rest of Canadian society (see also Stanbury, 1975). Similarly, Inuit find themselves caught in the vicious circle that now they require guns and snowmobiles to make a living, houses and convenience foods to be part of the Canadian culture. But, they also find that traditional occupations fail to provide sufficient income to pay for these things.

What is the solution? Some, including the Federal government, have from time to time advocated that the Reserve System be terminated. It seems that the situation of Indians offends the liberal ideology. On the one hand, education should be the panacea for Indian and Inuit problems in the same way it should be for everyone else. On the other hand, the special status of Indians is also offensive to this ideology because it sets them apart from the rest of Canadians and seems somehow to give them an advantage denied to others in the society. The result is lip service to cultural autonomy of native peoples and also impatience that they have not simply done like everyone else and become part of the mainstream culture. In practice, this has generally meant resocializing Indians and Inuit to Canadian culture and, in the process, denigrating native cultures, traditions and economies. For example, until recently, there has been little provision for teaching children in their own language. Nor have there been many native people trained as teachers and other professionals to service their own people on their own terms.[7]

It is evident that Indians and Inuit have been put in a particularly tense version of the assimilationist dilemma all ethnic groups face. To participate equally in the wider society means that members cannot expend scarce energies and resources in order to maintain a traditional culture.

Thus, education is two-edged. It is offered as the only hope of freeing native people from the wretched circumstances in which so many of them live. But, as McElroy (1974) points out, education and change are solutions from a White society perspective; the message is that if native people want jobs and houses and cars then they will have to change their ways and become North American. However, Indian students who do well in school and achieve high status roles must do so on White man's terms and must move wholly into White society. Mobility in White society deprives Indian and Inuit communities of leadership and stimulation. Without leadership, mobilization of collective interests is unlikely. The most able members are gone, unable to act as role models for following generations of young people who begin to ask themselves the recurring question of youth: "What do I want to be?" Marlene Brant Costelano (1970:54) argues that Indian children are caught at a personal level in this wider social dilemma:

The Indian pupil very early finds himself in a dilemma. The more capable he becomes in the White man's language and abstract concepts, the more he becomes alienated from the life style which provides continuity and sustenance for his inner life.

It is not even clear that if Indians are willing to pay the costs of "surrendering" their heritage, they will then be allowed to do so—they will be allowed to assimilate. Numbers of Indians, for instance, have left the reserve, usually for economic reasons, and moved to Canadian cities. Most, however, find themselves in low-paid casual and seasonal jobs, subject to indifference, and sometimes racism, by urban society. Those who do "make it," what Edgar Dosman (1972) refers to as "affluents," have often done so by becoming bureaucrats in the Department of Indian Affairs. They have, in effect, become ethnic brokers or mediators between Indian and White society. Alternatively, Frideres (1974:88) points out that "successful" Indians in the city are those who are able to "pass" as something else—Whites, French, in some instances, Hawaiian. They cannot be simply Indians if they want decent jobs and housing.

So, leaving the reserve has not been the answer for most Indians. Like other rural people, they lack occupational and urban skills and an effective social network or ethnic enclave in the city (see Clark, 1978). Thus, they quickly find themselves caught up in a cycle of poverty from which the only escape is to return to the reserve. It is, for instance, no accident that in doing research on urban Indians, Nagler (1970) found many of his interviewees in hotels and hostels bordering on Cabbagetown, a slum area of Toronto almost totally lacking formal or informal neighbourhood or community networks.

RED POWER

Racism, though having an individualistic or psychological component, arises out of structural conditions and arrangements, themselves ultimately the result of differences in power between two groups of people. Relative to Europeans, Indians were, from the beginning, in a powerless position, faced with the choice of annihilation or segregation. Frideres (1974) argues that Indians became a *colonized* people subject to exploitation and social control and it is as colonized people that they must assert, collectively, opposition to the dominant group. Thus, Frideres resolves the individual and collective dilemma facing Indians by proposing that:

. . . Natives must reject the notion of individual entrepreneurship or individual capitalism. Instead of seeking personal economic development they should aim at "native community development" which entails community ownership and control *of the economy (p. 162).*

Frideres agrees with most Indians that the clock cannot be turned back. But, Canadians can, for humane reasons, and at the same time sound sociological reasons, hand back to Indians control of their own lands, resources, and educational, bureaucratic and political institutions. They must, in other words, be given power over their own life chances and lifestyles. McElroy (1975:287) makes a similar though somewhat less militant argument in regard to the Inuit.

> *Inuit have been learning about change, and they realize that their children will inevitably be involved in northern development. But the nature of that involvement concerns them. They do not want their children to believe that the only way to achieve a sense of competence and self-esteem is to act like the* Kadloonat *(white person) seeking an end to political and economic subordination. Inuit leaders are asserting a sense of responsibility for directing change and for preserving the valuable aspects of their society and ecology.*

As the concept of Red Power implies, conflict is inherent in attempts at community control, conflict which will, no doubt, have additional teeth as Indians and Inuit collectively benefit from land claim and resource settlement and compensation as in British Columbia. It is not clear that the future development of native peoples will be in directions compatible with the "goals" of the rest of Canadian society or that it will always be in the best interests of all native peoples. Certainly, it is far better that native peoples suffer from their own collective mistakes and blunders than from those imposed from outside and above, by social scientists, bureaucrats or the elite.

This is not to say that social scientists who study native peoples, those who live among them, can have no role in facilitating change. The question of just what is the sociologist's role is, as we have seen, highly controversial within the discipline. At this point, it is enough to say that the sociologist can play an instrumental role in helping native peoples achieve their collective interests, not by imposing their own version of what this collective interest is, but rather by coming to understand the subjective life of the communities they are studying and by helping these communities link their private dissatisfactions to problems in the social structure. In other words, the sociologist must learn from the community its collective interest and return to that community this knowledge in a way that they may call upon it as a resource.

SUMMARY AND CONCLUSION

If we have devoted a good deal of space to ethnic relations in this book, it is because we think that ethnicity, historically and in the present, is very central to an understanding of Canadian society. As it happens, it is also a very interesting and vital part of Canadian sociology. What we have tried to do in this chapter is to understand ethnic groups and ethnicization within the context of inequality of power, wealth and status. Obviously, in a capitalist society these inequalities would not disappear if we were to become an ethnically homogenized society. But, often, because of nepotism, ethnic sponsorship, prejudice and discrimination, and perhaps because an ethnic group has not yet learned how to compete successfully in Canadian society, structured inequality cannot wholly be reduced to class inequality.

We have concentrated on ethnicization because, whether we are speaking of Quebec society, native peoples or immigrant groups in Canada, it seems to us that ethnic awareness and ethnic identity, rather than disappearing, have become more pervasive. Ethnicity persists even though an outsider may be unable to detect any differences between the ethnic group and the mainstream culture. Indeed, from an objective viewpoint, it may appear that everyone is assimilating towards a rather neutral middle-class society, a sort of watered-down version of the United States. Some would argue, then, that the much talked about tolerance in Canada for ethnic diversity is illusory, that while the so-called Anglo-Saxon majority may encourage ethnic folk festivals, arts and restaurants, it does not tolerate values, modes of thought and interpersonal behaviour which are different or alien. In other words, the mosaic ideology is only superficial; if you want to make it in Canadian society you had better learn to think and speak "White."

Is ethnicity, then, simply, "all in the mind," something which may once have existed but does so no longer? The concept of ethnicization implies that the answer is yes and no. It seems that we are subject to two simultaneous forces. One is the sheer experience of living in North America. No one, for example, is immune to the influences of television and of mass marketing of everything from movies and K-Tel records to hamburgers and Kraft Foods—what Isajiw (1978) refers to as the technological culture. There are, at the same time, strong diversifying forces as well. For various reasons, we also have strong identifications with the regions in which we live, with our ethnic group and probably with our nation. Difficult as it may be for outsiders to tell the difference, Canadians—English or French—do see themselves as somehow unique, set apart from Europeans, certainly, but also from Americans. As in the United States, Canadians make further distinctions; in some situations making regional identities salient and in other situations emphasizing ethnic differences. These have not disappeared and as sociologists we must accept this as a social fact. Ethnic groups are not static but are shaped and reshaped through the interaction within and with the larger society. At the same time as Greeks in Canada rapidly lose sufficient "Greekness" to almost be foreigners in Greece, present-day English and French Canadians become unrecognizable to their grandparents' generation. Nor, of course, are they English or French. Both host and immigrant group change and, in effect, become ethnic groups.

Ethnicity persists for at least two reasons. One is that it may serve as a partial counteractant to the tedium, sameness and impersonality of mass society. Ethnicity, then, may be one aspect of a more general quest by North Americans for a sense of community. Ironically, the business world, which contributes so much to the predictability and uniformity of contemporary life, is also very sensitive to the subjective aspects of ethnicity; brand new Holiday Inns and Hiltons, for example, often have an "Olde Englishe Pub," "Habitant Room" or an instant ethnic restaurant complete with waitresses in peasant costumes. Apparently, a good way to sell beer or cheese or Canadian wine, for that matter, is to give it a name and label which sounds and looks vaguely ethnic.

The second reason for the persistence of ethnicity is that the Canadian mosaic is, at least partially, a vertical mosaic—usually ethnic differentiation also means ethnic stratification. Ethnic diversity may give colour and flavour to a society, but it is also a focal point for conflicts over power, wealth and status. Ethnic identity rather than class turns out in many instances to be the more effective rallying point for the development of interests.

This is, of course, understandable. What, besides their poverty and powerlessness, do Indians and single female parents on welfare have in common? How much more convenient and simple it is for the Quebec working class to be able to see as the villains *Les Anglais,* thus lumping Canadian and American Anglophones together as exploiting capitalists. How much more it would dilute sentiments for social action to recognize, for instance, that, even in Quebec, there are English Canadians who are also living and working in poverty or who are simply wage and salary earners without wealth and power and who, in Marxist terms, are in the same predicament as themselves. Moreover, as Reitz (1974) had demonstrated, the very fact that the collectivity shares a language serves as a powerful force for group solidarity and group cohesiveness.

In short, as long as some ethnic groups find that, because of nepotism and/or outright discrimination, they are excluded or under-represented in the places where political and economic decisions are made, we can expect ethnicity to remain an important focus for social conflict. Rather than a survival from a previous age, ethnicity turns out to be a dynamic and flexible resource, capable of being called into action when needed and capable also of being transformed and re-invented as the situation demands.

SUGGESTIONS FOR FURTHER READING

We have been able to make only passing reference to the many ethnographic studies of the various ethnic groups which make up the Canadian mosaic. A recent and ambitious project sponsored by the Secretary of State has already published works on Japanese Canadians (Adachi, 1976); Portuguese Canadians (Anderson and Higgs, 1977); Polish Canadians (Radecki and HeydenKorn, 1977); and Scottish Canadians (Reid, 1977). More studies in this series are forthcoming. While we cannot list all of the many studies of ethnic groups in Canada, they include examinations of Hutterites, Doukhobors, Mennonites, Canadian Jews, Slavic Canadians, Italian Canadians and Dutch Canadians. To get a sense of the recent work on ethnicity, check the recently founded journal *Canadian Ethnic Studies*. A. Gregorovich's *Canadian Ethnic Groups Bibliography* (1972) is also a useful source. Of particular interest within the perspective we have presented is the study of Nova Scotia Blacks by Don Clairmont and Dennis Magill, *Africville: The Life and Death of a Canadian Black Community* (1974).

There is, understandably, a large body of research on Canada's native peoples. T. Abler and others have compiled a useful bibliography of works up to 1970, *A Canadian Indian Bibliography, 1960-1970* (1973), and Mark Nagler's *Perspectives on the North American Indians* (1972) gives a sample of this research. Two important works on Indians in Canada are James Frideres's *Canada's Indians: Contemporary Conflicts* (1974) and Edgar Dosman's *Indians: The Urban Dilemma* (1972). A provocative account of the destructive processes of colonialism on the Inuit is Hugh Brody's *The People's Land* (1975).

In addition to the many books we have already cited on Quebec society, an influential study on French-English relations outside of Quebec is John Jackson's *Community and Conflict: A Study of French-English Relations in Ontario* (1975).

The best general introduction to the processes of ethnicization are Andrew Greeley's *Ethnicity in the United States* (1974) and Nathan Glazer's and Daniel P. Moynihan's edited collection, *Ethnicity* (1975). Two recent Canadian collections also reflect what Greeley calls the "rediscovery of ethnicity": Leo Driedger's *The Canadian Ethnic Mosaic: A Quest for Identity* (1978) and W. W. Isajiw's *Identities: The Impact of Ethnicity on Canadian Society* (1976).

FOOTNOTES

[1]For further discussion of this, see Wangenheim (1968).

[2]Most of the studies we are describing here are based on the 1961 census. To the surprise of the authors, no one, to our knowledge, has updated these data using the 1971 census. We can suggest two reasons for this: (1) despite, or because of, computerization, the 1971 census has, as everyone puts it, "been a mess"; and (2) funds for research on ethnic inequality have not been as readily available as they were in the 1960s. Students interested in this issue should watch the major Canadian journals.

[3]Richer and Laporte (1971) have argued that English and French Canadians may, in fact, "think" quite differently.

[4]See, for example, Alfred Schutz's (1964) essay, "The Stranger."

[5]We should note, however, that while non-literate societies are as old, if not older, than industrial societies, some anthropologists view them as societies "frozen in time," inflexible and therefore highly vulnerable when faced with external social and ecological factors.

[6]A very thorough analysis of immigration and the Green Paper from various perspectives appeared in a special issue of *Canadian Ethnic Studies*, Vol. 7(1), 1975.

[7]A very readable and moving account of this process can be found in Heather Robertson's *Reservations are for Indians* (1970).

PART 4

Processes of Change

collective behaviour
CHAPTER XI

People scrambling over one another trying to get out of a burning cinema; students occupying the administration offices to demand a greater voice in university decision making; ghetto blacks participating in a "race riot"—these are examples of what sociologists have traditionally defined as *collective behaviour*. We say "traditionally" defined because recently a number of sociologists have questioned the usefulness of the term, arguing that it obscures the important differences between, say, panic and protest and exaggerates the differences between these actions and the behaviour of everyday life. Even among those who find the term useful, there is a good deal of debate over which activities should be included and which should not. In fact, this area of sociology seems to have produced more than its share of controversy and confusion.

Nevertheless, most sociologists would agree that the examples we have used share a few characteristics which distinguish them from most ordinary, everyday behaviour. First of all, of course, they involve large numbers of people. Second, the behaviour is transitory; that is, the activity is short-lived, even if its consequences are not. And third, the behaviour is relatively spontaneous; that is, much of the behaviour is improvised on the spot (Berk, 1974:7-8). There is, however, a good deal of disagreement about what other defining characteristics these examples may share. To understand these controversies, one should know something of the development of collective behaviour theory.

We have described how sociology arose largely in response to the two revolutions: the French Revolution and the Industrial Revolution. The eighteenth and early nineteenth centuries were a time of fear; sociological thought was the conservative reaction to the ghost of the French Revolution, to the fear of loss of community, to the fear of the anarchy supposedly unleashed in the new industrial city. And, the symbol of the end of the old order and of the new disorder was *the mob*. Radzinowicz (1948) probably catches something of the spirit of the times when he describes "the existence in London of a vast and unruly mob, always ready to take advantage of any incident to create disorder and endanger public safety" (p. 406). In Britain and France this was a time of mob riot and violence. Even as late as 1886, for example, the City of London placed itself in a state of alert against revolutionary mob violence; the city "was visited by something akin to the *grande peur*" (in Pearson, 1975:159).

Rudé (1970:34) writes that there exist two traditions of social thought which treat the mob either "admiringly as 'le peuple,' or, slightingly as 'la canaille,' " either as the people or as the rabble. Collective behaviour literature derives out of the latter tradition. In this tradition, the mob was seen as no more than the dregs of society who needed no motive to destroy, who destroyed for the pure pleasure of it. The mob was synonymous with the dangerous criminal classes which emerged in the new industrial city. For the bourgeois inhabitants of the new city, the rookeries of the city, where this riff-raff could be found living together in squalor and vice, spewed forth the collective violence which was so feared. Geoffrey Pearson captures well the language of nineteenth century thinking about the criminal classes:

> *Sewage and drains were guiding metaphors for those who depicted the deviance of this time. "Foul wretches" and "moral filth" lay heaped in "stagnant pools" about the streets. When they moved, they were seen to "ooze" in a great "tide". The population was "slime" which gathered in ghettos which were described as "poisoned wells", "canker-worms", "sinks of inequity", and "plague-spots". Their houses were described as "cess-pits"; and their way of life was a "moral miasma" . . . the city "reeked" of vice; the "scum" and the "dregs" of society was a* "moral debris". *. . . The words "pustule", "fever", and "wart" came readily to hand describing the moral condition of the labouring and dangerous classes (1975:161).*

In this passage, Pearson seems to be equating the labouring class and the criminal (dangerous) class. In fact, he is acknowledging the confusion of the times. It was during this period that social thinkers merged the notions of urban poverty and criminality in a way which was to dominate conceptions of crime and deviance to the present. But, perhaps more important, this confusion reflects the greatest fear of this period, that the chaos, the "senseless" violence, of the criminal classes would spread to the "respectable" labouring class.

Here we see the roots of the three dominant perspectives on collective behaviour. First, we can see the origins of the *mass society perspective* which holds that incidences of collective violence increase with the breakdown of traditional authority relations and with social disorganization. Second, we can find the roots of *convergence* theory which sees incidents of collective behaviour as a result of the coming together of the type of people predisposed to collective violence, for example, losers and riff-raff. Finally, out of this early fear of the mob has emerged the concept of *contagion,* the somewhat mystical notion that people can "catch" the irrational impulse to violence.

This is the context in which we must understand twentieth century attempts to build theories of collective behaviour. Sociologists have tried to throw off the moral and political language of these early works, to cast off the images of pathology and sickness and have tried instead to develop "scientific" theories of collective behaviour. However, as we shall see, American sociologists, until recently, continued in the conservative tradition. Included in their background assumptions was the belief that there must be better ways, more reasonable ways, to gain a more just society. Fired by the vivid images of the Communist revolutions and their aftermath, the Italian *fascisti* and Hitler rallies, the fear of the Horde persisted as a background theme in collective behaviour theory.

In the 1960s and the early part of this decade, however, along with the emergence of the youth movement, its New Left politics and counterculture values, perhaps as part of all this, a variety of approaches arose against the portrayal of collective behaviour as senseless and irrational. The challenges came from diverse sources, but what unified them was a sympathy with the participants in collective behaviour and a demand that their motives be understood, that their perspective be *appreciated.* Much of the impetus for the shift came from the labelling theorists we discussed in Chapter VI, who, in a similar way, challenged the background assumptions of deviant behaviour theory. Indeed, just as criminality, vice and collective violence were treated as one by the nineteenth century theorists, so again does collective behaviour and deviant behaviour merge. In an important contribution to the areas of deviance and collective behaviour, Horowitz and Liebowitz (1968:280) write:

> *The traditional distinction between social problems and the political system is becoming obsolete. Behaviour which in the past was perceived as social deviance is now assuming well-defined ideological and organizational contours; while political marginals are adopting a deviant lifestyle. This merger of social deviance and political marginality creates a new style of politics, based on strategies that are traditionally considered illegitimate. The result of this trend is estimated to be an increase in the use of violence as a political tactic, and the development of a revolutionary potential among the expanding ranks of deviant sub-groups.*

Certainly this means that campus demonstrations, urban race riots and violent labour disputes are to be viewed as rational, goal-directed and purposive. Collective behaviour comes to be viewed as the natural response of the oppressed (Marx, 1970). And, as we come to re-examine our own history through such an appreciative perspective, we come to recognize that Canada has a long tradition of collective and often violent protest. No longer, for example, can we view the Riel rebellion as an aberration inspired by a crazed leader. Increasingly, historians, social scientists—perhaps most Canadians—are coming to recognize the legitimate grievances and therefore the "rationality" of much of this collective action.

But, this approach also insists that deviants be accorded political status.[1] This is reflected, for example, in Taylor, Walton and Young's (1973) statement that juvenile delinquents are actually engaged in the redistribution of property. As well, vandalism comes to be seen as an inarticulate attempt to fight injustice and to right wrongs (Pearson, 1975:97). Ian Taylor (1971) makes a similar case for soccer hooliganism. What these writers are saying is what Karl Marx predicted—that the early collective actions of the revolutionary working class would be primitive, directed at the "wrong enemies." So too, the argument goes, should criminal and deviant behaviour be viewed as inarticulate or primitive political action. The "appreciative approach" of the 1960s and 1970s has been an important corrective to the taken-for-granted assumptions which had dominated the field. These sociologists were less likely to see change as "traumatic"; they sympathized with those who sought social change, and turned upside-down the area of deviance, seeing it not only as a sign of human diversity, but also as political protest. In the words of Stanley Cohen (1973:120):

> *There is much talk of alienation, dropping out, disaffiliation and youth on the streets. There is confusion about the line beyond which "stealing" becomes "looting", "hooliganism" becomes "rioting", "vandalism" becomes "sabotage". When do "reckless maniacs" become "freedom fighters"? Are the everyday encounters between the police and urban slum youth throughout the world somehow stripped of their political significance if what is happening is not defined as a "riot" or "disturbance"?*

But this approach has gone too far and not far enough. Sufficient time has passed since the anger and excitement of the student movement that we can reflect on the contributions of "misfit sociology." Some have argued that the emphasis on the politics of everyday life has led to a preoccupation with hipsterism and trivia. Paul Rock (1973) takes issue with the romantic version of criminals as political protesters. He argues that criminal behaviour is political only if the criminal himself regards his actions in these terms. Gary Marx (1970) raises a similar question, more directly relevant to collective behaviour, when he distinguishes political riots from issueless riots. Most important, however, are the limitations of any view that focuses solely on (a) the immediate circumstance of protest, and (b) the subjective perceptions and interactions of the participants. An understanding of collective behaviour requires that it be placed in a broader socio-historical context. For example, if we accept the view that collective behaviour is as "natural" as the powerful groups' adherence to the status quo, it becomes as important to explain why collective behaviour does not occur as why it does. We must take into account the role of powerful groups in inhibiting and shaping collective behaviour. And, we must account for the particular form that collective behaviour takes.

Robert Evans (1969:1) gives us a good sense of the range of possibilities:

Under the rubric "collective behaviour" are included theoretical and empirical treatises on riot, revolution, insurrection, rebellion, disorder, protest, strike, disaster, panic, flight, hysteria, fads, crazes, fashion, rumor, contagion, communication, mobs, crowds, audience, public, mass, social-political-religious patterns of behaviour, and other movements and cults.

Clearly "collective behaviour" includes very different forms of collective action. For example, while many people may engage in a fad, streaking, for example, they do so individually, probably without ever interacting with other streakers. This is obviously very different from the crowd, the gathering in interaction of a number of individuals with similar goals and interests. Moreover, not all forms of collective behaviour are political in the sense that they are directed towards changing the social structure. Not all riots can be characterized as ideological, nor do they all represent essential conflicts in the community.

. . . there are numerous occasions where, outwardly at least, men collectively seem to be doing many of the same things—battling authorities and each other, attacking symbols, looting, stealing, and destroying property—but where the elements of protest, ideology, grievance, strain, lack of access to channels for redressing complaints, social change . . . are relatively insignificant factors, if not absent altogether (Marx, 1970:23-24).

In fact, some forms of collective behaviour do seem to be *issueless* in that the people engaged in the behaviour may be acting out of expediency or opportunism rather than out of dissatisfaction with the social order and a desire to change things or bring in a new order. Riots during police strikes, for example, may be an instance of "issueless" collective behaviour, when people take advantage of a weakening in external social controls to violate traditional rules "mainly for fun and profit" (Banfield, 1970).

But how do we draw the line? Is a riot ever fully political or fully issueless? The difficulties in distinguishing these types of collective behaviour, the difficulties of rewriting history, are well illustrated by the Montreal police strike in 1969. One Montrealer reported: "You've never seen the city like this. It's like the war" (in Marx, 1970:31). Sniper fire, widespread looting and arson were reported in all the dailies. Certainly it is a safe guess that some of the participants were taking advantage of the absence of the police. But we all know, as well, that separatism, labour unrest and economic inequalities were hot issues at the time. It is also a safe guess, then, that some of the rioters were acting out of political concerns, expressing grievances. Not only are crowds likely to be composed of members with a wide variety of motivations, but these motivations may well change during the course of the activity. After all, collective behaviour inevitably involves social interaction; collective behaviour, then, may itself serve to socialize participants to new ways of thinking about themselves and their society.

We can differentiate forms of collective behaviour in the following terms:

1) Is the action "individual" (e.g., crime, fads) or collective (e.g.,

crowds, social movements)?

2) Is the instance of collective behaviour political or issueless? And how does this change in process?
3) How are the issues defined? That is, what kind of ideology unifies the participants and gives them direction?

We must ask why collective behaviour takes one form and not another and we must seek to understand the role of powerful groups in all of this. We shall return to these questions but first we shall examine some of the traditional perspectives on collective behaviour, in part because they provide a useful illustration of the role of values in sociological theory, but also because they offer important insights to the questions we have raised.

THEORIES OF COLLECTIVE BEHAVIOUR

Contagion

In its simplest version, contagion theory holds that, under certain conditions, people lose their capacity for critical thought. Their behaviour is no longer a rational calculation of the best means to achieve some ends, but rather the unthinking automatic imitation of the behaviour of others. This is often the kind of thinking which underlies the claims of law enforcement officers that a well publicized hijacking, say, will lead to a number of imitative crimes. A number of social scientists have concluded that this contagion is most likely to occur at times of crisis or stress (see Clark and others, 1975:2). Some variant of contagion theory is often used to explain the rapid spread of fads or crazes. Contagion theory also holds that the milling together of large groups of people may often lead to the spread of emotionality; crowds can exert pressures on people so that they do things they would never do alone. This notion that some distinctive process operates in crowds owes most to the work of the French sociologist, Gustave Le Bon.

Gustave Le Bon wrote *The Crowd* at the end of the nineteenth century. Despite its inaccuracies, lack of clarity and obvious conservative bias, it has remained one of the most influential works in the field. To appreciate Le Bon's work, it is useful to know at least a little about turn-of-the-century France and Le Bon's own sympathies. Le Bon was concerned about the rapid changes he was witnessing in his country. With accelerating industrialization and urbanization came new social classes and new lifestyles. Urban workers became, if not a powerful, at least a loud voice for social change. The power of the aristocratic classes was being challenged, particularly by the expanding middle class. Le Bon, however, wrote about the nineteenth century mobs we have discussed. He distrusted what he saw as the democratic tendencies in nineteenth century Europe where these new classes were increasing their participation in the political process. He did not like the changes he saw and he did not like the violent crowds that had helped to bring about these changes (Berk, 1974). Not only did Le Bon hold that crowds tended towards violence, he believed that the violence was typically irrational and unpredictable. Rarely is crowd behaviour anything more than aimless destruction.

He believed that crowds transform people into almost identical beings, incapable of rational thought, unable to exercise self-control, but able only to operate at a primitive, animalistic level. With the disappearance of individual differences, the crowd becomes a single entity characterized by a "group mind." The individual in the crowd, then, no longer acts and thinks as an individual, but acts and thinks simply as part of the crowd.

Le Bon's explanation for the emergence of this "group mind" is far from clear, but seems essentially to be based in the notion of *suggestibility*. People within a crowd are easily manipulated by leaders who almost "hypnotize" them. Crowd members will accept almost anything they are told by the leaders and will tend to copy each other's actions as well. They are suggestible, then, to leaders in particular, but also to other crowd members. A process of *contagion* is at work.

That this does not constitute an explanation of crowd behaviour should be fairly evident. Somehow, mystically, people in crowds supposedly "catch" crowd psychology from one another, lose their individuality and come under the control of leaders. Yet, this notion of the contagion effect of crowds has persisted. As recently as 1970, for example, Peter Berger, an influential American sociologist, wrote: "It seems to me that nothing very decisive has been added to Gustave Le Bon's insight that crowds act to destroy."[2]

Le Bon's influence is clearly evident in the work of the American sociologist, Herbert Blumer. Blumer accepted fairly fully Le Bon's description of crowds as irrational and unpredictable. More surprising, though, was Blumer's acceptance of the notion, albeit his own modified version, of contagion. Blumer's reliance on contagion to explain crowd behaviour is really rather ironic. Recall in Chapter IV we discussed Blumer's contribution to our understanding of social interaction. He has been most emphatic and articulate in his emphasis on the interpretive process in interaction. People think, imagine the future, and interpret one another's meanings before they act. Blumer has criticized "traditional" sociology and social psychology for failing to recognize the importance of this interpretive process. However, when he turns to collective behaviour, a subject he has written on extensively, he seems, often, to forget all about this. Supposedly something quite different is happening.

This "something quite different" Blumer (1952) calls *circular reaction*, where interpretation is replaced by something more like a reflex. Some *precipitating incident* catches people's interest and brings them together in one place. The people mill about observing the excited motions of the others in the crowd. They respond directly to this emotion without trying to interpret or evaluate it. Observing the intense excitement of others in the crowd makes one more excited which in turn makes the others in the crowd more excited and so on—circular reaction.

Blumer draws an analogy between the crowd and a herd of cattle. A cow, for some reason, may become agitated. As it begins to bellow and move wildly, it excites the other cattle who also begin to move about wildly. The excitement spreads throughout the herd. The excitement of the other cattle acts back on the first cow until the excitement reaches a point of frenzy and the cattle stampede. Many of us have probably experienced something like the contagious excitement that Blumer is talking about. For example, if you have ever been on an airplane and been confronted with some inexplicable smoke, you have no doubt witnessed the rapid spread of excitement. For Blumer, this circular reaction helps us understand crowd panic in the face of disaster. It also helps us understand violent mob action. When the collective excitement is directed at a common object, for example, an enemy to attack or a flag to burn, we see the acting crowd.

But, if you think about the airplane example, you will see that there is a fundamental flaw in Blumer's theory. While the people on the plane may become more tense, more fearful, they do not all act in the same way, they do not all panic. Indeed, even in situations which might be described as panic, people's actions, however distasteful we find them, could be seen as perfectly rational. For example, who is to say that it is irrational to push someone out of the way to get to the exit of a burning building? Individually, people will be acting on the basis of their definition of the situation. Not all of the people in a mob behave in the same way—some may loot, some may not; some may fight with the police, some may run; some may urge greater violence, some may urge moderation (see, for example, Rudé, 1964;

Graham and Gurr, 1969; and Berk, 1974). And, again, who can say that the acting crowd is not using "rational," perhaps the only, means to achieve its ends. Critics of contagion theory generally agree that Blumer, like Le Bon, exaggerated the differences between how people think within crowds and the interpretive process of everyday life. We shall return to these issues.

Convergence Theory

A somewhat more recent attempt to capture the nature of collective behaviour is what Ralph Turner (1964) has called "convergence theory." In essence, this approach offers a "type of person" account of collective behaviour. Certain groups of people carry around with them latent or unconscious antisocial drives; they bring these drives with them to the crowd. The crowd, then, does not create anything, it unleashes what was already there. Researchers within this perspective have tried to identify the psychological characteristics of participants in collective behaviour. The most famous attempt, and the most controversial, was Adorno's quantitative study of the authoritarian personality. His argument was that certain people had a psychological predisposition to obey authority and to enforce obedience on others. These people were also rigid, inflexible and unable to cope with change. And it is such people, Adorno argued, who are likely to give support to political extremism, particularly of the right.

A more pervasive theme, however, has linked political extremism to alienation. For example, Seymour Martin Lipset (1963) has argued that the lower classes, because they are *isolated* from the activities of democratic society, are most vulnerable to radical left-wing movements. Their isolation supposedly prevents them from gaining the political sophistication necessary to understand how democracies work. They lack the resources to use the political system effectively, if at all. They are undereducated and underexposed to the mass media, and are less likely to participate in formal organizations; their politics, therefore, are primitive. Similar and supporting arguments can be found in the writings of Fromm (1963), Hoffer (1951), Kornhauser (1959), and others in what we have identified as the "mass society approach." In a critical research article, Alejandro Portes (1971:821) summarizes the approach:

These authors have understood extremism as a consequence of an increasing lack of integrative bonds between individuals and the general social structure. Isolation, uprootedness, the anxieties of meaningless existence generate collective flights into the security of the totalitarian movements. The paternalistic appeal of the "leader" functions to comfort followers who at last find the peace of protection and belonging.

We have seen in the preceding chapter a similar explanation applied to the increasing importance attached to ethnicity in modern society.

Convergence, like contagion, emphasizes the unanimity in thought, feeling and action of those who engage in collective behaviour. These theorists have accepted the view of collective behaviour as normless; traditional norms which guide people's behaviour have supposedly broken down. If this is the case, what holds the people together? What accounts for the unanimity? Clark and others (1975:3) summarized the problem as follows:

By overemphasizing the breakdown in social norms, we can readily fall into the trap of regarding collective behaviour . . . as lacking in any kind of rules to govern what people do. . . . It is an easy step to the erroneous . . . notion that collective behaviour is totally uncontrolled, irrational, and senseless.

Emergent norm theory arose largely in response to these problems.

Emergent Norm Theory

Emergent norm theory, developed by Ralph H. Turner and Lewis M. Killian

(1972), holds that collective behaviour, just as the behaviour of everyday life, is governed by norms. In collective behaviour, however, the norms are new, created on the scene. According to this view, collective behaviour emerges in situations in which the everyday norms do not seem to work or to apply. The most obvious example may be the sudden disaster, a situation for which people have no routine norms. Strangers in a burning cinema are more likely to "panic" than, say, miners caught in a cave-in. The miners are likely to have thought about and discussed what they would do in a disaster and to have developed at least some normative expectations. As Lucas (1969) has shown, miners are likely to have a set of norms about how "real men" should act, how they should cope in a crisis, as well as a good deal of folklore wisdom about disasters. The people in the cinema, however, must react to a situation for which they have no clear norms. They must improvise.

Disaster events are only one example of the variety of situations in which people feel they must devise new ways of behaving. Clark and others (1975:7) provide a more general framework.

(1) People may be opposed to some aspect of the existing values, norms, or leaders in their society; or (2) they may perceive existing values, norms, or leaders as inappropriate, confusing, or insufficient. In either case, they are not content. They feel a sense of restlessness and an urge to do something to overcome the deficiency.

According to Turner and Killian, members of the crowd usually discuss among themselves how to define the situation and search for guidelines for action. Of course, some members of the crowd will be more willing to express their views and more forceful in making their opinions known. Turner and Killian do not assume that all members of the crowd come to agree. Surely unanimity is unlikely in a large collectivity. However, if someone in the crowd does not accept what he *thinks* is the "crowd's view," if he thinks he is very much alone, he is unlikely to oppose the crowd. He may even "go along." At first, then, many of the participants may conform to the new norms because of the power of the many others present to reward or punish their behaviour. Later, they are likely to conform routinely because they have come to accept the behaviour as appropriate in the situation.

This theory, then, proposes that behaviour in crowds can be understood through principles of conformity which apply to human behaviour more generally. All of us understand the power of group pressure and the importance of group support. No doubt we are more likely to succumb to group pressure if we think the group is unanimous.

David Matza (1964) offers a similar account in his explanation of juvenile delinquency. The juvenile, faced with the prospect of his first criminal act, often feels that he is the only member of his gang who is reluctant to break the law, the only one who feels guilt and fear. Therefore, he often conforms to what he thinks is the unanimous view of his gang; though, in actual fact, the gang may be far from unanimous. In any case, after participating in the illegal activity he may learn to define the behaviour as appropriate. At first, he conforms because of the group's power to reward and punish him; later he conforms because he has internalized the behaviour.

For Turner and Killian, the conformity in crowds is similar to the conformity in everyday life; the difference is simply a matter of degree. A similar emphasis can be found in the work of Tamotsu Shibutani (1966). Shibutani's focus is on communication within crowds. Faced with an ambiguous situation, people will use whatever information they have to arrive at some meaningful interpretation. In crowds, information is typically communicated through *rumour*. Although, in common sense terms, we generally think of rumour as inaccurate information, this need not be the case. Here we use the term simply to describe people's attempts to produce information, unavailable through formal channels (e.g., news media), to help them understand their situation.

Shibutani points out that members of a crowd are likely to play different roles in rumour formation. Some may be "messengers," who bring to the crowd bits of information, often what they have heard from others; some may be "interpreters," who try to weigh the information and put it in context; some may be "skeptics," who challenge the information, demand proof and express doubt about its validity; some may be "auditors," passive recipients of the information, while others act as "decision makers," active leaders in deciding what to do about the information. Shibutani identifies a number of other roles, but the important point here is that the participants in the crowd to not necessarily act unthinkingly. Rather, they may engage in careful and critical deliberation before they act.[3]

LIMITATIONS OF COLLECTIVE BEHAVIOUR APPROACH: PANIC AND PROTEST

The work of Turner and Killian and Shibutani is extremely useful, especially as it emphasizes the possibility that crowds, despite appearances, may not be homogeneous and what goes on in crowds may not be so very different from what goes on in everyday life. We need not posit any special process to understand the interaction. Moreover, the notion that norms are emergent allows us to consider crowds not as disorganized, but as in the process of organizing. This approach encourages us to ask how people in a crowd construct lines of action, how each comes to define the risks and rewards involved and how these definitions change through interaction. In other words, collective behaviour is symbolic interaction. The participants are no different from other people: "They fear punishment; they are vulnerable to economic and social pressures; they seek support and economic security; some can be co-opted, others corrupted" (Oberschall, 1973:160). As their definitions change, they may drop out or become more adamant, moderate their goals or become more extreme. And, as we shall see, how the participants come to define the risks and rewards depends in good part on how their initial attempts are dealt with by the state and its official representatives.

However, the perspectives we have discussed share at least one fundamental limitation. As we said at the outset, treating panic and protest as like phenomena obscures what are crucial differences between them. For example, when a community is struck by a natural disaster it makes good sense to talk about this as the "precipitating incident" which brought people together and focused their attention. Without the disaster, of course, there would be no panic, or no need for collective attempts to resolve the confusion created by the disaster. Here, the model is rather simple—a disaster occurs which disrupts routine practices and creates confusion, and people interact with one another working out new guidelines for their behaviour.

But, such a model is too simple to understand protest. Certainly some precipitating incident, usually some police action, will often bring together large numbers of people and give focus to their collective discontent. The discontent, however, is not caused by the incident, nor are the "battle lines" the mere accidental consequence of who happened to gather at that particular time and place. However much they may have overstated their position, the "misfit" sociologists of the 1960s no longer allow us to treat all forms of collective action as episodic and transitory. Specifically, to understand conflict groups and social movements, we must know something of the history and structure of the society in which they arise.

CONFLICT GROUPS AND SOCIAL MOVEMENTS

Conflict and Change

Throughout this book we have emphasized that social conflict is inherent in the very fact of social organization. Social structure implies conflict. Anthony Oberschall summarizes this:

At any given moment, there exists a certain distribution of scarce resources and of rewards—the good things desired and sought after by most, such as wealth, power and prestige—among the individuals, groups, and classes in a society. Some are better off, and others are worse off. Those who are favored have a vested interest in conserving and consolidating their existing share; those who are negatively privileged seek to increase theirs, individually or collectively. Social conflict results from this clash of opposing interests (Oberschall, 1973:33).

The structures which create impoverishment and oppression for some provide privilege and pleasure for others. It is not surprising that people are unwilling to give up their privileges and will resist the attempts of others to snatch them away. Disadvantaged groups, then, must take considerable risks and sacrifices when they collectively attempt to gain a greater share of the valued resources.

Overt conflict is not, of course, inevitable. After all, as we have seen, dominant groups are such because they have control of the resources of the society; they have at their disposal several lines of defence against structural changes which threaten their privilege. Frequently, because they control media and educational institutions, they are successful with their first and most subtle line of defence, ideology, the rationalization and justification of inequality. Poor people, for example, may, for a time at least, believe that they are better off spiritually than the rich, or that they are poor because they are stupid, or that they are freed of the "burdens" of power. They may also be diverted by fads and crazes—the contemporary equivalent of Roman circuses. At other times, subordinate groups may reject the ideology but still feel powerless to act. People know that there are other lines of defence—economic reprisals, arrest and, ultimately, soldiers, guns and tanks.

Between these extremes there are, of course, two other possibilities which make conflict less likely. First, people may strive individually rather than collectively to improve their position through the legitimate channels for upward mobility. When these are blocked, they may, in Merton's terms, innovate, attempt "illegitimately" to get a share of what privileged groups possess. Though viewed inevitably as a social problem by those in power, crime may also act as a "safety valve" which reduces some of the pressure which might otherwise be directed towards collective conflict. Clearly, if these defences of the dominant group were totally successful there would be no revolutions, uprisings and riots; collective behaviour would emanate only from immediate circumstances, never from long-standing structural grievances. History, of course, reveals that this is far from the case, that the lack of open conflict, the accommodative relationship which may be established between conflict groups, is always fragile, unstable and never permanent. And, as the fortunes of groups in society rise and fall, the accommodative structures are regularly challenged.

Hence, the relationships among collectives are continually shifting in our century of rapid and widespread change. Changes in the size and distribution of population, changes in the technology of production and communication and the changes we have been talking about throughout this book also find their counterpart in changes in our everyday lives. And, some will feel threatened; some will be given hope; some will entrench against these changes; some will try to speed them. Aspects of the culture long held sacred, perhaps taken for granted, may come to appear obsolete or at least open to challenge; new ideas may gain currency. As Barrington Moore (1972:56) points out, we have entered an age when people are more willing to "reject *in toto* the social system under which they live, the goals of their community and its moral standards." Clearly, social change and social conflict are intertwined; the relationship, however, is a complex one. In the following section, we shall examine more closely some of the economic and political changes which may create widespread discontent, but there is no mechanical relationship between this discontent and collective action. Groups characterized by widespread discontent might best be viewed as "publics," which may be mobilized to collective action. In this sense, a public is an amorphous and as yet unorganized collectivity (Mauss, 1975:12).

Structural Sources of Discontent

Understandably, most social scientists have focused on economic change—how economic trends are directly or indirectly related to grievance and protest. Two conclusions can safely be drawn from the very many studies: the relationship is important and it is most complex. Karl Marx, for example, argued that the increasing misery of the worker—deepening economic crises, lower wages, increasing impoverishment and so on—would produce a revolutionary potential. On the other hand, Tocqueville (1955) long ago argued that immediately preceding the French Revolution was a period of economic prosperity and it was this prosperity which promoted unrest. Some have looked at economic changes in absolute terms while others have focused on relative gains and losses, how some groups have fared relative to others. Some have examined long-term trends and others the short-term. As Shorter and Tilly (1974:4-11) rightly pointed out, it will make quite a difference whether we look at economic changes over a ten-year period or a hundred-year period. Long-term deprivation and short-term deprivation, for example, are likely to have different consequences. And the controversies continue.

One famous approach focuses on *relative deprivation,* a perceived gap between what people feel they should get and what they actually get, that is, between expectations and achievements. James Davies (1962), for example, argues that revolutions and rebellions are most likely in societies in which a period of economic improvement is followed by a sharp reversal. People's hopes and expectations will have been raised during the time of prosperity and then frustrated during the decline. For example, it was not until French Canadians had experienced some degree of economic prosperity that the Quiet Revolution began and demands for social change became more vociferous.

Relative deprivation occurs, then, if expectations outstrip achievements whether because expectations have risen, achievement has fallen or both. Subordinate groups may also feel deprived relative to the superordinate groups in society. For example, while it is no doubt true that the objective economic conditions of American Blacks have improved, particularly over the last 50 years, these improvements have been even greater for Whites; the gap between the groups has increased. Terrence White (1975) has used a similar argument to explain the growing opposition to international unions among Canadian workers who apparently feel that American workers have often been benefitting at the expense of their Canadian counterparts. White explains the decisions of Canadian locals to break away from the international unions in terms of the pervasive "feelings of relative deprivation in regard to union services (that is, bread and butter issues), rather than by nationalism alone" (p. 302).

Clearly, aggregate or overall economic trends will affect various groups in society in different ways. General economic prosperity may increase the gaps between rich and poor; prices may rise faster than wages; some regions may remain underdeveloped; some occupations may no longer be in demand; some industries may be caught with obsolescent technology. In fact, as we have shown in Chapter VIII, even with the dramatic increase in income in the past 20 years, those at the bottom of the class structure have been experiencing increasing impoverishment. In short, even in times of economic growth, some groups will suffer relative or even absolute deprivation. Furthermore, different kinds of changes will be important to different groups: those living a marginal or subsistence existence will be affected by food shortages and rising food prices; peasants will be affected by land shortage; commercial farmers will be affected by changes in world food prices; wage workers will be affected by wage cuts, declining purchasing power and unemployment; and so on. In sum, however complex the relationship, it is obvious that a real or perceived change in the distribution of resources will make some groups feel deprived. Nor are economic changes the only threat to accommodative structures.

Political discontent may arise from changes in the distribution and use of power. One example is provided by imperialism. As we indicated in Chapter VII, the history of imperialism and colonialism is a history of violence and conflict. The attempt to impose external authority on a previously autonomous people will always meet discontent and resistance. Similarly, Charles Tilly (1964), in a most influential study, explains the Vendée counter-revolution of 1973 in terms of the increasing interference by the revolutionary government in Paris in the affairs of the Vendée population. Grievances built up as the Paris government imposed military conscription, land reforms and other changes which usurped the authority of local influentials, and these grievances led eventually to the attempted counter-revolution.

Political discontent may also arise "from the demands for greater authority, rights, and recognition by those who are excluded from the polity and from full citizenship rights" (Oberschall, 1973:44). Allen Grimshaw (1970) points out that as these excluded groups gain in number, as they become organized and recognize their strength, they will increasingly participate in the struggle for power. The attempts of the ruling group to block them will increase their discontent. Political turmoil is likely to result if the ruling groups are perceived to be abusing their power—rigging elections, the continued use of force—in their attempts to block the excluded groups' demands.

The sources of political and economic discontent are too numerous and varied to be catalogued here. The important point to be taken from this discussion is that times of social turmoil and upheaval are likely to be characterized by some combination of economic and political discontent spread widely throughout the society while at the same time more concentrated in particular social strata. But such discontent, in itself, is not a sufficient condition for collective action. It is not enough that people know that something is wrong. Somehow, and this remains the most pressing question for collective behaviour theory, they must be mobilized into crowds, interest groups, pressure groups or social movements if they are to participate in the active pursuit of collective goals.

MOBILIZATION

There is nothing automatic in the transformation of collectivities, which share grievances and discontent and which objectively share common interests, into interest groups pursuing common goals. At the very least, the collectivity must develop common definitions of villains and victims, oppressors and oppressed, if they are to engage in collective action. However, if only these minimal conditions are present, collective action is likely to be episodic and coordinated much as Hobsbawm (1963) describes the "primitive rebels" in pre-industrial society. It is in this kind of collective action that it is, perhaps, hardest to distinguish between "social banditry" and "criminality." In his discussion of the soaring crime rates during Canada's Depression, Barry Broadfoot (1975) suggests that at least part of the reason for these inflated rates was just this kind of primitive protest, what he terms "rough justice." This protest was not guided by a full-blown counter-ideology or what Mannheim calls a "utopia." Rather, it was much more spontaneous, directed at little more than meting out punishment to those thought responsible for destroying the old order.

If protest is to be more sustained and coordinated, other conditions are necessary: (1) an ideology which can unify potential members; (2) willing and able leadership to articulate this ideology and to organize activities; and (3) channels for communication and a network of cooperative relationships (Clark and others, 1975:12-18). There has been a good deal of debate about the precise role of ideology in collective behaviour. In part, at least, the controversy stems from the fact that few participants in collective behaviour will hold a well-developed ideology (see Muller, 1970). Perhaps Heberle's (1951) term "constitutive ideas" is preferable here to the notion of ideology which implies a set of ideas more systematized and rationalized than is found in most instances of collective action. Ideologies are always emergent in collective behaviour but are rarely full-blown. In any case, counter-ideologies, always readily available in any society, are what give meaning to collective discontent.

Of course this is not to say, as conventional wisdom would have it, that "outside agitators" spread ideas which create grievances and collective outbursts. Such an image is often fostered by the powerful groups as a means of challenging the legitimacy of the grievances expressed through collective action. For example, in his description of the Estevan Strike of 1931, S. D. Hanson (1974) indicates that the authority's decision to blame "the troubles" on outside agitators allowed them essentially to break the strike. Ideologies or constitutive ideas do not create grievances, but they do identify and explain them, identify the heroes and the villains, define collective goals and strategies for achieving these goals and provide moral justification for the pursuit of these goals. The moral principles which justify collective action are almost always readily available within any society. In sum, ideas serve to translate private troubles into public issues and describe what must, practically and morally, be done. Such ideas do more than coordinate activities; they also promote commitment to the collective. Indeed, some aspects of the ideology may be directly intended to enhance the self-identity and pride of the protest group, both of which may be necessary for concerted political action. In any case, although obviously not all participants will accept all aspects of the proffered ideology, conversion to this ideology is an important predictor of commitment to and support for the protest group.

Sustained protest also requires leaders who are sufficiently motivated and skillful to articulate the ideology and to coordinate collective activities. Obviously such leadership is not always available and, because of this, much collective behaviour may not move beyond the primitive stage. Sometimes leadership comes from outside the strata which generated the collective protest; leadership may even come from men who have belonged to the social strata of the dominators. But, such leadership may often encounter "a certain aloofness and mistrust" which inhibits mobilization (Freire, 1970:162-165). Leadership is most likely to be successful if it emerges from within the collectivity, but even then it will encounter problems. Leaders of conflict groups are constantly open to challenge. Their positions are obviously less clearly defined than are conventional authority positions; they cannot so easily call upon shared norms of obedience or institutionalized sanctions to implement their decisions. There are, however, at least two conditions under which these problems may be minimized.

First, leadership may be drawn from an already existing organizational base. In fact, a good deal of evidence suggests that the leaders of collective behaviour are typically those who already have a legitimate authority base. This was the case, for example, for the leadership during the development of the CCF in Western Canada.

Though it was a new radical party, the CCF did not have to build up an organization from scratch. It was organized from the start by the "local" class and community leaders of rural Saskatchewan. The fact that the province was so well organized on an occupational basis enabled the new party leaders to obtain the support of the politically conscious community leaders. By the early 1940's, the CCF committees, composed in the main of the same people who were the officials of the other rural organizations, were operating in almost every district in the province (Lipset, 1950:252).

Second, protest groups may develop special kinds of leaders, what Weber has called *charismatic leaders,* whose authority rests on their personal characteristics, indefinable qualities which seem to endow them with exceptional powers. While we know little about charisma, it appears that the availability of such leaders can greatly facilitate mobilization. J. S. Woodsworth, the first leader of the CCF, has often been described in these terms (Zakuta, 1964). Perhaps the most obvious example in Canadian political life is William Aberhart, the founder of the Social Credit movement in Alberta. Much of the early success of this movement has been attributed to Aberhart himself, his physical presence, his oratorical skills, even his hypnotic powers (Clark and others, 1975:15).

Aberhart also serves as a good illustration of the importance of developing channels for communication and a network of cooperative relationships among the potential participants in collective behaviour. Aberhart first gained prominence as a religious figure. In the years between 1910 and the early 1920s he had developed such a large following that the audience for his weekly Bible lectures numbered about 2200.

Owing to the enthusiasm of his followers he was persuaded, in 1925, to broadcast his Sunday services over CFCN, known as "The Voice of the Prairies" and [for years] the most powerful radio station in Canada. In addition to his Bible Conference, he organized a Radio Sunday School which continued to function throughout the worst years of the Depression. By his use of radio, he built up a personal following that, according to certain estimates, numbered between two and three hundred thousand persons. In 1927 his organization was put on a more permanent basis when he and his followers constructed in the heart of Calgary, at a cost of $65,000, the large Prophetic Bible Institute, which thenceforth became the centre of all his religious activities (Irving, 1975:131-132).

In other words, Aberhart did not have to depend only on charisma. He already had access to communication media through which he could propagate his version of Social Credit ideology and he had created a network of cooperative relationships which enhanced communication and which provided a base for *block recruitment* to the movement. Aberhart's followers were, therefore, able to support and encourage one another in their decisions to participate in the movement.

Implicit in the preceding discussion is that the conditions for successful mobilization—ideology, leadership and communication networks—are most likely if the collectivity already has an organizational base. Anthony Oberschall (1973), in particular, has contributed to the development of a sociological theory of mobilization which emphasizes principles of social organization. He focuses on two aspects of social organization: the *organizational base* is the horizontal dimension describing the links within a collectivity; *segmentation* is the vertical dimension describing the links between the collectivity and other collectivities, particularly those higher up in the system of stratification (Oberschall, 1973:119).

A collectivity's organizational base may be rooted in either of two social structures. First, the collectivity may be held together by *communal ties*: traditional lines based in, for example, kinship or ethnicity. It is in this sense that, as we argued in the previous chapter, ethnicity can be seen as an effective rallying point for collective action. Second, the collectivity may be tied together through *associational ties:* secondary relationships, associations based on occupational, religious, economic and other interests. The CCF in Saskatchewan, for example, could draw on an organizational base provided by the many already existent farmers' cooperatives, civic associations and agrarian social movements. In general, "political protest in the west was greatly facilitated by the pre-existing dense network of ties which bound western farmers together" (Brym, 1978:6). Robert Brym and Barbara Neis (1978) make a similar argument in their examination of regional variation in support for the Fishermen's Protective Union of Newfoundland, a populist movement of the 1910s and 1920s. They show that mobilization of support for the FPU was most likely in those regions of Newfoundland where fishermen already had the "proper organizational foundations."[4]

This, of course, turns upside down "mass society theory" which argues both that collective behaviour is most likely in societies which lack organizational structures and that participants in collective behaviour are most likely to be those people least integrated into these structures, usually the desperately poor who are alienated from conventional society. On the contrary, communal or associational ties provide the horizontal links, social solidarity and established leadership necessary for the effective mobilization of collective behaviour. And, most studies agree that "misfits," "outcasts," the socially isolated and atomized, are unlikely to participate in *any* political activity—not in the ordinary political process nor in the formation of protest groups. They may sometimes jump on the bandwagon of a movement already well underway and established, but they will play little role in the formation and early stages of conflict groups or political activism generally (Oberschall, 1973:135-137).

It was precisely in these terms that Karl Marx (1971) explained the conservatism and political impotence of the nineteenth century French peasantry. Marx compared the peasantry to so many sacks of potatoes; nothing held the peasants together. There was little need for them to enter into mutual intercourse as each small isolated peasant holding was more or less self-sufficient; their mode of production, then, involved them in an exchange with nature rather than with others in society.[5] Robert Brym (1979) offers a similar explanation for the lack of agrarian radicalism in New Brunswick. He argues that because most farmers were involved in subsistence rather than commercial farming, they were socially atomized.

> *The preponderance of subsistence farming meant that there was no need in New Brunswick for the kinds of co-operative ventures which blossomed in the west, and therefore no social mechanisms within which a collective spirit could be generated. Why form an organisation to market crops when there are no crops to be sold on the market? For that matter, why come into contact with other farmers at all? Already in 1924 Louis Aubrey Wood noted that the "co-operative movements in the Maritime Provinces are now in a dormant state except in certain localities". He was certainly overly-optimistic to add that they "undoubtedly will flourish again" (Brym, 1978:9).*

A theory of mobilization, however, requires us to consider not only the links within a collectivity, but also the links between the collectivity and other collectivities, especially those higher up in the stratification system. The mobilization of a collectivity into some kind of protest group is most likely when the society is not only highly stratified, but also highly segmented. This simply means that the collectivity has few bonds or links with the powerful groups in society. This will be the case, for example, when the powerful groups

no longer exercise protective, political, judicial, administrative, and diffuse social leadership functions among the lower orders, yet still derive their economic livelihood from the subordinate collectivity as landlords or employers, often in an absentee capacity, and the lower orders are cut off from the upper-status groups (Oberschall, 1973:119).

A particularly important example from Canadian political life is the rise of class consciousness as expressed through militant unionism in Western Canada early in the century. The first decade of the twentieth century was a time of economic boom, a time when all Canadians seemed to prosper—all Canadians, that is, except the Canadian worker.

To him the twentieth century ushered in no new changes—or at least, no changes for the better. His conditions of work were still appalling, and his wages—though somewhat higher—could not keep up with spiralling living costs. Indeed, the influx of hundreds of thousands of hungry, penniless immigrants even made it difficult to hold a job. And what jobs! Stuffy, unventilated factories; sixty hours a week; back-breaking work; all for a dollar a day. These were the conditions of work for the men, women and children of Canada. And a dollar a day was considered excellent pay for the thousands of boys and girls, some not yet in their teens, who were forced to find jobs (Abella, 1975:3).

Irving Abella, a professor of history at York University, describes how a hostile government-employer alliance fought most legislation which might have protected the worker. The western worker was forcibly made aware that he was going to make no headway in the face of this powerful and hostile alliance, and out of this awareness emerged a new radicalism, a new commitment to industrial unionism and independent working-class politics. By 1920 the hositility, the class antagonisms, had erupted into countless bloody battles akin to class warfare (Abella, 1975:7-14).

When the bonds between the dominated and dominant are strong, the mobilization of collective protest is unlikely. If, for example, the most ambitious people in the collectivity are able to rise in the stratification system and become coopted by the dominant groups, the collectivity is deprived of leadership. It will look to the dominant group to solve its problems and provide leadership. For example, Raymond Hébert and Jean-Guy Vaillancourt (1971) speculate that a major reason for the failure of French Canadians in Manitoba to sustain their protest was the cooptation of much of their leadership by the elite. According to Hébert and Vaillancourt, this "circulation of elites" not only deprived the French Canadians of protest leaders, but also provided the traditional elite with new blood and therefore new vigour. Paulo Friere explains how the dominant groups use, as part of their programme of divide and rule, the "promotion of individuals who reveal leadership capacity and could signify a threat if they were not 'softened up' in this way" (1970:140-141).

Figure XI.1 summarizes the relationship between social structure and collective protest. Collectivities which are highly organized and have weak links to the power structure (Cell D) will be most rapidly and intensely mobilized to collective action. This is the basis, for example, for the history of agrarian radicalism in Western Canada. Collectivities which are weakly organized and which have an integrated relationship to the structures of power (Cell A) are unlikely to be mobilized for collective protest. This is probably true for the very poor, who are socially atomized and who may be so badly off that they fear any change, because it may mean things will become even worse. Saul Alinsky (1971), writing about how to organize the poor, argues that it simply is not true that the poor have nothing to lose. Rather, they have everything to lose, with the result that they may be afraid to protest at all. Alinsky goes on to suggest that if mobilization is to be successful and if the poor are to be organized, protest cannot be directed at abstract rights such as equality

Figure XI.1

COLLECTIVITIES CLASSIFIED ALONG VERTICAL AND HORIZONTAL DIMENSIONS OF INTEGRATION

HORIZONTAL DIMENSION: LINKS WITHIN THE COLLECTIVITY		
	Un- or Weakly Organized	Organized
VERTICAL DIMENSION: LINKS BETWEEN COLLECTIVITIES		
Integrated	A	B
Segmented	C	D

SOURCE: Adapted and simplified from Oberschall (1973:120)

or political representation, but must focus on concrete issues like bad landlords, dishonest merchants and so on. What we are suggesting, then, is that the very poor do not provide the basis for radical protests and, perhaps because they are objectively or subjectively dependent on a "protective" state, any protest generated is likely to seek change *within* the system rather than *of* the system.

If the collectivity is organized but has strong links to the power structure (Cell B), collective opposition is likely to be expressed through routine, institutionalized channels such as established lobby groups, political parties and trade unions. This describes, for example, much of the English-speaking political activity of middle-class Canadians fighting for their own special interest groups—against liberalized abortion laws, against the Spadina Expressway in Toronto, against spruce budworm spray programmes and so on. In fact, many of these movements, planned parenthood groups, for example, seem to have been brought to Canada and may be sustained by Americans in what might be seen as another example of cultural imperialism.

Finally, if the collectivity is segmented from the rest of society, particularly the power structures, but is at the same time relatively unorganized (Cell C), collective protest, when it does occur, is likely to be itself unorganized, short-lived and, often, violent (Rudé, 1964). Charles Tilly (1969) has pointed out that this kind of collective behaviour and violence is being replaced by "modern" collective conflict. His research points to the fact that the relatively unorganized and backward-looking rebellions of the past, protests in search of "rough justice," are being replaced by more complexly organized and forward-looking movements based in associational rather than communal ties and unified through already developed ideologies. Such conflict groups are perhaps best illustrated by Canada's political movements and its labour movement which we discuss more fully later on. In sum, collective behaviour is most likely in highly segmented societies, but whether this collective behaviour is sustained and organized will depend on whether the collectivity is internally organized.

Social segmentation, however, refers not only to the relationships of a collectivity to the structures of power, but also to the realtionships among collectivities more generally. Segmentation, in other words, refers to any social cleavages in society, cleavages which inhibit communication and cooperation between groups.

Such cleavages often serve to divide the working class and inhibit the formation of broadly based working-class movements. The questions here are obviously highly complex.[6] While we have suggested that the recognition of common interests in terms of ethnicity may eventually lead, for some, to class consciousness, ethnic identification may also serve to inhibit the development of class consciousness and cooperative relationships among the working class. Such internal divisions may often lead to competition and suspicion within the dominated class. We must also examine, then, the conflicts and coalitions among the various dominated segments of society. For example, Brym (1979) argues that to understand the emergence of left-wing populism in Saskatchewan and right-wing populism in Alberta, we must consider the "inter-class coalitions" in these two provinces. He suggests that part of the explanation rests in the fact that the Saskatchewan farmers had strong ties to the Saskatchewan working class, whereas the farmers of Alberta were most strongly tied to the urban *petite bourgeoisie.* Clearly, sharp divisions among the dominated make it less likely that they will be able, collectively, to organize for substantial structural change. We shall return to these issues.

Once a collectivity has been mobilized to form a conflict group of some kind, the course or direction of collective behaviour still remains in doubt. In Chapter VI, we described how labelling theory emphasized the role of law-makers, police and other powerful "labellers" in creating and shaping deviant behaviour. A number of theorists have also pointed out that we must examine how outsiders, especially authorities, react to initial attempts at collective behaviour and thereby help shape its course. Dick Gregory (1968:119), the comedian and political activist, for example, describes how the government's inattention to non-violent demonstrations or their too willing response of force can transform the demonstration into one of angry violence.

Societal Response and Confrontation

It seems evident that incipient conflict groups, crowds for example, will be influenced by how onlookers and the general public react. The consequences will be different depending, for example, on whether onlookers try to fight the crowd, ignore it or actively encourage it. In an influential article, Ralph Turner (1969) describes the dilemma faced by those participating in collective protest activities. Their actions must be sufficiently provocative to attract the attention of the general public (and the elite) but not so provocative that they are seen as threatening to the point that their message is "blocked out." In other words, while a minority group will be trying to call attention to some shared grievances, the general public, if it feels threatened, may not even interpret their actions as protest. So, very often, urban race riots and student demonstrations were defined by outsiders as criminal rather than political activities.

Similarly, those who feel most personally threatened by the prospect of Quebec separatism are most likely to oppose it. For example, a study of students at McGill University and the University of Toronto found that those who thought they would be most adversely affected by Quebec separation were least likely to see it as a real possibility, that is, to see it as credible, and were also least likely to see it as an expression of real economic grievances, perhaps *because* they felt more personally threatened by the prospect. However, it is interesting to note that this "head in the sand" tendency was less likely if the students were aware of the history of Quebec and separatism (Archibald, 1978:261).

According to Turner, protest activities are likely to receive the most sympathetic response from people who have themselves had similar experiences and who have participated in related activities. It is probably in this sense that the student movement of the 1960s has had its greatest impact. Now that we have witnessed the widespread participation of middle-class youth in protest activities, we can never view these activities in quite the same light. Most of your teachers, for instance, and probably your parents were involved either directly through their own participation or indirectly through the participation of those close to them. The 1960s protest is also part of your immediate history. Because of this, we are probably far less able to dismiss collective protest as the actions of extreme fringe groups, outside agitators or criminals. On the other hand, it is well to remember at the same time that most Canadians supported the invocation of the War Measures Act and severe treatment of the FLQ members and sympathizers after the kidnapping of Pierre Laporte and James Cross. Clearly, most Canadians saw the FLQ actions as more threatening than the government response.

Of course, the most important response to consider is that of the State. As we have already indicated, the State may often simply ignore some instances of collective behaviour if they are seen as posing no threat to the social order. For example, the rise of "Jesus freaks," Hare Krishna, Moonies and so on has been safely ignored by the State even while these movements are seen as threatening by many in the general public. And, as we have said, some forms of collective behaviour, what Blumer calls expressive crowds, may be tolerated because they are thought to perform an important safety valve function.

On the other hand, the State may enter into negotiation with the protest group. This will most likely be the case if the State feels that the demands of the protesters are credible and can be met within the system and if it fears that the protest could grow to threatening proportions. This may well be the case, for example, in the recent willingness by officials to enter into negotiations with Indians concerning land claims. In a sense, too, this is how we might view Mackenzie King's willingness to entertain a number of social reforms in the face of growing CCF strength.

Finally, the State may attempt to obstruct the collective behaviour through cooptation and manipulation or through the use of force. Ted Gurr (1969), for example, has shown that nations with a large and loyal coercive police force are able to keep political disturbances to a minimum. Most Canadians were probably surprised by the extent of the role played by Canadian police, particularly the RCMP, in controlling and harassing strikers, political protesters and radicals (see, for example, Brown and Brown, 1973).

One of the clearest examples of the importance of the response of the State in shaping collective behaviour is provided by Irving Abella (1974) in his discussion of labour struggles in Canada. He points out that most Canadians would be very surprised to learn that labour disputes in Canada were much more likely to be violent than those in Europe. Canada has a history of violent strikes, but to understand this violence, we must appreciate the "heavy hand of government" in attempts to thwart the growing Canadian labour movement. Abella discusses six key strikes in the history of Canadian labour between 1919 and 1949:

In each of [these] strikes . . . the heavy hand of government . . . grinds down upon labour. In each of these conflicts, the state comes down forcefully and aggressively on the side of capital. Labour was left to fend for itself against both business and government. Workers were to be crushed and unions destroyed whenever they posed a serious threat to industry. And to support business, the full resources of the state were always available. The army, police, legislation—all were at the disposal of industry in its efforts to keep labour weak and divided . . . this is a major theme of the history of the Canadian labour movement during those years. . . . In each of the strikes . . . violence, or the threat of violence, is a key factor. And usually, the violence is a direct result of the intervention of the state at the behest of industry to crush a strike (Abella, 1974:xv).

The climax of the Winnipeg General Strike of 1919, for instance, occurred on June 21 when the police response to the strikers created a panicking crowd very much like that described long ago by Gustave Le Bon. Twice the Mounted Police charged through the crowd and then were ordered to draw their pistols and fire a volley at the strikers. Their shooting continued for several minutes during which time one striker was killed and others were wounded. Not surprisingly, the crowd "panicked," a panic no doubt fed as well by the fact that the police were making mass arrests of the fleeing strikers. The monolithic response to the Winnipeg General Strike was to sap much of the energy and vigour of the, by then, powerful Canadian labour movement (Bercuson, 1974).

We cannot hope to understand collective violence or collective behaviour more generally without considering the consequences of official attempts at controlling the crowd, without considering the *confrontation* between the crowd and representatives of the State—the police, RCMP and army. Much work remains to be done in this area as the relationship between crowd behaviour and social control is difficult to sort out. On the one hand, the government's use of the police or military to disband a crowd may serve to prevent the crowd from developing into something more permanent and organized. On the other hand, it may also serve to politicize and even radicalize members of the crowd and sympathetic onlookers, thus planting the seeds of a more radical social movement.

Varieties of Social Movements

Social movements differ from crowds simply in degree: social movements are more long-lived and are at least somewhat more organized. One can classify social movements in terms of their orientation to social change. *Revolutionary movements* seek wholesale and immediate change in the social order. Such movements will often use violent means in their attempt to dislodge the established authorities from their positions of power. The FLQ in Canada illustrates well the impact that such movements can have even when there are few active members.

More often, however, social movements seek to change some specific aspects of society. Richard Allen (1975), for example, describes the Canadian *reform movements* which arose between 1890 and 1928 as largely a response to the social problems created by slums and immigration. The goals of reform movements generally involve specific legal reforms which they hope to achieve through influencing the power groups by some combination of manipulation and threat. While such movements as the Black Civil Rights Movement and youth movements of the 1960s and Women's Liberation are often successful in achieving certain limited objectives, they are unlikely fundamentally to alter the power structure. Often one aspect of these movements is the attempt to create, through consciousness-raising groups and the like, a subjective revolution, or what Reich (1971) described as "Consciousness III." In his highly popular book, *The Greening of America,* Reich tried to argue that a structural revolution would be the natural and inevitable consequence of a subjective revolution; that is, fundamental structural change would be achieved through the massive changes in people's perceptions and definitions. But, as Peter Archibald (1978) suggests, however valuable change in consciousness may be, people will encounter the weight of the structures of power when they try to realize their new ideals. However, it is not always easy to draw the line between reform and revolutionary movements. Clearly, many movements have elements of both and may even be divided internally on the issue of how much change is necessary. Such a split is nicely illustrated in Zakuta's (1964) discussion of the "right and left wings" of the CCF. Perhaps this split reached a climax with the emergence and "near success" of the Waffle group within the NDP. This group of nationalists and socialists surprised the party "old guard" by their show of strength at the 1969 federal convention in Winnipeg. Many of the established leaders within the "right" wing of the party tried to crush the Waffle group and expressed concern that these radical politics would tarnish the public image of the NDP.

Reactionary movements, on the other hand, seek to stop the changes they think are occurring in society and even to recapture a past way of life. For example, Women's Liberation seems to have spawned a number of counter-movements which hark back to the days when a woman "knew her place" and stayed home to raise and care for her family.

Whatever their differences, however, social movements are a major source of social change, of new values, of new ways of looking at the world. The Quebec separatist movement has obviously shown its influence in the last provincial election, but it has also demanded that we all consider the position in Canada of French Canadians and re-examine our old definitions and values. Surely most of us, men and women, have been changed by the Women's Liberation movement.

Of course not all movements are so successful. Most die a quick death; others barely persist in the face of fierce public resistance. Few conflict groups are able to muster the organizational base and continuous leadership necessary for sustained protest. Dependent as they are on the commitment of their members and the support of the public, most social movements eventually "water down" their ideology so that the public finds their ideas more palatable and the members see the goals of the movement as more readily attainable. Even movements which are successful in getting some of their goals accepted tend to become similarly watered down, more pragmatic and less idealistic. During this stage of *routinization,* a movement may evolve into a specialized association, for example, a political party or a union, and become an institutionalized part of the society it started out to change.

> *It will typically have a formalized leadership and administrative staff, holding clearly defined positions of authority and operating under explicit rules and regulations. Supporters of the association will usually be less enthusiastic than were supporters of the movement, but often more reliable because their participation will follow certain stable norms that obligate them to give a specific amount of time and money to the association (Clark and others, 1975:32).*

This is the main thrust of Zakuta's *A Protest Movement Becalmed* (1964) in which he traces the changes in the CCF as it evolved from a loosely organized social movement to a political party. We can also trace Canadian labour unions to their origins in a weak, but radical, social movement "whose members lived in constant fear of losing not only their jobs but perhaps even their lives" (Abella, 1974:xv). Right now, we can only speculate about the extent to which the PQ's electoral success may also lead to a decline in idealism and a more pragmatic orientation and increased routinization. The NDP, contemporary unions and the like are, in a sense, remnants of social movements. But they are much more. They serve as reminders of people who tried to change their society and to some extent succeeded.

CONCLUSION

It should be evident that no one theory offers a very convincing explanation of collective behaviour. It is an area which inevitably deals with sensitive and controversial issues—stability versus change, conflict versus consensus, violent versus peaceful change—and has therefore been particularly vulnerable to bias. Sociologists, perhaps more than most, care intensely about these issues and therefore have often found it difficult to be objective in their descriptions and explanations of collective behaviour. Furthermore, for obvious reasons, they have found it difficult to collect adequate data on crowds and crowd processes.

As soon as we introduce into our analysis the concepts of inequality and power and the conflict that this inevitably produces, we are forced to move away from the early theories of contagion, "group mind," the unthinking horde. The various recent approaches which we have considered no longer allow us to dismiss all instances of collective behaviour as simply deviant, criminal or mad. On the contrary, collective behaviour may be the concerted and deliberate attempt of a number of people to change their social environment. Many of the characteristics typically associated with collective behaviour, the confusion, the emotionality, the violence, may simply reflect the fact that trying to change one's social world is difficult and risky. And, as William Gamson (1975:143) asks, "If it costs so much to succeed, how can we be confident that there are not countless would-be challengers who are deterred by the mere prospect?" The study of collective behaviour reminds us that change does not happen independently of the actions of people. It is in large part the study of people actively shaping history and as such it must have a central place in sociology.

SUGGESTIONS FOR FURTHER READING

One of the major statements of collective behaviour theory is Neil Smelser's *A Theory of Collective Behaviour* (1962). He ties together much of the theoretical work and presents an accounting scheme for the analysis of all forms of collective action. His work is also an illustration of the conservative bias in functional approaches. The major symbolic interactionist statements are developed in Ralph Turner's and Lewis Killian's textbook *Collective Behaviour* (1972) and Kirt and Gladys Lang's *Collective Dynamics* (1961). A fine summary of these and more recent approaches is Richard Berk's *Collective Behaviour* (1974). Jerome Skolnick's *The Politics of Protest* (1969) provides an important critique of collective behaviour theory. Rudolf Heberle's *Social Movements* (1951) remains one of the most important statements on this aspect of collective behaviour.

Our own thinking has been most influenced by Anthony Oberschall's *Social Conflict and Social Movements* (1973) and Charles Tilly's fine historical work in *The Vendée* (1964) and Edward Shorter's and Charles Tilly's *Strikes in France: 1830-1968* (1974). A dramatic and committed discussion of working for revolution is Paulo Freire's *Pedagogy of the Oppressed* (1970). Armand L. Mauss has provided a rather unique and highly readable work which brings together the areas of deviance and social movements, *Social Problems as Social Movements* (1975). You could do no better than to read Barrington Moore Jr.'s *Reflections on the Causes of Human Misery and Upon Certain Proposals to Eliminate Them* (1972) for an understanding of the basis of collective action. Many of the most important statements on collective behaviour and collective violence can be found in a special edition of *The Annals of the American Academy* (1970), edited by James Short Jr. and Marvin Wolfgang.

For an account of collective behaviour in Canada during the very politically active period prior to 1840, see S. D. Clark's *Movements of Political Protest in Canada 1640-1840* (1959), as well as his account of religious movements in *Church and Sect in Canada* (1948). Samuel Clark and others have compiled a collection of studies of various Canadian social movements and also provide a good introduction to collective behaviour theory in *Prophecy and Protest: Social Movements in Twentieth-Century Canada* (1975). A good deal of fine work is available on the Canadian labour movement. You might start with Irving Abella's *The Canadian Labour Movement, 1902-1960* (1975) and his edited collection, *On Strike: Six Key Labour Struggles in Canada 1919-*

1949 (1974). Two particularly momentous strikes in Canadian history are the Winnipeg General Strike and the Asbestos Strike in Quebec. For accounts of these, see D. C. Master's *The Winnipeg General Strike* (1950) and Pierre Elliott Trudeau's edited *The Asbestos Strike* (1974). The Social Credit movement is examined in John Irving's *The Social Credit Movement in Alberta* (1960) and Maurice Pinard's Quebec study, *The Rise of a Third Party: A Study in Crisis Politics* (1971). Perhaps the best known study of agrarian social movements is James McCrorie's Saskatchewan based study, *In Union is Strength* (1965). Seymour Martin Lipset's *Agrarian Socialism* (1966) is an examination of the CCF in Saskatchewan; Leo Zakuta's *A Protest Movement Becalmed* (1964) is a study of the rise and decline of the national CCF.

FOOTNOTES

[1]An excellent and sympathetic account of this "misfit sociology" can be found in Geoffrey Pearson's *The Deviant Imagination* (1975).

[2]This passage can be found in the very interesting debate between Peter Berger and Richard Neuhaus, published as *Movement and Revolution* (1971).

[3]Despite this, Shibutani (1966) fails to rid himself of the influence of Blumer's notion of "circular reaction" and, therefore, fails to take his work as far as it might go.

[4]Brym and Neis also show how type of labour organization is related to patterns of economic underdevelopment.

[5]Their isolation, he argued, was increased because of their poverty and because of the poor means of communication in France.

[6]Gusfield (1962), for example, looks at the effects of intersecting segmentation on collective action.

the changing family
CHAPTER XII

The chapters which you have just read all deal with important aspects of Canadian society. Many of you, however, may feel that these chapters have not captured or touched your private lives. While you go to school and perhaps work in formal organizations and large bureaucracies, and while you may be vaguely aware of belonging to some of the collectivities we have discussed, you may at the same time feel that the most important part of who you are is not found in these contexts but in your intimate relations, particularly in the family. However outmoded the terms, dating and courtship probably grab much of your emotional commitment. And, among your most trying decisions will probably be those about marriage and family. In short, family seems to be regarded as a special and private realm. But, as we indicated at the outset, we believe that the primary task of sociology is to link the private and the public, to understand, for example, the relationship between the family and the broad socio-historical processes we have described. While it may seem remote to ask questions about how, say, the rise of capitalism has influenced family life, we shall argue, instead, that this is at the very heart of the matter.

At the same time, you should not think that what occurs within the family is some automatic response to these forces. Throughout this book we have tried to emphasize and illustrate the sociological paradox that people are not only created and constrained by society, they are also creators, able within certain limits to effect social change and to interpret in novel and unanticipated ways those large-scale changes which often seem simply to be happening to them.

The family and the way in which it is studied seem at first glance to highlight the first side of the paradox. Marriage and the family often appear to us as objective and taken-for-granted institutions which have always been there and always will be. This is strengthened by the fact that these relationships are also usually invested with considerable religious significance so that they appear to us as "God-given" and therefore beyond our control. Sociologists and anthropologists have also contributed to this impression by emphasizing how the family is almost completely subject to biological and functional constraints. Hence, approaches to the family have generally stressed its universality and the rather narrow limits within which change is possible. Yet, this has never stopped people from looking for alternatives, for new forms of family life and for different kinds of relationships between men and women.

For a number of reasons, we shall be focusing on change in this chapter. First, change is built into the family, more so than in other institutions we might study. The birth of a child creates a whole host of new relationships and roles. It turns husbands and wives into fathers and mothers. It creates grandparents, uncles and aunts and cousins. Aging brings other sorts of changes both within the family and in its relationship with others in the community and the kinship network. Indeed one of the predominant sociological perspectives on the family—the developmental approach—is premised on the notion that internal change is a central feature of family life, imposing, at different stages, different kinds of statuses and roles upon people, calling on them to assume different tasks, duties and obligations.

Another reason we need to keep social change in mind is that the family has most often been viewed as an institution which has things happen to it. That is, it has seldom been studied as an independent variable able to create changes in the wider society. It is usually depicted as adapting or failing to adapt to technology, to industrialization, to urbanization and to changes in societal values. So, it has often been argued that the small or nuclear family "fits" better into industrial society because it is more mobile geographically and socially than the extended family of the past. The family, goes the argument, was forced to adapt to the demands of industrial society. But, there is another way to look at these changes. Clearly, people chose to sever ties with close relatives because it would lead to a better job or a better social milieu. They also chose to reduce their fertility in order to improve their standard of living. Thus, it makes as much sense to argue that changes within the family structure made industrialization possible as it does to argue the opposite. Similarly, the idea of equality has begun to permeate a wide variety of relationships in Canadian society, including those between husbands and wives, parents and children. Is this a change which is occurring in the wider society which begins to affect family relationships or are changes which have been occurring in the family carried over into work relationships, teacher-student relationships and so on? As in the first example, the answer is probably that change is occurring in both directions; it is a two-way or interactional process. It is likely that the family is both a *dependent* and an *independent* variable, having things happen to it, certainly, but also creating and amplifying changes in the wider society.

Problems in Studying the Family

Paradoxically, the family is, at once, the institution we know most intimately and yet least well. We know what is happening in our own home, our own marriage, but we have only fragmentary and uncertain knowledge of what goes on elsewhere; we seldom know even what our best friends' marriages are *really* like. Nor do we have a clear-cut notion of what is a "normal" marriage. This is nicely illustrated by a British study of sex and marriage by Geoffrey Gorer (1969). He found that the frequency of sexual intercourse among married people ranged from twice daily down to once or twice a month with the median being about twice a week. Yet, at least three-quarters of the respondents in his survey thought of themselves as "about average." Nor was there consistency among those who thought that they departed from the norm; some with high rates thought of themselves as below average, some in the low category viewed themselves as above average.

Gorer's study demonstrates that it is not as difficult as we once imagined to obtain information even about something as intimate as sexual behaviour. Indeed, it looks as if once the researcher has been accepted inside the home very little is regarded as private information. But, like most studies of family and marriage, what he reports consists mainly of attitudes and statements about behaviour. While this is useful and probably fairly accurate information, it is no substitute for studies of the day-to-day life of families—whom they see, what they do or how family members interact with one another. Sociologists have not been as successful as novelists and film-makers in penetrating the interior of the family, the largely unexplored territory which we both "know" and do not know. The reason, of course, is that, more so than other aspects of social life, contemporary marriage and family life are almost exclusively "backstage" behaviour so that much of what we do within the family is "private and unrehearsed," not intended for an audience. We seldom "display our dirty linen in public," but seek rather to present to outsiders an image or performance which conforms as much as possible to our concept of the ideal and normal family.

Perhaps because the audience must collude with actors in sustaining the desired definition of the situation, "dropping in" is no longer very common. We dislike putting people in the embarrassing situation of being caught between scenes, as it were. We worry that the house will be messy, or that they will have nothing to offer by way of a drink or that they will be in the middle of a fight or sexual intercourse. Hence, we are likely to telephone first and even then to apologize for the short notice. In rural areas dropping in still seems to be a social custom, but here there is the long driveway and frequently a barking dog to give at least a few moments warning. In urban areas it is likely that only a few friends and relatives will have "back door" privileges, making them as much part of the "team" as audience, while these rights will seldom be available to the social researcher. In other words, the fact that the family has progressively become a private institution makes it more difficult to study than public institutions such as corporations, schools and prisons.

A second set of problems revolves around the question of social change: Are families smaller and less complex today than in the past? Is kinship no longer as important as it was in some previous era? It is only recently that social historians have devoted attention to these kinds of questions. Their research, however, has begun to call into question many of the conventional wisdoms which most people, sociologists included, took to be unquestionable truths. We have, it seems, wanted to believe in what William Goode (1963) calls the "classical family of Western nostalgia." That is, we "remember" the family of the past as the traditional rural family, an image which is strengthened, perhaps even created, by television commercials and programmes such as "The Waltons." Advertising agencies that promote beer and breakfast cereals seem to be especially attached to the family of nostalgia and are addicted to portraying scenes around the breakfast table or at the family gathering on Grandpa's farm. There are always lots of aunts and uncles, cousins, grandparents, children of assorted ages. Smiling, silver-haired Grandma is either dispensing home-made goodies (beer commercials) or is exclaiming how much better and nutritious is the packaged convenience food compared to her old-fashioned recipe for the "real thing." It is implied that all these relatives live in close proximity to one another, if not under the same roof, and that there is close communication between young and old.

Against this is the popular image of the modern family. It is small, urban, cut off from relatives and shorn of the basic values, functions and self-sufficiency which kept families together. In place of these good wholesome values and lifestyles, the modern family is seen as producing rebellious, ungrateful and uncommunicative youth, dissatisfied and bored housewives, philandering and over-worked husbands who have no time to be companions to their children, lovers to their wives.

How accurate are these images? Probably, suggests Goode, we need to be sceptical about both our present-day images of the family as well as those we hold of the past. In looking backward, the main point to remember is that by today's standards, the majority of people were poor. Because we do not know very much about that majority, our belief that change has occurred, our belief in a disappearing Golden Age, derives mainly from what we know of that minority who could afford large houses, servants and meals for more than the immediate family.

When we penetrate the mists of recent history, we find few examples of this classical family. Grandma's farm was not economically self-sufficient. Few families stayed together as large aggregations of kinfolk. Most houses were small, not large. We now see *more large old houses than small ones; they survived longer because they were likely to have been better constructed. The one-room cabins rotted away (Goode, 1964:7).*

The careful work by Peter Laslett (1967 and 1972), a British historian, and his colleagues in what is known as the Cambridge Group substantiates Goode's argument. They have found that large and complex families were never, in Europe, at least, in the majority. Rather, in the countries studied so far, about three-quarters of households were small, consisting of husband and wife and their children. Our common sense knowledge of families in the past, as conveyed in folk wisdom and art, is knowledge of the ideal. The nostalgia evoked by programmes like "The Waltons" and "Upstairs Downstairs" may be a nostalgia for a past that never was.

Perhaps the ideal in the past, too, was the large extended family under one roof. But, Michael Katz (1975) points out, as with cultural ideals in general, most people simply lacked the resources to actualize their notions of the ideal family. In part, then, our image of the large extended family of the past may be an accurate reflection of the family life of the rich, the only people who could afford to have and feed so many people. While Laslett is probably right about families in the past being smaller than we imagine, Katz shows that in Britain, as in Hamilton, Ontario, the richer people were, the more people there were in their household.

Clearly, we can never be entirely objective in our attempts to view the past and the trends of social change. Inevitably, we will smuggle in notions of good and bad in any discussion of change. When the subject of change is what has happened to the family and to marriage, values become even more blatant. For some, the "erosion" of the traditional family is but one more sign of the general "decadence" which is overwhelming us. From this standpoint, it seems that marriage and the vows which go with it have ceased to have meaning for people. Otherwise, why the high divorce rates of the past few decades? Why the increasing tolerance for "trial" marriages, group marriages, homosexual liaisons and so forth? Others counteract this pessimistic view of change by arguing that family and marriage have not become less important. Rather, they have, in an entirely new and different way than in the past, become crucial, perhaps *too* important. They are an institution in which people invest an unusual, perhaps unprecedented, amount of emotional involvement. From this perspective, a high rate of divorce and experiments in alternative family forms signify how much, not how little, people are attached to marriage and to making it work; they are willing to experiment and to try again and again in an effort to find happiness.

Obviously, there is no easy resolution of these positions, no one interpretation of whether changes and trends in family and marriage are for the best or the worst.

Probably the best we can hope to do is to try to distinguish between empirical statements (people marry earlier than 30 years ago; the divorce rate has risen steadily over the past few decades) and statements which use such value-laden terms as "evolution," "adaptation," "progress," "decline," "success" and "failure." In other words, before we can speak of progress, we have to specify where it is we want to go; before we speak of decline, we have to make clear why we believe the past to have been better than the present.

Similarly, to speak of a successful marriage is also to invoke a prescription about how marriages ought to be. If, for instance, we believe that marriage should be an intimate, intense and all-encompassing relationship, then many, perhaps most, marriages are unsuccessful and we have a real social problem on our hands. If, on the other hand, we believe that marriage should be based certainly on love and affection, but also on respect for individualism, personal privacy and openness, then success has a very different meaning. The successful marriage will be one which does not encroach entirely on the life space of the individual, which does not assume that we have only a finite amount of love to give out and which gives both partners equal opportunity for wider involvement and personal growth. Again, we are likely to find that only a minority of marriages reach our criteria of success.

In the rest of this chapter we shall be concerned with outlining some of the major changes which have occurred in family life over roughly the past two centuries. Keeping in mind these different value positions, we shall also look at some of the consequences and implications for the individual and society which seem to flow from these changes and at some of the reasons why the interpretations of these vary so widely. Before doing so, however, it is perhaps useful if we begin by defining the family and some of the kinship terminology which we have inherited largely from anthropology, and by looking at what various theorists believe are or ought to be the functions of the family.

What is a Family?

As with many concepts in sociology, we have a common sense idea of what a family is. Yet, the closer we come to a definition, the more likely we are to find exceptions. Historically, what we now think of as a household was often called a family; biologically related members, employees, apprentices and servants were at times considered part of the family. Philippe Aries's (1962) account of the development of family life suggests that this was especially the case in medieval society. But, even as late as 1851, the British census defined the family in terms which few of us would accept today:

> *. . . as persons under one head; who is the occupier of the house, the householder, master, husband, or father; while the other members of the family are, the wife, children, servants, relatives, visitors, and persons constantly or accidentally in the house (quoted in Katz, 1975:229).*

Cross-culturally, we also run into problems. In most societies husbands and wives and children live together either in a separate dwelling or in the home of one set of parents. But, there are a number of well-known exceptions; the Nayar of Northern India and the Israeli *kibbutz* in its early stages, for example, seemed in their lack of family structure to break every anthropological rule or generalization.[1] Moreover, there are, as Fallers (1965) points out, cultures where people "fictionalize" a biological kinship—at the death of senior generations, people join the household of distant kin and biologically unrelated persons and begin to address and treat them as "parents" and "siblings." Perhaps this is not so different from the many times we "adopt" aunts and uncles in an apparent attempt to invent an extended family. We have, also, more recent disputes about what constitutes a family. For instance, are two homosexuals living together a family? Are rural or urban communes families? What about single-parent families?

For Statistics Canada, the "family" is essentially the *nuclear family* consisting of "a married couple without or with sons or daughters who have never been married regardless of age; or a parent with one or more unmarried sons or daughters living in the same dwelling unit" (Canada, 1961:1-3). This stands in contrast to an *extended family system*. Strictly speaking, an extended family is created when a married couple joins the parents of one of the spouses and the three generations live under one roof or in close proximity to one another (Skolnick, 1973:12). The system is *patrilocal* when the married couple live with the husband's parents, *matrilocal* when they move in with the wife's parents. More generally, the concept of extended family is often used to refer to families in which married or unmarried sons and daughters, parents, grandparents, aunts and uncles, etc., live in the same household as the married couple. In fact, prior to 1941, the definition of family used by the Canadian census authorities included "such relatives of the head as brothers, sisters, nieces, etc." (Wakil, 1976:47).

After examining anthropological evidence from some 250 "human societies," George Murdock (1949) concluded that the nuclear or conjugal family is universal. Others have argued that the kinship structures of many societies are so complex as to render meaningless any discussion of the nuclear family as a distinct unit. Over the years, these positions have generated considerable controversy and debate. We can avoid this debate because it is apparent that in Canada, as in all other industrial societies, the nuclear or conjugal family is the predominant family form. By *conjugal*, we simply mean that it is the husband-wife relationship rather than the parent-child relationship which is the most common basis around which households are formed. As Table XII.1 shows, Canadian families are, for the most part, *neolocal* and have become even more so in recent decades. That is, the vast majority of Canadians, when they marry, prefer to set up economically independent households, separate from their parents and other relatives.

Single-Parent Families

Although the conjugal family obviously predominates in Canada and is for most people the desired family form, single-parent families, mainly female headed, comprise a growing minority of all families in Canada. In 1966, for example, one in 29 families was a single-parent family (Guyatt, 1971). Monica Boyd (1977) points out that the number of female-headed households increased by about 40% between 1961 and 1971, compared to an increase of 21% for husband-wife families, and appear to be following fairly closely the upswing in divorces and separations of recent years. Only about 20% of single-parent families are headed by males. One-parent families arise in a number of ways. Some, of course, are voluntary: unmarried mothers are increasingly choosing not to give up their babies for adoption (Pozsonyi, 1973; Guyatt, 1971) and, increas-

Table XII.1

THE PERCENTAGE OF FAMILIES NOT MAINTAINING THEIR OWN HOUSEHOLD AND RESIDING WITH RELATIVES

Year	1951	1956	1961	1966	1971
Families with Relatives	6.1	4.7	3.8	3.0	2.5

SOURCE: Wakil, 1976: Table 24, p. 76

ingly, adoption agencies are allowing single women (and men) to adopt a baby. However, the majority of single-parent families are headed by widowed females (41%) or are the result of deserted, legally separated or divorced females (31%) (Larson, 1976:223).

Given the ideals which underlie our conception of the conjugal family, it is not surprising that single-parent families are seen as problem families and as a deviation from the norm (Schlesinger, 1971). Part of the problem is of course economic, since, as we saw in Chapter VIII, women earn far less than men. Separated and divorced women are no exception to this rule (Boyd, 1977). The other part of the problem is that it is widely believed that children should not be deprived of a father unless it is absolutely necessary. Thus, the Anglican Church has come out against artificial insemination of single women on the grounds that no child should be born who has absolutely no expectation of ever having a father. It is, however, difficult to determine what, besides tradition and convention, underlies this assertion. As feminists point out, there is no scientific reason for concluding that single-parent families as such are somehow incomplete or, except for the fact that they are often poor, necessarily problem families. Rather, they suggest that, for many people, one-parent families are simply an alternative way in which the basic functions of the family can be fulfilled.

Adams (1960), an American sociologist, lends support to this view. He disagrees with Murdock about the universality of the nuclear family and suggests that the most basic unit is the mother-child dyad. Men must, of course, enter into dyads with women—the sexual dyad—for reproduction to occur at all. But, this can be, and often is, a rather fleeting relationship whereas the mother-child relationship seldom can be. According to Adams, it is not at all inevitable that a triad of mother, father and child will be formed or endure. Men, it appears, may only be permanent fixtures in the family when there is a sufficiently high standard of living that a community can be formed and when the father has something in the way of assets and position to pass on to the children.

In Western societies, the *matrifocal* or female-headed household has probably not been so much a desired pattern as a consequence of poverty. Generally, whenever employment for males is low paid, of low status and uncertain, women assume a dominant role in the family and men disappear or at least cease to have much of a role in child rearing and decision making. This seems to be the case in parts of the Caribbean, among lower-class Blacks in the United States and among some rural families in early twentieth century Quebec. Cruickshank (1971) has also found a similar pattern among the Athapaskan Indians in the Yukon Territory. As economic and technological changes have occurred in the North, Indian women have been better able to adapt than have their husbands. Jobs other than hunting and trapping require more education and skills than these men possess, with the result that they have gone from breadwinners to marginal roles in present-day Canadian society. Women, on the other hand, have experienced less discontinuity with their past since their traditional skills are more readily marketable and transferable to an industrializing and urbanizing society. This was almost exactly the situation for families who moved earlier in this century from the Southern United States to Northern cities. Needless to say, the jobs which these Black women can obtain—cleaning, cooking, sewing, waiting on tables, working in laundries—are also among the lowest paid jobs in society. We would expect, then, that as the economic situation for men improved, the matrifocal and single-parent family would begin to be less concentrated at the bottom of the class structure.

In the longer run, it is quite possible that as women begin to have an individual status based on their own occupational achievement and men are no longer the only ones who provide children with a place in the economic and status hierarchy, the single-parent family (of either sex) will not be so problematic. The way would then be opened for alternative and varied family forms of which the conjugal family as we know it might be only one variation. This, clearly, has little to do with the family *per se,* but a great deal to do with the status and situation of women in Canadian society. Until these change, single-parent families are, in effect, a social problem.

Other Variations

There are probably as many variations in Canadian family life as there are ethnic groups making up our society. Each of the 37 ethnic groups has brought with it traditions and values which give different weight to kinship relations, to the place of children in the family and to the role and status of single and married women. It may be futile, therefore, to try to speak of a typical Canadian family. Yet, we should not exaggerate these differences since, as Ishwaran (1976:23) points out, if there are forces leading to diversity in Canadian families there are also forces pushing towards uniformity. Clearly, the same social and economic forces—urbanization and industrialization, affluence and poverty—which have shaped and altered the family elsewhere have also been at work within Canadian society with very similar results.

With the possible exception of native peoples, Indians and Inuits, and some religious sects such as Hutterites and Mennonites, ethnic families seem to range along a continuum from traditional to modern, becoming more modern as they become second- and third-generation Canadians. Much the same is likely the case for the French-Canadian family; though it is often implied that it is a unique family form, it shares many of the same features found, for example, in Italian families and British working-class families. Recent studies suggest, as well, that the French-Canadian family, in Quebec and elsewhere in Canada, is moving in the same direction as are families everywhere in industrial society (Moreux, 1971).

Forces for diversity probably come as much from class, region and rural-urban factors as they do from ethnicity. In particular, poverty, uncertain employment and low status are factors which have a profound effect on the role and status of women within the family and which make kinship ties and relationships much more important for lower-class people than for middle-class people. Similarly, in rural areas the extended family remains an important family form. Kohl and Bennet (1965) argue that farms and ranches are too expensive for most people to buy on their own so that they must inherit one from their father. Daughters may be encouraged to emigrate to the city but sons are expected to stay at home, dependent for a very long period of time on their fathers. When they do marry, they bring their new wife to live on the farm, perhaps in the same household, but more likely in a separate house or trailer next door to their parents. Finally, families living in remote single industry communities seem to be extreme cases of the independent and neolocal nuclear family isolated for much of the year from any kin at all (Lucas, 1971; Himelfarb, 1977).

WHY KINSHIP?

As we have seen, those whom we now think of as classical sociologists were in various ways preoccupied with the implications of the shift from societies based on the primary ties of kinship to those based on the secondary relationships of industrial and capitalist society. Underlying their various dichotomies—mechanical-organic, community-society, traditional-legal rational, folk-urban—was a common belief that modernization was undermining, if not totally destroying, kinship and, as Karl Marx argued, the family itself.

However, later functionalists, notably Talcott Parsons (1954) and Parsons and Bales (1955), argued that the family was not disintegrating, it was merely changing and adapting to new values and new demands which were being placed upon it. The extended kinship structure was "evolving" into the *relatively* isolated and independent nuclear family. It was an adaptation because the nuclear family "fits" better into industrial and bureaucratic society and comes to have specialized functions.

According to this argument, people are freer to move where work exists or at the demands of their existing job when they are not so completely locked into a kinship network. Also, if they have no formal obligations to kin outside the nuclear family then upward social mobility is easier— they need not take a whole lot of relatives with them as they make their upward climb. Related to this is that, ideally, family type relationships ought not to enter into business and bureaucracy. Family influence, in other words, is not supposed to count. We are supposed to be hired and promoted not because we have family connections but because we have demonstrated ability and competence to do the job. As W. J. Goode (1963:108), another functionalist, summarizes it: "The extended family system with its standards of ascription, particularism and diffuseness is, ideally, not permitted to interfere with the efficient functioning of a modern enterprise."

Critiques of this perspective have come from two directions. First, while we have evidence about household size in the past, we have only fragmentary knowledge of the kinds of kinship relations which may have existed between people in pre-industrial society. Perhaps, as Katz (1975) speculates, kinship was not important prior to industrialization and is, in many respects, a relatively modern phenomenon. In any event, the second, and most telling, critique has come from those who have shown, empirically, that the nuclear family is not isolated and that kinship remains highly important in people's lives even in large urban settings.

One of the first of these studies was by Young and Willmott (1957). Using an essentially anthropological approach, they were able to show that in Bethnal Green, a working-class district in London, people were very closely linked into a kinship structure and were extremely reluctant to move from the area for that reason. For reasons which we shall explore later in this chapter, women depended a great deal on their own kin with the result that there was a strong desire to live very close to the wife's parents. Men, too, often got jobs through family connections. Since Young and Willmott, a large number of studies in Britain and North America have produced similar conclusions (cf. Adams, 1970). Indeed, the role of women as "kin keepers" and the particular importance of kinship to them seems in Quebec to be very similar to the British pattern. Philip Garigue (1957), for example, points out that in Montreal women have greater knowledge not only of the affairs of their own relatives but also of those of their husbands. The more recent study by Colette Moreux (1971:128) indicates that Quebec nuclear families remain embedded in a kinship structure.

> *Some people in Saint Pierre seem to be spatially surrounded by their kindred, living in a street which bears their name and which an ancestor had acquired so that his numerous children might live there. They may have a sister-in-law living above them, another across the street, their parents on their right, and a brother a little further away. . . . Contacts among relatives are usually frequent and often almost obligatory; so are the quarrels and related tensions. But, the ideal, which most people try to practice, is that quarrels must be patched up and that kin groups must be united at least* vis-à-vis *nonkin, which almost automatically means strangers.*

Studies in Toronto, Hamilton, Manitoba and Newfoundland conclusively show that these kinds of kinship ties are not restricted to Quebec but seem to be found among Canadians of various ethnic backgrounds and in different regions of the country (Piddington, 1961; Pineo, 1969; Boissevain, 1970; Irving, 1972; Martin-Matthews, 1976). Most of these are, however, studies of working-class or ethnic communities. The help of relatives in finding jobs, housing and babysitting is probably much more crucial for those new to the country or who lack economic resources. With the exception of *Crestwood Heights,* we know very little about the kinship structure of Canadian middle-class families.

The study, by Seeley and his associates (1956), found that nuclear families in Crestwood Heights were relatively isolated from kin. But, studies in Britain and the United States have shown that in the middle class, as well as in the working class, relatives play a very important role in helping young couples get started (Bell, 1968; Firth and others, 1969). However, what Sussman (1953) calls the "help pattern" does not necessarily take the form of finding jobs for young people; it is more directly economic help, often disguised as gifts, "loans" to buy houses and so on (Bell, 1968).

Nor does it seem that social mobility or geographical mobility have the dampening effect on kinship relations which the functionalist perspective had predicted (Litwak, 1960a; Bell, 1968; Richardson, 1977). It appears, rather, that working-class people, when they do move, migrate to places where they have relatives (Martin-Matthews, 1977; Tilly, 1967). Though middle-class people move, usually because of the job, improved communications and travel mean that they, too, keep in touch with their relatives. Litwak (1960), who has studied the effect of mobility on kinship in the United States, suggests that the appropriate term to describe modern kinship is *modified extended family.* He points out that "institutional segregation" makes it possible for people to be upwardly mobile and still keep in contact with kin. By this, he simply means that we are able to see relatives one day—what Goode (1964) calls "ascriptive" friends—and friends and acquaintances the next day. Who, for instance, has not at one time or another explained to a friend that "I'm busy Sunday, we have relatives coming." The unspoken implication is that no one would willingly choose to spend a day with someone else's relatives if it could be avoided. Indeed, when we offer to "subject" a boy-friend or a girl-friend to a family reunion, it is a sign that the relationship is beginning to get "serious."

There is the possibility, then, that we are able to move fairly readily between family-type relationships and the more impersonal and "objective" relationships which are supposed to characterize business and bureaucracy. Thus Colin Bell concluded, from his study of middle-class families in Wales, that the two types of relationships can coexist:

> *. . . a particularistic kinship ideology may be of great importance for the individual's emotional needs in an industrial society, though in his behaviour he may be completely committed to a universalistic pattern of relationships. Extended family ties become theoretically possible when universalistic and particularistic value systems are not seen as a continuum pervading all social systems but as applicable to different systems of society independently of each other. Extended family aid in the middle class has to do with standard of living and only in unusual circumstances with occupational appointments (1968:182).*

At this point, the debate about the isolated nuclear family begins to look like a non-debate. On the one hand, Parsons never said that the nuclear family would become totally isolated, only relatively isolated, and that kinship ties would tend to become based on *choice* rather than, as in the past, *obligation.* But, on the other hand, this does not seem very different from what proponents of the "modified extended family" and the "help pattern" concepts end up saying. Certainly, as they suggest, people at all class levels maintain some contact with kin. But, geographical mobility obviously lessens the amount and intensity of interaction possible. Telephone calls, letters and occasional visits, the kinds of contacts used to refute the concept of the isolated nuclear family, do not substitute for the day-to-day interaction and formal obligations found in traditional societies. The same is true for social mobility. Though there are fairly definite and unambiguous commitments between members within the nuclear family, how we should act, what we owe and can expect from other relatives, including our parents (and our grown-up children), is much less clear and far more open to negotiation, circumstances and, ultimately, choice. As one sociologist of the family puts it:

In our society there are no clear rules as to what we mean by "relatives" or "kindred." By definition, these are not bounded units since they are based on Ego's definition of the situation. Thus the picture of the kinship universe is one of increasing fuzziness at the edges and more definite, but still flexible, notions of duty, reciprocity, closeness (with the possibilities of conflict) nearer the centre. Moreover, this kinship universe is subject to change over time as a result of changes in one's life cycle as an individual and as a member of two intersecting and changing nuclear families . . . (Morgan, 1975:206-207).

What Morgan is suggesting is that we have a certain amount of leeway about whether to use the kinship structure either to seek help or to pass out benefits to others. If we have been successful financially, for instance, we do not have any clear-cut obligations to help out our unemployed brother-in-law or, to reverse the situation, any "legal" right to ask a wealthy brother-in-law for a job. But, we often do so. The unusual circumstances which Colin Bell refers to above may be more frequent than he implies. As it happens, both the isolated nuclear family concept *and* the modified extended family concept probably exaggerate the degree of conformity to norms of universalism and achievement which actually exists in most societies, including Canada.

It is likely that people will *use* the kinship structure as much as possible and whenever it is to their benefit to do so. For those at the bottom of the class structure, with little in the way of resources at their command, kinship itself is a resource which offers the possibility of mutual aid and exchanges and provides a measure of security against the uncertainties of the labour market. For those more favourably placed, extended family ties are important means of maintaining and enhancing high status. Thus, family influence, or "pull" as we more commonly put it, is not simply a carry over from a by-gone era but is, rather, a pervasive and persistent phenomenon in Canadian society. For instance, as we saw at the end of Chapter VIII, inheritance is more important today in forming the Canadian corporate elite than it was 20 years ago. Probably most people find jobs, not through impersonal or universalistic means—Canada Manpower or advertisements in the newspaper—but through family connections (Richardson, 1977:Ch. 4). It should also be remembered that in many societies "nepotism" openly and "unhypocritically" coexists with industrialization. For example, in Israel, as in parts of Africa, "protection," that is, family influence, is believed crucial in even the most routine of transactions such as applying for a driver's licence or social security. Similarly, Lucas (1971) points out that in single-industry towns nepotism is expected, indeed is often seen as desirable. Quebec society, too, seems to tolerate fairly openly what for English Canadians would be seen as conflict of interest and "corruption." Not long ago a Quebec minister who had awarded a contract to a relative explained to the press that if the bids were more or less equal, then why would he not choose his cousin whom he knows and trusts over a stranger. In sum, whether openly or "hypocritically," kinship remains an important resource—much like ethnicity—in our attempts to protect or improve our position in society.

FUNCTIONS OF THE FAMILY

An important assumption of sociologists and anthropologists is that if the family is a universal institution, it must serve some universal functions. What those who are speaking in terms of functions are saying, essentially, is that all societies must somehow cope with their present survival and their biological and social continuity. Somehow, people must be clothed, fed and sheltered, births need to be legitimated, infants and children require regular care and attention and the culture has to be transmitted to the next generation. Biological imperatives enter into the picture as well, restricting the range of possible social arrangements, making the nuclear family seem the only possible choice. For example, it takes a male and female to bring about reproduction. Women bear children so that, while the identity of the biological father is not always very crucial and may not even be known, the biological mother is always known. The family also provides the stability of relationships needed to cope with the fact that unlike baby fishes which arrive in the world ready to fend for themselves, human infants are born helpless, take a long time to mature and (apparently) require a good deal of sustained affection and stimulation. Also, the fact that there are about as many men as women in the world probably creates considerable pressure towards monogamy and makes polygamy the outcome of unusual circumstances or extreme inequality.

In sum, the nuclear family has seemed to many social scientists as universal because many of the functional requirements of society appear everywhere to be fulfilled by it. Thus, Kingsley Davis (1948) lists as universal family functions *reproduction, maintenance, placement* and *socialization*. Similarly, George Murdock (1949:10) argued that the nuclear family was basic and universal because it most adequately coped with all of the biological and social imperatives making survival possible:

> *In the nuclear family or its constituent relationships we thus see assembled four functions fundamental to human social life—the sexual, the economic, the reproductive and the educational. Without provision for the first and third, society would become extinct; for the second, life itself would cease; for the fourth, culture would come to an end. The immense social utility of the nuclear family and the basic reason for its universality thus begin to emerge in strong relief.*

Such a statement lends a kind of solidity to the family, a sense that it is inviolate and resistant to change. Yet, one of the ways in which to view change in the family is in terms of changes in its functions. Goode (1964), for example, suggests that the multiplicity of family functions can be distilled down to three basic ones: the *reproductive* or *replacement* function, the *status placement* function and the *child rearing* or *socialization* function. In this he does not differ very much from the earlier functionalists, Davis and Murdock. However, he suggests that these should not necessarily be seen as universals fixed for all time but as "variables" having more or less importance depending on the type of society, the position of the family within given societies and so on. For example, the class position of the family may have a significant effect on how much attention is paid to legitimacy. Higher status families have more in the way of property and status to pass on to their children than do those at or near the bottom of the class structure and will usually demand greater conformity to the norms of legitimacy. (Though much favoured over the legitimate son, Tom Jones, the "bastard," was not in line to inherit his father's estate.) Likewise, when most positions in a society are *ascribed*, "illegitimate" children pose a considerable threat to the social order since no one knows exactly how to treat them and what rights and obligations accrue to them. In contrast, when status is based at least partly (or ideally) on achievement criteria, the legitimating function may be relatively unimportant.

Scientific and technological change may also have an effect on the sexual and reproductive functions of the family. For instance, modern contraceptive devices (coupled with changing attitudes about women as property) reduce the need to contain and confine sexual activity within marriage. Even the reproductive function could, in principle, be divorced from the family. Artificial insemination is already technically possible and we may not be very far from "freeing" women from what Shulamith Firestone (1973) refers to as the "tyranny of the womb." This is not to suggest that test tube babies are either desirable or inevitable, but rather that we cannot assume that the family as we know it is the only possible alternative.

Of course, we do not have to enter into the world of science fiction to recognize that many of the family's traditional functions and tasks have, in industrial society, been split away from the family and "parcelled" out to other institutions. Smelser (1959) suggests that this is a specific example of a more general process of specialization and differentiation which occurs as societies undergo modernization. The most obvious illustration of this process is education which now is almost entirely the responsibility of the State. But we can add to this a long list of activities once carried out within the family and the kinship structure. Compared to, say, the pioneer family, food production, much of food preparation, part of child care and recreation are carried out by other specialized agencies and institutions. It is in this sense that we can speak of the family as moving from production unit to consumption unit—the paid work of family members takes place outside the home and is largely invisible to other members so that the major link between them comes to centre around leisure and the planning of consumption rather than work.

Modern Functions

At the same time, contemporary functionalists such as Talcott Parsons and Neil Smelser argue that we should not assume the modern family is an institution with nothing to do. Certainly, suggests Parsons, it is true that the family has lost some of its functions but this does not signify its demise or that it has become a useless survival from a by-gone age. Rather, it has, in his view, become specialized in socialization and the emotional support of adult members.

The kind of argument Parsons proposes—that "proper" socialization is necessary for the development of "healthy personalities"—is based upon a good deal of research. A variety of studies have shown, for example, that infants receiving good physical care, but insufficient cuddling, love, fondling and stimulation by a parent or some substitute can "waste away," even die. Similarly, many researchers have tried to demonstrate a link between delinquency and a lack of love and security during childhood; that is, "inadequate socialization" supposedly produces "unhealthy personalities." This is a murky area, indeed, given how little we know about what "ideal" socialization would look like and how immersed in moral and value judgement any discussion of "healthy" and "unhealthy" personalities must be.

According to Parsons, the other major function of the modern family is that it acts as a refuge from the pressures of the work-world. In a society where many relationships are secondary relationships and where status and self-respect depend on what one achieves (or fails to achieve), the nuclear family is a key primary group where one is a taken-for-granted member, where relationships are warm and affectionate and ends in themselves rather than means to other ends. At home, people can ideally be "themselves," free to recharge their emotional batteries for yet another encounter with the cold, impersonal world of work and bureaucracy. To a great extent, what is supposed to occur in the small private world of the modern family mirrors what occurs societally in traditional or tribal societies—we are taken as we are and can seldom improve or lower our ascribed status through our achievements or failures. Clearly, Parsons views the family in rather rosy terms.

As we might expect, this view has been subject to many criticisms. One of the most frequent is that while functionalists such as Parsons mean what they say to apply to families in all industrial societies, the model seems to be the American family and the middle-class American family in particular. He excludes, for example, rural families and upper-class and lower-class (especially Black) families which add up to a large body of exceptions within American society alone. Indeed, it often seems that for functionalists, lower-class families, where men have low-paid and low-status work and women are forced by economic circumstances to work outside the home, either do not exist or are "anomalies" which will pass in due course without any alteration of the status quo.

Feminists, too, have found in Parsons's analysis of the family much that is objectionable. In particular, they object to his assumption that the mother must inevitably take the expressive role in the family, the husband the instrumental or task role. Most would likely agree that this particular split is more or less historically accurate. But, they take exception to the implication that this dichotomy is somehow "natural" and therefore fixed for all time. They argue instead that with different or equal socialization experiences, men are capable of taking on the socio-emotional role, women can be task leaders or both can (and do) perform the two at different times. In other words, there is nothing besides traditional socialization and prejudice stopping men from staying home with children while women go out to work.

A much more fundamental criticism arises when we ask what the modern family is functional for. As we suggested earlier, any list of functions of the family is partly a value statement about what the family ought to be rather than an empirical statement about what it is. Moreover, as Bernard Farber points out, "when you start by saying 'here are the things which must be done for society to survive and these are the things which the family does for its society,' you are defining the goals of a society, as well as talking about tasks" (in Adams, 1975:84). Thus, Dorothy Smith (1973) argues that the problem with Parsons's analysis is not that it is inaccurate but that it is *ideological*—it takes for granted that industrialization is beneficial for everyone and that, therefore, the family ought to be performing the tasks which it does. Yet, if, as Smith suggests, we substitute capitalism for "industrialization," then we can begin to view the contemporary family and family relationships within the context of political economy. That is, we can begin to look at the way in which the modern family is functional in maintaining and upholding a system of class inequality and exploiting both men and women. The same functions, then, take on a very different cast when viewed from a radical or Marxist perspective:

> *. . . the home is a place where people are stored when they are not at work, where they are maintained and serviced, fed and cleaned, where they are psychologically repaired and the injuries of the daily routine and tensions generated on the job made good, and where the next generation of employees is produced and trained for their future occupational roles (Smith, 1973:22).*

Smith is not suggesting that the family does not perform certain functions in modern society. She is, rather, asking in whose benefit are these functions or tasks performed? The total society? Family members? Her answer is that the family largely serves the interests of capitalist society: although it was almost demolished during the early stages of capitalism, the family persisted because it seemed to offer a refuge in the face of the ravages of the industrial revolution and the rise of capitalism. The interests it serves, then, are not, as the functionalists maintain, values of the total society but of those who benefit from capitalism, the ruling class. Smith argues that the family does not really provide a sanctuary from the consequences of capitalism. As a feminist, it is not surprising that she has focused specifically on the situation of women. She describes their position in the family as essentially a double bind. They are asked, on the one hand, to love unconditionally their husbands and children and, on the other, to uphold the external moral order which demands that men be "productive" members of society, while women, in effect, stay home to tend the husband's needs.

A final question we can ask about the functional perspective on the modern family is whether in fact it is doing effectively what these theorists say it is doing—"organizing the process of socialization and tension management," to use Neil Smelser's terminology. That is, supposing that we accept the goals which underly these functions, then we still need to assess how adequately they are being performed in the family as we know it. We shall reserve most of this problem until our discussion of critiques of the modern family. But, we can note here that there is a growing body of theory and research which questions whether the "normal" middle-class family adequately fulfills either the socialization or affectional functions. In place of the conjugal family, these critics talk of the "brutality" of the modern family, the "deadly" family which generates violence, schizophrenia and other forms of mental illness and intense dissatisfaction for its members. Thus, divorce rates and remarriage rates *may* show how much people care about and expect from marriage, but they may also indicate just how difficult it is for people to find a measure of happiness in the modern family.

LOVE, MARRIAGE AND DIVORCE

One song tells us that love and marriage go together like a horse and carriage. But there is another song in another musical, *Fiddler on the Roof,* in which, after several decades of marriage, Tevye asks his wife, "Do you love me?" She evades his question and counters by reciting the many ways in which she has fulfilled the many duties which make up the role of the good Jewish wife. For her, as for most people in the world, love, or the lack of love, is irrelevant. What counts and what are grounds for complaint (or satisfaction) are how well each marriage partner has lived up to the role obligations which tradition has ordained. Indeed, throughout most of the world and most of history, love has seldom been regarded as having much to do with marriage; in fact the ancient cure for love—not always the most pleasant of emotional states—was to marry the object of one's devotion.

According to Hugo Beigel (1952), love has gone through three phases in Western societies, the courtly love of the twelfth and thirteenth centuries, its revival in the eighteenth and nineteenth centuries and finally the "romantic love complex" of the twentieth century. But, only in this last phase has it anything to do with marriage. We are all familiar with cartoons showing the lady in the tower bidding farewell to her brave knight who is about to ride off to battle, her "favour" tucked carefully in the sleeve of his armour. But, as Beigel points out, both are, in fact, married—to other people. It could not have been otherwise since their parents would have chosen their marriage partners, perhaps even before they were born. Nor was an "affair" in the offing. Like adolescent or puppy love (at least until recently), courtly love was based on celibacy, perhaps frustration and certainly idealization of the other partner. Men in the upper classes married in order to produce heirs, could and did rape peasant girls as they rode off to the crusades or other battles and could put certain women on "pedestals." Beigel suggests that when love re-emerged in the eighteenth and nineteenth centuries it was no longer celibate and idealistic. But, while sex and love had become intermingled, the love object was seldom, if ever, one's spouse—it was still someone else's. Hence the rise of "lovers" and "mistresses."

The third stage is one with which we are thoroughly familiar, the rise of what is usually called the romantic love complex. Richard Udry (1974:137) describes it as the myth that "for every girl there is a boy; when they know each other they will fall in love, experience bliss and live together happily ever after." Ralph Linton, an anthropologist, pointed out many years ago that American culture is unique in that it has attempted to capitalize on and make as the basis of marriage selection that which is in most cultures viewed as aberrant, irrational and undesirable—romantic love (Linton, 1936:175). Linton could, of course, quite easily have included Canada, the producers of Harlequin romances, in his generalization. Certainly, as Lyle Larson (1976:118) found, Canadian students appear to be at least as romance oriented as their American counterparts.

In short, love, a possibly universal psychological phenomenon, has usually been kept separate from the institution of marriage. Why, then, do attitudes differ so dramatically between our Western culture and others, past and present? William Goode (1959) has suggested that the answer is to be found in the degree of importance which marriage has for the society and the kinship structure. Marriage, according to Lévi-Strauss (1956:65), is an effective means of forming alliances with potential enemies. As he says, in many tribal societies, "one either marries out or gets killed out." The same principle was at work when even as yet unborn children of one European monarch were promised in marriage to the children of another, thereby turning possible war into an alliance.

More generally, suggests Goode, who marries whom can be disregarded and left to romantic attraction only when there is no property, power or titles to be passed through the kinship structure. Normally, he points out, "both mate choice and love . . . are too important to be left to children." In other words, it is only when parents or society have little to gain or lose by the union that marriage selection is "unrestricted" and not arranged by the parents on behalf of the children.

Throughout most of history, love relationships have been seen as potentially disruptive to stratification systems and to the existing social order based as it is on strong racial, ethnic and religious ties which define who is out-group, who is in-group. Increasingly, however, the importance of family as the formal unit of stratification is, for most segments of society, declining. Farmers and ranchers who pass on their property to sons are a notable exception. They have some interest in whom their sons choose as marriage partners. The "right" marriage may, eventually, create a consolidation of two properties into one; the "wrong" marriage may mean that if a divorce occurs the wife may demand her share of the assets, thus diminishing the family property. For similar reasons, those at the top of the class structure who have considerable wealth, prestige and power to pass on may be very concerned about who comes into the family. But, the vast majority of people have neither wealth nor power to preserve nor alliances to maintain and consolidate. So, suggests Goode, the precise nature of the marriage union is not so crucial as it was in earlier periods, in other societies.

Of course, marriage is never totally unrestricted. Our "field of eligibles" never includes everyone in the society. All societies, including our own, have formal and informal rules about *exogamy*—what group we must marry outside of—and *endogamy*—what out-groups are ineligible as sources of marital partners. For example, an exogamous rule is that it is illegal to marry anyone within our own kinship structure such as brothers, sisters, grandparents, an aunt, an uncle and so on.[2] These, by law, are declared *incestuous* marriages even when there is no "blood" relationship between the two people. Endogamous rules, formal or informal, also limit our choice of marriage partners. Traditionally, in India, for example, marriage outside one's caste was prohibited and until very recently it was illegal in most parts of the United States for Blacks and Whites to intermarry. In Canadian society there are few formalized rules about endogamy. Theoretically, we are free to marry virtually anyone who is outside of our kinship network. In practice, there is obviously considerable pressure from family and community for us to marry someone within our religious group, our community, our social class, our ethnic community and so on.

There is, then, a tendency in Canada, as elsewhere, towards *homogamy*—marriage to someone of roughly the same background and religion as ourselves. This suggests that falling in love is not as random and unpredictable as the "romantic love complex" implies. It seems that while people want to marry for love, the field of eligible mates and love partners is seriously curtailed by personal choice, family influences and beliefs about the consequences for marriages of too much mixture of backgrounds. Hence, people, consciously or unconsciously, may avoid situations where they run the risk of falling in love with the "wrong sort of person." Something of this process is caught in the statement, "I want to marry for love, but why can't I fall in love with someone who is rich?" The implication is that there are a lot of potential partners so that whom we fall in love with depends on whom we are exposed to. Parents who move to a better district or who encourage their children to belong to a religious youth group are, in effect, acting on this assumption, trying to stack the cards in favour of a "love match" which is also a "socially acceptable" match.

Of course, some may consciously go in the opposite direction, seeking out people of different backgrounds or religions than themselves, but these would seem to be

Table XII.2

RELATIVE DIFFICULTY OF CROSSING SELECTED SOCIAL BARRIERS IN MARRIAGE

Social-Structural Barriers	Source
Race	90.0
Religion	67.0
Ethnic Group	50.3
Economic Class	48.0
Nationality	46.1

SOURCE: Wakil, 1976: Table 5, p. 25

Table XII.3

PROPORTION OF PROTESTANT, CATHOLIC AND JEWISH BRIDES AND GROOMS MARRYING SPOUSES OF A DIFFERENT FAITH IN CANADA FOR SELECTED YEARS

Religious Affiliation	Year				
	1952	1957	1962	1967	1972
Jews	5.9	6.8	9.0	10.5	15.4
Catholics	11.4	11.5	12.0	16.1	20.5
Protestants	10.5	11.6	13.0	17.3	22.7

SOURCE: Wakil, 1976: Table 7, p. 27

in a minority. A study of University of Saskatchewan students, for example, reveals that there is still a very strong preference to marry someone of a similar background. As Table XII.2 from this study shows, there are still perceived barriers to intermarriage. Racial barriers are clearly viewed as the most difficult to cross, followed by religion. The actual behaviour of Canadians bears out these findings. Though there has been a steady increase in religious intermarriages, Table XII.3 indicates that the vast majority of Canadians still marry within their faith. Much the same seems to be true for inter-ethnic marriages: though on the increase, there is still a strong tendency for people to marry someone of the same ethnic background as themselves. Ethnic groups, however, vary considerably in their "propensity" for out-marriage. Scandinavians, for example, have the highest out-marriage (80.9%), the French, British and Jews have the lowest rates (Wakil, 1976:28). The stereotype that Asians and Italians are "clannish" is not true when it comes to intermarriage. In this, the British turn out to be the most endogamous of the various ethnic groups making up Canadian society.

The Popularity of Marriage

Whether based on a desire for love, or more "practical" considerations, marriage appears to be a very popular institution. Indeed, despite fears about the future of marriage, Tables XII.4 and XII.5 show that the marriage rate has generally increased, not decreased, over time. These tables also reflect the effect of economic conditions on marriage. During the Depression years of the 1930s, rates fell somewhat. This decline, however, was more than offset by the very high marriage rates at the beginning and end of World War II.

These relatively high rates of marriage, as well as the earlier age at which people marry, give Canada very much the look of a "married up" society. It seems apparent that single people form a much smaller minority of the population today than at any time in the past. In the nineteenth century, it appears that marriage was even more of a rarity, a bachelor subculture a more pervasive phenomenon. Ned Polsky (1969:22), for example, argues that in the last century "the heterosexual confirmed bachelor was a common American social type . . . the bachelor 'uncle'—sometimes a real uncle, sometimes an honorary one, but in any event a bachelor—was a fixture in hundreds of thousands of American families." He suggests that the earlier marriage age and the greater propensity for men to marry brought about the demise of a variety of institutions which served

Table XII.4

MARRIAGE RATES PER 1000 WOMEN, 1921-1971

	RATES		RATES EXPRESSED AS INDEXES	
	Per 1000 Women 15-44	Per 1000 Un-Married Women	Per 1000 Women 14-44	Per 1000 Un-Married Women
1921	35.7	82.8	100	100
1931	28.8	61.9	81	75
1941	45.9	99.7	129	120
1951	41.4	116.0	116	140
1961	34.5	106.8	97	129
1971	42.3	118.3	118	145

SOURCE: K. Ishwaran, 1976: Table 10, p. 59

Table XII.5

MARRIAGES (NUMBERS AND RATES) FOR CANADA, AT FIVE-YEAR INTERVALS SINCE 1901

	No.	Rate/1000 Popl'n
1971	189,240	8.7
1970	188,428	8.8
1969	182,186	8.7
1968	171,766	8.3
1967	165,879	8.1
1966	155,596	7.8
1961	128,475	7.0
1956	132,713	8.3
1951	128,408	9.2
1946	137,398	10.9
1941	124,644	10.6
1936	82,941	7.4
1931	68,239	6.4
1926	68,378	7.0
1921	71,254	7.9
1916	64,000	8.0
1911	63,000	8.6
1906	47,000	7.5
1901	38,000	6.9

SOURCE: Kubat and Thornton, 1974: Table H-5, p. 102

the bachelor subculture, notably the poolroom, but, also, the boarding house, fraternal orders, gentlemen's clubs and red-light districts. As he notes, "men today use prostitutes pre-maritally, extra-maritally and post-maritally, but hardly ever anymore as a way of maintaining life-long bachelorhood."

What of the minority of men and women who do remain single? Here we find a good deal of discrepancy between the actual situation and the images conveyed by *Playboy* and *Penthouse*. Myths die hard, it seems. Even today it is assumed that men will resist marriage, women are out to trap them—that it is the spinster rather than the bachelor who is to be pitied. But, a variety of evidence presents a contrary picture. For example, data put together by Jessie Bernard (1972) show single men are perhaps the most unhealthy group of people in society. They are far more prone to mental disorders and breakdowns than other groups and earn far less than married men and little more than single women at the same age and with the same qualifications. George Gilder (1974:31) points out that, in the United States, single White men with college degrees earned in 1973 an average of $10,500 whereas married men earned about $19,000. Single male college graduates earned about the same as married high school graduates. He concludes that "it would seem more important, then, for an ambitious young man to get married than to go to college." Nor does it seem that single men have a very exciting sex life which compensates for their relative poverty. Though more promiscuous than married men, single men have only about one-fifth as much sexual activity as married men of the same age and less than half as much as single females. Of course, we cannot be sure that the "unhealthy" features of single men are a result of their bachelorhood or a cause of it. Perhaps, for a number of obvious reasons, such men do not marry. However, it is clear that the *Playboy* myth of bachelorhood does not hold up.

Why have marriage rates increased so dramatically? One reason, certainly, is affluence. Also, the norm that a man must be able to support a wife "in the style to which she has been accustomed" seems to have disappeared. No longer do people remain engaged for what was often several years until the man could "afford" to get married. If Gilder is correct, men are, from an economic standpoint, wise to marry as soon as possible. People, today, can marry earlier and easier, in part, because of greater job security and higher salaries and, in part, because there is a good likelihood that at least until the first child arrives, wives will also be in the labour force. Chances are, too, that when the children are all of school age, she will return to paid employment.

A second reason for the popularity of marriage is that it has, for most people, come to be the principal source of intimacy, love and happiness. The result is that there has been a kind of turning inward, a growing tendency for marriage and family life to be "privatized" and insular. Skolnick (1978:115), for example, speaks of an "intimate environment," a possibly unique form of family and marriage.

Modern family life is different, but the size of the household is not what has changed. What seems to have changed is the psychological quality of the intimate environments of family life, and the relation between the family and the larger community. Within, the family has become more intense emotionally, while the ties between home and the outside community have become more tenuous.

Similarly, Richard Sennett (1970:32) depicts the modern family as a microcosm for its members to the extent that nothing really important in human relationships occurs outside the home.

It is small wonder, then, that young people move so quickly from the parents' home to the hoped-for intimacy, security and, above all, happiness which they have been led to believe marriage offers. Hence, we are caught in something of a vicious circle, a self-fulfilling prophecy. We are led to believe that the key to happiness lies in marriage and so we marry as quickly as possible. Those who do not find few institutional alternatives still intact which would substitute for family life. And, when they turn to former friends, now married, they are likely to feel left out and find that there is little space in the intimate and insular environment except, perhaps, for other married couples. Later, the birth of children excludes even further the single person from the institutions and lifestyle of the "married up" society.

Of course, the extent to which couples can afford the luxury of love is strongly influenced by their specific economic situation and the general economic position of women. Some years ago, Leo Zakuta (1963) pointed out that marriage based on love reaches its peak, as does divorce, in the Hollywood marriage. Where both partners are "stars" in their own right, there is little besides the desire for love and companionship to impel them to marry. Likewise, if things do not work out as hoped, there is little to stop them moving quickly into divorce and just as quickly back to the Registry Office for another try. We can contrast this with the situation of the "unskilled" housewife, that is, the woman whose skills are confined to domestic chores and child care. Whether or not she is in love with her husband may come fairly low in the list of factors which make her marriage satisfactory or unsatisfactory. Colette Moreux (1971), for instance, notes that for French-Canadian wives, a good husband is one who brings home sufficient money and who does not interfere too much in her activities. Indeed, as Safilios-Rothschild (1977:19) observes, lower-class people generally fear that love may interfere with the ability to assess whether the man is going to be a good provider, the woman a good wife and mother. Hence, in Southern Europe and in developing countries marrying for love is considered a luxury and privilege of the rich. But, as married women increasingly participate in the labour force, we can expect that the degree of love and companionship will also increasingly become the standard by which people judge the success of marriage.

Is this a good thing or a bad thing? As we might expect, opinions are divided. On the positive side, Beigel favours the romantic love complex because it has, in his view, done much to soften, humanize and equalize relations between the sexes and especially between husbands and wives. As is often the case, we do not know which came first, the chicken or the egg. Zakuta, for instance, feels that love becomes possible in marriage *because* there is greater equality between the sexes, thus allowing them to take each other into account as "real" human beings. Probably this is a two-way process. Because there is greater equality, couples begin the marriage as both lovers and "friends" and are able to negotiate roles and obligations rather than receiving them as part of the package of an arranged marriage, which may, in turn, lead to an even greater degree of equality between husband and wife. In the wider society, too, the romantic love complex may also play an important part in breaking down some of the endogamous barriers between race and race, class and class and religion and religion.

At the same time, the tendency for love and marriage to be synonymous means that people come to want intense and enduring involvement and are likely to judge the success of their marriage by the degree to which they can achieve and sustain that involvement. Compatability—emotional, intellectual and sexual—becomes of paramount importance. But, positive sentiments can as easily be turned into intense antagonism and hatred. If they do, the couple has fewer avenues of escape. The poolhall and club no longer exist as male sanctuaries; sympathetic relatives may not be so readily available for women to turn to. In centring their activities upon one another—what has become the ideal marriage—the couple also has cut off other meaningful relationships, ties which in a previous era might have compensated for an unsatisfactory marriage. It is not surprising, then, that when things do go sour, couples feel forced to enter into divorce. In placing such emphasis on marriage, in viewing it as the main route to happiness and fulfillment, they cannot live for very long with one which does not offer these things.

Some sociologists have argued that the high expectations people have of marriage put a very heavy strain on the social fabric. Ernest van den Haag (1974:141), for instance, points out that

> *Marriage was to cement the family by tying people together "till death do us part" in the face of the fickleness of their emotions. . . . Marriage differed from a love affair inasmuch as it continued regardless of love. Cupid shoots his arrows without rhyme or reason. But marriage is a deliberate rational act, a public institution making the family independent of Cupid's whims. . . .*
>
> *Instead of saying "till death do us part" we might say "till we get bored with each other"; and instead of "forsaking all others," "till someone better comes along." Clearly, if the couple intend to stay "married" only as long as they want to, they only pretend to be married; they are having an affair with legal trimmings.*

Van den Haag advocates that we substitute for romantic love, affection, a sentiment which comes not from the "chemistry" of a first encounter, but which emerges over time as people live and work together. Those who have studied "successful" and "unsuccessful" marriages lend support to this view. In the place of enduring love, intimacy and sexual attraction, they are forced to speak of processes of "disenchantment," "disengagement" and "corrosion." Pineo (1961), for example, argues that the free selection of mates means that the couple begin marriage with a maximum of love and compatability. The result is that they have nowhere to go but down. Hence, some degree of disenchantment may be an almost inevitable outcome of modern marriages. Marriages which do survive and which seem "healthy," then, are those in which people have somewhat lower expectations. They do not define "a good marriage as an intimate, intense, emotional relationship but rather as a practical, friendly, but business-like, way of arranging their lives" (Skolnick, 1973:215).

Divorce

If marriage is popular, so is divorce. Granted, in Canada, divorce rates are among the lowest in the Western world; in 1972 the crude divorce rate (number of divorces per 100,000) was only 148, compared to rates of 403 and 241 for the United States and the United Kingdom, respectively. But, as Table XII.6 shows, divorce has been steadily increasing, especially in the last decade, so much so that Monica Boyd (1977) refers to the change between 1968 and 1977 as a demographic revolution in divorce rates in Canada. The year 1968 was a crucial watershed because it was then that the grounds for divorce were expanded from almost exclusively adultery to some 16 different grounds (Pike, 1975).

Given the generally high expectations which people have of marriage, there is every reason to suppose that the divorce rate will continue to move upward. Accentuating this, probably, is the growing *secularization* in society generally, and in marriage specifically. We can expect, then, that marriage vows once regarded as

Table XII.6

DIVORCES (NUMBERS AND RATES) PER 1000 MARRIAGES FOR CANADA, AT FIVE-YEAR INTERVALS SINCE 1901

	No.	Rate/1000 Popl'n
1971	29,626	156.6
1970	29,063	154.2
1969	26,079	143.1
1968	11,343	66.0
1967	11,165	67.3
1966	10,239	65.8
1961	6,563	51.1
1956	6,002	45.2
1951	5,270	41.0
1946	7,757	56.5
1941	2,462	19.8
1936	1,570	18.9
1931	700	10.3
1926	608	8.9
1921	558	7.8
1916	—	—
1911	—	—
1906	—	—
1901	—	—

SOURCE: Kubat and Thornton, 1974: Table H-5, p. 102

sacred vows will more and more become secular contracts which, like any contract, can be terminated by failure of one party to live up to its terms or by mutual consent of both parties. It is likely, too, that divorce has ceased to have such close associations with "failure" and "personal tragedy." Today, it seems, one is as likely to congratulate the newly divorced as to commiserate with them. Also, as people begin to see that divorce does not necessarily ruin their friends, financially and emotionally, it becomes more feasible to imagine it as a possibility for themselves. Finally, the increasing participation of married women in the labour force is, as we mentioned above, likely to increase the probability of divorce.

Various sociologists have argued that we need not be alarmed about divorce since it indicates not a decline in the importance of marriage but is, rather, an indication of how central it is in most people's lives. As evidence, they cite the fact that though people get divorced frequently, remarriage rates are also quite high, suggesting that it is not marriage *per se* which is the problem but that *specific* marriage. On the other hand, divorce does create real problems. The economic consequences seem to fall heaviest on women; the "gay divorcee" is as much myth as the "playboy bachelor." If there are children, they usually are awarded to the mother, thus making her a single parent. The problem with this is that less than 7% of divorced women receive alimony. Most (74.4%) support themselves from paid jobs, whether they have children or not (Boyd, 1977:Table 2). But, as with married women, they also experience occupational segregation and receive lower incomes than do men. On the other side of this, of course, is the fact that men who are entertaining divorce must be aware that they are unlikely to gain custody of their children, however much they may want to.

Nor does remarriage always work the same for divorced women as it does for divorced men. In the United States, the latter remarry almost twice as frequently as do divorced women. According to Gilder (1974), men who divorce in their mid-thirties and forties do not, typically, marry a woman of comparable age, perhaps with children, rather, they "go back" and marry a "girl" in her early twenties. Their greater earning power and sexual experience plus the norms which make it acceptable for older men to be interested in and to marry women much younger than themselves allow them to compete successfully with younger men in the marriage market. The net result of this "serial polygamy," suggests Gilder, is that "American society is becoming filled with childless fathers and fatherless children," with no way for the two to come together. With our much lower divorce rate, this does not as yet seem to be a problem in Canada though trends in remarriage are in the same direction as in the United States. (From 1971 to 1973, 51,377 men remarried, compared to 46,967 women.)

WOMEN, FAMILY AND CHANGE

Whatever the verdict may be on the situation and function of the family today, it is fairly apparent that it has undergone a number of substantial changes. Various approaches to understanding and summarizing these changes have been attempted. One of the most famous of these is by Robert Winch (1971) who speaks of the family as having moved from *institution* to *companionship*. Others centre on the economic aspects of the family and suggest that it has gone from production unit to consumption unit. And, as we have seen, many have talked about the family in terms of changing functions. A useful attempt to pull these various approaches together is that by Young and Willmott (1973) who write about the growth of what they call the symmetrical family. Their approach is useful because it focuses on changes which have special significance for the situation of women in the family.

According to these authors, the family

has gone through at least three stages over the past 100 to 150 years—from *pre-industrial* to *industrial* to *symmetrical*. As the first label suggests, Stage 1 families predominated before the Industrial Revolution. These families were closely integrated because they were often units of production with the crucial division of labour being between members of the family who worked at different tasks, largely agricultural, later "cottage" industries. Essentially, the pre-industrial family was patriarchal. That is, it was presided over by the husband who legally and often in practice was the undisputed master. But, though women, like children, could be beaten and often were, they, as well as the children, were also crucial to the operation of the farm. Women were often able to earn more from their work than could their husbands. As Young and Willmott point out:

It was probably the exceptional wife who was not beaten by her husband, sometimes brutally; and her love, if she had any, was often alloyed with fear of her master. But when so much depended on the person to whom God had joined him, it would have been cutting his own throat to antagonize her too much (p. 67).

Gradually from the beginnings of the nineteenth century, the family lost its productive functions to industry much as it would later lose some of its educational ones to the school. This, in turn, had important consequences for relationships between family members. As E. P. Thompson, a historian, puts it:

Each stage in industrial differentiation and specialization struck also at the family economy, disturbing customary relations between man and wife, parents and children and differentiating more sharply between "work" and "life" . . . The family was roughly torn apart each morning by the factory bell (Thompson, 1963:416).

Of particular importance in the Stage 2 family, the industrial family, was that the situation of women in the working class worsened appreciably. Whereas in a Stage 1 family, women had some control over their economic situation, they became, in Stage 2, far more dependent upon their husbands, much more under their power. No longer could women produce food and clothing for themselves and their children, but now required cash for these things. As early as 1851, Mayhew, a British social researcher, wrote about the lot of costermongers' (street merchants') wives.

The costermongers strongly resemble the North American Indians in their conduct to their wives. They can understand that it is the duty of the women to contribute to the happiness of the man but cannot feel there is a reciprocal duty from the man to the woman. The wife is considered as an inexpensive servant and the disobedience of a wish is punished by blows. . . . Often, when the man is in one of his drunken fits—which sometimes last two or three days continuously—she must by her sole exertion, find food for herself, and him too. To live in peace with him there must be no murmuring, no tiring under work, no fancied cause for jealousy—for if there be, she is either beaten into submission or cast adrift to begin life again—as another's leavings (quoted in Young and Willmott, 1973:76).

We cannot, of course, be totally without sympathy to the situation of men during this long period, to the kinds of forces which apparently drove people to excesses of drink, to violence and to selfishness. While men may have been all-powerful within the home, their work-worlds were often abysmal. And, after long days in a factory, down a coal mine or on the streets selling, the pub was probably far more congenial than the squalor of a nineteenth century home. Also, as in most patriarchal societies, the company of men was probably felt to be more desirable than that of women and children, thus creating even greater separation between home, work and leisure. (One need only visit the Italian section of Toronto to see this still in operation—cafés and bars are almost exclusively filled with men. Similarly, in Quebec, taverns, until the introduction of *brasseries*, were legally restricted to men.) Even where men were more humane to their wives and children, they were still faced with low-paid and irregular employment, squalid living conditions and the constant threat of the poor-house which could fragment and eventually destroy families as successfully as the "factory bell."

The result, in any case, according to Young and Willmott, was that extended kinship relations became female-centred rather than male-centred. When husbands could not be relied upon to provide economic security, either because they were spending most of the income on alcohol and tobacco or because they were unemployed, women began to build an informal organization of women in their own defence and in the defence of their children. It was, as Young and Willmott put it, "an informal women's trade union" composed of strong ties between mother and daughter and, at times, sister and sister. Although nominally patriarchal, the family under capitalism became, in effect, *matrilocal*. That is, after marriage daughters brought their husbands home to live until suitable accommodation could be found in close proximity. Mothers provided their daughters with security, knowledge and practical assistance. Frequently, they freed daughters from child rearing and made it possible for them to work outside the home. In turn, as mothers grew old, the flow of services was reversed and they looked to daughters to support and care for them in their old age. Of course, contact with the husband's family was not cut off entirely. Indeed, various working-class studies have shown that men often depended on fathers and uncles to find them work (Young and Willmott, 1957). But, the majority of kinship interactions among working-class people are with the wife's family rather than the husband's family. Something of this is caught in the old rhyme:

A son is a son till he takes him a wife,
A daughter's a daughter for the rest of her life.

Young and Willmott are describing a family form typical in Britain up until about the 1950s, one which is insightfully caught in the cartoon strip *Andy Capp*. But, this same "union of women" has also been found in other societies where the position of men is particularly weak. This pattern was imported into English Canada by the nineteenth and early twentieth century British immigrants and developed independently in Quebec. There is also independent evidence in Canada and the United States that the Stage 2 family and its effect on the situation of women was very similar to what developed in Britain. For instance, universal suffrage is what we remember most about the feminist movement of the early decades of this century. But, equally, if not more, significant was the strong link between this movement and the temperance movement. Women such as Nellie McClung were less concerned with equal pay, child care and sexual inequality—issues central to Women's Liberation in the 1960s and 1970s—than they were with getting legislation passed which would give women some control over their own destiny, some protection for themselves and their children, some say over how their husband's pay cheque was spent (Roberts, 1976). One result was that beer parlours, at least in the Prairie Provinces, were forced to close over the supper hour—presumably so that men would remain sober enough to remember that they had better take home the pay cheque before it all went in one evening (see Gray, 1970).

As we move up the social hierarchy we would expect some differences in the position of women. Middle- and upper-class women, though better off economically, were in many respects in an even more vulnerable and defenceless position than their working-class counterparts. There were almost no places that they could go outside the family of origin or family of procreation; the rigid and patriarchal family structure of the nineteenth century, which in working-class families was, at times, probably diluted by men's general economic powerlessness, could flourish unchecked in the middle class.

The Symmetrical Family

The third stage, the symmetrical family, is essentially the conjugal family which we described earlier in this chapter. By "symmetrical," however, they are specifically drawing attention to the fact that, inside marriage, the roles of men and women have progressively become less segregated. Women are more likely to be in the labour force, men are more likely than in the past to "help out" around the home, doing work which was traditionally woman's work—changing diapers, washing dishes, cooking and so on. Second, family life has become more "privatized." That is, both men and women have turned inward to the conjugal family so that relatives and work friends count for less, immediate family members count for more. Zaretsky (1976) adds that people turned to the family for the sense of meaning and purpose lacking in most work. Young and Willmott argue that now there is much greater emphasis on companionship in modern marriage, a much greater emphasis on spending leisure time together and in planning and making purchases for the home jointly.

While the symmetrical family may be the predominant form, or perhaps an ideal form, we are likely to find, as did Elizabeth Bott (1957) some years ago, that, in practice, family structure runs the whole gamut from the patriarchal and highly segregated to the minority in which there is almost perfect equality between husband and wife, as in some dual career families (Rapaport and Rapaport, 1971). Probably, those at the middle of the class structure come closest to being symmetrical families. Ironically, those at the top and the bottom of the class structure are often alike in that there may be considerable segregation of roles. The reasons are, of course, very different. Families at the bottom of the class structure are still responding to many of the same economic issues that nearly undermined family life in the past. For men at the top, however, career and commitment to work seem to be more central than for men at the middle of the social hierarchy. Various studies suggest that these men marry women who are prepared to take charge of the family, including, sometimes, buying and selling homes and arranging the move when the company requires a transfer to a new locale. The husband, then, is freed to get on with the new job and his career (Pahl and Pahl, 1971; Seeley and others, 1957; Whyte, 1956). And, of course, we can still find examples around of the Stage 1 family, the production unit. Artisans and the minority who have returned to the land are two such voluntary groups; marginal farmers and fishermen are two, perhaps, involuntary groups which are essentially production units.

The Nuclear Family: Success or Failure?

Clearly, what all of those who have sought to describe the contemporary family have in mind are relative changes. Today's family does seem very different than it was in the past; from a contemporary perspective certainly, it seems a better place to be as a woman, as a child, or, for that matter, as a man. Though it is often hard to separate cause and effect, it can be argued that things do seem to be happening both within the family and in the wider society which push the marriage towards greater symmetry and more emphasis on love and companionship and intimacy. The nuclear or conjugal family does seem more split away from the extended family. But, it is, at the same time, a self-contained group with its own joint projects, leisure activities, "do it yourself projects," holidays and so on. House and home have become intertwined in a way which was inconceivable for most people in the nineteenth century.

Why have things changed? One obvious reason is that people, generally, are better off. They have more money to spend, more time to spend it in and a greater sense of security that illness, unemployment or other disasters will not leave them impoverished. Probably men are as selfish as ever, demanding that, whatever happens to the family budget, they are still entitled to their beer and tobacco. But, for most people, these demands do not eat drastically into the family budget as they apparently did in the past. In any case, the likelihood is that people drink at home rather than in the pub or club. For many people, too, the home has become a small business, a place to invest all one's spare cash and time. Second, while people are far from divorced from relatives, they have much greater latitude about how they choose to fit into the kinship structure; they are not so linked into it as in the past. Through choice or circumstance, couples are thrown together more and must depend from day to day on their own resources rather than on those of the extended family. Third, marriage and family have been part of, and may even have been the catalyst for, the Equality Revolution. Hence, relationships between husband and wife, and parent and child appear to be far more equal than in the past, more open to negotiation and less restrained by patriarchal or sexist norms. Certainly, love, as the basis of mate selection, has provided another push towards equality and a more "humanitarian" concept of family life. But, finally, even without love, the fact that women are more likely to be in the labour force gives them some measure of economic independence, some alternative to putting up with an unpleasant, even brutal, marriage and greater power in decision making within the family (Blood and Wolfe, 1960; Turk and Bell, 1972).

Women in the Family

However, many would argue that the symmetrical family and similar concepts paint too rosy a picture of the modern family and the situation of women in marriage and family. With respect to women, we encounter the old problem of assessing whether the glass is half empty or half full: should we congratulate ourselves on the progress we have made towards equality, or should we be concerned with the distance we have yet to go before we reach real equality between the sexes? Feminists have generally taken the second view and have pointed out that sociologists of the family (who are usually male) have exaggerated and overdrawn the advances which women have made within and without the family, economically, legally and socially (Huber, 1973). They are more likely to point to the unequal strains which marriage and child rearing place on women, how women's position within the family is essentially subservient and exploitative and what a good "deal" men get from marriage (Eichler, 1973). Jessie Bernard (1972), for example, describes what she calls *His* marriage and *Her* marriage, two radically different definitions of the same situation. Essentially what she is arguing is: smoke, and you raise dramatically the likelihood that you will get cancer; if you are a woman, get married and have children and you raise appreciably the chances that you will become mentally and physically ill.

Thus, marriage falls especially heavily on women and turns them into what Hannah Gavron (1966) called "captive wives." As we have seen, the insularity and relative isolation of the nuclear family mean that women are often denied their former "union of women." Without a mother or sister nearby, women are thrown on their own resources in a way unprecedented in Western history. As various studies reveal, women at home are trapped in colourless suburbs, their only intimate friend, their husband, who may or may not sympathize with their situation. Whether he is sympathetic or not, he is asked to take on the emotional burden formerly spread out over several people.

Others have concentrated on the problem that, in a society which places considerable emphasis on achieved occupational status, housework and being a mother seems to be a job with very low prestige (Eichler, 1973), or is subsumed by, made dependent on, the husband's occupation, be it of high or low status. Especially in the middle class, then, having to say that one is "just a housewife" is, indeed, problematic. It is not likely to make one the centre of attraction at a cocktail party, for instance, but, more crucially, the housewife role is one which seems purposely built to undermine the confidence of those who practise it. Morgan (1975:141-142 notes that:

> *The job is unpaid and carried out in relative isolation from others, with the exception of children who may be defined as "getting in the way." With a split between home and work we get a loss of an objective standard by which to measure oneself and one's actions. Status is not a fixed thing, a static evaluation, but an ongoing accomplishment. Where there are relatively few others who are in a position to evaluate one's work and activity, one's status and identity becomes much less certain.*

Thus, as we have seen, housewives may be compared to a class which has not become "aware of itself" or conscious of its objective interests. Isolated and separate from one another, housewives begin to view their problems—boredom and dissatisfaction, depression and low self-esteem, fear to try anything new and feelings of uselessness—as "private" troubles rather than as "public" issues.

Nor is the situation of working wives without problems. Research which has looked at what people *actually* do, rather than at what they say they do (as in the Young and Willmott study), shows that the egalitarian or symmetrical family is an overly optimistic concept. For instance, two Canadian studies, one on the East Coast, one on the West Coast, which have used time diaries[3], come up with the unexpected finding that when women go out to work, men's work and leisure time shows very little change (Meissner and others, 1975: Clark and Harvey, 1976). Rather, what seems to happen is that men go on much as they did when their wives were at home whereas women's work increases dramatically. Overall, the amount of time spent on housework declines somewhat, but men do not take on extra jobs around the house. They continue to do the same stereotyped jobs—washing the car, mowing the lawn, shovelling snow—that they have "always" done, while women simply work much harder. And, even when men do take on extra jobs around the house, this is usually in the form of "helping out": doing the dishes, putting the children to bed once in a while, reading them a story, cooking the odd meal. Rarely, it seems, do husbands take equal responsibility for planning the week's menu, setting up dental appointments for the children, redecorating the living room and so forth. In sum, while men are quite obviously more family oriented than in the past, more involved with child care and the running and maintenance of the home, we have some way to go before it can be said that the typical marriage is, in fact, a symmetrical marriage.

The Nuclear Family in Crisis

Many critics of the family have begun to look at the consequences of the modern family for all members, women certainly, but men and children as well. Richard Sennett (1970), for example, speaks of the "brutality of the modern family." He contrasts life at the turn of the century (in the United States) with modern suburban life. He suggests that, while what we have described as the Stage 2 family was often poverty stricken, it had a richer social life. People lived in overcrowded, often squalid slums but they, at any rate, were in close contact with one another. There were "escape valves" in the form of clubs, bars, coffee shops, relatives and the street itself. People had to come into contact with a lot of other people simply to get by at all. Of course, not all of these contacts were necessarily idyllic; one has only to read Mordecai Richler's accounts of growing up on St. Urbain Street in Montreal to realize that conflict with neighbours, rent agents and storekeepers was endemic. But, whether relationships between people were based on conflict or harmony, there was, nevertheless, contact, and with people of various ages, ethnicities, religions and temperaments. Sennett contrasts this with the situation of the average suburban nuclear family which is insular, isolated and segregated from the greater part of society.

Moreover, the contemporary nuclear family is premised on an ideal of equality which forces men and women for the first time in history to be "friends" together and with their children. Conflict, which is inevitable, is no longer acceptable. There is what Sennett calls a "guilt over conflict syndrome": one should not argue in front of the children; spats between husband and wife become grounds for divorce. For Sennett, the real "brutality" of the family lies in its insularity and privatization: people outside of the family, including relatives (especially old people), cease to be real, to be individuals to whom we owe sympathy or obligation.

The conviction that a family is the whole social arena in a microcosm stifles parents and children both in an obvious and in a subtle way. Clearly, no bond of four or five people represents the full spectrum of attitudes and human traits to be found in the wider society. The family as a world of its own can therefore become highly exclusive. . . . It is a short step from concentrating on one's own home affairs to sanctioning terrible repressions of disturbance from below: if the poor are silenced, then there need be no instrusions on the "meaningful" circle of one's own life, the intimate relationships between Pop, Mom and the kids (1970:33).

Is this an exaggerated, perhaps unduly pessimistic, view of the modern family? We would like to think so, but there is growing evidence that the family has its dark side as well as its "happy family" mode. Novelists and dramatists, too, often depict how family members conspire, consciously or unconsciously, to drive another member insane or how couples remain together through bonds of hate rather than of love. As Morgan (1975:103) concludes, art and social science are in accord that family life is two-edged: "one edge is warm, protective and fiercely loyal while the other edge is destructive, narrow and ultimately violent."

The dark side has emerged most clearly in the work of R. D. Laing and his associates, all psycho-analysts, who have sought to explore "the psychosocial interior of the family"—the system of relationships, of dyads and triads, of coalitions and conflicts, dramas and games, the "politics of family life"—which contribute to the development of "schizophrenia" and other forms of "madness." Whereas earlier theorists had separate theories to explain what goes on in "normal" families as opposed to "problem" families, Laing and others find that the line between the two is difficult to draw, the gap between normal and abnormal families not very large. For example, in attempting to understand the family backgrounds of schizophrenics, they are led to an investigation of everyday family life and find it to be not very different. Laing does not say that families, normal or abnormal, create schizophrenia. Rather, the strange and meaningless behaviour of schizophrenics can be rendered understandable and plausible when it is seen as a response to the kinds of double binds, the possessiveness, the definitions of the world outside, which the family imposes upon its members. Thus, for Laing, and especially for David Cooper (1970), the analysis of "schizophrenic families" easily extends into a critique of the institution of the family itself. For Cooper, the family is "deadly." It constantly assaults the self, places impossible demands upon people, encroaches on our "life space" and alienates us from any real sympathy and contact with others in society.

The "violence" which we have been speaking about is the unseen damage which modern family life does to the "psyche." Battered babies and wives, however, provide evidence of violence which is much more concrete. However much violence there may have been in the past, contemporary family violence has been made visible to all of us and we have come to see it as an important social problem. Steinmetz and Strauss (1974:50), who have studied violence in the family, conclude that "violence seems as typical of family relationships as love." Thus, various studies indicate that the "battered baby syndrome," once thought to be limited to broken and disreputable families, is probably the monopoly of no single type of family. Rather, it seems (like schizophrenia) to be the product of three or more generations of what culturally may be thought of as normal parent-child relationships. "The battering parent [then] is the battered child grown up" (Van Stolk, 1970), a view shared by others who have studied the parents of battered children.

Without exception in our study group of abusing parents, there is a history of having been raised in the same style which they have re-created in the pattern of rearing their own children. Several had experienced severe abuse in the form of physical beatings from either mother or father; a few reported "never having had a hand laid on them." All had experienced, however, a sense of intense, pervasive, continuous demand from their parents. . . . No matter what the . . . child tried to do, it was not enough, it was not right, it was at the wrong time, it bothered the parents, it would disgrace the parents in the eyes of the world or it failed to enhance the parents' image in society (Steele and Pollock, 1974:111).

Naturally, not all families generate or accentuate violence or madness. But, even without these, the nuclear family has appeared to many people to be in a deep state of crisis and perhaps decline. Generally, it seems no longer capable of encompassing the intense individualism, the concern with personal happiness and projects, which characterize contemporary society. Ironically, this has come at a time when there is also concern that the balance has shifted too far towards privatization and away from the collective interests of society. Yet, the nuclear family seems ill adapted to coping with either facet of this two-sided problem. On the one hand, people want to realize their own "projects," not have them subsumed by those of their parents (or in the case of women, by their husbands) and, on the other, there is socially and ecologically a need to open up family life to others in the community—single people, the aged—and to pool rather than to privatize our increasingly scarce resources. Why private swimming pools and not better public pools; why 20 lawnmowers when two or three to a street would suffice?

Family and Change

In recent years there have been many attempts to revitalize, restructure and reconstitute family life. We have seen trial marriages, open marriages, group marriages, communes and swinging, alternatives which, as we might expect, have usually benefitted men far more than women (Henshel, 1973). We have also seen homosexuals come out of the closet, lesbians assert their independence from men and from conventional family life, married couples admit openly that they *prefer* not to have children and women desert their husbands and children. Yet, even as outspoken a critic of conventional family and marriage as Robert Whitehurst has admitted that, as with other radical movements of the 1960s and early 1970s, people are retrenching even though the tensions and strains of family life have not been resolved. Unexpectedly, Birks and Eaton's bridal books and wedding packages have re-emerged, things inconceivable for young people less than a decade ago.

Where do we go from here? Predicting social change is a risky and uncertain enterprise. For example, even using hindsight, Robert Nisbet found that on the basis of 1920 data he could not "predict" World War II, let alone the great Depression of the 1930s. Nor did any "futurologist" in the 1960s predict the ecological movement which began at the turn of the decade. No sociologist in the 1950s reckoned on the rise of the civil rights or student movement; most in the 1960s were caught unawares by the rise and strength of Women's Liberation. Similarly, what science fiction writer could have foreseen that, after one moon landing, boredom would set in, that subsequent landings would be outdrawn by mediocre late movies?

We would be foolhardy, then, to make predictions about whether the present conservatism concerning marriage and family life is a trend or merely a respite, a collective gathering of breath before another onslaught on these institutions. What we can say with some certainty is that these institutions can no longer be seen as venerable, as fixed for all time. Whatever our present situation, we know that people have experimented, sometimes with good results, sometimes with drastic results, with marriage and family life. Knowing this is to lay bare the human nature of these institutions, to see them as human productions. Indeed, the fact that we can talk at all about the future of the family, whether in academic journals or in *Chatelaine* and *Weekend*, is to hold this institution up for scrutiny and questioning. Anthropologists, too, have obviously contributed to our uncertainty and questioning. Who, for instance, has not heard of polygamy, of matriarchal societies and of immensely complex and "bizarre" arrangements for child rearing? We become so blasé, so sophisticated, that anthropological reports are not "news" anymore; they do not shock students as they might have done not long ago.

If, as Berger argues, institutions are ruts or grooves which we are compelled to run in, then contemporary society is one in which there are several grooves confronting us, several alternatives theoretically and conceivably open to us. Of course, as we have seen in earlier chapters, this "openness" strikes people quite differently. For example, fundamentalists are likely to view the whole spectrum of alternative lifestyles as encroaching decadence, a sign that the apocalypse is nigh unto hand. Functionalists, as well, are likely to view contemporary marriage, divorce and family life as exhibiting signs of social pathology and as the breaking down of the social fabric. What may to some appear as openness, then, may appear to functionalists as an anomic society—one in which there are no clear-cut norms, and hence institutions, and where people are constantly faced with anxiety-producing decisions. Others, perhaps somewhat naively and non-sociologically, welcome the opportunity to experiment and to be liberated from the weight of tradition, of rules and norms set by people long dead who lived under social conditions very different from those of the present. They believe that society and, indeed, change are not simply things which happen to people and over which we have no control. Rather, from this view, people are creators and innovators who can act upon their physical and social environment, who are possessed of free will and who are able to say "no" to that which is seen as of no value or as irrelevant.

While we are sympathetic to this view, we also think that the sociological perspective shows us the limitations and constraints which bridle creativity, innovation and freedom—the degrees of freedom of human action are never as great as we might sometimes like to believe. As it happens, the perspective of both functionalists and conflict (or Marxist) theorists shows us that there are parameters to our freedom—we must cope with both biological and social constraints as well as those which emerge specifically from structured inequality.

With respect to the former, we can note by way of an example that in the literature on alternative family forms is a curious absence of children. Open marriage, dual career marriages, group marriages and liaisons of limited commitment all seem to be premised on there being no children on the scene. But, whereas one can change his or her marital status, the role of parent is, in our society, virtually impossible to change or shuck off at will. It may, then, be necessary to think of at least two types of marriage. On the one hand are voluntary childless couples (Veevers, 1973) who come together principally for companionship and for the economic advantages of a dual income. To such couples, and in a period when overpopulation is an issue, few if any of the functional imperatives need apply. With the right contract, childless couples could be free to marry and divorce and remarry with little harm done to the social structure or to family life. On the other hand, couples who *choose* to have children may well have to forsake, in the future, many of the expectations and norms which presently surround the conjugal or intimate family. They may have to contract for marriages of much longer duration; they may have to accept that for some fixed period *both* husband and wife will only be able to pursue their careers on a part-time basis. At the same time, we can imagine that the role of mother and father (though not necessarily housekeeper) might begin to take on a greater status in our society and that both would be somehow compensated for doing what was once taken for granted, but has become problematic and troublesome—child rearing.

Finally, we should note that many of the changes envisioned by those who criticize the contemporary family are not changes which can take place in isolation. As in the case of free schools, family reform is likely to founder unless there is also some basic change in the wider society. As we have seen, the isolated, privatized, nuclear family is an adaptation to industrialization. Marxists view contemporary family structure as the inevitable consequence of capitalism. As a consumption unit rather than a reproduction unit, it is a handy and manipulable target for advertisers. Women, once married, provide a cheap and variable reserve labour force (Connelly, 1977) and/or an effective support, physically and emotionally, for the male labour force. From this view, to change drastically the existing family form, to move, say, to communal living, can be little more than an escape for a favoured few without the demise of capitalist society. Functionalists understand that radical changes in the family structure must contend with the demands of complex industrial societies.

From any perspective, it is probably true that sociologists know least about processes of change, particularly the relationship between change *of* the system and change *within* the system. When conservatives explain their caution about social change, they are often asking questions such as what will happen to the family, interpersonal relations and individual freedom in the "new order." They are right that this is an area that requires a good deal of conceptual and empirical work. Such notions as social evolution, adaptation and the interdependency of parts do little to help us specify the important relationships; they do not provide the kind of explanation which allows for prediction. But, this uncertainty cannot paralyse us. It simply warns that social action cannot exist apart from theory.

FINAL THOUGHTS

Of all the concerns in sociology, none is more important nor more problematic than social change. Sociologists are not prophets; they cannot foretell the future. At most, sociologists have hoped to be able to predict a change in one variable when some other variable has also changed, for example, a change in family roles with increasing female participation in the labour force. But just what will this mean? How might such a change *within* the system influence change *of* the system? In the previous chapter, we rejected the notion that massive subjective changes—a subjective revolution—could produce fundamental structural change, that is, change of the system. Indeed, Harris (1973) calls this emphasis on a subjective revolution the "new witchcraft," dangerous because our attention is deflected from the issues of power and inequality. But, what is the relationship between changes in definition or lifestyle and structural change? As David Lockwood reminds us, values and ideologies must be taken into account because of what they tell us about how people orient and respond to objective inequalities (Lockwood, 1970). And just when do we decide that fundamental structural change has occurred? What criteria do we use to establish that the old order has become the new order or precisely to distinguish between change within the system and change of the system, or even between change that is real or only apparent? There is much we simply do not know about the relationship between order and change.

In a number of ways, the family serves as a magnifying glass for many of these conceptual and methodological problems. As we have said, the family is not a mere reflection of larger historical processes; nor is it simply the result of the creative attempts of people shaping their own destinies. It is the product of these sociohistorical processes *and* the creative actions of people trying to respond to what is happening to them. But we still do not know how much the family has changed in response to industrialization, nor can we be sure whether changes in family life may inhibit or encourage participation in collective action for more fundamental change.

One thing sociologists can do and have done is to imagine alternative futures, not to predict but to offer possibilities. This means more than to imagine what, for example, the family of the future might look like. It is more than simply drawing "scenarios" of what might occur; it is also asking questions about what ought to occur, raising questions about values. For example, can we tolerate the environmental and human costs of increasing technology and even economic growth? Fear that there will be a continuing deterioration in the quality of our lives and of our relationships and that the pursuit of economic growth will aggravate inequalities and further curtail our freedom have led a number of social scientists and philosophers to a critique of our values, to the search for alternative technologies and to the advocacy of a no-growth economy. What these thinkers share in common is the conviction that social forces do not operate independently of the actions of people and that a critical perspective encourages people to try to harness these forces for the deliberate pursuit of consciously chosen futures.

The 1960s were a time of protest, however chaotic and piecemeal. Cherished values—material success, Canadian unity, the authority of husbands, parents, teachers and governments—could no longer be taken for granted. The 1970s are often described as a decade of retrenchment and reaction; professors complain that their students are even more conservative than they. It is probably better described as a time of confusion and, for many, disappointed expectations. But obviously we cannot go back; the questions cannot be unasked. The attempts of people to change their condition are now part of our history. They cannot be ignored. It may well be a conceit of most people that the time that they are living through is somehow a crucial point in history. Nevertheless, it seems inescapable that Canada is at such a point and that it is now a time when sociologists or, better, Canadians must address themselves to social issues and commit themselves to social action and reform.

SUGGESTIONS FOR FURTHER READING

Given the importance of the family for society and the individual, it is understandable that all of the social sciences have been concerned with aspects of family, marriage, kinship and child rearing. This, in itself, has produced an immense body of theoretical and applied literature. Besides this, however, there is also a seemingly insatiable market for "functional" or "how to do it" books ranging from Alex Comfort's *The Joy of Sex* to Benjamin Spock's *Baby and Child Care* to Nena and George O'Neill's *Open Marriage*. American colleges often offer preparatory courses in marriage and family life. Henry Bowman's *Marriage for Moderns*, now in its eighth edition as *Modern Marriage* (Bowman and Spanier, 1978), is one of the better examples of the textbooks written for these courses.

Among the many textbooks on the *sociology* of the family, we particularly recommend Arlene Skolnick's *The Intimate Environment* (1978) and Bert N. Adams's *The Family: A Sociological Interpretation* (1975). D. H. Morgan's *Social Theory and the Family* (1975), a British book, is, in our view, one of the best textbooks we have encountered. Our discussions of kinship, women and the family and the "politics of the family" were heavily influenced by reading this book. Two comprehensive textbooks on marriage are Richard Udry's *The Social Context of Marriage* (1974) and Bob and Margaret Blood's *Marriage* (1978). John Scanzoni in his *Sexual Bargaining: Power Politics in the American Marriage* (1972) provides an excellent discussion of modern marriage and divorce.

Research on the Canadian family has, for the most part, appeared in articles rather than books or textbooks. S. Parvez Wakil's *Marriage, Family and Society* (1975) and K. Ishwaran's *The Canadian Family* (1976) provide edited collections of some of the major articles on family and marriage in Canada. Lyle E. Larson's *The Canadian Family in Comparative Perspective* (1976) combines text and readings. This book also contains an excellent bibliography of Canadian materials. A good source for statistical data on family and marriage is S. Parvez Wakil's brief book, *Marriage and Family in Canada* (1976). Benjamin Schlesinger and his students at the University of Toronto School of Social Work have, over the years, compiled a number of bibliographies on multi-problem families, single-parent families, the Jewish family and divorce and remarriage. For the precise titles, look in the card catalogue or in Larson (1976). He has recently edited a collection entitled *Sexual Behaviour in Canada* (1977) which has articles relevant to the family. Family violence in Canada is examined in a number of articles in Mary Alice Bayer Gammon's *Violence in Canada* (1978).

Aside from Philippe Aries's *Centuries of Childhood* (1962), the work which has done most to spur interest in the history and development of the family is Peter Laslett's *The World We Have Lost* (1965). The work he has stimulated is represented in a volume he has edited, *Household and Family in Past Time* (1972) and in Michael Anderson's historical work on kinship, *Family Structure in Nineteenth Century Lancashire* (1971). Michael Katz's *The People of Hamilton Canada West* (1975) is not only of obvious relevance to Canadian students, but is also an excellent book. Probably the major sociological work on family change under industrialization is William J. Goode's *World Revolution and Family Patterns* (1963). As is apparent, a major influence on our thinking about family and change is Michael Young's and Peter Willmott's *The Symmetrical Family* (1973). You might also want to read their earlier books, *Family and Kinship in East London* (1957) and *Family and Class in a London Suburb* (1960). These are now generally regarded as works which had a profound influence on the development of British sociology and on family and community research generally. Finally, Eli Zaretsky's *Capitalism, the Family and Personal Life* (1976) is an excellent Marxian analysis of the effects of capitalism on family life, an account which nicely complements and extends Dorothy Smith's article which we cite in this chapter.

For an introduction to the family in cross-cultural perspective, we recommend Stuart Queen's and Robert Habenstein's *The Family in Various Cultures* (1974). You might also read, in this connection, Marion Levy's important essay, "Aspects of the Analysis of Family Structure," in a book by the same title edited by Ansley J. Coale (1965).

There is, as we might expect, a large literature on women and the family. A good starting point into this area is the papers written in special editions of *The Journal of Marriage and the Family* (November, 1971), *The American Journal of Sociology* (January, 1973) and *The Canadian Review of Sociology and Anthropology* (November, 1975). Two important books on the housewife role are Ann Oakley's *The Sociology of Housework* (1974) and H. Z. Lopata's *Occupation Housewife* (1971). A very complete bibliography by Margrit Eichler and her associates appears at the end of Marylee Stephenson's edited collection, *Women in Canada* (1977).

Along with feminist literature, the early 1970s saw a massive upswing in writing on alternatives to conventional marriage and family life. One influential collection of articles is *Family, Marriage and the Struggle of the Sexes*, edited by Hans Peter Drietzel (1972). Two collections edited by Roger Libby and Robert Whitehurst provide what is probably the most representative sampling of this literature, *Renovating Marriage* (1973) and *Marriage and Alternatives: Exploring Intimate Relationships* (1977). We also recommend to you Arlene Skolnick's and Jerome Skolnick's *Family in Transition* (1971 and 1978). Finally, as an antidote to all of the pessimistic prognoses of books about the nuclear family in crisis, etc., read Mary Jo Banes's optimistic and sensible book, *Here to Stay* (1976).

FOOTNOTES

[1]For a useful description of the Nayar, see Adams (1975:33-37). Family life in *kibbutzim* is described by Spiro (1956) and Talmon (1972).

[2]For a complete list of "ineligibles," see Saunders (1975:45).

[3]People are asked to keep an hour by hour record, usually for one or two weekdays and a weekend day, of all their work and leisure activities.

bibliography

Abella, Irving, ed.
1974 *On Strike: Six Key Labour Struggles in Canada 1919-1949.* Toronto: James Lewis and Samuel.
1975 *The Canadian Labour Movement, 1902-1960.* Ottawa: Canadian Historical Society. Historical Booklet No. 28.

Abler, T., and others.
1973 *A Canadian Indian Bibliography 1960-1970.* Toronto: University of Toronto Press.

Acheson, T. W.
1972 "The Social Origins of the Canadian Industrial Elite, 1880-1885." In *Canadian Business History, Selected Studies, 1497-1971,* edited by D. S. Macmillan. Toronto: McClelland and Stewart.
1973 "Changing Social Origins of the Canadian Industrial Elite, 1880-1910." *Business History Review* XLVII (2) Summer.
1977 "The Maritimes and 'Empire Canada'." In Bercuson (1977:87-114).

Acker, J.
1973 "Women and Social Stratification: A Case of Intellectual Sexism." *American Journal of Sociology* 78 (4): 936-945.

Adachi, K.
1976 *The Enemy that Never Was: A History of the Japanese Canadians.* Toronto: McClelland and Stewart.

Adams, Bert N.
1970 "Isolation, Function and Beyond: American Kinship in the 1960's." *Journal of Marriage and the Family* 32 November.
1975 *The Family: A Sociological Interpretation.* Chicago: Rand McNally College Publishing Company.

Adams, Ian.
1971 *The Poverty Wall.* Toronto: McClelland and Stewart.

Adams, Ian, W. Cameron, B. Hill, and P. Penz.
1971 *The Real Poverty Report.* Edmonton: M. G. Hurtig.

Adams, Richard N.
1960 "An Inquiry into the Nature of the Family". In Skolnick and Skolnick (1971: 72-82).

Alexander, David.
1977 *The Decay of Trade: An Economic History of the Newfoundland Saltfish Trade, 1935-1965.* No. 19. St. John's: Institute for Social and Economic Research, Memorial University of Newfoundland.

Allen, Richard.
1975 "The Social Gospel and Reform Tradition in Canada, 1890-1928." In Clark and others (1975: 45-61).

Alinski, Saul.
1971 *Rules for Radicals.* New York: Random House.

Ambert, Ann-Marie.
1976 *Sex Structure.* Toronto: Longman Canada.

Ames, Michael M., and Joy Inglis.
1975 "Tradition and Change in British Columbia Sikh Family Life." In Ishwaran (1975: 77-91).

Anderson, Charles.
1974 *The Political Economy of Social Class.* Englewood Cliffs, N. J.: Prentice-Hall.

Anderson, G. M., and D. Higgs.
1977 *A Future to Inherit: The Portuguese Communities of Canada.* Toronto: McClelland and StewarT.

Anderson, Michael.
1971 *Family Structure in Nineteenth Century Lancashire.* Cambridge: Cambridge University Press.

Andreski, Stanislav.
1974 *Social Sciences as Sorcery.* London: Penguin Books.

Apostle, Richard.
1977 "Subjective Dimensions of Social Class in Canada." Paper presented at Atlantic Association of Sociology and Anthropology, St. John's, Newfoundland.

Adorno, T. W., and others.
1950 *The Authoritarian Personality.* New York: Harper & Brothers.

Archibald, W. Peter.
1978 *Social Psychology as Political Economy.* Toronto: McGraw-Hill Ryerson.

Ariès, Philippe.
1962 *Centuries of Childhood: A Social History of Family Life.* New York: Random House.

Armstrong, Pat, and Hugh Armstrong.
1975 "The Segmented Participation of Women in the Canadian Labour Force." *Canadian Review of Sociology*

and Anthropology 12 (4) November: 370-384.
1978 *The Double Ghetto.* Toronto: McClelland and Stewart.

Aron, Raymond.
1965 *Main Currents in Sociological Thought.* Vol. I and II. London: Weidenfeld and Nicolson.

Atkinson, J. W., and D. C. McClelland.
1948 "The Protective Expression of Needs." *Journal of Experimental Psychology* 38.

Atwood, Margaret.
1972 *Survival: A Thematic Guide to Canadian Literature.* Toronto: House of Anansi Press.

Auerback, Lewis, and Andrea Gerber.
1976 *Implications of the Changing Age Structure of the Canadian Population.* Ottawa:Science Council of Canada.

Baldwin, Elizabeth.
1977a "The Mass Media and the Corporate Elite: A Re-analysis of the Overlap between the Media and Economic Elites." *Canadian Journal of Sociology* 2 (1) Winter: 1-28.
1977b "On Methodological and Theoretical Muddles in Clement's Media Study." *Canadian Journal of Sociology* 2 (2) Spring: 215-222.

Bane, M. J.
1976 *Here to Stay.* New York: Basic Books.

Banfield, E.
1970 *The Unheavenly City.* Boston: Little Brown.

Banks, Olive.
1968 *The Sociology of Education.* New York: Schocken Books.

Banton, Michael.
1965 *Roles.* London: Tavistock Publications.

Barber, Bernard.
1957 *Social Stratification.* New York: Harcourt, Brace and World.

Barrett, Michael, and Chris Taylor.
1977 *Population and Canada.* Toronto: Faculty of Education, University of Toronto.

Barth, Fredrik.
1969 "Introduction." In *Ethnic Groups and Ethnic Boundaries.* Boston: Little Brown: 3-98.

Becker, Howard S.
1958 "Problems of Inference and Proof in Participant Observation." *American Sociological Review* 23 (3): 652-660.
1963 *Outsiders.* New York: Free Press.
1964a "Social Interaction." In *A Dictionary of the Social Sciences,* edited by J. Gould and W. L. Kolb. London: Tavistock.
1964b *The Other Side: Perspectives on Deviance.* Glencoe: Free Press.
1967 "Whose Side Are We On?" *Social Problems* 14: 239-247.

Beigel, Hugo.
1952 "Romantic Love." *American Sociological Review* 15 (1951): 326-324.

Bell, Colin.
1968 *Middle-Class Families.* London: Routledge and Kegan Paul.

Bell, Daniel.
1973 *The Coming of Post-Industrial Society.* New York: Basic Books.

Bendix, Reinhard.
1963 *Work and Authority in Industry.* New York: Harper Torchbook.

Bendix, Reinhard, and S. M. Lipset.
1967 *Class, Status and Power.* New York: Free Press.

Benedict, Ruth.
1934 *Patterns of Culture.* New York: Mentor Books.

Bercuson, David.
1974 "The Winnipeg General Strike." In Abella (1974: 1-32).

Bercuson, David, ed.
1977 *Canada and the Burden of Unity.* Toronto: Macmillan.

Bereiter, Carl.
1972 "Schools Without Education." *Harvard Educational Review* 42 (3): 390-413.

Berg, Ivor.
1970 *Education and Jobs: The Great Training Robbery.* New York: Beacon Press.

Berger, Peter L.
1963 *Invitation to Sociology: A Humanistic Perspective.* New York: Doubleday Anchor.
1971 "Sociology and Freedom." *American Sociologist* 6: 1-5.

Berger, Peter, and Hansfried Kellner.
1964 "Marriage and the Construction of Reality." *Diogenes,* Summer: 1-24.

Berger, Peter, and Thomas Luckmann.

1966 *The Social Construction of Reality: A Treatise in the Sociology of Knowledge.* New York: Doubleday.

Berger, Peter, and Richard Neuhaus.
1970 *Movement and Revolution: On American Radicalism.* Garden City, New York: Doubleday.

Berk, Richard A.
1974 *Collective Behaviour.* Dubuque, Iowa: William C. Brown.

Bernard, Jessie.
1972 *The Future of Marriage.* New York: World Publishing Co.

Berne, Eric.
1964 *Games People Play.* New York: Grove Press.

Bernstein, Basil.
1961 "Social Class and Linguistic Development: A Theory of Social Learning." In *Education, Economy, and Society,* edited by A. H. Halsey, Jan Floud, and C. Arnold. New York: Free Press: 288-314.

Berry, J. W., and G. J. S. Wilde.
1972 *Social Psychology: The Canadian Context.* Toronto: McClelland and Stewart.

Berton, Pierre.
1975 *Hollywood's Canada.* Toronto: McClelland and Stewart.

Beyer Gammon, Mary Alice.
1978 *Violence in Canada.* Toronto: Methuen Publications.

Bieler Brettel, Carol.
1977 "Ethnicity and Entrepreneurs: Portuguese Immigrants in a Canadian City." In Hicks and Leis (1977: 169-180).

Birnbaum, Norman.
1971 *Toward a Critical Sociology.* New York: Oxford University Press.

Blau, P. M.
1955 *The Dynamics of Bureaucracy.* Chicago: University of Chicago Press.
1956 "Social Mobility and Interpersonal Relations." *American Sociological Review* 21 (3) June: 290-295.
1964 *Exchange and Power.* New York: Wiley.

Blau, P. M., and O. D. Duncan.
1967 *The American Occupational Structure.* New York: Wiley.

Blishen, Bernard.
1967 "A Socio-Economic Index for Occupations in Canada." *Canadian Review of Sociology and Anthropology* 46: 1-53.

Blishen, Bernard, and Hugh McRoberts.
1976 "A Revised Socio-Economic Index for Occupations in Canada." *Canadian Review of Sociology and Anthropology* 13 (1): 71-79.

Blood, Bob, and Margaret Blood.
1978 *Marriage,* 3rd ed. New York: Free Press.

Blood, R. O., and D. M. Wolfe.
1960 *Husbands and Wives: The Dynamics of Married Living.* New York: Free Press.

Blum, Alan F., and Peter McHugh.
1971 "The Social Ascription of Motives." *American Sociological Review* 36 (1): 98-109.

Blumer, Herbert.
1957 "Collective Behaviour." In *Review of Sociology: Analysis of a Decade,* edited by J. B. Gittler. New York: Wiley.
1969 *Symbolic Interactionism: Perspective and Method.* Englewood Cliffs, N. J.: Prentice-Hall.

Boas, F.
1940 *Race, Language and Culture.* New York: Macmillan.

Bodemann, Y. Michael.
1978 "A Problem of Sociological Praxis: The Case for Inventive Observation in Field Work." *Theory and Society* 5: 387-420.

Boissevain, J.
1970 *Italians of Montreal.* Ottawa: Queen's Printer.

Borovoy, A. A.
1966 "Indian Poverty in Canada." *Canadian Labour* 12, December: 13-15.

Bott, Elizabeth.
1971 (1975) *Family and Social Network.* London: Tavistock.

Bottomore, T. B.
1965 *Classes in Modern Society.* London: George Allen and Unwin.

Bottomore, T. B., and Maximilien Rubel, eds.
1963 *Karl Marx: Selected Writings in Sociology and Social Philosophy* London: Pelican Books.

Bowen, Elenore Smith.
1964 *Return to Laughter.* Garden City, New York: Anchor Books.

Bowles, Samuel, and Herbert Gintis.

1976 *Schooling in Capitalist America.* New York: Basic Books.

Bowman, Henry A., and Graham B. Spanier.
1978 *Modern Marriage.* New York: McGraw-Hill.

Boyd, Monica.
1977a "The Forgotten Minority: The Socio-Economic Status of Divorced and Separated Women." In Marchak (1977: 46-71).
1977b "Occupational Attainments of Native-Born Canadian Women: Results from the 1973 Canadian National Mobility Study." Paper presented at the CSAA meetings, Fredericton, N.B.

Boyd, M., M. Eichler, and J. R. Hofley.
1976 "Family: Functions, Formation, and Fertility." In Cook (1976: 13-52).

Boydell, Craig, and others, eds.
1972 *Deviant Behaviour and Societal Reaction.* Toronto: Holt, Rinehart and Winston.

Boydell, Craig, and others, eds.
1974 *The Administration of Criminal Justice in Canada.* Toronto: Holt, Rinehart and Winston.

Breton, Raymond.
1964 "Institutional Completeness and Ethnic Communities and Personal Relations to Immigrants." *American Journal of Sociology* 70 (2): 193-205.
1972 *Social and Academic Factors in the Career Decisions of Canadian Youth.* (with J. McDonald and S. Richer) Ottawa: Information Canada.

Brim, O. G., Jr., and S. Wheeler.
1966 *Socialization After Childhood: Two Essays.* New York: Wiley.

Brittan, A.
1973 *Meanings and Situations.* London: Routledge and Kegan Paul.

Broadfoot, Barry.
1975 *Ten Lost Years, 1929-1939.* Don Mills, Ontario: General Publishing Company Paperjacks.

Brody, Hugh.
1975 *The People's Land.* London: Penguin Books.

Bronfenbenner, Urie.
1970 *Two Worlds of Childhood.* New York: Russell Sage.

Brown, Lorne, and Caroline Brown.
1973 *An Unauthorized History of the RCMP.* Toronto: James Lewis and Samuel.

Brown, Roger.
1965 *Social Psychology.* New York: Free Press.

Bryant, Clifton D.
1974 *Deviant Behaviour: Occupational and Organizational Bases.* Chicago: Rand McNally.

Brym, Robert.
1978 "Regional Social Structure and Agrarian Radicalism in Canada: Alberta, Saskatchewan and New Brunswick." *Canadian Review of Sociology and Anthropology.*

Brym, Robert, and Barbara Neis.
1978 "Regional Factors in the Formation of the Fishermen's Protective Union of Newfoundland." *Canadian Journal of Sociology* (3).

Burke, Edmund.
1790 (1955) *Reflections on the Revolution in France.* Indianapolis: Bobbs-Merrill.

Burke, Kenneth.
1965 *Permanence and Change.* 2nd rev. ed. Indianapolis: Bobbs-Merrill.
1969 (1945) *A Grammar of Motives.* Berkley: University of California Press.

Caldwell, Gary.
1974 *A Demographic Profile of the English-Speaking Population of Quebec 1921-1971.* Québec: Centre International de Recherches sur le Bilinguisme.
1978 *Out-Migration of English Mother-Tongue High School Leavers from Quebec 1971-76.* Lennoxville: Bishop's University.

Caldwell, G., and D. Czarnocki.
1975 "Interpreting Social Change in Post-War Quebec in a Quebec-Ontario Comparative Perspective." Paper presented at the CSAA meetings, Edmonton.

Carlton, Richard A., Louise A. Colley, and Neil J. MacKinnon, eds.
1977 *Education, Change and Society.* Toronto: Gage Educational.

Caplow, T.
1956 "A Theory of Coalitions in the Triad." *American Sociological Review* 21, August: 489-493.

Carnoy, Martin.
1974 *Education as Cultural Imperialism.*

New York: David McKay.

Carstens, Peter.
1971 "Coercion and Change." In Ossenberg (1971: 126-145).

Castaneda, Carlos.
1968 *The Teachings of Don Juan: A Yaqui Way of Knowledge.* New York: Ballantine Books.

Castellano, Marlene Brant.
1970 "Vocation or Identity: The Dilemna of Indian Youth". In *The Only Good Indian,* edited by Waubageshig. Toronto: New Press.

Chirot, Daniel.
1977 *Social Change in the Twentieth Century.* New York: Harcourt Brace Jovanovich.

Chomsky, Noam.
1957 *Syntactic Structure.* The Hague: Mouton.

Cicourel, Aaron V.
1964 *Method and Measurement in Sociology.* New York: Free Press.
1970 "Basic and Normative Rules in the Negotiation of Status and Role". In *Recent Sociology, No. 2.,* edited by Hans P. Dreitzel. New York: Macmillan, 4-45.

Clairmont, Don, and Dennis Magill.
1974 *Africville: The Life and Death of a Canadian Black Community.* Toronto: McClelland and Stewart.

Clairmont, Don, and Fred Wien.
1974 "Segmentation, Disadvantage and Development: An Analysis of the Marginal Work World, Its Linkages with the Central Work World and Its Role in the Maritime Provinces." Halifax: Institute of Public Affairs, Marginal Work World Program.

Clark, Burton R.
1960 "The Cooling-Out Function in Higher Education." *American Journal of Sociology* 65, May: 569-576.
1962 *Educating the Expert Society.* San Francisco: Chandler.

Clark, Lorenne, and Debra Lewis.
1977 *Rape: The Price of Coercive Sexuality.* Toronto: The Women's Press.

Clark, S. D.
1948 *Church and Sect in Canada.* Toronto: University of Toronto Press.
1959 *Movements of Political Protest in Canada, 1640-1840.* Toronto: University of Toronto Press.
1968 *The Developing Canadian Community.* 2nd ed. Toronto: University of Toronto Press.
1976a *Canadian Society in Historical Perspective.* Toronto: McGraw-Hill Ryerson.
1976b "The Issue of Canadian Identity." Paper presented at St. Thomas University, Fredericton, N.B.

Clark, Samuel D., J. Paul Grayson, and Linda M. Grayson.
1975 *Prophesy and Protest: Social Movements in Twentieth-Century Canada.* Toronto: Gage Educational.

Clark, Susan, and A. S. Harvey.
1976 "The Sexual Division of Labour: The Use of Time." *Atlantis* 2 (1): 46-66.

Clarkson, Stephen.
1976 "The Ambiguities of Analysis: The Problem of Knowing Ourselves." *Journal of Canadian Studies* XI (4): 50-54.

Clement, Wallace.
1974 "Inequality of Access." *Canadian Review of Sociology and Anthropology* 12 (L): 33-52.
1975 *The Canadian Corporate Elite.* Toronto. Macmillan Co. of Canada.
1977a "The Canadian Bourgeoisie: Merely Comprador?" In Saul and Heron (1977: 71-84).
1977b *Continental Corporate Power.* Toronto: McClelland and Stewart.
1977c "Overlap of the Media and Economic Elites." *Canadian Journal of Sociology* 2 (2) Spring: 205-214.

Clivio, Gianrenzo.
1977 "Italiese Glossary." Report of research in *University of Toronto Graduate* V (2) Winter: 1, 7.

Cloward, R. A., and L. E. Ohlin.
1960 *Delinquency and Opportunity.* New York: Free Press.

Coale, Ansley J., and others, eds.
1965 *Aspects of the Analysis of Family Structure.* Princeton, N. J.: Princeton University Press.

Cohen, Albert F.
1966 *Deviance and Control.* Englewood Cliffs, N. J.: Prentice-Hall.

Cohen, Percy S.
1968 *Modern Social Theory.* London: Heinemann.

Cohen, Stanley, ed.
1971 *Images of Deviance.* London: Penguin.

Cohen, Stanley.
1973 "Protest, Unrest and Delinquency: Convergences in Labels and Behaviour." *International Journal of Criminology and Penology* I: 117-128.

Cohn, Werner.
1976 "Jewish Outmarriage and Anomie." *Canadian Review of Sociology and Anthropology* 13 (1) February: 90-105.

Coleman, James, and others.
1966 *Equality of Educational Opportunity.* Washington, D.C.: U.S. Government Printing Office.

Colfax, J. David, and Jack L. Roach, eds.
1971 *Radical Sociology.* New York: Basic Books.

Collins, R. H.
1971a "Functional and Conflict Theories of Educational Stratification." *American Sociological Review* 36 (6) December: 1002-1019.
1971b "A Conflict Theory of Sexual Stratification." *Social Problems* 19 (1): 3-21.
1974 "Where are Educational Requirements for Employment Highest?" *Sociology of Education* 47 (4) Fall: 419-442.

Collins, R., and M. Makowsky.
1978 *The Discovery of Society.* New York: Random House.

Comte, Auguste.
1893 *The Positive Philosophy of Auguste Comte.* Translated by Harriet Martineau. London: Bell.

Connelly, M. Patricia.
1977 "The Economic Content of Women's Labour Force Participation in Canada." In Marchak (1977: 10-27).

Connelly, M. Patricia, and Linda Christiansen-Ruffman.
1977 "Women's Problems: Private Troubles or Public Issues." *Canadian Journal of Sociology* 2 (3): 167-178.

Cook, Gail, ed.
1976 *Opportunity for Choice.* Ottawa: Statistics Canada and C. D. Howe.

Cook, Shirley J.
1969 "Canadian Narcotics Legislation, 1908-1923: A Conflict Model Interpretation." *Canadian Review of Sociology and Anthropology* 6: 36-46.

Cooley, Charles H.
1902 *Human Nature and the Social Order.* New York: Scribner.
1909 *Social Organization.* New York: Scribner.
1926 "The Roots of Social Knowledge." *American Journal of Sociology* XXXII, July: 59-79.

Cooper, David.
1970 *The Death of the Family.* London: Penguin Books.

Copp, Terry.
1974 *The Anatomy of Poverty.* Toronto: McClelland and Stewart.

Corwin, Ronald.
1965 *A Sociology of Education: Emerging Patterns of Class, Status and Power in the Public Schools.* New York: Appleton-Century-Crofts.
1974 *Education in Crisis: A Sociological Analysis of Schools in Transition.* New York: Wiley.

Coser, Lewis A.
1956 *The Functions of Social Conflict.* London: Free Press.
1971 *Masters of Sociological Thought: Ideas in Historical and Social Context.* New York: Harcourt Brace Jovanovich.

Coxon, Anthony, and Charles Jones.
1978 *The Images of Occupational Prestige: A Study in Social Cognition.* London: Macmillan.

Crawford, Elizabeth, and Stein Rokkan.
1976 *Sociological Praxis: Current Roles and Setting.* London: Sage.

Crozier, Michel.
1964 *The Bureaucratic Phenomenon.* Chicago: University of Chicago Press.

Cruikshank, J.
1971 "Matrifocal Families in the Canadian North." In Ishwaran (1971: 39-53).

Crysdale, Stewart, and Christopher Beattie.
1977 *Sociology Canada: An Introductory Text.* 2nd ed. Toronto: Butterworth.

Curtis, James, and William Scott, eds.
1973 *Social Stratification in Canada.* Scarborough: Prentice-Hall.

Dahrendorf, Ralf.
1958 "Out of Utopia: Toward a Reorientation of Sociological Analysis." *American Journal of Sociology* 64, Sep-

tember.
1959 *Class and Class Conflict in Industrial Society.* Stanford: Stanford University Press.
1969 "On the Origin of Inequality between Men." In *Social Inequality,* edited by A. Beteille. London: Penguin: 16-44.

Danziger, Kurt.
1974 "The Acculturation of Italian Immigrant Girls in Canada." In *Sociology Canada: Readings,* edited by Christopher Beattie and Stewart Crysdale. Toronto: Butterworth.

Davies, James C.
1962 "Toward a Theory of Revolution." *American Sociological Review* 27, February: 5-19.

Davis, A. K.
1971 "Canadian Society as Hinterland Versus Metropolis." In Ossenberg (1971: 6-32).

Davis, Fred.
1964 "Deviance Disavowal: The Management of Strained Interaction by the Visibly Handicapped." In Becker (1964b).

Davis, John.
1975 "Learning the Norm of Universalism: The Effect of School Attendance." In Pike and Zureik (1975: 84-98).

Davis, Kingsley.
1948 *Human Society.* New York: Macmillan.

Davis, Kingsley, and W. E. Moore.
1945 "Some Principles of Stratification." *American Sociological Review* 10 (2): 242-249.

Dawe, Alan.
1970 "The Two Sociologies." *British Journal of Sociology* 21 (2) June: 207-218.

De 'Ath, Colin E., and Peter Bradbury.
1977 "Brokers and the Social Ecology of Minority Groups." In Hicks and Leis (1977: 181-200).

Denis, Ann B.
1975 "CEGEP Students: Varieties in Socialization Experience." In Pike and Zureik (1975: 209-238).

Denzin, Norman K.
1969 "Symbolic Interactionism and Ethnomethodology: A Proposed Synthesis." *American Sociological Review* 34, December.
1970 *The Research Act.* Chicago: Aldine.

Djilas, Milovan.
1959 *The New Class: An Analysis of the Communist Systems.* New York: Praeger.

Dosman, Edgar.
1972 *Indians: The Urban Dilemma.* Toronto: McClelland and Stewart.

Douglas, Jack D.
1967 *The Social Meaning of Suicide.* Princeton: Princeton University Press.

Douglas, Jack D., ed.
1970 *Understanding Everyday Life.* Chicago: Aldine.

Douglas, J. W. B.
1964 *The Home and School.* London: Granada.

Drache, Daniel.
1976 "Rediscovering Canadian Political Economy." *Journal of Canadian StudIEs* XI (3) August: 3-17.
1977 "Staple-ization: A Theory of Canadian Capitalist Development." In Saul and Heron (1977: 34-47).

Dreeben, Robert.
1968a "The Contribution of Schooling to the Learning of Norms." *Harvard Educational Review* 37 (2) Spring 1967: 211-237. Reprinted in *Socialization and Schools.* Harvard Educational Review, Reprint Series No. 1.
1968b *What Is Learned in School.* Reading, Mass.: Addison-Wesley.

Dreitzel, Hans Peter, ed.
1970 *Recent Sociology, No. 2: Patterns of Communicative Behaviour.* New York: Macmillan.
1972 *Marriage, Family and the Struggle of the Sexes.* New York: Collier-Macmillan.

Driedger, Leo, ed.
1978 *The Canadian Ethnic Mosaic: A Quest for Identity.* Toronto: McClelland and Stewart.

Dumont, Louis.
1970 *Homo Hierarchicus: The Caste System and its Implications.* Chicago: University of Chicago Press.

Durkheim, Emile.
1893 (1960) *The Division of Labour in Society.* Glencoe, Ill.: Free Press.
1895 (1938) *The Rules of the Sociological Method.* Chicago: University of Chicago Press.

1897 (1951) *Suicide.* Glencoe, Ill.: Free Press.
1912 (1915) *The Elementary Forms of the Religious Life.* London: Allen and Unwin.

Dutton, Donald G.
1972 "Reactions of Restaurateurs to Blacks and Whites Violating Dress Requirements." In Berry and Wilde, eds. (1972: 320-324).

Easto, Patrick C., and Marcello Truzzi.
1974 "The Carnival as A Marginally Legal Work Activity: A Typological Approach to Work Systems." In Bryant (1974).

Ehrlich, Paul R.
1968 *The Population Bomb.* New York: Ballantine Books.

Eichler, Margarit.
1973 "Women as Personal Dependents: A Critique of Theories of the Stratification of the Sexes and an Alternative Approach." In Stephenson (1933: 36-55).
1977 "The Prestige of the Occupation Housewife." In Marchak (1977).

Elkin, Frederick.
1971 "Mass Media, Advertising and the Quiet Revolution." In Ossenberg (1971: 184-206).

Elkin, Frederick, and Gerald Handel.
1973 *The Child and Society: The Process of Socialization.* 2nd ed. New York: Random House.

Elliot, Jean, ed.
1971 *Immigrant Groups.* Toronto: Prentice-Hall.

Ellul, Jacques.
1967 *The Technological Society.* New York: Vintage Books.

Evans, Robert, ed.
1969 *Readings in Collective Behaviour.* Chicago: Rand-McNally.

Eysenck, H. J.
1971 *Race, Intelligence and Education.* London: Temple Smith.

Fallers, Lloyd A.
1965 "The Range of Variation in Actual Family size: A Critique of Marion J. Levy, Jr's. Argument." In Coale and others (1965: 70-82).

Fanon, Franz.
1968 *The Wretched of the Earth.* New York: Grove.

Farberman, H. A., and G. P. Stone.
1970 "On the Edge of Rapprochement: Was Durkheim Moving Toward the Perspective of Symbolic Interaction?" In *Social Psychology Through Symbolic Interaction,* edited by Farberman and Stone. Wattham, Mass.: Ginn-Blaisdell.

Felt, Lawrence E.
1975 "Nationalism and the Possibility of a Relevant Anglo-Canadian Sociology." *Canadian Journal of Sociology* 1 (3) Fall: 377-386.

Ferguson, T.
1975 *A White Man's Country: An Exercise in Canadian Prejudice.* Toronto: Doubleday.

Festinger, L., and others.
1956 *When Prophesy Fails.* Minneapolis: University of Minnesota Press.

Feuer, Lewis A., ed.
1959 *Marx and Engels: Basic Writings on Politics and Philosophy.* Garden City, New York: Anchor.

Firestone, Shulamith.
1973 *The Dialectic of Sex.* New York: Morrow.

Firth, R., J. Hubert, and A. Forge.
1969 *Families and Their Relatives.* London: Routledge and Kegan Paul.

Foot, R. N.
1951 "Identification as the Basis for a Theory of Motivation." *American Sociological Review* 16, February: 14-21.

Forcese, Dennis.
1975 *The Canadian Class Structure.* Toronto: McGraw-Hill Ryerson.

Forcese, Dennis, and Stephen Richer.
1975 *Issues in Canadian Society: An Introduction to Sociology.* Toronto: Prentice-Hall.

Frank, André Gunder.
1969 *Latin America: Underdevelopment or Revolution.* New York: Monthly Review Press.

Freire, Paulo.
1970 *Pedagogy of the Oppressed.* New York: Seabury.

Frideres, James.
1974 *Canada's Indians: Contemporary Conflicts.* Toronto: Prentice-Hall.

Fromm, Erich.
1963 *Escape from Freedom.* New York: Holt, Rinehart and Winston.
1966 *Marx's Concept of Man.* New York: Frederich Ungar.

Frye, Northrup.
1977 "A Summary of the Conference." In Conference on the Future of the Canadian Federation. *Options.* Toronto: University of Toronto Press: 435-448.
Fullan, Michael.
1972 "Overview of the Innovative Process and the User." *Interchange* 3 (2/3): 1-46.
Gamson, William A.
1961 "A Theory of Coalition Formation." *American Sociological Review* 26, June: 565-573.
1975 *The Strategy of Social Protest.* Homewood, Ill.: Dorsey.
Gans, Herbert J.
1962 *The Urban Villagers.* New York: Free Press.
1968 "The 'Equality' Revolution." *New York Times Magazine* November 3: 36-39.
1972 "The Positive Functions of Poverty." *American Journal of Sociology* 78, September: 275-289.
Garfinkel, Harold.
1956 "Conditions of Successful Degradation Ceremonies." *American Journal of Sociology* 61, March: 420-424.
1967 *Studies in Ethnomethodology.* Englewood Cliffs, N. J.: Prentice-Hall.
Garigue, P.
1956 "French-Canadian Kinship and Urban Life." *American Anthropologist* 58, December: 1090-1101.
Garry, Carl
1975 *Administrative and Curriculum Change in a Canadian Community College.* Canadian Sociology and Anthropology Association Monograph Series.
Gartner, Alan, Colin Greer, and Frann Rieshan, eds.
1974 *The New Assault on Equality, I.Q. and Social Stratification.* Toronto: Harper and Row.
Gavron, Hannah.
1966 *The Captive Wife: Conflicts of Housebound Mothers.* Middlesex, England: Penguin Books.
Geertz, Clifford.
1963 "The Integrated Revolution." In *Old Societies and New Societies,* edited by Clifford Geertz. Glencoe, Ill.: Free Press.
Gerth, Hans H., and C. Wright Mills
1953 *Character and Social Structure.* New York: Harcourt, Brace and World.
1958 *From Max Weber: Essays in Sociology.* New York: Oxford University Press.
Gertler, Len, and Ron Crowley.
1977 *Changing Canadian Cities: The Next 25 Years.* Toronto: McClelland and Stewart.
Giddens, Anthony.
1971 *Capitalism and Modern Social Theory: An Analysis of the Writings of Marx, Durkheim and Max Weber.* Cambridge: Cambridge University Press.
Giffen, P. J.
1966 "The Revolving Door: A Functional Interpretation." *Canadian Review of Sociology and Anthropology* 3 (2): 154-166.
Gigeroff, Alex K.
1968 *Sexual Deviations in the Criminal Law.* Toronto: University of Toronto Press.
Gilder, George.
1974 "In Defense of Monogamy." *Commentary* 58 (5) November: 31-36.
Glaser, Barney G., and Anselm Strauss.
1976 *The Discovery of Grounded Theory: Strategies for Qualitative Research.* Chicago: Aldine.
1971 *Status Passage.* Chicago: Aldine.
Glazer, Nathan, and Daniel P. Moynihan
1963 *Beyond the Melting Pot.* Cambridge, Mass.: M.I.T. Press and Harvard University Press.
Glazer, Nathan, and Daniel P. Moynihan, eds.
1975 *Ethnicity.* Cambridge, Mass.: Harvard University Press.
Goffman, Erving.
1959 *The Presentation of Self in Everyday Life.* New York: Doubleday Anchor.
1961a *Asylums.* Garden City, New York: Doubleday Anchor.
1961b *Encounters.* Indianapolis: Bobbs-Merrill.
1963a *Behaviour in Public Places.* New York: Free Press.
1963b *Stigma: Notes on the Management of Spoiled Identity.* Englewood Cliffs, N.J.: Prentice-Hall.
1974 *Frame Analysis.* New York: Harper and Row.
Gold, G. L., and M.-A. Tremblay.
1973 *Communities and Culture in French*

Canada. Toronto: Holt, Rinehart and Winston.

Goode, W. J.
1959 "The Theoretical Importance of Love." *American Sociological Review* 24 (1) February: 38-47.
1960 "Norm Commitment and Conformity to Role-Status Obligations." *American Journal of Sociology* 66, November: 248-261.
1963 *World Revolution and Family Patterns.* Glencoe, Ill.: Free Press.
1964 *The Family.* Englewood Cliffs, N.J.: Prentice-Hall.
1973 *Explorations in Social Theory.* New York: Oxford University Press.

Gorer, Geoffrey.
1967 *Sex and Marriage in Britain Today.* London: Heinemann.

Goslin, David A.
1969 *Handbook of Socialization: Theory and Research.* Chicago: Rand McNally.

Gouldner, Alvin W., and Richard A. Peterson.
1962 *Technology and the Moral Order.* Indianapolis: Bobbs-Merrill.
1970 *The Coming Crisis in Western Sociology.* New York: Basic Books.

Government of Canada
1961 *1961 Census General Review: Canadian Families.* Ottawa: Dominion Bureau of Statistics. (Statistics Canada).
1968 *Fifth Annual Review.* Ottawa: Economic Council of Canada.
1970 *Report of the Royal Commission on the Status of Women in Canada.* Ottawa: Information Canada.
1971 *1970-1971 Canada Year Book.* Ottawa: Dominion Bureau of Statistics. (Statistics Canada).
1977 *Perspective Canada II.* Ottawa: Supply and Services.

Goyder, J. C., and J. E. Curtis.
1977 "Occupational Mobility in Canada Over Four Generations." *Canadian Review of Sociology and Anthropology* 14 (3): 303-319.

Graham, Hugh D., and Ted R. Gurr, eds.
1969 *Violence in America.* New York: Bantam Books.

Grant, George.
1965 (1970) *Lament for a Nation.* Toronto: McClelland and Stewart.
1969 *Technology and Empire.* Toronto: House of Anansi.

Gray, James.
1972 *Booze.* Toronto: Macmillan.

Greeley, Andrew M.
1974 *Ethnicity in the United States.* New York: Wiley.

Gregorovich, A.
1972 *Canadian Ethnic Groups Bibliography.* Ottawa: Queen's Printer.

Gregory, Dick.
1968 *The Shadow that Scares Me.* New York: Doubleday.

Grimshaw, Allen D.
1970 "Interpreting Collective Violence: An Argument for the Importance of Social Structure." In Short and Wolfgang (1970: 9-20).

Gross, Edward, and Gregory P. Stone.
1970 "Embarrassment and the Analysis of Role Requirements." In Stone and Farberman (1970: 174-190).

Gross, R., and B. Gross, eds.
1969 *Radical School Reform.* New York: Simon and Schuster.

Gurr, Ted Robert.
1969 "A Comparative Study of Civil Strife." In *Violence in America: Historical and Comparative Perspectives,* edited by Hugh David Graham and Ted Robert Gurr. Report submitted to the National Commission on the Causes and Prevention of Violence. New York: Bantam Books: 572-632.

Gusfield, Joseph R.
1962 "Mass Society and Extremist Politics." *American Sociological Review* 27, February: 19-30.
1972 "Moral Passage: The Symbolic Process in Public Designation of Deviance." In *An Introduction to Deviance: Readings in the Process of Making Deviants,* edited by W. J. Filstead. Chicago: Markham.

Guyatt, D.
1971 *One-Parent Family in Canada.* Ottawa: Vanier Institute of the Family.

Haas, Jack, and William Shaffir.
1974 *Decency and Deviance.* Toronto: McClelland and Stewart.
1978 *Shaping Identity in Canadian Society.* Toronto: Prentice-Hall.

Hagan, John.
1977 *The Disreputable Pleasures.* Toronto: McGraw-Hill Ryerson.

Hagan, John, and Jeffrey Leon.

1977 "Rediscovering Delinquency: Social History, Political Ideology, and the Sociology of Law." *American Sociological Review* 42, August: 587-598.

Hall, Edward T.
1959 *The Silent Language.* Greenwich, Conn.: Fawcett.

Hamilton, Richard, and Maurice Pinard.
1977 "Poverty in Canada: Illusion and Reality." *Canadian Review of Sociology and Anthropology* 14 (2): 247-252.

Hamilton, Richard, and James Wright.
1975 *New Directions in Political Sociology.* Indianapolis: Bobbs-Merrill.

Handelman, Don, and Elliott Leyton.
1978 *Bureaucracy and World View: Studies in the Logic of Official Interpretation.* St. John's: Institute of Social and Economic Research.

Hanson, S. D.
1974 "Estevan 1931." In Abella (1974: 33-46).

Hardin, Herschel.
1974 *A Nation Unaware: The Canadian Economic Culture.* Vancouver: J. J. Douglas.

Harrington, Michael.
1965 *The Accidental Century.* Baltimore: Penguin Books.

Harris, Marvin.
1968 *The Rise of Anthropological Theory.* New York: Thomas Y. Crowell.
1974 *Cows, Pigs, Wars and Witches: The Riddles of Culture.* New York: Random House.

Hartz, Louis, ed.
1964 *The Founding of New Societies.* New York: Harcourt, Brace and World.

Harvard Educational Review
1969 *Environment, Heredity and Intelligence.* Reprint Series No. 2. Cambridge, Mass.: *Harvard Educational Review.*

Harvey, Edward.
1974 *Educational Systems and the Labour Market.* Toronto: Longman.

Harvey, Edward, and Ivan Charner.
1975 "Social Mobility and Occupational Attainments of University Graduates." *Canadian Review of Sociology and Anthropology* 12 (2): 134-149.

Hawthorn, Geoffrey.
1970 *The Sociology of Fertility.* LoNdon: Collier-Macmillan.

Heberle, Rudolph.
1951 *Social Movements: An Introduction to Political Sociology.* New York: Appleton-Century-Crofts.

Hébert, Raymond, and Jean-Guy Vaillancourt.
1971 "French-Canadians in Manitoba: Elites and Ideologies." In Elliott (1971: 175-190).

Henry, Frances.
1971 *Forgotten Canadians: The Blacks of Nova Scotia.* Toronto: Longman.

Henshel, Anne-Marie.
1973 "Swinging: A Study of Decision Making in Marriage." *American Journal of Sociology* 78 (4): 885-891.

Henshel, R. L., and A.-M. Henshel.
1973 *Perspectives on Social Problems.* Don Mills, Ont.: Longman.

Herrnstein, R.
1971 "I.Q." *Atlantic Monthly,* December.

Hicks, George L.
1977 "Introduction: Problems in the Study of Ethnicity." In Hicks and Leiss (1977: 1-20).

Hicks, George L., and Philip E. Leiss, eds.
1977 *Ethnic Encounters: Identities and Contexts.* Belmont, Calif.: Wadeworth.

Hiller, Harry.
1976 *Canadian Society: A Sociological Analysis.* Toronto: Prentice-Hall.

Himelfarb, A.
1975 *"Fat Man, Thin World: A Participant Observation Study of Weight Watchers."* Ph.D. dissertation, University of Toronto.
1977 *The Social Characteristics of One-Industry Towns in Canada.* Ottawa: Supply and Services.

Himelfarb, A., and J. Evans.
1974 "Deviance Disavowal and Stigma Management: A Study of Obesity." In Haas and Shaffir (1974: 221-232).

Hobsbawm, E. J.
1965 *Primitive Rebels.* New York: W. W. Norton.

Hoffer, Eric.
1931 *The True Believer: Thoughts on the Nature of Mass Movements.* New York: Harper and Row.

Hoffman, Lois.
1972 "Early Childhood Experiences and Women's Achievement Motives." *Journal of Social Issues* 28 (2).

Hofley, John.

1971 "Problems and Perspectives in the Study of Poverty." In *Poverty in Canada,* edited by J. Harp and J. R. Hofley. Toronto: Prentice-Hall: 101-116.

Hogarth, John.
1971 *Sentencing as a Human Process.* Toronto: University of Toronto Press.

Hollander, Edwin, and Raymond Hunt.
1971 *Current Perspectives in Social Psychology.* New York: Oxford University Press.

Holt, John.
1964 *How Children Fail.* New York: Pitman.
1967 *How Children Learn.* New York: Pitman.
1969 *The Underachieving School.* New York: Pitman.

Holzner, Burkhart.
1968 *Reality Construction in Society.* Cambridge, Mass.: Schenkman.

Homans, George C.
1950 *The Human Group.* New York: Harcourt, Brace and World.
1958 "Social Behaviour as Exchange." *American Journal of Sociology* 62, May: 597-606.
1961 (revised 1974) *Social Behaviour: Its Elementary Forms.* New York: Harcourt, Brace and World.

Hopper, Earl.
1971 "Educational Systems and Selected Consequences of Patterns of Mobility in Industrial Societies: A Theoretical Discussion." In *Readings in the Theory of Educational Systems,* edited by E. Hopper. London, Hutchinson.

Horowitz, Gad.
1965a "Creative Politics." *Canadian Dimension* 3 (1): 14-15, 28.
1965b "Tories, Socialists and the Demise of Canada." *Canadian Dimensions,* May-June: 12-15.
1966 "Conservatism, Liberalism and Socialism in Canada: An Interpretation." *Canadian Journal of Economics and Political Science* 32, May.

Horowitz, Irving Louis.
1973 "The Hemispheric Connection: A Critique and Corrective to the Entrepreneurial Thesis of Development with Special Emphasis on the Canadian Case." *Queen's Quarterly* 80: 327-359.

Horowitz, I. L., and M. Liebowitz.
1968 "Social Deviance and Political Marginality: Toward a Redefinition of the Relation between Sociology and Politics." *Social Problems* 15, Winter: 280-296.

Huber, Jean, ed.
1973 "Changing Women in a Changing Society." Special Issue of *American Journal of Sociology* 78 (4) January.

Hughes, D., and E. Kallen.
1974 *The Anatomy of Racism: Canadian Dimensions.* Toronto: Harvest House.

Humphreys, Laud.
1970 *The Tearoom Trade.* Chicago: Aldine.

Hyman, H. H., and E. Singer, eds.
1968 *Readings in Reference Group Theory and Research.* New York: Free Press.

Illich, Ivan.
1970 *The Celebration of Awareness.* Garden City, New York: Doubleday.
1971 *Deschooling Society.* New York: Perennial Library (Harper Row).

Inkeles, Alex.
1964 *What Is Sociology?* Englewood Cliffs, N.J.: Prentice-Hall.

Innis, Harold A.
1930 *The Fur Trade in Canada: An Introduction to Canadian Economic History.* New Haven: Yale University Press.
1940 *The Cod Fisheries: The History of an International Economy.* New Haven: Yale University Press.
1956 *Essays in Canadian Economic History.* Toronto: University of Toronto Press.

Irving, H. K.
1972 *The Family Myth.* Toronto: Copp Clark.

Irving, John A.
1960 *The Social Credit Movement in Alberta.* Toronto: University of Toronto Press.
1975 "The Evolution of the Social Credit Movement." In Clark and others (1975: 130-152).

Isajiw, W. W.
1974 "Definitions of Ethnicity." *Ethnicity* 1: 111-124.
1976 *Identities: The Impact of Ethnicity on*

Canadian Society. Toronto: Peter Martin.

Isajiw, W. W., and Norbert Hartmann.
1970 "Changes in the Occupational Structure of Ukrainians in Canada." In *Social and Cultural Change in Canada,* Vol. 2., edited by W. E. Mann. Toronto: Copp Clark.

Ishwaran, K.
1976 (1971) *The Canadian Family.* Toronto: Holt, Rinehart and Winston.

Jackson, Brian.
1964 *Streaming: An Educational System in Miniature.* London: Routledge and Kegan Paul.

Jackson, Brian, and Dennis Marsden.
1962 *Education and the Working Class.* London: Routledge and Kegan Paul.

Jackson, John D.
1975 *Community and Conflict: A Study of French-English Relations in Ontario.* Toronto: Holt, Rinehart and Winston.

Jencks, Christopher.
1972 *Inequality: A Reassessment of Family and Schooling in America.* New York: Harper and Row.

Jensen, Arthur R.
1969 "How Much Can We Boost I.Q. and Scholastic Achievement?" *Harvard Educational Review* 39 (1): 1-123.

Johnson, Leo A.
1973 *Disparity and Improverishment in Canada since W.W. II.* Toronto: New Bytown Press.

Johnson, Terrence.
1977 "The Professions in the Class Structure." In *Industrial Society: Class, Cleavage and Control,* edited by Richard Scase. London: Ruskin House.

Jones, Frank E., and Hugh A. McRoberts.
1977 "Social Origins, Education and Occupational Attainment: Some Preliminary Findings." Paper presented at CSAA meetings, Fredericton, N.B.

Kalbach, Warren E., and Wayne W. McVey.
1971 (1979) *The Demographic Bases of Canadian Society.* Toronto: McGraw-Hill.

Kaplan, Abraham.
1964 *The Conduct of Inquiry: Methodology for Behavioural Science.* San Francisco: Chandler.

Karabel, Jerome.
1972 "Community Colleges and Social Stratification." *Harvard Educational Review* 42 (4): 521-563.

Katz, Michael B.
1975 *The People of Hamilton Canada West: Family and Class in a Mid-Nineteenth-Century City.* Cambridge, Mass.: Harvard University Press.

Kaufman, Bel.
1964 *Up the Down Staircase.* Englewood Cliffs, N.J.: Prentice-Hall.

Kelner, Merrijoy.
1970 "Ethnic Penetration into Toronto's Elite Sturcture." *Canadian Review of Sociology and Anthropology* 7, May: 26-35.

Key, William.
1973 *Subliminal Seduction.* Englewood Cliffs, N.J.: Prentice-Hall.

Kirk, Russell.
1961 "Is Social Science Scientific?" *New York Times Magazine,* June 25. Reprinted in *Social Realities,* edited by George Ritzer. Boston: Allyn and Bacon, 1964.

Kluckhohn, Clyde.
1949 *Mirror for Man.* New York: McGraw-Hill.

Kohl, S., and J. W. Bennett
1965 "Kinship, Succession and the Migration of Young People in a Canadian Agricultural Community." *International Journal of Comparative Sociology* 6, March: 95-116.

Kohlberg, Lawrence.
1963 "The Development of Children's Orientations toward a Moral Order: A Sequence in the Development of Moral Thought." *Human Development.*
1964 "The Development of Children's Orientations toward a Moral Order: Social Experience, Social Conduct, and the Development of Moral Thought." Human Development.
1970 "Moral Development." In *Adolescents and the American High School,* edited by R. F. Purnell. Toronto: Holt, Rinehart and Winston.

Kornhauser, William.
1959 *The Politics of Mass Society.* New York: Free Press.

Kozol, Jonathan.
1967 *Death at an Early Age.* Boston: Houghton-Mifflin.

Kroeber, A. L., and Talcott Parsons.
1958 "The Concept of Culture and of Social System." *American Sociological Review* 23, October.

Kubat, D., and David Thornton.
1974 *A Statistical Profile of Canadian Society.* Toronto: McGraw-Hill Ryerson.

Kuhn, Thomas.
1962 *The Structure of Scientific Revolutions.* Chicago: University of Chicago Press.

Laing, R. D.
1967 *The Politics of Experience and the Bird of Paradise,* London: Penguin.

Lang, Kurt, and Gladys E. Lang.
1961 *Collective Dynamics.* New York: Thomas Y. Crowell.

Larson, Lyle E.
1976 *The Canadian Family in Comparative Perspective.* Scarborough: Prentice-Hall.

Laslett, Peter.
1965 *The World We Have Lost.* New York: Scribner.

Laslett, Peter, and Richard Wall.
1972 *Household and Family in Past Time.* Cambridge: Cambridge University Press.

Lasswell, Harold D.
1950 *Politics: Who Gets What, When, How.* New York: Peter Smith.

Lautard, Hugh.
1978 *"Occupational Segregation by Sex and Industrialization in Canada: 1891-1971."* Unpublished Ph.D. thesis, University of British Columbia.

Laxer, Robert, ed.
1973 *Canada Ltd: The Political Economy of Dependency.* Toronto: McClelland and Stewart.

Lazarsfeld, Paul F., and others, eds.
1972 *Continuities in the Language of Social Research.* New York: Free Press.

Le Bon, Gustave.
1895 (1960) *The Crowd: A Study of the Popular Mind.* New York: Viking Press.

Lemert, E. M.
1951 *Social Pathology.* New York: McGraw-Hill.
1972 *Human Deviance, Social Problems, and Social Control.* Englewood Cliffs, N.J.: Prentice-Hall.

Lenski, G. E.
1966 *Power and Privilege.* New York: McGraw-Hill.

Levesque, René
1968 *An Option for Quebec.* Toronto: McClelland and Stewart.

Lévi-Strauss, Claude.
1956 "The Family." In *Man, Culture, and Society,* edited by Harry L. Shapiro. New York: Oxford University Press, 142-170.
1963 *Totemism.* Translated by R. Needham. Boston: Beacon Press.
1969 *The Elementary Structures of Kinship.* Boston: Beacon Press.

Levitt, Kari.
1970 *Silent Surrender: The Multinational Corporation in Canada.* Toronto: Macmillan.

Levy, Marion J., Jr.
1965 "Aspects of the Analysis of Family Structure." In Coale and others (1965: 1-63).

Libby, Roger W., and Robert N. Whitehurst.
1973 *Renovating Marriage: Toward New Sexual Life Styles.* Danville, Calif.: Consensus.
1977 *Marriage and Alternatives: Exploring Intimate Relationships.* Glenview, Ill.: Scott, Foresman.

Lieberson, Stanley.
1970 *Language and Ethnic Relations in Canada.* New York: Wiley.

Lindesmith, A. R.
1965 *The Addict and the Law.* Bloomington, Ind.: Indiana University Press.

Lindesmith, A. R., and A. L. Strauss.
1968 *Social Psychology.* New York: Holt, Rinehart and Winston.

Linton, Ralph.
1936 *The Study of Man.* New York: Appleton-Century-Crofts.

Lipset, Seymour M.
1963a *Political Man.* New York: Doubleday Anchor.
1963b "The Value Patterns of Democracy: A Case Study in Comparative Analysis." *American Sociological Review* 28, August.
1966 *Agrarian Socialism: The Cooperative Commonwealth Federation in Saskatchewan, A Study in Political Sociology.* Revised 1968. Berkeley: University of California Press.

Litwak, E.
1960a "Occupational Mobility and Extended Family Cohesion." *American Sociological Review* 25: 9-21.

1960b "Geographic Mobility and Extended Family Cohesion." *American Sociological Review* 25: 386-394.

Lockwood, David.
1970 "Social Integration and System Integration". In *Modern Sociology,* edited by P. Worsley. London: Penguin, Chapter 66.

Lofland, J.
1969 *Deviance and Identity.* Englewood Cliffs, N.J.: Prentice-Hall.

Lofland, Lyn H.
1975 "The 'Thereness' of Women: A Selective Review of Urban Sociology." In Millman and Kanter (1975: 144-170).

Lopada, H. A.
1971 *Occupation Housewife.* New York: Oxford University Press.

Lopreato, J., and E. Hazelrigg
1972 *Class Conflict and Mobility.* San Francisco: Chandler.

Lorimer, James, and Myfanwy Phillips
1971 *Working People.* Toronto: James Lewis and Samuel.

Lower, A.
1964 *Colony to Nation.* Toronto: Longman.

Lucas, Rex A.
1969 *Men in Crisis: A Study of a Mine Disaster.* New York: Basic Books.
1971 *Minetown, Milltown, Railtown: Life in Canadian Communities of a Single Industry.* Toronto: University of Toronto Press.

Luce, R. D., and H. Raiffa.
1957 *Games and Decisions.* New York: Wiley.

Lukes, Steven.
1967 "Alienation and Anomie." In *Philosophy, Politics and Society,* edited by Peter Laslett and H. G. Runciman. Oxford: Oxford University Press.

Lumsden, Ian.
1970 *Close the 49th Parallel Etc.* Toronto: University of Toronto Press.

Lurie, Alison.
1967 *Imaginary Friends.* London: Pan Books.

MacDonald, L. R.
1975 "Merchants Against Industry: An Idea and Its Origins." *Canadian Historical Review* LVI.

Macpherson, C. B.
1962 *The Political Theory of Possessive Individualism: Hobbes to Locke.* Oxford: Clarendon.

Malinowski, B.
1945 *The Dymanics of Cultural Change.* New Haven: Yale University Press.

Mann, W. E., ed.
1970a *The Underside of Toronto.* Toronto: McClelland and Stewart.
1970b *Social and Cultural Change in Canada.* Toronto: Copp Clark.
1971 *Social Deviance in Canada.* Toronto: Copp Clark.

Manis, Jerome, and Bernard Meltzer.
1967 (1972) *Symbolic Interactionism: A Reader in Social Psychology.* Boston: Allyn and Bacon.

Manzer, Ronald.
1974 *Canada: A Socio-Political Report.* Toronto: McGraw-Hill Ryerson.

Marchak, Pat.
1975 *Ideological Perspectives in Canada.* Toronto: McGraw-Hill Ryerson.

Marchak, Pat, ed.
1977 *The Working Sexes.* Vancouver: The Institute of Industrial Relations.

Marris, Peter.
1973 *Loss and Change.* London: Routledge and Kegan Paul.

Marsden, Lorna.
1972 *Population Probe: Canada.* Toronto: Copp Clark.
1975 "Population Issues in the Immigration Debate." *Canadian Ethnic Studies* VII (5): 22-29.

Marsden, Lorna, and E. B. Harvey.
1979 *Social Change in Canada.* Toronto: McGraw-Hill Ryerson.

Martel, George, ed.
1974 *The Politics of the Canadian Public School.* Toronto: James Lewis and Samuel.

Martin, F. M.
1954 "Some Subjective Aspects of Social Stratification." In *Social Mobility in Britain,* edited by David Glass. London: Routledge and Kegan Paul, 51-78.

Martin, Wilfred B.
1976 *The Negotiated Order of the School.* Toronto: Macmillan.

Martin, Wilfred B. W., and A. J. Macdonnel.
1976 "Aspects of Educational Opportunity in the Atlantic Provinces." Paper presented at the 11th annual

meeting of the Atlantic Association of Sociologists and Anthropologists, Fredericton, N.B.
1978 *Canadian Education: A Sociological Analysis.* Scarborough: Prentice-Hall.

Martin-Matthews, Anne
1977 "The Newfoundland Migrant Wife: A Power Versus Powerless Theory of Adjustment." *Atlantis* 2 (2): 152-166.

Marx, Gary T.
1970 "Issueless Riots." In Short and Wolfgang (1970: 21-23).

Marx, Karl.
1971 "Peasantry as a Class." In *Peasants and Peasant Societies: Selected Readings,* edited by Teodor Shanin. Harmondsworth: Penguin: 229-237.

Marx, Karl, and Frederich Engels.
1965 *The German Ideology.* New York: International.

Masters, D. C.
1950 *The Winnipeg General Strike.* Toronto: University of Toronto Press.

Mathews, Robin.
1973 "Canadian Culture and the Liberal Ideology." In Laxer (1973: 213-231).

Matthews, Ralph.
1976 *There's No Better Place Than Here: Social Change in Three Newfoundland Communities.* Toronto: Peter Martin Associates.

Matza, D.
1964 *Delinquency and Drift.* New York: Wiley.
1969 *Becoming Deviant.* Englewood Cliffs, N.J.: Prentice-Hall.

Mauss, Armand L.
1975 *Social Problems as Social Movements.* Philadelphia: Lippincott.

McCall, G. J., and J. L. Simmons
1978 (1968) *Identities and Interactions: An Examination of Human Associations in Everyday Life.* New York: Free Press.
1969 *Issues in Participant Observation.* Reading: Addison-Wesley.

McCrorie, James N.
1964 *In Union is Strength.* Saskatoon: Saskatchewan Farmers Union.

McDonald, Lyn.
1975 "Wages of Work: A Widening Gap Between Women and Men." *Canadian Forum,* April-May, 4-7.

McElroy, Ann.
1975 "Ethnic Identity and Modernization: The Biculturation of Baffin Island Inuit Children." In Pike and Zureik (1975: 262-290).

McGrath, W. T., ed.
1975 *Crime and Its Treatment in Canada.* 2nd ed. Toronto: Macmillan.

McHugh, Peter.
1968 *Defining the Situation.* Indianapolis: Bobbs-Merrill.

Mcluhan, Marshall.
1965 *Understanding Media: The Extensions of Man.* New York: McGraw-Hill.

Mead, George Herbert.
1934 *Mind, Self, and Society.* Chicago: University of Chicago Press.

Mead, Margaret.
1928 *Coming of Age in Samoa.* New York: Morrow.
1955 *Cultural Patterns and Technical Change.* New YorK: Mentor.

Meadows, D. H., D. L. Meadows, J. Randers, and W. W. Bahrens, III.
1972 *The Limits to Growth.* New York: New American Library.

Meisel, John.
1977 "Who Are We? Who Are They? Perceptions in English Canada." In Conference on the Future of the Canadian Federation, *Options.* Toronto, University of Toronto: 13-34.

Meissner, Martin, and others.
1975 "No Exit for Wives: Sexual Division of Labour." *Canadian Review of Sociology and Anthropology* 12: 4 (1): 424-439.

Merton, Robert K.
1939 "Social Structure and Anomie." *American Sociological Review* 3: 672-687.
1961 "Now the Case for Sociology." *New York Times Magazine,* July 16. Reprinted in *Social Realities,* edited by George Ritzer. Boston: Allyn and Bacon.
1968 *Social Theory and Social Structure.* Chicago: Free Press.

Merton, Robert K., Ailsa P. Gray, Barbara Hockey, and Hanan C. Selvin.
1952 *Reader in Bureaucracy.* New York: Free Press.

Metzger, L. Paul.
1971 "American Sociology and Black Assimilation: Conflicting Perspectives." *American Journal of Sociology* 74 (4) January: 643-644.

Michels, Robert.
1915 (1959) *Political Parties.* New York: Dover.

Miller, S. M.
1960 "Comparative Social Mobility." *Current Sociology* 9 (1): 1-80.

Millman, Marcia, and Rosabeth Moss Kanter, eds.
1975 *Another Voice: Feminist Perspectives on Social Life and Social Science.* Garden City, New York: Anchor.

Mills, C. Wright.
1942 "The Professional Ideology of Social Pathologists." *American Journal of Sociology* 6: 165-180.
1949 "Situated Actions and Vocabularies of Motive." *American Sociological Review* 5, December.
1951 *White Collar.* New York: Oxford University Press.
1956 *The Power Elite.* New York: Oxford University Press.
1959 *The Sociological Imagination.* New York: Oxford University Press.
1967 *Power, Politics and People: The Collected Essays of C. Wright Mills.* Edited by Irving Louis Horowitz. London: Oxford University Press.

Milner, Sheilagh H., and Henry Milner.
1973 *The Decolonization of Quebec.* Toronto: McClelland and Stewart.

Miner, Horace.
1939 *St. Denis: A French-Canadian Parish.* Chicago: University of Chicago Press.
1956 "Body Ritual among the Nacirema." *American Anthropologist* 58 (3): 503-507.

Minifie, James M.
1971 "Mass Media and their Control." In Ossenberg (1971: 169-183).

Mitford, Jessica
1977 *The American Way of Death.* New York: Fawcett World Library.

Montagu, Ashley.
1969 "The Concept of Race in the Human Species in the Light of Genetics." In *The Concept of Race,* edited by A. Montagu, London: Collier-Macmillan, 1-11.

Moore, Barrington, Jr.
1972 *Reflections on the Causes of Human Misery and Upon Certain Proposals to Eliminate Them.* Boston: Beacon.

Moore, Steve, and Debi Wells.
1975 *Imperialism and the National Question in Canada.* Toronto: S. Moore.

Moreux, Colette.
1971 "The French-Canadian Family." In K. Ishwaran, ed. (1971: 126-147).

Morgan, D. H.
1975 *The Family and Social Theory.* London: Routledge and Kegan Paul.

Morris, R. N., and C. M. Lanphier.
1977 *The Three Scales of Inequality: Perspectives on French-English Relations.* Toronto: Longman.

Mouzelis, Nicos.
1967 *Organisation and Bureaucracy.* London: Routledge and Kegan Paul.

Mueller, Claus.
1970 "Notes on the Repression of Communicative Behaviour." In Dreitzel (1970).
1973 *The Politics of Communication.* New York: Oxford University Press.

Mumford, Lewis.
1934 *Technics and Civilization.* New York: Harcourt, Brace and World.

Murdock, G. P.
1949 *Social Structure.* New York: Free Press.

Nagata, Judith A.
1969 (1977) "Adaptation and Integration of Greek Working Class Immigrants in Toronto: A Situational Approach." *International Migration Review* 4 (10) Fall. Reprinted in *Sociology Canada: Reading,* 2nd edition, edited by Christopher Beattie and Stewart Crysdale. Toronto: Butterworth: 148-157.

Nagler, Mark.
1970 *Indians in the City.* Ottawa: Canadian Research Centre for Anthropology, University of Saint Paul.

Nagler, Mark, ed.
1972 *Perspectives on the North American Indians.* Toronto: McClelland and Stewart.

Naylor, R. T.
1972 "The Rise and Fall of the Third Commercial Empire of the St.

Lawrence." In Teeple, ed. (1972: 1-42).

Neill, A. S.
1960 *Summerhill: A Radical Approach to Child Rearing.* New York: Hart.

Nelsen, Randle W., and David A. Nock.
1978 *Reading, Writing and Riches: Education and the Socio-Economic Order in North America.* Kitchener, Ont.: Between The Lines.

Nettler, Gwynn.
1974 *Explaining Crime.* New York: McGraw-Hill.

Newman, Peter C.
1975 *The Canadian Establishment.* Vol. 1. Toronto: McClelland and Stewart.

Nie, Norman H., and others.
1975 *Statistical Package for the Social Sciences.* New York: McGraw-Hill.

Nisbet, Robert A.
1967 *The Sociological Tradition.* London: Heineman.
1969 *Social Change and History.* London: Oxford University Press.

Novak, Mark W.
1975 *Living and Learning in the Free School.* Toronto: McClelland and Stewart.

Nyquist, E. B., and G. R. Hawes, eds.
1972 *Open Education.* New York: Bantam.

Oakley, Ann.
1974 *The Sociology of Housework.* New York: Pantheon.

Oberschall, Anthony.
1973 *Social Conflict and Social Movements.* Englewood Cliffs, N.J.: Prentice-Hall.

Ogburn, William F.
1922 (1950) *Social Change with Respect to Culture and Original Nature.* New York: Viking.

Olmstead, Michael S.
1959 *The Small Group.* New York: Random House.

Ondrack, Dan A.
1972 "The Generation Gap: Attitudes Toward Authority." *Canadian Personnel* 19 (1) January: 31-32.

O'Neill, John.
1972 *Sociology as a Skin Trade: Essays Towards a Reflexive Sociology.* New York: Harper Torchbooks.
1975 "Facts, Myths, and the Nationalist Platitude." *Canadian Journal of Sociology* 1 (1) Spring: 107-124.

O'Neill, Nena, and George O'Neill.
1972 *Open Marriage.* New York: Avon Books.

Ontario, Province of.
1972 *The Learning Society.* Toronto: Commission on Post-Secondary Education.

Opie, I., and P. Opie.
1959 *The Lore and Language of School Children.* London: Oxford University Press.

Ortega y Gasset, José.
1932 (1961) *The Revolt of the Masses.* London: Unwin.

Ossenberg, R. J., ed.
1971 *Canadian Society: Pluralism, Change and Conflict.* Scarborough: Prentice-Hall.

Ostry, Sylvia.
1967 *The Occupational Composition of the Canadian Labour Force.* Ottawa: Dominion Bureau of Statistics.

Packard, Vance.
1957 *The Hidden Persuaders.* New York: D. McKay.

Pahl, J. M., and R. E. Pahl.
1971 *Managers and their Wives.* London: Allen Lane, Penguin.

Panitch, Leo, ed.
1977 *The Canadian State: Political Economy and Political Power.* Toronto: University of Toronto Press.

Parkin, Frank
1971 *Class Inequality and Political Order.* London: Paladin.
1976 "Ethnic Conflict and Social Theory." Paper presented at the annual meeting of the Canadian Sociology and Anthropology Association, Fredericton, N.B.

Parkinson, C. Northcote.
1957 *Parkinson's Law.* New York: Ballantine.

Parsons, Talcott.
1951 *The Social System.* Glencoe, Ill.: Free Press.
1954 "The Kinship System of the Contemporary United States." In *Essays in Sociological Theory,* by Talcott Parsons. New York: Free Press.

Parsons, Talcott, and R. F. Bales.
1955 *Family, Socialization and Interaction Process.* Glencoe, Ill.: Free Press.

Paul, Gurbachan.
1975 "The Green Paper and Third World Immigrants: A Subjective Analy-

sis." *Canadian Ethnic Studies* VII (1): 40-49.

Pearson, Geoffrey.
1975 *The Deviant Imagination: Psychiatry, Social Work and Social Change.* London: Macmillan.

Peers, Frank.
"Oh Say Can You See?" In Lumsden (1970: 135-156).

Pelletier, Gérard.
1971 *The October Crisis.* Toronto: McClelland and Stewart.

Perrow, Charles.
1972 *Complex Organization: A Critical Essay.* Glenview, Ill.: Scott, Foresman, and Co.

Persig, Robert M.
1975 *Zen and the Art of Motorcycle Maintenance.* New York: Bantam.

Peter, Karl.
1976 "The Dialectic of Family and Community in the Social History of the Hutterites." In *The Canadian Family in Comparative Perspective,* edited by Lyle E. Larson. Scarborough: Prentice-Hall.

Peter, Lawrence J., and Raymond Hull.
1969 *The Peter Principle.* New York: Morrow.

Phillips, Charles E.
1957 *The Development of Education in Canada.* Toronto: Gage.

Piaget, Jean.
1948 *The Moral Judgement of the Child.* New York: Free Press.
1952 *Judgement and Reasoning in the Child.* New York: Humanities Press.
1954 *The Construction of Reality in the Child.* New York: Basic Books.

Piddington, Ralph.
1961 "A Study of French-Canadian Kinship." *International Journal of Comparative Sociology* 2, March: 3-22.

Pike, Robert M.
1970 *Who Doesn't Get to University—and Why: A Study of Accessibility to Higher Education in Canada.* Ottawa: Association of Universities and Colleges of Canada.
1975 "Legal Access and the Incidence of Divorce in Canada: A Sociological Analysis." *Canadian Review of Sociology and Anthropology* 12 (2) May: 115-133.

Pilisuk, Marc, and Thomas Hayder.
1965 "Is There a Military Industrial Complex which Prevents Peace?" *Journal of Social Issues* 21, July: 67-117.

Pinard, M.
1971 *The Rise of a Third Party: A Study in Crisis Politics.* Englewood Cliffs, N.J.: Prentice-Hall.

Pineo, Peter.
1961 "Disenchantment in the Later Years of Marriage." *Marriage and Family Living* 23 (1) February: 1-11.
1969 "The Extended Family in a Working-Class Area of Hamilton." In *Canadian Society,* edited by Blishen and others. Toronto: Macmillan.
1977 "The Social Standings of Ethnic and Racial Groupings." *Canadian Review of Sociology and Anthropology* 14 (2): 147-157.

Pineo, P. C., and John Porter.
1967 "Occupational Prestige in Canada." *Canadian Review of Sociology and Anthropology* 4: 24-40.

Platt, Anthony M.
1969 *The Child Savers: The Invention of Delinquency.* Chicago: University of Chicago Press.

Polsky, Ned.
1969 *Hustlers, Beats, and Others.* New York: Anchor.

Pomfret, Alan.
1976 "Conceptual Issues in the Study of Planned School Change." Paper presented at the annual meetings of the Canadian Sociology and Anthropology Association, Laval, Quebec.

Porter, John.
1965 *The Vertical Mosaic: An Analysis of Social Class and Power in Canada.* Toronto: University of Toronto Press.
1967 "Canadian Character in the Twentieth Century." *Annals of the American Academy of Political and Social Science* 370, March: 48-56.
1968 "The Future of Upward Mobility." *American Sociological Review* 33 (1) February: 5-19.
1975 "Ethnic Pluralism in Canadian Perspective". In Glazer and Moynihan, eds. (1975: Chapter 9).

Porter, Marion R., John Porter, and Bernard Blishen.
1973 *Does Money Matter? Prospects for Higher Education.* Toronto: Institute for Behavioural Research.

Portes, Alejandro.
1971 "Political Primitivism, Differential Socialization, and Lower-Class Leftist Radicalism." *American Sociological Review* 36, October: 820-835.

Posgate, Dale, and Kenneth McRoberts.
1976 *Quebec: Social Change and Political Crisis.* Toronto: McClelland and Stewart.

Postman, Neil, and Charles Weingartner.
1969 *Teaching as a Subversive Activity.* New York: Dell.

Pozsonyi, Judith.
1973 "A Longitudinal Study of Unmarried Mothers Who Kept their First-Born Children." London, Ontario: Family and Children's Services of London and Middlesex.

Prentice, Alison.
1977 *The School Promoters: Education and Social Class in Mid-Nineteenth Century Upper Canada.* Toronto: McClelland and Stewart.

Prentice, Alison, and Susan Houston, eds.
1975 *Family, School and Society in Nineteenth Century Canada.* Toronto: Oxford University Press.

Queen, Stuart A., and Robert W. Habenstein.
1974 *The Family in Various Cultures.* 4th ed. Philadelphia: Lippincott.

Radcliffe-Brown, A. R.
1952 *Structure and Function in Primitive Society.* New York: Macmillan.

Radecki, H., and B. Heydenkorn.
1977 *A Member of a Distinguished Family: The Polish Group in Canada.* Toronto: McClelland and Stewart.

Radzinowicz, L.
1948 *A History of English Criminal Law.* Vol. 1. London: Stevens.

Ramu, G. N., and Stuart D. Johnson.
1976 *Introduction to Canadian Society: Sociological Analysis.* Toronto: Macmillan.

Rapoport, R., and R. Rapoport.
1971 *Dual Career Families.* Middlesex: Penguin.

Ray, M. B.
1961 "The Cycle of Abstinence and Relapse among Heroin Addicts." *Social Problems* 9, Fall: 132-140.

Reich, Charles A.
1971 *The Greening of America.* New York: Bantam.

Reid, S., ed.
1977 *The Scottish Tradition in Canada.* Toronto: McClelland and Stewart.

Reiss, Albert.
1961 "The Social Integration of Peers and Queers." *Social Problems* 9: 102-119.

Reitz, Jeffrey G.
1974 "Language and Ethnic Community Survival." *Canadian Review of Sociology and Anthropology.* A special publication on the occasion of the VIIIth World Congress of Sociology: 104-122.

Reusch, Hans.
1951 *Top of the World.* Richmond Hill, Ont.: Simon and Schuster.

Richardson, C. James.
1977a *Contemporary Social Mobility.* London: Frances Printer Publishing.
1977b "Education and Social Mobility: Changing Conceptions of the Role of Educational Systems." *Canadian Journal of Sociology* 2 (4) Fall: 417-433.
1977c "The Problem of Downward Mobility." *British Journal of Sociology* 28 (3) September: 303-320.

Richardson, Ken, and David Spears.
1972 *Race, Culture and Intelligence.* Middlesex: Penguin.

Richer, Stephen, and Pierre Laporte.
1971 "Culture, Cognition and English-French Competition." In Elliot (1971: 141-150).

Richert, Jean Pierre.
1974 "The Impact of Ethnicity on the Perception of Heroes and Historical Symbols." *Canadian Review of Sociology and Anthropology* 11 (2) May: 156-163.

Richmond, Anthony H.
1967a *Post-War Immigration in Canada.* Toronto: University of Toronto Press.
1967b *Immigrants and Ethnic Groups in Metropolitan Toronto.* Toronto: Institute for Behavioural Research, York University.
1970 "Immigration and Pluralism in Canada." In Mann (1970: 81-95).
1975 "The Green Paper: Reflections on

the Canadian Immigration and Population Study." *Canadian Ethnic Studies* XII (1): 5-21.

Riesman, David, and others.
1950 *The Lonely Crowd.* New Haven: Yale University Press.

Rioux, Marcel.
1971 *Quebec in Question.* Toronto: James, Lewis and Samuel.
1973 "The Development of Ideologies in Quebec." In *Communities and Culture in French Canada,* edited by G. A. Gold and M. A. Tremblay. Toronto: Holt, Rinehart and Winston: 260-278.

Rioux, Marcel, and Yves Martin.
1964 *French-Canadian Society.* Vol. 1. Toronto: McClelland and Stewart.

Ritzer, George.
1972 "Sources of Controversy in Sociology." In *Issues, Debates and Controversies,* edited by G. Ritzer. Boston: Allyn and Bacon.

Roberts, Wayne.
1976 *Honest Womanhood.* Toronto: New Hogtown Press.

Robertson, Heather.
1970 *Reservations Are for Indians.* Toronto: James, Lewis and Samuel.
1973 *Grass Roots.* Toronto: James, Lewis and Samuel.

Rocher, Guy.
1970 "L'Avenir de la Sociologie au Canada." In *The Future of Sociology in Canada,* edited by Jan J. Loubser. Montreal: Canadian Sociology and Anthropology Association.
1972 *A General Introduction to Sociology.* Translated by Peta Sheriff. Toronto: Macmillan.
1975 "Formal Education: The Issue of Opportunity." In Forcese and Richer (1975: 137-161).

Rock, Paul.
1973 *Deviant Behaviour.* London. Hutchinson.

Rock, Paul, and Mary McIntosh.
1974 *Deviance and Social Control.* London: Tavistock.

Rogers, David.
1968 *110 Livingston Street.* New York: Random House.

Roth, Julius.
1971 "Hired Hand Research." In *Sociological Methods,* by Norman K. Denzin. Chicago: Aldine: 531-539.

Roussopoulos, Dimitrios I.
1973 *Quebec and Radical Social Change.* Montreal: Black Rose.

Rousseau, Jean-Jacques.
1762 (1973) *The Social Contract.* London: J. M. Dent.

Royal Commission on Bilingualism and Biculturalism.
1968 *Report.* Vol. 2. Ottawa: Queen's Printer.

Rubington, E., and M. S. Weinberg.
1968 *Deviance: The Interactionist Perspective.* London: Macmillan.

Rudé, G.
1964 *The Crowd in History.* London: Wiley.
1970 *Paris and London and the Eighteenth Century: Studies in Protest.* London: Fontana.

Runciman, W. G.
1966 *Relative Deprivation and Social Justice.* London: Routledge and Kegan Paul.
1968 "Class, Status and Power?" In *Social Stratification,* edited by J. A. Jackson. Cambridge: Cambridge University Press, 25-61.

Ryerson, Stanley.
1972 "Quebec: Concepts of Class and Nation." In Teeple (ed.), (1972).

Safilios-Rothschild, Constantina.
1977 *Love, Sex and Sex Roles.* Englewood Cliffs, N.J.: Prentice-Hall.

Saturday Review of Education.
1973 "How Will We Raise Our Children in the Year 2000?" Symposium. *Saturday Review of Education,* March. Reprinted in *Social Realities,* edited by George Ritzer. Boston: Allyn and Bacon.

Saul, John, and Craig Heron.
1977 *Imperialism, Nationalism, and Canada.* Toronto: New Hogtown Press.

Saunders, Iwan.
1975 "Canadian Law and Marriage." In Wakil (1975: 43-58).

Sawchuk, P.
1974 "Becoming a Homosexual." In *Decency and Deviance,* edited by J. Haas and B. Shaffir. Toronto: McClelland and Stewart: 233-245.

Scanzoni, J. H.
1972 *Sexual Bargaining: Power Politics in the American Marriage.* Englewood

Cliffs, N.J.: Prentice-Hall.

Schermerhorn, Richard A.
1970 *Comparative Ethnic Relations: A Framework for Theory and Research.* New York: Random House.

Schlesinger, Benjamin E.
1971 "Remarriage as Family Reorganization for Divorced Persons." In K. Ishwaran, ed. (1971: 377-395).

Schlesinger, Benjamin, ed.
1977 *Sexual Behaviour in Canada: Patterns and Problems.* Toronto: University of Toronto Press.

Schur, Edwin.
1965 *Crimes Without Victims.* Englewood Cliffs, N.J.: Prentice-Hall.
1971 *Labeling Deviant Behavior: Its Sociological Implications.* New York: Random House.

Schutz, Alfred
1964a *Collected Papers.* Edited by M. Natanson. The Hague: Nijhoff.
1964b "The Stranger." In Schutz (1964: 91-105).

Scott, M. B., and S. M. Lyman
1968 "Accounts." *American Sociological Review* 33, February: 46-62.

Seeley, John R., and others.
1956 (1963) *Crestwood Heights: A Study of the Culture of Suburban Life.* New York: Wiley.

Selltiz, Claire, Lawrence S. Wrightsman, and Stuart W. Cook.
1976 *Research Methods in Social Relations.* New York: Holt, Rinehart and Winston.

Sennett, Richard.
1970 "The Brutality of Modern Families." *Transaction: Social Science and Modern Society* 7 (4): 29-37.

Sennett, Richard, and Jonathan Cobb.
1972 *The Hidden Injuries of Class.* New York: Random House.

Shackleton, Doris.
1977 *Power Town: Democracy Discarded.* Toronto: McClelland and Stewart.

Shaw, Martin.
1972 "The Coming Crisis of Radical Sociology. In *Ideology in Social Science,* edited by Robin Blackburn. London: Fontana: 32-44.

Shibutani, Tamotsu.
1955 "Reference Groups as Perspectives." *American Journal of Sociology* 60: 560-569.
1966 *Improvised News: A Sociological Study of Rumor.* Indianapolis: Bobbs-Merrill.

Shibutani, Tamotsu, and Kian M. Kwan.
1965 *Ethnic Stratification: A Comparative Approach.* New York: The Macmillan Company.

Short, James F., Jr., and Marvin E. Wolfgang.
1970 *Collective Violence.* Special Edition of The Annals of The American Academy of Political and Social Science, 391 September.

Shorter, Edward, and Charles Tilly.
1974 *Strikes in France, 1830-1968.* London: Cambridge University Press.

Silberman, Charles E.
1970 *Crisis in the Classroom.* New York: Random House.

Silverman, R., and J. Teevan, eds.
1975 *Crime in Canadian Society.* Toronto: Butterworth.

Simmel, Georg.
1964 *The Sociology of Georg Simmel.* Translation and Introduction by K. H. Wolff. New York: Free Press.

Singelmann, P.
1972 "Exchange as Symbolic Interaction: Convergences between Two Theoretical Perspectives." *American Sociological Review* 37 (4) 414-423.

Skidmore, William.
1975 *Theoretical Thinking in Sociology.* Cambridge: Cambridge University Press.

Skoda, L., and J. C. Robertson.
1972 *Isodemographic Map of Canada.* Ottawa. Information Canada.

Skolnick, Arlene S.
1973 (1978) *The Intimate Environment.* Boston: Little Brown.

Skolnick, Arlene, and Jerome H. Skolnick.
1971 *Families in Transition.* Boston: Little Brown.

Skolnick, Jerome H., ed.
1969 *The Politics of Protest.* New York: Simon and Shuster.

Smelser, Neil J.
1959 *Social Change in the Industrial Revolution.* Chicago: University of Chicago Press.
1962 *The Theory of Collective Behaviour.* New York: Free Press.

Smith, Dorothy.
1973 "Women, the Family and Corporate Capitalism." In M. Stephenson, ed. (1973: 5-35).

Sorokin, Pitirim.
1927 (1959) *Social and Cultural Mobility.* New York: Free Press.

Spiro, Milford E.
1956 *Kibbutz: Venture in Utopia.* Cambridge: Harvard University Press.
1958 *Children of the Kibbutz.* Cambridge: Harvard University Press.

Spray, W. A.
1972 *The Blacks in New Brunswick.* Fredericton: New Brunswick.

Sprott, W. J. H.
1958 *Human Groups.* London: Penguin Books.

Stanbury, William T.
1975 *Success and Failure: Indians in Urban society.* Vancouver: University of British Columbia.

Stebbins, R. A.
1967 "A Theory of the Definition of the Situation." *Canadian Review of Sociology and Anthropology* 4 (3): 148-164.

Steele, Brandt F., and Carl B. Pollock
1971 "The Battered Child's Parents." In Skolnick and Skolnick, eds. (1971: 356-365).

Steinmetz, S. K., and M. A. Strauss.
1974 *Violence in the Family.* New York: Dodd Mead.

Stephenson, Marylee, ed.
1977 *Women in Canada.* Don Mills: General Publishing.

Stolzman, James, and Herbert Gamberg.
1975 "The National Question and Canadian Sociology." *Canadian Journal of Sociology* 1 (1) Spring: 91-106.

Stone, G. P.
1962 "Appearance and the Self." In *Human Behaviour and Social Processes,* edited by A. M. Rose. Boston: Houghton-Mifflin: 86-118.

Stone, G. P., and H. A. Farberman
1970 *Social Psychology Through Symbolic Interaction.* Waltham, Mass.: Ginn-Blaisdell.

Stone, Leroy O.
1967 *Urban Development in Canada.* Ottawa: Dominion Bureau of Statistics (Statistics Canada).

Stone, Leroy O., and Claude Marceau.
1977 *Canadian Population Trends and Public Policy through the 1980's.* Montreal: McGill-Queen's University Press.

Strauss, Anselm L.
1971 *The Contexts of Social Mobility: Ideology and Theory.* Chicago: Aldine.

Stub, Holger R., and Robert R. Bell.
1968 *The Sociology of Education: A Sourcebook.* Homewood, Ill.: Dorsey.

Stymeist, David H.
1975 *Ethnics and Indians.* Toronto: Peter Martin.

Sudnow, David, ed.
1972 *Studies in Social Interaction.* New York: Free Press.

Susskind, M. B.
1953 "The Help Pattern in the Middle-class Family." *American Sociological Review* 18, February: 22-28.

Sutherland, Edwin H.
1939 *Principles of Criminology.* Philadelphia: Lippincott.
1949 (1961) *White Collar Crime.* New York: Dryden.

Symons, T. H. B.
1975 *To Know Ourselves: The Report of the Commission on Canadian Studies.* Ottawa: Association of Universities and Colleges of Canada.

Synge, Jane.
1977 "The Sex Factor in Social Selection Processes in Canadian Education." In Carlton and others (1977: 298-310).

Szasz, Thomas.
1960 "The Myth of Mental Illness." *American Psychologist* 15: 5-12.
1961 *The Myth of Mental Illness.* New York: Harper.
1965 Psychiatric Justice. New York: Macmillan.

Talmon, Yonina.
1972 *Family and Community in the Kibbutz.* Cambridge, Mass.: Harvard University Press.

Taylor, Ian.
1971 "Soccer Consciousness and Soccer Hooliganism." In Cohen (1971: 134-164).

Taylor, Ian, Paul Wilson, and Jock Young.
1973 *The New Criminology: For a Social Theory of Deviance.* London: Routledge and Kegan Paul.

Teeple, G., ed.
1972 *Capitalism and the National Question in Canada.* Toronto: University of Toronto Press.

Tepperman, Lorne.
1975 *Social Mobility in Canada.* Toronto:

McGraw-Hill Ryerson.
1977a *Crime Control: The Urge Toward Authority.* Toronto: McGraw-Hill Ryerson.
1977b "Effects of the Demographic Transition upon Access to the Toronto Elite." *Canadian Review of Sociology and Anthropology* 14 (3): 285-293.
forthcoming "Sociology in English-Speaking Canada: The Last Five Years." *Canadian Historical Review.*

Thompson, D. C.
1973 *Quebec Society and Politics.* Toronto: McClelland and Stewart.

Thompson, E. P.
1963 *The Making of the English Working Class.* London: Pelican.

Thornton, Leonard M.
1975 "People and the Police: An Analysis of Factors Associated With Police Evaluation and Support." *Canadian Journal of Sociology* 1 (3): 325-342.

Tilly, Charles.
1964 *The Vendée.* Cambridge, Mass.: Harvard University Press.
1967 "Migration to American Cities." In *The American City,* edited by Daniel P. Moynihan. New York: Basic Books.
1969 "Collective Violence in European Perspective." In Graham and Gurr (1969: 12-24).

Tocqueville, Alexis de.
1955 *The Old Regime and the French Revolution.* New York: Doubleday.

Toffler, Alvin.
1971 *Future Shock.* New York: Bantam.

Troost, Cornelius J., ed.
1973 *Radical School Reform: Critique and Alternatives.* Boston: Little, Brown.

Trudeau, Pierre E.
1968 *Federalism and the French-Canadians.* Toronto: Macmillan.

Trudeau, Pierre E., ed.
1974 *The Asbestos Strike.* Toronto: James, Lewis and Samuel.

Truman, Tom.
1971 "A Critique of Seymour M. Lipset's Article, 'Value Differences, Absolute or Relative: The English-Speaking Democracies'." *Canadian Journal of Political Science* 4 (4) December.

Tucker, Robert C., ed.
1978 *The Marx-Engels Reader.* 2nd ed. New York: Norton.

Tumin, Melvin.
1953 (1967) "Some Principles of Stratification: A Critical Analysis." In Bendix and Lipset (1967: 53-58).

Tumin, Melvin, ed.
1967 *Comparative Perspectives on Race Relations.* Boston: Little, Brown.

Turk, J. L., and N. W. Bell
1972 "Measuring Power in Families". *Journal of Marriage and the Family* 24, May: 215-222.

Turner, Jonathan H.
1977 *The Structure of Sociological Theory.* Homewood, Ill.: Dorsey.

Turner, Ralph H.
1960 "Sponsored and Contest Mobility and the School System." *American Sociological Review* 25 (6) December: 855-867.
1964 "New Theoretical Frameworks." *Sociological Quarterly* 12, April: 122-132.

Turner, Ralph B.
1969 "The Public Perception of Protest." *American Sociological Review* 34, December: 815-831.

Turner, Ralph, and Lewis M. Killian.
1972 *Collective Behaviour.* 2nd ed. Englewood Cliffs, N.J.: Prentice-Hall.

Tylor, E. B.
1958 *Primitive Culture.* New York: Harper Torchbooks.

Udry, J. R.
1974 *The Social Context of Marriage.* 2nd ed. Philadelphia: Lippincott.

UNESCO.
1974 *Man and the Environment: New Towns in Isolated Settings.* Kambalda, Australia.

University of Toronto.
1977 *Options: Proceedings of the Conference on the Future of the Canadian Federation.* Toronto: University of Toronto Press.

Vallee, Frank, and Norman Shulman.
1969 "The Viability of French Groupings Outside Quebec." In *Regionalism in the Canadian Community 1867-1967.* Toronto: University of Toronto Press.

Vallieres, Pierre.
1971 *White Niggers of America.* Toronto: McClelland and Stewart.

Van den Berghe, Pierre L.
1974 "Introduction" to *Class and Ethnicity in Peru,* by Pierre L. Van den Berghe. Leiden: E. J. Brill.

Van Den Haag, Ernest.
1974 "Love or Marriage." In *The Family: Its Structure and Functions,* edited by Rose Laub Coser. 2nd ed. New York: St. Martins Press: 141-142.

Van Stolk, Mary.
1972 *The Battered Child in Canada.* Toronto: McClelland and Stewart.

Vaz, Edmund W.
1965 "Middle-Class Adolescents: Self-Reported Delinquency and Youth Culture Activities." *Canadian Review of Sociology and Anthropology* 2.
1976 *Aspects of Deviance.* Toronto: Prentice-Hall.

Veevers, Jean.
1973 "Voluntary Childlessness: A Neglected Area of Family Study." *The Family Coordinator* 23: 199-205.
1977 "The Child-Free Alternative: Rejection of the Motherhood Mystique." In Marylee Stephenson (1977).

Vercors.
1953 *You Shall Know Them.* Translated by Rita Barisse. Toronto: McClelland and Stewart.

Vinacke, E. W.
1969 "Variables in Experimental Games: Toward a Field Theory." *Psychological Bulletin* 71: 293-318.

Vonnegut, Mark.
1975 *The Eden Express.* New York: Praeger.

Wakil, S. Parvez, ed.
1975 *Marriage, Family and Society: Canadian Perspectives.* Toronto: Butterworth.
1976 *Marriage and the Family in Canada.* Calgary: *Journal of Comparative Family Studies.*

Wangenheim, Elizabeth.
1968 "The Ukranians: A Case Study of the Third Force." In *Canada: A Sociological Profile,* 1st ed., edited by W. E. Mann. Toronto: Copp Clark: 178-189.

Warner, Lloyd.
1963 *Yankee City.* New Haven: Yale University Press.

Warnock, John W.
1970 "All the News it Pays to Print." In Lumsden (1970: 117-134).
1974 "Metropolis/Hinterland: The Lost Theme in Canadian Letters." *Canadian Dimension* 10 (2) June: 42-27.

Warriner, C. K.
1970 *The Emergence of Society.* Homewood, Ill.: Dorsey.

Watkins, Mel.
1973 "Contradictions and Alternatives in Canada's Future." In Laxer, ed. (1973: 250-269).

Watson, G. Llewellyn.
1975 "The Poverty of Sociology in a Changing Canadian Society." *Canadian Journal of Sociology* 1 (3) Fall: 345-362.

Webb, Eugene J., and others.
1966 *Unobtrusive Measures: Nonreactive Research in the Social Sciences.* Chicago: Rand McNally.

Weber, Max.
1958 *The Protestant Ethic and the Spirit of Capitalism.* New York: Scribner.

Weinstein, Jay A.
1976 *Demographic Transition and Social Change.* Morristown, N.J.: General Learning Press.

Weiss, Carol H.
1972 *Evaluation Research: Methods for Assessing Program Effectiveness.* Englewood Cliffs, N.J.: Prentice-Hall.

Werthman, Carl, and I. Piliavin.
1967 "Gang Members and the Police." In *The Police,* edited by D. J. Bordua. New York: Wiley.

Westergaard, John.
1974 *Class in Capitalist Society.* London: Heinemann.

Westhues, Kenneth.
1975 "Inter-Generational Conflict in the Sixties." In Clark and others (1975: 387-408).

White, T. H.
1975 "Canadian Labour and International Unions in the Seventies." In Clark and others (1975: 288-305).

Whyte, William F.
1943 (1955) *Street Corner Society.* Chicago: University of Chicago Press.

Whyte, William H., Jr.
1956 *The Organization Man.* New York: Doubleday Anchor.

Whorf, Benjamin L.
1956 *Language, Thought, and Reality.* Cambridge, Mass.: M.I.T. Press.

Willey, Basil.
1962 *The Eighteenth Century Background.* London: Penguin.
Willmott, Peter.
1969 *Adolescent Boys of East London.* London: Pelican.
Willmott, Peter, and Michael Young.
1960 *Family and Class in a London Suburb.* London: Routledge and Kegan Paul.
Wilson, Thomas P.
1970 "Normative and Interpretive Paradigms in Sociology." In Douglas (1970: 57-79).
Winch, R. F.
1971 *The Modern Family.* 3rd ed. New York: Holt, Rinehart and Winston.
Wirth, Louis.
1938 "Urbanism as a Way of Life". *American Journal of Sociology* 44, July: 1-24.
Wise, S. F., and Robert Craig Brown.
1967 *Canada Views the United States, Nineteenth Century Political Attitudes.* Toronto: Macmillan.
Woods, John.
1976 "Repatriating the Canadian University." *Journal of Canadian Studies* XI (4): 56-66.
Wrong, Dennis.
1961 "The Over-Socialized Conception of Man in Modern Sociology." *American Sociological Review* 26, April.
1964 "Social Inequality without Social Stratification." *Canadian Review of Sociology and Anthropology* I (1): 5-16.
1977 *Population and Society.* 4th ed. New York: Random House.
Young, Jock.
1971 "The Police as Amplifiers of Deviancy." In Cohen (1971).
Young, Michael.
1958 *The Rise of the Meritocracy.* London: Penguin.
Young, Michael F. D.
1971 *Knowledge and Control.* London: Heinemann.
Young, M., and P. Willmott.
1957 *Family and Kinship in East London.* Baltimore: Penguin.
1973 *The Symmetrical Family.* London: Routledge and Kegan Paul.
Zakuta, L.
1963 "Equality in North American Marriages." *Social Research* 30, Summer: 157-170.
1964 *A Protest Movement Becalmed.* Toronto: University of Toronto Press.
1970 "On 'Filthy Lucre'." In *Human Nature and Collective Behaviour,* edited by T. Shibutani. Englewood Cliffs, N.J.: Prentice-Hall: 260-270.
Zaretsky, Eli.
1973 *Capitalism, the Family and Personal Life.* New York: Harper and Row.
Zeitlin, Irving.
1968 *Ideology and the Development of Sociological Theory.* New York: Prentice-Hall.
Zureik, Elia, and Robert M. Pike, eds.
1975 *Socialization and Values in Canadian Society.* Vols. I and II. Toronto: McClelland and Stewart.

author index

subject index